MARSHALL LOEB'S

1989 Money Guide

MARSHALL LOEB'S
1989 Money Guide

by Marshall Loeb

Managing Editor of Fortune *Magazine*

LITTLE, BROWN AND COMPANY • BOSTON • TORONTO • LONDON

FIRST EDITION

The Library of Congress has catalogued this serial title as follows:

Marshall Loeb's Money Guide. — [1984]- — Boston: Little, Brown,
   c1983-

   v.;24 cm.

   Annual.
   ISSN 8755-1586 = Marshall Loeb's Money Guide.

   1. Finance, Personal — Periodicals.   I. Loeb, Marshall.   II. Title:
Money Guide.
HG179.M342   332.024'005—dc19   84-646730
                                              AACR 2   MARC-S

Library of Congress

HC: 10 9 8 7 6 5 4 3 2 1

PB: 10 9 8 7 6 5 4 3 2 1

RRD VA

Published simultaneously in Canada
by Little, Brown & Company (Canada) Limited

PRINTED IN THE UNITED STATES OF AMERICA

For my family:
Peggy, Michael, Margaret, Henrietta, Gail, Michael II,
Kate — and more TK

Contents

Contents | xv

Preface

THIS book is a greatly revised and completely updated version of the annual *Money Guides* that have been published since 1983. It is based largely on the work of my distinguished present and former colleagues — the writers, reporters and editors of *Fortune* and *Money* magazines. To them it is dedicated. As Managing Editor of *Fortune*, one part of my job is to choose articles from the magazine to which I am assigned, abridge and rewrite them, then present them on the CBS Radio Network in daily broadcasts, titled "Your Dollars." Previously, I did the same as Managing Editor of *Money*. I have re-edited and updated a selection of those scripts to create the more than 350 chapters in the book.

A quite special note of thanks belongs to Carolyn Tasker. She has been my researcher throughout the preparation of this book. She and Mildred Lenhardt also checked the manuscript, as did Patricia Lynch, Eileen Einfrank, Jeanne Reid, Robin Micheli and Leslie Lawrence with earlier editions. Without their organizational skills and constructive criticism, this would have been a much lesser work.

Warren M. Bergstein, a senior manager with the accounting firm of Ernst & Whinney, and his associate Sandra Price were surefooted guides through the maze of tax reform. I am very grateful for their expert insights and suggestions.

My deepest appreciation as well to Anne Gut, my highly talented and dedicated administrative assistant, who has been so exceptionally helpful in so many ways.

Ray Roberts of Little, Brown, an editor and a gentleman, worked wonders to bring this book to publication. Betsy Pitha did a smoothly expert job of overseeing the copyediting.

James B. Hayes, *Fortune*'s publisher, gave the project enthusiastic support. Marilyn Sahner and Patricia A. Straus, invaluable colleagues at Time Inc., made it possible for me to broadcast material from *Fortune* and *Money* on the CBS Radio Network. At CBS, my particular thanks go to Frank Murphy and David Kurman.

Let me express my gratitude to Jason McManus, Editor-in-Chief of Time Inc., a brilliant journalist and a deeply caring man; to Ray Cave, Editorial Director of Time Inc., who has taught me more about being a managing editor than he can ever imagine; to Gilbert Rogin, Corporate Editor of Time Inc., who has been a source of inspiration; and to Edward L. Jamieson, Executive Editor of *Time*, my friend and colleague for the better part of thirty years.

MARSHALL LOEB'S
1989 Money Guide

Introduction

Ten Ways to Preserve and Protect Your Money and Make It Grow

PEOPLE enjoy more personal freedom and can make better choices about their lives if they learn to handle their money sensibly. Just as a financially sound company has more opportunity to do great things than a strapped and worried organization does, so a financially sound person has more opportunity to act imaginatively and expansively. Certainly, money is not an end but a means: a means to help make the most out of ourselves by being able to pay for education, travel, medical care and a worry-free retirement. The more we earn, quite obviously, the more we can spend to enhance and secure the lives of ourselves and of our families, to enrich our communities, to aid our favorite causes. The more we save and invest, the more we also provide the seed capital that helps create new enterprises and jobs.

Each and every one of us has the opportunity — and the obligation — to preserve and protect our money, and make it grow. This book speaks to our opportunities — our opportunities to earn more money, to invest it more profitably, to spend it more sensibly and more pleasurably, to save it more prudently and to improve our careers.

We have better chances than any other people at any other time to do all that. Chances to put our money into forms of investments, savings, insurance that did not exist just a few years ago. Chances to build our careers or start businesses in fresh forms of industry, services or commerce, in newly expanding regions of the country. Chances to borrow capital through rather novel means.

The trouble is that chances mean choices, and making choices is hard. We have new freedoms to decide whether, when, how and how much to invest, save, spend. Tough choices. Many people dodge those decisions. They take life as it comes and then lament their missed opportunities. That is practically always a mistake. Almost invariably, it is better to make some decision than no decision. A bad decision can be reversed; making no decision leaves you in limbo, uneasy, frustrated.

Thus, my aim is to outline your money choices and to urge you to seize your opportunities. Let me start by explaining 10 ways in which you can act immediately to preserve and protect what you have and help it to grow. Many of these steps will sound familiar, but few people have taken advantage of all of them, and they provide a sound base on which to begin. All of them — and many more — are elaborated upon in later chapters of this book.

STEP ONE: *Build up a cash cushion to protect yourself against emergencies.*

That way, if you unexpectedly need money, you will not have to borrow at exorbitant interest rates or sell off investments at what may be unfavorable prices. Try to accumulate and maintain easily tapped liquid savings equal to three months of your after-tax income. Put that money into a money-market deposit account or a savings certificate at a federally insured bank or savings institution. Another sound choice is to place your savings in a money-market fund.

STEP TWO: *Start investing regularly and faithfully, come rain, come shine.*

After you have established your necessary liquid savings, begin deploying your money into a diversity of investments. Your insured savings are secure; they grow at a measured pace, depending on the level of interest you collect, and you can tap into them at any time. Your investments carry some risk, but they can grow at a faster rate than your savings.

You reduce your risks by diversifying. Markets have become so volatile that you no longer can buy only one stock or bond and confidently hold it for a lifetime. Thus, it is wise to start investing by buying into a diversified, professionally managed mutual fund; then branch out into some stocks and bonds, and later perhaps some real estate investment trusts (REITs) and income-producing real estate or conservative, income-oriented limited partnerships.

Resolve to invest the same amount of money every month or from every paycheck. That's known as dollar-cost averaging, but you can think of it as investing on the installment plan. When your investments rise in value, you can congratulate yourself for having earned some paper profit. When they fall, at least you can take advantage of your new opportunity to pick up some bargains: a short while ago, your regular monthly investment could buy perhaps only two shares, but now it can buy three!

Above all, don't despair; all investments decline sometimes. Wise investors position themselves for the long term. If you believe that the country and its economy will do well over the long term, then your investments will do well. That is, they will do well if you don't become greedy and rush to buy when markets surge to their tops, and if you don't panic and rush to sell out when markets plunge to their bottoms. The discipline of dollar-cost averaging helps you avoid those two common errors.

STEP THREE: *Act now to further reduce your taxes for this year — and future years.*

Probably nobody takes all the deductions to which he or she is legally and legitimately entitled. So resolve now to use your tax-saving opportunities and to keep better records of your deductible expenses. Remember: pack rats always save more.

Here are a few of many money-saving steps you still can take:

Buy municipal bonds. The federal government does not tax the interest you collect on most of them, and if the bonds are from your home state, you will probably escape state and local taxes, too. Also invest in supersafe U.S. Treasury securities, or U.S. government bond funds, or U.S. Savings Bonds, the yields on which are exempt from state and local taxes.

Deposit money in your company's profit-sharing or stock purchase plans; taxes are deferred on any contributions made by your employer and on any earnings made by those contributions and by your own deposits. Take advantage of a so-called 401(k) salary-reduction plan if your company offers one; for 1988 you can contribute up to $7,313 tax-free.

Deduct expenses incurred for charitable work, such as making phone calls or driving your car to and from the place where you do volunteer work (the allowance for your 1988 income taxes is 12 cents a mile). Give your old clothes, books or furnishings to charities and collect receipts for the gifts' estimated value. You can also donate shares of stock or other securities. Note: You must itemize your return in order to take charitable deductions.

STEP FOUR: *Open an Individual Retirement Account* (IRA).

Even though one of its most important tax-saving features has been limited or eliminated for many people by tax reform, an IRA can be a valuable device both for reducing your taxes and for increasing your capital. Everyone under 70½ years old who earns money from a job can have an Individual Retirement Account, and almost everyone should. But some 60% of those who are eligible have not opened an IRA. That's a money-losing shame.

The dividends, interest and capital gains on your investment compound tax-free until you withdraw the money, probably when you retire and are in a lower tax bracket. It's remarkable how fast your money will grow when it is unencumbered by taxes. If you put away $2,000 every January and it grows by a reasonable 8% annually, you will have some $31,300 after 10 years, $98,800 after 20 years, $244,700 after 30 years and $559,600 after 40 years.

That significant characteristic of IRAs remains even after tax reform. But it is quite likely that you may no longer be able to subtract your annual contribution from your taxable income. True, anyone who is not covered by an employee pension plan can deduct the full IRA deposit. If, however, you are covered by a plan — whether or not you are vested — you will be able to deduct your contribution only if you earn a rather moderate income. Under the law, if you are a single person covered by an employer, you can take the full deduction if you earn $25,000 or less annually in adjusted gross income. Married couples filing jointly keep the full deduction if their combined income is $40,000 or less. Singles who earn between $25,000 and $35,000 and joint filers who earn between $40,000 and $50,000 can deduct part of their contribution. The deduction tapers off as you earn more money. It vanishes altogether when your income tops $35,000 or $50,000.

As described later in this book, you can put your IRA money into almost any form of savings or investment except for art and other collectibles. My own favorite repository for an IRA, particularly for young people who are confident of the future and willing to take sensible risk, is the no-load growth mutual fund that invests in stocks and other securities. Funds with the best performance records are named in the mutual-fund chapters of this book, and you can get an updated list of the top performers in the "Fund Watch" column of *Money* magaine.

It is wise to make your annual IRA contribution as early in the year as possible. You can put in your deposit anytime from January 1 of the current year to April 15 of the next one. Let's say you deposit $2,000 every year for 10 years and earn 10% annually on it. Put that money in every January 2, and in 10 years you will have $35,000. But if you regularly wait until April 15 of the following year, your money will grow to only $29,000. Over a period of 20 to 30 years, the compounding of tax-deferred earnings on early contributions can add tens of thousands of dollars to your account.

STEP FIVE: *If you are eligible, also open a Keogh account.*

Keogh plans work much like IRAs, but you can put much more money into them and deduct it all from your taxable income. You can open a Keogh if you are self-employed full- or part-time. It's surprising how many people are eligible for Keoghs but don't know it — or don't take advantage of this large and liberal tax shelter. You qualify just so long as you work for yourself. You can work full-time, part-time or free-lance. You can work at one job for an employer but still contribute your earnings from a second, self-employed moonlighting job. Among those eligible for Keoghs are most small-business people, lawyers, doctors, dentists, carpenters, plumbers, actors and directors, free-lance writers, waiters, taxi drivers and the like.

You can contribute 20% of your income from self-employment, up to a maximum contribution of $30,000 a year. Also, you can have both an IRA and a Keogh (although you may not be able to *deduct* your IRA contribution). Between them, some high-income individuals can put away as much as $32,000 a year. If both spouses are self-employed, they can shelter up to $64,000 annually, provided their Keogh contributions do not exceed 20% of their self-employment income.

One warning: Unlike an IRA, which you can open as late as April 15 of next year, you have to open a Keogh plan by December 31 of this year in order to contribute any of this year's earnings to it. However, you can make those contributions up to the time you file your income taxes — as late as April 15, or August 15 if you get an extension.

STEP SIX: *Be sure you have a will — a sound, valid, hard-to-shake and up-to-date will.*

There is no way without a will to make sure that whatever you leave goes to whomever you wish. If you do not have a will, your heirs could be clobbered by taxes and your children could be raised by someone you don't want. Yet it is shocking how many adult Americans do not have this basic document — almost two-thirds of them do not.

Estate laws change fairly often and sometimes radically, so it is important to review your will regularly. The last major change was in 1981; if you made out your will before the end of that year, your money may not be distributed the way you wish it to be. Therefore, check right now to see if your will is current. If it is not, make an appointment with a lawyer to prepare a new one as soon as possible. It is best to have your will drafted by an attorney and updated at least once every three years.

STEP SEVEN: *Save money on your life insurance and make sure you have the right kind of policies.*

For basic insurance protection, the least expensive policy is still annual renewable term. If you are, say, 40 years old, $100,000 of coverage at one company will cost you $300 for annual renewable term and $1,500 for traditional whole life. But if you want to protect your family and simultaneously build up tax-deferred savings, your best means may well be whole life.

Or, you might be wise to buy term insurance and then put the money you save into mutual funds or some other sound investment. And you can save still more by buying only the life insurance you need. How much do you need? Remember this: If no one is relying on you for financial support, you probably don't need any life insurance at all.

STEP EIGHT: *Save money by giving it away.*

Put money in the names of your close relatives who earn less than you and thus are taxed at lower rates, especially your minor children and grandchildren. Four years of college can easily cost $60,000 or more, but careful tax planning can cut your bill a lot.

Even after tax reform, the interest, dividends and capital gains on money given to children aged 14 or over will be taxed at *their* low or nonexistent tax rate, not at the giver's higher rate.

STEP NINE: *Buy a personal computer and learn to use it.*

If you invest your money and, more important, your time in purchasing and mastering a computer, it will pay you dividends many, many times over. With the sophisticated new programs, the computer can help you pick out the best stocks. For example, from the thousands of issues, you can segregate those few that are priced well below their book value or that have especially modest price/earnings ratios or that are selling far beneath their recent peaks. A computer also can help you chart and graph the movements of specific stocks. It can keep track of the investments you have and alert you to any that are starting to go sour. Not least, a computer can help you mightily to plan your tax strategy, keep the records that will simplify the chore of paying taxes, and legitimately reduce what you have to pay.

STEP TEN: *Keep up with the news that affects your money.*

The world is changing very rapidly, and almost every event of consequence close to home or in some distant corner of the world influences your investments, your savings, your personal balance sheet. A drought in Africa, a coup in Latin America, a technological breakthrough in Asia — not to mention a new bill passed in Congress or a policy shift by the Federal Reserve Board — can alter the price of everything from chocolate bars to new cars or lead to sharp gyrations in the values of your investments and the levels of the interest rates you pay or collect. It is important, then, to become an avid reader of the daily financial pages and of business magazines. One rather immodest but heartfelt comment: I think you will find *Fortune* to be particularly valuable and enjoyable.

So there you have the 10 initial steps. There are more, many more, that each of us can take in order to seize the moment, make the right choices and take advantage of our opportunities. For an explanation of them, read on.

— MARSHALL LOEB

Your Personal Finances

How to Become Financially Independent

FINANCIAL independence means having the wherewithal to say to yourself: "If I wanted to, I could quit what I'm doing today and live comfortably for the rest of my life."

Millions of Americans can achieve that dream.

You do not have to marry well or choose your parents wisely to reach financial independence. More likely, you will gain it by investing — shrewdly and boldly. Or by starting your own business. Or by working for a generous company and taking advantage of all the corporate savings plans, stock purchase programs and profit-sharing plans that you can.

Say that you have a good job and you figure on getting fairly substantial raises. You would like to retire in 20 years, but you want your retirement income to equal your final salary, counting your expected raises and inflation. You usually can achieve that goal by saving 10% of your salary every year for the next 20 years and earning 10% compounded on your money.

The sooner you start saving, the easier and faster you will be able to accomplish independence. And you will have help along the way. Banks and a bewildering variety of investment firms are all clamoring for your money, and offering high real rates of return to get it. In many cases, the government will even let you shelter your savings from taxes. One of the smartest ways to begin is to put the $2,000 maximum each year into a tax-deferring Individual Retirement Account. If you start doing that in 1989 and earn 10% compounded annually on the money between now through the year 2009, you will have $128,000.

Even if you cannot deduct your contribution, an IRA is still a great tax saver. Your money can grow at a surprising clip. Thanks to the law of compound interest, you earn returns not only on your original stake but on your accumulated gains as well. At a 10% rate of return, which you should be able to get, your investment would double in just over seven years.

As a start to becoming financially independent, pick the safest high-growth investment you can find — and then give it your undivided attention. Probably it will be in the stock market or in real estate.

Real estate demands more hours and energy. You must scout around for the best property, negotiate the deal to buy it, fix it up if necessary and maintain it. But if you have some money to begin with, it can be most attractive to invest in single-family houses that you rent out. With perhaps $10,000 down and a 30-year mortgage, you might get a $100,000 property. Later, as your earnings accumulate, aim to buy another house, then another. Eventually, try to sell off your oldest houses and use any after-tax profits to pay the debt on the rest.

If you have less money and time to commit to your investment program, you are better off to concentrate on stocks. Choose growth stocks, including some blue chips, scattered in several industries. If your capital base is not large, your best investment is probably a mutual fund that automatically diversifies your portfolio. Over the last 10 years, the typical growth fund has had a total return of 16.74% a year.

You can also achieve financial independence long before retirement age simply by taking advantage of the liberal employee-benefit plans offered by many corporations. Job hopping from company to company is not the way to build a reserve of capital. Most programs do not go into effect until you have been with a company for at least a year. But an employee earning, say, $35,000 who stays with the same firm for 20 years can amass as much as half a million dollars from generous benefit plans.

The most important capital-building corporate benefits are profit-sharing and savings plans. In both, your employer usually contributes money above and beyond your regular salary to an account that is turned over to you when you quit or retire. In a profit-sharing plan, the contribution depends on the company's annual earnings — and in the best years usually amounts to about 10% of your salary. In a typical savings program, the company will match each dollar you invest with 50 cents of its own. And remember: Everything the company tosses into the pot, plus all the earnings on both your own and the company's contributions, will get the huge boost of tax deferral. The money grows free of taxes until you withdraw it.

A relatively new kind of savings program — called a salary-reduction, or 401(k) plan — offers a great tax break. You put part of your pay in the plan and it is not considered immediate income — so it is tax-deferred and can grow with extra speed. One drawback, though: It is hard to take out any of your money before you leave the firm. Under tax reform, if you withdraw money before age 59½, you may have to pay a 10% penalty on top of any income tax you owe.

Probably the most common way to try to become financially independent is to start your own business. You still will find the widest range of opportunities in the fast-growing Sun Belt states, but there also are pockets of prosperity in the Pacific Coast region, New England and the rebounding Rust Belt. As more large industrial firms move into these areas, they will need smaller companies to supply them with parts and with secretarial, accounting, advertising, computing and many other services.

Before you launch any business, take a hard look at its real market potential. Do not try to start too big. The safest course is to create a firm small enough for the money you have and then make it larger. A small success is better than a big failure.

Be sure you start with enough money. Underfinancing is as bad as overborrowing. It can choke a promising enterprise or force you to give up control to your backers. A little financial help from your friends and relatives is fine, but treat such loans as strictly business deals, complete with signed legal agreements. Handshake deals often lead to bitter quarrels.

To launch and maintain almost any enterprise, you need a credit line from a bank. When you first go to a bank and begin to establish a relationship, do not rush to the highest officer. Instead, find a younger employee who has time for you. Ask him or her to review your ideas and refer you to a lawyer or accountant who can help you to write an intelligent business plan. In at least three or four pages, it should describe your product or service; the staffing, space and equipment you will need; and the reasons that your business should succeed. The plan will help you to define your objectives — and to get a line of credit.

Draw from it as you need the money, not in a lump sum that would saddle you with unnecessarily large repayments.

Still another way to gain financial independence is to go to work for a start-up company and persuade the founders to give you some stock in the firm in lieu of a large salary. But before you count your gains, bear in mind that one-quarter or more of start-ups fail to survive even two years. They tend to be undercapitalized and shorthanded, so you often work long hours for little pay.

You can find many start-ups among newly deregulated businesses, in fields such as airlines, trucking and other transportation; real estate and personal financial services; health services, especially geriatric care; and in software and other computer-related businesses. To locate start-ups, watch the help-wanted columns in trade periodicals and newspapers. You also can learn about new ventures in national magazines such as *Venture* and *Inc.* and in regional ones such as *California Business*. High-tech ventures cluster around universities, so a business school professor may know of some. Another source is the management-assistance officer at your district Small Business Administration office.

Before you join a new venture, be sure to consider certain questions: Is the new product or service really worthy? For evidence, read the founder's business plan. What is the founder's business record of past success? For information, consult his or her business associates and rivals. Who is putting up the money? A token of an entrepreneur's commitment is the amount of his or her own money invested in the new venture.

The more complicated your employment arrangement, the more you will want a contract or at least a letter of understanding. Get as much down on paper as possible, then show the agreement to your lawyer.

Avoiding Mistakes with Your Money

E VERYONE makes financial mistakes — like the man who died before he told his new bride the location of his safe-deposit box, or the low-income fellow who invested the family savings in tax-exempt bonds instead of corporate bonds, which would have paid him much more.

The most common financial mistake is a failure to define your goals. Few people know what they really want their money to do. Several years' accumulation of savings or a sudden inheritance or other windfall leaves them with money to invest and no idea of how to make it best work for them.

What is *your* goal? For example, are you saving for college tuition, or future security? A necessary first step to accomplish your goal is to estimate just what you want your money to do and how much you will need to do it. The next step is to figure out how much you must put away each week — or month — to reach your goal.

Another common mistake is failure to follow through on your financial goal. The cost of not making investment moves immediately can add up. Say that, after a check of your personal finances, you decide to shift some money from your low-paying savings account into higher-yielding Treasury bills. If you delay just a few months, your procrastination will cost you a bundle of money.

A third financial mistake is the failure to maintain careful records. You have to keep — and keep updated — lists of your investments, your bank accounts and any financial advisers you might have. Your personal financial file should list names and amounts of all your securities, money-market funds, hard assets and life insurance policies. It also should give the location of your safe-deposit boxes and contain your tax records and credit-card information, as well as wills and deeds.

Keeping it is not only a wise precaution in case anything happens to you; it is also a constant reminder of your financial position. If you are always aware of where your money is, you can take advantage of tax changes and map out new investment strategies. Keeping such information complete and correct makes it easier for you to switch around your investments and eases the burden on your family if you become ill or injured.

Still another common financial mistake is greed. Some people are so obsessed with making tax-exempt or sheltered investments that they often miss much more lucrative, if taxable, investments. You should look for good, sound economics in an investment before you weigh the tax benefits. This is especially true now that reform has eliminated or reduced the tax advantages of many investments.

It is a mistake to heed advice from people who are not qualified to give it. Amateurs — like your next-door neighbor or your cousin's son-in-law — can do more damage than good. You are better off soliciting and then carefully considering professional advice from brokers, bankers, attorneys, accountants or financial planners. Fees should be agreed on in advance, but sometimes the advice is free.

Another common mistake is a failure to keep an open mind about investment opportunities. Many people invest in just one thing and stick with it. Huge sums of money are still locked away in passbook savings accounts, many of which pay interest of only 5½%. Higher-yielding money-market funds, Treasury bills, short-term income trusts or tax-deferred annuities are safe as well as rewarding, but many people are — in the words of one savings bank president — too lazy or afraid to move their money.

One of the biggest mistakes most people make with their money is not hedging their assets and not diversifying their investments. If you have a variety of investments, you stand a better chance of riding out any financial storm.

The worst mistake an investor can make is to assume he or she will not make a mistake. It may be comforting to learn that some of the most knowledgeable people in the world of finance have made some awful gaffes with their own money.

Recent presidential candidate and former Senate Finance Committee chairman Robert Dole, for example, once invested in what was called a sure thing — a piece of an oil well. The only problem was that there was no oil in the hole. Senator Dole is still trying to figure out what his percentage of zero is. The lesson here: Investigate carefully before you put your money into an investment, and if the person selling it calls it a sure thing, hang onto your wallet.

You wouldn't expect former New York State banking commissioner Muriel Siebert to be easily fooled. Yet she once bought a real estate tax shelter because it seemed like a decent tax write-off. Some of the biggest people in the country were in on the deal. The shelter turned out to be a fraud, and the IRS disallowed it. Siebert had to pay back taxes and interest. Since that experience, she studies every shelter she plans to invest in backward and forward.

Barbara Thomas, a former member of the Securities and Exchange Commission, once saw a nicely priced co-op apartment that she wanted to buy. But she chose instead to spend the down payment on a vacation trip to China. Well, China is still there, but the apartment is now worth at least five times what Thomas could have bought it for — and she vows in the future that when she sees a well-documented good deal, she will grab it.

Wayne Nelson, a Merrill Lynch vice president, once saved some money for a swimming pool but instead sunk it into a speculative stock that he bought on margin, with borrowed money. The stock plunged, and he lost his entire investment in a week. Nelson says that taught him that buying stock on margin is a double whammy. It can buy you twice the trouble for half the money.

Douglas Casey, the best-selling author of *Crisis Investing* and *Strategic Investing,* admits to ignoring his own advice. In his second book, he predicted that the stock market would surge by the end of 1982. He was right. But instead of buying stocks as he told his readers to do, he remained an aggressive short-seller right through December of that year. The moral: When you have a well-thought-out plan, be sure to follow it.

Just think of all those newspaper stories about other successful men and women who have been duped into bad business deals or tax shelters that bombed. Why is it that smart people so often make dumb investments? These victims seem incapable of leaving money lying around in the bank, earning nice interest. Highly acquisitive by nature, they are willing to go out on too long a limb with their capital. Then, too, they tend to be busy people whose schedules are packed to the max. So they turn over the details of their financial lives to someone else. But the stewards they choose are often extreme risk-takers like themselves.

To recapitulate, here are ways you can head off serious losses in your personal finances:

—Define your goals. Give careful thought to what you want your money to do for you. Then follow through, by saving and investing.

—Keep careful records, and review and update your financial plans regularly.

—Don't be carried away by tax-sheltered investments. They make sense only if they would be worthwhile investments even without the tax breaks.

—Get your advice from professionals — stockbrokers, bankers, attorneys, accountants, insurance agents and financial planners. Make sure they coordinate all the advice they give you.

—Keep your knowledge of investments up-to-date by reading widely.

—Put your money in a variety of investments that can flourish in different financial climates. That way you can minimize the cost of any errors.

—Push yourself hard to ask questions — of yourself, your advisers and anybody trying to sell you an investment. Remember: Nobody is infallible, and there are no dumb questions — only dumb answers.

Facing Up to Your Fears

LET's admit it: many people's personal finances are a mess. They don't keep records, their savings are scattered and not earning nearly as much as they could and their family budget is all bull and a yard wide. But you *can* get your personal finances together.

Your greatest obstacle is fear. Yet when people recognize their fears of finance, they often choose to confront and conquer them. Fortunately, the three most common fiscal fears are easy to identify. They are fear of responsibility, fear of risk and fear, believe it or not, of wealth.

Victims of fiscal irresponsibility are plagued by inaction. What they really yearn for is someone who will make their financial decisions for them. So, often they unquestioningly invest in what some broker or banker — or even some fairly successful friend — advises them to invest in. And often they get stung.

Then there is fear of risk. Victims are afraid to do anything with their assets for fear of doing the wrong thing. So they keep their money in low-yielding passbook savings accounts when they could easily earn much more interest by transferring at least some of it to higher-paying money-market funds or U.S. Treasury securities or federally insured bank certificates of deposit or bank money-market deposit accounts.

As for fear of wealth, people sometimes feel undeserving of increased incomes or substantial inheritances. If they have investments, they're afraid to change them even when a security plummets. They feel guilty about earning more than their parents did. Their guilt translates into immobility.

Facing up to your fears about money and then taking steps to act and put your finances in order is one way to sleep free of worry or guilt. And, in a world where so much seems to be sliding out of control, it's reassuring to know that, if you're willing to make the effort, it's still possible for you to determine your own financial destiny.

Calculating Your Net Worth

THE first step toward taking control of your personal financial life is to calculate your net worth. That is what you own minus what you owe. Once you figure out what you are worth, you can set your goals — for example, to take a vacation, buy a house or secure a comfortable retirement. Then you can devise strategies to reach those goals.

Your net worth is your financial mirror image — what you look like on a given day. Anyone with a simple pocket calculator can figure net worth. Add up the current value of all your assets. Start with your checking and savings accounts and money-market funds. Don't forget the current market value of any stocks, bonds or other securities you may own. Your insurance agent can supply the current cash value of your life insurance if it is not in the policy. To find out what your house or condo is worth, consult a real estate broker or note the asking prices of similar homes for sale in your neighborhood.

When adding up, do not overlook the current worth of your employee benefits, such as profit-sharing and thrift programs and unexercised stock options. Often these assets are second in value only to your house.

If you own some art, antiques, jewelry or other collectibles, you may need to call in an appraiser to give a good estimate of their current resale price. No matter what kind of collectible you have, you can expect to pay an appraiser an hourly fee of $100 to $300. If you do not have many collectibles, you do not need an appraiser. Just ask a knowing dealer what he thinks you could sell them for. But remember: Your possessions are worth what you could get if you had to sell them immediately — not what it costs to replace them.

You should recalculate your net worth at least once a year. Some debt counselors urge their clients to take their financial reading immediately before they start Christmas shopping. But if you have never drawn up a personal balance sheet or yours is as old as a 6% fixed-rate mortgage, the best time to start is now. You might discover that you are better off than you thought.

Making — and Sticking to — a Budget

ONE of the surest moves to financial security is to create — and stick to — a budget. You need this all-important personal balance sheet whether you are a student whose money runs out long before the month does or an executive with a comfortable income. A budget will quickly tell you whether you are spending too much and how you can save. Having a real budget — not one that you pretend to keep in your head — allows you to sleep at night without agonizing over how you are going to keep up with ordinary expenses and pay for the unexpected.

If you do not have a budget, start one now. In just three months' time you can win the battle of the budget. If you devote only a few hours during each of those months to considering and correcting your income and outgo, you can reduce overspending, free up money for savings and investments and build a cash reserve for that sudden urge — or need — to splurge.

During the first month, figure out precisely what you earn and what you spend. Add up your salary and any other money you receive, such as dividends, interest, allowances or child support. Then examine how you spend your money. You do not have to exhume all records dating back for years. It is more than enough to analyze your expenses — and your income — for, say, the last 12 months. This will enable you to calculate routine monthly expenses as well as sums that you must pay at irregular intervals, such as insurance premiums, school tuition and gifts. One purpose of your analysis is to help you plan for these irregular but necessary expenses so that you will never again have to invade your investments to pay for unexpected bills.

You may find that you just cannot account for a large share of your spending. To get a handle on that, try to keep a journal and jot down all expenses as they hit you, day by day, for a week.

Devote the second month of your budget program to figuring out how you can trim any excesses in your spending so that you can build savings and investments. Calculate what percentage of your total income goes to each expenditure, from clothing to commuting costs to mortgage payments or rent.

Some financial advisers recommend that you allocate no more than

65% of your take-home pay for fixed monthly expenses, including food, utilities and rent or mortgage payments. Allow another 20% for such variable outlays as household repairs, recreation and clothing. Put aside 10% for necessary expenses that hit at different intervals, such as insurance premiums and property taxes, and the last 5% — or more, if possible — for savings.

Take a close look at your monthly installment debt. You are in good shape if 10% or less of your after-tax income is spent on car payments, department-store and credit-card charges or bills for furniture and appliances that you bought on time. If the figure is 10% to 15%, you are creeping toward the danger zone. If those expenses stretch beyond 15% to 20% of your income, you are losing the battle of the budget.

To correct that, allocate a set amount of money each month for debt repayments. Pay as much as you possibly can afford. Figure out what indulgences and luxuries you can sacrifice — temporarily. It may be sensible even to raid your savings to pay your debt. You will never get rich keeping cash in a passbook account paying only 5½% while your credit-card or other installment debts cost you more than twice that amount.

Particularly if you have a checking account that pays interest, you may be tempted to wait till the last minute to pay your ordinary bills. After all, the longer you delay, the more interest you earn. But be careful! If you cut it too close, you could end up paying finance charges on your installment debts. They probably would cost you far more than the interest you would earn on your checking account. Interest-bearing checking accounts pay 5.5% annual interest or less, but credit-card charges typically are 18.3% annually.

How can you make sure your bill payments will be on time? Keep this in mind: It is the day of *receipt* that counts, not the postmark. Federal law requires creditors to mail bills to you at least 14 days before you are supposed to pay them. But companies have to rely on the Postal Service to deliver them on time. And then you have to allow enough time for your payment to arrive by the due date. Postal delays do not entitle you to an extension.

In the third month of your budget-making schedule, carefully re-evaluate your income-and-outgo statement and make any changes so that you can live on your budget. Do not get carried away. Everybody needs some luxuries, so you and each person in your family should be allowed to keep at least one indulgence. If you are passionate about movies and want to see three or four films a week, then adjust your spending in some other area. Successful budgeting depends on being neither too rigid nor too loose. If your budget is too lean, you will not stick to it. Your purpose is to make a budget that you can keep.

Once you have created a workable budget and conquered your debt problems, you should start saving a fixed amount each month. Deposit that sum in a money-market fund, a bank money-market deposit account, short-term bank certificates of deposit, U.S. Treasury bills or other liquid savings. Put that cash away as regularly and as faithfully as you meet your mortgage payments or rent. Aim to build up savings that eventually will amount to three months of your after-tax income.

One of the surest and simplest ways to save is to have a regular amount automatically deducted from each paycheck. If your employer offers a company savings or investment plan, grab it. Happily, the interest, dividends and capital gains on such accounts are tax-sheltered: you pay no taxes on the growth of your money until you withdraw it, probably many years from now. And it is remarkable how fast your money will grow if it is tax-sheltered. Also, you frequently can arrange for a fixed amount of each paycheck to be deposited in a bank savings account, a money-market fund or a credit union. To find out how you can best accomplish that, just ask an official of your payroll department or the financial institution where you want your money deposited.

Another way to save is to bank each pay raise until the next one comes along. Or sock away any minor windfalls, such as bonuses, gifts, tax refunds, profits from your investments or free-lance fees.

Sticking to a budget requires work. Primarily, you will have to continue keeping sound records. You can do that by paying for all items over $10 with checks and letting them serve as your expense ledger. Put an asterisk on a corner of each check that you later might charge off as a tax deduction.

You also will have to keep working to hold your spending in line. Figure out what are your biggest expenditures, and how to restrain them. Probably most formidable are your income taxes. You may be able to cut them by setting up an IRA — plus a Keogh plan if you have some self-employment or moonlighting income — and by switching from some taxable investments to tax-free ones, such as municipal bonds. Make certain that you are using all legitimate deductions, notably those in the Introduction and under the heading of "Your Taxes: How to Cut Your Taxes."

Your second major expense is housing. It varies greatly, depending on where you live. If you buy a house in or around New York City, for example, you probably will pay at least 125% more than you would for a house in Phoenix. Wherever you reside, if you bought your house or condo in the early 1980s — when mortgage rates soared to historic peaks — you may be spending as much as 40% of your take-home pay on the loan. That is clearly too much. Now that rates are lower, check with a banker or some other housing lender to see if it makes sense to renegotiate your loan. Usually it does if you do not plan to sell your property soon and can get a mortgage with rates three percentage points below the one you now have. Anything less than that probably would not cover your closing costs and penalties for a new loan. But with a favorable new mortgage, you may be able to reduce your monthly expenses by more than $100.

A third budget-breaker is your car loan. If the total size of your loan is more than 15% of your annual net income, it might be time to trade down to a less expensive model — or scrap the second car.

The Charms of
Asset Management Accounts

To PULL your personal finances together and make the most of what you have, you can get considerable aid from a relatively new service offered by brokers, bankers and mutual funds: an asset management account. It is a combination money-market and brokerage account that usually lets you earn high interest on your spare cash, buy and sell securities, borrow more money than you otherwise could and write an unlimited number of checks at no extra charge. You also get a single monthly statement listing all your financial transactions, and that can be a convenience.

So what's the catch? You generally need cash or securities worth $10,000 or more to get into the tent. And you have to pay an annual fee, which can range from $25 to $120.

If you think convenience is worth the price, your first decision is to choose where you want your asset management account to be. A banker and a broker are equally safe: they offer plenty of insurance for your assets.

If you are primarily interested in investing in stocks and you see the account as a way to simplify your investing paperwork, you should find an excellent broker. But if you are not an active investor and want mainly to organize savings and checking transactions, you may be better off with a bank.

Look carefully at the standard features these accounts offer. One of their greatest charms is the so-called sweep. It automatically reinvests dividends and bond income, typically in a money-market fund. So your cash earns interest from the day you get it until the day you spend it. Find out whether the sweep is done daily or weekly, and whether it includes all your cash or just the amount above a certain minimum.

Asset accounts let you write checks against your money-market deposits. Checking typically is free, and you can write as many drafts as you wish with no minimum checking amount. The big issue here is whether or not you will get your canceled checks at the end of the month. Banks generally return asset-account checks, but most brokers simply note the payee, amount and date on your monthly statement.

Usually asset accounts offer a free Visa, MasterCard or American Express card. But find out whether it works more like a credit card, which sends you a monthly bill and lets you pay after some delay, or a debit card, which has the disadvantage of immediately deducting your charges from the cash in your account. Many asset management accounts come with debit cards.

You can borrow against your cash and securities in an asset management account. Shop around to see where you can get loans with the lowest interest rate. Often that is from a broker. With a brokerage asset management account, you can borrow as much as half the value of your stocks at the so-called margin rate, which is usually much lower than consumer loan rates charged by banks. And the larger the brokerage loan, the lower the rate.

When picking an asset management account, also study the kind of brokerage service you can expect. An asset account with a bank or a mutual fund gives you access to discount brokerage service, with commissions as much as 90% lower than the fees charged by full-line brokers. But traditional brokers will give you something for their extra charge: investment advice.

Take a close look at the monthly financial statement you will get with your asset management account. Some are jumbles. Make sure you can understand the statement.

Also find out exactly who will service your account. Many banks promise that if you open an asset management account with them, you will be assigned a personal banker. With a brokerage asset account, you will be assigned an account executive to handle securities trading. But he or she most likely will be underjoyed when you call about a lost check or a statement error, since an account executive doesn't earn commissions by solving such problems.

In sum, a bank may offer you better personal service and lower brokerage commissions, but a broker may offer you lower interest rates on loans and more investment advice.

Where to Get Help

DOES the thought of organizing your personal financial affairs still overwhelm you? Take heart. You need not — indeed, should not — do it all by yourself.

Help in getting your finances together ranges from books that can motivate and educate you to professional financial planners who can compile voluminous studies of your economic life. Or you can enroll in courses, attend public seminars and ask the advice of a stockbroker, an insurance agent, attorney, accountant or banker.

There is no reason why you cannot at least decode the basic ciphers of money management in a few weekends of dedicated reading. Among the best books are *The Money Book of Money* by Robert Klein and the Editors of *Money, The Power of Money Dynamics* by Venita VanCaspel and *The Money Encyclopedia,* edited by Harvey Rachlin. *The Lifetime Book of Money Management* by Grace Weinstein explains clearly and in great detail how to develop and carry out a long-term financial planning strategy.

For tax planning, it is hard to beat *Julian Block's Guide to Year-Round Tax Savings,* which uses actual IRS case studies to explain the tax laws — without jargon. Another sound choice is *Miller's Personal Income Tax Guide,* which has work-sheets to lead you step by step through IRS forms.

Finding a useful guide to investments is harder, because there are so many bad ones around. Your top choice for a broad-ranging work is *The Complete Guide to Investment Opportunities* by Marshall Blume and

Jack Friedman. Each of the book's 58 chapters is written by a specialist in a particular type of investment, be it Art Nouveau furniture or Treasury notes. Two outstanding guides to Wall Street are Louis Engel and Brendan Boyd's *How to Buy Stocks* and Charles Rolo's *Gaining on the Market.* The latter explains in layman's terms the strategies of professional investors. If you plan to buy a house or invest in property, *The Real Estate Book* by Robert L. Nessen will tell you just about everything you need to know.

Courses on personal finance are offered by more and more colleges, universities, community service organizations and other sponsors of adult education programs. The charge is often as little as $75 or less, or even free for senior citizens. The chance you take is that your teacher is merely a salesperson in the guise of an educator, so check his or her credentials closely. Avoid instructors whose expertise is limited to selling stocks, bonds, insurance or other so-called investment products.

If you want extensive personalized advice about investing, budgeting and pulling your finances together, you should hire a professional financial planner. People who have trouble getting started discover that the help of a financial planner — even just at the beginning — can make the difference between success and failure. You can get names of recommended planners from bankers, accountants and stockbrokers.

Financial planners sometimes offer public seminars to expand their market. These meetings usually are advertised in local newspapers, and they can be worthwhile. Often the planners charge nothing for the first hour or two of consultation, then $75 to $200 for each additional hour.

Finally, you can get an inexpensive education by enrolling in one of the thousands of investment clubs. (See "Your Investments: Starting an Investment Club.")

What a Financial Planner Can Do for You

IF YOUR only financial plan is to stay one jump ahead of the bill collector, and you hardly have time to balance your checkbook, you may need help from a planner. This professional sells everything from general advice on your taxes, budgeting, retirement and estate planning to specific investments, such as mutual funds, life insurance and real estate, energy and other tax shelters. Most planners work independently in a solo or group practice. Others are on the staffs of brokerage houses, banks, insurance companies and mutual funds.

The majority charge an initial fee to devise a written comprehensive plan diagnosing your financial ailments and prescribing monetary medications to achieve financial health. The plan generally will cost from $2,000 all the way up to $10,000, depending on three factors: your net worth or income; the planner's reputation; and whether the planner also charges a commission on any investments you buy from him or her. After you get the plan, you and your planner should review your finances at least once a year. This will cost you 30% to 50% of your original bill. However much you pay a planner, the cost is relatively modest compared with the potential long-term rewards — and risks — of following his or her recommendations.

What can you reasonably expect from a financial planner? For starters, he or she should be able to calculate your net worth and devise a workable budget to help you meet your goals. After that, a planner should coordinate the specialized help you will need from such other professionals as a securities broker, accountant, insurance agent and lawyer. But do not expect a planner to take responsibility for running your everyday finances. That is still your job.

A planner will advise you to direct your investments into broad areas. For example, he or she may suggest that you should put half of your capital into stocks or stock mutual funds, one quarter into tax-sheltered investments and one quarter into safe and predictable savings certificates. But because most financial planners are not stockbrokers or securities analysts, they tend to shy away from recommending individual stocks. Instead, they suggest mutual funds and limited partnerships that are professionally managed.

A planner suggests what you should do, but first he or she has to ask you several questions. How much risk are you willing to take? How important to you is it to reduce your taxes? How do you feel about borrowing to invest? As you answer, you often begin to realize that your attitudes toward money may not square with the way you actually spend and invest it.

Once the planner has a fix on your goals and how you want to reach them, he or she begins to make recommendations. For example, the planner will examine your insurance policies and your mutual funds to determine whether you have the right kind and enough of them. At that point, you are free to head for your nearest insurance agent or mutual-fund dealer to do your buying. Or you can allow the planner to sell you the financial "products" he or she thinks you need. On such sales, the planner collects commissions of 1% to 10%, and sometimes more.

Your planner is likely to turn next to your taxes. If you decide you really want a tax shelter, there is no reason not to buy it from the planner. But make sure that the shelter has economic as well as tax benefits, and that the planner has first explored other ways of reducing your taxes. Always ask what the chances are that you will be audited if you buy into the shelter that has been recommended. Find out whether the IRS has audited earlier tax deals that were offered by the sponsors of the shelter that the planner is now recommending. If audits have occurred, how often have investors been slapped with back taxes and penalties?

How to Find a Good Financial Planner

THERE are no licensing requirements or laws to protect the consumer, so anyone can hang out a shingle and call himself a financial planner regardless of education, experience or ethics. Even planners admit that too many who claim the title are incompetent or worse. But first-rate financial planners are increasingly available — if you know how to identify them. You can find some by asking for recommendations from an accountant or lawyer, by attending the free seminars that planners often hold to recruit clients, and by requesting names from the institutes that train planners.

You are probably best off with a planner who also has experience as a lawyer, an accountant or a licensed insurance, securities or real estate salesperson. Such credentials show that the planner has specialized training and can be made to answer to some body of regulators. The initials CLU after the planner's name stand for Chartered Life Underwriter and mean that he or she is expert in life insurance. The CPA pedigree — for Certified Public

Accountant, of course — suggests considerable knowledge about tax planning.

Good practitioners also usually have credentials as Certified Financial Planners from the International Board of Standards and Practices for Certified Financial Planners. Most CFPs graduate from the College for Financial Planning (9725 East Hampden Avenue, Suite 200, Denver, Colorado 80231-4993). People who have completed its study program and passed its series of examinations on taxes, estate planning, investments and other subjects have the initials CFP after their names. Two hundred and fifty thousand people purport to be financial planners, but some 19,000 are registered CFPs. Another respected certification is that of Chartered Financial Consultant (ChFC), awarded by the American College (270 Bryn Mawr Avenue, Bryn Mawr, Pennsylvania 19010). Cross off any candidates who have not bothered to get at least this much training. Be sure to check the planner's credentials with the organization that issued them. Pretending to be a Certified Financial Planner is considerably easier than pretending to be a lawyer or CPA.

The International Association for Financial Planning has compiled a rather elite registry of some 1,000 financial planners. Among the requirements for admission are a degree in a field related to planning, at least three years' experience as a planner and a passing grade on a tough, all-day test. Once admitted to the registry, planners must put in 30 hours of continuing education each year to retain their membership. To find out whether any of the registry's members work in your area, write to the International Association for Financial Planning (Two Concourse Parkway, Suite 800, Atlanta, Georgia 30328) for *The Directory of Registry Financial Planners* and enclose $2.50 for handling and postage.

You should assemble a short list of prospects, and be sure to interview each one. Any reputable planner should talk to you for at least an hour free of charge. Ask for samples of plans he has prepared, and the names of clients you can call.

If a plan is all that you want, there is a flourishing and inexpensive plans-by-mail industry. You fill out a questionnaire and back comes a computer-generated report with some recommendations. For generic advice but not specific investment recommendations, the Consumer Financial Institute (51 Sawyer Road, Waltham, Massachusetts 02154) charges $300. Major brokerage houses and some large banks and insurance companies also offer these canned plans, for free or as much as $250.

Questions to Ask Your Financial Planner

BEFORE you hire a planner, ask some tough questions. That's the best way to separate the crack advisers from the quack advisers.

Be sure to ask how the planner earns his or her money. As mentioned, many planners charge fees of $75 to $200 an hour. Others give free advice but earn commissions by selling you mutual funds, tax shelters, insurance or other financial products. The advantage of hiring a fee-only planner is that you know he or she will not recommend an investment to you just to collect a commission. But fee-only planners are costlier than those who accept commissions. Most planners combine fees and commissions.

Always ask how much money a planner makes on everything he or she tries to sell to you. If you know that someone stands to pocket a 10% commission on one investment and only 3% on a less expensive alternative, you will have reason to ask why you are being steered toward the costlier one. The commissions are usually the highest on life insurance and tax shelters.

Most consumer complaints about planners involve those who earn their keep solely by commissions, especially those who peddle just one line of goods. The biggest beef is against salespeople who call themselves financial planners to disguise their true calling. This is especially true of unscrupulous purveyors of tax shelters. Promising extravagant write-offs, they often underemphasize the risks you take. A reliable planner will offer you a choice of shelters as well as other investments and specific advice, such as ways that you may defer compensation or shift income to your children in order to legitimately reduce taxes. The planner who claims he can cut your taxes without risking an audit has to offer you more than a "once in a lifetime" chance to invest in a worm farm for an eight-to-one write-off.

Financial planners are notoriously partial to selling you insurance because many of them earn enticing commissions on policies. If your planner recommends that you buy whole life insurance, ask why you should not purchase a much less expensive term policy. The money that you save on it you then can invest in annuities or municipal bond funds. They provide high yields *and* tax advantages.

A conscientious planner should channel your assets into a variety of investments so that your returns will be stable despite market or interest rate fluctuations. Ask your planner to draw up a pie chart of his recommendations. If one type of investment swallows more than a quarter of your pie, request an explanation.

Ask the planner how much wealth you can reasonably accumulate in five years. Most investors do well if their returns consistently outpace inflation by 4% or 5% a year. If your planner claims to be able to top those rates, he or she may be misleading you or steering you into high-risk ventures.

If you are within 10 years of retirement, ask your planner to estimate how much money you will need to meet your retirement goals. He or she will estimate how much you can expect from Social Security, company pension and savings plans and your own investments. With this information in hand, your planner should tell you whether you will need to save more or work longer to meet your objectives. He or she should also suggest a schedule for gradually shifting your investment priorities to increase your monthly income.

Ask how much time the planner will spend with you, and who will write your plan. In large firms, your case may be consigned to junior staffers, and you may not get the experience you want. Expect a planner to spend three or four hours with you, gathering facts and discussing ideas. Take time to consider the planner's recommendations before you buy any financial products. And do not feel you have to buy anything. What you need may well be insights instead of new investments.

The final clue to a financial planner's caliber is commitment. Your planner should be ready to work over the long term with other professionals you may hire, such as a lawyer or tax accountant. No one person can master all of the technical information that goes into preparing a well-designed financial plan. Have your planner arrange for you and all your advisers to sit down together at least once. That way everyone will know what everyone else is supposed to do.

The Separate Role of the Investment Adviser

SOME people, particularly active investors, find it worthwhile to hire not only a financial planner but also an investment adviser. This is the professional who recommends specific stocks and sometimes bonds in which to put your money. The investment adviser thus differs from the financial planner, who gives you broad advice on your taxes, investments and insurance but usually does not recommend specific stocks.

Until recently, investment advisers wouldn't even look at you unless you had investments worth $100,000 or more. But competition has forced many to accept much smaller accounts, sometimes $10,000. Fees on the smallest accounts typically are about 2% of the assets being managed. On larger accounts, they vary from ½% to 1%. No longer are these fees fully tax-deductible. You can deduct them and your other miscellaneous expenses only to the extent that they exceed 2% of your adjusted gross income.

To find an investment adviser, start by asking for recommendations from your lawyer, accountant or stockbroker. If you are one of the fortunate few who have $1 million or more to invest, you also can write to the Investment Counsel Association of America, 20 Exchange Place, New York, New York 10005. That is a professional organization of advisory firms, and it will mail you a free list of its members.

To determine whether or not any adviser is up to managing your assets, check his or her record. Ask for figures going back at least 10 years, so you can determine how the adviser performed during falling markets as well as rising markets. He or she should have done at least as well as the Dow Jones Industrial Average and the Standard & Poor's 500 stock index.

It is crucial to find out what an adviser's investment philosophy is before you hire one. Advisers follow one of several strategies. Some aim for high growth, others for safety. Still others are the so-called contrarians. They look at which stocks are in fashion and then assume that they are overpriced. The contrarians avoid those stocks and steer you into more neglected issues that are often undervalued.

If you hire an adviser, you generally will have to sign a contract giving him or her discretion over your account. The adviser then will be free to buy and sell securities without further authorization from you. If this makes you uncomfortable, perhaps you should not have an adviser.

Once you have contracted with an adviser, be patient. In general, wait at least a year before you judge the record — but sometimes less than that. If the value of your holdings drops 20% from the high of the previous quarter, and the adviser fails to take remedial action, it may well be time to fire him.

Windfalls: Handling Unexpected Wealth

M ANY people joke about it, some even cry over it, but, in fact, the odds are improving that one day you will receive a windfall. Twenty-nine states now have lotteries, and the jackpots are huge. Most sudden money comes less spectacularly, from estates and court settlements; this year alone *millions* of Americans will inherit some wealth. If you are one of them, you face a nice problem: What do you do with your fresh fortune?

Unless you already have considerable money and know how to manage it, sudden wealth will require a new financial strategy. Your goal should be to preserve that hefty capital and make it work for you. Taking large risks with your riches is not only unnecessary but also unwise.

When that first check arrives, stash the cash for six months or so in a money-market fund, a Treasury bill or some other short-term investment. There it will remain, liquid and safe, while you sort out your options.

A primary priority is minimizing taxes on your treasure. All windfalls are taxable as ordinary income. To reduce Uncle Sam's take, set up an Individual Retirement Account if you are eligible to deduct the contribution from your taxable income each year. If you are self-employed, also start a Keogh account to defer taxes on up to $30,000 a year. All your contributions to a Keogh are deductible.

If you have minor children, transfer at least part of your inheritance to them. Just go to a bank or brokerage house and open accounts in each of their names, under the Uniform Gifts to Minors Act. Each child under age 14 can earn $1,000 a year in interest, dividends and other investment income and pay taxes on it at his or her low rate. Income above $1,000 will be taxed at the parents' rate. Children aged 14 and older pay taxes at their own rate on all their unearned income.

When investing your hoard, the main rule is to diversify, so that you do not blow the whole wad on a single mistake. Consider a mix of a no-load mutual fund, Treasury securities and municipal bonds or unit trusts. Such trusts are sold by brokers, and they invest in a variety of municipal bonds. In mid-1988 they were yielding about

8% interest — and you do not pay federal income taxes on that income.

Seek professional help. You probably will need an accountant for tax advice and a financial planner to devise a strategy for conserving your money and making it grow.

Many of the suddenly rich feel uneasy, not to say guilty, about their new wealth. Others make the mistake of quitting their jobs in euphoria, and some suffer by altering their life-styles, changing too much about their lives too soon. A windfall can catapult you from one economic position to another, but attitudes, values and behavior change more slowly. So ease into your enviable new status gradually.

Your Investments

How to Start Investing and Do It Right

M ANY people who have not done it before are wondering how to start investing — and do it right. If you are in that position, you need an investment strategy.

Start by analyzing yourself. Define your financial goals and how you plan to reach them. Is your goal to pay for college or for a house or for a comfortable retirement — and just how much money will you need to achieve that objective?

Before you invest in anything that has the slightest risk, be sure you have enough insurance and savings to protect yourself against an emergency. It is smart to hold savings equal to three months of your after-tax income. Do not worry if it takes you two or three years to accumulate that amount.

It is also important to assess your tolerance for risk. If your fear of losing money is stronger than your desire to make large profits, stick with a conservative investment philosophy. Conservatives invest for safe and steady returns of income. More adventurous types invest for future growth.

People younger than 50 years old probably should not be too conservative. One top adviser recommends that they put no more than 20% of their spare cash into investments that promise steady income returns from dividends and interest. He says that 80% or more of their investment should be aimed at growth.

If you are over 50, however, you will probably want to put a large share of your spare cash into income-producing assets. If you want steady income payments plus the possibility of growth, consider Treasury and top-grade corporate bonds. You can get instant diversification by investing in a bond mutual fund or unit trust.

Whether you buy bonds or stocks, do not get too caught up in the race for quick profits. Most investors do best by picking several stocks as a way of cushioning the loss of one flier that takes a dive. And be prepared to live with the rule of five. It says that out of every five stocks you own, probably one will be a loser, three will do nicely and one will do much better than you expected.

Stocks and bonds are, of course, your basic tools of investing. Before you invest, you should determine just what you want your tools to accomplish and which ones to use to reach your goals.

When you buy common stocks, you become part owner of a corporation. A stock can increase your wealth in two ways: by paying you regular dividends and by rising in price. If it does indeed rise, you can sell out at a profit. It is this growth, not the dividends, that gives stocks their investment edge. Over the long term, since 1926, the 500 stocks in the Standard & Poor's index have produced an average return — from price appreciation plus dividends — of 9.9% a year. That is double the average 5% annual return that investors got from corporate bonds.

You can choose from different types of stocks depending on your investment goals. Growth stocks are shares in companies that often expand faster than the overall economy. In rising markets, the stocks of young and growing companies tend to do at least one-third better than the broad stock indexes. But when the market falls, they are also likely to plunge faster.

Income stocks place an emphasis on dividends, so their prices are more stable. In a prolonged market rise, income stocks do not climb as fast as growth stocks. Utility shares are a foremost example. In the 12 months after the bull market began in August 1982, the Dow Jones Utility Average rose 24%, which was less than half the gain of the Dow Jones Industrial Average. But top-rated utilities pay high dividends — 6% to 8% in 1988.

Most investment advisers believe the stock market should do well over the long term. But if you are unsure of how to start an investment program that will take advantage of a favorable future, you should consider buying shares in a mutual fund. Funds offer just what beginning investors need: professional management and instant diversification. You can get in with an investment of $1,000 or less. Once you own shares in a fund, you typically can add as little as $25 at a time. You can find the addresses and phone numbers — often toll-free 800 numbers — of various funds in advertisements on the business pages of newspapers and also in financial magazines.

What if you want to start investing, but you have only a small stake, say $100? Will any brokerage houses or mutual funds welcome your business?

Yes indeed, *many* will. At least 150 mutual funds will accept an initial investment of $100 or less — and in some cases there is no minimum at all. For a description of more than 1,650 funds, look in your public library for a book called *Wiesenberger Investment Companies Service.*

As for stockbrokers, many have such large minimum commissions — at least $30 every time that you buy or sell — that it does not make sense to start an account with just $100. But as an alternative, you can try Merrill Lynch's so-called Blueprint Program. It charges 10% on trades up to $200. After that, commissions decrease on a sliding scale. Trades exceeding $7,500 are charged at Merrill's regular rates.

If you find it hard to set aside money regularly, try this: have a mutual fund automatically deduct a set amount from your checking account every month. Many employers also let you have a specific amount taken out of your paycheck and invested in a company-sponsored profit-sharing or thrift plan. Such programs usually let you choose from at least two types of funds. You can put your contribution in a stock mutual fund or a fixed-income bond-and-savings fund.

The drawbacks are that your money is likely to be conservatively managed, and you may have some trouble if you want to withdraw the whole amount before you leave the company. But that is balanced by the nice fact that all the earnings on your money compound tax-free, until you withdraw it when you leave the company.

Some employers will match part of your contribution. This gives you an immediate profit. If that is the case, be sure to accept this company offer — and save or invest as much as you possibly can.

After you have built up some mutual-fund shares, you may get the itch to start picking stocks on your own. You will have an advantage over major financial institutional investors, those who tend to buy conservatively for bank trust departments, corporate investment plans and pension programs. The institutions' investment managers generally stick to the shares of 500 or so fairly substantial companies, but you can choose from more than 6,000 stocks. It is easier for small investors to buy shares in young, unproven, fast-growing firms. If the business becomes large enough to attract big investors, the stock's price — and your profits — may jump dramatically.

Anyone with more than $2,000 to invest in stocks should put it in two or more companies. You will want to diversify among industries too. That will help protect you. If, for example, mortgage rates rise and you own nothing but housing stocks, you could be pummeled.

Ultimately, you should aim to own five or more stocks. That is a small enough number to be manageable and large enough for diversity. When you reach that point — and you want to strike a balance somewhere between the young, daring investor and the older, conservative investor mentioned earlier — you may want to aim for the following division of your money:

A quarter of your stock portfolio should consist of small and promising companies producing goods and services that are unique or stand to be in strong demand even in periods of recession. Another quarter should be invested in the largest, most conservative companies; they can offer stable growth. The remaining half should be in medium-size concerns that are growing faster than the economy as a whole. Among the current growth fields are telecommunications and capital goods.

You will have to do your homework. Before buying a stock, look up its record in *The Value Line Investment Survey* or *Standard & Poor's Corporation Records* or *Moody's* manuals, available in many public libraries. You also can ask a broker to send you a copy of the company's annual report and the even more detailed 10-K statement that must be filed every year with the Securities and Exchange Commission.

Finally, deciding when to sell your shares is as important as choosing when and what to buy. Do not rush to dump a long-term growth stock just because it hits a temporary sinking spell. In fact, that is when smart investors consider buying even more shares — at bargain prices.

In sum, here are three sensible rules for investors, beginners and veterans alike:

First, put aside a fixed amount of money each week or each month, no matter how small. Then save or invest it regularly, come rain, come shine. When markets fall, you can figure you are at a bargain sale because you will be able to buy more shares for your money. And when markets rise, you can congratulate yourself, because your investments will rise too.

Second, diversify. No longer can you buy just one stock or bond and confidently hold it for a lifetime. The world changes too fast for that. So, even if your investments are modest, spread out to several kinds of stocks — or into a widely diversified mutual fund.

Third, do not wait to buy in at the very bottom of the market and do not try to sell out at the very top. Nobody — but nobody — is smart enough to do that. Remember: Bulls make money and bears make money, but hogs never make money.

The Prospects for 1989

WHERE, more specifically, should you put your savings and investment money in 1989? There is uncertainty about what Congress may do about the federal budget deficit. But a positive element is that inflation stands to remain reasonable. Most of the major causes of the 1970s inflation — the leaping price rises for fuel, other raw materials, services and labor — are either heading down or increasing at a slower rate than before.

Thus, you might be wise to shape your savings and investment strategy for the immediate future around the expectation that relative price stability will continue. So long as the inflation rate stays at about 6% or below, you would be wise to avoid investing much in the traditional hard assets that in the past profited from scary inflation — among them gold, silver, collectibles and commodities. Similarly, times of only moderate inflation figure to be lean times for the common stocks of the producers of commodities.

But moderate inflation tends to lift many other stocks. It allows the Federal Reserve Board to continue making credit fairly easy and to hold interest rates fairly stable. Stable rates help almost all stocks and notably those of companies that are borrowers, such as utilities.

Relatively modest inflation also means that the *quality* of corporate profits is higher than before. The reason is that the purchasing power of the dollar is stronger than during inflationary times. With their profits, companies can buy more in the way of new plants, equipment and raw materials. Consequently, when the quality of profits rises, the prices of company stocks should rise.

Money magazine asked leading stockbrokers and financial planners to recommend the best ways to invest $10,000.

For a working couple in their mid-20s, much depends on whether you own your own home. If you don't, most advisers suggest applying your money toward the down payment on a house or condominium. Real estate values are not expected to rise as fast as in the past, but they should keep pace with inflation. And switching from rent to house payments will remain a good deal, since you get tax deductions for your mortgage interest payments and property taxes.

Many dual-income couples should put $4,000 every year into his-and-her Individual Retirement Accounts, even if not all of it is deductible. A sensible buy for your IRA or any other investment might be a fairly aggressive stock mutual fund. To cite just one example, the Twentieth Century Select fund, headquartered in Kansas City, has gained an average 21.9% a year over the last 10 years.

Couples with fairly young children should aim to build up a major sum for college tuition. Tax reform has made saving for your child's education more difficult. But if you plan wisely, you can still find ways to limit taxes and increase your college fund. One way is to transfer wealth to the tot in the form of tax-exempt securities, stocks in fast-growing companies, life insurance, or Series EE U.S. Savings Bonds with maturities after your child's 14th birthday. Once he or she turns 14, all earnings on the taxable assets will be taxed at your child's lower rate.

Couples in their 50s should aim to enlarge their retirement nest egg without increasing their tax bill. One solution is to buy tax-exempt municipal bonds that will mature about the time you plan to retire. In mid-1988, 10-year munis were yielding about 7% to 7½%.

Retired couples should invest conservatively for income. They might consider bank-issued certificates of deposit sold through stockbrokers. Such CDs in mid-1988 yielded about 8.6% when held for five years.

Strategies to Meet Your Own Goals

INVESTING is as much an art as a science. That's especially so if you are trying to pick the right mix to pay you a rather large sum at a time that is far off. Many forecasters with eminent records predict relatively low inflation and slow, stable growth between now and the year 2000. That would provide a climate in which stocks and bonds should do well.

If you are a conservative investor looking for a place to put money you may need some years from now, you might divide your cash into four equal parts and then apportion it this way: put one-quarter of it in 10-year Treasury bonds; another quarter in 15-year corporate bonds rated AA or better; still another quarter in mutual funds that buy stocks; and one-quarter in real estate and precious metals.

A word on the often-overlooked virtues of bonds: If long-term interest rates drop, the prices of your bonds will rise. You then could sell them for a tidy profit. If rates climb, bond prices will decline; if you hold your bonds until they mature, you will collect every penny you paid for them. But be aware that you will get less than you paid if you have to sell before the maturity date at a time when the market value of your bond is down.

So much for a portfolio for the conservative investor. What if you are willing to accept more risk in hopes of earning more profits? Then put 50% of your investable cash in growth stocks or the mutual funds that buy them. Place another 20% of your money in long-term Treasury bonds and 20% in corporate bonds rated AA or higher. The remaining 10% of your moderate-risk portfolio might be in precious metals, which are sound hedges against inflation.

Let's say you know you will need retirement income in 15 years or so. Or you will have tuition bills to pay. Or perhaps you are looking for a sensible long-term investment for your IRA or some other tax-deferred account. What then should you buy? One investment to use as a base may well be zero-coupon U.S. Treasury bonds. You might put as much as 90% of your IRA money in them. With "zeros," you don't collect your interest payments in semiannual installments but in one big lump sum when the bond matures or comes due. (See "Your Investments/Bonds: Zero-Coupon Bonds.")

A potential problem is that you are liable for income taxes on that interest even though you do not collect it right away. So zeros belong only in a tax-deferred account such as an IRA or Keogh plan, or in the hands of a lightly taxed person such as a child.

If you want high yields outside of a tax-sheltered account, you might carve up your money this way: 40% in municipal zero-coupon bonds that are exempt from federal taxes; 50% in 10- to 15-year tax-exempt unit trusts, which you can buy from brokerage firms; and 10% in precious metals. True, gold probably will not rise in value so long as inflation remains under control. But platinum, which has done well lately, could jump further because of increased industrial demand, plus turmoil in South Africa.

What if you have already put away enough money for emergencies, your children's education and your retirement? Congratulations! Now you have a bit of excess cash you want to invest. Why not speculate?

You might start with stocks in depressed industries. Some of the most successful investors do just that, figuring that stocks in battered businesses have nowhere to go but up. For example, shares of many steel companies, which had plunged deeply, made a remarkable recovery in 1987. Some analysts now think that the earnings of long-depressed oil companies will rise in the not-distant future, and so will their stocks.

Another interesting speculation is currency futures. They allow you to bet on whether the dollar will go up or down compared with an index of foreign currencies. These contracts are traded on the Cotton Exchange in New York City, but you can buy them from most brokers. For example, if you put up a typical $2,000 for a contract, you earn $500 for every point that the dollar rises or falls against the index of foreign moneys. That is, you earn $500 if you bet right on whether the dollar will rise or fall. Of course, if you are wrong, you lose $500. And you may have to put up extra cash to meet margin calls. So to play this game, you need a strong stomach — and a fairly fat bankroll.

Investments for Different Stages of Your Life

YOU need different strategies for investing at different stages of your life. Say you are a young, single adult. Now is the time to start saving to build a cash cushion to protect yourself in case of emergency. Now is also the time to begin investing to make your money grow for the future.

If you have all your money tied up in a passbook savings account paying only 5½%, try to shift some of it into a higher-yielding certificate of deposit (CD). You can get a federally insured CD for a minimum of $500 at most banks, savings and loan associations and stock brokerage firms.

Aim to build up your insured savings until they amount to three months of your after-tax income. Once you have that security blanket, you can take some measured risks and begin investing. A sensible way is to put aside a fixed amount every month. You might invest in a growth mutual fund or a few conservative stocks.

There are many good mutual funds, of course, and you can get their names and toll-free 800 numbers in financial publications. Four funds that had average total returns of 20% or more a year over the past five years are the Merrill Lynch Pacific, Putnam OTC Emerging Growth, Vanguard High Yield and Fidelity Magellan.

If you are willing to take a bit more risk in hopes of getting more reward, consider buying shares in a real estate investment trust from a broker. These trusts invest in buildings, land and mortgages, and they are like mutual funds of real estate. Their shares trade just as stocks do and they pay dividends.

If you are married and do not have children, you have a special opportunity to build up some savings and investments. Financially, a married couple can be more than the sum of its parts. When you have only each other to look after, you have an obvious edge over singles and parents. One spouse can work steadily while the other goes for a college degree or launches a promising business. Or if both spouses hold jobs, you can try to live on the income from one and save or invest the other paycheck.

But couples do face financial problems. While you have more investment opportunities, you also confront more complex choices than ever before. Above all, avoid making devastating mistakes. The worst disasters often involve leaping into tax shelters or other high-risk investments that crash. If you want to be safe, don't put too much reliance on any one investment. Here's a list of financial dos and don'ts for married couples without children:

—Do buy life insurance and disability insurance to protect both spouses in case anything happens to one of you. But don't buy more insurance than either mate will really need; your employers may already provide enough. If you do buy, your best bet is probably term insurance.

—Do build up your savings. But don't keep money in a low-yielding passbook savings account. As mentioned above, you are better off with a money-market fund, which you can find through a mutual-fund company or a brokerage house, or with a certificate of deposit or money-market deposit account, both of which you can get at a bank or savings and loan association.

—Do put money away in savings or investment plans that your employer offers. Not only do such programs give you tax breaks, but often the employer kicks in 50 cents or so for every dollar you put in, and that's "found money."

—Do be financially nimble enough to change course suddenly when baby makes three.

Financial planning for parenthood is a bit like laying in for a long siege. As parents, you may have to stretch your budget to accommodate pediatrician bills, piano lessons and pilgrimages to summer camp. For a middle-income couple, the cost of rearing a child until the age of 18 will be over $100,000. And that estimate does not include the special parenting costs faced by two-income couples: they must choose either to pay for day care or to lose a paycheck while one parent stays at home with the child. Nor does that figure include the towering burden of college. In the 1988–1989 school year, the average total annual bill for a student at a private university is about $11,330, up 8% from last year.

When negotiating the route from diapers to diplomas, your first financial need is to establish an emergency cash reserve. Next, you can turn to your long-term goal of building capital. You might want to consider investing in a steady-performing growth mutual fund and, for diversification, in growth-oriented real estate or a high-yield income mutual fund. To stockpile money for a child's education, contribute to a bank or brokerage account in your child's name under the Uniform Gifts to Minors Act. Be aware that once you give this money, it belongs to your child. So if he or she decides to buy a car instead of a college education, you cannot demand the money back.

When your children are grown and leave home to strike out on their own, you are suddenly relieved of a great financial burden. No more bills to pay for everything from food and clothes to visits to the dentist. Your immediate temptation may be to spend all your new extra money on yourselves, on many of the things you have been waiting so many years for. Purge that urge to splurge! Instead, now is the time to put money away in a savings and investment plan. After all, you will need it soon enough for retirement.

Figure out just how much those tuition bills and other child-rearing expenses have cost you. Then aim to save and invest just about that much for at least the next several years.

It's also wise at this stage of life to re-examine whether you are taking full advantage of all your opportunities to reduce your tax bills. You will want some additional deductions because you will have fewer dependents to claim.

Perhaps you have put off opening up an Individual Retirement Account because you felt you did not have enough funds to do it while you were still supporting your children. Consider opening an IRA now. And if you are self-employed or earn some free-lance income, seriously consider also opening a Keogh plan, which allows you to shelter much more money than an IRA alone.

Reducing Your Risks

An investor, by definition, is a person who takes risks — but only sensible risks, the kind that will not endanger his or her financial health. And there are ways that you can reduce your risks in the market.

When you invest, as the late Wall Street writer Charles Rolo has observed, there are seasons for courage as well as for caution. So a strategy for all seasons must be one that decreases or increases your exposure to risk, depending on what kind of investment weather you expect. Managing risk does not mean dumping all stocks or other investments when you see storm clouds — or rushing in to buy at the glimpse of a rainbow. Controlling risk usually calls for making a few adjustments in your investments rather than for a sweeping change.

To develop a strategy for all seasons, you first must ask yourself a basic question about your investment goals: Are you more interested in seeing your investments grow in value for the long term, or in collecting immediate income from dividends and interest payments? Obviously, betting on future growth is riskier than collecting fairly well-assured dividends and interest payments.

The degree of risk that you choose to take should be determined by your age, family situation, current and prospective earning power, net worth, tax bracket — and temperament. A 30-year-old single person with bright career prospects can take larger risks than a middle-aged couple with children or retired persons living on their savings.

An aggressive investor who aims for high growth but does not demand immediate income from dividends might put all his money into high-growth, high-risk stocks. Or he could pick medium-risk growth stocks but simultaneously increase both his risks and his potential rewards by using leverage. That is, he borrows money from his broker to buy stocks on margin.

Meanwhile, a more conservative investor — one who is aiming for moderate growth combined with dependable income — might divide his investments almost equally among high-yielding blue-chip stocks, corporate or municipal bonds, and a money-market fund or bank money-market account.

When calculating how to manage risks, it pays to bear in mind that there are three kinds of investment risk:

First, the risk that is related to the overall behavior of the securities market is called, not surprisingly, *market risk*. The standard yardstick of a stock's market risk is its volatility — that is, the extent of its price fluctuations in relation to those of the Standard & Poor's 500 stock index. A stock that historically has risen or fallen more sharply than Standard & Poor's index is considered riskier than the market as a whole. To find out a stock's historic record of volatility, ask your broker to look it up in *The Value Line Investment Survey*. (For more on *The Value Line Investment Survey*, see "Your Investments: Choosing Advisory Services.") When you think it's time to be cautious, you can cut your market risk by reducing the portion of your assets that is invested in common stocks, eliminating the most volatile issues.

Second, stock prices also fluctuate because of industry and company developments. This type of risk is called *diversifiable risk* because you can reduce it if you diversify your investments. Small investors can achieve good diversification by owning only five stocks, provided they are in different industries that are exposed to different types of economic and political risk. For example, some stock groups that are not likely to behave in the same way at the same time are: airlines, banks, computers, cosmetics, energy exploration, gold mining and hospital management.

Third, investors also face what is called *interest-rate risk*. It stems from changes in interest rates and it applies primarily to bonds. But it can also affect the shares of corporations whose earnings are hurt when interest rates rise — and helped when they fall. These firms include utilities, banks, finance companies and savings and loans.

Ideally, you would buy these interest-sensitive stocks just before interest rates started to turn down — and then switch into money funds or Treasury bills just before the next uptrend begins. Calling the turns on interest rates right on target is an impossible dream, but anybody who reads the financial pages carefully should be able to get a handle on which way rates are likely to head.

Before you make any decisions about your investments, watch the relationship between short-term and long-term interest rates. The stock market always has trouble making headway when short-term rates, such as those available on Treasury bills, are higher than long-term rates, the kind offered on bonds. When short-term rates fall significantly below long ones, a bull market quite often follows in a few months.

However, if unexpected bad economic news sends the market down, then be sure to avoid companies with big debts. Look instead for stocks of large growth companies with low price/earnings ratios that are selling at low prices. Because of their low base, even a modest rise in price would mean a big percentage gain for you.

Your Safest Investments

ALMOST all investments have some risks, but don't let that stop you from investing. Sometimes the riskiest strategy of all is to do nothing. If you had just let your cash sit in an ordinary savings account in the 1970s, inflation would have drastically cut the value of your money. Smart people analyze their own situations and decide which risks they are willing to take, and which they want most to avoid.

Above all, you will want to protect your principal — that is, to make sure that you don't wind up with less cash than you start out with. One safe haven that guarantees your principal is a money-market fund or a money-market deposit account.

Finally, you will need safety against inflation. When inflation kicks up, tangible assets, such as real estate or gold, tend to rise in value. So if you put some money into them, you will be protected if hyper-inflation strikes again.

You will get the most safety by diversifying. Put your money in a variety of investments. If some of them tumble, the others may well stand up — and you won't lose everything. As a rule, place no more than 10% of your investment money into the stock of any one company. And don't sink more than 20% into stocks belonging to any one industry. That way, trouble in any single stock or industry won't derail your holdings.

Choose stocks based on their value, not on their price alone. Begin by comparing a stock's price against a measure known as its book value per share. You can find that figure in the firm's annual report, or ask a broker. Stocks that sell *below* their book value may well be bargains.

Next, check the stock's price/earnings ratio. You can find this number in the financial pages of most major newspapers. If the price/earnings ratio is below 10 to 1, and the company's earnings are rising, you may have found solid value.

Other relatively safe stock-market strategies include buying so-called convertibles. These are hybrids — part stock, part bond. They offer higher profit potential than is typical with conventional bonds. They are also less risky than common stocks. (See "Your Investments/Bonds: Convertible Securities.")

If you go looking for a mutual fund and safety is your prime concern, keep in mind performance rankings of mutual funds done by Lipper Analytical Services.

Two outstanding examples of low-risk stock funds are the Lindner Fund and Sogen International. Over the past 10 years, investors gained an average of 21.7% in Lindner Fund and 20.1% in Sogen International. Among income funds, Lipper cites Income Fund of America and Lindner Dividend. Over five years, Income Fund of America averaged an annual gain of 14.6%, and Lindner Dividend had an annual gain of 14.5%.

One way for a fund to minimize risk is to move its money between the securities markets and the money market as the economy goes through its cycles. Two funds that successfully employ this flexible approach are Strong Investment and Strong Total Return.

Another strategy is for a fund to diversify its holdings among a variety of investments, such as stocks, gold, real estate and currencies. For example, the Permanent Portfolio Fund allocates a never-changing 35% of its assets to long- and short-term Treasury securities, 20% to gold, 15% to speculative stocks, 15% to real estate and natural resource stocks, 10% to Swiss francs and 5% to silver.

You can be sure that your money will be protected if you put it in one of the money-market deposit accounts. You get them at federally insured banks or savings institutions, and most require that you keep a minimum balance of $100 to $500. All your deposits up to

$100,000 are guaranteed either by the Federal Deposit Insurance Corporation or by the Federal Savings and Loan Insurance Corporation.

If you have less than $1,000 to put away, look into one of the money-market funds. They are sponsored and sold by mutual-fund companies, and they put your money into an array of so-called money-market instruments, including Treasury and government agency issues, bank certificates and short-term corporate debt. They are not federally insured, but only one fund has failed to pay off in full in their 18-year history. Many money funds require an initial minimum investment of $500, but in most cases you need not maintain any set balance to earn the fund's full yield.

The safest short-term investments are Treasury bills. As long as you hold these federally backed issues until they mature — in either 13, 26 or 52 weeks — you will get back your entire principal, plus interest. The interest is exempt from state and local taxes. The trouble is, the price of admission is steep. You need $10,000 to buy a Treasury bill.

Buying on Margin

BROKERS are only too happy to lend you money to buy stocks and bonds if you open a so-called margin account. You have to put up only part of the securities' price and you borrow the rest from your broker.

You just sign a couple of forms and your broker runs a routine credit check on you. Brokers are eager to approve your application because margin accounts lead to additional business and higher profits for them. You can come out ahead in rising markets because you put up only 50% of the cost of your stocks, and 25% of your bonds. So your money works at least twice as hard for you. The interest that you pay on your margin loan is not only low, but it is also deductible from your taxable income up to the amount of your net investment income for the year.

In mid-1988 the interest rates charged for margin loans ranged between 9% and 10½% compared with just about 16% for personal loans at a bank. Sound easy? Maybe too easy. Margin accounts can be a lot more risky than you might expect.

Let's say you want to buy 100 shares of a stock that costs $40 per share. Normally you would pay $4,000 plus commissions. But with a margin account, you must put up only 50% of the purchase price, or just $2,000. Your broker would lend you the remaining $2,000, and the stock that you bought would act as the collateral for your loan.

If the value of your stock rises — great! If it rises enough, you could sell some shares, pay off the loan, and come out ahead. But if the gains in your stock do not cover your net interest payments, then you lose money. And if the stock price falls, you could suffer in two ways. Not only would your investment dwindle, but you could receive a call from your broker — a so-called margin call.

A margin call occurs when the value of your collateral falls below a certain percentage of your total purchase — usually 30% to 35%. If the worth of your holdings drops below that level, your broker will demand that you deliver enough cash or other securities to bring your collateral back up to the required amount. If you can't deliver — sometimes by the next day — the broker will sell your stock, take back what he lent you and collect interest.

Before you decide to borrow on margin, the key question to ask yourself is: Do you believe in the shares so wholeheartedly that you would be willing to borrow money even from a bank in order to own them? If not, a margin account is not for you.

If you do invest on margin, keep a close watch on your stocks. Check the closing prices at least twice a week, or more often if the shares tend to fluctuate widely. You don't want a margin call to take you by surprise.

To protect yourself, you can buy what's called a put option. It is the right to sell a stock at a specified price to the seller of the put. If the price of your stock drops enough, the put option will become more valuable. Then you can sell the option to offset the losses on your stock.

For extra insurance, you can instruct your broker to sell your stocks automatically if they fall to a certain price, by using a so-called stop order. Choose the price at which you would no longer want to own the stock and advise your broker to sell at that level. Then, if your shares fall without your noticing, your broker will sell them anyway to prevent you from losing more money.

One little-known tip: You can use margin loans to buy more than stocks or bonds. Say you want to purchase a house or apartment that costs $100,000. If you are fortunate enough to own $200,000 worth of stocks, your broker will lend you $100,000 against them. You continue to own those securities, and you avoid the up-front costs that you would have to pay on a mortgage loan. For a $100,000 mortgage, those so-called closing costs — for taxes, origination fees, lawyers' fees, title search and the like — can easily run $3,000 to $5,000. Just remember that you ultimately have to pay off your margin loan, and you will have to pony up more securities if their price drops in a falling market.

How to Act When Interest Rates Move

NOTHING affects the prices of your investments more than changes in interest rates. Here are answers to some common questions about consequences of those changes — and how to act on them.

Can you make profits on bonds when interest rates fall?

Yes, you can. Since bond prices rise when interest rates decline and vice versa, a skillful trader can make money by buying bonds at the top of the interest-rate cycle — and then selling at the bottom. The trouble is those once-steady interest rates have been bouncing down and up quite quickly — and this new volatility makes bond trading riskier than ever.

When interest rates fall, does it make sense to buy stocks?

Yes, it often does. Lower interest rates reduce a company's costs and thus lift its profits — and often its stock price.

What stocks do best when rates fall?

Many stocks do well at those times. Among them are the shares of banks and savings and loan associations, because they can pay lower interest rates to depositors. Utilities are big borrowers, and so they stand to gain when their interest costs decline. Lower rates also help boost the housing market, so real estate investment trusts, lumber companies and appliance manufacturers also prosper.

Do any stocks perform well despite high interest rates?

High rates reflect expectations of steep inflation, and investors turn to natural resources as inflation hedges. So oil, gas and mining company stocks tend to rise.

Should you buy stock on margin when rates are high?

Not unless it's a very promising stock. The interest you pay is tax-deductible up to the amount of net income you earn from your investments. But when rates are high, your stock still would have to rise quite a bit for you to break even after taxes.

If you want to play absolutely safe, where can you invest your money when rates are high?

Four financial instruments offer a safe return at close to top interest rates: money-market funds; bank money-market deposit accounts; six-month money-market certificates; and U.S. Treasury bills with maturities of 90 days to a year.

But do these four have any disadvantages?

Yes, they do. Since these investments are short term, you can't lock in high rates for very long. Also, remember that the minimum investment for Treasury bills is $10,000.

Should you borrow on your life insurance to invest when rates are high?

Yes, if you have a whole life policy that you bought before 1980. You often can borrow against the cash value of such a policy at a rate between 5% and 6%, put the cash in a money-market fund and earn considerable profit with little risk. But since you decrease the value of the policy by the amount you borrow, you should be sure to make your beneficiary the heir to the investment.

Should you buy gold or silver when rates are steep?

No. When Treasury bills and other safe alternatives offer high yields, precious metals lose their luster for many investors, and prices tend to drop sharply.

Which Economic Indicators to Watch

You are always hearing about the latest change in this or that economic indicator. Unemployment is down. The prime rate is up. But which among all these economic weathervanes will help you understand — and foretell — the direction of the economy and the fate of your investments? Here are five of the best:

To predict the direction that interest rates in general will take, look at the *interest rate on three-month Treasury bills*. You usually can find it every Tuesday on the business pages of major newspapers. The three-month Treasury bill rate is particularly sensitive because it is based on the rate that investors demand in return for putting up their own money.

To figure out whether inflation will rise or fall, keep a close watch on *major labor contracts.* Any settlement that increases wages by more than 10% is a danger sign.

Another gauge of future inflation is the relative *strength of the dollar.* If the dollar drops in value against other currencies, prices for foreign goods will rise. This will stir up inflation and cut into corporate profits.

An excellent indicator of the economy is the *payroll employment* figure. This counts the number of employees currently on company payrolls around the country. As this figure rises, so probably will consumer spending and, along with it, the stock market.

Probably no statistic is more closely watched as an indicator of the financial future than *the stock market* itself. When the market rallies, it is a good sign for the economy in general. People and companies become more willing to invest and create jobs. The best meter by which to read the market is the Standard & Poor's 500 stock average. Its broad sampling of 500 companies makes it more useful than the Dow Jones industrial average, which is based upon the stock prices of only 30 companies.

Beware of Boiler-Room Scams

D ID you ever get a phone call from a smooth-talking salesman who wants you to buy into a federal oil and gas leasing lottery that he claims is "guaranteed" to bring you big profits? Or perhaps a sure-thing investment in precious metals? Watch out. You could be getting a snow job straight from America's sunny capital of fraud.

Much of the selling that goes on over the telephone is legitimate, but you should be wary of get-rich-quick schemes, a remarkable number of which originate in southern Florida. Boiler-room operations there generally depend on corps of salespeople working out of a cramped office — hence the term "boiler room." They reach you on specially rigged telephones that filter out the background din and give you the impression of someone calling from a quiet suite.

The pitch is smooth and grabby, and usually read straight from a carefully prepared script. You will be offered *certain* profits with no risk of loss. And often the salesperson will falsely claim that you'll be able to deduct the entire investment from your income taxes. Sadly, this last claim might come true. If you lose your entire investment, you may be able to deduct that amount as a capital loss.

Among the favorite schemes of these operators is to sell to the unwitting investor chances of obtaining drilling rights on potential oil properties owned by the federal government. The government charges $75 to enter one of its lotteries, but boiler-room hucksters will try to squeeze up to $400 a chance out of their customers with the false promise that they have inside information.

Boiler-room victims rarely get their money back. So *never* buy *any* investment that is pitched to you in a cold call over the phone unless and until you carefully — *very* carefully — check out the company making the offer. The place to begin checking is with your own state-government department of securities.

Choosing Advisory Services

W HEN you read all those ads offering investment newsletters and other advisory services for anywhere from $50 to $500 a year, just remember: They vary enormously in quality. The best of the stock advisory services often beat the market averages. But many others are worthless and potentially harmful.

Almost anyone can do some research and put out a stock-market advisory letter. In fact, the publishers have included high-school dropouts, an electrician and a hairdresser. Some of the investment services are addicted to self-congratulation, often making ambiguous forecasts and then boasting that they have been "right on target." Published performance records often overstate gains and understate losses because they don't take buying and selling commissions into account. For example, if a service advises buying a stock at $10 and then decides it should be sold at $11, the service credits itself with a 10% gain. In fact, after brokerage commissions on a trade of 100 shares, the investor's real gain might well be closer to 3%.

If you don't know much about the market and have a few hundred or few thousand dollars to invest, you might be better off letting mutual funds manage your money. But a good service might be helpful if you have, say, $15,000 to invest.

Before committing yourself, it's wise to sample as many services as you can. Most will offer a one- to six-month trial subscription for a low price, and some will send you a sample copy at no charge. The best way of getting to know a variety of services is to write for the free catalogue published by Select Information Exchange (2095 Broadway, New York, New York 10023). It describes hundreds of services and offers a trial subscription to 20 of your choice for $11.95.

The major advisory services that focus mainly on fundamentals often are the most useful. They provide earnings estimates, industry and company analyses, investment strategies, stock recommendations and model portfolios — a package of investment materials that you cannot find assembled elsewhere in one place.

One of the largest advisory services is *The Value Line Investment Survey* (711 Third Avenue, New York, New York 10017). This weekly service costs $495 a year, or you can try 10 issues for $60. For those who learn to use the vast amount of information and guidance it offers, *Value Line* can be very valuable. Every week its staff of 100 analysts, economists, and statisticians evaluates 1,700 stocks. Each issue also includes a comprehensive overview of the market.

Another major service is *The Outlook,* published weekly by Standard & Poor's Corporation (25 Broadway, New York, New York 10004) for $240 a year; a 13-week trial subscription costs $29.95. *The Outlook* is cautiously bullish. It's easy to read and digest, does not encourage taking great risks and is backed by the large analytical staff of Standard & Poor's. It lists the best- and worst-acting stock groups and gives about 40 recommended issues graded on the basis of risk and investment objectives.

United & Babson Investment Report (210 Newbury Street, Boston, Massachusetts 02116), which costs $215 a year ($119 for six months), is similar to the Standard & Poor's *Outlook* but gives more space to Washington news and business trends. *United & Babson's* advice tends toward the conservative.

In choosing an investment service, remember this: The best of them don't claim to be right all the time but readily admit when they have been wrong. Beware of any service that promises you the moon. The most that you can expect from a service is that it provides a sound basis for your own decision-making.

Beyond looking into the advisory services, you would profit from reading several books on investment. A pair of classics are *The*

Intelligent Investor by Benjamin Graham and *The Battle for Investment Survival* by Gerald M. Loeb (no kin, incidentally). A modern companion to these is *Gaining on the Market* by Charles Rolo.

Also, for information on specific stocks, you can call almost any corporation's shareholder-relations department for information. Request the annual report, the 10-K form that public corporations file with the Securities and Exchange Commission, all recent corporate reports to shareholders and transcripts of presentations the firm has made to brokerage societies or analysts' groups.

How to Read an Annual Report

A N annual report can give you a load of useful intelligence about a company and the value of its stock — if you know where to look. You should not only read a corporation's most recent report but also scan its reports from the past three years. To get them, simply call the firm's investor relations department and request that it mail you the free brochures.

Ease into the latest report by way of the chief executive's letter. It should explain briefly and clearly why the firm had a good or bad year and describe precisely how management intends to move the company ahead. To assess management's ability to meet such goals, compare the promises made in the chief executive's past letters with the company's subsequent performance.

Next, turn to the consolidated balance sheets in the back of the report. These list the figures for the company's total current assets and liabilities at the end of its fiscal year. The "current ratio" is total assets divided by liabilities. Most analysts consider a ratio of between 1½-to-1 and 2-to-1 to be safe. Anything less could be a warning that the company has more debt than it can handle safely.

Also look at the income statement for signs that the company is inflating its earnings to hide management problems. Be suspicious if profits have continued to rise in recent years despite a dip in sales. Examine the income statement for entries called extraordinary or nonrecurring gains. Such one-time gains could mean the firm is selling off assets to cover up operating losses.

Some companies exaggerate their earnings by reporting sales

before money is actually received. To detect this type of financial juggling, turn to the annual report's footnotes. That is where a company is required by the Securities and Exchange Commission to disclose its accounting methods. The footnotes may also tip you to the threat of major lawsuits pending against the company.

Finally, you will want to spot-check the auditor's statement in the report. Take heed if this letter from the company's accountant is more than two paragraphs long. The third paragraph could contain disclaimers by an auditor who has reservations about the report.

Starting an Investment Club

INVESTMENT clubs are becoming more popular than ever among the people who want to learn about the stock market — and make a little money while they are at it. New clubs are being formed in college classrooms, corporate offices, condominium living rooms and even church basements. The National Association of Investment Clubs, which helps the new ones get started, estimates that there may be as many as 30,000 of them across the country with perhaps 600,000 members.

Each club typically has about 16 members, and for them the monthly meetings are an opportunity to learn about investing and dabble in stocks at an affordable price. Clubs usually require members to ante up from $10 to $45 a month.

At some meetings the atmosphere is relaxed and informal; at others it's almost as intense as a session of a billion-dollar mutual fund's portfolio committee. In successful clubs, members usually do their own research rather than rely on brokers or investment analysts. The members spend long hours poring over annual reports and such resources as Standard & Poor's *Corporation Records* and *The Value Line Investment Survey*. Both of those are often available free in public libraries. Some clubs even send members to interview the chief executives of local firms that look like promising investments.

Only a few clubs determine by majority rule whether to buy or sell a stock. Most use a weighted voting system so that long-term members with the most money at stake have the biggest say. No one seriously expects to grow rich solely through a club. According to the National Association, the average club's portfolio contains 15 to 20 stocks with a total value of less than $55,000 — meaning about $4,000 a member. But some clubs have impressive growth rates on their investments.

Because most investment clubs are partnerships, individual members must pay capital gains taxes on their share of any profits. New investment clubs with only small amounts to invest may find brokerage costs running more than 10% of their trades. As a result, some of them use discount brokers, who charge considerably less but give you no advice on where to put your money.

Most investment clubs do not want new members, and a few have stiff entrance requirements: you sometimes have to put in as much money as the other members have. Therefore, if you want to become a member of an investment club, you are probably better off starting a new one than trying to join an existing group. The majority begin simply, with two friends deciding to start a club, and they each sign up two or three other friends, and the chain grows. If you want to create a club of your own, you can get valuable help from the National Association of Investors Corporation. It will send you a handbook with advice on organizing a club, and for $12 a primer on the fundamentals of stock analysis. Write to: The National Association of Investors Corporation, 1515 East Eleven Mile Road, Royal Oak, Michigan 48067. The NAIC's annual dues are a modest $30 per club, plus $8 for each member.

The NAIC recommends that all clubs, especially new ones, follow these conservative principles:

— Invest regularly, preferably monthly, no matter where you think the stock market is heading — because a club that tries to predict broad stock trends is often wrong.

— Reinvest all earnings so that your club's portfolio can rise faster through compounding.

— Invest in growth companies. The association defines them as firms with both earnings and dividends outperforming their industry average.

Clubs should aim for 15% annual growth in their investments. To start you toward your goal, the association will send you a model portfolio, which is updated quarterly by its professional stock selection committee. The organization also provides work-sheets to help members analyze stocks on their own.

Investment clubs tend to do well, but when they fail it is often because they allow a trading attitude to sweep away the more reliable accumulation attitude. When the market moves sideways or down, impatient members often urge the club to follow an in-and-out strategy. It is much wiser — and more profitable — to hold on to sound investments for long-term growth.

STOCKS

Beginning in the Market

REGARDLESS of whether the stock market rises or falls in the days and months ahead, it probably makes sense for you to have a well-thought-out program of cautiously and gradually investing in the market. If the nation generally does well in its domestic and foreign policies in the future, its economy should do well; and if the economy prospers, the stock market should go up over the long term. It is indeed the long term that most of us should be thinking about when we invest.

History's lesson is that stocks tend to perform better than most other investments. From 1926 to 1987, common stocks of the Standard & Poor's 500 returned an average 9.9% a year — or 6.6% after adjusting for inflation — according to R. Ibbotson and R. Sinquefield, *Stocks, Bonds, Bills and Inflation* (SBBI), updated in *SBBI 1988 Yearbook* (Ibbotson Associates, Chicago). In the period from June 1982 to June 1988, these stocks returned an average of 16.6% a year after adjusting for inflation. Some people earn much more than the market averages, particularly if they read widely of economic trends and other developments that affect markets, and if they choose their brokers wisely. (For more, see "Your Investments/ Brokers: How to Choose One.")

More and more young people are setting aside part of their paychecks to invest in the market. That is partly because they can no longer assume that Social Security and a company pension will ultimately take care of their retirement needs. They also recognize that when you begin investing while young, you can still afford to take some risks in search of great profits. But, regardless of your age, how can you best get started in the stock market?

Your first decision is whether to aim for income (that is, for high dividends) or for growth (that is, for stocks that pay little or no dividends but have good reason to rise in price). Most investment counselors agree that young people should choose a strategy of capital growth.

As a start, you might consider investing in a mutual fund. For $1,000, or sometimes less, you can buy shares in a pool that is invested by the fund's professional managers in a wide range of stocks. That way you get a diversified investment that you probably could not afford on your own. Many funds grow nicely and, on the down side, few conservative funds lose very much.

There are two basic types of funds: load and no-load. You buy load funds through brokers or financial planners, and they charge you a sales commission, as much as 8½%. You buy no-load funds by mail or telephone, and you pay no commission for them. Since both kinds of funds perform about the same, it often makes sense to save the commission by buying the no-loads. (For more, see "Your Investments/Mutual Funds.")

Another way to begin is to join an investment club. Since members jointly choose stocks to purchase, a club offers you an opportunity to invest and to get experience in researching the market. Determining when to sell and when to hold onto a stock is another valuable lesson that can be learned in such a club. Most members ultimately gain enough confidence to do their own investing. Studies show that after five years, 85% of members invest independently as well as through the club. (For more, see "Your Investments: Starting an Investment Club.")

Once you strike out on your own, you probably will be able to afford only one or two stocks at first. But ultimately you should aim to own five to 10. That is enough diversity but not too much for you to keep watch over.

Balance is important. As suggested previously, a quarter of your investments might be in very small companies that give you a chance for big gains — and, of course, the possibility of big losses. Another quarter could be in the largest, most conservative companies for stable growth. The remaining half might be medium-size concerns that are growing faster than the economy. In every case, try to spot companies whose share prices are relatively low compared with their current earnings and future prospects.

Keep your eye on investing's early-warning system. The market as a whole usually moves about three to six months *ahead* of changes in the economy. On average, the market begins to rise about six months *before* a recession ends. Typically, the climb lasts 2½ years, followed by about 1½ years of downturn.

Bear in mind that business conditions affect various stock groups differently. Basic industries such as autos and housing rise and fall along with the economy. So they prosper when an economic recovery begins. But when the recovery is a year or more old, the strongest companies tend to be consumer-goods firms such as retailers, clothing makers and home-furnishing manufacturers. That is because consumers finally feel secure enough to spend freely.

In picking stocks, you probably can benefit from buying some sophisticated market information guides. A popular one is Standard & Poor's *Security Owners' Stock Guide,* which gives the vital statistics on over 5,300 common and preferred stocks and 430 mutual funds; it costs $93 a year. You can get still more in-depth information from *The Value Line Investment Survey* for $495 a year. To save money as well as earn it, just remember that these advisory-service guides often are available at your public library. (See "Your Investments: Choosing Advisory Services.")

When you buy stocks or bonds, you can choose either to hold the certificates yourself or keep them in so-called street name. That means they are held by your broker. Which is better for you?

There is one clear drawback to holding your stocks in street name. If the brokerage firm runs into severe financial troubles, your holdings could be tied up for months. You will, however, get them back eventually, because they are insured by the Securities Investor Protection Corporation.

But keeping your stocks and bonds in street name has many advantages. It is certainly convenient. You do not have to worry about losing your certificates or sending them through the mail. If you want to borrow on margin — that is, take out a loan from your broker — your securities in street name easily serve as collateral. Brokerage houses also maintain up-to-date records on the value of your holdings, and will reinvest your dividends automatically in, say, a money-market account.

How to Pick Them

ARE you tired of hunting frantically for tomorrow's hot stocks? If so, you should consider investing in *undervalued* stocks — and waiting patiently for their market prices to rise.

Many of the professional stock pickers who have done best in fair markets and foul alike are known as value hunters. They believe that the only sound investment strategy is to buy a stock when it is selling below the company's true value. Then they wait — perhaps for years — for other investors to recognize this value and bid up the stock's price. To succeed with such a strategy, you will need discipline and a willingness to buck the prevalent opinion of the Wall Street herd.

As a small investor, you might think you just cannot compete in a stock market dominated by large financial institutions. But there is a sound reason why amateurs like you can humble the institutional investors. Because so many of them have to concentrate on safety and the ability to sell out quickly if they have to, they choose their stocks largely from among 500 or so of the nation's biggest and best-known companies.

Professional managers are reading and hearing the same good or bad news about the same stocks at the same time, so they often buy and sell in a pack. This makes investing in the institutions' relatively few favorites increasingly risky for the rest of us: the bottom could drop out of stocks that fall from favor. But individual investors do not have to worry about causing market turbulence or justifying their stock picks to a fickle clientele. They can go prospecting in a market of 6,000 or so stocks that most of the institutions ignore and few, if any, analysts bother with. As a class, these shares produce the biggest profits. In a study of the market behavior of 510 stocks between 1970 and 1980, issues with virtually no institutional ownership rose an average of almost 21% a year versus 10½% for institutional favorites.

Before you make your stock selections, learn what investment analysts — the ones who have the best records of forecasting and picking winners — think will happen in the market. You can get a reasonable idea of that by reading the financial press and investment advisory newsletters.

If you want to develop winning stock strategies, it is wise to follow certain guidelines:

Scout for stocks owned by fewer than five big institutional investors. These shares, while risky, often tend to rise faster than others. You can find out how many institutions hold an issue by looking it up in Standard & Poor's *Stock Guide,* which all brokers and many libraries have.

Also, search for stocks whose prices are low relative to their earnings. Newspaper stock tables show the price/earnings ratios based on the *previous* 12 months' earnings. For a better guide, use the ratio based on analysts' estimates of *future* earnings. You can find such estimates in *The Value Line Investment Survey.* Or ask your broker to send you Standard & Poor's stock reports for specific companies.

Look also for shares of well-established firms that have high dividends relative to stocks in general, notably relative to stocks of companies in the same industry.

One popular strategy among small investors is to concentrate on issues selling for $3 or less. These cheap thrills can be fast-growing small companies. Another tactic is to try to catch a fallen star, a stock that has fallen victim to bad news. You can spot these unfortunates in daily newspaper lists of stocks reaching 52-week lows.

To find out whether the company is reeling from only a temporary setback instead of a terminal problem, look for long-term debt that is not greater than 40% of the company's total capitalization and less than 10% of annual sales. Aggressive new management, significant cost reductions and the introduction of potentially profitable products are other signs that the corpse may be coming back from the grave.

Sometimes you can find hot stocks on Wall Street by making a cool evaluation of the people, products and services you encounter on Main Street. Many successful small investors discover that personal experience leads them to stock-market winners. For example, your children might direct you to a new fast-food chain that is packed with hungry youngsters. Perhaps the firm's stock is worth a nibble. Or you might detect a changing pattern in sales at your job. An investment opportunity may be behind it.

Investing in what you know firsthand lets you exploit two of your best assets — your experience and your own good judgment. But do not invest without first finding out more facts. Superb products and services can come from poorly run, unprofitable companies. And a close encounter with a single product tells you nothing about a firm's other lines of business. They may not be so terrific. In other words, use your experience, but do not let it overimpress you. You should do the same kind of research you would do with any investment. For example, does the company have cash hoards, real estate, oil reserves or other assets that might catch the eye of a takeover artist or make the market take a second look? The most convenient source of answers is usually *The Value Line Investment Survey.*

Ask a stockbroker for a copy of the firm's latest annual report, or write the company for one. Look for steady growth in revenues and net income over a five-year period. See how current assets compare with current liabilities, and hold out for close to a two-to-one ratio in favor of assets.

Also, see how the company measures up to others in the same industry. You can find reliable comparative data in Standard & Poor's annual industry surveys. One of the key figures to compare is return on equity. If your firm's return is lower than that of its competitors, beware. The company probably is not being managed as well as it might be.

Strategies for Buying

ALTHOUGH nobody can be sure whether the stock market will go up or down over the next few months, you should aim to recognize the few really major, long-term turning points in the market, such as the huge rebound that began in August 1982 and the crash of October 1987.

Stocks generally move in expectation of changes in the economy and in corporate profits. The market is always looking ahead. If both inflation and interest rates are heading down, that's bullish news. But when the consumer price index and interest rates on Treasury bills show sustained increases, watch out. It's a clear and present danger signal.

Fortunately, your own decisions about the stock market do not have to be perfect to be profitable. Just watch for the major turns in the market. You can buy somewhere *above* the bottom and sell out some time *after* the market has hit its peak — and still make more money than the investor who ignores the market's long-term gyrations.

One old belief about the stock market is called the "efficient market theory." It holds that all new information about any stock spreads too quickly for ordinary investors to profit from the news before the stock rises. But that's not really so, according to a study by the Institutional Brokers Estimate System, a service of the brokerage firm Lynch Jones & Ryan. It found that after several stock-market analysts sharply increase their earnings estimates for a company, its stock probably will do *better* than the major market averages for the next six months. In other words, you can benefit from good news.

Over the six years to 1980, if you put money into the 20 stocks with the highest upward revisions of earnings estimates, and then sold them a year after you bought them, you would have earned almost 28% a year. That's far more than the 11% annual rise during the same period in the Standard & Poor's 500 stock index. Lynch Jones & Ryan reports that much the same pattern has held true in the years since 1980. The moral: It pays to shop around for stocks of companies on which several stock-market analysts have recently increased their future earnings estimates.

At the other extreme, you also can do well buying stocks that recently have plunged as a result of disappointing earnings or other sour news. A number of them become good bargains. In fact, some of the shrewdest investment professionals study each day's stock-market tables just to find shares that have hit new lows. They figure that if these stocks have intrinsic values, they may have nowhere to go but up.

If you decide to buy stocks, you must determine their basic values, as previously discussed. To help you gauge that, you would be wise to look at four measures:

Number one is the stock's *historic trading range*. You should consider buying on bad news when a stock nears its lowest price in the last three to five years.

Number two is *earnings*. Look at how well a company has done in the last 10 years for an idea of what it is capable of earning. If the most recent results are at the low end of the range, ask a broker for his firm's estimate of earnings for the next six or 12 months. If a turnaround is expected, you may consider buying the stock.

Number three is *book value per share*. That is the company's net assets divided by the number of shares. If the stock is selling for less than book value per share, it may be underpriced — and thus a good buy. If the price is less than half the book value, you have little to lose.

Number four is the *balance sheet*. Be suspicious of an unusually large amount of long-term debt. The ratio of a firm's debt to the market value of its stocks should not be significantly above the average for its industry.

Once you have picked out some undervalued stocks, don't buy right away. It is axiomatic that turnarounds generally take longer to materialize than anyone expects. So spend some time watching those stocks. But also don't plan to wait until a stock hits its very bottom. Nobody is smart enough to pick that. Instead, set target prices, and buy if and when the stock reaches them. By doing that, you might do well buying bad-news stocks.

Strategies for Selling

ANYONE can buy a stock, but the real test of smart investing is knowing when to sell it. Almost from the moment you purchase a stock, you should be thinking about what will be the right time to unload.

For many investors, however, selling a losing stock is like shaking some bad habit. It's a painful step you know is good for you, but you keep putting it off. In fact, deciding when to sell a stock is harder — and more important — than deciding when to buy. If you do not buy a stock and the price rises, all you lose is an opportunity. But if you fail to sell a stock and then the price falls, you lose real money.

Here are some guidelines to help you decide what to do when the stock you love no longer loves you back:

Set a goal. You might aim to sell if a stock rises 50% above the price you paid — unless you have sound reason to believe it will climb a lot more.

Cut your losses. Never hesitate to sell because you are behind. You could wind up further behind. Consider dumping a New York Stock Exchange issue if it declines 15% from the price where you bought it. American Stock Exchange and over-the-counter stocks are more volatile, so give them more rope. But sell them if they decline 20% to 25%. You can instruct your broker ahead of time to sell a stock automatically if and when it declines to a certain price. You do this by placing a so-called stop-loss order every time you buy a stock.

If you bought a stock expecting favorable developments that then do not occur within a reasonable time, bail out. And if the expected does happen, but the price of the stock does not move, unload promptly.

Another sell signal is a sudden spurt in the price/earnings ratio of a stock. This means that buyers are becoming too wildly optimistic. In falling markets, stocks with price/earnings ratios that have soared are likely to come tumbling down if earnings are at all disappointing.

Some advisers suggest you consider selling if a stock's price/earnings ratio rises more than 30% above its average for the past 10 years. For example, if the price historically is about 10 times earnings per share but suddenly jumps to 13, that may be the time to clear out. You can get these figures from a broker or from *The Value Line Investment Survey*.

If you learn of a significant deterioration in a company's sales growth or profitability or financial health, then it is time to kick the stock out. The same applies if the prospects for the industry that the company is in no longer seem so bright, or if the company itself loses its competitive edge.

Sometimes the behavior of the stock itself will tell you that your love affair with it is getting too hot not to cool down. One sign is if the stock market is rising and trading volume in the issue is heavy, but still it fails to advance in price. Another is when a stock is not making gains similar to those of others in its industry.

Many people put off selling when it's time to sell because they don't like the idea of paying taxes on their gains. But it's much wiser to take a taxable short-term gain than wait and suffer a long-term loss.

Losing some money is inevitable. No investor buys only winners. But as Martin Zweig, a top investment adviser, says, "You can be right on your stocks only 40% of the time and still do fine — if you cut your losses short."

How Technicians Spot Trends

Some professional stock watchers called technical analysts have several theories worth knowing about. To judge when the market is ready to make a major move, technicians study a number of indicators. One is called *momentum*. This means the speed with which market averages, such as the Standard & Poor's 500 stock index, rise or fall. If the index continues rising, but at a slower and slower rate every day, it may be heading for a fall.

Another technical measure is *trading volume,* the number of shares changing hands. It is a good sign when volume is large on days that the market rises and small on days that it sags.

Yet another measure is called *on-balance volume.* For example, if the market rises on volume of 100 million shares one day and then falls the next day on only 60 million, the on-balance volume is plus-40. That is a bullish omen. But when the on-balance volume turns down, watch out. It could be a signal that the pent-up buying power is nearly exhausted and that stock values are about to sag.

Then there is the *advance/decline line.* Very simply, it is a daily count of the number of stocks that rise and the number that fall. When the gainers outnumber losers, the advance/decline line goes up; that is a sign that the market is getting stronger. When losers predominate, the advance/decline line goes down. That is a sign of weakness in the market.

One sign that a rising market could be heading for a fall is when different stock-market indexes say conflicting things. For example, if the Dow Jones Industrial Average is rising at the same time that the Standard & Poor's 500 stock index is falling, that is a cautionary indication.

Another so-called technical indicator is how much money mutual-fund managers are keeping in cash instead of in stocks. If they have more than 7% of their assets in cash, it is a favorable sign for the market: the money might go into stocks.

Market peaks also are marked by clear signs of speculation. Two of the surest occur when small investors start borrowing heavily to buy on margin and when small-company stocks all seem to be scoring huge gains.

The Wisdom of Dollar-Cost Averaging

I T NEVER fails. Every time you plunge into the market, you find yourself buying in at the top. Then, stocks stumble and you get so discouraged that you sell — precisely at the bottom. You can avoid these expensive errors by investing a set amount of money each month — regardless of whether the market is heading up or down. This is a canny and often profitable investment strategy called dollar-cost averaging.

Think of it as investing on the installment plan. You regularly invest, say, $50 or $100 each month. If stock prices then go up, you can congratulate yourself for having earned some profits. But what if prices go down? Well, you congratulate yourself on your new opportunity to pick up some bargains. Several months ago, your $50 monthly investment could buy, say, only two shares; now it can buy three!

Many people find that a sound way to practice dollar-cost averaging is to buy the shares of a mutual fund at regular monthly intervals, particularly a no-load mutual fund with a record of having done better than the broad market averages over the last several years. No-load mutual funds give you professional management of a diversified portfolio of securities for a small fee.

Dollar-cost averaging also can be used to buy shares of individual stocks, but brokerage fees on small transactions can be prohibitively high — often at least $30 to $35 a trade. And because mutual funds have diversified portfolios, they tend to bounce back from market disasters — when the market ultimately recovers. But an individual stock can fall through the floor and stay in the cellar for years.

True enough, if you sink all of your money into the stock market in a lump sum, and then the market proceeds to rise like a rocket and continue climbing for many years, you will do better than if you put in your money bit by bit, month after month. But look at dollar-cost averaging as a defensive strategy. It will keep you from getting crushed in the wild up-and-down market swings.

The discipline of investing fixed amounts in regular installments helps you to avoid two common errors: putting all your money into the stock market at a time when it might be getting ready for a sharp tumble, and selling out at big losses when stocks are deeply depressed.

Watch the Insiders

Do you want an inside tip on the stock market? Then watch for those times when high executives buy or sell shares in the company they work for. Information on such insider trading is easy to find and simple to use.

When officers of a company trade its stock, they often know something you don't know, and their deals have to be reported to the Securities and Exchange Commission. When they *buy* a lot of their own stock, it usually does much better than the market averages. The five New York Stock Exchange issues that corporate insiders bought most heavily in the six months before the market surged in August 1982 soared 87% by the end of 1983.

When insiders *sell*, watch out. Heavy sales by insiders preceded many of the market's disasters, including, for example, Digital Equipment, Warner Communications and Coleco, in 1983. At the end of that year, insiders were selling four times as many stocks as they bought. Sure enough, despite many optimistic predictions, the market proceeded to plummet early in 1984.

Thus, when you see heavy significant insider selling of a stock, consider cashing in your own shares in the company. The situation is particularly dangerous when insider selling suddenly increases after a stock has started to decline. You can protect yourself with a stop-loss order. That way, if disaster does strike, you can escape with limited damage. That doesn't mean you have to stay out of the market. It's a good time to look at the stocks those knowing insiders have been *buying*.

You can follow the trading of high company officers by subscribing to newsletters that follow the subject. Two top letters are *Consensus of Insiders*, a weekly (P.O. Box 24349, Fort Lauderdale, Florida 33307-4349; $199 a year); and *The Insiders*, a biweekly (3471 North Federal Highway, Fort Lauderdale, Florida 33306; $49 a year).

Buying What the Big Winners Buy

HAVE you ever heard of a 13D filing? No, it is not something that you would find in a dentist's office or on a clerk's desk. It is one of those obscure government reports that might give you a clue to making some money in the stock market.

For that clue, recall what Damon Runyon used to say: "If you rub up against money long enough, some of it might rub up against you." Some of it might rub off on you — if you follow the purchases of the handful of multimillionaire investors who make audacious bids in the stock market to take over whole companies. Their names are often in the headlines, names like T. Boone Pickens, Carl Lindner and others.

Quite a few smaller investors closely study this smart-money group. One who does is Kiril Sokoloff, publisher of the newsletter *Street Smart Investing.* In a five-year survey completed in June 1983, he measured the investment results of 150 of these big capitalists and found that of nearly 300 stocks in which they took major positions, 95% rose in price.

You can follow the trades of these large investors fairly easily. Many of their deals are a matter of public record because of the size of their purchases. By law, any investor who acquires more than 5% of a company's shares must report that transaction to the Securities and Exchange Commission within ten days on a form called 13D. The SEC publishes a daily summary of these so-called 13D filings in the *SEC News Digest,* which you can study at the SEC's public libraries in Chicago, New York and Washington, D.C. Or for a fee, you can get this information more conveniently from several computer services and investment newsletters. In addition to *Street Smart Investing* (2651 Strang Boulevard, Yorktown Heights, New York 10598; $350 a year), newsletters include *SEC Today* (655 15th Street, NW, Washington, D.C. 20005; $375 a year); *Special Situation Report and Stock Market Forecast* (P.O. Box 167, Rochester, New York 14601; $230 a year); and *Insiders' Chronicle* (P.O. Box 272977, Boca Raton, Florida 33427; $350 a year).

The Best Market Newsletters

OVER 750 newsletters claim to tell you which stocks to buy to make money, and the editors of some of them have done amazingly well over long periods. But such advice does not come cheaply. Most newsletters cost about $150 a year, though some are only $40 and others are $1,000.

Of course, many newsletters also have done poorly, and their numbers may soon increase. The Supreme Court has ruled that newsletter publishers no longer must register with the Securities and

Exchange Commission as investment advisers. So now practically anyone who wants to start an investment letter can do so. And the newsletters can publish anything as long as it is not misleading or fraudulent information.

Thus, the need for weeding the good newsletters from the rotten is more important than ever. To find the best, you can read services that keep score on them. *The Hulbert Financial Digest* (643 South Carolina Avenue, SE, Washington, D.C. 20003; $135 a year) rates about 100 advisory services on the success of their stock selections. Another service, *Timer Digest* (P.O. Box 7700, Greenwich, Connecticut 06836-7700; $175 for 18 issues every three weeks or $95 for nine issues), monitors 70 newsletters that claim to call the major turning points in the market and reports on the 10 best. These publishers may give you a free copy if you call or write, or you can probably see a copy for free at a stockbroker's office.

Money magazine has named seven of the stock-market newsletters that are generally outstanding:

Market Logic (Institute for Econometric Research, 3471 North Federal Highway, Fort Lauderdale, Florida 33306; $95 a year, two months' free trial) counsels subscribers on almost every aspect of investing, from stocks and mutual funds to options and gold.

Growth Stock Outlook (P.O. Box 15381, Chevy Chase, Maryland 20815; $175 a year) is one of only a handful of publications whose recommended stocks have made money every year since 1980.

The Zweig Forecast (P.O. Box 5345, New York, New York 10150; $245 a year) is a successful newsletter for investors who trade stocks frequently.

The Gordon Market Timer (P.O. Box 938, Englewood Cliffs, New Jersey 07632; $252 a year) is designed primarily to help mutual-fund investors decide when to switch between stock funds and a money-market fund.

Robert Kinsman's Low-Risk Growth Letter (Kinsman Associates Incorporated, 899 Northgate Drive, 3rd Floor, San Rafael, California 94903; $175 a year) has made money every year since 1980.

The *California Technology Stock Letter* (155 Montgomery Street, Suite 1401, San Francisco, California 94104; $270 a year) covers the computer industry.

Finally, the *Dick Davis Digest* (P.O. Box 2828, Ocean View Station, Miami Beach, Florida 33140; $120 a year) reprints excerpts, including specific recommendations, from some 300 market letters.

The Hidden Dangers of
Too-Big Dividends

I F YOU are collecting dividends on your stocks now, you should review your investments to see if you are really getting a good deal. Shares that offer the possibility of hefty price appreciation often provide a bigger return than those with dazzling dividends. In fact, the shares of some large companies that pay no dividends at all have achieved a much greater total return than high-dividend companies of the same size.

Many experts contend that big payouts simply signify bad management. Smart managers should be reinvesting profits in new equipment, research or other productive activity. In an analysis of 1,000 companies over five years in the late 1970s and early 1980s, the financial advisory firm of Mitchell & Company found that corporations which reduced by 20% the portion of their earnings allotted to dividends enjoyed stock price gains averaging 38%. Meanwhile, companies that increased the portion of their earnings spent on dividends showed an average 39% decline in stock prices.

Be wary of an issue that pays substantially higher dividends in relation to its price than other companies in the same industry. The high yield may be the result of a recent decline in the stock's price. That could be a sign of serious problems in the company. Also watch for changes in corporate strategy that could result in lower dividends. Such was the case in 1984 with ITT, which cut its annual dividend from $2.76 to $1.00, partly to pay for an ambitious research and development program.

If you do not need a steady stream of income, you might be wise to look for growing companies in expanding industries — and let the dividends go hang. If, on the other hand, you want some price growth along with the security of dividends, choose stocks selling at low price/earnings ratios. And if you do not want to pick your own stocks, you can aim for a high total return by investing in a mutual fund that combines dividend income with a chance at capital gains. For the ordinary investor a so-called growth-and-income mutual fund that does not charge a load may well offer the best opportunity to achieve that high total return.

Beware of Last Year's Stars

OH, how the mighty fall. At least they do in the stock market. If you keep that in mind, you will avoid the mistake of investing in a stock just because it recently had a spectacular gain. Quite often last year's overpuffed superstars become this year's disappointing dogs. For just one example, take a look at the sorry records in 1984 of what had been the 10 best-performing issues on the New York Stock Exchange in 1983.

Among them, only one finished even in the top half of New York Stock Exchange issues in 1984. This was a semiconductor manufacturer, International Rectifier. Its stock climbed a meager 2% and placed 611th among the 1,484 stocks that were analyzed and ranked by *Money* magazine. International Rectifier may have been helped by the fact that it was in the midst of its first profitable year in several years and analysts were predicting still higher earnings ahead.

For most of the rest of 1983's top 10, just staying out of the cellar in 1984 was tough enough. In 1983 an oil service and farm equipment maker named Hesston was the third-fastest-growing stock, with gains of 216%. In 1984, after expected sales failed to materialize, the stock tumbled 74% and it ended up ninth from the *bottom* of all stocks ranked. Lehigh Valley Industries, a conglomerate in shoes, steel products and car parts, was ninth from the top in 1983. But in 1984 it lost money and slipped to number 760.

Most of the other 1983 winners did manage to increase their sales and profits in 1984. Among these were Rymer, a food processor; Wyle Laboratories, a high-tech industrial supplier; Kysor Industrial, a conglomerate; and Arkansas Best, a trucking concern. But fears that these stocks were about as high as they would go apparently led investors to withdraw their winnings. All four of these companies fell to rankings below the top 1,000 and wound up in the bottom third of the market.

How to React to Takeover Bids

CORPORATE takeovers, buyouts and spin-offs occurred by the thousands in the past year, and no end appears in sight. The effects aren't felt just on Wall Street. Investors all over the country need to know how to react as well. Suppose you wake up one fine morning, turn on the radio or look in the business pages of your newspaper, and find that a company in which you own stock is supposedly a takeover target. What should you do?

The primary rule is: Don't chase rumors. There are far more false stories out there than real deals. But if a stock you own does become an active takeover target, your choices are many.

You may be asked to consider what is known as an equity buyback plan. If you are, break out the bubbly and hold on to your shares. Maybe even buy some more. When a company announces that it is buying back its own common stock, chances are strong that the price of the shares will rise.

Another form of corporate maneuver that investors increasingly must ponder is the leveraged buyout. This basically means that the firm's own management or an independent investor proposes to buy up the shares owned by the public and take the company private. If a leveraged buyout proposal comes your way, do nothing until you have read the official offering statement. Then see what you are really getting for your shares.

Do accept the deal if you figure out that over the long term the transaction will yield you a substantially higher return than would selling at the current market price. But be wary of offers in which you will be paid in low-quality "junk bonds" as well as cash. Often the bonds in these deals are riskier than the stocks you are holding.

If a company whose stock you own decides to spin off one of its divisions, you have to answer a couple of questions:

First, should you hold on to your shares in the parent firm, or perhaps even buy more? The best answer is that the parent firm is often worth keeping — if the spin-off rids it of unprofitable, debt-laden divisions, or if the deal unloads businesses that the parent lacks the expertise to manage.

Second, should you get rid of the stock you receive in the spun-off enterprise? The answer is: Don't automatically sell those shares. Give the company a year or so to prove itself. If it does not do well within that period, then sell.

A more difficult deal to decipher is a hostile takeover bid. Basically, you have to decide whether to hold on to your shares or to sell out. The primary piece of advice is: Don't get greedy. Sell out if the stock rises to within 10% of the price the raider proposes to pay.

But say the shares have not risen quite that high yet. Then you still might consider selling and taking whatever profits you have earned as a result of the takeover bid — if the management seems to stand a fighting chance of beating back the takeover offer. It usually does so if it owns more than 10% of the firm's stock. If management seems too weak to resist, you would be wise to hold on to your stock, wait for the raider's last offer, then get out.

You also want to delay selling if the target firm actively seeks a so-called White Knight to pay a still higher price or if it announces an offer to buy its own shares. A bidding war could result and kick up the price of your stock. Of course, do not sell if you think the price of your shares will eventually rise anyway, with or without the takeover.

How to Find Takeover Candidates

TENS of thousands of investors have been blessed with bonanzas from the surge in corporate mergers and takeovers. Because the stocks of the acquired companies have been bid up to giddy highs, many investors now are trying to guess which firms will be acquired next — so they can buy those companies' stocks and ride them up.

In a takeover deal, the acquiring company typically pays a premium of 30% or even more over the market price for each share of the company it wants to acquire. So it's small wonder that many investors are rushing to buy the stocks of companies that they think are candidates for takeovers. According to the late Wall Street writer Charles Rolo, here are some guidelines for finding them:

First, look where the bargain-hunting corporations shop. Acquirers prefer companies that have large cash holdings. The buying company then can recover part of the purchase price by using the selling company's very own cash. Acquisition-minded corporations also look for stocks selling appreciably below book value — that is, total assets minus total liabilities per share.

Second, look where owners may want to sell. Deal makers often search out companies whose principal owners have reasons to want a merger — for example, if they are elderly, own the controlling interest and have most of their eggs in that one corporate basket. A sellout would enable them to diversify their holdings and perhaps get some stock that is more readily marketable.

Third, look where takeover and merger activity is already strong. It has been intense in the broadcasting, publishing, oil, and software industries.

Stock Splits

W HEN the stock market soars, it's time to watch for stock splits. A company subdivides its stock to keep it attractive to investors. They generally prefer shares in the $10-to-$40 range. If a stock rises to, say, $60, then the company may issue three new shares in exchange for two old shares. That usually brings the price per share down to about $40.

The most recent New York Stock Exchange study shows that stocks splitting at least three shares for two between 1963 and 1980 rose an average 2½ times more than stocks that did not split. The study compared prices three years before the split with those three years after it.

Firms most often declare stock splits when their earnings are strong. Splits thus can be good news for shareholders, bringing increased dividends and favorable growth prospects. So it may be wise to ask a broker for his recommendations of stocks that seem likely to split.

Investing in Tomorrow's Products

T HE classic way to grow rich is to get in on the ground floor of a new product — not necessarily by making it or selling it, but by investing in it. You do not have to be an Eli Whitney or an Alexander

Graham Bell to invest profitably in the products that will create the fortunes of the future. What you *do* need is information, patience and an eye for the products and processes that can make life easier, more efficient, longer or more enjoyable.

Which fields are most likely to produce the next generation of successful new companies? If you ask venture capitalists, business school professors, bankers and owners of small enterprises for their list of the potentially fastest growing areas of the economy in the coming years, they most likely will recommend these:

First, data processing: Bruising competition has brought a series of failures, but many survivors of the shakeout should do well. The future looks bright for those companies that manufacture or service computers and software — provided they bring unique products or special capabilities to this crowded field. A number of computer companies, for example, are working on "artificial intelligence" software systems that would enable machines to make decisions, diagnoses and conclusions beyond a human being's capability. Any company that develops such a system would be hugely promising.

Second, health: Americans spend over $400 billion a year on personal health and medical services. One reason for this high bill is that it costs so much to stay in a hospital. So there will be plentiful opportunities for making, selling or servicing medical equipment for use in the home.

Third, genetics: Some of the best possibilities for smaller firms in this area are in support fields — for example, manufacturing lab equipment or producing enzymes for use in genetic research.

Fourth, communications: Opportunities can be great for entrepreneurs who make, sell or service cable TV and satellite transmission equipment.

There are, of course, still more opportunity areas: for example, extracting valuable metals from material before disposing of it, or helping companies become more productive and efficient. For a really far-out investment, you can put some cash in space companies. Private firms are beginning to launch extraterrestrial projects. You can buy stock in companies that already have earthbound businesses but are planning space ventures. Or you can contemplate investing in one of a few space-only companies that are now privately held but plan soon to go public. Most opportunities at present are in the dozens of space firms that seek money directly from individual investors, and promise in return a share of future profits.

In *all* these areas, you have to be particularly careful when selecting stocks. Few investors know enough about technology to judge whether or not any wildly trumpeted product represents a genuine profit-making opportunity.

The worst method for investing is to be seduced by hot tips from unknowing in-laws and friends. As one top mutual-fund manager warns, there is no faster way to the poorhouse, other than pursuing slow horses and fast women, than following tips in the new technologies.

But a sober and sensible way to invest is to first pick out an emerging field in the new technology and then follow it carefully. Subscribe to specialty magazines and trade journals. Some good ones are *Electronic News* (7 East 12th Street, New York, New York 10003; $40 a year); *Electronic Business* (275 Washington Street, Newton, Massachusetts 02158; $50 a year); *High Technology Business* (P.O. Box 2886, Boulder, Colorado 80322; $30 a year); and *California Technology Stock Letter* (155 Montgomery Street, Suite 1401, San Francisco, California 94104; $270 a year).

Once you have done some homework, you can consider putting cash into those companies that are most effectively pioneering new products. Conservative people might wager 10% or so of their investment money on such ventures; more aggressive types might put in 30% or even 40%.

The most glamorous way to invest in the companies that are turning out revolutionary new products is to buy the shares of firms that are going public for the first time. That is not always easy. Since supplies are often limited, most new issues are offered first to a broker's best clients. But do not despair if you cannot get the crisp new shares on the initial offering. If you like a company, there is no reason not to buy its stock later on. You may even get it cheaper. Many new issues drop below their initial offering price sometime within a year.

Before you buy, learn all you can about a company that is going public. Ask your broker for copies of newsletters that discuss new issues. Among the leading letters, one is *New Issues* (3471 North Federal Highway, Fort Lauderdale, Florida 33306; $95 a year); and another is Standard & Poor's *Emerging & Special Situations* (25 Broadway, New York, New York 10004; $175 a year).

Look to see if responsible analysts say the company's product has the potential for capturing a 20% share of a market that itself could grow very large within a decade. Favor concerns that have 20% to 30% annual growth in both sales and earnings over the past several years and that are plowing 10% to 15% of annual revenues into research and development.

Above all, read the prospectus. You owe it to yourself to slog through it before you put up a penny. Check out who the company's officers are — they're listed in the prospectus — and how much experience they have had marketing other products in the same or related fields. Make sure that the underwriters and the venture capitalists who are backing the firm have sound records of success. If the venture capitalists are not selling their entire stock holdings in the offering, that could be a favorable sign that they think the company has a strong future. (For more, see "Your Investments/Stocks: The Pleasures and Pitfalls of New Issues.")

You also can invest in tomorrow's products by buying shares of one of the mutual funds that concentrate on purchasing the stocks of small, promising companies. A sound method of choosing among the funds is to get a subscription to one of the many newsletters that rate mutual-fund performance. Two of the best letters are *United Mutual Fund Selector* (210 Newbury Street, Boston, Massachusetts 02116; $110 a year), and *NoLoad Fund*X* (235 Montgomery Street, San Francisco, California 94104; $95 a year).

Among the funds that invest chiefly in small stocks are the Nova Fund (260 Franklin Street, Boston, Massachusetts 02110; 617-439-9683, or 800-572-0006 from outside Massachusetts); the Eaton Vance Nautilus Fund (24 Federal Street, Boston, Massachusetts 02110; 617-482-8260, or 800-225-6265 from outside the state); Vanguard Explorer II (P.O. Box 2600, Valley Forge, Pennsylvania 19482; 800-662-7447); and Twentieth Century Ultra (P.O. Box 419200, Kansas City, Missouri 64141-6200; 816-531-5575).

Many of those funds are heavily weighted with high-tech issues. But if you want still more specialization, you might look into the Alliance Technology Fund (140 Broadway, New York, New York 10005; 800-522-2323, or 800-221-5672 from outside New York) or the Fidelity Select-Technology Portfolio (82 Devonshire Street, Boston, Massachusetts 02109; 617-523-1919, or 800-544-6666 from outside the state).

Another way to invest is to buy into publicly traded venture capital companies and small-business investment companies. They often sell shares that are traded over the counter or on exchanges and use the money to invest in promising new ventures. When you are evaluating them, the best measure of their performance is their net asset value per share — of course, it should be rising. (For more, see "Your Investments/Stocks: SBIC and Venture Capital Shares.")

Fast-Growth Stocks

ONE route to profit in the market is to find fast-growth companies while they are still too small to attract wide attention. But before buying, examine growth stocks by five important measures:

First, there's earnings. Ideally, they should have increased an average 20% or more a year for the last five years.

Second, check into the capitalization — that is the value of all common shares. If the capitalization is under $100 million, the stock often sells for a bargain price.

Third, consider the price/earnings ratio. Usually, a stock should sell for no more than 20 times its earnings per share.

Fourth, look at return on equity. It shows how effectively management is using the money it has received from shareholders. A return of 15% on equity is good; 30% is extraordinary. You can arrive at the figure by dividing a company's net income by its net worth, but it's much easier just to ask your broker.

Your final test is a low ratio of debt to equity. Usually a company's long-term debt should be no higher than the total market value of its common stock.

Some of the most sought-after growth stocks, of course, are those of companies on the cutting edges of technology. High-tech stocks were bid to crazy heights after the market surged in August 1982. The inevitable day of reckoning came in mid-1983, and the overpriced shares went down in smoke. By mid-1984, the price/earnings ratios of high-tech stocks were back to where they had been two years earlier, before the market exploded. But these stocks still carried price/earnings ratios about 50% higher than that of the market. That was because investors continued to believe high technology would be the economy's major source of long-term growth. They still have sound reasons to do so, even though young companies in overcrowded, highly competitive fields are especially risky.

You can reduce your risk by concentrating on underpopulated industries where one or two companies have found a profitable market niche. One such field is computer-aided engineering, which, among other things, allows engineers to design silicon chips directly on a computer screen. One company at the forefront of this business is Mentor Graphics of Beaverton, Oregon.

The human side of high technology is the speculative but exciting biotech or health-technology industry. Biotech stocks are *not* for the timid. Most of the companies have yet to show any earnings. And profits could be a long time coming because years of clinical testing are required before a medical product can be sold. Ask a stockbroker for firms whose products are well along in the clinical testing phase. In mid-1988 one such company was Amgen.

Over-the-Counter Stocks

I F YOU are willing to buy stocks that are risky but may offer some outsized rewards, you might want to shop on the over-the-counter market. Shares on the OTC market tend to be those of companies that are too small and too new to be listed on the major exchanges. They also have fewer shares, so even a small amount of buying or selling can cause sharp moves, up or down.

OTC issues are listed on what's called NASDAQ, which stands for the National Association of Securities Dealers Automated Quotations system. That's a computer-linked network of about 500 competing broker-dealers who electronically post the prices at which each of them will buy or sell certain OTC stocks. The NASDAQ listings are loaded with small, glamourless companies, some of which are selling for a bargain price of only 10 times earnings — or even less. They may be undervalued simply because few people have bothered to look at their financial statements.

If you want to invest in this market, swear off hot tips. Think instead about small companies that have caught your eye — say, by selling a product or service you admire or by expanding in a market you understand. Candidates might include new firms that are major competitors in emergent fields and seasoned concerns that are prospering in otherwise troubled sectors, such as computers or savings banking.

Also popular are mutual funds that specialize in over-the-counter stocks. One of the best is Fidelity's OTC Portfolio (82 Devonshire Street, Boston, Massachusetts 02109; 617-523-1919, or 800-544-6666 outside the state). It got started only in December 1984, but as of mid-1988 it had gained nearly 130%.

SBIC and Venture Capital Shares

Only rich people used to be able to ante up the venture capital that got new companies going. But you can invest in beginning businesses too, and you don't have to be a millionaire to do it. One way to get in on the ground floor is to find a promising firm that is just starting out and put money directly into it. In exchange you will be given some of that company's stock, and you can call yourself a venture capitalist.

Trouble is, you have to search hard for these opportunities because they are rarely publicized. Your best leads will come from local bankers. Ask them what ventures are just beginning and need some cash. Look for companies in businesses you know something about. It is also wise to start with ventures that are near your home so that you can maintain close contact with the people running the company.

But let's face it: most people who sink their money directly into start-ups will lose at least part of it. Even successful ventures rarely show a payoff within five years. Arthur Lipper III, chairman of *Venture* magazine, recommends that you place no more than 20% of your investment cash in such companies.

You can improve your odds by buying shares in small-business investment companies, or SBICs, that are open to public investment. These companies raise capital and invest it in businesses with a net worth of $6 million or less. There are 307 all-purpose small-business investment companies and another 128 that specialize in minority enterprises. Most are owned by banks or groups of private individuals, but a few have public shares that can be bought or sold over-the-counter or on the American Stock Exchange. Among them are First Connecticut and Allied Capital.

SBICs concentrate on small business that creates jobs. They are licensed by the Small Business Administration, which guarantees them up to $4 for each $1 of private capital they raise. Some of the money is invested in start-ups that offer little more than potentially workable concepts. The rest is in second- and third-round financings to help spur the growth of companies that are already marketing a product or have moved solidly into the black.

A number of SBICs prefer to cut out as much risk as possible. They invest only in companies that are mature enough to provide them with some current income, which they in turn pay out to their shareholders in dividends.

What kind of SBIC you invest in depends on whether you want immediate income or longer-term capital gains. But whatever kind you select, ask yourself two questions: Do you think that the companies supported by the SBIC are sound businesses? And what is the investment record of the SBIC's manager? You can draw much of this information from the SBIC's quarterly and annual reports.

Another way to get in on start-up businesses is through a venture capital company. This is essentially a mutual fund that invests in nonpublic concerns. Venture capital firms tend to put their money in riskier enterprises. But some of them have produced big winners. For example, Boston's Nautilus Fund is best known for its investment in Apple Computer back in 1979. Apple soared and made many shareholders happy — notably those who took their profits near the peak before it eventually plunged. Venture capital companies are traded over-the-counter or on the American Exchange.

Before you buy shares in a venture capital company, read the annual and quarterly reports carefully. You want to know what new companies they are financing and how well — or poorly — the investment manager has performed in the past.

Lately, a few brokerage companies have offered for public sale some partnerships that invest in new businesses, among them Merrill Lynch and Boettcher & Co. Investors can buy into the partnerships for $5,000 plus a sales commission. Unfortunately, there is no public marketplace where you can sell your units if you suddenly should need the money. All Merrill Lynch will do, for example, is try to match up sellers with buyers through brokers.

You also can try to buy the shares of new companies when they first go public. It is not easy to get in on a popular new issue. And the price may shoot to the stratosphere when all the people who could not buy it try to pick it up from those who could. Within a year, however, many new issues slip back to their offering price — or go even lower. Investors who wait for such a decline usually have gains as big as those who got in early.

If you want to buy a company that is going public, ask a broker for a prospectus. See who is doing the selling. If all the original backers are now backing out, beware. The public offering of stock may be rescuing them from a bad investment. But if the original investors are hanging on to their shares, that could be a sign the company has a very bright future.

The Pleasures and Pitfalls of New Issues

INVESTORS seem to be passionately eager to get in on the hot new issues of stocks that are coming to market for the first time. But before plunging in, examine them closely. Offering prices are often inflated, and companies that are too questionable to win the financial support of blue-ribbon underwriters have little trouble finding unexacting sponsors. As one long-established underwriter warns: "Anyone who ventures into new issues needs to be rigorously selective. A lot of real junk is being brought to market, and that's scary."

On the other hand, quite a few companies of real substance are selling their issues to the public for the first time. The new-issues market is presenting the public with a chance to invest in some youthful companies that are trailblazers in applied technology. Out of such companies will emerge the top growth firms of the late 1980s and the 1990s. Again, the key is selectivity, and its importance is shown by the performance statistics.

Getting information about new public issues is not difficult. Some brokerage houses publish weekly calendars of forthcoming offerings. Most brokers subscribe to *Investment Dealers' Digest,* a weekly that covers the new-issues market. The prospective investor should ask his or her broker for the stock's prospectus, the so-called red herring, and scrutinize it carefully.

Look for the passage that lays bare the holdings of the top officers of the company that is selling its stock to you. To repeat, if they are unloading a lot of their own shares, you should shun the issue.

Check the prospectus to see that the underwriter of the issue is a well-established firm. Even the best underwriters make errors of judgment, but they will not knowingly market the stock of a company that is likely to damage their reputation. Some of the highest-quality new issues are brought to market by such blue-chip investment firms as L. F. Rothschild & Co.; Ladenburg Thalmann; Alex. Brown & Sons; and Morgan Stanley. Yet these companies, too, can fall victim to cyclical downturns in the market or unexpected competition from lesser-known firms and suddenly find their deals and reputations souring. The bottom line is to be careful not to depend too heavily on any one underwriter.

See who is providing the venture capital financing. Strong backing by venture capital entrepreneurs suggests that the new company has been well groomed to go public and probably has genuine promise. You can breathe easier if the prospectus lists such respected venture capital firms as Kleiner Perkins Caufield & Byers, DSV Partners, Sutter Hill Ventures or Venrock Associates.

Examine the balance sheet in the prospectus. Are the new company's finances strong enough to keep it going even if profits do not meet expectations — or, if profit growth is on target, to provide capital for continued expansion? If you don't trust your own judgment on these matters, don't invest in new issues without reliable professional guidance.

Penny Stocks

HAVE you been told that you can make easy money by investing in penny stocks? Well, you might, but it's unlikely.

Penny stocks are securities that are issued at $1 or less a share. Sometimes they quadruple in price within days after they are first sold as speculators bid them up. But when a penny bubble bursts, there is often little or nothing left of your investment.

Penny issues don't trade on an exchange but in markets made by small regional brokerage houses. A typical penny-stock company can be a shaky firm that prices its stock at rock bottom to attract naive investors. These are the people who assume that buying 10,000 shares at 10 cents each is a better deal than buying 100 shares at $10.

Investors who come out ahead on these stocks not only pick the right ones but also quickly dump them after their early rise. There is less chance to profit if you buy penny stocks after their initial offering.

Buying Shares of Bankrupt Firms

BUSINESS failures have been running at high rates, and that's a shame. But many investors are finding bargains in bankrupt firms. They buy up the stocks and bonds of big, bankrupt corporations at distress prices. These speculators hope that the companies will come out of their court-directed reorganizations slimmed down and comparatively debt-free, and that the increased value of their securities will amply reward investors for the steep risks they are taking.

Investors' eyes glisten at memories of the huge fortunes that were made on such bankrupt companies of the past as Penn Central and Interstate Stores, which later became Toys "Я" Us. Of course, many investors in bankrupt firms have lost considerable money: W. T. Grant is just one example.

The potential for gain springs from the nature of the bankruptcy laws. They are designed to give moribund companies a new lease on life, to let them work out a plan to pay off creditors. Among those creditors, bondholders have the first claim on a company's assets. Common stockholders' rewards are much less assured. They are entitled to whatever assets are left — if any — after the bondholders and other debt holders are paid.

So, bankruptcy investors tend to stick with secured debt. At times they will venture further down the pecking order to buy preferred or common stock. But usually they will do that only after a company has just come out of reorganization, shining with such virtues as a clean balance sheet, an accumulation of tax losses that can be carried forward to offset future earnings and a talented management with definite ideas about where it's heading.

Investing in bankrupts is not for the faint of heart or short of pocket. Even situations that look promising often do not pan out. Since the bankruptcy investment game is dominated by the professionals, it would be foolhardy to sit in without coaching from the experts at a brokerage house such as Bear Stearns or another of the firms that invest in bankrupt companies. One mutual fund that does this is Mutual Shares (26 Broadway, New York, New York 10004).

Foreign Shares

THE sweeping rise in the value of the dollar earlier in the 1980s increased Americans' purchasing power for foreign goods. But bargain hunters may have overlooked one interesting if chancy buy: foreign *stocks*. These investments stand to do well if the dollar continues to drop against the currencies of Germany, Britain, Switzerland, the Netherlands and other countries. Even if the stock you pick doesn't rise but the dollar declines against the currency of that country, you will come out ahead when you sell. The reason: the foreign currency you collect from the sale will convert into more dollars than it cost you to buy the stock. And if the stock rises, you will get a double lift.

On the negative side, Americans who invest in foreign stocks run the risk that a foreign currency decline will cut into any stock gains. In the specific case of Japan, that country's currency has risen so fast against the dollar, and Japanese stocks have soared so high relative to corporate earnings, that many analysts would not be surprised to see a fall. Also, different accounting standards make it hard to evaluate foreign companies, and information is not as quickly available as it is for U.S. stocks. For those reasons, money managers believe you should probably limit your international investments to at most 10% or 15% of your stock holdings.

You can buy individual foreign stocks yourself. Most Canadian shares are traded in the U.S. just like American securities. So are the stocks of about 700 other foreign companies. They are sold in the form of American Depositary Receipts, or ADRs. Each ADR is issued by a U.S. bank and represents one to 10 shares of a foreign stock held abroad at a custodian bank. ADRs generally trade over-the-counter, though a few are listed on the New York Stock Exchange.

Experienced investors seeking a wider choice can buy and sell shares directly on foreign stock markets. Your U.S. broker should be able to handle the transactions. But don't expect him or her to offer expert advice on which foreign stocks look particularly attractive.

An easy way to get your feet wet is with American mutual funds specializing in foreign stocks. Among them, Merrill Lynch Pacific and G. T. Pacific concentrate on Far Eastern stocks. For stocks of companies in Europe and elsewhere, you might consider Kemper International, Scudder International, Transatlantic and Fidelity Overseas.

Seeking Safe Utilities

PARTICULARLY if you are looking for high yields, electric-utility stocks may have a place among your investments — provided you realize that the dividends are not certain and the stocks' prices are subject to swift change without notice. That is because volatile oil prices and the debate over nuclear power cause many electric-utility stocks to be as risky as some high-tech issues. Nuclear facilities are staggeringly expensive to build, and the Soviet disaster at Chernobyl will add fuel to efforts to stop the building of new ones. Whenever construction is halted, billions of dollars can be lost. It is precisely to compensate you for the possibility of such a short circuit that utilities usually pay substantial dividends.

If you are shopping for utilities stocks, many analysts recommend that you stick to those companies that either have no nuclear plants at all or have no plans to build more. Among those stocks recommended by analysts are TECO Energy, which was once known as Tampa Electric, and IPALCO Enterprises, which was formerly called Indianapolis Power & Light. Both of them have no nuclear plants and both are rapidly diversifying into other fields. TECO is expanding into coal mining and hauling, and IPALCO has acquired Indianapolis Cablevision.

Then there are the utilities that are already operating nuclear plants safely but have no plans to build more. Some of them that analysts have been recommending include Consolidated Edison in New York, Northern States Power, Wisconsin Energy, Wisconsin Public Service, Baltimore Gas & Electric and the FPL Group in Florida.

Dividend-Reinvestment Plans

You rarely get something for nothing, particularly when it comes to buying stocks. But one exception is the dividend-reinvestment plan. It lets you buy shares *without* paying a broker's commission — and often at a discount price.

When you buy stock in certain companies, they offer you these reinvestment programs. They automatically let you use your stock dividends to buy more shares in the company free of a brokerage commission. More than 1,000 companies have reinvestment plans. Better yet, at least 64 of them also give you discounts on the price of the stock. Discounts generally amount to 3% to 5%. However, Acme Electric gives its investors 10% off the market price.

Once you are on record as a shareholder, you simply sign a form authorizing the company to put all of your dividends in additional shares. For example, if you reinvest $100 of dividends in a company that also offers a 5% discount, you get $105 worth of stock. When you don't have enough to buy a full share, the company credits you with a fractional share.

In short, dividend reinvestment is an easy, money-saving way to build up more stock. A good broker can give you the names of companies that offer reinvestment plans. Or you can get a list of them by sending $2 to Standard & Poor's, Public Relations Department, 25 Broadway, New York, New York 10004.

Index Options

WHEN you invest in only one or two stocks, you are taking the chance that *they* might not go up when the market does. Most people cannot afford to buy a variety of stocks wide enough to fluctuate with the entire market. But now there is an investment designed to let investors profit from the rise or fall of the total market: index options.

Index options are like stock options. They give you the right to buy or sell securities at a predetermined price any time before the option expires. An option to buy is a call; the right to sell is a put.

When you buy such an option from a broker, you place a bet that some broad index of stocks will rise or fall, usually within the next 90 days. An index option usually costs only a few hundred dollars, but you could reap the same profits as if you had invested $15,000 to $20,000. That is because a small move up or down in the index can cause a much bigger change in the value of the option. This enormous leverage accounts for the thrills of index-options trading. And the chills. Because if you wager wrongly you lose everything you had invested. That happened to many sad investors in the crash of October 1987.

The most popular index option is called the Standard & Poor's 100. It is a weighted average of the current market value of 100 blue-chip stocks selected by the Chicago Board Options Exchange. Seven other stock indexes are also used for options trading, including the New York Stock Exchange composite and the American Exchange's major market index.

If you are optimistic about the market, you buy a call option. It surges in value when the market goes up. If you are pessimistic, you buy a put option. It surges when the market goes down.

Remember, investing in stock index options is tempting but very chancy. One top brokerage officer recommends this strategy: First, determine how much capital you are willing to risk. Then, invest it all in supersafe one-year Treasury bills — except for an amount equal to the interest that you will collect on your Treasuries. Next, place *that* amount into stock index options. Even if you lose it all, the interest you collect on your Treasuries will cover your losses.

You also can use puts to protect any profits you already have made on the stocks that you own but do not want to sell just now. If the market should fall, your stocks also would probably fall, but your put option would rise. That gain would offset at least part of the losses on your stocks.

Tax-sheltered Shares

IS THE tax man taking a big bite out of your stock dividends? Then you may want to consider a form of stock whose returns are at least partly sheltered from taxes. They go by such odd names as REITs and FREITs.

REITs are real estate investment trusts. They own income-producing properties or make mortgage loans and pay regular dividends to shareholders. Some of these payments may be considered a return of capital and therefore are not directly taxable. Eventually, of course, you will have to pay taxes on your accumulated profits when the REIT sells some of its properties.

Some investors prefer a second type of investment called finite-life REITs, or FREITs. They sell off their properties or distribute the profits according to a fairly fixed schedule, typically starting in the sixth year after they are set up. (For more, see "Your Investments/ Real Estate: REITs and Limited Partnerships.")

BONDS

Sizing Up the Market

Bonds used to offer secure income from interest, a safe harbor for your money and no excitement whatever. Oh, how that has changed. Jagged rises and falls in interest rates have sent bond prices plunging and leaping like a bronco with a burr under its saddle. Rates now fluctuate more in a day than they once did in a year. Since bond prices move as fast as interest rates, but in the opposite direction, the bond market is no longer a calm haven for the faint-hearted.

Despite the uncertainties in the market, Americans have gone on a bond-buying binge. But many of the professionals who manage investments for banks, insurance companies and pension funds are apprehensive about buying long-term bonds. They are afraid to commit money for decades ahead at fixed rates. What has the bond market on edge is worry that the U.S. Treasury must borrow so much to finance 12-digit federal budget deficits that interest rates may surge once again, causing bond prices to plunge. Of course, many other forecasters believe that the deficits will soon narrow and inflation will subside permanently, thus pushing interest rates lower.

If rates do head down, the prices of bonds will go up. In that case, the bond that you buy today you can sell for a nice gain in the future. The risk you run, of course, is that interest rates could turn the other way around, and climb back up. In that case, if you ever had to sell before your bond matured, you would take a loss.

Bold investors who are willing to trade actively may be able to profit handsomely from volatile interest rates. The principles of trading in fixed-income investments are simple: To get the highest yields you should invest for as short a term as possible when rates are rising. Once you are convinced that rates have peaked, you should move into longer-term securities — to lock in those high yields and to reap any capital gains.

Prudence dictates caution in the bond market. But you can make sound use of bonds provided you understand the risks. For in-and-out speculators seeking quick capital gains, trading can be as attractive in bonds as in stocks. If you seek steady income, you can still find that old-time safety, perhaps by buying the bonds of reliable, major corporations that are selling at deep discounts from their face values. And if you are willing to take a risk with your principal, there may be an opportunity now to lock up 20 or 30 years of reasonable yields by buying long-term bonds.

How They Work

IF YOU are thinking about investing in bonds, you have a vast smorgasbord of choices. You can buy ordinary, individual bonds, just like Mother and Dad did, or you can buy into whole portfolios in the form of a bond fund or a unit trust.

A bond is a long-term IOU, and it pays a fixed rate of interest. Usually, you collect your interest checks every six months. Then when the bond comes due, your capital is repaid in full. So you can choose to tuck your bond away in a safe-deposit box and collect regular interest payments until the bond matures. But it is precisely those far-off maturity dates and the fixed interest rates that make bonds risky.

Say you buy a new 30-year corporate bond at its face value of $1,000. Say also that it pays 10% interest, so you collect $100 a year every year until the date when the bond matures, or comes due. But if long-term interest rates in the meantime rise — say, to 20% — your bond will fall in value. It will be worth only about $500 in the open market, because that is the amount that makes your $100 annual return equal to a 20% yield. If you had to sell your bond to raise money before it matured, you would lose cash.

On the brighter side, however, if interest rates fall below 10%, your fixed-interest bond is obviously worth more than $1,000. That is because an investor would have to pay more than $1,000 in the market to buy a bond that would yield the guaranteed $100 a year that you collect. You may want to speculate in bonds if you think that interest rates will fall, thus pushing prices up.

When you buy a bond, you should consider four factors: First, there is the so-called coupon rate. That is the percentage of interest you collect. Second is the maturity date. That is the date when you will be paid the face value of the bond, usually $1,000. Third, there is the tax status. The interest paid on bonds issued by government bodies is usually exempt from certain taxes. Finally, there is the quality rating — AAA or B-minus or such — which tells you the financial soundness of the issuer.

Most investors should stay with bonds that have a quality rating of AAA or AA. Indeed, U.S. Treasury securities, which are guaranteed by the federal government, are even safer than AAA corporate or municipal bonds. Prices of top-quality issues of all kinds fall less than those of other long-term bonds when interest rates rise.

But adventurous buyers might consider lower-quality issues. A bond rated BBB offers a yield two or three percentage points higher than one rated AAA. And yields for so-called junk bonds — which are rated BB+ or lower — are still richer. These low-rated bonds have real risks. While few bond issuers have ever defaulted on the principal, interest payments could be deferred or the bond's quality rating could be lowered further, and that would depress the price.

Your Choices

FOR small and substantial investors alike, bonds now appear to offer an unusual opportunity. In mid-1988, corporate AA-rated industrial bonds were paying interest that was more than five percentage points higher than the rate of inflation. And that was two to three times as much real interest as bonds historically pay.

You will probably do best buying U.S. Treasury issues or perhaps AAA-rated corporate bonds. Yields on 30-year Treasuries in mid-1988 were about 9.4%. That compared with the 10.18% available on top-rated corporates. This was a spread that made T-bonds the wiser choice of the two. Corporate bonds yield more to reward you for taking a chance that the company that issues the bond might get into trouble and be unable to pay the interest or principal when it comes due. Not only are Treasuries safer — the U.S. government would have to fall before they default — but also the interest they pay is exempt from state and local taxes. Sorry, you *do* have to pay federal taxes on it.

There is another important difference: when interest rates drop, private companies often "call" — that is, buy back — their high-yielding bonds. By contrast, 30-year Treasury bonds are "noncallable" for at least 25 years, and some are protected for the full 30 years; all other Treasury bonds are totally "noncallable." So you can hold on to these high-yielding bonds for a long time — usually until they mature — with no fear that the government will force you to sell out. When you buy any kind of corporate or municipal bond, you should check to see whether it can be called in early by the issuer. Some corporate bonds guarantee against calls for up to 10 years.

You can find some particularly good values among the general obligation bonds of heavy industrial states in the so-called Rust Belt, such as Pennsylvania and Michigan. Such bonds are sometimes rated only A or AA, but their ratings and relatively bargain prices do not yet reflect the increased tax revenues that the economic recovery poured into state coffers.

Municipal bonds are hard to buy in units smaller than $5,000. They are equally tough to sell without paying a high commission if you own fewer than 25 bonds. So the best way for most people to buy these securities is through one of the tax-free bond municipal funds. (See "Your Investments/Bonds: Tax-exempt Municipals.")

Investors who yearn for that old-fashioned bond market religion — that is, for a faithful return without much risk — should shop for a bond that is way down in price. These deep-discount bonds were issued 25 years ago, when interest rates were only 4%. Naturally, nobody would buy a bond today that pays only 4%. So the prices of these bonds have tumbled deeply in the market. Consequently, you can go to a stockbroker and for much less than $1,000 buy a bond that will pay you back $1,000 when it matures some years from now — and in the meantime pay you its regular, though modest, interest.

Many analysts say that among the best deep-discount bonds are those that were issued by the old telephone company. For example, in mid-1988, you could buy $1,000 worth of AT&T's 4¾% bonds maturing in 1992 for only $815. The interest that these bonds pay is small, which is why they are cheap. But you can use a discount bond to build a college fund for the children.

Deep-discount bonds should not be confused with low-quality

bonds, those rated BB+ or lower, which are rather affectionately known as junk bonds. They reflect weak spots in the issuer's financial armor and behave more like stocks than bonds. Their prices tend to rise in line with improvements in the economy or in the fortunes of the issuing company.

Speculators who aim for maximum capital gains — but are willing to take maximum risk, too — might consider convertible bonds. They are called "convertible" because they can be swapped for a stated number of shares of the issuer's stock. A convertible's price swings not only with interest rates, but also with the issuing company's underlying shares. When share prices rise or fall, so do convertible prices.

Bond Funds and Unit Trusts

B ECAUSE prices of individual bonds are so unsteady, investors are looking for less risky ways to get into the bond market. You can spread the risk of default by buying bond mutual funds and unit trusts, which give you a small share in a large number of bonds. Professional managers relieve you of worries about which bonds to buy and sell, and when to purchase or unload them, by performing those tasks for you.

A bond mutual fund will always redeem your shares at the present worth of the underlying bonds. If the prices of bonds in the mutual fund's portfolio go up, then your shares immediately go up. Of course, it works the other way around, too. Brokers sell bond funds and collect commissions of up to 8½% from you, but you easily can buy commission-free, no-load bond funds by mail.

As an alternative, of course, you can buy individual bonds. And you can sell them back in the market at any time. But whether you are buying or selling, you will usually take a beating on the price because commissions are high unless you are dealing with very large amounts. So you stand to get a better deal on commissions with no-load bond funds than with individual bonds.

Individual bonds do have some advantage over funds. If interest rates rise and a bond's price drops, you know that your bond eventually will be paid off at its face value — when it matures, or comes due. But bond funds never mature. So, if interest rates surge and stay high, your bond fund shares may never again be worth what you paid for them.

Unit trusts are usually huge bond portfolios assembled and sold by brokerage houses in small slices of $1,000 to $5,000. They give you the combined benefits of diversification and fairly good prices. After you have paid commissions, you generally get about $950 to $960 worth of securities for each $1,000 you invest. The yields are slightly bigger than those of bond funds because the portfolios are usually riskier.

The trust's sponsor almost always will buy units back from you at a price equal to their net asset value. The advantages of liquidity and diversification, however, come at some cost; you run a risk that interest rates will rise, and the price of your units will decline. Also, the sponsors usually buy long-term bonds maturing in 30 years and do not sell any of them unless the issuer is revealed to be in imminent danger of default. By then, of course, it is usually too late.

True, you will not be too badly clobbered because the trust owns many different bonds, and it is highly unlikely that more than a few bond issuers would default at any one time. Still, the way to safe-guard yourself against turkeys in your trust — before you send in your money — is to read the trust's prospectus. It lists each bond in the portfolio along with its credit rating and tells you about any provisions that the bonds may be called in early by the issuer if interest rates fall.

You also can buy tax-exempt unit trusts. In mid-1988, they were paying interest of about 8% — tax-free. Investors who are especially safety-minded can put some money into an *insured* tax-exempt trust. The bonds are backed by an insurance company guarantee that interest and principal will be paid on schedule, but the cost of the insurance reduces the yield to a shade less than you would get on an unsecured trust. (See "Your Investments/Bonds: Insured Municipals.")

Taking all these factors together, the easiest and safest way for most persons of moderate means to buy a diversity of bonds is to invest in a no-load bond mutual fund. The interest income is reasonably steady, there are no commissions when you buy or sell and the annual fees are modest. Unlike unit trusts, bond fund portfolios are actively managed. The issues in them are constantly being traded, and presumably the managers know enough to escape from a troubled situation and sell out well before a bond encounters the danger of default.

Tax-exempt Municipals

MUNICIPAL bonds have become Everyman's tax shelter. The federal government does not tax the interest you collect on most of them, and if the bonds are from your home state, you probably will escape state and local taxes, too. This exemption is not the only reason to buy munis. They also yield high interest. Often they pay about 80% to 85% as much as U.S. Treasury bonds do, but your income from Treasuries is not exempt from federal taxes. In May 1988 solid 30-year municipals were paying around 8.3%, which was four points higher than the compounded annual rate of inflation.

Tax reform has made many municipal bond owners nervous. Since reform puts almost all people in lower tax brackets than they were in before, their effective return from tax-exempt bonds is lower than in earlier years.

But do not rush out and sell your tax-free bonds. Even if your tax rate falls, your return from municipals could still be quite good. For example, if you were in the 33% tax bracket for your 1988 income, a top-rated 30-year municipal yielding 8.32% would have paid you the equivalent of a 12.4% taxable yield. If you were in the 28% tax bracket, your yield would have been 11.3%.

Municipals have the usual risk: if interest rates climb, the prices of the bonds fall. Then, if you had to sell off your investment to raise money, you would get less than you paid for it. Another risk is that the state or city agency that issued the bond could go broke and default on its payments of principal and interest. To avoid this danger, small investors should stick with the highest-quality bonds — those rated AAA or AA by Moody's or Standard & Poor's.

You can buy individual bonds from a stockbroker; as discussed, he or she usually will require you to purchase at least $5,000 worth. But it is unwise to buy them unless you plan to hold them until they mature and the issuer pays you back the full face value. If you sell out earlier, you could lose as much as 5% of the value of your bond on sales commissions and the spread between the higher "asked" price at which the broker sells you the bond and the "bid" price at which he will buy it from you. You are at the broker's mercy for what he will pay because the vast majority of municipal bond prices are not even published in newspapers.

One new investment is a tax-free municipal bond that has no certificate. Buying or selling this bond is merely a computer transaction, and your record of ownership is a monthly brokerage statement. One plus is that the interest is paid directly into your brokerage account on the day it is due. You do not have to wait for a check to arrive or clear. And there are no worries about certificates being lost or stolen.

Another fairly new wrinkle in tax-exempt securities is the single-state municipal bond fund or unit trust. You usually pay no federal, state or local taxes on the interest from this investment. Residents of high-tax New York and California have been buying single-state funds for years, and investor demand has been rising throughout the country. Single-state funds or trusts are available in about half the states, including Connecticut, Massachusetts, Michigan, Minnesota, Ohio, Pennsylvania and Virginia.

Such funds give you the advantage of diversification: you get different bonds, all issued by agencies within one state. The higher your tax bracket, of course, the more you can benefit from a single-state tax-exempt fund.

Another smart long-term investment is tax-exempt municipal put bonds. The issuers of put bonds offer to buy them back from you at face value at least once a year, sometimes after an initial holding period. For example, in mid-1988 you could buy AAA-rated 20-year bonds yielding 5.35% and "puttable" in one year.

You can reduce your risks as well as your cost by buying shares in a municipal bond fund or a unit trust, whether single-state or not. Probably the best tax-exempt investments for most people are the shares of no-load tax-exempt bond mutual funds. For annual management fees and expenses of only about one-half of 1% of your investment, the funds give you a share of a professionally managed portfolio of bonds that you can sell at any time.

You can buy funds directly from mutual-fund companies. Their toll-free numbers and addresses are found in advertisements in the financial press. The municipal bond funds with the highest total returns for the 12 months ending June 30, 1988, were UST Master Tax-Exempt Long, with a total return of 13.2%; Alliance Tax-Free Income–High Income, 10.7%; and Nuveen Insured Tax-Free Bond–National, 9.7%.

Insured Municipals

I F YOU are thinking about investing in municipal bonds, you may be worried that many states and localities are severely troubled by federal budget cutbacks and shrinking tax revenues. But there is a new way that you can invest in municipals and insure yourself against any losses from defaults.

You can profit from the oversize yields and still be able to sleep at night by investing in *insured* municipal bond funds or trusts. The portfolios of insured bond funds and trusts are backed by a number of private insurance companies, and all are rated AAA by the authoritative Standard & Poor's rating service. The insurance guarantees investors full payment of interest and principal when due, and costs about $1.25 a year for every $1,000 you invest. This has the effect of reducing your annual yield from a fund or trust by only one-eighth of 1%.

Insured trusts are sponsored by many brokerage firms. You can buy units through your broker, who will deduct a sales commission of roughly 5%. That means that if you put up $1,000, you get about $950 worth of bonds.

Merrill Lynch's Municipal Bond Fund Insured Portfolio is insured principally by AMBAC Indemnity Corporation and Bond Investors/Guarantee Insurance Company. The fund offers an extra: you can write checks of $500 or more against your money.

Beware of Unwelcome Calls

Y OU MAY have an unpleasant surprise in store if you own high-paying bonds that were originally issued in the early 1980s: those securities could soon be called in and paid off. Yes, you would get back all the money you paid for the bonds, but you would lose those nice, high regular interest payments.

Interest rates on municipal bonds, for example, hit their highs of more than 13% in 1982. From then until mid-1988 their yields fell by about five percentage points. Because of this decline, state and local government agencies still stuck with paying those 13% rates have been eager to redeem their older bonds as soon as they could and then sell new bonds at today's lower rates. These early payoffs are known as "calls."

Investors generally are protected from calls for at least 10 years after the bond is issued. But some bonds may be redeemed within five years, or even less. A stockbroker or a financial planner can tell you whether your bond is among the ones at risk of an early redemption.

If you are considering buying a new bond, it's probably wise to pick one that offers you call protection for at least 10 years. That way you can lock in today's interest rates for well into the future. This would become especially valuable if and when interest rates decline.

Investors in bond unit trusts also need to watch call provisions, especially if the trust touts an extraordinarily steep yield. Such trusts often are invested in many of the older high-interest bonds, which may be called. You would be wise to check the call dates on bonds listed in the prospectus of the trust to see if you are adequately protected. Otherwise, you could end up with a much lower yield than the trust advertised.

Variable-Rate Option Municipals

A RATHER new investment that allows you to earn tax-free income without tying up your money for more than a year is the variable-rate option bond. It is a long-term municipal bond, but the interest rates it pays are adjusted annually — up or down — to whatever the current market rate is. And once a year or, in some cases, more often, you will have the option to cash in the bond and collect what you paid for it.

Variable-rate option bonds, sold by many brokerage firms, were paying, averaged over time, approximately one-half to one percentage point more than tax-exempt money-market funds in mid-1988. True, the variable-rate yield was about three points below the rate available on conventional long-term municipal bonds. But if investors in those regular bonds sell out early, they have no assurance of getting back the full amount they have invested.

If you plan to hold onto your tax-free bond for many years, you are probably best off buying a regular municipal bond. But if you think you will need your money back in a year, you might be well advised to consider variable-rate option bonds.

The Glories and Dangers of Junk

ALL that glitters on Wall Street is not gold, but it may be junk—junk bonds.

These are bonds that are rated low by the official bond rating services: BB+ or lower by Standard & Poor's, BA1 or lower by Moody's. As a trade-off for their risk, junks pay higher yields than do top-quality bonds, and often sell at a discount. In mid-1988 junks were yielding between 11¾% and 20%, compared with 10.18% for long-term industrial AAA issues.

You can lessen your chances of choosing a bond that may default if you diversify, by buying a bond mutual fund. Look for a fund that in its name has the term "high-yield" — that means junk. Along with the yields, junks offer you a better chance for capital gains than do high-rated issues. When interest rates drop, or bond ratings are upgraded, the prices of junk bonds often shoot up faster than do better-quality issues.

When you shop for junk, you should distinguish between two types: genuine trash and quality junk. Bonds whose quality ratings have recently been downgraded are genuine trash. Pass them up. But other bonds may be diamonds in the rough. The companies that issue the bonds may be simply too young to have a long and favorable credit history. In other cases, the ratings services may not yet have recognized turnarounds in the issuing companies. And still other bonds may be quality junk because they are found in out-of-favor lines of business, such as gambling. So you may do well by scouting for glitter amid the junk.

Recently a new and far riskier type of trashy junk bond has been flooding the market. Many of these new debt issues are being used to finance corporate takeovers by outsiders or so-called leveraged buyouts by company insiders. Either way, many corporations are overburdened with more debt than they safely can support.

If there is a recession or a miscalculation by the dealmakers, some of these corporations could take a dive and drag bondholders down with them. In a major bankruptcy, a defaulting junk bond could lose more than half its value overnight.

To be on the safe side, avoid junk bonds issued in connection with such takeovers and buyouts. Some of them may be sound, but it's almost impossible for amateurs to evaluate. Also, diversify your holdings to reduce your risk. The best way is to invest in a corporate bond mutual fund that actively manages 70 to 140 issues. These funds in mid-1988 were returning about 8.6%. The following bond funds have had the best results during the past five years: Kemper High Yield, 101.9%; First Investors Special Bond, 92.5%; and Fidelity High Income 90.4%.

Convertible Securities

CONVERTIBLE securities are part bond and part stock. In today's uncertain financial climate, they can be a sensible buy — provided you are an experienced investor.

A convertible is a bond or preferred stock that pays a fixed rate of interest or a preset dividend. And it has a unique advantage: it can be exchanged for the issuing company's common shares — if and when they rise to a certain price. So an investor in convertibles might have it both ways. He collects high interest or dividend income now — and maybe he pockets big profits later on by converting into the common stock.

But you must pay a price for this flexibility. The cost of a convertible is higher than the value of the stock you can exchange it for. Also, the interest or dividends you collect on a convertible are usually three or four percentage points below what you can get on the same company's bonds or preferred stock.

If the issuing company's common stock rises steeply, a convertible reaches what is called its conversion price. It then pays to switch into those common shares — and earn a profit. But what if the stock market goes down? The convertible is still attractive because it usually holds its value better than the common stock will.

Gerald Appel, editor of *Systems and Forecasts* newsletter, says that the ideal convertible is one that costs about $1,000, pays you 7½% to 8% in interest and costs you only 10% to 12% more than the value of the common stock that you can switch it into. Such a convertible will tend to keep pace with the common stock in an up market and fall only half as fast as that stock will in a down market.

You might also consider convertible bond funds. They pay about as much interest as money-market funds do. But since you can trade in the bonds in a fund for stocks, you can still reap big gains when stocks start to rise again.

Convertible bond funds are less risky than stock mutual funds, in part because bonds are safer than stocks. The total returns of convertible bond funds for the first six months of 1988 averaged 12.7%. The best performer was Dreyfus Convertible Securities. It returned 19.8%. Three other funds that did well were Convertible Securities and Income, with a return of 18%, Integrated Income–Convertible, with a return of 17.9%, and Rochester Convertible–Growth, with a return of 17.4%.

U.S. Savings Bonds

THE Treasury Department has overhauled good old U.S. Savings Bonds to make them more enticing. Are the bonds better investments than before? They certainly are — and they offer often overlooked tax breaks.

Until fairly recently, series EE bonds, which you can buy for $25 to $5,000, weren't paying much interest compared with other bonds. To get the maximum annual yield of 9%, you had to keep a bond for eight years. You would earn less if you cashed it in earlier.

Now, however, the return on EE bonds held five years or longer fluctuates with market interest rates. The bonds' return is 85% of the average yield of five-year Treasury notes and bonds. There's also a nice extra: to protect you against sharp interest-rate drops, EE bonds are guaranteed to pay a yield of at least 6%, provided you hold them for the full five years. Trouble is, you collect no semi-annual interest checks. All the interest is paid when you cash in the bond — in five years.

But that interest is exempt from state and local taxes, and you pay no federal tax until you cash in the bonds. Even then, you can defer the tax by swapping series EE issues for series HH bonds, which you can get for $500 all the way up to $10,000. The interest on series HH bonds — 6% paid twice a year — is taxable annually, but you are still postponing payment of taxes on your series EE bonds' interest and using tax-deferred dollars to earn interest on series HH bonds.

Zero-Coupon Bonds

You might think that zero-coupon bonds are the real nothings of the investment world. They pay you no interest now nor will they do so for years to come. Worse, *you* are liable for income taxes on the interest you have not even received. What kind of an odd investment is this — and who would want to buy it? Well, *you* might.

Zeros are not without their attractions. With a zero-coupon bond, you can invest as little as $50 and be assured that it will grow to a specific sum when the bond comes due. The term generally ranges from six months to 30 years. These securities sell at really deep discounts. Example: for only $590 you could buy a corporate zero-coupon bond in mid-1988 that would pay you $1,000 in 1994; for $245 you could get one that would pay you $1,000 in the year 2003.

When the bonds mature, you collect all the accrued interest. If you own a zero-coupon, you are not confronted every six months or so with the problem of reinvesting the interest income to maintain the high yield. So you make as few investment decisions as possible.

And you can escape the necessity to pay taxes on the phantom interest year by year. Just buy zero-coupon corporate bonds for your Individual Retirement Account or your Keogh plan or some other tax-sheltered account. Or invest in tax-free municipal zero-coupon bonds.

Watch out for brokers' hidden markups. They can cause the prices — and yields — of zeros to vary. Many brokers don't disclose the commissions you pay. Take, for example, a $1,000 zero-coupon bond maturing in the year 2008. One regional broker, A. G. Edwards & Sons, in St. Louis, sold the bond in mid-1988 for $168.

But another broker, Butcher & Singer, in Philadelphia, charged $165. In the former case, you would collect a yield of 8.96%. In the latter, you would collect 9.04%. Other spreads may be wider. So, shop around among brokers to make sure of getting your very best deal.

Ginnie Maes

MEET my friend Ginnie Mae. She's quite attractive, not a racy type at all, but safe and most rewarding for those who know and love her.

Ginnie Mae is really a security, issued by the Government National Mortgage Association and backed by the mortgages that the quasi-federal organization holds. When you invest in one, you are buying a share in a pool of fixed-rate home mortgages insured by the Federal Housing Administration or the Veterans Administration. You also get your principal returned in monthly installments because homeowners pay off their mortgages monthly. You probably want to reinvest that principal right away, so you do not deplete your capital. Since you get both interest and principal paid in installments, you collect higher regular payments from a Ginnie Mae than from a bond or a certificate of deposit or some other interest-bearing security.

One problem with Ginnie Maes is that you can never be certain how much money you will receive each month and how long these installments will last. That's because homeowners often pay off their mortgages ahead of schedule. Prepayments are so common that Ginnie Maes backed by 30-year mortgages actually have an average life of only 10 to 12 years. To compensate investors for the uncertainty, Ginnie Maes offer a higher interest rate than Treasury issues of comparable maturities. For example, the "bond equivalent yield" on Ginnie Maes backed by 10.5% 30-year mortgages in mid-1988 was 10.28%, versus 9.02% on the 10-year Treasury bonds with which they are most often equated. The bond equivalent tells you how much you would have to get from other bonds that pay interest only twice a year to equal the yield of a Ginnie.

Ginnie Maes are as safe as U.S. Treasury securities because the government protects you against late payments and foreclosures; so they are particularly attractive for conservative investors. But, as mentioned, Ginnie Maes will give you about a point or two more yield than comparable Treasuries will.

Trouble is, Ginnie Maes cost a bundle — $25,000 each. But for $1,000, and in some cases as little as $100, you can go to a mutual-fund dealer or a stockbroker and buy Ginnie Maes in the form of bond mutual funds or unit trusts. In mid-1988, the mutual funds were yielding interest of about 9.2%. But beware: If homeowners prepay their mortgages, the yield *and* share price of a Ginnie Mae fund will likely fall.

Some unit trusts even let you write an unlimited amount of checks against your money; the minimum check is usually $500. You also can reinvest your monthly payments of interest and principal. That allows your money to compound and keep continually working for you. And you can cash in your units at any time, without fees or penalties.

Fannie Maes and Freddie Macs

SAY that you are looking for a place to park a good bit of money, and you desire safety as well as high yields. Then you might want to consider securities known as Fannie Maes and Freddie Macs.

Fannie Mae is the nickname of the Federal National Mortgage Association, and Freddie Mac stands for the Federal Home Loan Mortgage Corporation. Both issue mortgage-backed securities similar to the more famous Ginnie Maes. The difference is that when you buy a Fannie Mae or a Freddie Mac, you invest in a pool of conventional home loans, and not the Federal Housing Administration and Veterans Administration mortgages that you get with Ginnie Maes.

Like Ginnie Maes, Freddie Macs and Fannie Maes pass along to investors on a monthly basis the interest and principal payments made by homeowners on mortgages in the pools. Even if homeowners do not meet their obligations, Fannie Mae guarantees that you will receive your fair share of interest and principal every month. Freddie Mac, however, guarantees only the interest. If homeowners do not make their mortgage payments on schedule, you might have to wait as long as a year to receive your rightful share of principal.

Newly issued certificates from Freddie Mac and Fannie Mae require a minimum investment of $1,000. But these certificates are usually not available to the individual investor. You can, however, buy into a mutual fund that has invested in these securities. One such fund is USAA Income Fund of San Antonio.

Both Freddie Mac and Fannie Mae are corporations chartered by Congress, though they are not officially part of the federal government. In mid-1988 Freddie Macs were yielding 9.9% and Fannie Maes, 10.01%; while Ginnie Maes were yielding 10.07%.

Sonny Maes and Sallie Maes

IF YOU are in a high tax bracket, Sonny Mae can help you out. Sonny Mae stands for the State of New York Mortgage Agency, which issues bonds that are backed by fixed-rate mortgages. It uses the proceeds to subsidize housing loans at below-market interest rates for first-time home buyers.

Sonny Mae bonds are exempt from federal income taxes for most investors. But if you are subject to the alternative minimum tax, you will have to pay taxes on a Sonny Mae. For residents of New York State, these bonds are also exempt from state and local taxes. In mid-1988, a Sonny Mae maturing in 2018 was yielding 8.38%.

Many other state housing agencies issue similar mortgage revenue bonds. Check to see whether your state offers double- or triple-tax-exempt issues at an attractive price, selling at or below face value.

Then there is Sallie Mae. That is the nickname of the Student Loan Marketing Association, a government-chartered, publicly owned corporation that buys federally guaranteed student loans and issues its own securities. For steady income, you might consider buying Sallie Mae bonds. Each one is backed by Sallie Mae's assets, rather than by a specific pool of loans, so it is almost as risk-free as a bond guaranteed directly by the government. But Sallie Mae bonds usually pay nearly a third of a percentage point more than U.S. Treasury issues. Alas, the minimum investment is just under $10,000. So you might prefer Sallie Mae stock, which is traded on the New York Stock Exchange. Sallie Mae shares were first issued in September 1983, at $20; in mid-1985 they were $30; and in mid-1988 they were $73.25.

MUTUAL FUNDS

How to Make Money in Them

JUST as there is no perfect person or painting or poem, so there is no perfect investment. But the one that comes closest for most people is the mutual fund.

What you get from a mutual fund, at relatively low cost, is professional management of your money. Your investments are handled by people who devote their full time and attention to them.

You also get diversification. A fund buys a wide variety of securities and then sells its own shares to the public. The price of a share rises or falls every day, along with the rises and falls of the total value of the securities the fund owns. And you can sell your shares back to the mutual fund at any time.

Funds offer you an increasingly broad range of investment choices to meet your specific objectives. You can buy anything from aggressive but risky funds that aim for maximum capital gains to more conservative funds that hold bonds or tax-exempt securities and aim to pay you high regular interest. Then there are money-market mutual funds, which give you an escape hatch once readily available only to the rich professional investors. If you think there is trouble ahead for stocks, you can switch out of the stock market and into the safe money market, just by making a phone call to the mutual-fund company. To have this flexibility, just be sure that the company you choose offers a variety of stock, money-market and other mutual funds.

Mutual funds often beat the broad market indexes. From 1973 to 1988, funds that invest primarily in stocks gained more, with all dividends reinvested, than the Standard & Poor's index of 500 stocks. But *short-term* investments in mutual funds can be very risky, particularly in declining markets. Too many people learned that lesson in the crash of 1987, when many funds — though by no means all of them — plunged.

Once you invest in a fund, you receive dividends every quarter and capital-gains distributions annually, if the fund has earned either. A fund earns and distributes capital gains if and when it sells securities at a profit. Almost all mutual funds offer to reinvest your earnings automatically in additional shares. You can also use mutual funds for your Individual Retirement Accounts and Keogh plans.

What kind of mutual fund should you choose and how should you choose it? The answers are explored in later chapters, but in sum the choice depends on your objectives and on how much time you are prepared to spend regularly studying the stock market. Perhaps you follow the financial news but you certainly do not want to reexamine and make changes in your investments as often as every week. What you need is a mutual fund that over the years consistently climbs more than the stock-market averages during good times while not falling more than the averages in bad times. Quite possibly that will be one of the so-called growth funds, which invest in the stocks of expansive but well-established companies, or growth-and-income funds, which favor bonds and the stocks of large companies that yield big dividends. Pick with care because many of these funds do *not* do as well as the market averages. Those that do usually have managers whose records of success go back five or 10 years.

On the other hand, what if you are willing to pay really close attention to your investments and try for spectacular gains during bull markets? Then you are a candidate for so-called maximum-capital-gains funds. They are aggressive funds that search for the fast-moving stocks of small, potentially rapidly rising companies. But be ready to bail out of such a high flier quickly. Maximum-capital-gains funds tend to climb fast — and then tumble fast when the market starts to turn down.

You can specialize — and hedge your bets — by buying so-called sector funds, which concentrate on specific areas of the economy. Let us say you are essentially optimistic about stocks but also a bit wary about a possible resurgence of inflation. In that case, you can invest part of your assets in a technology-stock fund, which buys into promising though risky technology companies. But simultaneously you would keep another part of your money — say, 10% — in a fund that buys gold-mining shares. They most likely will jump if inflation threatens.

A major decision is whether to buy a fund from a stockbroker or a financial planner — or directly from one of the mutual-fund companies. The broker or planner will charge you a load, or commission, usually 2% to 8½%. But for that, he or she will also give you considerable advice. If you feel you need that counsel, it makes sense to buy a load fund. But if you do not need hand-holding, you might as well buy a so-called no-load fund directly from a fund company and save the commission. For a directory of no-load funds, send $5 to the No-Load Mutual Fund Association, P.O. Box 2004, JAF Building, New York, New York 10116.

Even with the commission taken into account, the strong long-term performers tend to be split fairly evenly between load and no-load funds. However, if you want to put your money in a mutual fund for only a short time — a year or less — you should go with a no-load fund. A load fund always has to earn a higher total return to perform as well as a no-load. And one year is seldom long enough for a load fund to do that.

Some previously no-load funds are charging fees of 1% to 3% when you buy, and others impose exit fees. More than 1,000 funds are using yet another method: under what is called the 12b-1 plan, fund managers take money directly from shareholders' assets to pay for advertising, marketing and distribution. Funds charge anywhere from $\frac{1}{100}$ of 1% to 1.25%. To discover if you are paying a 12b-1 levy, look in your fund's prospectus for the table that lists annual operating expenses.

Whether you choose load or no-load, market professionals advise that you not necessarily buy the hottest fund of the moment. As mentioned earlier, the funds that do spectacularly well when the market is rising often do spectacularly badly when it begins to fall. In short, this year's heroes can easily turn into next year's bums.

So it is wise to look for funds that have been consistently profitable over the years, those that have outperformed the broad stock indexes in both up and down market cycles. This provides the best test of fund managers' ability to handle money over the long term. To compare the performances of 750 mutual funds over the current year and the previous five years, you can buy *Mutual Fund ProFiles*, a quarterly published jointly by Standard & Poor's and Lipper Analytical Services. The four issues appear in November, February, May and August and cost $145. To subscribe, write to Standard & Poor's Corporation, 25 Broadway, New York, New York 10275-0123.

Ten Top Long-Term Performers

Money magazine has identified 10 all-weather mutual funds that consistently produced high returns in the five years through June 1988 and did so with comparatively low risk. Herewith, in order, are their records for five years — and for 10 years, if they have been in business that long.

Mutual Qualified Income (26 Broadway, New York, New York 10004; 212-908-4048). A growth-and-income fund whose primary objective is capital appreciation, Mutual Qualified had a gain, with all dividends invested, of 148.2% over the five years.

Mutual Shares (26 Broadway, New York, New York 10004; 212-908-4948). Another growth-and-income fund, Mutual Shares rose 141.4% in five years and 555.7% in 10 years.

Merrill Lynch Phoenix (P.O. Box 9011, Princeton, New Jersey 08543-9011; 609-282-2800). This fund, also designed for growth and income, gained 128.4% in the past five years.

Alliance Balanced Fund (1345 Avenue of the Americas, New York, New York 10105; 800-221-1662 or 212-902-4160 in New York). This fund rose 121.9% in five years and 305.4% in 10 years.

Fidelity Puritan (82 Devonshire Street, Boston, Massachusetts 02109; 800-544-6666 or 617-523-1919 in Massachusetts). A fund whose primary objective is current income, Puritan rose 107.4% in the past five years and 383.8% over the past 10 years.

IDS Mutual (1000 Roanoke Building, Minneapolis, Minnesota 55474; 612-372-3131). Another balanced fund, IDS Mutual gained 106.9% over five years and 297.2% over 10 years.

Phoenix Balanced Series (One American Row, Hartford, Connecticut 06103; 800-243-4361 or 203-278-8050 in Connecticut). Its gains were 104.5% over five years and 369.3% over the past 10 years.

Evergreen Total Return (550 Mamaroneck Avenue, Harrison, New York 10528; 800-262-4471). This current income fund rose 102.9% in five years.

National Total Income (605 Third Avenue, New York, New York 10016; 212-661-3000). Another current income fund, this one gained 99.3% in five years and 327.5% in 10 years.

Strong Total Return (815 East Mason Street, Milwaukee, Wisconsin 53202; 800-368-3863 or 414-765-0620 in Wisconsin). This fund, whose primary goal is growth and income, gained 97.8% over five years.

Choosing the Best Ones for You

B EFORE you invest in a mutual fund, write or phone the fund company for its prospectus. You can find the addresses and phone numbers of most widely available funds in advertisements in financial magazines or the business pages of newspapers.

Read the prospectus to learn how much the fund has gained — or lost — not only over the past year but also over the past five or 10 years, and how well it has held up over periods of major market downturns. The prospectus also should clearly define the fund's investment objectives and list the securities it holds. Make sure you are comfortable with them. Look also for the section that says whether the fund's managers are allowed to shift out of stocks and into, say, U.S. Treasury bills or certificates of deposit as market conditions change. This flexibility to switch into fixed-income investments gives you added protection against losses when stocks turn down.

The prospectus will also tell you whether the fund carries a load, up to 8½%, or is a no-load. Some funds also charge fees of 1% to 5% when you sell your shares; be sure to check in advance whether the fund you are considering levies such redemption fees.

You buy a no-load fund directly from a mutual-fund company and a load fund from a broker or financial planner. In return for the commission, the broker or planner should be able to give you investment advice and tell you the fund's objectives, what it invests in and how it has performed in both up and down markets. If he or she does not know or refers you to the prospectus instead, find another salesperson. Better yet, particularly if you do not need ongoing advice from a broker or planner, buy a no-load fund and save the commission.

A load fund's strong performance over time can make up for the commission. But there is no evidence that load funds as a group outperform no-loads. Above all, remember this: a far more important consideration than the size of the commission, if any, is how well the fund has performed compared with others.

Be aware that funds on a roll are sometimes swamped with new shareholders and more money than they can wisely invest. Make sure you note the size of a fund's total assets. Generally, smaller funds are nimbler than their larger brethren. That is because funds managing less than $100 million of capital are better able to invest a significant portion of their assets in a promising company with a slim amount of outstanding stock. The larger a fund, the more difficulty it has buying a lot of those thinly traded stocks of small companies. If the fund's total assets have risen to $500 million or more over the past several years, you have to wonder how profitable it will be in the future. Many mutual-fund firms manage a "family" of funds. They let you switch your money from one fund to another, usually just by making a telephone call. This convenience can be important if you buy into a fund that invests aggressively for maximum capital gains. When the fund is rocked by a declining market, you can quickly switch to a steadier income-oriented fund.

A superb way to invest in mutual funds is to buy the shares of not just one but several of them. This increases your chances of scoring consistent gains. For example, over the three years to mid-1985, you would have done well if you had divided your money between two distinctly different types of mutual funds that invest in stocks. Funds that specialize in *small* company stocks scored impressive gains from August 1982 until June 1983, when they slumped for a while. But then *big* company stocks, and the funds that buy them, performed well enough to make up for more than those losses.

You can get even greater diversification by investing in other kinds of funds that specialize in single industries or geographical regions. But because these so-called sector funds concentrate in one economic area, you should limit your investing in any one of them to about 10% of your assets. That way you will not be hurt too badly if that sector turns down.

Whichever types of funds you choose, you should consider following a strategy called dollar-cost averaging. You just put an equal amount of money into the same fund at regular intervals. That way, you buy most of your shares when stock prices are down, and you avoid the temptation to invest heavily near a market peak.

The choices you make among funds will depend on your career and your financial and family situations. You need to ask yourself what your financial commitments will be in the future for college costs, retirement or other necessities. Can you afford to take some risks now, or is preserving your money supremely important to you?

Once you have answered such questions, look for a package of different mutual funds that suits your needs. Many strategists recommend putting 20% to 40% of your investment money into corporate or tax-exempt bond funds. That's because bonds pay unusually high interest rates. Also, some bond funds have done well in recent times. Among top-ranked corporate bond funds in mid-1988 were Putnam Income, which was returning 9.2%, and United Bond Fund, with a return of 9%.

You might also consider one of the municipal bond funds. Their dividends are usually exempt from federal taxes. For a list of the top-performing high-yield tax-exempt funds for the five years ending June 30, 1988, see "Your Investments: Tax-exempt Bond Funds."

You also have to decide how much money to put into the different types of funds. If you are young and confident and have few obligations or dependents, you might want to emphasize aggressive funds that aim for maximum capital gains. But if you are saving for college bills or an approaching retirement, you probably would be more comfortable with so-called growth funds, which are less volatile, or still more conservative growth-and-income funds.

If you are planning to buy and *hold* your mutual-fund shares, you will most likely turn away from the most aggressive stock funds. They are better suited to people who are fund switchers. Such investors dump their stock-fund shares and buy money-market-fund shares when the stock market turns down.

Always remember that you will make the wisest selections if you consider such changing personal factors as your age, your family situation and your financial responsibilities. Take a fairly young couple, earning comfortable salaries from their two jobs. They would be smart to aim for long-term growth of capital. To get it, they might put one-third of their mutual-fund assets into aggressive-growth or long-term-growth funds. Another third would go into a growth-and-income fund, and the last third into a bond fund.

A couple in their 40s and with two or more teenage children would take a different tack. College costs probably would be on their minds. So such a couple would want to keep a fair amount of their mutual-fund money — say, 10% — in a money-market fund, where they could withdraw it swiftly and without fear that their shares had lost value. Our mid-life couple would also be concerned about building a nest egg for retirement. Thus, they probably would want to put half of their fund money into growth and growth-and-income funds, a third or more of their investments into bond funds and perhaps 5% in a gold fund as a hedge against inflation.

Still older couples who need to concentrate on preserving whatever wealth they have built for retirement in a few years might put 20% of their fund assets into growth funds with strong records in weak stock markets. Another 35% might go into growth-and-income funds, and still another 35% would be put into bond funds, including one that invests in tax-exempt bonds. The remaining 10% should go into a money-market fund.

The Specialty Funds

PERHAPS you think a certain sector of the economy is about to surge, and you want to cash in on its rise. Then you might want to consider buying into a specialty mutual fund that invests in that part of the economy.

About 50 funds buy stocks in particular economic sectors. They may concentrate investors' money in specific industries, such as health services, high technology or banking. Or they may focus on individual commodities, such as gold or oil and gas. They may buy foreign stocks or shares of companies operating in a particular region of the U.S. or the world.

Some mutual-fund companies, such as Fidelity, Vanguard and Financial Programs, Inc., have funds that offer investors the choice of several sectors. Fidelity's Select portfolio, for instance, contained separate mini-funds for 30 different sectors in mid-1988. An investor can switch money around among the sectors simply by phoning the company and requesting the change. Other companies may offer only one sector, but almost all will give the investor a choice of switching out of it and into a money-market fund. That way, whenever you sense danger in the sector, you can immediately move your investment to a safe money fund.

Unlike regular mutual funds, specialty funds are not for beginners. Since they concentrate on a single type of stock, they are highly volatile and risky. Their prices usually move up — and down — much more sharply than the market as a whole. Energy funds, for instance, rose faster than most other mutual funds in 1979 and 1980, after the fall of the Shah of Iran sent oil prices into orbit. But in 1981 and 1982, when oil prices dropped, so did shares of energy funds.

Technology funds, among other specialty funds, have taken it on the chin in recent years.

Gold funds have been even more mercurial. They invest in gold-mining shares. Both the funds and the stocks are really surrogates for owning gold metal. Because they diversify your investments, gold-fund shares are safer than individual mining stocks, and both the funds and the mining stocks are easier to sell than gold ingots. In addition, they require no storage fee and — unlike the metal itself — often pay substantial dividends. Be aware, though, that many of the gold-mining companies are in South Africa, and a political explosion there could severely damage their stocks.

During 1980, when inflation was in double digits, gold funds rose faster than all other mutual funds. They soared as much as 64%. Later, when gold prices fell, they plunged; but then they rose again. So, if you think inflation will get out of hand once more, and are willing to take big risks for the possibility of big gains, you might put some money into gold funds.

On the other hand, if you believe that inflation will not run away and the economy and the stock market will do well for the next few years, now may be the time to invest in mutual funds that aim for aggressive growth. While these funds are not, strictly speaking, specialty funds, they do concentrate their investments in a particularly incendiary area: small companies that have large potential. Such firms tend to be involved in high-tech, biotech, health-care and other services. Like the companies they invest in, the funds usually jump, and tumble, faster than the market itself. After the bull market began in August 1982, quite a few of them rose more than 100% in less than a year. But in mid-1983, the overpriced high-tech stocks cracked — and so did these funds, many of which dropped substantially. Even the most optimistic analysts stress that you must be prepared to move out of highly speculative aggressive-growth funds at the first sniff of decline.

Tax-exempt Bond Funds

FOR a sound investment on which you will not have to pay federal income taxes, consider buying shares of a tax-exempt bond mutual fund. You also will not have to pay any sales commission if you purchase shares in a no-load bond fund directly from a mutual-fund company. But the sponsors may charge fees of 1% to 3% a year.

Managers of these funds constantly buy and sell a large variety of tax-free municipal bonds, and this diversification helps protect you against loss. The managers aim to unload any bonds that may be going sour. And they can make gains through trading. The risk is that fund managers may guess wrong and sell bonds when prices are low and buy them when prices are high.

The top high-yield tax-exempt bond funds for the five years ending June 30, 1988, were IDS High Yield Tax-Exempt, which averaged an annual gain of 11.7%; Merrill Lynch Municipal Bond–High Yield, which gained an average of 11.6%; and Vanguard Municipal Bond–High Yield; which averaged 11.4%.

"Humanistic" Funds

I F YOU are concerned about social issues such as the spread of armaments or pollution, should you apply your ethical standards to your investments? That's your decision, of course. Many people think that trying to "do good" with your investments will keep you from doing well. But in fact, you *can* profit both financially *and* spiritually. Over the past 10 years, some of the mutual funds that are guided by their own ethical criteria have performed better than stocks in general. Other such funds have not done as well, so you have to be particularly selective.

Naturally, picking investments to match your ethics limits your choice. If you want to avoid arms makers, as well as alcohol, tobacco and gambling enterprises, you will not be able to invest in 60% to 70% of the stocks listed on the New York Exchange. You can achieve reasonable results, but you may not get the highest return possible.

Then too, choosing stocks to meet your standards can be troublesome. Consider the question of South Africa, in which drawing lines between specific companies may be difficult. For example, a corporation that has closed its operations in South Africa may still do business there through a middleman. And a company that has chosen to continue in South Africa may well be providing jobs and opportunities for blacks.

The first question to ask yourself is what you really hope to achieve. If you want to influence corporate or government policy, you may be disappointed. Chances are your investments just will not be big enough. You would probably be better off investing for maximum returns and donating some money to an action group. But if your goal is to keep a clear conscience, social investing can work for you.

If you want advice, an organization called the Social Investment Forum (711 Atlantic Avenue, Boston, Massachusetts 02111; 617-423-6655) will send you a list of brokers who use social criteria.

Besides being highly selective in the stocks you buy, you can employ a sound method of letting your ethics guide your investments by putting your money in a mutual fund that judges companies by certain moral standards. For example, the Dreyfus Third Century Fund (800-645-6561) avoids corporations that have operations in South Africa or that are involved in alcohol, tobacco and gambling. Dreyfus Third Century rose 14.5% in the first six months of 1988.

The Managed Growth Portfolio of the Calvert Social Investment Fund (800-368-2748) keeps its money away not only from companies that do business in South Africa but also from those involved in nuclear power or weapons systems. It looks to invest in companies that practice equal-opportunity hiring and have what the fund's managers consider to be strong community and environmental records. In the first six months of 1988, this fund went up 9.5%.

If you are concerned about energy development, you might want to try the New Alternatives Fund (516-466-0808). It searches for firms that conserve and produce alternative sources of energy, excluding nuclear power, and it will not invest in arms makers, South Africa or companies with poor environmental records. The fund gained 18.9% from January 1 to July 1, 1988.

The Pax World Fund (603-431-8022) also avoids arms makers, companies with gambling, alcohol or tobacco interests and those that it believes discriminate against minorities or women. In the six months ending June 30, 1988, it increased 8.4%.

The Parnassus Fund (415-362-3505) is both a socially conscious and a contrarian fund. It invests in out-of-favor companies that its managers think make quality products, treat their employees well and are community-minded. It rose 39% in the first six months of 1988.

If you want to avoid companies involved in South Africa, alcohol, tobacco and gambling, you might also consider one of the Pioneer Group funds (800-821-1239 or 617-742-7825 in Massachusetts).

They were the first to adopt social criteria, and in the six months ending June 30, 1988, their funds rose anywhere from 16.9% to 26.4%.

A money-market fund that applies very strict rules is the Working Assets Money Fund (415-989-3200). It avoids not only companies doing business in South Africa but also banks that lend there. And it shuns U.S. Treasury securities as part of its antiweapons policy. The fund also searches for firms that support environmental-protection measures, equal-opportunity and worker health and safety rules. In the six months ending June 30, 1988, it yielded 6.1%.

Switching Among the Funds

SINCE today's fast-rising mutual fund can easily turn into tomorrow's loser, one way to make money in mutual funds is to be a fair-weather friend. You get out of the losers and into the winners by switching around from fund to fund, always aiming to move just before big up or down swings in the stock market. When it is advancing rapidly, you invest in the speculative funds. Then at the merest flutter of danger, you can switch to the safety of a more secure money-market fund. Investors also quite often have the option of moving to tax-free municipal bond funds or corporate bond funds within a group managed by the same fund company.

But you need to know when to switch and more specifically which fund to switch to. For this reason it probably pays to subscribe to a monthly newsletter advisory service that tracks the performance of the various funds. Among those newsletters are *United Mutual Fund Selector* (210 Newbury Street, Boston, Massachusetts 02116; $110 a year); *Growth Fund Guide* (P.O. Box 6600, Rapid City, South Dakota 57709; $85 a year); *Mutual Fund Specialist* (P.O. Box 1025, Eau Claire, Wisconsin 54702; $79 a year); *NoLoad Fund∗X* (235 Montgomery Street, San Francisco, California 94104; $95 a year); *Switch Fund Advisory* (1385 Piccard Drive, Rockville, Maryland 20850; $140 a year); and *Telephone Switch Newsletter* (P.O. Box 2538, Huntington Beach, California 92647; $117 a year).

The letters rank the mutual funds according to how much the prices of their shares rise or fall in value over one-month, three-month, six-month and one-year periods. The strategy of switching is to (1) buy into the mutual fund that is on top of the rankings for performance over the past year, and (2) keep your money in that fund as long as the advisory service tells you it is among the top five in its category for the past year. The various categories that the funds are divided into include growth, aggressive-growth, and growth-and-income.

When your newsletter arrives — usually a week to 10 days after the end of the month — a quick glance will tell you if the fund you are invested in is still on top. If it is not, the rankings will show you which one is.

An easy way to switch is to put your money into a mutual-fund company that offers a variety of kinds of funds. Then when your advisory service tells you just which one is the company's current star, you can move your money into it by phoning the company.

You often can do even better at switching if you are willing to go to the trouble of closing your account with one mutual-fund company and opening a new account with another company that offers the currently best-performing fund in its category. According to one study, if you had followed such a switching strategy between August 1976 and July 1982, your money could have grown at an annual compounded rate of almost 28%.

Leapfrogging from fund to fund in search of the best return does require a bit of work. The first step is to call the toll-free 800 number of the new fund you want to invest in. You can get these numbers from mutual-fund newsletters or mutual-fund companies' ads or merely by dialing toll-free information at 800-555-1212.

When you reach the mutual-fund company, ask for shareholder services. Tell the person with whom you speak that you want to open an account and then request an account number for yourself.

Next, write to the head of the shareholder services at your old fund, that is, the one you are currently invested in. Your letter should say, "Please sell all full and fractional shares in the account of . . ." and then give your name and your old account number. Ask that the redemption check be made payable to, and sent to, the new fund you are moving to. And be sure to request that the words "for the benefit of" appear on the check, followed by your name and your new account number.

Probably it will take one to two weeks for your money to arrive at your new mutual fund. You can short-circuit this process if you have a money-market account with the mutual fund that you are leaving.

Tell that fund to switch all your assets to your money-market account. Then write a check for the full amount you have in the account and mail it to your new mutual fund.

Fortunately, there is one way to skip that paperwork. All you have to do is open an account at any office of Charles Schwab & Co., the San Francisco-based discount broker. Then, by making a single toll-free phone call to Schwab you can switch in and out of more than 270 mutual funds. Schwab will charge a fee based on the size of your order, so this will cost you more than if you shift assets on your own.

Borrowing Against Your Mutual Funds

THE Securities and Exchange Commission not long ago repealed a long-standing ban on using mutual-fund shares as collateral when you borrow money from a stockbroker. That means you now can use your mutual funds to get a personal loan from your broker or to buy securities on margin.

Should you take advantage of this opportunity? Probably not — if you are a conservative investor who likes to buy steady and sound securities and just put them away in a safe-deposit box without trading them. But if you have a high tolerance for risk, margin buying can increase your potential rewards.

The margin requirements vary from time to time, but in mid-1988 to borrow $4,000 to buy *stocks,* you would need to pledge fund shares worth at least $2,000. To borrow $2,000 as a *personal loan,* you would have to put up $4,000 in such shares. Either way, you would pay a variable interest rate, usually one-half to two and a half percentage points above so-called broker loan rates. You do not have to make regular payments on the interest or the principal. You can repay whenever you want, just as long as the market value of the fund shares you pledge as collateral remains above a certain percentage of the loan amount. Usually it's 30% or 35%.

As a margin buyer you will be at greatest risk when interest rates are rising. That means you will have to pay higher rates on your loan. Also, the value of securities tends to fall at such times, so you may get a margin call from your broker and thus have to put up additional collateral. The good news is that mutual funds are less volatile than many stocks and bonds. When markets turn down, fund shares are not likely to drop dramatically in price and trigger a margin call.

Wise Ways to Withdraw Your Money

SOME people are in the enviable position of being able to live off their mutual-fund investments. But to do that wisely, you should know the best ways to withdraw your income from a fund.

In fact, what many investors — particularly those who have retired — like best about mutual funds is that you can get at your money whenever you want it, without inconvenience or penalties. Quite a few stock or bond mutual funds will set up an automatic withdrawal program for you, so you can live off regular payments. To do this, you ordinarily must have at least $10,000 in your account. Then you can choose one of two forms of automatic withdrawals.

You can have a *fixed amount* sent to you monthly or quarterly. The fund will sell the shares necessary to get the amount you predetermine. Or you can take a regular payment based on a *fixed percentage* of the value of your fund assets. That way, even if the total value of your investment changes because of market conditions, you will be withdrawing the same proportion of your assets with each payment. The T. Rowe Price mutual-fund organization reports that this so-called percentage method of withdrawing money is best. It is more likely to let your principal grow over time than having a fixed amount sent to you periodically.

Another way to withdraw money from a stock mutual fund is to have the dividends and capital-gains distributions sent to you as a regular payment. The advantage is that none of the fund shares are sold off.

BROKERS

How to Choose One

B ACK in the bullish months of 1987, it almost did not matter whether your stockbroker was a genius, a guru or simply somebody's smiling son-in-law. The momentum of the market was so strong that you were fairly well assured of making money.

That's no longer true in today's volatile market. So, choosing a brokerage firm for the first time, or switching to a new one, becomes a key decision. It isn't easy, particularly for small investors. Some firms don't want to bother with accounts of less than $15,000. Not many will turn you down flat, but your account is likely to get serious attention only if it can generate sizable commissions.

If you are a small investor, you will find that big, national brokerage houses generally are more hospitable than lesser outfits. These large companies stand to make a bit of profit from the sheer volume of their small accounts. Look for the major firms that offer special services, such as cut-rate commissions.

But if you want to concentrate on investing in companies located in your own area, you might do better with well-established regional brokerages. Their traditional strength has been in spotting small local companies that have gone on to become great winners. True, they also have a disadvantage: they often are less familiar with companies located far away, and with complex stock strategies, than are the larger national houses.

If you follow the market very closely yourself and feel you do not need regular, professional advice, then consider using discount brokers. They generally offer no frills and no hand-holding, but they often charge commissions of less than 1%.

Once you have picked the brokerage house that you like, how do you select the salesperson in that firm just right for you? Choosing the right broker is not quite as important as selecting the right spouse or the best boss, but since the broker will do much to determine whether you are affluent or financially uncomfortable in the future, it is a decision to be taken seriously.

The first thing to do is to solicit recommendations. Ask friends who are themselves successful investors. Ask accountants and tax preparers. They have inside knowledge of how well their clients are doing in the market, and legally and ethically they can tell you who some of the winning brokers are.

If referrals don't produce enough candidates, write letters to the branch managers of some brokerage firms listed in your local Yellow Pages. Set forth your financial situation and investment goals. When replies come in, interview not just one but several brokers. Ask each one: How long has he or she been a broker? Where does he get his information? In what areas have his greatest successes been? What does he think is his biggest weakness? At the time he suggests buying a stock, does he also prudently recommend a price at which you should sell out in the future?

You are generally better off with a veteran, well-experienced broker — one who has been through a few market reverses, who knows that stocks can go down as well as up — than with an eager newcomer who will learn his lessons with your money.

Instead of looking for a broker who will tell you what to do, search for one who can use his knowledge and experience to help you make *your own* decisions. Read financial publications and perhaps subscribe to an investment advisory service. Get various research reports from your brokerage house. Use them to learn the factors that professional analysts employ to evaluate stock.

Before doing business with a broker, don't be shy about asking him for the names of people whose accounts he handles. Then call up two or three of them. You might uncover some unexpected blemishes, such as a tendency to overtrade. Too much trading may produce high commissions for your broker but very small returns for you.

Be sure to evaluate your market performance coldly after you have been with the broker for six months. And then do it yearly. Compare your gains and losses with the Standard & Poor's index of 500 stocks. If your portfolio's performance, before commissions, falls below the Standard & Poor's, don't hesitate to take your money and run — to another broker.

Be Careful of Securities Analysts

I F YOU are like many investors, you buy stocks because your broker recommends them. But did you know that most brokers get their tips from someone called a securities analyst? How reliable is his or her research?

Securities analysts are highly paid investment sleuths who work for brokerage houses, banks and other financial institutions. They spend their time finding stocks that they think will make a profit. But many analysts are too often bullish on the wrong stocks. Michael O'Higgins, president of his own investment counseling firm in Albany, New York, compared the records of professional analysts. He checked their forecasts from 1973 to 1987 on the 30 stocks that make up the Dow Jones industrial average. O'Higgins found that you would have earned three times as much money investing in the firms that analysts predicted would have only slow earnings growth than you would if you had taken their recommendations of companies that they expected to have faster earnings increases.

Analysts often fall in love with their stocks, just as novice investors do. And they occasionally fear that gloomy forecasts will alienate the managements of the companies they follow. Sometimes an analyst is under pressure to give a company a good report because the analyst's parent firm is acting as the well-paid underwriter for that company's new stock issues. Therefore, it is smart to ask any broker who recommends a stock to you if his firm has an investment banking relationship with the company he is pushing. If it has, you should be extra careful.

Analysts also tend to pass news along first to big, institutional customers and then to the retail brokers who do business with smaller investors. This puts you at the rear of the information line and, in many cases, that is too far back to take any profitable action on the tip. In general, it is wise to patronize brokerage houses that freely publish their analysts' recommendations and keep track of the resulting profits or losses in those stocks.

The Discounters

You can save as much as 90% on commissions by dealing with a discount broker. But you pay some penalties for these price cuts. So, should you use a discount broker?

If you do, you will have plenty of choice. There are more than 100 independent discount brokerage firms plus some 3,000 discount offices associated with banks. You can find discounters through ads in newspapers and financial magazines, and you can reach them over toll-free phone lines.

The appeal of discount brokers goes well beyond thrift. More and more of them offer special customer services, and a few even supply that most touted of full-commission services — stock-market research.

Whether or not you decide to use a discount broker should depend on your investment behavior. You may want to forget about discounters if you usually buy or sell fewer than 100 shares at a time and lean toward lower-priced shares. In that case, you will be better off dealing with full-commission firms that have lower minimum charges on such deals. For example, buying 10 shares of a $15 stock would cost you less than $30 in commissions at some full-service brokers, but $30 to $40 at most discounters. There also may be no savings at all on trades below $1,500.

If you are fairly new at investing and don't know your way around Wall Street, a traditional broker is also the right choice for you. He will advise you what to buy, what to sell and when to buy or sell it. Just one winning stock recommendation from a full-service broker's research staff could more than make up for his higher commission. If you want cut-rate commission but feel hesitant to end your relationship with a full-service broker, try asking for a discount. Your broker probably can offer as much as 30% off the typical full fee on any substantial transaction.

On the other hand, you might do well to move to a discount broker if you feel confident enough to make your own stock-market decisions. In choosing the discounter, it is paramount to select a company that can weather precipitous ups and downs in the stock market. If a firm has at least seven years of service, then it already has survived two market downturns, and you are probably safe.

Your chief consideration may well be commission rates. Generally they vary with the kind of trading you do.

So-called value brokers charge rates that are a percentage of the dollar value of each transaction. This usually works out best for you if you deal in low-priced stocks.

Then there are the so-called share brokers. They offer bigger discounts when you trade large numbers of shares. Share brokers work to your advantage if you buy or sell 500 shares or more and if you deal in high-priced stocks.

To cite a couple of examples of the wide variances in commissions charged by discounters:

If you wanted to buy 100 shares of a $10 stock, Marquette de Bary in New York City would charge you $25. But Whitehall Securities in New York City would charge $50. That's about the same as a full-commission broker.

If you wanted to buy 500 shares of a $50 stock, Whitehall's commission of $63 would be less than half the fee charged by Marquette. And a full-service broker might charge as much as $400.

The major discount brokers are licensed to do business in most states and have nationwide toll-free numbers that you can find in newspapers and financial publications. All have Securities Investor Protection Corporation insurance of at least $500,000 per client and are subject to the same regulations as are traditional brokers. In sum, discounters are safe.

Many offer specialized services that set them apart. For example, Charles Schwab & Co. insures the value of its securities up to $10 million. And when you phone in an order to buy or sell, at least two discounters, Schwab and Rose & Co., will execute it immediately. Before you hang up, you will learn the price you paid or received. That is information you normally don't get as fast from regular brokers.

When picking a discounter, choose on the basis of not only the size of the commissions but also the scope of the services. You should be free to trade more than just stocks, or to buy stocks on margin — that is, to borrow up to 50% of the cost from your broker. You also should expect a discounter, like a full-service broker, to pay you interest on cash in your account and to give you stock quotes during market hours.

In the past, discounters have provided impersonal service. Now they increasingly offer you the choice of dealing with one representative or a team of them. Many discounters will take custody of your

Individual Retirement Account or Keogh plan. And a few offer the combination of credit-card service, margin trading and free checking available in a full-fledged asset management account. So read the financial press closely to see the various deals and extras being dangled by discounters, and shop around.

Using Your Bank as a Broker

C AN your banker also be your stockbroker? Well, he or she could not until the government began to allow such double duty a few years ago. Now some 3,000 bank holding companies and savings and loan associations have either bought or linked up with stockbrokers. Just about every large bank in the country has brokerage operations. And it's almost impossible to find a city where some bank doesn't sell stocks. So, the one-stop financial shop may be right down your block.

At a number of banks, the brokerage is nothing more than a self-service computer terminal with a telephone. Sometimes it's a counter with a bank clerk to help you fill out applications and phone in orders. At others, it's a fully staffed mini-brokerage office, complete with trained broker.

Most banks sell stock through their own or an affiliated discount broker. So their commissions are usually lower than those at full-service brokers. But the banks' discounters often are 10% to 15% more expensive than independent discounters are. The reason is that only a handful of banks execute their own trades. The rest just take your order and must hire — and pay — another company to do the buying and selling of securities.

Still, banks are more likely than independent discounters to offer a wide range of so-called financial products. Bank-affiliated discounters often sell everything from bonds to gold bullion, while some independents confine themselves to stocks and stock options. On other counts, bank-affiliated brokerages score well too. They can execute trades almost as swiftly as any discounter — and perhaps get the money to you even faster.

But if you want detailed investment research or advice, your best bet is still a full-service broker. Most banks will give you only current stock quotes and basic investment information.

Regional Brokers

J UST about everyone is familiar with Merrill Lynch's thundering herd, and you may recall that when E. F. Hutton talked, you were likely to get the soup in your lap because your waiter was listening. But a growing number of investors are turning their ears to lesser-known regional brokerage houses. They can get you into the stocks of small local companies that are among the fastest growing in the country.

Regional firms often specialize in fairly small companies with strong managements. Some firms limit their bailiwick to a single city; others specialize in regions — for example, growth companies of the Midwest or Southwest. Analysts read the local papers, understand the local economy and continue to follow local companies even if they temporarily fall out of favor with investors.

These brokers tend to have strong and deep ties to their region. Many began as municipal bond houses handling underwritings for towns and small cities too insignificant to be noticed by national firms. Gradually, the regionals branched out into selling common stocks as well.

If you think the economic prospects are bright for companies in a specific part of the country, a long-distance call to a regional broker will get you a sampling of current research reports. If you like what you see, you can open an account, also by phone, and start receiving monthly market letters with regional economic forecasts and lists of recommended stocks.

Many regional brokerage houses have notable records of performance. In the East, for example, are Advest in Hartford, Connecticut; Legg Mason Wood Walker in Pittsburgh; and Baker, Watts & Co. in Baltimore. In the South are Interstate Securities in Charlotte, North Carolina, and Robinson-Humphrey in Atlanta. In the Midwest are Cleveland's Prescott, Ball & Turben, and Milwaukee's Robert W. Baird & Co. In the West and Southwest, there are Rauscher Pierce Refsnes of Dallas, Boettcher & Co. of Denver, and Crowell, Weedon & Co. in Los Angeles.

To find other regional firms, one good source is a Standard & Poor's guide called *Security Dealers of North America*. It lists securities firms, their addresses and phone numbers, by city and state.

When these firms venture out of their regions, it usually is to cover the competitors of local companies. Their analysts keep turning up small companies that have fast-expanding markets and earnings. Gradually the glitter of these little stars will attract attention by national firms. That is the regional analyst's dream: finding stocks, getting clients into them early, then waiting until a big national firm discovers them, recommends them — and sends the price up.

Questions to Ask Your Broker

STOCKBROKERS are salespeople, and so they can sell hard. If you feel uncomfortable when a broker urges you to buy a stock, be sure to ask some pointed questions.

One of the first should be: How has that stock done lately? A more important question, particularly if you are a long-term investor who plans to buy and hold: What are the long-range earnings forecasts for the stock? If your broker doesn't have the answers immediately, tell him that's all right — that he can call you back when he gets them. Patience pays.

Did your broker or an analyst at his or her firm do the research on the stock? If it was an analyst, ask to see his or her report on the company. And find out how well other stocks that this analyst has recommended have done.

Is the stock undervalued? One sign that a stock could be a buy is that its price is near the bottom of its trading range of the past few months. But a stock could be cheap because the company faces serious problems. Ask what makes the stock such a bargain.

What is the company's profit margin? If it is above its industry average, the company is probably well run.

Why should you buy this stock *now*? Obviously you don't want to bother with a concern when its business cycle is about to turn down. Most industries have predictable cycles of earnings declines and recoveries. Ask when to expect the next longer-term upswing or downswing and when the stock price is likely to reflect that change.

What are the chances that, near-term, the stock will go down instead of up? Ask if the company faces strong competition, is involved in expensive litigation or is laden with debt. Heavy interest payments may cut into earnings. Get your broker to help you set a price at which you might be wise to sell and cut your losses. The price he names will help you gauge the risk he sees in the investment.

How does this stock fit in with your overall strategy? Make sure that your broker knows whether your investment objective is long-term growth or high-dividend income or a quick killing. Tell him how much risk you are willing to shoulder to achieve your aims. If you are a buy-and-hold investor and your broker keeps suggesting ideas suited to frequent traders, then trade brokers.

Who are the large shareholders in this company? What you would like to hear is that some wealthy private investors have just bought a lot of the stock and are thinking of attempting a takeover. Or that the firm's management owns a sizable portion of the shares. Top managers who are also substantial stockholders have an added incentive to see that a firm does well.

Is this stock better than the one the same broker urged you to buy last week? Most brokers have several stocks to sell, so get yours to compare some of the other issues on his list with the ones he's flogging now.

Remember: if you invest in a stock and its price plummets, you will lose money, but your broker will still pocket a commission. Unlike you, he or she is guaranteed to profit if you follow his or her advice.

How Safe Is Your Brokerage Account?

WHENEVER a stock brokerage firm fails, investors start wondering, "What happens if *my* broker goes broke?"

Despite the market frenzy in 1987, only four brokerage firms went under, and it is very unlikely that yours will collapse. But if it does, your stocks, bonds and money fund shares are protected by the Securities Investor Protection Corporation against losses up to $500,000. This government-chartered private corporation — nicknamed "Sipic" — oversees liquidations of brokerages and restores securities to clients. To do this, SIPC has a $390 million fund raised by assessing the brokerage firms. It also can tap a $1 billion line of credit at the U.S. Treasury, and a $500 million credit line with private banks.

But commodity futures contracts are not covered by SIPC, nor is cash left with a broker specifically to earn interest. Options are covered, although they are usually too short-lived to survive the freeze put on customer accounts when a firm fails.

One problem is that providing customers with access to their accounts usually takes from one to six months. In the meantime, customers cannot sell any securities in their accounts. Customers first receive any securities held in their own names. If their stocks or bonds are in the firm's name — that is, in "street name" — clients will be given a prorated share of any street-name securities that the firm can produce. SIPC then will make up the difference between what the clients got and what they are owed.

If you are worried about your broker's financial health, there are signs of trouble to watch for. Does it take a long time for your broker to execute your orders to buy and sell? Do confirmation slips fail to square with transactions? Are your monthly statements inaccurate? Problems like these suggest the firm could be having back-office snarls, and it might be time to move your account.

Even if you are confident of your broker's stability, you should take steps to protect yourself. Certainly, don't hold more than $500,000 worth of securities at any single brokerage house. If you are really skittish, you can hold securities in your name instead of the firm's name or even keep the certificates at home or in a safe-deposit box. In a liquidation, you will get the shares in your name back faster than shares in a street name. And you will have them back in no time if they never leave your possession.

Selling Without a Broker

D ID you know that you can sell stock that you own without using a broker? That way, you can save the money that you would normally spend for the sales commission.

The procedure for transferring ownership of stock is not all that hard. First, sign the back of your stock certificate and have your bank guarantee your signature. That is to protect you against forgeries. Then, fill in the new owner's full name, as well as his or her Social Security number and address. Next, get the name and address of the transfer agent of the company in which you own stock. To obtain it, simply write to the corporate secretary of the company. Finally, send the stock certificate by registered mail to the transfer agent. Attach a letter explaining that you are selling the shares. The transfer agent then will issue a new certificate in the new owner's name.

And what is the charge for this? Nothing at all.

PRECIOUS METALS

Gold

THE price of gold hit a modern low of $284 an ounce in 1985, then reached a plateau around $450 for much of 1987 and the first half of 1988. Despite an increasing fear of inflation in mid-1988, the demand for gold as a hedge was not strong. As writer John Curran has noted in *Fortune*, longer-term results from owning gold are not encouraging. The first day that Americans could legally own gold bullion was January 1, 1975. Anyone who bought gold bars the next day would have seen each dollar he invested rise to $2.49 by July 1, 1988. But each dollar invested in *stocks* would have bounded ahead to more than $6.55.

Gold pays no dividends. That may seem trifling when its price is streaking ahead, but over many decades it matters a lot. Since 1926, dividends have accounted for more than one-third of the return from owning stocks. A further shortcoming of gold is that it cannot compound investors' gains as a company can when it retains earnings and uses that fuel to grow.

Even gold buyers who want to hedge against inflation may get less than they bargain for. Though an ounce of gold today still has the same purchasing power as it did hundreds of years ago, gold's shorter-term record as an inflation hedge is not so good. Since 1980 inflation has reduced the purchasing power of a dollar by 30%. Gold has not only failed to offset that loss, but its price has actually fallen nearly 50% during that period.

Still, if you believe that double-digit inflation, oil-supply interruptions and world monetary crises will strike yet again, you might be inclined to invest in precious metals. You then would have a series of choices of how and what to buy.

Extreme pessimists who have no faith in any country's currency probably would prefer gold bars. But owning such bullion can be a nuisance. You have to pay for storage and insurance, and you also may have to transport the metal to and from dealers, and perhaps lay out more money for assay costs when you sell.

A simpler way to invest in gold — or silver and platinum — is to buy certificates of ownership. They signify that you own a specified amount of the metal stored in bank vaults. When the time comes to sell, a phone call is all that is necessary. Your minimum initial purchase might be $1,800. After that, you make subsequent investments for as little as $100. Commissions range from 1½% to roughly 3% when you buy, depending on the quantity. You also pay a ½% annual storage charge when you buy and 1% when you sell. Choose your dealer carefully: a couple of metals certificate programs have been exposed as scams.

Instead of certificates, many people prefer to buy one-ounce gold coins, such as South African Krugerrands, Canadian Maple Leafs, Chinese Pandas, and the American Eagle, which the U.S. Mint introduced in October 1986. Although you pay 3% to 6% more than their gold content is worth, and sales tax on top of that, coins are easier to resell than gold certificates or bars. The easy portability and worldwide acceptance of coins appeal to the so-called refugee mentality. But you should bear in mind that neither gold coins nor bars nor certificates pay any dividends.

Shares of high-quality South African mining companies do offer high dividends and a chance at capital appreciation. But mining stocks are typically more volatile than bullion. That's because mining profits balloon once the price of the metal moves above the cost of extracting and refining it. A price rise of a few percentage points can double the earnings of a mining company. When gold prices decline, however, shares also drop more sharply than the metal itself.

This volatility also carries over to the dividends that the companies pay. In 1988, when gold was selling for about $450 an ounce, the dividends were roughly 6% to 8%. At $600 an ounce, dividends would likely be 12% or 14%. One warning: Buying gold stocks subjects your investment to political and economic risks, notably racial explosions in South Africa. Indeed, South Africa's troubles cast doubt over the future of all its gold offerings, including Krugerrand coins, whose import is presently banned.

You can minimize the risks of gold stocks by diversifying. For example, you can balance South African mining shares with North American ones such as Campbell Red Lake, a company listed on the New York Stock Exchange.

If you do not wish to make a big investment but you want broad diversification, you could meet your needs by buying into one of the gold mutual funds. They acquire the shares of various gold-mining companies, and so they provide some diversification. These funds soared in the early 1980s, then slumped, recovered strongly, and then took a nosedive in the crash of 1987. Even so, they led other fund groups for the year.

Seven funds that performed best during recent years are Oppenheimer Gold & Special Minerals (2 Broadway, New York, New York 10004), Lexington Goldfund (Park 80 West, Plaza 2, P.O. Box 1515, Saddle Brook, New Jersey 07662), Bull & Bear Gold Investors (11 Hanover Square, New York, New York 10005), International Investors (122 East 42nd Street, New York, New York 10168), Keystone Precious Metals (99 High Street, Boston, Massachusetts 02110), Vanguard Special Portfolio-Gold and Precious Metals (Valley Forge, Pennsylvania 19482) and Franklin Gold (155 Bovet Road, San Mateo, California 94402).

Before you buy, remember: Just as gold stocks generally rise faster than gold when the market is up, so too they usually plunge faster than the metal when its price falls. Whether you choose to purchase gold funds or gold stocks or the metal itself, the amount you buy should be only a relatively modest share — perhaps 5% to 10% — of a well-diversified investment portfolio.

Platinum

WHEN people think of investing in precious metals, they often think only of buying gold or silver. But have you ever considered platinum? In some recent years, its price has bounded.

A reason is that almost all platinum in the non-Communist world has been produced by just three companies, in South Africa. Their mines are believed to be producing at nearly full capacity. While there are plans to develop ten new mines in South Africa, it will be some time before increased production can affect this country's output.

What this means for investors is that the non-Communist world's supply of platinum will probably fall short of demand for the next few years at least. In 1987, South African mines provided a record 3.1 million ounces of platinum, but demand also set a record, of 3.32 million ounces, exceeding 3 million ounces for the first time. As in previous years, the shortfall was made up on sales from the Soviet Union's supply. If the Soviets should decide to limit their sales, prices would surge.

Much of the demand is coming from the U.S. and Japanese auto industries, which are the world's biggest users of platinum — largely for pollution-fighting catalytic converters. Several European countries now also require converters, and all of Europe's cars will have them by 1991.

People who invest in the metal often choose to buy so-called platinum futures, which bet on future price trends. But futures are extremely risky. You can lose many times your stake if the market goes against you. The safer approach is to purchase the metal outright. The least expensive way is to buy one- or ten-ounce bars from either of the North American refiners: Engelhard Corporation of Edison, New Jersey, or Johnson Matthey of Toronto, Canada. Or consider buying platinum coins. In August 1988 one-ounce platinum coins, called Nobles, were selling for around $560.

COMMODITIES

Playing the Riskiest Game

For those who yearn for the fastest, toughest, highest-risk financial game of all, there are commodities. As many as 90% of all amateur traders lose money and drop out within a year, and the only consistent winners are the brokers who charge you commissions. Still, if you crave excitement and have a cast-iron stomach, commodities trading can offer impressive gains for that tiny portion of your investable funds that you are willing to put completely at risk — your mad money. But unless you are an expert, never put more than a nickel or dime out of every investment dollar into commodities.

The reason that commodities futures trading offers both outsized losses and outsized gains is leverage. When you buy commodities contracts, you do so on margin. The contracts give you the right to buy a specified commodity at a set price for a limited time. Let's say the price of gold is $450 an ounce, and you think it will rise in the next six months. Then you can invest in a contract to buy 100 ounces of gold at about $450 an ounce. That's $45,000 worth of gold. But speculating in gold futures costs less than 10% of the price of the metal. If gold goes up to, say, $500 an ounce by the time your contract expires six months from now, you win. On an outlay of less than $4,500, your profit will be $50 an ounce, or $5,000 — minus commissions.

But if prices move strongly against you, your broker will demand that you put up still more money. Unless you produce the cash immediately, the broker will sell out your position, at a potentially bone-chilling loss. To avoid that, give your broker a stop-loss order on each futures contract. That way, you establish in advance a price at which you will automatically sell out a position rather than take further losses.

In the early 1980s, some commodity prices suffered their longest decline in 15 years. Blame Mother Nature. She gave us bountiful harvests, which lowered prices of many farm commodities. Also blame the sluggish economy, which curbed demand for metals, and high interest rates, which lured investors out of commodities and into money-market funds. Commodity prices did start to revive when the economy pepped up and interest rates returned from their trip to the moon. Also, the tax law of 1982 helped commodities traders since it lowered the maximum tax on their profits from 70% to 32%. Profits are now taxed as ordinary income as a result of tax reform.

It cannot be stressed too much that commodities are risky. Small investors who speculate in commodities make two major mistakes. Many of them operate on the basis of tips; they are often wrong, and the amateurs cannot hope to match the professional traders for access to updated, accurate information about markets. Small investors also tend to be undercapitalized. To stay in this game, you should have five dollars in reserve, ready to commit, for every dollar you put up.

You can make do with less money by buying mini-contracts on the Mid America Commodity Exchange, which is located in Chicago. Mini-contracts control smaller quantities of commodities than do regular futures, but they are just as volatile as full-size contracts, and you will still get margin calls. But because you put up proportionately less money, you have less to lose.

A reasonable way for small investors to get into the market is to buy one of the 130 or so publicly traded commodity funds. The advantage is that the funds are professionally managed and diversify your investment among many types of commodities. More important, any losses are limited to the amount of money you put up; you are never subject to a margin call. But before you invest, you should know that 15% to 20% of your dollar goes to fees and commissions. Also, you should make sure that the trading advisers of the fund have proved that they can make money. If you are interested in commodity funds, you can follow them in a newsletter called *Managed Account Reports* (5513 Twin Knolls Road, Suite 213, Columbia, Maryland 21044; 301-730-5365). A subscription costs $225 a year.

Financial Futures

E VEN for the experts, the commodities futures market has always been a gamble. But now there are futures contracts for people who don't know beans about soybeans. The so-called commodities in this case are good old stocks and bonds, and they are traded in the fast and furious financial futures market.

The financial futures include contracts in Treasury bills, bonds and notes, bank certificates of deposit and a variety of other interest-bearing securities. When you buy one of these contracts, you are betting that, for example, interest rates will go down in the future and thus the prices of the bills, bonds or notes covered by the contract will go up.

You can buy financial futures through commodity firms or through brokers who specialize in commodities at large stock brokerage houses. But if you are a would-be buccaneer in the financial futures market, take a tip from the experts and do your trading on paper for a while, until you get your sea legs. If and when you are ready to start wheeling and dealing for real, then pick active markets, such as those trading in Treasury bill and Treasury bond futures. The more trading that is going on, the more likely you are to find a buyer or a seller for your contract at the price you want. And don't forget to place stop orders with your broker. They instruct him to close out your position when the price reaches a certain level — and they can help you limit any losses.

But any way you play it, futures is a highly leveraged business. So this kind of investment — while increasingly popular — is not for those who aren't prepared to take substantial risks.

OTHER INVESTMENTS

Art

I T takes art to invest intelligently in paintings, sculpture, photographs and prints. The key is to avoid faddish junk and have patience. Even when you buy with extreme selectivity — and with the close advice of a reliable dealer — you may not make a profit for five years or more, unless you were able to afford one of the few sought-after masterpieces. For these, the market is unlike anything in the past, and no one knows how high prices will soar. Fortunately, though, there are areas of the art world that are not so overinflated and in which art can be a smart investment.

Three fields are particularly promising and reasonably inexpensive for beginning collectors: prints, photographs and contemporary works of painting and sculpture by little-known artists. Some of them may become tomorrow's great stars. Fine pieces in these fields may be had for as little as a few hundred dollars. Buyers on limited budgets do not have to settle for obscure artists. For example, some of the 4,000-plus lithographs by 19th-century French social satirist Honoré Daumier can be had for less than $200 each.

A factor that has nothing to do with an image's beauty can boost the price of a print or photograph. People sometimes pay 100% more for a work that has the artist's signature on it. For less affluent collectors, the absence of a signature is a small price to pay for the opportunity to acquire a superb print for little money.

Among the most reputable sources of prints are major auction houses and the galleries that belong to the Art Dealers Association of America. For their names and addresses, write to the Art Dealers Association at 575 Madison Avenue, New York, New York 10022.

To find the best sources of photographs, write to the Association of International Photography Art Dealers at 93 Standish Road, Hillsdale, New Jersey 07642. You can order its $5 booklet, *On Collecting Photographs*, or, for $3, its membership directory.

In assembling a collection of contemporary paintings and sculpture, it is sometimes fun to try to discover new talent on your own. But the safest path for the neophyte is to develop long-term relationships with professional dealers who are closely associated with emerging artists. These dealers can offer much expertise and advice.

The major galleries and auction houses are concentrated in New York City, still the undisputed capital of the U.S. art trade. If you cannot make fairly regular trips to New York, then seek out local dealers as your agents to establish relationships with other dealers and auction houses.

The place *not* to buy works by lesser-known contemporary painters and sculptors is at an auction. Auction houses rarely offer such works anyway because they sell poorly there.

By contrast, auction houses are often excellent sources of prints and photographs. First, go to dealers to see what the prices are. Then, if something you want comes up at an auction, you may be able to get a better price.

When you are ready to buy, deal only with galleries and auction houses whose directors and employees have well-established reputations for honesty. Make sure they're willing to disclose all the facts about the art they sell. No reputable dealer should object to your consulting other experts before you make a purchase.

In the course of buying from a dealer, it's customary to *negotiate* the prices. Many dealers routinely add 10% to their asking prices for bargaining purposes. But don't badger a dealer who insists that his price is firm. Quite a few dealers allow buyers up to a year to pay, interest-free, and sometimes even longer than that.

Even though you are buying art on a low budget, there are some so-called bargains you will want to avoid. Stay away from World War I and World War II posters that are more interesting as historical curiosities than as art objects. Also avoid any contemporary prints that were produced in huge numbers and photographs that are neither rare nor of high quality. And remember: Nothing is a good buy, unless you really want it and have a passion for it.

Folk Art

EVERYTHING from diamond rings to Oriental rugs has declined in real value from the peaks of some years ago, but one family of collectibles that has held up well — and even risen to new records — is American folk art. But it is a crazy-quilt world with whirligig prices, so you have to love it — or leave it alone. Not even the experts agree on what domestic folk art is, and nobody can say for sure what it is really worth. Generally, as writer Gus Hedberg has observed, American folk art can include any tangible rudiment of daily life in the 18th, 19th and even 20th centuries that has been enhanced by a touch of art — everything from a gravestone to an old rag doll. Indeed, 19th-century weathervanes can cost more than the average meteorologist earns in a year, and some patchwork quilts are so rare and valued that no one would ever dream of sleeping under them.

The best examples of American folk art will continue to command high prices, but you can still get investment-grade American folk art for less than $1,000 — and even more that is just fun to own, for much less than that. Above all, the best folk art buy is something that truly delights you, aesthetically and personally. It should figure as a wise investment only secondarily.

A reliable guide to the shops, auctions and regions where a fledgling collector might begin looking for American folk art is the *Maine Antique Digest*. It costs $29 a year. Its address is P.O. Box 645, Waldoboro, Maine 04572.

If you want to buy folk art, it is wise to concentrate on a particular category. That will help you to establish a sense of confidence and expertise.

Among the most enduring investments are quilts. That is partly because there is a growing international demand for them. When buying for investment, look for the quilt with complex, intricate stitching and with unusual features, even a one-of-a-kind pattern. Top-quality old examples range all the way from $1,000 to $20,000, and the exceptionally beautiful and rare ones can go at auction for $100,000 and more. However, handsome contemporary quilts that you can actually sleep under without depreciating your investment are available for less than $300.

When buying a basket, check the bottom to see if it is still strong. But if the rest of the basket looks well-worn, yet the bottom has hardly been scuffed, that's a sure sign of a forgery. The best investments in baskets are those with unusual forms or those with handpainted decorations. It's hard to find one in sound condition for less than $100. To get bargains, avoid shops with expensive business cards, and head for stores and auctions in the back hills. There you sometimes can come across an oak splint basket from the late 19th century for as little as $75.

With a weathervane, older is considered better. If wood, it should be dulled and weathered; if gold leaf, it should have lost much of its gilt; if copper, it should be green. A vane with a beautifully aged patina is worth considerably more than one that has been repainted.

If you buy a painting as an investment, be wary of heavy restoration. And an anonymous folk painting may be just as valuable as one by a recognized artist.

If you are buying furniture, rely on the eye of an experienced dealer to avoid counterfeits. Once you get home with your piece of furniture, stifle any ambitions that may arise in you to fix it up. One woman who bought an 18th-century painted chest a few years ago for $25,000 then proceeded to refinish the piece. As a result, it's now worth no more than a few hundred dollars.

Collectibles: Plates, Books and Medallions

ADVERTISEMENTS breathlessly proclaim that limited editions of porcelain plates, books, medallions and china dolls offer terrific investment opportunities. In fact, companies that make and sell these purportedly limited editions of collectibles tend to exaggerate their investment value. Still, a careful collector can come out ahead. If you are tempted to buy, you would be wise to follow four rules:

First, buy only what you love. If it takes 20 years to sell your four Finnish Christmas plates, at least you will enjoy looking at them in your china cabinet.

Second, make sure that a manufacturer announces how many items constitute an edition before he begins taking orders. Avoid companies that will sell to anyone who orders within a fixed period, usually six months or a year. That means everybody who wants the item will get it, thereby killing the potential for a resale market.

Third, buy the finest material and craftsmanship that you can afford.

Finally, keep your collectibles in mint condition. You can't dine off collector's plates or let your children play with limited-edition porcelain dolls. If you eventually try to sell them, such factors as how clean they are or whether or not you can provide the original box they came in can make all the difference.

Each type of limited edition has its own characteristics and peculiarities. For example:

Plates: Seven million Americans — more than for any other limited-edition item — collect plates made of porcelain, pewter, crystal and even silver. About 150 manufacturers, including Royal Doulton and Rosenthal, bring out some 500 new issues a year. Single plates generally cost between $18 and $125, although some go for as much as $350. But if you ever try to sell, you may not get what you paid. Only about 30% of those who want to sell ever find buyers.

The most publicized place to buy and sell plates is the Bradford Exchange in Niles, Illinois. The toll-free number is 800-323-8078. Sellers phone in their asking prices and buyers call in bids. If a trade is made, sellers pay a 30% commission, and buyers pay a minimum of $4. All transactions are guaranteed by the Exchange.

Books: You may get both pleasure and profit by collecting books and selling them to other collectors at high prices some years from now. But be careful to buy only top-quality volumes with handmade paper, handset type and illustrations commissioned for the book.

Bibliophiles scorn many mass-produced reprints of classics. Though they claim to be limited editions, thousands of such books are printed, and their quality is often mediocre. But serious collectors admire and have bid up the prices of volumes published by some quality limited-edition presses. Among them is the Limited Editions Club in Manhattan. For example, its edition of Joyce's *Ulysses* sold for $10 in 1935; recently it brought $2,200 at auction.

A few hundred small presses irregularly publish well-crafted books in editions of fewer than 500 volumes. You can find reviews of small-press books in a quarterly magazine called *Fine Print* (P.O. Box 3394, San Francisco, California 94119; $48 a year).

Medallions: Beware of buying gold and silver medallions that are minted not by governments but by private companies. Interest in these novelties peaked in the 1970s, when private mints rushed to capitalize on gold fever. They turned out tokens commemorating all sorts of events and personalities. But collectors' ardor for them has cooled along with gold and silver prices. Even in the best of times, such ceremonial wampum has been hard to resell. For example, one 12-medallion set honoring the poet Robert Frost was issued in 1974 for $275; today, coin dealers will pay only about $65 for it.

Perhaps 10% of the medallions can be resold at more than the intrinsic value of the gold or silver in the piece or set. With very few exceptions, those issued by private companies in so-called limited editions are actually mass-marketed and thus are worthless as either investments or collector's items. And unless you are an expert at evaluating the age of those issued by a government, it is best to stay away from them also as investments. They are rarely dated, and thus the buyer has no way of knowing whether the piece was minted in the early 1920s or 1986 — the government often uses the same mold over and over again, perhaps with time lapses between each minting.

Richard Doty, a numismatic curator at the Smithsonian Institution in Washington, warns: "When you sell them, limited-edition medallions tend to be worth no more than the silver and gold they contain. Your only hope of selling them at a profit is if you have a very dumb brother-in-law."

Coins

COLLECTING genuine coins can be rewarding, whether you buy buffalo-head nickels or metal money from ancient Rome. U.S. coins alone have returned about 13% a year over the past decade. But particularly for the novice, investing in numismatic coins — those no longer being minted — is risky.

If you are new at the game, your first step should be to find a dealer you can trust. Look for one who has been in business at least 10 years. Ask him for references from customers and from a local bank if you plan to invest seriously in coins.

Dealer markups are about 15%. So if you try to sell a coin back, expect to get about 15% *less* than its stated market value at the time. Usually, you will have to hold a coin at least three years, and possibly 10 years, before turning a profit. That's why dealers and financial planners recommend that you commit no more than 10% to 15% of your investment money to your collection.

You will stand a better chance to profit if you concentrate on coins of a particular period or country. For example, so-called ancient coins — those minted before the fall of the Roman Empire in the fifth century A.D. — have appreciated about 10% to 20% annually in recent years. You can still get some bargains on ancient coins sold in the U.S. and Europe. Prices range from about $10 to $20 for common, fourth-century A.D. bronze coins to many thousands of dollars for rare gold or silver pieces.

As for U.S. coins, their prices tend to rise rapidly in inflationary times and drop as inflation declines. While coins of relatively recent mintage often fetch only a few cents over face value, a gold doubloon made in New York in 1787 recently sold for $725,000. The U.S. coins that dealers recommend most often to investors are Morgan silver dollars, which were minted between 1878 and 1904 and again in 1921. For example, a nearly perfect 1885 Morgan dollar made at the Carson City mint has risen in the past decade from $200 to around $1,150.

Even if you are not a coin collector, after a 1984 ruling by the Internal Revenue Service you may want to own at least one kind of coin. The IRS has decided that coin dealers must now report sales of South African Krugerrands, Canadian Maple Leafs and Mexican gold coins. The government wants to be sure that any profits that collectors make on them will not go unreported and untaxed.

But the rule does not include numismatic coins, scarce or rare coins that usually are worth far more than the gold, silver or bronze they contain. Because sales of them still do not have to be reported, goldbugs are trading in their Krugerrands for numismatics. That has driven up the price of one numismatic in particular — the double-eagle $20 gold piece, minted in the 19th and 20th centuries. The old double-eagle may well continue to be a profitable speculative investment.

Gems

DIAMONDS, rubies, emeralds, sapphires — ah, what romance! But as investments, those luscious gems are quite chancy. Before you try to profit from your jewelry box, remember that gems that have been bought to wear are seldom of investment quality. When you buy them, you rarely pay wholesale prices. The dealer takes a substantial markup — sometimes as much as 100%. And if you ever try to sell the stone, dealers usually will offer you even *less* than wholesale prices.

Unlike stocks and bonds, there is no easily quoted market for gems because no two stones are identical in quality or value. Diamonds are evaluated by four measures: carat (or weight), color, clarity and cut. Even the color of white diamonds is graded from D for the whites, to Z for dingy yellow. The difference of just one letter grade can amount to thousands of dollars per carat in the price.

If you do invest in diamonds, insist on receiving a certificate from an independent laboratory that has graded the stone within the last 12 months. Even with that, you also should get a recertification by having your jeweler send the stone, insured, by registered mail, to the Gemological Institute of America. It has offices in New York City and Santa Monica, California.

In short, if you are acquiring jewelry for pleasure, fine. But don't deceive yourself into believing you are making a sure-thing investment. Unless you are an expert, gems are for buying, not for selling. With occasional exceptions, colored stones are less costly than diamonds — but more risky. That's because a world diamond cartel usually keeps a floor under prices, but there are no cartels to hold the prices of rubies, emeralds or sapphires.

Among the colored stones, fine rubies have risen the fastest lately. Supplies are short because few rubies are being exported by Burma, the source of the richest and reddest stones. The next most valuable rubies come from Thailand, while the lighter Sri Lanka rubies are less coveted. Sapphires are almost as rare as rubies, and some of the best and the bluest are from Kashmir. Emeralds may be a safer investment because they are easier to resell than sapphires.

The steep price of precious stones is stirring interest in much more speculative semi-precious stones, notably aquamarines and topaz stones, which come in shades of orange and yellow. The finest opals are too fragile to be a solid long-term investment; they can crack fairly easily.

There is no universally accepted grading system for colored stones, as there is for diamonds. But before buying, an investor should insist on independent written appraisal of the gem's quality, weight, color — and, of course, its dollar value.

Toys

Toys of the 1950s and early 1960s aren't kid stuff anymore. Now they are called contemporary collectibles, and many command precious prices. Collectors are paying hundreds — and sometimes thousands — of dollars for toys that sold for a few dollars when new. The buying and selling is done at antique toy auctions. You can find auction locations and dates advertised in a monthly magazine called *Antique Toy World* (4419 Irving Park Road, Chicago, Illinois 60641).

Collectors covet dolls of the 1950s and early 1960s for their beauty and wardrobes. Among those that have appreciated the most are the eight-inch Madame Alexander Brand Romeo and Juliet dolls. They cost $3.50 each when they came out in 1955. Now a pair in good condition can fetch up to $3,500. Barbie can bring you bounty, too. An original Barbie, first sold for $3 in 1959, today can command as much as $1,400 in pristine condition and preserved in her original box.

The 1950s era techno-toys, such as robots and satellites, also can command high prices at auction. Other valuable toys include small metal trucks and cars of the 1950s. Originally $5 or so, they now sell for $100 to $300.

So-called character toys, often from cartoons or kids' TV shows, are also surging. A 14-inch Popeye doll that first sold in 1935 now brings $800.

You may be able to find toys that have more than nostalgic value and sell them for high prices. Where to look? Garage sales are one place. Before you buy, inspect the toy carefully. Make sure it functions properly, has no missing parts, peeling paint or other signs of corrosion. Top bids are usually reserved for toys in mint condition with their original boxes. The best place to find toys worth a bundle is at home. Just think: the joys may be in your attic.

Rock 'n' Roll Memorabilia

SOME of the hottest collectors' items now are rock 'n' roll memorabilia. They are bought and sold at auction houses that deal in collectibles.

Rock 'n' roll collectibles include original recordings, posters, souvenirs, even old magazines. The October 27, 1975, editions of *Time* and *Newsweek* with cover stories about Bruce Springsteen sold for $25 each just a decade later.

If you want to be a collector you should specialize in items related to a single band, or in a particular category of items, such as backstage passes. The most valuable collectibles are likely to be those associated with musicians who marked a turning point in rock history, such as The Beatles. A military tunic that John Lennon wore on concert tours fetched $850 at auction. But keep in mind that assets like these are not very liquid. As with most collectibles, you are best off buying an item because you want to own it, not because you expect to make a profit.

REAL ESTATE

Your Prospects for Profit

R EAL ESTATE has been the source of more great fortunes than any other investment, but its future is clouded because tax reform has reduced its lavish tax benefits. At the extreme, alarmists prophesy that property values ultimately will plunge, that rents will soar and that so many investors will walk away from their buildings they will need a parade permit.

Don't be taken in. If you adjust your investment strategy, you should come out all right. Buy real estate investments for income and capital appreciation, but don't insist that every nickel you spend is a deduction. Here's why:

The new tax law does not allow you to deduct so-called passive losses from other income, such as your salary or income from stocks and bonds. Generally, limited partnerships and rental real estate investments qualify as passive investments under the new law. You can use passive losses only to offset income from passive investments. Thus, if you own rental property, you will be allowed to deduct your mortgage interest, property taxes and expenses only up to the amount of your rental income plus any other limited partnership income you may have.

One exception to the rule covers owners of rental real estate who meet three tests: You own at least 10% of the property; you make, not merely approve, the management decisions; and your taxable income is less than $100,000 a year. Then you can deduct up to $25,000 in losses against any other income. If you earn more than $100,000, the $25,000 limit will be reduced by 50% of the amount that your income exceeds $100,000. For example, if your income is $130,000, you could use up to $10,000 in losses from your rental property (half of $30,000 equals $15,000; and $25,000 minus $15,000 equals $10,000).

The new rules will be phased in over five years for properties bought before President Reagan signed the law on October 22, 1986. On your tax return for 1988, you can use 40% of your losses to offset any other income. The figure drops to 20% in 1989, 10% in 1990 and none in 1991.

The wise choice for real estate investors is to acquire property that, because of location and other attributes, has intrinsic value above and beyond the tax benefits. The key to success now is patience, with an eye toward long-term gains and consistent annual income.

That advice holds true whether the investment you are considering is part of an office building, a shopping center, an apartment house or even your own home. In fact, do not count on making any profit from buying a house or condo now for your own use if you are likely to move within three or four years. The increase you can expect in the value of your home probably will not offset the cost of borrowing and the real estate commissions you will have to pay when you sell. The increase in property values is expected to average 5% or so annually, though it will be much higher — or lower — in some regions and neighborhoods than in others.

If you want to own and manage property directly, your best investment today would be a single-family house or, if you could afford it, a multi-unit apartment building. But for a lot less money, you can become a limited partner in a real estate syndication or a shareholder in a real estate investment trust, or REIT. You can buy limited partnerships from stockbrokers and financial planners, and you generally have to put up at least $5,000.

The Tax Benefits

THOUGH reform has reduced the tax benefits of owning rental real estate, you may still qualify for a host of deductions. Remember, if you own at least 10% of the property, actively manage the building (making, not just approving, all decisions) and earn less than $100,000 a year, you can use up to $25,000 in losses to offset any type of income — including wages or earnings from securities. Investors who earn between $100,000 and $150,000 a year may qualify for losses subject to a lower limit.

But be aware that being a landlord is not for everyone. Many busy people simply do not have the time or temperament to cope with tenant complaints and broken boilers. Instead these people can buy into REITs or limited partnerships.

Within the limits of the new tax law, landlords can deduct not only mortgage interest and property taxes but also fire and liability insurance premiums, expenses for finding and screening tenants, commissions for collecting rents, the cost of traveling to and from the property and, best of all, depreciation.

Tax reform has stretched out the depreciation of residential rental real estate from 19 years to 27½ years for property placed in service after 1986. And you can use only what is called straight-line depreciation. To get your annual depreciation allowance, divide the cost of the property by 27½.

Investors who fix up old buildings also can do well. To qualify for the tax benefits, you must sell or rent out the building for nonresidential commercial or industrial use, which does not include apartment rentals. Also, the improvements must cost at least $5,000, or more than the price you paid for the building. Reform has eliminated all but the tax credits for very old buildings. Beginning with your 1987 income taxes, you could take a credit equal to 10% of the cost of renovating a building that is more that 50 years old, although the total amount is subject to limitation. If you own a building that is a "certified historic structure" or is located in a historic district, you get a tax credit for 20% of the renovation costs, again subject to limitations. In this case, you can also take the credit for apartment buildings. To find out whether a building qualifies, check with the U.S. Department of the Interior or your state's historic-preservation office. And to learn what your tax credit might amount to, be sure to consult your tax adviser.

The Ideal Property Investments

You no longer can assume that just about any real estate will automatically increase in value, but property still can be a terrific long-term investment — if you know what to buy. Novice investors should avoid commercial properties such as stores and office buildings. Managing them requires special expertise such as, for example, knowing how to handle business leases. Stick with residential properties; they are easier to handle.

According to most experts, the ideal investments today are three-bedroom, two-bath houses. They are large enough for small families, which tend to be the most stable tenants. There is great demand in many communities for these single-family homes. That means they usually can pay you enough in rents to cover your mortgage and maintenance costs — and give you a nice profit. They are also relatively easy to sell if you need to cash in your investment in a hurry.

If you are a first-time investor, you would be wise to stick close to your own community. The market will be familiar, and the travel time will be less than if you buy a far-off building. By investing in your backyard, you are in a good position to anticipate what will happen to real estate prices. Wherever you buy, talk with other property owners and visit many properties to get a feel for real estate values. Make sure the neighborhood is economically stable. There is no quicker way to lose your money than to purchase a house on a block that is about to be engulfed by crime. Look for solid construction and sturdy appliances before you worry about charm.

If you do not have much time to spend on repairs, buy real estate that is in ready-to-rent condition. But if you do have hours to spare and are handy with a saw and paintbrush, look for structurally sound houses in less than sterling condition that can profit from a moderate amount of fix-up.

One sensible rule is to buy the *worst* house on the *best* block. A property that can be pulled into rentable condition with a fresh coat of exterior paint could be an excellent investment. Bringing this home up to par with its neighbors by later adding a room or doing some landscaping can pay big dividends in rental profits. It also can produce a fat gain when the property is sold.

Another choice is to look for a deteriorating house in a turnaround neighborhood. You will stand your best chance of locating such a property by searching in a community that you know well. As mentioned, you can save taxes by renovating properties that are considered to be historically significant. But use caution. Such investments require rehabilitation skills and a sharp sense of timing. If you are too early, you will not get enough rent to pay for its upgrading.

How to Buy

O NCE you decide to invest in rental property, you probably will be eager to buy something quickly and put your money to work. *Resist* the temptation. Many new real estate investors underestimate the complexity of the field and overestimate how much they know about it.

Immerse yourself in a study of real estate as you would any new business venture. Talk with other investors and brokers; that will help you pinpoint the neighborhoods with the best investment potential. Seek out areas that have begun to gain favor among young householders as an alternative to more expensive established neighborhoods. Look for good transportation, shopping and schools and a strong, diversified employment base.

Then you can narrow your search to specific properties. Your best ally is likely to be a broker who is knowledgeable about your chosen area. Check his or her reputation with local bankers and attorneys. Discuss with the broker your debt limits and investment standards. Other obvious sources of sale properties are newspaper real estate sections, posted "FOR SALE" signs, city auctions of buildings in arrears and word of mouth. Plan to inspect dozens of buildings before you make a bid.

If you find a property that approaches your standards, investigate it thoroughly. Unless you are versed in building construction and mechanics, take along a construction engineer whose judgment you trust. The $175 to $400 fee will be worth it. You also can use the engineer's report to negotiate a better deal.

Look for a modern furnace and a water heater that has a capacity of at least 40 gallons for each family. And ask when that water heater was purchased. Be alert for signs of trouble. Stains on ceilings might mean plumbing or roof leaks and sagging floors could indicate structural defects. Your biggest worry will be the condition of the roof — replacement costs are high. Particularly with a large building, check the condition of the central air-conditioning plant and that of the asphalt parking lot, if there is one. You can confirm the stated age of a building by looking inside the toilet tank; most are stamped with their date of manufacture. Or look for a city building inspector's sticker.

Before investing in a rental house or apartment building, always ask yourself: Does it make financial sense for you? Can you *really* afford the initial cash outlay? Rental units average about $70,000, but, of course, many are much costlier. You will have to put 10% to 25% of that down — or $7,000 to $17,500 on a $70,000 house. Legal fees, advance property taxes and mortgage surcharges will add another $2,000 to $4,000 on the medium-priced home.

Make sure the property can pay you enough rental income to cover mortgage payments, taxes, utilities and maintenance costs. A property that does not is especially risky in low-inflation periods. You cannot count on its price to rise steeply enough to make up the losses.

When calculating the economics of a property, pay particular attention to financing. Do not go to just one bank or other lender, but shop around to several of them to get the largest possible mortgage at the lowest interest rate.

In many cases, the best source of financing is the seller. If the owner is anxious to unload the property, he or she may offer terms that are far more attractive than those at the banks. Many real estate ads will mention the availability of owner financing.

If the price of the property is more than you can afford, you may want to look into a type of cost splitting called a shared-equity financing agreement. With it, you will not buy the property for yourself, but you will share the ownership — and the cost — with the occupant. (For more, see "Your Home: Shared-Equity Mortgages.")

How to Be a Landlord

POSSIBLE tax breaks and potential capital gains might well tempt you to consider becoming a landlord. But be warned: The migraines are multiple, and the investment is not the instant winner it once was. Whether the property you rent to outsiders is a vacation cottage or the home you have lived in, to succeed as a landlord you need patience.

Steep real interest rates and lofty purchase prices make it extremely tough to turn an immediate profit. In some cities, you will have to wait for rents to rise, and that could take years. And do not forget that values for existing homes are expected to increase only 5% or so annually for the next several years.

Before you leap into landlording, be sure you can afford to tie up your money for as long as it will take for the investment to become profitable. The new restrictions on deducting losses virtually require that the building you buy produces a positive cash flow — that is, its rents must exceed your maintenance and financing costs. If it does not do so immediately or at most within a year, the property will merely wring cash out of you. For this reason, when you are stalking the positive-cash-flow property, confine your search to a tight rental market where the vacancy rate is 6% or less and rents reasonably could be increased.

Take a hard look at the troubles of being a landlord. Do you really want to hunt for tenants? How do you feel about being rousted out of bed by a phone call telling you that a pipe has burst? Of course, you can hire a management firm to take care of those chores. Its services will cost you 6% to 10% of the rent and could go as high as 20% if you have a single-family house.

If you are new at managing property, take a tip from experienced landlords: use great caution in screening prospective tenants. The hours you spend can save days of grief later on. Check each applicant's references. Call his or her employer to confirm job tenure. Ask the applicant's present landlord if he or she would gladly continue renting to the applicant. You may want to run a credit check, and you would be wise to get a security deposit of two months' rent.

Once the tenant has moved in, inspect the premises often, looking for little problems that could cause big troubles later on. Then fix them. If you do not want to be bothered by frequent minor repairs, you can offer the tenant a rent break to do his or her own maintenance. Your periodic checks will let you know whether the work is being done properly.

All in all, landlording has its rewards. It just takes longer now than before to realize them.

Renting to Your Parents or Children

I F YOU have older parents who need shelter, there is a superb way for you to help them and enjoy the tax benefits of being a landlord. The IRS used to outlaw most tax deductions when you rented your property to a close relative, but Congress eliminated that restriction starting in 1981. Now you can buy a condo or house, lease it to your elderly parents and take deductions for maintenance, mortgage interest and depreciation — provided, of course, that your deductions are within the limits set by the new tax law. The IRS also insists that you charge your kin a fair market rent. You can easily document that by asking a local real estate broker for a written estimate of what rent the property should command.

In fact, if you have parents who are 55 or older, you may want to buy their house. That way, you *both* can get tax breaks. Your folks do not have to pay any federal income taxes on their profits from the sale — up to $125,000. And now that you own the house, you can take the normal real estate tax deductions for property taxes and mortgage interest payments. Furthermore, when you rent the house to your parents, you can take the additional deductions for depreciation on your property.

The same tax breaks apply, of course, when you buy a house in a college town and rent it out to your son or daughter, the student. Many parents are managing to make money on their children's college education by buying houses for them — and perhaps a few classmates — to live in. Be sure you charge a fair market rate in order to get a passing grade from the IRS. But if you hire your child as the building superintendent, you can give him or her a 10% rent rebate.

Just one real-life example: When Bill Nelson was a sophomore at the University of California at Santa Barbara, he and three of his classmates could not find a house to rent. So his mother bought one. The boys got a nice deal. For a four-bedroom house, they paid $450 a month — exactly what they had paid for a rather cramped three-bedroom apartment the year before. The $450 almost entirely covered Mrs. Nelson's monthly mortgage payments, and the boys also promised to handle the repairs. After Bill Nelson graduated, he rented the house out for $775 a month. The house originally cost Mrs. Nelson $85,000; five years later it was worth $250,000.

Buying a house in a college town can be an excellent investment, but it does present risks. Not all students are really cut out to be landlords. Some are too immature, or may see their parents' real-estate venture as an opportunity to shelter friends. These youngsters may be reluctant to collect rent from their pals. Besides, owning a house requires constant attention. Occasionally the student landlord has to make a tough choice between mopping up a flooded basement or studying for an exam.

If you like the idea of buying a house or condominium for your college-bound youngster, you may be wise to let your child spend freshman year getting used to his or her surroundings before you commit your money. If you then decide to buy, choose a larger, five-bedroom house over a smaller, two-bedroom one; the extra rental income is often worth the additional expense.

Some other tips:

— Avoid a rattletrap house that needs a lot of work — unless you are prepared to spend a lot of money to fix it.

— Pick a property as close to the campus as possible. But if housing demand is really high, do not rule out anything up to five miles away.

— Think twice about buying in a small town that does not have many year-round residents. After all, you have to find people who will be temporary tenants during the summer vacation.

Buying — and Selling — Condominiums

A S MENTIONED earlier, real estate investments can offer a mix of rental income, tax benefits and capital gains. But ownership of a condo — that is, a dwelling unit in a group-owned building or on group-owned land — has additional advantages. Condos generally require less capital and have fewer maintenance problems than single-family houses do.

You can start by buying a unit for personal use. Condo owners can deduct mortgage interest and real estate taxes from their taxable income. People who rent out units also can deduct monthly maintenance and depreciation — up to the limits set by tax reform. In 1988, about 15% of the condos in the U.S. were held as investments.

Some investors convert whole apartment houses into condos. You can invest in one of these deals either directly, by buying a building and converting it, or indirectly, as a limited partner who supplies some of the capital but stays on the sidelines. Of course, if you buy into a limited partnership, you will be able to use any losses only to offset income from passive investments.

If you are a tenant in a building that is being converted, you generally will have to pay twice as much per square foot to buy your apartment as the converter did. Even so, that "insider's" price is almost invariably well below the market value of similar homes. Some tenants make a profit by immediately reselling. That's known as flipping.

Tenants who buy and stay on commonly have to pay more per month in maintenance fees and mortgage expenses than their previous rent, but much of that extra cost may be offset by tax deductions.

Recently condo sales have shown a healthy upturn in the country as a whole, and especially in the Northeast. In some parts of the country, however, the condominium market is still as soft as ice cream. From 1983 to 1987, prices of many units dropped 15% to 35%. So what do you do if you own a condo in a depressed market and want to sell?

Above all, don't panic. If possible, try to wait a year or two to see whether the condo glut subsides and prices rebound in your area. A recent cutback in construction in some places could balance out the current oversupply. Even during the slump elsewhere, prices have held up strongly in a number of cities, including New York and San Francisco.

Besides waiting, another choice for a condo owner is to move and rent out the unit. You might consider offering a tenant a lease with an option to buy at a prearranged price in, say, 12 months. That way, if real estate values rise, the tenant will be delighted to buy your condo at what will then be a discount.

If you must sell now, list your condominium for 10% to 20% less than the price of a single-family house in a comparable location. Historically, that's the difference needed to attract buyers to condos. Also, put some buzzwords in your newspaper classified ads. The words "overlooking pool" appeal to singles. Young couples might be lured by the phrase "Can't Afford a House?" And phrases such as "safe, no kids" and "carefree living" might attract empty-nester parents in their 50s or 60s.

Buying Vacation Homes

SECOND homes are bought primarily for recreation, relaxation and retirement, but they can be profitable real-estate investments, too. If you buy in the right place at the right time, the value of your vacation retreat can go through the roof. You stand the best chance for gain if your second home has two characteristics.

First, it has to be fairly easy to get to. The choicest turf is no more than a gas tank away from a big population area. If you can afford it, buy on or near the water. This is the surest bet for both high rentals and capital appreciation.

Second, the land surrounding the property should have limited potential for development. That automatically limits the supply of houses. Environmental laws that put a lid on construction have made waterfront properties especially attractive, though costly, investments. The state of New Jersey, for example, stopped a developer from filling in and building on some wetlands. In the three years after that ruling, prices of second-home plots in the area surged 300%.

Stay away from idiosyncratic vacation homes. The dwellings that hold their value best are those with exteriors that are in keeping with the area. And look for communities that have stable growth, strong zoning and a distaste for go-go construction projects.

If you are considering a development that is under construction, grill the developer and the real estate agent about the timetable for installing such amenities as recreational facilities, community water supplies and sewage disposal. Get guarantees in *writing*. Check with the local real estate commission or with an office of the federal Department of Housing and Urban Development to see if the developer has registered for interstate land sales and has posted a substantial bond to pay for anything he inadvertently omits.

When you have located a property you are interested in, bargain vigorously. Bid at least 20% less than the asking price — especially in areas where the market is sluggish.

Timing is critical in both the purchase and sale of vacation real estate. Because it is a discretionary purchase, prices fluctuate more widely in economic booms and busts than the prices of other houses do. Lately, buyers with cash in hand have been finding quite a few bargains. Prices have dropped 10% to 20% since 1981 in some areas. The reasons include overbuilding and low inflation.

Finding a mortgage should be easier than it's ever been. The Federal Home Loan Mortgage Corporation has joined the Federal National Mortgage Association in buying vacation-home mortgages held by banks. That has made credit more readily available. Also, many sellers will take back the mortgages themselves. This means they, in effect, agree to receive payment for the house over a period of 10 years or so.

But it is important to shop around for financing. Many banks demand not only a ½% premium for such loans but also 20% to 40% down, plus points and fees that can amount to 3½% of the total mortgage. Check with a local real estate agent or title company to find which banks grant the best vacation-home mortgages.

One way to beat the cost of second houses is to divvy up the ownership — and expenses — with several families. For example, four couples share a $100,000 ski condominium in Keystone, Colorado. Each couple arranged their own financing and borrowed from private sources, since banks do not give mortgages on a quarter of a house. Under a legal agreement, if one couple wants out, the others get first crack at buying their share.

To help pay for the mortgage, taxes and upkeep, more and more owners are renting out their second homes. Local real estate agents find tenants, and keep an eye on the property once it is rented. The agents' fees range from 10% to 20% of the rent. For higher fees, managers of some resort communities not only find tenants but also collect the rent and take care of repairs.

Like owners of any house, you can deduct the mortgage interest and property taxes on your vacation home — as long as the IRS deems your pleasure palace a second home. If you do not use it for more than 14 days a year, the house may qualify as rental real estate. Then you must meet the requirements of any rental real estate owner in order to deduct up to the maximum $25,000 allowed beyond the amount of any passive income you may have.

The Special Incentives for Renovation

PEOPLE have been fixing up old buildings for profit practically since cave dwellings went out of style. But tax incentives and special financing can make renovation a better deal than ever.

The federal tax credit for rehabilitation expenses is particularly valuable since it reduces your income tax dollar for dollar. Beginning with your 1987 income taxes, you could get a credit of 10% of your expenses for restoring buildings more than 50 years old that you use to generate income. If you renovate a building that is located in a historic district or is certified by the Department of the Interior as having historical significance, the credit could rise to 20% of the costs. Your state historic-preservation office can tell you if a building is eligible for certification, and then can help you get it approved.

Many cities and states also have passed tax abatements that for several years exempt owners of restored structures from the higher property taxes that would normally follow from a building's increased assessed value.

When you are looking for ways to invest in older buildings, the best places to start are preservation groups, landmarks foundations and historical societies. Preservationists also have up-to-date information about tax incentives as well as about money available from federal, state and local sources. (For more, see "Your Investments/Real Estate: The Tax Benefits.")

REITs and Limited Partnerships

FEW small investors can afford to spring for an office building, a large apartment house or a shopping center. Yet you can get in on these potentially lucrative investments, and it is easier than you might think. You can become either a limited partner in a real estate project or a shareholder in a real estate investment trust, commonly known as a REIT.

Limited partnerships are sold by brokerage houses, insurance agents and financial planners. You generally have to put up a $5,000 minimum. That entitles you to shares, or units, in a major real estate investment. You can choose from basically two types of partnerships — those that stress tax breaks and those that emphasize income and the prospect of capital gains when the partnership's properties are sold. Remember that under the new tax law all limited partnerships are passive investments. That reduces their tax benefits and enhances the appeal of income-oriented partnerships.

So much money has poured into partnerships that sponsors are competing with each other for prime properties. As a result, the quality and yields of some investments may suffer. You will do best to stick with sponsors who spread risk among several properties and who have a record of profit. Such sponsors include JMB Realty Corporation and the Balcor Company, a subsidiary of American Express.

Real estate investment trusts are very different from limited partnerships. A REIT operates somewhat like a closed-end mutual fund, but one that invests in a diversified portfolio of real estate or mortgages instead of stocks and bonds. Shares of REITs are traded just like those of closed-end funds or common stocks, on the exchanges or over-the-counter. This means you can sell your REIT shares in the open market. REITs thus offer the advantage of being a liquid form of investment in real estate, which is traditionally an illiquid asset.

You can buy 100 shares in some REITs from stockbrokers for $2,000 to $3,000. You then collect the income that the trust earns from rent and other sources. In fact, REITs are required by law to distribute 95% of their taxable income as dividends to shareholders. Because they pay out so much of their earnings, they pay no corporate income tax. That means, unlike companies that issue stock, their earnings are not taxed before they are distributed. Thus, investors get a bigger share of the profits than they do with stock. When you collect those dividends, you also may be exempt from paying taxes on a portion of them. Yet for all these breaks, tax reform has little effect on REITs because they do not qualify as passive investments.

When the trust sells off the properties it owns, you get the profits from the sale. You collect them either in the form of special dividends or increased earnings per share, which often boosts the price of your REIT stock.

If properties owned by a REIT rise in value, the market probably also will bid up its shares. REITs soared in the early 1970s, then crashed when many construction loans failed. But these trusts made a comeback in the early 1980s. With the combination of dividends and price appreciation, they earned an average compounded annual rate of return of 14% a year from 1980 through 1987, almost matching the 14.6% a year for common stocks in the Standard & Poor's 500 stock index.

In the first half of 1988, the REITs' rate of return continued to be 14%. Many were trading at close to their all-time highs, especially those invested in properties in their own regions. Still, you can find some bargains. In mid-1988, some real estate investment trusts were selling at 23% below the appraised value of the properties and mortgages they held.

One of the most common types of these trusts is so-called equity REITs. In mid-1988, they were paying dividends of 5% to 13%, and as much as half of their cash distributions may be sheltered.

The most successful REITs often specialize in one type of property, such as shopping centers or apartment buildings. But many recently offered REITs are so-called blind pools, and market analysts tend to warn you against them. Blind pools don't own any properties at the time of the offering, and it may take them a year to complete their acquisitions. Meanwhile, your investment money is put into a money-market fund, and if interest rates decline, your yields will go down while the blind pools wait to buy.

To choose a REIT, read the prospectus. Find out what property is owned and where it is located. Avoid REITs that charge high front-end fees of 10% or so. Make sure the trust has been in business at least eight years. Older REITs own the most deeply undervalued assets: the ones that can be sold at the largest profit. Also, you will be able to make a considered investment judgment on the basis of those REITs' long performance records and their history of dividend increases.

Buying Into Second Mortgages

A LMOST everybody complains about daunting mortgage rates, but those rates are a cause for rejoicing for one kind of person. He is the sophisticated investor who is willing to take the risk of putting his cash into second mortgages.

Second mortgages are loans made to homebuyers whose down payments and primary mortgages still don't add up to the purchase price. Anyone with a fairly large sum to invest can grant such second-mortgage loans and earn an annual return of 10% or more.

With most second mortgages, the borrower makes monthly payments only on the interest. The investor — that is — the lender, gets his principal back in a lump sum when the loan expires; typically, that is in three years. The interest rate is negotiated by the lender and borrower. As a rule, it is about two percentage points above the rate local banks charge on first mortgages.

Recently there has been an alternative to the second-mortgage formula called a shared-equity financing. Here an investor puts up part of the down payment on the house. Technically, this is not a loan; the investor becomes a co-owner. (For more, see "Your Home: Shared-Equity Mortgages.")

Say that you want to invest in a second mortgage or a shared-equity deal. You can get leads to people who need such financing by asking builders, real estate agents or mortgage loan brokers. Beware, however, of shady brokers, who lure investors with promises of suspiciously high returns of 18% to 24%. In New Mexico, two mortgage brokers recently were sentenced to prison for, among other things, failing to tell investors that one-third of their borrowers defaulted.

With either a second mortgage or a shared-equity investment, it is easier to get in than get out. If the investor in a second mortgage needs his money before the term of the loan is up, he can sell the note. But if interest rates are higher than at the time the loan was made, he will have to sell the note at a discount.

So if you are prospecting for high annual returns, you may want to consider the second-mortgage investment market. But be prepared to keep your money locked up for the length of the loan.

Making Tax-free Exchanges

I F YOU hold some land or a house for an investment, there may come a day when you will want to sell it for a profit. You would get a better deal if you do not sell it, but swap it for another piece of property. That way, you delay paying any taxes on your capital gains. You do not pay until you ultimately make a sale. This rule applies to all kinds of real property, so long as you use it as an investment. It could be a house or a condo, a plot of land on which you plan to build or even barren land that you are holding for possible future development.

For example, one couple living in Utah long owned 100 acres of idle farmland way off in North Carolina. Because they bought it many years ago, when prices were cheap, they would have a big profit if they sold it — and they would have to pay large capital-gains taxes. But they can avoid that if they find someone with whom to make a tax-free exchange for other property, perhaps closer to home in Utah.

The properties you exchange do not have to be identical or even of the same value. You could swap farmland for an apartment building or a condo. But you would be taxed on any additional cash you received at the time of the deal. And the swap has to be simultaneous. You cannot sell your property first and then buy another.

How do you find some other property owner to swap with? Just write to your state board of realtors for a list of brokers who are certified commercial investment members. That means they have received special training in real estate transactions and passed state exams. Be sure to seek the help of a tax attorney who is knowledgeable about real estate to make sure that your swap contract meets all the requirements of a tax-free exchange.

Your Home

The Outlook for Housing Prices

A s AMERICANS, we expect nothing less than life, liberty — and a house that appreciates in value year after year. But median prices of existing houses have increased less than the Consumer Price Index in four of the past eight years. Median prices also show little or no gains in some cities from year to year. For example, prices have been flat recently in Miami, Tulsa and Albuquerque. And in a few, such as Houston, Dallas and Oklahoma City, the median sales price of existing single-family houses actually fell in 1987.

Economists and other analysts who watch this market say the message is that it's high time for homeowners to lower their expectations. Many reckon that houses in general will appreciate only about as fast as the inflation rate. Therefore, it's quite likely that they will not rise more than some 5% a year for the next five years — though, of course, there will be greater and smaller appreciation in some communities.

The prospect of modest gains has broad implications for mobile Americans who have come to depend on their houses as their best overall investments. For example, you would be wise to refrain from stretching for a second mortgage or home-equity loan on the expectation that the eventual sale of your house will bail you out. And unless you live in a house for at least three to five years, closing costs, brokerage fees and other expenses may wipe out any profit you can expect when selling.

Looking at the positive side, even though mortgage rates in mid-1988 were heading up, they were still lower than they had been for most of the past 10 years. Also, today's economy is far healthier than it was in the early part of the decade. It was then that the recession and mortgage rates above 13% sharply reduced the number of house shoppers and prevented sellers from raising prices.

If you are a homeowner, don't be overly concerned about tax reform. Although a drop in your tax rate would make real estate write-offs less valuable to you, you can still deduct your mortgage interest payments and property taxes.

Cities Where Prices Are Highest — and Lowest

FOR HOMEOWNERS, real estate prices lately have not been cause for raising the roof. Median prices for existing houses rose little more than inflation in 1987, up roughly 5% from the year before. But the picture varies from city to city.

According to a nationwide survey of home sales by Coldwell Banker, a three-bedroom, two-bath house ranged from a low of $66,833 in Oklahoma City to $636,557 in "super elite" Beverly Hills. The median price for such houses in the 172 markets that Coldwell studied was $125,900. Among other elite and upscale areas, the same kind of house cost $417,333 in San Francisco, and $364,333 on the north shore of Long Island's Nassau County.

Cities whose housing costs hover around the median include Cincinnati, Ohio ($122,467), Greensboro, North Carolina ($122,967), Harrisburg, Pennsylvania ($124,633), Cheyenne, Wyoming ($124,500) and St. Paul, Minnesota ($127,800).

And what about renting a house? Except for small exclusive pockets, rents are highest in the suburbs of New York, Boston and the San Francisco/Oakland area — the typical three-bedroom there costs $1,000 to $1,800 a month and even more. But rents are below average in Baton Rouge; Spokane; and Portland, Oregon.

When Is the Right Time to Buy?

I s NOW a good time to buy a house? The answer is yes — if you really need a house to live in and if you have found one that you like.

Don't wait for mortgage rates to come down. Though they may well decline in the future, you certainly cannot bank on that happening. Mortgage rates tend to decline much less than interest rates in general do. But what will happen if rates really plunge? Then demand for houses will heat up and prices are likely to surge. So, either way, you are probably best off buying your dream house now.

How much of your income can you afford to spend when you are buying a house or an apartment? A little less than you used to. A few years ago, it was sensible to reach financially to get the biggest house in the best neighborhood that you possibly could manage. Inflation then was running away, meaning that your house was likely to spurt in value, and you would be paying off your mortgage debt in ever-depreciating dollars. Now that inflation is moderate, real estate professionals advise you not to buy more house than you can handle. They say you may spend a little more than you are comfortable with because real estate stands to remain a sound — although not a runaway — investment. Beware, however, of buying a house well beyond your means. Once you own it, you will not be able to keep it up, and that will hurt you when you are ready to resell. If you don't have the money to paint your house or otherwise repair it, you will never get top dollar for it.

Choosing a House to Purchase

A MERICA's favorite investment is still the family house. It is also by far the biggest investment that most people make. By July 1988, the median price had climbed to $123,500 for a new house and to $91,600 for one that had been previously occupied. In little more than a decade, those figures had jumped from, respectively, $55,700 and $48,700.

As mentioned previously, chances are that prices will not soar nearly as fast in the next 10 years. Still, today's smart buyers can expect to earn a profit when they sell. You probably *will* sell your home at some point, unless you feel sure that you will remain in it for the 30 years it will take to pay off the mortgage. Thus, when choosing a house, you should select one that not only appeals to you but also stands to be a worthwhile investment. Whether it's a small starter home or a spacious family dwelling, the same factors affect the resale value of a house:

Medium-sized houses are better long-term investments than very large or small ones. Those with three bedrooms are easier to sell than those with four or more. Houses in the strongest demand also have at least two full baths.

Houses are better than condominium apartments. Most people prefer single-family detached houses. Of course, there are exceptions; condos or co-ops are solid investments in popular areas of many cities, including New York, Boston and Washington.

Conventional styles sell more easily — and for higher prices — than do unconventional ones. In the East, conventional means split-levels and colonials; in the South and West, contemporaries are more common; in the Heartland, a style known as Midwestern traditional is most appealing. Remember: Today's trendy style may be tomorrow's out-of-fashion oddball.

Standard interiors attract more buyers and higher prices than unusual configurations do. If you want to sell a pink Cadillac, you will have to find someone who dotes on pink Cadillacs. Two rooms add the most to resale value: the kitchen and a second bathroom. The kitchen should have plenty of light and modern appliances. It does not have to be equipped for Julia Child, but it should come with a dishwasher and a garbage disposal. And even if you live in the Deep South, buy a house with a fireplace. Though wasteful of energy, fireplaces are romantic accessories that usually hold their value in all parts of the country.

The houses in a neighborhood should be of roughly equal value. Stay away from places where there is a wide disparity, because smaller, cheaper dwellings depress the prices of their more elaborate neighbors. If you do find yourself in a neighborhood where house values differ substantially, look for the ugly duckling on a street full of swans. Even if you do not improve the property, the neighborhood will lift its value. So remember: the least expensive house in a neighborhood is a much better buy than the most expensive one. The former will be pulled up by surrounding values; the latter will be held down by them.

Location is paramount. It's hard to beat a house in a neighborhood where the homes and lawns are well cared for. Check the zoning laws. You don't want to see auto body shops or mobile homes springing up among standard single-family homes.

One way to pick the right neighborhood, as writer Robert Runde has observed, is to see how other buyers are voting with their dollars. A second gauge is the variation between asking and selling prices. In choice neighborhoods, the difference is small, often only 3% to 5%.

Another measure is how quickly houses have been selling. If the average length of time on the market is less than three months, the area is strong and in demand. Similarly instructive is the percentage of houses put up for sale that are actually sold within 90 days. In an undesirable place, two-thirds of all the homes listed with real estate firms might not change hands within that period or might even be taken off the market without being sold. To get this information, call either a local board of realtors or a home builders' association.

A smart way to start your search is to look for a community or part of the city that has superb schools, whether or not you have school-age children. Parents are willing to pay premium prices to move to an area that offers excellent education. Check to see how much the community budgets for school expenses *per child* and compare that figure with other school districts in the area. Also find out what percentage of the high-school graduates go on to college; 80% or more is excellent. Before you buy, be sure to visit a local school and speak with the principal. Simply by asking him or her what distinguishes the school, you can gain some valuable impressions. For example, if the principal boasts, "Our school is almost as good as Smithville's," you might then want to search for a house not in that school district but in Smithville's.

You also can make a sound investment by putting your money in a brand-new tract house. Builders are very anxious until they get those first few houses off their hands and see that the development will sell. Savvy buyers can capitalize on those fears to knock down the asking price or squeeze such extras out of the contractor as better-quality kitchen fixtures.

Before you buy a house anywhere, you may want to find out about the record and reliability of the firm that built it. One way to gather information is to call the nearest branch of an organization called Home Owners Warranty and get a list of its members to see if your builder is one of them. (To find the nearest branch, call 800-241-9260 if you live east of the Mississippi River, or 800-433-7657 if you live west of it.) More than 12,000 builders belong to HOW. They are required to build according to approved standards and to carry a 10-year protection against major structural defects in the houses they construct. You can also get free brochures on how to protect your biggest investment, and what to do to maintain it or remodel it, by writing to Home Owners Warranty, 2000 L Street, NW, Washington, D.C. 20036.

How you buy can be as important as what you buy. The success of an investment depends largely on getting favorable financing. Put down as little of your own money as possible and try to get as much financing as you can from the seller. Ask for as long a term as the seller will accept. Assume the seller's mortgage if you can. You will normally be able to do so if it is a Federal Housing Administration– or Veterans Administration–backed loan, or if the mortgage has been in effect for many years.

In summary, here are some tips for selecting a home that will pay off:

— The best way to buy a house is to buy the neighborhood. Look for a superior school system. That is what potential buyers will want when you sell your house.

— If your house has one bathroom, one of the best improvements you can make is adding a second bathroom. Another profitable remodeling project is redoing the kitchen.

— You stand to earn more profit in a new dwelling than in an old one. From 1980 to July 1988, prices of new single-family homes rose 91%, versus 47% for old ones.

— If you want to build onto your house, do not plan an addition that raises the value of your property more than 20% over the value of other houses in the neighborhood. It will not pay in the end, when you sell your house.

— When it comes time to sell, try to make the sale before you buy and move into another house. Empty houses seldom command their asking prices.

How to Get the Most from a Real Estate Agent

BEFORE you search for a house or apartment, you should hunt for a real estate agent. Do not rely on luck and newspaper ads but start with recommendations from friends who have recently moved.

Call the board of realtors in the community you are moving to and ask for names of several former Realtors of the Year; agencies earn this designation because they sell a lot of houses and know much about the market. If the board of realtors is not listed in the phone book, a local realtor should be able to direct you to the nearest board. Also, go to open houses where the public is allowed to view some of the homes listed for sale with various brokerage firms.

The agent you choose should have access to the local multiple listing service. It is a computerized network that gives him or her a complete rundown of all the houses listed for sale in the area. He or she also should know the local mortgage market and help you figure out how much house you can carry based on your income and expenses. Once you have found a house you want to buy, the agent will help you negotiate the price and close the sale.

A brokerage firm usually earns a commission of 6% of the selling price of the house for listing it — that is, putting it on the market — and selling it. If your agent works for another firm, the commission is split 50-50 between the firm that lists and the firm that sells. But the bottom line is that the seller of the house, not the buyer, generally pays the commission.

Almost all agents really work for the seller. For this reason, when you have found a house you would like to make a bid on, never tell your agent: "Let's offer the Smiths $100,000 — but we'll go as high as $110,000 if we have to." The agent is obliged by the custom of the trade to repeat that information to the seller. So wait until the seller refuses your offer before you volunteer that you are willing to pay more. And remember: It is generally in the broker's interest to downplay whatever faults lie in a house or neighborhood.

Some agents, however, have set themselves up to represent only the buyer. The buyer often pays this kind of broker a flat fee or by the hour. That way the broker will not steer the buyer to more expensive houses in order to get a fatter commission. If the buyer does not find a house he or she likes, the broker usually refunds part or all of the fee.

The broker who works for a buyer will examine houses listed through agencies as well as those advertised directly by owners. He or she will also inspect the house for flaws in construction and check the neighborhood for potential changes in assessments or problems in the schools. Such a broker is likely to strike a much tougher bargain for his or her customer, the buyer, than a conventional broker. The broker might demand, for example, that the seller guarantee the integrity of the roof or the plumbing for a period of up to one year. When serving the buyer, some real estate agents submit questionnaires to sellers requesting specific details about a house's condition. This tends to flush out the costly little surprises.

What if you are selling your house? You will find that the competition among real estate brokers for your business has become fierce, partly because nationwide companies are fighting to expand in the market. Thus, you can make some particularly good deals now.

The large, national organizations claim to offer more tempting services than small, independent agencies can. For example, one national agency, Electronic Realty Associates (ERA), promises to buy your house if it can't make a sale within 210 days *and* if you buy another house from ERA.

Independent real estate brokers have been fighting back, sometimes offering to work for less than the prevailing commissions. But the kind of deal you get from any agent depends overwhelmingly on how desirable your house is. If you have a sound, attractive structure in a sought-after location, you might be able to offer a broker a commission of 4% or 5% instead of the conventional 6%.

Occasionally you can persuade a broker to give up part of his or her commission just to get a stalled deal moving again. If a buyer and a seller are only a few thousand dollars apart, the broker may agree to cut his or her fee if the seller accepts a lower price. In effect, the broker absorbs some of the seller's loss.

Some brokers have unbundled the traditional package of services and provide, at an hourly rate, only what customers need. Other brokers — the discounters — are charging commissions of about 2%. But these agents use color slides to let the potential buyer screen properties in their offices, and then they expect sellers to show their own houses to prospects.

Count On Those Extra Costs

WHEN you buy a home, you will discover that the price is much bigger than what the seller is asking. Behind the down payment and the mortgage installments lurk nettlesome expenses known as closing costs. They can amount to 3% to 6% of the size of the mortgage. On a typical $80,000 mortgage, that means you will have to pay an additional $2,400 to $4,800.

Among the extras you have to fork over are points. A point equals 1% of the mortgage amount, and your lender is likely to demand one to four points at closing. That is meant to protect him in case he did not charge you enough interest to make a profit.

And buyers who cannot put down at least 20% of the purchase price in cash are usually required to buy private mortgage insurance to protect the lender against default. For this insurance, you will be charged a one-time fee of half a point plus annual premiums of a quarter-point or more.

Mortgage lenders also want proof that the seller has a clear title to the property you are buying. That is why you will have to pay for the cost of a title search. You also will have to buy insurance to cover the possibility that the search missed something. Figure on the two fees running you a third to a half a point.

It is up to you to insure the house. At the closing you must show that you have a policy and that the first-year's premium has been paid. That will come to between $300 and $600 for a single-family house and slightly less for a condo.

Of course, many towns, counties and state governments also muscle in on the closing, demanding their due in the form of sales or transfer taxes. These are usually based on the selling price of the house or the size of the mortgage and can run a couple of points or more.

Just when you think you have paid every conceivable tithe, tariff and tax, a few more bills will crop up. If you need an attorney to represent you at the closing, for example, that will be $500 to $1,500. But you will know you have finally reached the end of the line when you have to pay to have your deed recorded. That usually will be only $40 to $60.

Raising Money for the Down Payment

EVEN IF you are struggling to come up with a modest down payment, you can still buy a home. Do not automatically assume you have to raise 10% to 20% of the purchase price in cash.

If you have served with the armed forces, you may be able to get a Veterans Administration–insured mortgage for 100% of the cost of the house or apartment — and pay nothing. You do not have to be a vet to qualify for a Federal Housing Administration–insured loan that can cover up to 95% of the purchase price. You can apply for VA and FHA loans at banks and savings and loan associations.

You also can qualify for a 95% loan without government backing. But your income must be high enough to meet the payments, and your credit rating has to be impeccable. A good repayment record on auto and student loans is essential.

To raise cash for a down payment, consider selling off your own IRA. You will have to pay ordinary income tax and a 10% penalty on the money you withdraw early from your IRA, but these costs may be outweighed by the tax deductions the house will generate.

If your employer allows it, you can borrow against your contributions in a corporate profit-sharing program or a salary reduction plan. You will be charged interest at a rate that is often lower than a bank would charge.

If your parents want to help you out, they can give $40,000 each year to a married child and spouse without having to pay federal gift taxes. In return for making the down payment, your parents could become co-owners of the house. That way you could buy a more expensive place than you could otherwise afford, and your folks might qualify for significant tax breaks.

The seller of the house you want to buy also can be the source of the down payment. One possibility to explore with him or her is renting the house for a period with an option to buy. A portion of your rent could go to building a down payment.

Finding the Best Mortgage

THE excitement of home buying involves not only the hunt for the right house but also the search for the right mortgage, sometimes *any* mortgage that will fit your budget. Now that interest rates have come tumbling down from their peaks earlier in the decade, millions of families are finding ways to finance the home of their dreams. You should be able to do it too — if you are willing to explore the vast new world of mortgages.

It is a good time to get a mortgage, but it is up to you to find the right one. Mortgage lenders have a large supply of cash and they are eager to lend it to you, and they are offering many new kinds of loans. You will find analyses of different types of mortgages in the following chapters. Here is a quick guide:

If you are buying your second or third home and plan to stay a few years, you may well want a *fixed-rate* mortgage. Its virtue is predictability. The rate you pay will be slightly higher at first than those you would get with other kinds of mortgages, but it will remain constant, and the equity from your previous home should help you afford it. Rates on fixed-rate 30-year mortgages in mid-1988 averaged 10½%. On a $75,000 loan, for example, the monthly payments worked out to $686, excluding taxes and insurance.

Then there is the initially more affordable *adjustable-rate* mortgage. It is inviting for younger buyers who expect their salaries to grow rapidly. The interest on it goes up or down, usually every one to three years, in line with an overall index of interest rates that you and your lender agree on. To draw customers, lenders generally offer adjustable mortgages at interest rates below fixed-rate loans. This enables you to start off paying low rates. But after the first interval, the monthly payment will change.

If you cannot decide between an adjustable-rate or a fixed-rate loan, the solution may be the increasingly popular offering called a *convertible* mortgage. It starts out with an adjustable rate that is usually several percentage points lower than that on a fixed-rate mortgage. But if, for example, interest rates drop in the future, you can convert to a fixed-rate mortgage at the then-current rate for such loans. In August 1988, if you took out a convertible mortgage the interest rate might have started at 8%, which was far lower than the available 10.5% on a fixed-rate loan. Say that after three years your adjustable rate drops to 7.5% but your lender is offering fixed-rate mortgages at 7%. You would be able to convert to that 7% fixed-rate loan. There is a price for convertibility, of course. If you convert, lenders commonly charge a fee of between $100 and $250.

When you go shopping for a mortgage, start by looking in your newspaper to see what local lenders are offering. Then look for a real estate broker who uses a computerized service, which can make comparison shopping a lot easier and faster. In many cities and suburbs, a broker will punch into a desktop computer the size of the loan you are looking for, the amount of your income and other details of your finances. The computer then displays on its screen descriptions of different mortgages that are available from various lenders. It also displays the latest interest rates being offered and tells you if you are likely to qualify for a particular loan. In some cases, these services permit you to apply for the mortgage electronically. You never deal with the lender in person and the papers are simply mailed to you for signing.

The most valuable matchmaking services are clearinghouses for mortgages from many lenders, including those in faraway places where money is more easily available and interest rates are more competitive than in your own area. One big computerized service is Rennie Mae, from the American Financial Network, in Dallas. The service, which allows you to make an application for a mortgage on the computer once the appropriate one has been found, is available in 20 states and Washington, D.C. For information call 800-447-3898. Among other services are Compufund, which you can find at 55 mortgage and real estate brokers in Southern California, 28 in Northern California, 30 in Dallas and Fort Worth and 8 in Seattle; and HSH Associates (10 Mead Avenue, Riverdale, New Jersey 07457; 201-831-0550), a mortgage-search service that you must contact directly. For $12, you can get a kit for homebuyers that includes the latest HSH weekly report on the terms of loans from dozens of institutions in your state. HSH publishes regional editions for 36 states and 50 major metropolitan areas. Before you send your check, call and see if they cover your area.

Adjustable-Rate Mortgages

IF YOU plan to buy a house or an apartment, you may be inclined to lock in today's interest rates by taking out a long-term fixed-rate mortgage. Don't be too hasty. A loan with an adjustable rate could turn out to be a better deal.

When you get an adjustable mortgage, the initial rate you pay is usually two or three percentage points lower than on a fixed-rate loan. After a year or so the rate rises — and then it goes up or down periodically along with interest rates in general.

Adjustable-rate mortgages once were limited mainly to less affluent first-time homebuyers who could not qualify for the higher-priced fixed-rate loans and needed that first-year break on interest payments. But now so-called ARMs are becoming popular among people who are trading up to second and third houses and who can afford whatever loan they want. The reason: If interest rates fall —or just hold steady — then these borrowers can save thousands of dollars in interest costs compared with what they would have to pay with a conventional mortgage. One study has shown that people who took out adjustable-rate mortgages in recent years have done significantly better than those who had fixed-rate loans. For example, on a typical 30-year $72,000 mortgage granted in 1981, you would have saved some $24,000 with an ARM by early 1988.

Many homeowners are even paying off their old fixed-rate mortgages and trading them for new adjustable-rate loans. Generally, it does not make sense to do such refinancing unless the average long-term cost of your new mortgage is three or more percentage points below your old one.

It pays to get an ARM if you expect to remain in your house or condo no more than three years before you sell out. The benefit you get from your first-year discount should more than make up for any rises in interest rates in the next few years.

You also should take out an ARM if you are willing to shoulder the risk of higher rates later on in return for the immediate use of the cash you will save right now.

In any event, you will have to negotiate with your lender to get the terms you want.

What's the ideal adjustable mortgage? First of all, the interest rate should be pegged to the one-year U.S. Treasury security rate. It tends to rise or fall rapidly. Second, the interest rate and your monthly payments should be adjusted every year, not every several years. Also, the loan agreement would include caps that limit the interest rate changes to no more than two percentage points a year and five to six points over the life of the loan. Third, your initial interest rate should be about two to three percentage points below that of fixed-rate loans. Fourth, when you get your mortgage, you should have to pay no more than two points in loan fees — a point being equivalent to 1% of your mortgage principal. Fifth, if you are worried that interest rates may soar in the future, you may want to ask your lender for an option to convert your adjustable mortgage to a fixed-rate loan in anywhere from two to five years at the then-prevailing interest rate. You might also want to ask for a waiver of any penalties for repaying your mortgage ahead of schedule.

Unfortunately, the perfect mortgage does not exist, but you should be able to trade some features for others that are especially important to you. For example, to get a lower interest rate, you can agree to pay additional fees up front. Whatever horse trading you do, however, never accept a cap on your monthly payments. When interest rates rise but your payments don't, the size of your loan grows because the unpaid interest is added to your mortgage.

The Federal Reserve Board and the Home Loan Bank Board have produced a free booklet to help you understand adjustable-rate mortgages and read behind the fine print. It is called *The Consumer Handbook on Adjustable Rate Mortgages*. You can get it from mortgage lenders and real estate agents or by sending 50 cents to Consumer Information Center–F, P.O. Box 100, Pueblo, Colorado 81002.

Shared-Appreciation Mortgages

A YOUNG couple in Phoenix spotted a house they wanted to buy. The price: $98,500. They figured that after putting 20% down they could get a $78,800 mortgage at interest rates then at 13½%. But monthly payments would have come to $950 a month, and that was more than the couple could afford. Their solution was to go to a mortgage company that offered them what is known as a shared-appreciation mortgage.

This type of loan lowered their payments by one-third. In return the buyers promised to give the lender one-third of the profit they make whenever they sell the house. Because housing values have risen so dramatically in the past, offering to share your appreciation might sound like a pact with the devil. But by agreeing to share profits, the Phoenix couple was able to buy as their first house one that otherwise might have taken years to acquire. And when they do sell, even though they will have to give the lender a third of the profit, they still stand to come out ahead. That's because their two-thirds share will probably amount to just as much as the full profit on a cheaper property.

Generally, these shared-appreciation mortgages help not only first-time buyers, but also elderly buyers who cannot afford to make big payments and who expect to own their houses for the rest of their lives.

If you consider a shared-appreciation mortgage, be aware of the risks. Under some agreements, a lender can collect his share of the appreciation after 10 years, even if the homeowner has not sold. If the homeowner does not have the cash to pay, he will have to borrow and perhaps take out a new mortgage. This could zap him with exploding monthly payments.

The shared mortgage is also a poor choice for a do-it-yourselfer. If you make home improvements yourself, the value that you add to your house is shared with the lender.

Shared-Equity Mortgages

WOULD you like to help your grown child buy his or her first house? Then you might want to consider a so-called shared-equity arrangement. It allows you to split the costs of buying and maintaining a home and combine two incomes to qualify for the mortgage.

A shared equity deal works like this: Two people purchase a house, but only one lives in it. The other partner is solely an investor. The occupant of the house must pay a fair market rent to his or her partner but keeps the proportion of the rent that represents his or her ownership. Meanwhile, the partner who does not live in the house typically pays a portion of the monthly carrying costs, including the property taxes and first-mortgage installments, and does not collect monthly interest payments. He or she gets to split the deductions for interest and taxes with the co-owner who occupies the house. Eventually they divide the value of the property, including any appreciation. Usually after a period of three to 10 years, the owner-occupant must buy out the investor.

Unfortunately, the investor who wants out of a shared-equity arrangement is really stuck. There is no secondary market at all for such investments — not yet, anyhow. But if you want to set up such an agreement, have a real estate lawyer with experience in this field draft a contract. The fee is typically $200, depending on what your lawyer charges per hour.

Still More Mortgages

A N INCREASINGLY popular method of reducing your mortgage payments is the so-called buy-down. That happens when desperate builders who have a house to unload make a lump-sum payment to the lender — and the lender in turn reduces his or her mortgage interest enough to tempt people to buy the house.

For example, when mortgage rates were much higher in the early 1980s, a California developer spent $4,600 to reduce the interest rate on a mortgage to 9¾%. The rate rose one percentage point every year, until it leveled off at 12¾%. In that period, the buyer's monthly payment went up by $300. But the couple who bought the home hoped that it would rise in value by then — or that they would be able to refinance at a lower rate.

Another type of home mortgage that could save you much money over the life of the loan is the biweekly mortgage. It allows a bank to deduct your house payments every two weeks from your checking account. Each payment is half of what you would turn over every month under a conventional mortgage. Since all months except February are a few days longer than four weeks, you make 26 payments a year, not 24. That, in effect, is an extra month's payment.

This could produce a big savings. Take a $100,000 mortgage at 11%. Your biweekly payments would be $476 and you would wind up paying $952 more a year than if your payments were monthly. But you would be able to retire your mortgage in about 20 years rather than 30. That works out to a savings in your interest payments of $95,000.

Particularly if you are a first-time homebuyer or are returning to the housing market after many years, you will need to educate yourself further about the myriad types of mortgages and real estate terms. A sensible way is by reading a booklet called *The Mortgage Money Guide,* published by the Federal Trade Commission. It defines the 14 most popular types of mortgages without endorsing any one of them and lists the pros and cons of each. The booklet helps prospective buyers understand the fine print in mortgage contracts. There is also an easy-to-read page of mortgage payment tables. To get a copy of the guide send $1 to *The Mortgage Money Guide,* Consumer Information Center–F, P.O. Box 100, Pueblo, Colorado 81002.

The Profits and Perils of
Swapping Your Mortgage

I F YOU are one of the boatload of people who still have not refinanced the high-interest mortgage you took out in the early 1980s, this may be the time to switch to one that lets you lop a lot off your monthly payments.

You may be carrying a mortgage with rates as hefty as 14% or more, perhaps because you have just not bothered to look around to see what's available. In mid-1988, lenders were offering a bewildering array of loan choices at reasonable, sometimes sharply discounted, rates. For example, you could get an adjustable-rate mortgage with an interest rate of 7%, or even less.

Swapping a peak-interest loan may or may not be a smart move. Everything depends on your up-front costs and how long you plan to keep your home.

Looked at over the full term of the loan, a saving of even one point in the interest rate on a 30-year, $100,000 mortgage saves you nearly $13,000 in total payments. But unless you can reduce your mortgage interest rate by three points or so, it is probably not worth the hassle and the immediate costs. For example, if there is a prepayment penalty clause in your mortgage, you will have to pay plenty to get out of the loan agreement — as much as 3% of the unpaid balance. That's on top of the usual costs of refinancing, which often can be almost as much as the closing costs on the original mortgage.

So check carefully to see what these real front-end costs will be, after you figure in your income tax deductions for them. Then compare them with the immediate and long-term savings you can expect by refinancing. You also should be planning to live in your house for at least three more years. Otherwise, the costs most likely will exceed the amount that you would save in monthly payments.

One quick way to see how long it will require for refinancing to pay off is to divide your closing costs by the reduction on your monthly payment. The result will equal the number of months it will take you to break even. For example, if your closing costs are $6,000 and your monthly saving is $150, you will need to keep your home 40 months to break even (6,000 divided by 150 equals 40).

Buying a House at Auction

THE auctioneer's familiar chant of "going, going, gone!" now can mean not that paintings or antiques have been sold — but a new house. To unload homes, more and more builders and real estate developers have been auctioning them off to the highest bidders. Texas is a center of the auction action, and houses are also being auctioned in Florida, Oklahoma, Colorado and many other states.

An auction could be your chance to pick up a bargain in a house or a vacation condo. Most houses are auctioned off in desperation only after they have languished on the market for a time. Usually they will go for less than the original asking price — often 5% to 30% below. In addition, developers often arrange favorable financing for such purchases.

But watch out. Savings can be illusory. Sellers sometimes jack up the asking price before the auction to encourage higher bidding. Be sure you find out whether the pre-auction price was in line with the asking price of similar homes in the area. A local real estate broker should be able to tell you.

Fortunately, most developers advertise auctions in local newspapers at least a month in advance. The Friday edition of the *Wall Street Journal* also carries ads for auctions of condos in popular resort regions, as well as other properties. If you study the ads in advance, you will have plenty of time to talk to agents and comparison-shop. Make certain you inspect any property you are thinking of buying and find out if there is any minimum bid.

Once your auction bid is accepted, you will be asked to sign a standard sales agreement and fill out a mortgage application on the spot. Be prepared to leave $2,000 to $3,500 as a deposit. But if you change your mind, the seller is not obligated to return your money unless you fail to qualify for a mortgage. So look carefully before you leap into an auctioned house. And before you bid on any property, be sure you set a limit on what you want to spend.

You also may want to look into buying a foreclosed house. Until recently, few homebuyers considered purchasing foreclosed and other distressed properties because such dwellings tended to be poorly maintained and in run-down neighborhoods. But that has been changed by the soft real estate market in many parts of the country. In 1987, lenders and government agencies repossessed more than 100,000 houses and condos, some in the $100,000-and-up price range.

Banks, other lenders and financially plagued builders are so anxious to get foreclosed properties off their hands that they tend to sell them for prices below comparable homes in the same area. You often can buy foreclosed homes directly from banks or savings and loan associations. Most lending institutions will gladly give you a list of their foreclosed houses.

Assembling a House from a Kit

You can buy almost anything from a catalogue today. But did you know that you can buy a new house from a catalogue? And it could be a much better deal than you think.

Some 30,000 people bought so-called kit houses in 1987. The basic components are pre-cut and marked in the manufacturer's factory. Then they are shipped to you with instructions for assembling by you or your contractor.

Kits can cost as much as a third less than comparable custom-built homes. A modest home with two bedrooms, two baths and living, dining and kitchen areas usually starts at $75,000. That includes the cost of the kit and of putting it together, but not the land.

Kits also let you put up a house faster than you could by hiring an architect and a contractor to design and build a house. And we are not talking here of a shack in the box. The materials are usually as good as — or even better than — those in a standard home.

You can order kits that are complete — right down to the poles in your closets — but most include only the materials to construct a weather-tight house shell. That means the framing, lumber, roof, walls, exterior siding, windows and doors. You then pay a general contractor to buy and install everything you want to finish the house, such as the wallboard, wiring and plumbing.

You can save as much as 10% to 15% on construction costs by acting as your own contractor. Then you would have to find the various subcontractors needed to finish the house, and you would monitor their work schedules. That, of course, takes a lot of your time.

Anyone can get a list of 215 kit makers by sending $1 and a stamped self-addressed envelope to the Building Institute, 70 North Broadway, Nyack, New York 10960. Advertisements for kit homes also appear in housing and building-trade magazines.

The first step in buying a kit is to steep yourself in manufacturers' catalogues. When you see something you like, phone the company to find its local dealer. Check with your local Better Business Bureau or state consumer-affairs office to see if any complaints have been filed against the company. Also ask the firm for names of local builders who have assembled its kits and for homeowners who have bought them. Interview them and visit their houses.

Once you know that you are dealing with a reliable company, you are ready to sit down with its representative to discuss the details of the house you want. Most buyers choose log houses. They are a far cry from Abe Lincoln's boyhood home, and they are sold by such firms as Rocky Mountain Log Homes (2301 State Street, Hamden, Connecticut 06518), Rocky Mountain Log Homes (3353 Highway 93 South, Hamilton, Montana 59840) and Southland Log Homes (P.O. Box 1668, Irmo, South Carolina 29063).

Many people work up their own designs. Of course, the more you depart from a standard plan, the more you will have to pay.

Selling Your House

BEFORE you buy a house or apartment, be sure to sell the one you now live in. Otherwise, you can run the risk of paying two mortgages and being forced to sell out at fire-sale prices. In any case, do not assume that your present house will sell as quickly or for as much money as you think it is worth. Get an appraiser's estimate of its value and ask a real estate agent how rapidly homes in that price range are turning over in your area.

If houses stay on the market for more than two months, do not even look for a second home until you have a firm contract of sale on the first. And continue living in the house, if possible, while it is on the market. Untenanted houses give buyers the impression that the owners are desperate to sell.

To put your house into shape for selling, figure on spending at least $300 and several weekends of your time. Start with your home's so-called curb appeal, or how it looks from the street. A househunter's first impression can make or break the sale. You do not need to spring for a major paint job unless the outside walls are blistering and peeling. But touch up the trim. The $75 or so you spend on paint for outer doors and window trim often makes your house look freshly painted.

Do not forget to wash the windows, inside and out. When the glare of the sun hits dirty panes, you can see the streaks from the street. Patch cracks and potholes in your driveway. Finishing touches such as a bright red mailbox or tubs of pink geraniums flanking the front door sometimes can do more for the house than any major expenditure.

You also should spruce up the interior. Thin out your possessions before you show your house. The fewer things you have in a room or closet, the larger it will appear. Repaint rooms that need it, such as those that your kids have graced with unusual colors. Kitchens and bathrooms always must be immaculate. A rusty sink or a ring around the toilet bowl can scare off prospective buyers who might think the plumbing needs repair. All homebuyers are conscious of energy costs, so your heating system must appear to work well. Wipe the boiler and the area around it to remove soot or oil stains.

You are probably better off not trying to sell your house yourself. Real estate agents can market it through a multiple listing service, which alerts nearly every agent in the area that your home is up for sale.

Before your house goes on the market, make sure it is correctly priced. It is worth hiring a professional appraiser, but shop around because fees vary. To find several candidates in your area, write or call the American Institute of Real Estate Appraisers (430 North Michigan Avenue, Chicago, Illinois 60611).

While you are awaiting the sale, investigate the area you will be moving to. Drive around and see what neighborhoods best suit you. Survey the prices quoted in real estate ads in the Sunday paper. But do not actually househunt. You could fall in love with a new homestead while you are still wedded financially to your old one.

By selling first, of course, you may have to move out before you have found another house. Try to avoid that possibility in your negotiations with a prospective buyer. For example, you might be able to postpone the closing date to give yourself time to find a new place.

Such an extended closing period also gives the buyer more time to change his or her mind. So, a better solution, if the buyer is amenable, is to close the deal as soon as possible but rent your house back from him until you find another one. If the buyer balks at such a provision, resign yourself to renting elsewhere, preferably in or near your future neighborhood. Though a temporary inconvenience, this strategy will acquaint you with the market and make you a smarter buyer.

Financing Your House Sale

A RE you trying to sell your house or apartment but just cannot get rid of it? Then consider lowering your asking price rather than offering to lend some of the money to a buyer. So-called seller financing should be your last resort.

Six years ago, when interest rates were much higher, one of every four people who sold their homes had to help provide the buyer with some financing. Today far fewer homeowners are being forced to act as bankers by taking back a first or second mortgage from the buyer.

Sellers typically make loans at rates as much as two percentage points below market rates. But you should not subsidize the buyer unless you cannot sell your house any other way. Most people do not have the time or skills to manage such an investment successfully.

Say that you decide to help provide the financing for the buyer of your house. Your first problem could be neglecting to do a thorough credit check on him or her. Although you might be planning to get tough the moment your buyer misses a payment, there is not much you can do.

You might figure you could threaten to foreclose — that is, take back your house. Just try it! Foreclosure can drag out for months. All the time, your debtor can enjoy the comforts of your old home — and you cannot exactly expect him to treat the house with tender loving care during the whole nasty affair.

After any foreclosure, your house probably will be sold at auction. Chances are the auction price will be considerably less than the house is really worth. And, you will have to pay around 5% of that winning bid to the foreclosure trustee.

Even the best-referenced creditor can go belly-up. Whatever you can do to make that option as unpleasant as possible for him or her will stand to your advantage. So demand a healthy down payment, at least 10% and preferably more. For an insolvent buyer, it is a lot less painful to walk away from a mortgage contract with nothing to lose but a good credit rating than to lose both his credit rating and, say, $10,000.

If you want to finance the sale of your house yourself, you can enlist help from officers at your bank or savings and loan association. For a fee of 1% to 2% of the loan amount, they will service the mortgage you give to a buyer. The banker will do a credit check on the prospective buyer, collect payments and handle a foreclosure — if one becomes necessary. In addition, the bank or savings or loan will sell you insurance against default. Typically, the cost is $400 for a $40,000 loan.

Once a mortgage contract is signed between seller and buyer, it is usually too late to make adjustments. So a mortgage contract always should be drafted by a professional — usually a lawyer — to meet the specific needs of both buyer and seller. Real estate agents, who are often involved in arranging owner financing, generally use blank forms that are filled in by the buyer and seller and later checked by the agency's lawyer. If the contract turns out not to be what you want, too bad.

In many states, for example, if a mortgage contract does not say that the loan you give to the buyer of your house is nonassumable, it is legally considered to be assumable. Thus, by simply promising in writing to make a loan in these states, you have agreed to make it assumable. If the buyer decides to sell the house, you will have to accept as your debtor whomever he or she chooses.

If you ever need money before the note comes due, you will have to sell the loan to a mortgage banker for less than its face value. But you will get a better price if you arrange the loan at the outset through the Federal National Mortgage Association's Home Seller program. A Fannie Mae–approved bank or savings institution processes your buyer's application. The fee, which is negotiable, is usually paid by the buyer. To get the names of participating lenders in your area, write to the Federal National Mortgage Association (3900 Wisconsin Avenue, NW, Washington, D.C. 20016).

One form of seller financing that some buyers find attractive is the so-called balloon mortgage. With a balloon, repayment of a large part of the principal is deferred. So monthly payments are low until the loan period ends, when you, the lender, get one big payment. A common problem with giving the buyer a balloon mortgage is that it ties up your money until the note matures and he or she has to pay you back. But an arrangement known by the dismaying name of hypothecation allows you to negotiate a way around that grim obstacle to liquidity. Essentially you use the money owed you as collateral for a new but smaller loan that you get from a bank or savings and loan association. Then you can use the loan money to add to the down payment on your new house.

With hypothecation, you might well work out the figures so that the homebuyer's monthly payment to you will be exactly the same as what the bank asks you to pay on your smaller loan. Your buyer could send his or her check directly to your bank and, in one stroke, be paying an installment on both your loan and his or hers. In any case ask your bank or savings and loan about the possibility of using hypothecation.

If you are thinking of financing the sale of your own house, here is what you should do:

— Get a lawyer to write *all* your contracts — even if you use a real estate broker.

— Cover in writing everything that could possibly happen.

— Do a property credit check on the buyer.

— Make sure you get a big enough down payment to keep your buyer from hightailing it.

— And insure your loan.

Giving Your House Its Semi-annual Physical

Every spring and autumn is the time to save some money, and protect what is probably your biggest investment, by giving your house its semi-annual top-to-bottom physical examination. No matter how invulnerable your home may look, hazards to its health lurk almost everywhere. So it pays to head off problems in the early stages by practicing preventive maintenance. If you take care of your house, it will take care of you. In sum, you will get more for it when you sell it.

The best way to handle maintenance chores is to put them on a schedule. For newer houses and those in mild climates, an annual inspection tour should suffice. But if your house is more than 10 years old or has to weather ice and snow, you are wise to make quarterly checkups.

In most parts of the country, the worst enemy of your house is water. The place where it does its earliest damage is the roof. The most vulnerable roof areas are the flashings — the metal sheeting that covers the joints where chimneys and vent pipes rise through the roof. Cracks and gaps in the sheeting sealant should be recoated with tar or latex sealer, which will cost you only about $10. Other trouble spots include gutters and downspouts. A handyman usually can clean, patch and adjust them in an hour or two for about $60.

Check that your shingles are well maintained. If your shingles are loose or cracked, leave any repairs to a professional. He should charge $20 to $25 per shingle for any replacements. But a $3 tube of latex caulking compound should be enough for you to fill any gaps in the seal around windows and doors and the junctures between the foundation and patios and walks. Such steps can save you hundreds, even thousands, of dollars in emergency repairs later on.

It is tempting to postpone brick, concrete and asphalt repair jobs. However, you should not underestimate the damage that can be done by water freezing in masonry cracks. The repair work is often back-straining, but the consequences of not doing it promptly can be costly.

You also can save both time and money by repairing your house in stages rather than all at once. The south side usually needs painting every three to six years. The other sides require it only every eight to ten years.

The indoor preventive maintenance you should perform most often is to change or clean the filters in air conditioners and hot-air furnaces. Tend to furnaces about three times a year and central air-conditioning systems twice as often. Filthy filters can reduce their efficiency 10% to 25%. Yet you can get new ones for only about $1 each. An oil-fired furnace should be professionally cleaned and serviced once a year. The charge should be about $40. You may be able to save up to 25% of your energy costs simply by caulking windows and putting weather stripping around doors.

It is prudent to inspect your smoke detectors and any burglar alarms once a month. And check your electrical panel every several months. If you detect a burning odor, you may simply have a blown fuse, which you can take care of yourself. But you may have loose wires or a power overload. When in doubt, call an electrician.

You do not need a professional, however, to fix your dripping faucets. Usually you can do that with just a wrench and a 10-cent washer. Your subsequent savings on water can be surprising.

Fortunately, there is a wealth of books that can help you do many repairs yourself. One way to choose among the wide variety is to focus on a project you know something about. Say it is repairing a faucet; then check that section in several books and get the one that describes it most clearly.

Among the best is *The New York Times Complete Manual of Home Repair* by Bernard Gladstone. The 36-volume home repair and improvement series published by Time-Life Books also gets high marks from do-it-yourself advisers. Each volume concentrates on a particular subject — for example, masonry, plumbing or wiring. For $10.99 you can buy the specific volume you need.

Which Improvements Pay Off?

I F YOU own a house, you would not remodel a kitchen, add a bathroom or install a swimming pool solely to enhance its resale value. But you will get back most of what you spend — if you choose the right home improvement projects. As writer Robert Runde has pointed out, some of them stand to pay off dramatically better than others when the time comes to sell your house.

Energy efficiency improvements have begun to pay for themselves — but only since the oil price shocks of the 1970s. Earlier, homebuyers often could not care less about insulation or energy-saving windows. Now, most people are concerned about saving on their energy bills. But trendy innovations — for example, solar heating panels — offer a less certain return.

The more personalized a project, the more chancy the return. Remodeling a kitchen usually adds sales appeal. But if you put in a deluxe gourmet kitchen and wind up with a buyer who is a canned-soup cook, do not expect to get your money back.

An extravagant improvement can make your home harder to sell. Not every prospective homebuyer will love a $15,000 pleasure center with a custom-made whirlpool, hot tub, steam bath and built-in stereo system. Indeed, it could be a turn-off. So do not spend too much on your home improvement, especially if you are thinking of moving in a few years.

The limits on what a house can sell for are well defined in any neighborhood. If the houses range from $90,000 to $120,000, your top resale price still will not be much more than $120,000, no matter how many rooms, baths, hot tubs or skylights you add. You are not likely to recover any costs that raise the value of your property to more than 20% over that of similar homes in your neighborhood. People tend to want the *least* expensive house in an area. If yours is the *most* expensive, it will be less marketable.

Just as you should not invest too much in improvements, you should not make them yourself, either. Hiring professionals to do the entire job usually gives you the soundest investment. If you are less than craftsmanlike, your botches can subtract from the value of your house.

The most profitable interior home improvement is to remodel your kitchen. That is because the kitchen again is becoming the nerve center in many homes, a combination family room and workplace. So it should be sunny and spacious. It also should have new appliances, plenty of storage and a step-saving layout that positions the stove, sink and refrigerator close together. But try to confine your remodeling expenses on it to 10% of the estimated value of your home. As mentioned, if your renovation is sensible and not extravagant, there is a strong chance you will recoup almost your entire investment when you sell.

Another project that should return almost its entire cost is to add a second bathroom. A third bathroom is popular, too, but most prospective homebuyers consider more than three unnecessary. Since decor is so much a matter of taste, elaborate bathroom *remodeling* is less likely to pay for itself. But do not skimp on finishing touches. An elegant ceramic tile floor creates a far better impression than vinyl.

Fireplaces can be one of your best investments. That is rather surprising; people know that fireplaces usually waste more heat than they provide but figure they can afford it. A fireplace that you install will return much of what you paid. As for central air conditioning, it helps you sell your house if it is in the Sun Belt. But in colder regions buyers are reluctant to pay extra because air conditioning is so expensive to operate.

Since people crave a comfortable place to lounge outdoors, another worthy investment is a deck or patio. Yours could return 40% to 70% of its cost. When you sell out, you also can get back 40% to 70% of the cost of adding a conveniently located family room. But an addition that disrupts the traffic pattern, or fundamentally clashes with the style of the house, can detract from its worth. If you convert the garage to a game room, you eliminate all the buyers who want a garage.

As investments, swimming pools do not add much to the market price of a house in cooler regions of the country. Many people worry about the time and trouble it takes to maintain a pool, as well as the potential danger to children. Even in warm areas, recovery of your outlay is uncertain.

If you make big, important improvements that add to the value of your house, you can subtract the costs from your profit when you sell your house. That will cut your tax bill. Beware, though: Ordinary home repairs and replacements do not qualify.

Tax-saving Home Improvements

ARE you spending money to improve your house? Be sure to keep track of exactly how much you are paying. When the time comes to sell your house, you should be able to get significant tax deductions. Not only can some renovations boost the price of your home, but the Internal Revenue Service might count them in the total cost of your residence.

When you sell your house, you usually have to pay a tax on any profit — the difference between what the house originally cost you and what you sell it for. But the IRS will let you include in your cost the price of major improvements made after you bought the home. And the higher your total cost, the lower your profit — and the lower your taxes.

For example, if you have put in some new shrubs or trees or a lawn, a new fence or a porch, you can list any or all of them as part of the total cost of your residence. Many internal improvements count as well: storm windows, lighting fixtures, air conditioners — even wall-to-wall carpeting is recognized by the IRS. So are termite-proofing and waterproofing. The key word is *improvement*. The tax people will not let you count things that are normal repairs and upkeep.

It pays to keep accurate records of *all* your improvements and renovations. That way you can avoid having to guesstimate when the time comes to pay the IRS.

One more tip: You also can add to the cost of your house any commissions or legal fees you pay when the time comes to sell.

Raising Capital for Home Improvements

THIS year alone, Americans will spend more than $60 billion on major improvements and additions to their homes. How will they raise all that money? They will do it the old-fashioned way: they will *borrow* it.

Your best deal when seeking money for a major home improvement project is to borrow from your company profit-sharing plan or against the cash value of your whole life insurance policy. You will pay below-market interest rates and you will not be hit with rather hefty loan origination fees. If you cannot tap these sources, you can apply for a variety of loans offered by banks, credit unions and finance companies. Interest rates are lowest at credit unions, higher at banks and highest at finance outfits.

Most homeowners finance their remodeling projects by taking out a second mortgage on top of the one they already have. You can borrow up to 80% of the appraised value of your house — minus the unpaid balance on your first mortgage. Bankers charge one to two percentage points more for second mortgages than for first mortgages, and you can repay over 30 years. As with any loan that is secured by real estate, you must pay closing costs — usually several hundred dollars.

You might do better financing your improvement if you paid off your first mortgage and took out a new, larger loan. This is known as refinancing. It makes the most sense if you bought your house between 1979 and 1982 when interest rates were at nosebleed levels. You will face stiff closing costs, and possibly a prepayment penalty of up to six months interest for paying off your first mortgage early. But refinancing usually will be worth it if it lowers your interest rate three percentage points or so.

Many affluent borrowers are using home-equity lines of credit to pay for home renovations. You can get these loans from brokerage firms as well as banks, savings and loan associations and some credit unions. You open a line of credit equal to 75% to 80% of the appraised value of your house, minus the unpaid portion of the mortgage principal. Then you simply write your own loans by writing out checks as you need the money. The interest rate is adjustable, varying monthly with whatever index the loan is tied to. But you do not pay any interest until you actually borrow the money, and then only on the amount that you borrow. You will have to pay closing costs, but you can use the borrowed money for any purpose — not just remodeling.

The interest that you pay on a mortgage or home-equity loan remains deductible under the new tax rules. But Congress has put on some limitations. These restrictions apply primarily to affluent people and are quite complex. So they take some explaining:

Beginning with the 1988 tax year, you will be able to fully deduct only the interest you pay on your first $1,000,000 of debt whether you are single or married. (If you're married and filing separately, you may deduct interest on the first $500,000.) This covers debt that you incur when you acquire, construct or substantially improve your principal and/or second residence and that is secured by such property. But wait: There's a further wrinkle. The million-dollar limit applies only to debt taken out after October 13, 1987. Interest on all debt that you had taken before October 13, 1987, will be deductible even though it exceeds the limit. However, the amount of this previous mortgage debt will reduce the $1 million limit on all new debt.

Say you had bought a house or apartment with an $800,000 mortgage two years ago and you want to buy a vacation home this year with a $400,000 mortgage. Then you will not be able to deduct the interest on your entire debt of $1,200,000 but only the interest on your first $1,000,000 of it. But if you already had incurred the $1,200,000 in debt before October 13, 1987, you could deduct the total interest on the mortgage debt.

Also, starting with the 1988 tax year, you can fully deduct the interest incurred on $100,000 of a home-equity loan regardless of the purpose of the loan or the original cost of your home. This applies to all home-equity loans taken out on or after October 13, 1987. A home-equity loan taken out before October 13, 1987, is subject to the tracing rule — that is, a taxpayer must trace how the proceeds of the loan were used.

You can deduct *some* of the interest incurred on a debt that exceeds the $1,000,000 mortgage limit or the $100,000 home-equity loan limit as personal interest. But you will be able to take deductions on only 40% of this excess interest in the 1988 tax year, 20% in 1989 and 10% in 1990. Starting in 1991, you will not be able to deduct any of this excess interest.

Finding Repairmen You Can Trust

FINDING craftsmen to repair or remodel your house calls for almost the same degree of care you would employ in looking for a family doctor. To do otherwise is to jeopardize the value of your most cherished investment.

For small home-repair and remodeling jobs you can get by with the name of a craftsman plucked from the phone book. But make sure your nominee has been in business locally for three years or so and will supply references. Be certain to call these people and have them give you an account of the person's workmanship, prices, reliability and character.

If you are planning a project that calls for superlative craftsmanship, ask for referrals from building materials wholesalers, such as plumbing supply houses and lumberyards.

For major remodeling jobs, you will probably need a general contractor. He or she will assume command of the entire project. That means finding designers to draw up your plans, hiring subcontractors to do the work and arranging for building permits and inspections. The fee: roughly 10% to 15% of the entire cost.

Coping with Contractors

A MAJOR home improvement project is not likely to be a tranquil experience, but it should not be a calamity either. Your satisfaction with the job may depend more than anything else on how skillfully you choose and deal with the carpenters, plumbers, electricians and any other contractors you hire to work on your house.

To get the best deal from a contractor, first of all be careful whom you hire. You can get names of financially sound workmen from bankers and storekeepers who deal with them. Local chapters of such trade groups as the National Association of Home Builders and the National Association of the Remodeling Industry also can point you to reliable contractors. And the Better Business Bureau keeps files on tradesmen who have drawn complaints.

Once you have located several candidates for a substantial job, evaluate them carefully. One consideration is rapport. It's a mistake to hire a workman just because he is engaging; yet it's also wrong to dismiss personal chemistry. Pick someone you can communicate with. And visit one of his job sites. If the place is messy and disorganized, it is reasonable to wonder whether the tradesman takes meticulous care of his work.

When picking a contractor, ask yourself the following questions:

— Was he recommended by a trustworthy source?

— Has he supplied the names of previous customers whom you can check for references?

— How long has he been in business under the same name? More than 10 years is a definite plus.

— Will the contractor give you his home address and phone number?

— Has he agreed to include starting and completion dates in the contract?

— Does a check with his bank indicate that he is financially sound?

— Did he offer you a *written* guarantee?

Finally, if you answer yes to the next two questions, perhaps you should look for another contractor:

Has he made oral promises that he will not put in the contract? And, did he offer you a discount for signing up at once? If so, those are danger signals you cannot afford to ignore.

For your big home improvements, try to get at least three bids. When all have come in, discard any astronomical ones. But you may want to choose the contractor who comes highly recommended even if his bid is *not* the lowest.

No bid is set in concrete. So negotiate with the contractor you really want. Contractors expect their profit to be 10% to 25% of a project's total cost. But if they need work, they will accept less.

Whether you are renovating your whole house or simply adding kitchen cabinets, following some basic rules will help you get the most from your contractor:

Before hiring any workmen for a major project, write a tight contract that cites the details of the job practically to the last nut and bolt. In remodeling a bathroom, you would designate the brand name, model number and color of appliances and fixtures. You would also specify materials for cabinetry, countertops and hardware.

Start with a standard form, called an owners and contractors construction agreement, to spell out your expectations. The forms are available at many stationery stores. Be sure to put down the particulars of your job, including the following: a precise list of all work to be done and appliances and fixtures to be installed; the starting and approximate completion dates of the work; a stipulation that all work must be done to the highest standards and a guarantee to provide replacement materials and additional labor, if necessary; and, finally, a provision that the contractor is responsible for obtaining any required building permits.

Pay the contractor in stages. Turn over 10% at the start and 30% as each third of the job is finished. Hold off paying the last installment until two weeks after the project has been completed. This way you can make sure there are no surprises.

Do not skimp on materials or workmanship. As one Houston stonemason remarks: "Cheap workmanship is like cheap wine. The price is right, but you'll regret it later."

Putting Your House in the Movies

IF YOU have always dreamed of being in the movies but never made it, consider making a star out of your house. Putting your home in the pictures can be thrilling and fairly lucrative — and it is easier now than it has ever been. More and more moviemakers and TV producers are looking for real-life settings for their extravaganzas. Many pay $1,000 a day and sometimes more to rent houses with that lived-in look.

Your chances are best if you live in or near areas where most commercials, TV shows and movies are filmed, meaning New York or Los Angeles. But many production companies and advertising agencies are also active renters in Atlanta, Boston, Dallas, San Francisco and other cities.

If you would like to make your home a star, first list it with your state and local government film commissions. They help producers find locations. Also register with at least one of the nationally known location services. For example, in New York City there are such companies as Judie Robbins Locations, Location Locators and Wild Locations. And in Los Angeles, try Cast Locations. Some of them are listed in the Yellow Pages under "Motion Picture Location Service."

Beware of any service that promises to use your home if you pay a registration fee. The company should keep a description and photo of your house on file at no charge, even if you live out-of-state. Send color photos that emphasize your home's fascinating and distinctive details, such as a tennis court, circular staircase or cathedral ceiling.

Putting your home in pictures may mean that a cast and crew of up to 100 people — with countless pieces of equipment — may be trooping over your property and upsetting family routines. They might want to repaint or even completely redecorate your house. So make sure the producers sign a contract that spells out the filming dates and makes the company responsible for any damages.

Your Taxes

How to Cut Your Taxes

ALMOST anyone now can reduce his or her taxes by using some techniques that the rich have been employing for years. You do not have to be wealthy to take advantage of them. But do not wait until the eve of April 15 to think about ways to save. Start looking today for deductions and credits that will cut your tax bill for this year — and well into the future. The earlier you act, the more you stand to save.

As you read this chapter, you may recognize tax savings that you failed to consider when you filed your most recent tax return. You can correct these omissions by filing an amended return. (See "Your Taxes: The Best Time to File.")

Of course, it will not pay to increase your write-offs if you do not itemize them. So the first thing to do is add up any expenses that you can write off for the year. On your 1987 income, the IRS automatically gave you deductions of $2,540 if you were single and $3,760 if you were married and filing jointly. For your 1988 income, tax reform increases the standard deduction to $3,000 if you are single and $5,000 if you are married and filing jointly. If your total deductions top the standard deduction, then it pays to itemize.

The following chapters elaborate on the major ways to reduce your tax liability, but here is a summary of some of them:

You can give money and other assets to your children. Under the new rules of tax reform, children under 14 years of age will be taxed at their parents' rate on investment income above $1,000. But children who are 14 and over will pay taxes on all their income at their own rate, which is probably much lower than your own.

Congress also has provided that some investments legally and quite effectively shelter you from taxes. Municipal bonds yield tax-exempt current income. Real estate investment trusts can provide tax-sheltered income. But anyone mulling over investments that will save taxes is a little like a teenager pondering marriage: you had better be sure that the lust to avoid taxes is not leading you into a disastrous long-term commitment.

The surest and simplest way for many people to reduce taxes is to contribute to an Individual Retirement Account. If your adjusted gross income is $35,000 or less ($50,000 if you are married and filing jointly), and if you are not covered by an employee pension plan, you can deduct part if not all of your contributions to an IRA. In any case, IRA savings grow tax-free.

If you want to set up an IRA for this year's income, you can do it any time before you file this year's tax return — that is, as late as April 15. But self-employed people who want to establish a tax-saving Keogh plan have to do it by December 31 of this year — or their Keogh contributions this year will not be tax-deductible. You can make contributions to your IRA as late as April 15. And if you ask the IRS for an extension, you can contribute to a Keogh until the extended due date of the tax return, as late as October 15 if a valid extension is obtained. This is not true for the IRA.

Taxpayers can take write-offs for rooms in their homes that are used exclusively for a profit-making business. You also can take some deductions for the purchase of home office supplies, phone bills, utilities, repairs and even maid service and other operating expenses. You can depreciate such assets as file cabinets, desks and typewriters. If you have a home computer that you use half or more of the time for your business, you can either deduct that portion of the cost from your taxable income in one year or depreciate it in installments over five years. Your business software also may be deductible. Be aware, however, that the IRS sets a limit on these write-offs. Beginning with your tax return for 1987, you could not deduct more than the *net* income.

You still can deduct a number of unreimbursed business and job-related expenses and miscellaneous expenses, but reform has tightened the rules. You must lump your expenses together and write off only the amount by which they exceed 2% of your adjusted gross income. Deductions in this category include union dues, tax preparation fees, job uniforms, job-related educational expenses and the cost of business publications — including this book.

If you use your car while on the job, you can write off your operating expenses as part of the miscellaneous deductions. Your regular commuting costs to and from work are not deductible. But if you drive your car on business — say, to make sales calls — the IRS lets you deduct 21 cents a mile for the first 15,000 miles and 11 cents for each additional mile. Unfortunately, this can fall far short of what it costs to keep your car running. Remember, however, that instead you can deduct your *actual* auto expenses — as long as you have the proper documentation. In short, you can fatten your deductions by maintaining thorough records. Start by keeping a log of the miles you drive for business purposes and note your total mileage for the year. Also, keep track of your outlays for gas, repairs and insurance. Then figure out what proportion of your driving is for business. You can deduct that percentage of your costs.

Resolve to keep better records of all your tax-deductible expenses this year. As mentioned, at tax time pack rats always pay less. Silly little deductions have a way of becoming impressive big ones. Keep even your grocery receipts when the purchases are for business entertaining.

In 1987, you started to say good-bye to your nonmortgage interest-payment deductions. That includes credit-card finance charges, auto, college and any other consumer loans. Only home-backed and margin loans remain deductible. The new rule will be phased in by 1991. You can write off only 40% of your nonmortgage interest in 1988, 20% in 1989 and 10% in 1990.

Frequently overlooked write-offs include the fair market value of property you give to charity, such as clothing (you must itemize your return in order to deduct charitable gifts). If you are itching to change jobs within your current field, you can deduct most travel and other expenses connected with your job search — as long as you itemize your return. And do not forget to deduct this year any investment losses from previous years that exceeded the $3,000 annual limit.

Tax credits are much better than tax deductions. Deductions reduce only the adjusted gross income on which your taxes are calculated, but credits reduce your actual taxes, dollar for dollar. So if you have a chance to gain any credits, take it.

If you get an income tax refund this year, there is no reason to feel smug. You just gave the government an interest-free loan last year. Had you invested that yourself, you could be hundreds of dollars richer by now.

You can reduce your withholding by going to your employer's payroll office and changing the number of so-called allowances on your W-4 form. In 1987, each allowance exempted $1,900 of your pay from withholding. The exemption went up to $1,950 in 1988 and will be $2,000 in 1989. You get an automatic allowance for yourself, for each of your children and for your spouse, if he or she does not work for pay. If you are single and have only one job, you get two allowances. But you may be entitled to more. Caution: Beginning in 1988, personal exemptions will be phased out for certain high-income taxpayers.

To find out how many exemptions you can claim, use your tax return for last year to estimate your deductions for the current year. Then check the table on the W-4 to calculate the number of allowances your deductions generate. But do not go overboard. Your withholding and any estimated tax payments have to total at least 90% beginning with your tax return for 1988. Otherwise, you could be liable for an underpayment penalty of 10%.

Remember: There is nothing wrong with employing legal tax-avoiding tactics. Every one of them was put into the tax code by act of Congress or judicial decision for some purpose — at best to encourage Americans to save, invest and become homeowners, which in turn enables businesses to start, to grow and to expand employment. As the late Judge Learned Hand said in a 1947 tax decision: "Nobody owes any public duty to pay more than the law demands: taxes are enforced exactions, not voluntary contributions."

The New Tax Rates

UNDER the new tax law, most people could expect a drop in their tax bill. As a group, individuals would pay an estimated $130 billion less over the next five years. But tax reformers who spoke of simplifying the tax code must have been humming "The Impossible Dream." Most of the new tax law is anything but simple. Still, one thing will be easier to figure: your tax rate. Beginning in 1988, you fall into one of two brackets: 15% or 28%. Married couples who file jointly will pay 15% if they have up to $29,750 in taxable income. Above that, the rate is 28%. Single taxpayers will owe 15% if they have taxable income of up to $17,850. Over that, the rate rises to 28%.

Congress has thrown in one hitch: upper-middle-income and wealthy taxpayers have to pay an extra 5% on part of their taxable income. Hence, married couples who file jointly will pay 33% on income from $71,900 to $149,250. Singles will pay 33% on income from $43,150 to $89,560. Above those levels, the 33% tax rate applies until all personal exemptions are phased out. After that, the rate returns to 28%. In effect, such people lose the advantage of being taxed at 15% on part of their income.

One note of caution: Some taxpayers, mainly wealthy ones, may be subject to a special set of rules known as the alternative minimum tax (AMT). If so, certain tax strategies and some deductions may be disallowed or worth less than before. Your accountant or tax lawyer can advise you on this. Due to the reduction in rates, the AMT for income earned in 1988 will be more prevalent than in the past.

Company Thrift Plans

WHEN bureaucratic-sounding memos come around explaining your company's savings, stock purchase or profit-sharing plans, do you just toss them? Then you are making a money-wasting mistake. If your employer offers you a chance to get into such a program, seize it.

You get two big tax breaks on company thrift plans. Taxes are deferred on all contributions your company makes to your account *and* on all the earnings on the money put in by both you and the company. You do not pay any taxes on the dividends, interest or capital gains.

One type of company thrift plan is the profit-sharing program. The company makes annual deposits in employee accounts based on the size of each year's corporate earnings. On top of that, employees may be able to add voluntary contributions of their own.

Usually you have a choice of investing the money in stocks or bonds and perhaps an interest-paying savings account. Happily, some companies now offer a family of mutual funds as an alternative. Stock mutual funds have, on average, earned more than the conservative bank trust departments and investment counselors who usually manage profit-sharing funds.

Another type of company plan is the stock purchase program. In this, you might have the option of contributing between 3% and 6% of your pre-tax salary. Often the company will kick in one dollar for your two. All that money goes to buy stock in the company itself. You may have to wait three years or more to become vested — that is, to have title to the stock bought by the company matching funds.

If you have a choice of several company plans, the best place to park your voluntary contributions is where the company puts in the highest proportion of matching funds. That is "found money." But how much you want to contribute to a company stock plan will also depend on how optimistic you are about your employer's future. Beware of buying your company stock so heavily that most of your assets wind up in that one issue. A reverse in the firm's fortunes could jeopardize both your nest egg and your job.

Whichever plan you select, you generally cannot withdraw your money until you quit or retire or reach age 59½. Otherwise, you may have to pay a 10% penalty on top of the ordinary income tax you will pay. But many plans allow you to borrow against your accumulated balances at market interest rates.

When you leave the firm, you may be able to use a tax-saving maneuver regarding your lump-sum distribution. Favorable treatment of lump-sum distribution under the tax reform of 1986 is generally limited to a one-time election of five-year forward averaging, only after you reach age 59½. If, however, you reached 50 before 1986 and you receive a lump-sum distribution, you can elect five-year forward averaging under the new tax rates or 10-year forward averaging under the 1986 rates, regardless of the age requirement of 59½. Your IRA funds are not eligible for averaging. You pay income tax on them at ordinary rates.

401(k) Plans

I F YOU like your Individual Retirement Account, you may love the misleadingly named "salary-reduction plan." Actually, it could reduce your income tax bill. It used to be the best tax shelter of all — until reform reduced its benefits. But a salary-reduction plan —

officially known as a 401(k) — is still an attractive, long-term, tax-deferred investment, particularly for people who can no longer deduct their IRA contributions.

The salary-reduction plan is like a super IRA. Yes, you can have both an IRA and a 401(k). But you can put more into a 401(k) — up to $7,313 in 1988. None of the money is taxed until you withdraw it. Meanwhile, all the dividends, interest and capital gains that you earn on the money grow untaxed until withdrawal.

Many companies offer these plans to their employees. Instead of collecting all your pay, you can choose to put part of it into a 401(k). Often, for every one dollar that you put up, your employer kicks in another 50 cents — and that is a bonus nobody should pass up. You can put the money into savings or investments, where it presumably grows, tax-free. Let's say that you earn $35,000 a year, and you choose to put $3,000 into a 401(k). You pay no federal income taxes on that $3,000 until you withdraw it. You then pay taxes at your ordinary rate on your contributions and the income and gains they have earned.

You can take out your own contributions, your account's earnings and, in some cases, even your employer's contributions, if you retire, leave the company, become disabled or can prove hardship. In the past, hardship has been loosely interpreted to include buying a house or paying college tuition.

Beginning in 1989, however, if you plead hardship you will be permitted to withdraw only your own money from a 401(k), and you will have to pay a 10% tax penalty as well as income tax on the sum. The penalty is waived if you use the money to pay medical expenses that exceed 7½% of your adjusted gross income.

When you leave the company, you can take advantage of forward averaging: when you withdraw all the money, you are taxed on it as if you got it in either five or 10 smaller, equal annual installments.

Keogh Plans

WHAT marvelous tax-saving device is available to most doctors, plumbers, movie directors, taxi drivers, lawyers, architects, actors, artists, authors and moonlighters of all kinds? It is the Keogh plan. Many people who are eligible to start a Keogh do not even know it. Maybe you are one of them.

Keoghs are tax-deferred pension accounts designed for those who are self-employed either part-time or full-time and for employees of unincorporated businesses that do not offer their own pension plans. So you can put money into a Keogh if you own your own business, or in many cases if you work for someone who does, or if you are self-employed in almost any way. Even if you have just a small sideline business or earn only a few hundred dollars from a hobby, you can set up a Keogh account and thereby both save on taxes and write your own ticket for a first-class retirement.

A Keogh is much like its smaller cousin, the Individual Retirement Account. You can have *both* a Keogh and an IRA, but you usually can shelter more money in a Keogh than in an IRA. An eligible person can invest in a Keogh as much as 20% of his or her income earned from the job, up to a maximum contribution of $30,000 a year. Thus, if you have a Keogh as well as an IRA, you can shelter as much as $32,000 annually.

Remember that if you wish to put away any of this year's income, you must open your Keogh by December 31 with a nominal contribution of $100. But then you can make the balance of your contributions up to the time you file your income taxes, as late as April 15, or the extended due date if you get an extension.

You can start your Keogh at the same places as an IRA: at a bank or brokerage firm, a mutual fund, an insurance company or some other financial institution. You can stock it with the same savings certificates or investments as an IRA. All your assets will grow free of income tax until you withdraw them after the age of 59½.

There are several varieties of Keoghs. The most generous are called *money-purchase* plans. They let you put away as much as 20% of your annual self-employment income, up to a maximum contribution of $30,000. The drawback is that you must agree to contribute the same percentage of your income to the plan every year, unless your business shows a loss. If you fail to make a contribution, you could face an IRS penalty of up to 100% of the shortfall.

If you are not sure you can keep up such payments, you may be better off with a second type of Keogh, called a *profit-sharing* plan. You can put in only 13% of your income, up to the $30,000 ceiling. But you can change your contributions from year to year or not contribute at all.

If you are 55 or older, you can save and deduct much more than the usual maximum amount — up to 100% of your self-employment income — with a *defined-benefit* Keogh. It lets you put away as much as it takes to provide yourself with a retirement income equal to your very highest paid years, up to certain maximums. Starting in 1987, the new tax law set a maximum annual withdrawal of $90,000 for people who retire at age 65. The maximum annual benefit drops substantially if you decide to retire before age 65. Benefits that you accrued before 1987 are exempt from the new limits. You have to hire an actuary to make the official calculations for your plan every year and submit them to the IRS. In general, the later you open the account, the more you will need to contribute each year to meet your retirement goal.

You can take advantage of another special Keogh program if you earn less than $15,000 a year from all your sources of income. You are then allowed to contribute 100% of your self-employment income or $750 — whichever is less — to a Keogh plan. For example, if you earn $750 from your own small sideline business and make less than $14,250 from a paid job, you can put the entire $750 in a Keogh.

How should you invest your Keogh money? Your strategy should mesh with your needs and goals. If you are a professional or an entrepreneur and you figure that your Keogh funds will be a main part of your retirement income, you will want to put a premium on safety. So, diversify to reduce your risk, and stick to top-rated bonds and stocks.

If you are financially secure and willing to take some risks in hopes of higher gains, you might buy speculative growth stocks and perhaps some high-yielding, low-quality bonds.

If you eventually plan to take all the money out of your retirement fund in a lump sum, your Keogh may be less heavily taxed than your IRA. If you have contributed for at least five years, your withdrawal may qualify for forward averaging. With forward averaging you are taxed on the money as if you drew it out in smaller equal amounts stretched over either five or 10 years. You pay much less in taxes than if you had to report the entire sum as ordinary income for the year in which you received it. IRAs, alas, do not qualify for this tax break. (For more, see "Your Retirement: Making the Most of Your Nest Egg.")

Remember: after age 59½, you can take advantage of forward averaging only *once*. So if you use it on, say, a lump-sum distribution from a company pension plan, you will not be able to use it for your

Keogh. Fortunately, there may be a way out of this problem. You can deposit your lump-sum company pension payment into your Keogh and take forward averaging on the combined total whenever you choose to withdraw it.

Do not set up a Keogh if you think you will need to pull out the money before you reach age 59½. If you do, the government will penalize you 10% of the amount you withdraw. Soon after you reach age 70½, you must start withdrawing funds from your Keogh. But unlike an IRA, you can continue to contribute to your Keogh for as long as you earn self-employment income — even after you begin withdrawals at 70½.

Simplified Employee Pensions

THE TROUBLE with Keogh plans is that they require a tremendous amount of paperwork. If you want to avoid that swamp, consider depositing your savings instead in a Simplified Employee Pension. A SEP is just like an Individual Retirement Account but allows you to put away much more. You can contribute $2,000 plus 15% of your self-employment income, up to a total contribution of $32,000 a year.

You can open a SEP at the same places that handle IRAs and Keoghs — at banks, brokerage houses, insurance companies and mutual funds. But be sure the institution knows that you want a SEP. Otherwise, you may have trouble placing more than $2,000 a year into the account. That, of course, is the annual maximum for an IRA.

Just as with an IRA, you can set up a SEP as late as April of the next year and still get the tax deduction for the present year. And you can invest in the same things, such as stocks, bonds and mutual funds. You also can start taking money out of a SEP at age 59½, but you must start withdrawing soon after you turn 70½.

The disadvantage of a SEP is that you cannot use the neat device of forward averaging on your withdrawals as you can with a Keogh. If you take a lump sum out of your Simplified Employee Pension, you have to pay taxes on all of it right away.

Saving from Sideline Businesses

PARTICULARLY if you are a young adult, you should be looking for ways to increase your income rather than merely avoiding taxes. In that case, you might start a small sideline business of your own. It can be both a tax haven and a nice investment that eventually may turn into a profitable full-time enterprise. Look to your hobby for something you really enjoy doing — and turn it into a spare-time occupation. As tax expert Paul Strassels notes, "It could be anything: chartering a fishing boat, dealing in antiques, selling real estate, catering parties."

If you have your own business — or a part-time business — you can take some of the juiciest tax deductions the IRS will allow. Beginning with your return for 1987, you had to earn a profit in three out of five years. You could deduct all *business* expenses for your car, equipment, travel — even any magazines or books that you could demonstrate were necessary for research in your field of business, or the expense of attending out-of-town seminars directly related to your enterprise. You also could deduct 80% of your business-entertainment expenses.

A sideline business has another major tax advantage. If it loses money, the loss is deductible from income that you earn elsewhere, say from your full-time salaried job. In this case, too, the IRS will let you deduct such losses if you report a profit in just two out of five years. But be careful. If you report only minuscule earnings, the IRS could assume that you are not serious about making the business succeed. So keep meticulous records that document the place and purpose of all business expenses. They will help you show that you spend considerable time and effort looking for clients and making the business go.

Unfortunately, the IRS audits the owners of small businesses more than any other taxpayers. Do not get carried away and deduct too much for your sideline. Deductions for what the IRS deems unnecessary or unreasonable business, travel and entertainment expenses come in for close scrutiny. And the taxmen are especially watchful for such cardinal sins as failure to report income or neglect in paying withholding taxes.

Saving by Giving Money Away

UNLESS your child is a rock star, his or her tax bracket probably is lower than yours. So it pays to shift income from your name to your minor child's, where it may be taxed less harshly. The interest, dividends and capital gains earned on that money may have many years to compound at the youngster's modest or nonexistent tax rate.

Tax reform has stiffened the rules on gifts to children. But you still have ample opportunity to enjoy the tax advantages. Children who are under age 14 will be taxed on any investment income over $1,000 at their parents' rate. Once a child reaches age 14, however, the income will be taxed at the child's rate.

A parent who invests for his or her child's future without transferring the money to the child may be letting the government take an unnecessary share of it. Similarly, an adult who owns stocks or bonds that have appreciated in value and sells them to pay for a child's education is just plain foolish. Instead, *give* the securities to the child, and let him or her sell them. Profits from the sale may be taxed at the child's rate instead of at your much higher one.

The easiest way to give money to your child is to set up a custodial account under the Uniform Gifts to Minors Act. You just get a Social Security number for the child, then ask a banker, a broker or a mutual-fund manager to open an account in the child's name. You can give each of your children up to $10,000 a year this way without incurring any federal gift taxes. Couples can give away $20,000 a year to each of their children. Whoever is custodian of the account — usually a parent — can spend the money and the earnings on it for any purpose that benefits the youngster. This commonly includes private school, summer camp or violin lessons — but not some frivolous activity like a trip to Disney World. You also lose the tax break if you spend the child's money on anything that constitutes an ordinary parental obligation, such as clothing or food or shelter, except in the case of college room and board. (For more, see "Your Education: How to Save for College.")

To keep the money on a string so you can yank it back in the future, you can set up a Clifford Trust. But the broom of tax reform has swept away the tax advantages of Cliffords. With such a trust, you transfer money or stocks or other assets to your children for 10 years and a day.

Under the new law, all income from newly created Cliffords will be taxable to whoever sets up the trust, whether they be parents, other relatives or friends. If you have already established a Clifford, its tax treatment will depend on when you did so. Income from trusts created before March 1, 1986, will be taxed at your rate until your child reaches age 14. Then his or her tax rate will apply. But if you set up a trust after that date, the income will be taxed at your rate even after your child hits 14.

Parents who set up Cliffords before the March 1, 1986, deadline should load the trust with tax-deferred investments, perhaps including U.S. Savings Bonds, that will mature after the child turns 14. For a trust established after the deadline, tax-exempt municipal bonds are the best bet.

Investment Deductions

INVESTMENTS can give you some of your best tax breaks.

Municipal bonds will pay you tax-exempt income. You will not pay any federal tax on the money, and if you invest in bonds issued in your own state, you will not pay state or local taxes either. You can get municipals from brokers, or you can buy them indirectly as shares in mutual funds or unit trusts.

You also can get some partially tax-exempt income by investing in supersafe U.S. Treasury bonds, notes or bills. You will have to pay federal tax on your earnings, but states and localities cannot touch your income. To buy these securities, simply call the nearest Treasury Department regional office or Federal Reserve Bank.

Even old reliable U.S. Savings Bonds can provide tax breaks. Your interest is exempt from state and local levies, and no federal tax is due until you redeem the bonds. Series EE bonds held five years or more return at least 6% a year — or 85% of the average yield on five-year Treasury securities, whichever is higher. In mid-1988, this worked out to 7.09%.

You can deduct up to $3,000 a year in losses you have suffered from the sale of stocks, bonds or other assets. If you have had a larger loss than that in any previous tax year, you can save the excess, carry it over to later years and then use it to offset income.

Capital Gains

LONG-TERM capital gains have long been the lightly taxed darlings of investors. Alas, they have lost their tax-favored status — beginning with the return you file for income that you earn in 1988.

Until 1987, if you sold any investments that you had owned for at least six months, Uncle Sam taxed you at the long-term capital gains rate, which was a maximum of 20%. For your return for 1987, that maximum rose to 28% even if your tax rate for ordinary income was in the top 38½% for the year. And if your ordinary income tax bracket was below 28%, your capital gains were taxed at your ordinary income tax rate.

Beginning in 1988, the IRS will tax all capital gains as ordinary income. The distinction between long-term and short-term holding periods will no longer be relevant for purposes of computing the tax on the gain. Your rate thus will be 15% or 28% — or up to 33% if your income is high enough to be hit by the 5% surcharge. Married couples who file jointly will pay 33% on income from $71,900 to $149,250. Single filers will pay 33% on taxable income from $43,150 to $89,560.

Capital losses are fully deductible against capital gains but still may offset only $3,000 of ordinary income in any taxable year. Any amounts over that you can carry forward and deduct in future years.

Medical and Dental Deductions

IN ORDER to take tax deductions for your medical bills on your 1987 income taxes, they had to total more than 7.5% of your adjusted gross income for the year. That is quite a lot, of course, but you may have more deductible medical expenses than you realize.

Are you paying to support a child in college? Then your medical costs include any portion of college fees that covers his or her prepaid group health care. Among other frequently overlooked expenses are your travel costs on your way to visit a doctor, a hospital, or just about any place you go to get medical services. If you buy or rent equipment that your doctor prescribes, such as a whirlpool or dehumidifier, that cost, too, is a deductible expense. And do not forget to count in your expenses for insurance premiums on policies covering dental care, or for replacement contact lenses.

Remember to add to your medical expenses those you also pay for adult dependents, such as elderly parents or relatives. You can claim these bills if you provide more than half of the dependent's support. A lump-sum payment for lifetime medical care of a dependent can be claimed in the year you made it. The annual cost of institutional care for a mentally or physically handicapped dependent qualifies — so long as the care is primarily medical. By this measure, nursing-home fees can qualify as deductible expenses.

Finally, are you thinking of revamping your image with cosmetic surgery, hair transplants or behavior modification programs such as diet workshops? Consider creating the new you in one calendar year. Some procedures and programs that improve your well-being can be claimed as medical expenses, especially if your doctor prescribes them. Paying for them in one year will enhance your chances of exceeding the 7½% medical deduction threshold. Be sure to keep statements from your doctor and maintain accurate records of your expenses.

Home Office Deductions

THE Internal Revenue Service is increasingly tough on tax returns that include deductions and depreciation write-offs for home offices. If you want to set up a home office that the IRS can live with, you should do so for business-related reasons first and tax benefits second. Before you can claim any deductions, you must be able to prove that the area of the house or apartment you work in is used regularly and exclusively for enterprise. But you need not devote an entire room to your business. If you can prove a part of a room was used just for work, that will do. Partitioning the room with a divider will help support your case, but it is not necessary.

You also must make certain your home workplace meets any of three IRS tests:

One, the office is your primary location for any trade or business.

Two, the office is the place used by your clients, customers or patients in meeting or dealing with you in the normal course of your business. And you must meet or deal with business contacts in person — not by telephone.

Three, the office is a separate structure, such as a garage, that is not attached to your dwelling unit but is used in connection with your business.

Once your home office passes any one of these three tests, you can start counting your deductions. In fact, you can claim deductions for a part-time business operated out of your house even if you work full-time somewhere else in another job. But there is a limit to the generosity of the IRS in becoming your silent business partner. Beginning with your tax return for income you earned in 1987, you cannot deduct more than your *net* income. And you usually are not entitled to deductions if you use your home office just to manage your investments.

Your list of allowable deductions should begin with your direct business costs — those solely attributable to your work space. They include expenses as diverse as painting or repairs and supplies that have a useful life of less than a year. If you own your home and itemize, you can deduct the portion of the mortgage interest and real estate taxes that correspond to your home office. If the office makes up 25% of your house, one-fourth of your interest and property taxes are deductible. If you rent an apartment and use one room as an office, you can deduct the portion of the rent that is equivalent to the size of the work area.

Homeowners and renters can deduct a prorated portion of their utility bills, including electricity, gas, oil, telephone, water and trash collection. Also deductible are insurance premiums paid to protect your home office from a casualty loss or theft. But you cannot deduct the cost of landscaping around your house.

Your juiciest write-off may be depreciation. If you own your house or condo or co-op apartment, you can depreciate the part used as an office over 15 to 30 years, depending on when you bought your home. If you bought your home on or after January 1, 1987, you can depreciate the office over 27½ years. Better yet, you can depreciate over five to seven years any office equipment and furniture, from a personal computer to a coffee table.

The IRS does not give any guidance on how lavish a home office can be and still be deductible. As a rule, however, writing off a Persian carpet or a crystal chandelier is out. But you can depreciate and take the tax credit on, say, a $15,000 computer system if it is necessary for your business.

Last-Minute Deductions

As CHRISTMAS approaches, taxpayers eagerly if belatedly start shopping for deductions they can take before the year draws to a close. Normally, the golden rule of such year-end tax maneuvering is to claim all the sensible exemptions, credits and deductions you can in the current year and, simultaneously, to delay receiving as much income as you can until next year. That way, you quite legitimately can put off paying taxes on it for a full 12 months. Self-employed people aften delay billing their customers or patients until the very end of December so that the money will not arrive until early the following year. Companies put off paying their year-end executive bonuses until January.

You, too, can follow the same tactics. If you make estimated payments of state income or local property taxes, send in your fourth-quarter installment in December, instead of January when it is due, and you will be able to deduct it from your tax bill for the current year. For the same reason send in your December home mortgage payment before January 1. You might consider squeezing two years' worth of charitable contributions into this year to increase your deductions.

You can get extra write-offs for business expenses by prepaying next year's subscriptions to business publications and dues to professional groups. But remember that the IRS counts these as part of your miscellaneous deductions — which must equal more than 2% of your adjusted gross income in order to qualify for a deduction.

If you are self-employed, open a Keogh account at a bank, brokerage house or mutual fund before December 31. A Keogh is like a super IRA and will save you taxes. (For more, see "Your Taxes: Keogh Plans.")

One warning: If income tax rates go up next year, you may well be better off collecting income this year — and then paying the lower rate on it. The information in the previous paragraphs is applicable to those years in which tax rates are stable.

Here are a few more tips, which are useful regardless of changes in tax rates:

If you need a tax loss and are willing to boot out a few dogs among your investments, there is a way to do it without altering your basic investment strategy. Swap lagging bonds for similar ones that you think will rise soon. You can do the same with stocks, but it's harder to find shares that are almost identical to the ones you already hold. Generally you carry out the swaps late in the year. But do not wait until late December to make these exchanges. It may be difficult then to find just what you want.

Mutual-fund investors can consider taking a few losses as well. What you do is redeem only those shares that are worth less than you paid for them. You will need to review carefully your records of purchase, with their dates and prices, and it is drudgery. Pick out the losers, and send a list of them to the bank that serves as the fund's transfer agent, instructing the bank to redeem only those particular shares.

Finally, be particularly cautious of buying limited partnerships toward the end of the year. That's when hustlers tend to come out of the woodwork and unload inferior partnerships on panicky investors who are desperate for ways to reduce their taxes. Quite a few of these end-of-the-year offerings could be dangerous to your wealth.

The Best Time to File

WHEN should you file your income tax return? The earlier the better after January 1 — if you expect to get a refund. If you file by the end of February, you should receive your check in the mail within six weeks. But if you delay and file in April, when the Internal Revenue Service is deluged by forms from other last-minute taxpayers, you could face a 12-week wait for your refund.

As mentioned earlier, do not congratulate yourself too enthusiastically if you are in line for a refund. That just means you gave the government free use of money that was rightfully yours. If you want to put that extra cash to work for you instead of for Uncle Sam, simply reduce the amount withheld from your paycheck. You do that by asking your payroll department at work for a W-4 form and increasing your number of allowances on it.

If you have the money to pay but just cannot complete your tax return by the April 15 deadline, the IRS will extend your day of filing to August 15. What you have to do is send in an extension form — IRS Form 4868 — and an *estimated* payment of your taxes by April 15. Just estimate your income for last year and subtract any deductions and credits you expect to take. Then refer to the tax tables in the 1040 instruction booklet for the amount you owe.

If you underestimate the bill, you may have to pay the ½%-a-month penalty — plus interest — on your balance outstanding. But if you send in your return late without having filed for an extension, the IRS will be much less forgiving. (See the next chapter.) Another matter to watch: Even if you file an extension form, you must make your past year's contribution to your IRA by April 15.

If you have omitted information or would like to add information to your tax return after you have filed it, you may prepare amended federal and state returns. Generally, the IRS allows you up to three years from the original filing date to amend your return.

What If You Can't Pay on Time?

ALMOST one out of four people who owe the government taxes on April 15 cannot pay. What should you do if you come to the cold discovery that you owe the government more than you can possibly raise in cash?

Don't panic. What you should do is file your *tax return* on time and send in whatever amount you can. Otherwise, you will be stuck with stiff penalties.

First, you will be liable for a fine of at least 5% and not more than 25% of your tax liability *each month* for late filing of your form plus ½% *each month* for late payment. Second, you may be charged about 10% annual interest, compounded *daily*.

You can avoid tax fines by filing a timely extension and paying at least 90% of your total tax liability. You still will have to pay interest on any balance due.

The IRS can attach your paycheck and seize your bank accounts and house. But it almost never takes such drastic action — if you earnestly try to pay your debts.

The key is communication. If you do not enclose a check when you file your return, you eventually will receive a letter demanding payment within 10 days. Do not ignore this notice: the IRS gets tougher with every passing day. Just be sure to telephone or visit the IRS office listed on the delinquency notice. Do that immediately after receiving the first notice instead of waiting for the fourth and final one about three months later. If you have a professional tax adviser, bring him or her along to the tax office. Your adviser probably will charge you at least $100, but he or she can get the IRS to agree to better terms than you can.

Several hundred delinquent taxpayers each year manage to persuade the IRS to reduce the amounts they owe. But such deals are reserved for people who the tax collectors think will never be able to pay their bills in full. For example, an elderly person with few assets and little chance of earning much might be a candidate for such a compromise.

Once this ordeal is over, make a point of preventing it from happening again. If you are a wage-earner, take fewer withholding allowances at work so more money for taxes will be deducted from your pay. If you are self-employed, increase your quarterly estimated tax payments.

How the IRS Sizes Up Your 1040

IT IS always a bad idea to try to cheat on your income tax, and it is even worse now. Thanks to their powerful computers, the tax collectors are checking up on much more of your income than ever before. Until recently, about the only lines on your tax return that the Internal Revenue Service could check and verify without an audit were those for interest income, dividends, salaries and wages. But the list is growing fast.

Since 1983, the IRS has been corroborating against other sources such income as any state and local tax refunds you may have received, proceeds you collected from any sales of investments, your

Social Security benefits and IRA and pension payouts. With your return for 1985, the IRS also began verifying mortgage interest deductions and alimony income. By law, companies, banks, brokerage firms and government agencies that pay various types of income must fill out IRS forms stating the amounts distributed to you during the year. Banks and other institutions have to declare how much interest they collect and any IRA contributions they receive from you.

It may take about 18 months for the IRS to finish matching the information it gets from these sources with what you declare on your 1040 tax forms. When there is a discrepancy that does not look like a harmless error, an IRS computer will fire off a letter demanding that you explain the difference or pay up. If you under-report interest or dividend income, the letter also will say that you owe a 5% negligence penalty. Other discrepancies do not involve an automatic fine, although the IRS could try to prove in court that you intentionally tried to misrepresent your earnings or deductions.

How to Avoid an Audit

LITTLE more than 1% of all personal income tax returns are audited. So, chances are you are safe. But if you are called in by the IRS for one of those troubling and time-consuming procedures, you can take some comfort from these facts:

One of every five audited taxpayers emerged from the process in 1986 owing no more than when he or she filed. Indeed, in 1985, one in 200 people who were audited came away with refunds averaging about $1,400. And many thousands of others negotiated settlements with the IRS that left them paying more taxes, but less than the agency originally had demanded.

Generally the IRS begins sending out audit notices in July of the year in which the returns in question are filed. If you receive a letter saying your return will be audited, you typically have up to six weeks to get ready for a meeting at a local IRS office. There is one exception: If the deductions in question can be easily documented, you can respond by mail.

Who gets audited? Anyone can, of course. Whether or not your return will be audited depends mostly on how closely your tax data compare with the average deductions, exemptions and credits claimed by taxpayers with your income. The bigger your income, the more likely you will be audited. High-income people who make the greatest use of sophisticated tax breaks are the most likely to claim the kinds of debatable write-offs that the IRS likes to challenge. Also prime candidates for audits are people who are paid mostly in cash, such as waiters, taxi drivers and beauticians.

To prevent a tax audit, beware of some treacherous write-offs. Steer clear of tax-shelter partnerships that promise suspiciously high write-offs — for example, deductions that equal two or more times your investment in the first year. They will almost surely provoke the IRS. Also audit-prone is a tax shelter financed with a note that the promoter says you will never have to repay. The IRS will not let you deduct money that you are not really risking. Be wary of shelters in such highly speculative ventures as records or gold mines. The deduction might be sound, but you could lose your investment.

Deductions for what the IRS deems unnecessary or unreasonable business travel and entertainment expenses also come in for close scrutiny: for example, taking a trip to Europe for a management course that is available locally. So be sure to document the time, place, cost and purpose of all business travel and entertainment.

How to Survive an Audit

I F YOU become one of the million or so unfortunate taxpayers who are audited each year, keep cool. The damage probably will be minimal, unless you have engaged in outright fraud.

After the audit notice arrives in the mail, try to get some idea of how extensive the examination is going to be. One way is to phone the IRS and say you want to schedule an appointment on a day when no one will be rushed. If the IRS agent responds that the interview should not take longer than a couple of hours, relax. It is likely to be a hasty one-hour job. That is the kind most people get. But if you are told to set aside a week, then you know it will be a serious review — and you have trouble.

If you find that you are repeatedly audited for the same

deductions — say, higher-than-average dental bills — and these deductions have been allowed in the past, have your tax preparer write to the IRS to ask that the latest audit be canceled. When he points out that in past years these deductions have been allowed, you have a better than 50% chance of avoiding an audit this year.

Before you go into any audit, be sure you are well briefed. Confer in advance with your tax preparer. You probably will have to pay his or her usual fee for the strategy session, but getting him or her to explain the reasoning behind any challenged deductions, exemptions or credits is well worth the expense.

Always bring a tax professional along to help explain your return. Your preparer can even appear instead of you, though only if he or she is a CPA, an attorney or someone who has passed a tough IRS test to become a so-called enrolled agent. That rules out most storefront preparers. Insist that the audit take place at the IRS or at the office of your preparer, but not at your own home or office. There is no point in giving the tax collector a more complete picture of your economic situation than he will get from your written return.

The most important factor in deciding the audit's outcome will be the evidence you present to support your deductions. A dossier of receipts, bills and diaries will help you document your write-offs. You will do best if you offer a sound defense without appearing defensive. You might even ask for additional deductions at your audit. If you can document them, you may improve your overall bargaining position.

Your attitude will do a lot to determine how tough or lenient the auditor will be, so be polite. Answer all questions simply and directly, but never volunteer any information. If the auditor assigned to you is abusive, you have the right to demand another. But do not act belligerently toward your IRS examiner. Do not speak loudly. Do not smoke, and do not wear clothing or jewelry that might cause the auditor to think that your income is higher than you reported.

If you are not satisfied with the outcome of your audit, you can appeal on the spot to the examiner's supervisor. That person will come to his or her own conclusion. If you then are still dissatisfied, you have 30 days to ask that an IRS appeals officer hear your case. You might find him or her more willing to concede some or all of the issues than your auditor was. Unlike auditors, appeals officers are allowed to weigh the cost of a possible court battle in determining how much, if anything, you should pay.

You can appeal further to the U.S. tax court, district court or

Claims Court. But before you take that step, you should decide whether the battle is really worth it. Tax court cases are typically long, often expensive and rarely successful. (For more, see: "Your Taxes: How to Complain to the IRS.")

How to Get the Tax Adviser Who Is Best for You

Suppose you are salaried, earn less than $30,000 a year, perhaps own a little stock and pay a mortgage. Chances are your tax profile is simple. If so, you should be able to handle your own forms with the help of a do-it-yourself tax preparation book. Or you can take your forms to one of the national storefront chains such as H&R Block or Beneficial Income Tax Service. They all charge set fees, depending on the complexity of your form. The average price of a Block preparation comes to a little less than $50.

If your personal finances are more complex — say that in the past year you have sold a house, started a business or had active stock trades — you will find that no professional is better trained to handle your taxes than a certified public accountant. It is best to hire a CPA who specializes in taxes, rather than one who does general accounting. Accountants charge $50 an hour and up. Merely having your forms filled out probably will cost at least $100.

If your income is large enough to warrant an accountant's help, you probably will need tax planning, too. At one of the so-called Big Eight accounting firms, that could include estate planning, several meetings with a personal adviser on tax strategies and shelters, updates on relevant IRS rulings, monthly projections of your taxes and an array of tax reports. The cost is generally more than $3,500. But an experienced CPA in a small firm should be able to approximate this royal treatment for $300 to $500.

A group of professionals who offer expertise in areas where even accountants fear to tread are tax attorneys. They are great for handling specialized tax problems such as those related to divorce and the sale, purchase or start-up of a business. These lawyers usually work for taxpayers in, or close to, the top tax bracket who want to shelter part of their income. Tax lawyers can argue your case before the IRS and into tax court. Their rates typically are $200 an hour.

Whomever you choose to prepare your taxes, he or she should sign your return, and should be willing — unequivocally willing — to appear along with you at the IRS in the event you are audited.

Before you sign the completed return yourself, read over each line and check to see the figures correspond with your records. When you do not understand how your preparer came up with a certain number, ask. If the IRS finds an error, it is you who will have to pay any back taxes, interest and penalties. So do not just dump your financial records on your accountant's desk and run.

Also make sure your return will be completed before April 15. Recently, one taxpayer's attorney had prepared his forms but sent them in three months late because of a clerical oversight. The Supreme Court ruled that the taxpayer was indeed liable for a late-filing penalty. Tax expert Julian Block advises that you should ask your preparer "early and often" how work is coming along on your return. And if you think there is a chance he will not finish on time, file for an extension.

How can you evaluate the quality of help you will get from an accountant or tax lawyer or storefront tax preparer whom you are contemplating hiring? Start by asking what kind of clients his or her firm handles. See if its members are experienced with people in your shoes. Beware of firms that operate on "pool arrangement" in which your tax forms float among a number of accountants, each of whom handles a few lines.

Listen to the questions the tax adviser asks *you*. If he or she neglects to inquire about the basics of your tax situation — whether you own a home, have a pension plan or contribute to an IRA — you have drawn a dud. Be particularly suspicious if he or she starts steering you into such exotic tax shelters as jojoba-bean partnerships without first finding out your needs. He or she may be trying to sell you a product rather than providing a service.

The vast majority of tax professionals are competent and honest, but the number of incompetent, negligent and fraudulent tax preparers is much higher than the Internal Revenue Service's estimate of only a few thousand, out of roughly 200,000 in the country. According to the government's General Accounting Office, the IRS is not doing enough to find or penalize the wrongdoers.

How can you tell if your tax preparer might be a problem? Watch out for one who demands a percentage of your tax refund as payment. Especially steer away from a preparer who guarantees you a refund. Also, avoid anyone who says he or she will give you a refund right away and will later endorse and cash your IRS check. That is illegal — and subject to a $500 penalty.

How to Get Quick Answers

WHOM do you call when you have a question or two about your taxes? Try the IRS. It provides recorded, dial-a-deduction tax information that is accurate, reasonably clear, and free.

For the number to call, turn to page 35 of your 1040 instruction booklet. Then look on page 36 for the list of 150 tax subjects and their corresponding three-digit codes. Once you place the call, you punch one of these codes on your touch-tone phone to get a tape-recorded discussion of the selected subject. If you have a rotary-dial phone, wait until someone answers and then state the code for the tape you want to hear.

In most cases, the recordings also refer you to free IRS publications for more information. If you want to talk directly to an IRS staff member, you can find the appropriate phone number on page 37 of your 1040 booklet. You stand your best chance of getting through to IRS staffers if you phone early in the morning or late in the week. But recorded help is available around the clock seven days a week for taxpayers with touch-tone phones. (All the page numbers given above come from the instruction booklet for 1987 income and are subject to change.)

How to Complain to the IRS

SAY that you are entitled to a tax refund but it does not arrive, or it is smaller than expected, or you receive a bill to pay additional tax. If you have a complaint about your taxes, there are a few secrets for getting action — and satisfaction — out of the IRS.

Get in touch with one of the agency's specially designated problem-resolution officers, or PROs. There are 73 of these merciful missionaries, one in each IRS district office and service center. If you call a PRO, he or she usually can sweep away weeks or months of potential bureaucratic frustration.

If your complaint isn't settled in five working days, the problem-resolution officer is supposed to advise you of the status of the case and give you the name and phone number of the person down the line who can solve it. And if you don't get satisfaction even then, you can ask that your case be sent to the IRS appellate division. If you lose there, you have 90 days to take one of three further steps:

First, you can withhold payment on a claim of less than $10,000 and take your case to the small-claims division of the U.S. tax court.

Second, you can pay a disputed tax of any amount and file for a refund with your IRS office. If it's disallowed, you then can sue in a U.S. district court or the Claims Court.

In 1987 the government won 80.4% of the cases brought in the district courts; taxpayers won complete victories in 16.8% of the cases and partial victories in 2.7% of them.

In the Claims Court during 1987 the government won 85.2% of the cases, while taxpayers won 11.1% and gained partial victories in 3.7%. The Claims Court has several drawbacks for aggrieved taxpayers. Fighting a case there requires you to make a trip to Washington. Before your case is even heard, you must pay not only the taxes in dispute but also any interest and penalties. Yes, you do get a refund if you win. But only when you can afford the cost and inconvenience should you resort to the Claims Court.

Finally, you can sue in the U.S. tax court without paying the tax in advance. In 1987 the government won a full 38.1% of all cases there, while taxpayers had full victories in only 5.2%.

You probably can avoid the courts if you have a legitimate claim. Indeed, if an IRS problem-resolution officer cannot help you, go to your congressman. Often, he or she or an aide can break a logjam in your case in a matter of hours.

Tax Shelters after Reform

J UST mention tax shelters, and many people get anxiety attacks. No wonder. Tax reform has demolished large numbers of shelters by wiping out what was often their biggest appeal: quick, high write-offs.

The new tax law does not allow you to deduct "passive losses" from your other income, notably your salary income or what you earn from securities. You can use losses from passive investments only to offset "passive" income. Generally, limited partnerships and rental real estate investments qualify as passive investments under the new law. So tax reform spelled death for the common practice of using big losses on paper to offset other income.

As mentioned earlier, one exception to the rule covers owners of rental real estate who meet three tests: You own at least 10% of the property; you are active in the management decisions; and your taxable income is less than $100,000 a year. Then you can deduct up to $25,000 in losses against any other income. If you earn more than $100,000, the $25,000 limit will be reduced by 50% of the amount that your income exceeds $100,000. For example, if your income is $130,000, you could use up to $10,000 in losses from your rental property (half of $30,000 equals $15,000; and $25,000 minus $15,000 equals $10,000).

The new rules are being phased in over five years for investments made before President Reagan signed the bill on October 22, 1986. On your return for your 1987 income, you were able to use 65% of your passive losses to offset any other income. The allowable amount drops to 40% in 1988, 20% in 1989, 10% in 1990 and none in 1991. If you are stuck with pre-1987 passive losses, one strategy is to seek shelters with good, long-term growth prospects that generate passive income. Beware, though, of shelters that carry high personal risk. It's not worth committing yourself to large financial obligations just to get tax savings.

Shelters usually have been set up as limited partnerships. The sponsors, who are the general partners, are responsible for all business decisions. And the investors, who are limited partners, advance most of the money. If the venture makes money, the investors share in the profits. If it fails, their liability is limited to the amount they have agreed to invest.

When searching for a shelter, your first choice will be between a public limited partnership and a private one:

Public partnerships are registered with the Securities and Exchange Commission, which requires the sponsors to disclose their records. Each of these partnerships has scores, and often hundreds, of investors. To invest, you most often have to put up at least $5,000, though the minimums can range from $2,000 to $10,000. You buy public partnerships through securities brokers or financial planners.

Private partnerships are sold by planners and others, but the sponsors do not have to register with the SEC, although they do have to make some disclosures to that agency. They can accept up to 33 investors. As you might guess, the stakes are higher — usually a minimum investment of $25,000 or more. Your risks of being audited by the IRS are greater with a private partnership than a public one. In the first years of a real estate limited partnership you might earn income from rent. After anywhere from five to 15 years, the shelter sponsor would aim to sell the properties and distribute the profits, if any.

Oil and gas shelters use your money to lease land and equipment and then pay for drilling or producing. These shelters usually last about 15 years. Naturally, the sharp decline in oil prices has reduced the income from many energy shelters and caused some to go broke.

Bear in mind that if you fall to a lower bracket as a result of tax reform, any deductions you take will be less valuable. In the 50% tax bracket — the top tax bracket for 1986 income — $1 of deductions saved you 50 cents in taxes. Beginning in 1988, with the top rate at 28%, those in the top bracket get just 28 cents in tax savings. People in lower brackets also have their tax rates reduced and thus profit less from shelters. For some people in the higher income tax bracket, however, the rate in 1988 can be 33% because of the 5% surcharge on taxable income between $71,900 and $149,250 for joint returns and between $43,150 and $89,560 for single individuals.

It is particularly important for you to hire an accountant, a tax lawyer or a knowledgeable financial planner to examine the prospectus for any shelter you are considering. Have your professional adviser assess the accuracy of the assumptions behind the program's projected write-off and cash distributions. Then have him or her calculate what your after-tax return would be in your tax bracket.

Make sure the shelter's sponsor is experienced — and successful. Consider only those sponsors who have a solid financial position and at least a five-year record of consistent returns. In judging financial strength, look at the sponsor's net worth. It should be close to the amount he or she intends to raise through the partnership.

Questionable shelters are even more likely than ever to draw the IRS's attention. The tax act passed in 1984 requires most shelter sponsors to register each of their programs with the IRS and to keep lists of investors. The law also requires you to provide the IRS with the registration number of the shelter you are investing in. So, if you buy a shelter, get the registration number from the stockbroker or financial planner who sells it to you. Then, when you file your income tax return, you will be ready to file a relatively new form, No. 8271, which gives the IRS your shelter's number.

When considering a shelter, the old rule is truer than ever: make sure it is a strong investment with solid prospects for offering profits. Here are some dos and don'ts to help you evaluate a shelter:

— Never consider any investment proposed in a classified ad or by an unknown caller on the telephone.

— Be particularly wary of shelters in such highly speculative ventures as phonograph records or gold mines.

— Shun any deal financed with a note that the promoter says you will never have to repay. The IRS just will not let you deduct money that you are not really risking.

— Reject any program that fails to provide detailed information on the sponsor's prior performance. Examine closely the records of the general partners to make sure they have a proven, successful history. Ask for bank and credit references and for audited reports of previous projects.

— Check the prospectus to see that the general partners collect their share of the profits at the same time as you, the limited partners, do. You want to make sure there is no skimming.

Several monthly newsletters evaluate public partnership tax shelters and sponsors, and they can point you in the direction of reliable programs. Two that assess deals of all types as well as tax-planning strategies and economic factors are the *Stanger Report* (1129 Broad Street, Shrewsbury, New Jersey 07702) and *Brennan Reports* (P.O. Box 882, Valley Forge, Pennsylvania 19482).

To find shelters, you can ask brokers or financial planners for prospectuses, but many of these professionals sell partnerships only from concerns they know well. If you contact the general partners directly — you can find their names in the newsletters — they will sell you a shelter or point you to a broker or planner who will.

All shelters are chancy ventures, but some offer surer profits than others. To recapitulate how to boost your return and cut your risk:

Determine whether you want to buy into a so-called public partnership or a private partnership. The public ventures have to be registered with the SEC, and rules governing them tend to be stricter. A private partnership, by contrast, might offer you the comfort of dealing with your own family lawyer or accountant. But just because someone is a sharp accountant does not mean that he or she is an expert in the fine points of real estate or oil and gas drilling. Impartial experts tend to agree that the most consistently successful results come from investing in public programs.

Ask your stockbroker what public shelters he or she might recommend. Dealing with a solid broker helps you to avoid jerry-built shelters. Also, hire an expert accountant, tax attorney or financial planner to analyze any shelter before you sink your money into it. Study closely the prospectus covering the shelter. It will help tell just what you are buying and whom you are buying from.

Examine the financial picture of the general partners. Look for the section in the prospectus on prior performance. It is a bad sign if the sponsors of real estate deals have waited more than a year to start the cash distributions. On oil and gas ventures, payouts should begin within two years.

Watch out for unusually high or low fees. High charges mean that you will get less investment for each dollar that you put up. On the other hand, suspiciously low charges up front may disguise inflated operating costs or other expenses later on. But do not worry if 80% or preferably 85% of your money is actually being invested.

Your IRAs

How They Work

I F YOU were limited to just one investment a year, what would it be? For many people, a sound choice still would be a tax-saving Individual Retirement Account. Forty million Americans can't be wrong. That's the number who have opened IRAs since Congress made them available to just about everyone in 1982.

True enough, tax reform has taken away from many people one of the two major benefits of IRAs: your ability to deduct from your taxable income every dollar you invest. But even if you lose that major benefit, IRAs still offer what could be a more important advantage: both your contributions *and* the interest and dividends and capital gains you earn on them will grow tax-free in your account until you make withdrawals, presumably after you retire. Then you will pay income tax at your ordinary rate — but only on the cash you remove. If you are like many retirees, your tax rate at that time will be lower than it was when you were working.

Employed people who are not covered by a pension plan can deduct all contributions to an IRA. But if you are in a company plan — whether you are vested or not — you can deduct your contribution only if you meet certain income requirements. Married couples who file jointly can deduct their full IRA deposit if their adjusted gross income is $40,000 or less a year. Single filers can deduct up to $2,000 if they earn $25,000 or less. Couples who earn between $40,000 and $50,000, and singles who earn between $25,000 and $35,000 can write off part of their contribution. The amount you can deduct tapers off as you earn more money.

Even if your earnings put you above the $35,000 to $50,000 ceilings, you may be able to claim at least part of an IRA deduction. One way is to take advantage of a 401(k) plan if your company offers one. With a 401(k), you can instruct your employer to put away up to $7,000 of your annual salary toward retirement. For each dollar you contribute, some employers add 25 cents to your account.

Because the money you put away under a 401(k) is not considered taxable income, your contributions lower your adjusted gross income. Say that you and your spouse earn $52,000 and thus are not eligible for an IRA deduction. But if you put $7,000 into a 401(k) plan, your adjusted gross income would decline to $45,000. In that case you would be able to deduct up to $1,000 in contributions to your IRA. Similarly, you may qualify for a full or partial IRA deduction if you put money into a Keogh plan or a Simplified Employee Pension.

The fact that IRAs compound tax-free means that they are government subsidies to investors. If you put the maximum $2,000 a year into an IRA for 20 years and earn 10% annually on the money, your $40,000 in contributions will turn into $126,000. By contrast, if you put the same amount of money into nonsheltered investments and earn 10% on them, your total after 20 years will be significantly less. It will be reduced by your annual payments of income taxes on your dividends and interest, plus taxes on any capital gains that you take.

IRAs do not have many drawbacks. Yes, you may have to pay between $10 and $30 a year in fees to the bank, savings and loan association, brokerage firm, mutual-fund or insurance company where you keep your account. Plus, you cannot withdraw the money before age 59½ without being assessed a 10% penalty by the tax collectors. But both are small prices to pay for what can be a really terrific tax shelter.

You have until the time you file your income taxes — as late as April 15 — to open your IRA and put some of your previous year's pay into it. You can invest your money in bank certificates of deposit, stocks, bonds, mutual funds, annuities, limited partnerships, stock options, futures contracts, real estate, Ginnie Maes and U.S. Treasury securities. Off limits are life insurance, precious metals, gems, art and other collectibles and investments bought on margin. But you are allowed to buy U.S. Treasury gold and silver coins.

The further you are from retirement, the more an IRA's tax-deferred compound earnings can do for you. If you are 35 and start depositing $2,000 a year for the next 30 years and your money earns 10% — which is a reasonable figure — you will be richer by a full $362,000 when you turn 65.

Your IRA will grow much faster if you put in your contributions as early each year as possible. Let's say you make the maximum $2,000 contribution, but you wait until the very last minute — that is, until every April 15 — to make your contribution for the prior year. If your investment earns 10% annually, in 20 years you will have $110,000. But if you make that same contribution as soon as each new tax year begins on January 1, you will end up with $16,000 more in the same amount of time. And after 30 years, you will have $42,000 more than you would have if you waited until the last minute.

Remember that you do not have to put the maximum $2,000 in your account every year. Legally, you can open an IRA with as little as $1, but most banks require at least $25. Your contribution need not be made all at one time. You can make periodic deposits, as with any other account — as long as you meet the April 15 deadline. You can even skip a year, but you cannot make up for it by putting in more than $2,000 the next time. You also can open as many IRAs as you please and divide deposits among them, just so long as your total contribution in one year does not exceed $2,000. You also can switch your IRAs from one financial institution to another without forfeiting the tax benefits.

Once you have made an initial contribution, you can leave your account at that level or you can build it up with weekly or monthly deposits, just so the total does not top $2,000 a year. Often you can have these deposits automatically deducted from your paycheck and deposited in a bank or in a mutual fund. Even small deposits grow nicely. Put away just $9.60 a week, for instance, and in 12 months you will have a tax-sheltered nest egg of $500 — plus whatever interest, dividends and capital gains you may have earned on it.

Some employers offer payroll-deduction plans for IRA contributions. These periodic deductions are a convenient method of forced savings. One disadvantage is that they do not let you accumulate the maximum amount possible in your IRA, because your total allowable contribution is not made in one lump at the beginning of the year and is not working for you the entire year.

When you start to withdraw your IRA money, it will be taxed as ordinary income. But presumably you will be retired by then and in a lower tax bracket than you are now.

Unless you are disabled, you will face stiff consequences if you *permanently* withdraw the money before you turn 59½: the IRS will claim as a penalty 10% of any funds you take out, and you will also owe income tax on them at your regular rate. But you can *temporarily* withdraw money from your IRA once a year, without paying any tax or penalties. You just have to roll over and replace the money within 60 days. So, if you are careful, you can use your IRA money for a short-term emergency loan. The only extra cost may be a fee imposed by some banks or mutual funds when you withdraw and replace your IRA funds this way.

You are allowed to start permanent withdrawals anytime after age 59½, but you *must* begin making them soon after you turn 70½ — to be precise, by April 1 of the next calendar year — taking out at least the minimum amounts decreed by the IRS on the basis of life-expectancy tables. For instance, if you are a 70-year-old man, you are expected to live 12 more years, so you must withdraw at least one-twelfth of your funds in the first year. If you are dependent principally on the IRA income, it might be safest when you retire to transfer the entire sum into an annuity that provides lifetime payments for you and your spouse.

When you die, the money you have in an IRA goes to any beneficiary you have named. The beneficiary may defer paying income taxes on the money until he or she withdraws it, and that can be done anytime during his or her lifetime.

If only one spouse is employed or if one spouse has a very small income, the couple can contribute a total of $2,250 annually under the "spousal" IRA provision. But each partner must have a separate account. The $2,250 spousal IRA can be divided as the couple wishes, so long as no more than $2,000 goes into either account in a given year. For example, one partner may contribute $2,000 and the other $250; or each may contribute $1,125. In case of divorce the ex-spouses keep individual control of the funds already in their separate accounts.

If you own a small business, you can increase your nonworking spouse's IRA deduction. Just hire your beloved part-time. As long as the service he or she performs is legitimate and the compensation is reasonable, you can put up to $2,000 of the spouse's salary in the IRA every year. But you also will have to make other federally mandated tax payments for your spouse, such as for Social Security.

True enough, some people should not open IRAs. As a rule, children ought not to put earnings from summer or after school jobs in an IRA, because they are already in a very low tax bracket or pay no taxes at all. And if you think you will need your savings in a few years to buy a house or send a child through school, that money should not go into an IRA. The penalty for early withdrawal will probably exceed what you would gain in tax-sheltered earnings on several years of IRA contributions. But almost anyone else who has earned some income from a job, and can afford to put aside savings that he or she will not need until at least the age of 59½, should think seriously about opening an Individual Retirement Account.

Where to Invest Your IRA Money

INVESTING the cash you put in your Individual Retirement Account is like shopping in a well-stocked financial supermarket. You can choose from many thousands of securities, bank instruments, mutual funds, annuities and income-producing limited partnerships. But your decision will be considerably easier if you answer these four questions:

First, how old are you? The closer you are to retirement, the less risk you can afford. The stock market might be a terrific investment for someone under 50. But at age 63 you might be asking for trouble, since a market slump could leave you short-changed at a critical time.

Second, what other investments do you have? You want to diversify. If your non-IRA assets are mostly in common stocks, you might balance them by filling your tax-deferred account with high-yielding fixed-income investments, such as bank certificates.

Third, how daring are you? If an investment is going to keep you awake at night, it is not for you. One fairly painless way to learn your tolerance for risk is to put a small part of your IRA money into a growth stock or an aggressive growth mutual fund. As the price swings, the lining of your stomach will tell you how much risk you feel comfortable with.

Fourth, what do you know? Do not invest in something you do not understand. Unless you are an experienced investor, you would probably be wise to avoid limited partnerships in real estate, oil and gas or other areas. It is hard for anyone but an expert in such investments to tell a good deal from a bad one. Other investments that demand caution include options and commodities futures.

Over the years your IRA should grow — and change — just as you do. The younger you are, the more you should go for growth. Let's say you are 30 and have some safe investments outside your IRA. In that case, you might do well to place almost all of your IRA money in long-term growth mutual funds.

By contrast, if you are in your 50s and plan on dipping into your IRA within 10 years or so, you would be well advised to start moving out of stocks and into such safer staples as money-market funds and short-term bonds. Specifically, you might be wise to invest 50% of your money in certificates of deposit, U.S. Treasury securities, Ginnie Mae funds and short-term or intermediate-term corporate bonds. Another 25% might be in money-market funds. The remainder could go into high-dividend stocks or so-called income mutual funds — the conservative kind that pay you regular installments of cash.

To repeat, if your IRA investment strategy emphasizes safety, fixed-income securities are hard to beat. Short-term certificates of deposit are the best-known type, but they may not be the best choice now that interest rates have come down so much. Other fixed-income investments offer higher returns with comparable risks. Among them: Ginnie Maes, which are home mortgage securities backed by the federal government.

You can take more risk — and possibly earn a bigger return — by buying shares in a mutual fund. There are some 2,400 funds, and you can choose one whose strategy fits your own.

If you have accumulated at least $10,000 in your IRA and are willing to do your own investment research, you may want to open a self-directed account at a brokerage house or a mutual-fund company. Such accounts let you trade stocks, bonds, certificates of deposit and other securities at will. Self-directed IRAs can cost about $25 to open, $25 a year to maintain and $50 to close.

If you are undecided how to divvy up your IRA funds between stocks and income-oriented investments, consider the new breed of mutual fund that will make the decision for you. Known as asset allocation funds, these funds strive to get the best return by dividing their assets among stocks, bonds and money market securities.

No one asset is ideal for an IRA, despite what its sponsor might say. By contrast, some investments are truly unsuitable for the accounts. Be skeptical of mutual funds that claim they are especially designed for tax-deferred accounts. Such funds often emphasize short-term trading, and there is no evidence that they actually achieve superior performance in the long run.

Question any rate of return that seems seductively high. There is probably a reason for the steep yield, such as excessive risk. Be especially wary of CDs that offer split rates — a lofty one for 60 days and a lower one for the duration of the term. Insist on having the annual yield calculated for you. It is the best basis for comparison.

In evaluating an IRA investment, first consider how it scores for preservation of principal. Ask yourself how great a chance there is that you could lose some, or even all, of the money you invest. But remember that you generally pay for high safety by accepting relatively low returns.

Another key characteristic to watch for in your IRA account, once you are 59½, is liquidity. The more quickly you can convert an investment into cash, the more liquid it is. The more liquid your IRA assets, the easier it is to plan withdrawals and adjust your investments in response to economic changes.

Also consider volatility. If investments that jump and fall sharply make you nervous, then play safe. But if you have a strong gut, go for growth and don't worry too much about volatility.

Consider also how well an investment stands up to inflation. A locked-in 7% interest on a certificate of deposit looks nice enough when inflation is only around 4%. But that unchanging rate loses much of its luster if inflation rises toward double-digit levels. The message: include in your IRA some investments, such as stocks, whose value tends to go up when inflation is on the rise.

Mutual-Fund Plans

THE best place to invest your IRA money may well be in a large mutual-fund group — that is, a company that operates several kinds of mutual funds. When you put your cash in one or more of these groups, your fees are low, your investment choices are numerous and at many fund families you can move your money around from one investment to another simply by making a telephone call.

No fewer than 80 mutual-fund companies have funds that invest in stocks, bonds and the money market — plus an astonishing array of permutations and combinations of the three — and let you switch your money among them. A big mutual-fund company may offer as many as 75 choices, ranging from a money-market fund that invests exclusively in federal government securities, to a fund that buys stocks of fast-growing high-tech companies, to a highly specialized fund that buys into companies in a specific line of business. The primary advantage of such variety is that you are not locked into one type of investment. That is important when you are putting money aside for a retirement that is possibly decades away.

The discount brokerage firm of Charles Schwab & Co. has a special deal. With your IRA money, it lets you buy, sell and switch among more than 270 no-load and low-load mutual funds as well as stocks, bonds, options and government securities. The brokerage fee is about $35 for a $2,000 IRA transaction.

When you buy a so-called load mutual fund, you pay a commission — as much as 8½% — most of which goes to the salesman or broker who sells it to you. But you can save a lot by investing instead in a no-load fund family. In that case you will generally pay only an annual charge of $5 to $10 and a management fee, normally ½% to 1½% of the value of your account. You buy directly from the fund group instead of from a broker. There is no evidence that either load or no-load funds outperform the other.

You can use an IRA's tax advantage to the fullest if you invest the entire $2,000 at the beginning of each year. But you also can arrange to have your bank automatically deduct an agreed-upon amount from your checking account — say, $25 or more a month — and send it to the fund group. And if your employer offers an IRA program, you can have your IRA investment deducted from your paycheck.

What kind of mutual fund you invest in should depend on your age, income, temperament and your view of how the economy will fare in the future. A young person with many working years ahead can afford to think seriously about taking some risks and putting his or her IRA money into a maximum-capital-gains fund that tends to invest in the shares of relatively new, small companies. But as you near retirement, you cannot afford such gambles. So at some point in your 50s, you should move that nest egg into more conservative growth or income funds, money-market funds or bank certificates of deposit.

How much you decide to invest in various kinds of funds depends partly on how large a portion of your retirement income your IRA will constitute. If you expect to rely only on your IRA fund and Social Security, then be very conservative. On the other hand, if you have a generous pension and other investments, you can take some chances in your IRA.

As an IRA investor, give a lot of thought to the amount of stress you are willing to accept. It does you no good to be in a mutual fund that goes up 300% in a decade if it is so volatile that it loses most of the gain during a down market and scares the wits out of you. For this reason, the ordinary IRA investor might feel more comfortable with a fund that aims at long-term growth rather than maximum capital gains. (For more, see "Your Investments/Mutual Funds: Switching Among the Funds.")

Bank and S&L Plans

I F WHAT you want is a worry-free and very nearly decision-free Individual Retirement Account, then you may be wise to open your IRA at a bank, a savings and loan association or a credit union that is federally insured. An IRA account at any of these institutions has several advantages. You deal face-to-face with your banker; the fees are modest to nonexistent; you can get started by depositing as little as $25 at some institutions; and the federal government insures your balances up to $100,000. When your account gets near the insurance limit, just open *another* IRA at a different savings institution.

But there is a reason why not everybody is beating a path to his or her local banker. If you need to withdraw your money for some emergency, you may have to forfeit at least three months' interest on bank certificates of more than a year, and one month's interest on those of a year or less. However, if you are 59½ or older, most banks will waive this penalty when you cash in certificates of deposit on your IRA. (For more, see "Your IRAs: A Break at Banks for Older Savers.")

The closest equivalent to a bank or credit union is a money-market fund. Money funds are considered quite safe, although they are not federally insured. You can get almost the same interest rates as the funds pay and federal insurance up to $100,000 by putting your cash into a bank or savings and loan money-market deposit account.

Banks and S&Ls also offer two types of longer-term IRA savings certificates:

First, there are fixed-rate certificates. They guarantee you both preservation of capital and predictable returns. This they do by locking you — and the bank — into the same interest rate for anywhere from three months to 10 years. The shorter a CD's life, the lower the rate. You would want a short-term CD if you believe interest rates will rise in the future; then you fairly soon could cash in your CD and buy a new one that pays the higher rate. But if you think that interest rates will decline in the future, you would want a certificate with a fairly long-term fixed rate. That way you would continue to enjoy today's relatively high real rates.

Then there are variable-rate certificates. The initial yield is a percentage point or so lower than on fixed certificates, but the yield moves up or down every few weeks, in line with interest rates in general. Consequently, you would choose variable certificates if you think rates will rise.

Stock brokerage firms also sell — or, rather, resell — CDs that they have bought from a bank or savings and loan association. Most brokerages sell them without charging a commission, and the interest rates they pay you are often higher than at banking institutions. That's because brokers can scour the market for the steepest returns.

Because of deregulation, the interest rates that banks and S&Ls pay on IRA accounts vary widely from plan to plan, from bank to bank, and from state to state. Rates are often highest in fast-growing states, where bankers are eager to get your money and then lend it out. So be sure to shop around. The only accurate way to compare is to ask for the compounded annual yield, also known as the effective annual yield. Trouble is, bankers are likely to quote you the so-called nominal interest rate, which does not reflect the differences in the way the interest is compounded. To repeat: Always ask for the effective annual yield; and do not open an IRA in a bank or S&L that will not tell you what it is.

When shopping for CDs, be wary of advertising hype. A "bonus of 2%," for example, may turn out to be exactly what it says it is — a premium of only 2% of the base rate, not a bonus of two percentage points above the base rate. Another lure is the split-rate CD. It pays an extraordinarily high rate for a millisecond or two before reverting to a rate that may be lower than prevailing ones.

A Break at Banks for Older Savers

You may be in line for some profitable privileges at your bank if you are at least 59½ years old and have an Individual Retirement Account. The government already allows people in this age group to withdraw money from their IRAs without paying the usual 10% tax penalty. And now most banks will let you cash in any certificates of deposit in your IRA before they mature, without imposing their own usual penalty of three months' worth of lost interest.

That means you could buy, say, a 2½-year CD paying 8%. If interest rates fell, you would continue to collect that relatively high yield. But if rates went up, you could cash in your CD with no penalty and buy another at the steeper rate.

The reason for this no-penalty policy is keen competition for your IRA dollars. Because it is so easy for older investors to take their IRA money and run, banks are offering them special incentives with the hope that these depositors will keep their cash in the same institution.

Insurance Company Annuity Plans

Your friendly insurance agent probably will be calling you soon — if he has not already — to tell you all about his company's annuity plans for your Individual Retirement Account. It might be wise to listen.

An IRA annuity that you take out with an insurance company is a contract promising to pay you income for a specified time, usually from the day you retire for the rest of your life. Insurance companies offer you two kinds of IRA annuities.

First, there are fixed plans. They guarantee to pay you back all the money you put into them, plus either a variable or fixed rate of interest.

Second, many insurance companies are offering variable annuities. The value of the money you put in fluctuates along with the ups and downs of the stock market. So, you get a crack at capital gains, which you don't get in a fixed annuity. Of course, you can also suffer capital losses if the market goes down. Some of these variable plans allow you to move your money at will from one type of investment to another, typically into a stock investment fund, a bond fund or a money-market fund.

On fixed annuities, some insurance companies have been guaranteeing relatively high effective one-year yields, after management fees. But watch out: a number of insurance companies announce a guaranteed rate on your *new* IRA contribution each year, but say nothing about the rate that they will pay on your deposits and reinvested earnings from previous years. So make sure you ask the insurance agent which rate he is quoting: the new money rate or the so-called portfolio rate, which applies to your recent contributions *and* all the money in your account.

The disadvantages to annuity plans are the high sales charges you will face if you want to withdraw more than 10% of your funds during the first few years. These charges come on top of the IRS penalties for early withdrawal. And yearly management fees on variable annuities can run high. But annuities offer you the largest choice of payout plans once you do retire, and most insurance companies have a good record for safety in managing pension money. (For more, see "Your Retirement/Annuities: Savings with a Tax Shelter.")

Bond Plans

IT IS easy to see why bonds have proved most seductive to IRA investors. They offer steady, fixed rates of return. Plus, if you hold a bond until it matures, you are almost guaranteed to get back every penny you put in.

Bonds are issued by corporations, by the federal government and by state and local authorities. But for your IRA, you should consider only bonds issued by Uncle Sam or by companies. That is because interest on municipal bonds is tax-free. So if you spend your IRA money on a muni, you would be paying for tax breaks you cannot use.

Unless you are willing to take chances with your money, you are best off picking bonds rated A or BBB or higher by the major bond-rating services. There is little risk that the borrowers will not be able to pay back your interest and principal.

The safest bonds, bar none, are issued by the U.S. Treasury and other federal agencies. If Uncle Sam gets into a pinch on his debts, he simply raises taxes, prints new dollars or issues new securities. But safety has its price. Treasury bonds usually yield a percentage point or two less than do corporate bonds with comparable maturities.

You generally buy corporate bonds and government agency certificates from brokerage firms. Banks and brokers sell Treasury securities. Be sure to shop around for the lowest commissions.

Real Estate Plans

REAL ESTATE can play an important role in your IRA. True, it may not be the very top investment for your Individual Retirement Account this year. The value of real estate in 1988 is generally expected to rise no more than 5% or so. But eventually nearly everyone should have some real estate investments in his or her tax-saving IRA. That's because tangible assets such as land and buildings provide a good hedge. If inflation rises again, they will tend to jump in value, while such paper investments as stocks and bonds usually slump.

The best way to get real property into your IRA is to buy shares in real estate investment trusts, commonly known as REITs. Their shares are publicly traded, just like stocks, and you can buy them from brokers. REITs invest in such projects as apartment complexes, office buildings and shopping centers. Some REITs also make mortgage loans.

By law, REITs must distribute at least 95% of their taxable income to their shareholders. So, shareholders can collect high regular payments if the trust performs well. In mid-1988, yields ranged from 5% to 13% for so-called equity REITs — the kind that invest in property. And yields were 9% to 13% for REITs that exclusively make loans.

Equity REITs are usually best for IRA investors, despite their somewhat lower yields. The reason is that they are the ones that will grow in value if inflation kicks up.

Before you buy, study the annual financial statements of several equity REITs and look for those that actively try to improve their properties. Shares in such REITs are more likely to outperform inflation. For safety, lean toward REITs that have bought their properties outright with all cash. That means they will not be saddled with tough-to-meet mortgage payments in hard times. It is wise to stay away from REITs that own mainly urban office buildings. Such properties have been overbuilt in many areas, especially in the South and Southwest.

Your Own Company Plans

EMPLOYERS often have automatic payroll-deduction programs that enable you to contribute regularly to an IRA. If your company does not offer such a plan, you can arrange for your bank to deduct a fixed amount from your checking account every payday. Either way, you will be automatically saving — and possibly sheltering from taxes — up to $38.46 a week to reach the IRA maximum of $2,000 a year.

While payroll-deduction plans are convenient, they do cost you a little money. If you spread your contributions over a year instead of investing the whole $2,000 in January, you will be investing as late as December money that could have been earning tax-deferred income 11 months earlier.

Some employers let you invest your IRA money in company retirement programs. Others will allow you to decide whether to put it in mutual funds, bank certificates or annuities.

A better choice than an IRA for many people would be an ordinary company thrift or savings plan. Employees typically invest up to 6% of their pay in a mutual fund through automatic payroll deductions. Then the company matches some of that investment. Most plans offer a 50% match — if you contribute $3,000, say, the company adds $1,500. Immediately, then, your investment earns a 50% return.

A consulting firm that has compared company thrift plans and IRAs discovered that an employee who can't afford to put money in both of them will earn more, after taxes, with a company savings plan. That assumes that both investments pay the same rate of interest and that the company matches at least 25% of the employee's contribution.

Of course, if you can afford to invest in an IRA *and* a company savings plan, by all means do so. Both enable you to make more of your money — often *much* more.

Self-directed Plans

SOME 40 million taxpayers have Individual Retirement Accounts, but only a quarter of them actively manage their money. The rest just hand their IRA money over to banks or other financial institutions. But if you just tried, perhaps you could make your IRA grow faster than the big boys can. Particularly if you read the financial press and take the time to study investment markets, you should consider opening a self-directed IRA, for it will give you a nice variety of investment choices.

Of course, you can buy stocks for your IRA, selecting either shares that pay high, dependable dividends or growth stocks that offer the chance for fat profits — along with, alas, the risk of big losses. You also can fill your account with mutual funds, ordinary bonds, zero-coupon bonds, bond trusts, Ginnie Mae unit trusts, commodity funds, promissory notes, certain kinds of options and income-producing limited partnerships. About the only things you cannot do through a self-directed IRA are buy stocks on margin, borrow to buy any other investment or invest in life insurance or such tangible items as gold, silver, Oriental rugs or diamonds. U.S. Treasury gold and silver coins came off the forbidden list beginning in 1987.

You can open your self-directed IRA at almost any brokerage house. It usually costs at least $25 to start such an account. Besides that, you will have to pay commissions on any trading you do. For example, they will run to $70 or so on a $2,000 transaction with a full-service broker. So if you plan on heavy trading, consider a discount broker who will trim a few dollars off relatively small transactions — and as much as 75% off the posted commission rate on trades of $10,000 or more. But some discounters limit their business to stocks and bonds. If you want to invest in, say, limited partnerships or commodities, you may have to go to a full-service broker.

When weighing whether to open a self-directed account, consider how aggressive you want to be with your investments. If a conservative strategy appeals to you, one of the best ways to invest IRA money is in ultra-safe corporate or government bonds. AA-rated long-term industrial bonds in mid-1988 were paying 9.7% interest, and corporate bond unit trusts very nearly that much.

But there is another way to look at IRA funds, especially if you are in your 20s or early 30s. Over the long run, conservative investments such as bonds and bank certificates of deposit probably will not grow nearly as much as stocks in up-and-coming industries. If so, you stand to earn higher profits from such shares, even after taxes.

Consequently, an investor who will not be needing cash for 30 or 40 years most likely would do better to invest in a diversified portfolio of the shares of high-technology and other innovative companies than to tie up money in fixed-interest securities. Indeed, almost anyone who feels optimistic about the future of the stock market should keep at least some IRA money in growth-oriented stocks or mutual funds that invest in them.

Comparing the Fees

DEPENDING on where you invest your IRA money, you can pay practically nothing in start-up fees and annual maintenance — or quite a lot. Generally, banks and savings and loan associations have the lowest fees — from nothing to only a few dollars a month. The banks often sell you a certificate of deposit for your IRA. If you decide to transfer your money to another kind of investment, there is only a modest charge, providing you do not switch out of your CD before it matures. At most banks, if you cash in your IRA certificate early, you will forfeit at least three months' interest.

No-load mutual funds also charge minimal fees, usually $10 a year. These funds are the kind that you buy directly from the mutual-fund company rather than from brokers. But if you choose a so-called load mutual fund, the kind that is sold through brokers and some financial planners, add a fat 8½% sales commission.

You can set up your own self-directed IRA at a brokerage house. Both full-service and discount brokers commonly charge $25 to start one, plus $25 a year or more to maintain it. But there are exceptions; discount brokers Rose & Co. and Charles Schwab & Co. allow you to open an IRA for no charge. Both have branches across the country. Wherever you open your account, you will have to pay commissions on all of your stock trades for the IRA.

Annuities that you buy from insurance companies tend to have the heaviest fees. If you put $2,000 into an annuity plan, and then withdraw it in less than a year to switch to another form of IRA investment, the experience could cost you as much as $176.

Most institutions subtract your fees from your account. But if you do not want to drain assets from your IRA — and if you want the maximum tax deductions it offers — you can arrange to make separate payments of your fees. Then, on your income tax return you can itemize them under "miscellaneous" and Uncle Sam may share the cost with you.

How to Switch Your Account

MANY people who have put their IRA money in a bank, a brokerage firm or a mutual fund figure that they have to keep it there until they retire, many years from now. But that's really not so. You can move your Individual Retirement Account from one financial institution to another — but it takes some doing.

Say you have your IRA invested in stocks but you figure that the stock market is in for a tumble. What to do? Simply switch your account out of stocks and into a bank account or some other place that pays a safe, fixed rate of interest.

You just tell your broker to sell the stocks. Then you can take all the proceeds yourself and deposit them in a bank IRA. This is called a rollover.

Similarly, if you already have your IRA money in a bank but figure the stock market will go up, you can switch your money into stocks or mutual funds. This also is a rollover. Usually, you can make only one rollover a year. If, however, you have three or more separate IRAs in your name, you can make one rollover annually from each of the accounts.

To make a rollover, you can write for withdrawal instructions or go in person to the institution that now holds your IRA and just take out the funds. Then you deliver them to your new custodian.

One big caution: Be sure that you transfer all the money to your new account within 60 days of withdrawing it from your old account. Otherwise, it no longer will be treated as a tax-exempt IRA, and you will have to pay a tax penalty to boot.

You can avoid this problem by making a so-called direct transfer. Just ask the institution to which you want to transfer your IRA money to have it sent directly from the institution that is now holding it. For example, if you have your IRA invested in a mutual fund, you can ask the fund to transfer it to a bank or vice versa. This way, you can move your IRA as often as you wish.

But you will face some hassle. You will probably have to write a letter to your old company and get your signature guaranteed. And then you will have to fill out more forms at the new firm, and be prepared to wait. If you feel the switch is taking too long, then protest — loudly and often. And be sure to have your new company prod the old one.

Although major banks whisk millions around the globe in seconds, they typically require 30 days' prior notice for IRA transfers. Why do they take so long? Chiefly because many financial institutions are inundated by more accounts than they can efficiently handle. Also, moving an IRA from one place to another requires a costly load of paperwork.

So don't be overly hasty to transfer. You may have to pay brokers or mutual funds a switchover fee of $5 to $50. Switch only if you have a genuine grievance or feel you can earn a lot more elsewhere.

Rolling Them Over

YOU can save a bundle of taxes on the lump sum of cash or stock that you collect from your company savings or profit-sharing fund when you leave the firm. You do that by putting much of the proceeds immediately into a tax-deferring Individual Retirement Account. This transaction is called an IRA rollover.

You thus postpone paying taxes on your earnings from these company plans, and on your employer's contributions, until you start withdrawing the money from the IRA. If you then expect to be in a lower tax bracket, it is probably wise to make this IRA rollover.

But be careful: The taxman won't allow you to roll over any contributions that you made to the company plan, since these are not subject to income tax when you leave the company. However, if your employer made any contributions for you, you are liable for income tax on them — unless you roll the money over into an IRA within 60 days of receiving it.

You do not have to roll over all the money; you can choose to put only part of it into an IRA and pocket the rest immediately. But if you roll over less than half the money, then you will not be eligible for favorable forward tax-averaging treatment on the rest of it. In brief, if you pocket half or more of the money, you may be subject to fairly stiff taxes on it.

Some Better Alternatives

ALTHOUGH Individual Retirement Accounts are a worthy way of saving money and reducing your taxes, they are not the only way. You might do better not only with a company savings plan but also with a nonprofit-group annuity, a salary-reduction plan or a Keogh plan.

To repeat: if your company has a savings plan, chances are you will be able to accumulate more money, after taxes, by contributing to it than by opening an IRA.

Another nice shelter is the nonprofit-group annuity. It can be bought by teachers, hospital nurses, social workers and other employees of nonprofit organizations. If you work for an eligible group, you can tell your employer to put as much as 20% of your pay into an untaxed annuity or some other investment. You get all the advantages of an IRA but usually can shelter more than $2,000 of your salary per year. There is no tax penalty for withdrawals.

Some companies are going the tax-sheltered annuities one better by offering their employees a so-called salary-reduction plan. Again, a portion of your salary is withheld — untaxed — and the money is invested in an annuity, in the company's stock or in some type of mutual fund. (See "Your Taxes: 401(k) Plans.")

If you are self-employed, you can have both a Keogh plan and an IRA, so you need to decide which to contribute to if you cannot afford both. The Keogh wins hands down because you can shelter much more income in it than in an IRA.

Your Family

Wedding Costs: The New, Sensible Sharing

Nowadays couples are back to marrying, or remarrying, in old-fashioned ways, even if they have been living together for years. This return to basics, alas, makes a considerable dent in the family's finances.

Traditional weddings, with white satin gowns and three-tiered wedding cakes, are in style again, but it is expensive to let them eat cake. The cost for food, drink and dancing — along with flowers, invitations, clothing and church or synagogue fees — comes to an average of $10,000. It is easy to spend much more than that — perhaps $15,000. One-third to one-half is spent at the reception. The dinner or buffet ranges from $20 to $50 a person; add 50% for kosher catering. If you want an open bar, figure on another $3 to $10 per guest, plus up to $30 for each bottle of champagne. So it is not hard to spend close to $100 a guest.

Sensible planning can reduce the bill. Some couples getting married on the same day agree to share the cost of flowers at the scene of the ceremony. Others save a few hundred dollars by skipping such reception giveaways as printed matches and napkins. Friends can contribute their photographic or musical talents, or even their cake-baking and flower-growing abilities. Traditionally, members of the wedding paid for their own dresses and tuxedo rentals. Now some couples and their families sensibly handle these bills instead of giving their attendants expensive gifts of jewelry as keepsakes of the wedding.

It used to be that the wedding bills were paid by the father of the bride, but that old etiquette is giving way to the new economics. Today, families of the bride and the groom commonly split the costs. Often the expenses are divided four ways — among both sets of parents and the bride and groom.

Splitting the costs seems natural to many of today's career-minded brides. After all, their parents paid for educations that were intended to prepare their daughters to pay their own way — or at least a good part of it. So parents of the bride can take heart: you may be losing a daughter, but at least you are not obliged to pay the whole bill.

Even pre-wedding festivities are more practical. Gone are the days of a group of women giggling over a sexy negligee at a bridal shower. Today friends often give "couples showers." Guests are expected to bring gifts that both members of the pair can use, like gardening tools. Couples who start out willing to share gardening chores can probably count on sharing many years together.

It is no longer considered crass to give cash. Authorities on etiquette say that the preferred gift of many of today's young brides and grooms is money. A check is also the gift of choice for more mature newlyweds who already have fully stocked households. At some ethnic weddings, custom dictates that you give cash to the bride or groom at the reception. Or you can mail your check to the couple's home within a week after the ceremony.

Many wedding guests base the size of their gifts on the elaborateness of the reception. One reliable guide is your estimate of the per-person cost of the party. For example, a sitdown dinner with dancing might call for $50 or $100. But if you are a distant friend or a college classmate who has recently graduated, it would not be gauche to give the bride and groom less.

Prenuptial Agreements

FOR many modern couples who plan on marriage, only one deeply intimate, often embarrassing subject remains taboo: money. It seems indelicate, if not downright greedy, to ask "What's your net worth?" before saying "I do." Nevertheless, more and more engaged people are overriding their inhibitions and writing prenuptial contracts. These specify who owns what property and what should become of it in various contingencies.

Almost all couples should prepare and sign a prenuptial contract. You will create a happier union if you spell out in advance just who owns what — and which financial obligations each partner has to the other. Such an agreement is particularly important in cases where the bride as well as the groom has a career, with her own income, assets and obligations, or if one partner has children from an earlier marriage and wants to protect their inheritances. Love may be lovelier the second time around, but marriage finances are messier. If one mate-to-be is studying for a profession, a contract can help you pin down how much the other partner's working contributes to his or her future earnings. Finally, an agreement can clarify who owns what property and how pooled assets would be split if the marriage dissolves. A doctor or accountant, for example, may stipulate that his spouse accept a lump-sum settlement instead of a share in his practice or business.

Courts in most states now recognize a contract that tries to head off a battle in the event the marriage breaks up. Such agreements can save hundreds of hours of fact-finding and testimony and thousands of dollars in legal and other fees. More important, a prenuptial agreement can help you set the financial ground rules for a fair and lasting marriage and resolve ahead of time any mismatched expectations over money.

You can work out the details of your prenuptial agreement on your own, of course. Each partner should have his or her own lawyer review the contract, however, because judges often suspect that without an attorney to protect the interest of each side, one party may too easily sway the other. But not many prenuptial pacts have had to be tested in court. Happily, the people who have them tend to stay married.

What Finances to Settle Before Marriage

WHETHER or not you sign a prenuptial agreement, you and your mate-to-be should thoroughly discuss the subject of money before you step up to the altar. Take inventory of your separate assets and liabilities. Decide what property you want to keep in your own name and what you want to merge. For example, most financial advisers suggest that you keep separate as well as joint bank accounts.

Be sure to familiarize yourself with the law. Each state has its own laws governing marital and separate property and stipulating what happens if the two are mingled. One tip: If you want to put property in your spouse's name, avoid the federal gift tax by transferring ownership *after* the marriage. The marital gift tax deduction is unlimited.

You and your intended should discuss the advantages and disadvantages of joint ownership. An accountant or financial adviser can explain the nuances. For example, in one form of joint ownership, the title specifies that if one of you dies, the property goes automatically to the spouse. In another form, however, each of you owns half of the property, and you can leave your share to whomever you wish, such as a child from an earlier marriage. If a married couple takes title to a house as *tenants in common,* then either partner can leave his or her share of the house to whomever he or she names in his or her will. (For more, see "Your Family: The Perils of Holding Your Assets in Joint Name.")

Be certain to update your will. If you die without a will, your spouse generally receives only one-third to one-half of your separate property. The rest is distributed among other relatives.

Consolidate or coordinate your medical insurance. If you both have group plans where you work and you are paying part of the premiums, you may be able to save money by dropping one plan and having the other cover you as a family. Or you may be able to keep both policies, naming each other as dependents, and get more of your medical costs covered. And do not forget the obvious: Be sure to change the name of your beneficiary on your life insurance, pension, profit sharing and annuity.

One of the best approaches for divvying up household bills when both spouses hold paying jobs is to have three bank accounts — his, hers and theirs. The common pot might go for food, maintenance of the house or apartment, recreation and joint savings. Then, each partner's individual account could be used to pay for his or her share of the rent or mortgage. And how should a working couple divide up their joint income tax bill? Well, if one spouse earns, say, 60% of the couple's total income, then he or she should pay 60% of the taxes.

What Every Spouse Should Know

IN finance, as in love, it is what spouses do not tell each other that hurts. Talking to your mate about what you own and what you owe seems such a simple thing to do. Yet many people are reluctant to do it. Some husbands still assume their wives do not understand finances or are not interested in them. And some married partners do not trust each other. But keeping your mate in ignorance can be dangerous to your wealth.

A sensible time to review your assets is when you are writing your will — and *both* spouses should have wills. Use the occasion to make or update lists of all the valuable possessions you own separately or in common. Include all real estate, bank and brokerage accounts, cars and boats, precious stones, works of art and life insurance policies. Keep the separate lists of your assets in the same secure place you keep your wills.

You should know the names and addresses of the financial professionals in your mate's life. This includes any stockbroker, accountant, personal banker, attorney and financial planner. You also should learn the details of your spouse's job benefits and work history, such as whether you have survivor's rights to his or her pension. If your mate held a previous job long enough to earn a pension, you could be eligible for additional retirement funds.

Military service often endows survivors with financial rights in the event of a spouse's death. If your husband or wife was in the armed forces, you might be eligible for G.I. life insurance, a pension, burial expenses, even a VA mortgage loan. To apply for these benefits, you will need the veteran's discharge papers.

That is one reason why couples should exchange written lists of documents and where they are kept, including military discharge papers. Also birth certificates, marriage license, wills and insurance policies.

Rent *two* safe-deposit boxes and put in your own box the papers you will need if your spouse dies. Banks in some states will seal the box of the deceased upon notification of death, and you may have to wait weeks or months for a court to grant permission to open that box. Also leave copies of all necessary documents with a lawyer, an adult child or some other trusted third party.

The Perils of Holding Your Assets in Joint Name

A T some point in your life you will almost certainly want — or need — to own an asset jointly with your spouse or with your parents, siblings or friends. But before you make that very important decision, you should know a few things about the complex laws of ownership. Sometimes, even for the happiest of married couples, joint ownership is not so smart.

True enough, joint ownership can simplify estate planning and the eventual disposition of your wealth. On your death, your share of jointly held real estate, stocks or other property usually passes *automatically* to your surviving co-owner. That means it bypasses probate — the often lengthy and expensive process by which a will is proved valid in court.

Yet joint ownership can lead to feuds among co-owners and heirs and daunting tax bills. For example, a childless couple may think they can do without wills because they hold all of their property jointly. Not so. If the husband dies, everything passes to his wife without complication. But if the wife then dies later without a will, every cent would go to her relatives under state laws known as laws of intestacy. The husband's relatives would be left with no legacy at all.

You can avoid such problems by writing a will that describes how you want the assets disposed. Trouble is, you would not avoid probate this way.

But you can sidestep probate if you set up what is called a *revocable living trust.* For several hundred dollars an attorney will draw up the trust. In it, you agree to transfer ownership of your assets, while you are still alive, to a trustee. That person then manages the property on behalf of the people whom you name as beneficiaries. You can retain control of the assets in the trust, and, if you name yourself as a beneficiary, even receive income from them.

You can have the trust written so that, after your death, its assets go automatically to your heirs. Or the assets can remain in the trust, with the income from them going to your beneficiaries. Either way, the assets avoid probate.

Joint ownership is also dangerous for individuals who own highly appreciated assets — such as a house that has jumped substantially in value — or whose estate is worth more than $600,000 this year. They would be vulnerable to heavy income or estate taxes.

Take a couple who bought a house for $50,000 in 1970 and held it jointly until the husband's death. At that time, let's say the house was worth $200,000. Half of the house's value would pass automatically to the wife, leaving her with both her husband's $100,000 share plus her own equal share. If she then sells the house for $200,000, the IRS would tax her on a $75,000 capital gain on her share. But she could have avoided the tax if her husband *alone* had held title to the house and had passed it to her in his will. The reason: Married couples can leave estates of any size to each other tax-free. Because she inherited a house worth $200,000, she would not have any taxable gain if she sells it at that price.

Of course, many spouses object to putting the house in one partner's name. They fear that their mate might divorce them and keep the house. Contrary to popular belief, however, you usually cannot keep goods out of your spouse's reach simply by registering them in your own name. Judges just will not stand for it.

Despite the tangles that can occur, there are times when joint ownership does makes sense. You might elect to own property jointly if you want to shift income to a family member in a lower tax bracket. If, say, a mother and her young child owned stock together, the child's share of the earnings might be lightly taxed — if it was taxed at all. That is because the child presumably would have little or no other taxable income. The new tax law makes this harder to do because investment income over $1,000 is now taxed at the parent's rate if the child is under age 14.

Joint ownership also can help you shield assets from creditors. And it can have psychic rewards for a mate who feels happy just holding half of the family's riches. But remember: While joint ownership can give you or your spouse a warm feeling, it can give you or your heirs the chills when it comes time to settle up with the almighty IRS.

Protecting Your POSSLQ

OVER 2 million American couples fit the Census Bureau description of POSSLQ. That stands for Persons of the Opposite Sex Sharing Living Quarters. They have special financial problems, which they can solve by taking some sensible steps.

The facts of unmarried life are that the law is muddy about the financial rights of two people living together without benefit of clergy. Take inheritance, for example. When one member of a *married* couple dies without a will, state laws typically assure that the bulk of the person's property will pass to the surviving spouse. But when an *unmarried* person leaves no will, all of his or her earthly goods can be claimed by the next of kin. Even a loathsome great-aunt thousands of miles away stands before a live-in partner in the inheritance line.

The message is clear: If a person is living with someone to whom he or she would like to will his or her worldly goods, that person had better put his or her intentions in writing. That may sound terribly unromantic. But the harsh fact is that putting your financial intentions in writing is the best way to protect a joint venture of the heart. Written contracts can protect your interest if disputes arise with your partners — or with an ex-spouse or government authorities — over such matters as insurance, inheritance or debts that you have to pay.

Couples with few major assets can get by with the fill-in-the-blanks legal forms usually found in books on living together. If your finances are more complicated, you may need a lawyer's assistance to draw up a financial agreement. If you choose to do it yourself, your agreement at least should be notarized. Contracts between unmarried couples generally are recognized by the courts as long as they violate no laws and both partners enter into them freely.

Unmarried couples should always own things separately. For example, he buys the car, she buys the computer. They should acquire as little as possible together and keep receipts or other records of what each buys. Doing that will prevent bitter battles if and when they split up.

For much the same reason, unmarried couples should not have joint bank accounts or credit cards. In joint charge accounts, each person is 100% responsible for debts incurred by the other, and creditors can seize bank assets that are deposited in either name.

The tidiest way to split household expenses is down the middle. Many POSSLQs simply put their initials on receipts of bills they pay, toss them into a drawer and square accounts once a month. An exception, of course, is if one partner is enrolled full-time in college or is too ill to work. Then the other, working partner pays the bills. But records should be kept and, ultimately, he or she should be paid back — at least in part.

For example, a young woman in Raleigh, North Carolina, returned to college. Her live-in partner underwrote her expenses with a 7% loan. She signed an agreement to repay him, whether or not the two continue living together.

Unmarried partners also should be sure to do the following:

— Buy medical insurance if either partner isn't covered by a group health plan.

— Name your long-term POSSLQ as a beneficiary of your life insurance policy.

— Sign a so-called medical power-of-attorney permitting your POSSLQ to visit you and to make medical decisions if you're seriously ill.

— And, perhaps most important, write a will leaving to your POSSLQ what you think he or she deserves.

Financial Planning When You Are Expecting a Child

MANY young two-career couples do not worry excessively about their financial future. But once they are expecting a baby, they find they have a compelling reason to think ahead. They need investments that will help them build up their net worth as quickly as possible.

If you are expecting your first child, you should open a money-market account at a bank or in a money fund and try to build a cash reserve of at least $5,000. Only after you have this secure cash cushion should you think about investing — because all investment involves some risks.

One of the best ways to start investing is by putting money in a growth mutual fund. It invests in stocks of solid companies that offer better-than-average opportunities to multiply money. If you choose a no-load fund, you will avoid paying a sales commission, which often runs 8½%.

A sensible way to invest in a mutual fund is to put in the same amount every month, whether the market rises or falls. That is known as dollar-cost averaging. Your money buys fewer shares when the market goes up, and more shares when it goes down.

If either the husband or wife works for a company that has a stock purchase plan or a savings plan, you would do well to contribute part of your salary. This forces you to put money away and can spare you some taxes. It is a particularly smart way to invest if the company matches part or all of your contribution, which most do.

If both partners work, each should consider putting the maximum of $2,000 a year into an Individual Retirement Account. Even if you cannot deduct your contribution, an IRA is still one of the best ways to invest for the long term. Remember: *All* your earnings grow tax-free.

You might wisely invest your IRA in a mutual-fund family. Many companies that offer a variety of different mutual funds let you move your money readily from one fund to another to take advantage of swings in the stock and bond markets.

Be sure to review your insurance — preferably before your baby is born. Your total disability coverage, including that from Social Security, should replace about 60% of your income. Both spouses also should buy enough life insurance so that the survivor could invest the proceeds and live off the interest. Assuming that the money can earn a 10% yield, that means if you need $30,000 a year, you should take out a policy for $300,000.

If you do not have a will, sit down with a lawyer and have one drawn up. It will cost about $200 for each parent. Make sure you carefully choose a guardian of your child in the unlikely event that both of you die before your heir apparent reaches 18. Most lawyers advise that you choose a brother or sister instead of your aging parents.

The Real Cost of Kids

FOR most married people in the baby-boom generation, having children is not just a fact of life but a matter of choice. Often they are postponing children because they worry that kids cost too much. What is the real cost of raising children?

Bringing up baby is more expensive today than at any other time in history. That is partly because the luxuries of a generation ago are considered middle-class birthrights today. The U.S. Department of Agriculture concludes that raising a child to age 18 costs anywhere from $45,000 to $139,000. But the Urban Institute in Washington, D.C., is more generous than your kid's Uncle Sam. In its latest survey the institute calculates parents would spend $150,000 in the first 18 years. If parents are in a higher income bracket, those costs can go as high as $232,000.

If Mom stays home until Junior toddles off to kindergarten, her lost income from a job could amount to another $100,000 or more. And that dollar cost may be compounded by atrophying skills and evaporating seniority.

Knowing when the expenses of childhood rise and fall can help you prepare for them. Newborns come into the world at considerable cost. Routine hospital and delivery fees run about $2,800 in a metropolitan area, and an untroubled cesarean birth adds some $1,650. But from age one to five or six, the costs of child-rearing are relatively low. This is the time parents should put away cash in deep-discount bonds, zero-coupon bonds, U.S. savings bonds and other investments to pay for the expenses that start moving up as soon as the child goes off to school and really climb with the teenage years.

Puberty is pricey, due in part to dating and all its accoutrements. The annual insurance premium on your car can more than double with a 16-year-old son at the wheel. At 18, child-rearing costs are three times higher than the costs in the birth year. Welcome to the groves of academe and the most expensive years in a child's life.

If you have — or plan to have — children, you can prepare now for those predictable costs ahead. Start by checking what your health insurance covers. A good maternity package in a group policy will pay two-thirds of the hospital and physician's fees for the birth of a child. Later on, most policies do not cover the routine examinations of a healthy baby. So, unless you belong to a health maintenance organization, you will have to budget at least $275 for those monthly visits to the pediatrician during a baby's first year.

Where to Adopt a Child

I F YOU are childless — and not by choice — you have many new options in adoptions. Today almost anybody can adopt a child, but it may be a rather special one.

Only a decade ago public and private adoption agencies had many more healthy American-born babies than they do now. The reason, of course, is the wide availability of birth control devices and abortion. Also, unmarried mothers are more willing to keep their children. You can get a directory of agencies that place healthy American-born children by writing to the National Committee for Adoption, 1930 17th Street, NW, Washington, D.C. 20039.

Would-be parents are becoming increasingly interested in adopting foreign children and kids whom social workers categorize as "hard to place" or as having "special needs." They include youngsters with physical, mental or emotional handicaps, as well as nonwhite children, older children of all races, and brothers and sisters whom adoption agencies do not want to split up. Special-needs youngsters account for nearly all the children now available for adoption in the U.S.

Agencies are finding it easier than ever to place them, often with people who formerly did not qualify as adoptive parents. Single, handicapped and low-income people — even couples in their 50s and 60s — are now allowed to adopt.

About two-thirds of all parents adopt through agencies; the rest get children through doctors or lawyers. Public adoption agencies, operated by state and local governments, generally do not charge fees. Private agencies, commonly sponsored by religious and charitable groups, charge an average of $7,700, which often includes lawyer's fees. If it doesn't, you will usually have to pay $1,000 to an attorney for preparing adoption papers.

The fees are often reduced or waived for parents who adopt hard-to-place children. Almost all states also have subsidy programs for parents who adopt such youngsters. Moreover, parents who adopted these children in 1986 could deduct up to $1,500 of their expenses. Beginning in 1987, tax reform replaced the deduction with a government subsidy to cover part of the adoption costs.

A small but growing number of corporations are granting maternity leaves and other benefits to employees who adopt children. For example, Procter & Gamble gives unpaid leaves plus up to $2,000 for adoption-related expenses. Time Inc. gives up to one year unpaid leave plus a onetime cash payment of $2,100. So, if you are an adoptive parent or are considering becoming one, check to see if your company will provide any benefits.

Your city or state department of social services can give you a list of licensed adoption agencies in your area. For help in finding special-needs children in states beyond your own, write to the National Adoption Center (1218 Chestnut Street, Philadelphia, Pennsylvania 19107; 215-925-0200).

If you want to adopt a healthy child fairly fast, you can seek help from American agencies that specialize in foreign adoptions. The wait is usually no more than 18 months. Most of the children come from Asian countries, especially the Philippines and South Korea, and many also come from Latin America. Babies available for adoption in Western Europe are as scarce as in the United States.

Adopting a foreign child usually costs between $4,000 and $8,000, and the investment is not without risk. There have been more than a few recent cases of fraud. In some instances, children have been illegally smuggled out of their native countries. And in 1983, 31 Americans lost about $2,500 each when a Chilean attorney fled his country without honoring his promise to locate babies for them. If a private foreign adoption goes awry, you will have small chance of recouping any money you handed over in advance.

So, it is best to work only through well-established organizations. You can find many of their names and addresses in *The Report on Foreign Adoption*, a book that costs $15 and is available from the International Concerns Committee for Children (911 Cypress Drive, Boulder, Colorado 80303). For a list of lawyers, social-services agencies and orphanages in Central and South America, you may write to the Latin America Parents Association (P.O. Box 72, Seaford, New York 11783). A group called Holt International Children's Services (P.O. Box 2880, Eugene, Oregon; 503-687-2202) can direct you to agencies specializing in children from South Korea, India, Thailand, the Philippines and Latin America.

You might also get the government's booklet on foreign adoption, called *The Immigration of Adopted and Prospective Adoptive Children.* It is available from the Superintendent of Documents, U.S. Government Printing Office, Washington, D.C. 20402-9325, and costs $1.75. The booklet is especially good in outlining the red tape involved in a foreign adoption. For example, you must get a U.S. visa for the child, naturalization papers and a final decree of adoption.

Another way to avoid waiting years to adopt a child is through private placement — that is, adoption without an agency's help. People who use independent placement find the birth mother on their own and take the baby straight home from the hospital. Many consult relatives, friends, clergymen, teachers, social workers, lawyers and doctors — any person who might help locate a pregnant woman who chooses not to keep her child. This way, you can bypass the demands and restrictions that adoption agencies may impose on your age, religion, and marital status *and even* the adoptive mother's employment. Sometimes agencies also demand proof of infertility. Independent adoption is often faster than using an adoption agency, which might take four years or longer. The cost of an independent adoption is anywhere from $3,000 to $20,000.

Independent adoption does have drawbacks. It is not permitted in Delaware, Michigan, Minnesota and North Dakota. Even where it is allowed, you must find a pregnant woman willing to give up her child and then, typically, pay her medical and legal expenses. There is always the chance that the mother will change her mind and try to reclaim her child in the courts.

To find out more, write or phone the adoption office of your state's department of social services. You also can get in touch with local adoption groups by contacting the National Adoption Center in Philadelphia and an organization called RESOLVE (5 Water Street, Arlington, Massachusetts 02174).

Finding Reliable Day Care

MORE than half of all mothers with children under the age of six are working outside their homes. Many have trouble finding decent care for their kids. Full-time nannies are too expensive; they can cost $250 to $350 a week. Baby-sitters are cheaper but not always reliable. Increasingly, parents conclude that the best solution is to put their children in a day-care center.

Many new day-care centers have opened in recent years, but the number still has not kept up with demand. Shortages are especially critical in metropolitan areas such as Boston, Denver, Los Angeles, Minneapolis and New York, particularly for children under age two. Day-care centers just cannot find and hire enough capable staff members at fees that are within most parents' reach.

About half of the 63,000 licensed day-care centers in the U.S. are run by churches and other nonprofit organizations. Private operators make up the rest. They range from small independent centers to larger chains. More than 300 corporations now sponsor child-care centers for their employees. And about 3,500 companies provide child-care help in some form.

The employee does not have to pay any income taxes or Social Security taxes on such reimbursements up to a maximum deduction of $5,000. And the employer can deduct them as regular business expenses. The company can pay employees directly for child-care costs until their children reach 16. Care for disabled dependents of any age also can be covered. Since it costs less for a company to pass out child-care subsidies than to build and run a day-care center, many firms may be inclined to adopt them. If you are a working parent looking for help with child-care costs, you might ask your personnel office to consider sharing your payments.

Revelations of child abuse at some day-care centers are appalling, but it would be a sad mistake to write off *all* such centers. Many of them offer quality, convenience and affordable prices. Happily, reported incidences of child neglect or abuse are quite rare. Still, providers of group care vary widely.

People who operate small group care centers in their own homes usually are not subject to — or do not bother with — state licenses. But larger centers, which look after 50 to 200 kids, are almost all licensed. State licenses help ensure that the centers meet minimum standards for health, fire safety and staffing.

The other advantages of large day-care centers over the small, home-based ones are greater flexibility of hours and broader curriculums. The larger chain operations and other commercial day-care centers typically have more modern facilities than do nonprofit providers, which are sponsored by churches, universities, cooperatives and companies as a service to employees. But the nonprofit operations often allocate a higher percentage of their budgets to attract better teachers and reduce staff turnover — which can be a problem at some chains that pay minimum wages.

The cost of group care depends largely on a child's age and on the size and experience of the staff. Monthly fees for children under age five average about $300, but monthly fees of $400 to $600 are not unusual. Uncle Sam helps to defray day-care expenses with a tax credit for working couples and single parents. Depending on your income, the credit may be worth as much as $720 for one dependent and $1,440 for two or more.

Selecting a good center is not child's play, but your task will be easier if you ask a few important questions of fellow parents and of the professionals who provide child care.

Question one: How large are the classes? Big groups tend to be too confusing for babies and toddlers. The maximum number of babies under two years should be eight per group. Toddlers aged two to three should not be placed in groups larger than twelve.

Question two: What is the ratio of staff to children? There should be at least one adult for every three or four babies — or for every six toddlers.

Question three: Can you meet with the teachers easily and often? Most centers encourage parents to drop by anytime for a visit. Be wary of those that do not. And formal conferences to evaluate your child's progress should be scheduled at least twice a year.

Question four: Is there a wide variety of toys designed for your child's age group? Infants like colorful mobiles, mirrors and plastic boxes. With preschoolers, look for musical instruments, games and costumes.

Question five: Are teachers conscientious about sanitary conditions? Kids under age three in day-care centers are more likely to contract gastrointestinal ailments than those who stay at home.

Question six: Have arrangements been made for medical emergencies? A nurse or doctor should be available nearby, ready for a call. Parents should be informed promptly when there are outbreaks of illnesses such as chicken pox or measles.

Once you have settled on a day-care center, keep monitoring it for changes in its programs or personnel. But your best indicator of quality may be your child's enthusiasm. If your son or daughter hates to leave the center at the end of the day, chances are you made the right choice.

Parents often assume that all branches of a day-care chain meet uniform standards of quality, but this is not always the case. The difference between sound and sloppy centers is determined mainly by the quality of the local director and staff.

Sometimes parents overstress the importance of teaching academic skills in a day-care center. In fact, teaching everyday living skills to children may be more important than drilling them in the alphabet and numbers. But the main point is this: Before placing a child in any center, parents must check it out thoroughly, by visiting it and by speaking both with staff members and with parents of other children who attend.

Is Early Training Worth the Price?

TODAY'S young parents want their kids to be such super-achievers that many of them spend large sums of money on lessons and activities designed to give their children an edge in life. Sometimes these well-meaning parents go too far.

This year more than 2.5 million youngsters will enter nurseries and preschools. For example, in Atlanta at the Suzuki Learning Center, children as young as three years old learn to play the violin in all-day classes costing $5,100 annually. Other toddlers of the same age are taught reading and math, and take lessons in gymnastics. Even babies barely able to hold up their heads do 45-minute exercise workouts.

Only in recent years have parents adopted the idea that kids can start improving themselves so young. Never mind that no conclusive evidence exists that the relentless application of learning skills early on ensures better performance in school or in life later. Parents are still willing to pay handsomely on the promise that it might. And the prices *are* steep. At Suzuki, lessons that teach children to play the violin or piano cost $10 a half hour. Computer classes for young children average about $20 an hour. So do Suzuki-type lessons that teach children to play musical instruments. Cooking classes and language classes for toddlers cost around $13 an hour. For between $8 and $10 an hour you can send your child off to learn karate, dance, swimming, art and early reading.

But eager parents should be wary. Benjamin Spock, the venerable pediatrician, warns parents that pushing kids ahead too soon could do more harm than good, by creating unnecessary anxiety and stress. Furthermore, Professor David Elkind, author of the books *The Hurried Child* and *Miseducation: Preschoolers at Risk,* believes that formal training in reading and mathematics should be saved until a child is at least five and a half or six. Anything earlier than that, he warns, is too tough for kids.

Setting Your Child's Allowance

WITH ice-cream cones often costing $1 and more, children are being pinched by high prices, just like Mom and Pop. So they are getting jobs a lot younger, doing their own comparison shopping for toys and clothes, and turning to a price-fighting tactic as time-honored as the tooth fairy. Kids are clamoring for increases in their allowances.

What principles should parents follow when giving an allowance?

Experts in child-rearing suggest that children should start getting allowances early, along with some basic lessons in cash management. Even preschoolers can figure out that a quarter is worth more than a dime.

The amount of the allowance should grow along with the child and his spending needs. According to a 1981 survey of 600 young people by *Money* magazine, children seven and under typically received 25 cents to 75 cents a week; eight- and nine-year-olds collected $1 to $2.50; 10- to 13-year-olds, $1.50 to $5. Those figures have more than doubled since 1981.

A youngster's spending money should be large enough to cover fixed expenses — school lunches and bus fares, for example — and still leave something to save or spend as he or she chooses. If he or she blows it all, parents only hurt the child by giving more, except in very special cases. A child must be taught to manage well and live within his or her income.

Child psychologists also warn parents to beware of inadvertently causing children to confuse money with less tangible family gifts, such as love and attention. Sometimes divorced parents pay their kids hefty allowances to compensate for their absence — and that does the youngster no good at all.

But children can profit from a special clothing allowance as soon as they are old enough to spend large sums wisely, usually by age 12 or 13. How much to give? One guideline is what the government figures a middle-income family spends to clothe a child — about $40 a month for a 14-year-old, $50 for a 17-year-old.

The recent inflation-age psychology of many adults — buy now, save later — seems to have permeated children's minds, too. By many measures, teenagers are saving less than they ever did. So, to encourage thrift, many parents open bank accounts for their kids. Wise parents also believe that just as kids must be taught to save, they must learn to give to charity. As a small child, David Rockefeller, retired chairman of Chase Manhattan Bank, was required by his father to save 10% of his $1 a month allowance for charity. His childhood financial training served him well.

Teaching Your Child to Invest

D o you have a child who is curious about the stock market? With your encouragement, your budding T. Boone Pickens can learn the ABCs of investing and perhaps earn a little pocket money.

Some children fare quite well managing their own investments. Take Trevor Nelson, the teenage son of a Merrill Lynch stockbroker in Washington, D.C. Trevor has been an avid stock-picker since 1982, when he was 11 years old. Among his winners was Coleco, which he bought at $14.25. After a stock split that turned his four shares into eight, Trevor sold at $44.50.

Like Trevor, most kids who are keen on the stock market get their inspiration from investment-minded parents. To interest your children in the market, it is best that they invest real money — yours or theirs. Investing is not child's play. And it is hard to capture a kid's imagination with hypothetical stock picks.

Investing can be fun when kids buy into companies they know, such as fast-food chains or computer makers. You also can tap your youngsters' enthusiasm by suggesting that they follow and select stocks of highly visible firms in your hometown.

Of course, investing real money means real money may be lost. One of Trevor Nelson's pals, Byron Schulze, now 18, was excited about the stock market until he lost all but $10 of his $180 investment in Pizza Time Theaters. The company went bankrupt in 1984, and Byron now keeps his money in a bank account.

Despite such risks, children are usually best off investing in individual stocks rather than a mutual fund. Funds offer diversification and professional management. But they are not necessarily well suited to teaching your youngsters about the market. With stock, children are introduced to the idea of owning a piece of a company. This concept will become increasingly important to them as they grow older. You, however, will have to buy, sell and register the stock in your name as the child's custodian. Under state laws, a minor legally can own securities — but not trade them by himself or herself.

How to Choose a Legal Guardian

CHANCES are your minor children will never need a guardian, but you should make provisions for their future in case anything happens to you and your spouse. Most people put off the grim chore of selecting someone to look after their children if they become orphans. Yet if you should die and there is no one ready to assume responsibility for them, the surrogate's court or the probate court will appoint a guardian. Often it is a relative. The judge will not be able to consult your wishes since you won't be around to express them.

The way to avoid this is to name a guardian in your will. There are two kinds of guardianships: first, guardianship of the person; and second, guardianship of the property or the estate.

A guardian of the person handles the children's day-to-day upbringing, while a guardian of the property manages whatever money you have left for the kids. A guardian of the property must submit an annual accounting to the court of how he is managing the assets and often must request permission to make various expenditures on behalf of the kids.

Although this system protects the children's interests, the guardian gets tangled in red tape. He also must post a bond to protect the estate in case he absconds with the money. A bond on a $250,000 estate would run about $1,000 a year, and the estate foots the bills, somewhat diminishing what you leave for your children.

To avoid these complications and expenses, lawyers recommend that, unless your estate is unusually large, you nominate only a guardian of the person and pass any assets along to your kids in a trust. The trust document, which should be drawn up by a lawyer, should spell out how you want the money spent — on schooling, clothes, music lessons and so forth. A trustee then can write checks up to limits set by the trust without having to ask the court for approval. Ideally, the guardian should be a trustee, perhaps along with a bank officer.

The hard part about selecting a guardian is picking the right person. Choose someone who is about your age and, preferably, related to you. If you are not close to your relatives, pick a person who would bring up your children the way you would. Make sure you ask the people you have in mind whether they would be willing to take on the responsibility of guardianship. Discuss with the guardians the financial arrangements you have made for the children and how you want them brought up.

A guardian named in the will is under no legal obligation to accept the responsibility and can refuse it. If he does, the court will have to find another person, who may not be someone you would choose. For that reason, attorneys recommend that you also name a back-up guardian in your will.

Children, too, have the right to know who their guardian is going to be. So consult at least your older children before you make a decision.

Every few years, or whenever personal or financial circumstances change, review the guardianship provisions in your will. The brother you have named may have been divorced or your best friend may now run a head shop in Malibu. If you think you should name a new guardian, tell the current one and draft a new will.

If someone asks *you* to be a guardian, think hard about whether you should accept. Find out what the parents expect of you and whether the children are to live with you. Ask how the parents want the children educated and if there are any restrictive conditions, such as a statement in the will that the children cannot be moved out of the country. Inquire about money. You should be told what funds are available for the kids' day-to-day upkeep and to carry out any special wishes, such as sending Junior to Harvard.

Ask the lawyers who drew up the will to explain your obligations and rights. And, if you have children of your own, find out how they would feel about having other children in the household.

Discussing Finances
with Your Aging Parents

IF YOUR parents are approaching or beyond retirement age, there are certain sensitive subjects that you should broach now to help ensure their well-being. Raising matters of money and mortality with them requires delicacy. But it is crucial that you have an understanding of your parents' financial affairs in the event you are called on to manage them.

Start by asking your parents to make a list of their assets and liabilities. They should note whether these assets are held in joint tenancy, tenancy in common or in one person's name. Then an accountant or a lawyer who is expert on tax matters should evaluate whether their forms of ownership are the most advantageous ones for estate purposes. If your parents refuse to discuss their finances, suggest that they draw up the list in private and keep it in a sealed envelope or a locked box at home. Make sure you know where it is.

Next, you should determine whether your parents' income is sufficient to meet their retirement needs. For example, do they have low-interest-bearing passbook savings accounts and World War II–vintage savings bonds that could be cashed in and used to buy bank CDs paying more? Their house also could be a source of income even while they live in it. Ways to unlock this equity include so-called reverse mortgages, sale leasebacks, charity life agreements and home equity credit lines.

If your parents are 65 or older, they qualify for Medicare. But they also need supplementary health insurance that pays the deductibles and the percentage of doctor and hospital bills not reimbursed by Medicare. Discourage your parents from piling on one policy after another. They cannot be reimbursed more than once for the same bill.

Most nursing-home costs are not covered by Medicare or private health insurance. But your parents may be eligible for two government programs designed to supplement income and cover the medical costs of the needy. They are Supplemental Security Income and Medicaid. To qualify for this aid, a married couple cannot own more than $2,550 in real and personal property exclusive of the family home, auto and a specified amount of life insurance.

Do *both* of your aging parents know how to handle financial matters? Often in marriages one person manages the money. If that spouse dies first, the survivor may be at a loss to assume the task. While both parents are alive, you might suggest that the partner who is unaccustomed to balancing the checkbook take over the bill paying one month a year. Both your parents should know where important papers are kept.

Senility, illness or accident could leave one or both of your parents unable to manage. If no provisions have been made, a court will appoint a guardian or conservator — even if one partner is still competent. So each of your parents should have a durable power-of-attorney agreement. This is an inexpensive way to ensure that people whom your folks trust will manage their affairs when they cannot. Your parents give this power of attorney to each other — and also name a successor, either you or one of your brothers or sisters.

Also ask your parents how they feel about life-prolonging hospital procedures. To protect against extraordinary measures to keep your parents alive, the power-of-attorney agreement must give you charge over the person's health care.

If your parents' wills are older than the 1981 tax law, or if your folks moved to another state since their wills were written, these documents probably should be reviewed. A lawyer can update the wills to take into account such changes in estate tax law as the increased marital deduction.

Finally, you should know where your folks keep their important papers. The best place is in their attorney's office. They and the executor of their estates should have copies as well. Your parents should keep these papers in triplicate — with one copy in a safe-deposit box, one in a fireproof box at their home and another at one of their children's homes.

When a Parent Needs Your Money

As people live longer, more and more grown children will be called upon in the future to give financial help to their aging parents. But how much support should you provide, and how can you do it without making grave sacrifices yourself?

A wrenching dilemma arises when the financial needs of the older generation conflict with those of the young generation. Nobody has developed a formula for resolving it. Even clergymen provide varying responses.

Rabbi Stanley Schachter, former vice-chancellor of the Jewish Theological Seminary of America, says: "Children have an obligation to maintain their parents at a level of their *highest* dignity, ideally in the manner to which they are accustomed."

John Rhea, a Presbyterian minister who is an expert on the subject, has another view: "The top priority for an adult child is not to make the parents happy but to make them comfortable, to make sure their *basic* needs are met."

And Monsignor Charles Fahey, a former chairman of the Federal Council on Aging, says: "There is a strong responsibility to care for and love your parents, but that does not necessarily equate with economic support. Your primary responsibility is to your *own* children."

These different outlooks mean that each individual has to decide for himself or herself. Still, you *can* get guidance from a trained social worker or other professional. A hospital, nursing home or senior-citizen center can refer you to such a counselor.

Most people want to take care of their parents, and they do an admirable job of it. In 80% of cases, any help the elderly require comes from family members.

Helping to support an aging parent need not mean the end of your dream of educating your own children or retiring comfortably or leading a reasonably good life. What you need is to give in ways that cut the burden on you by sharing it with Uncle Sam.

The key is to transfer assets from you to your parents *temporarily*. Then have your folks invest the money in *their* names, so that any dividends, interest or capital gains are taxed at *their* rate, which is presumably lower than *your* rate. In fact, a couple 65 or older filing jointly pays no federal tax if their taxable income in 1988 is $10,100 or less. An individual 65 or over is exempt on sums of $5,700 or less.

Finally, you can buy your parents' house and rent it back to them, a move that may entitle you to some tax deductions for property taxes, mortgage interest and depreciation. (For more, see "Your Investments/Real Estate: Renting to Your Parents or Children.")

Giving direct financial aid is not the only way to help your aging parents. A whole new network of sources has sprung up to provide care and support for the aged. To find out what is available locally, consult your city or state department of aging, listed in most phone books. Also try Family Service America, a nonprofit group representing 280 agencies. It will direct you to its local agency. Write to Family Service America at 11700 West Lake Park Drive, Milwaukee, Wisconsin 53224.

How and Where to Get
Good Care for Aging Relatives

JUST about everyone has heard an aged parent or grandparent plead: "Whatever you do, don't send me to a nursing home." Take heart. You have newer and better choices than the old nursing home.

Health care at home can solve the financial and emotional problems that bedevil ailing elderly people and their families. Services available to the elderly in their own homes are expanding rapidly, and so is the number of government, charitable and for-profit agencies that provide such care.

Limited services by a registered nurse normally are 100% reimbursable by Medicare if related to a hospital stay. Medicare also pays for the services of a home health aide, though only in conjunction with skilled nursing care. But even if an old person doesn't require skilled nursing, some private health insurance policies will pay for personal care and homemaking services. One way to determine whether the agency providing home care is a good one is to find out whether it is certified by Medicare. About 5,800 agencies are.

To find one of these services, get in touch with either your state's local office for the aging or your community's family-service bureau or a religious organization. You might also call a neighborhood senior-citizen center; its employees can guide you to programs for old people.

For a nationwide listing of accredited services that provide care for the elderly in their own homes, write to the National HomeCaring Council at P.O. Box 20508, New York, New York 10017. Another source is the National League for Nursing, 10 Columbus Circle, New York, New York 10019. You can receive a publication called *How to Choose a Home Care Agency* by sending a stamped, self-addressed envelope to the National Association for Home Care, 519 C Street, NE, Washington, D.C. 20002.

In-home services for the aged are improving as they expand. Growing numbers of home health-care workers now help more old people to live on their own. Also, special geriatric day-care centers enable old people to spend many hours there but sleep in their own homes. Through a New York State program called Nursing Homes Without Walls, old people eligible for placement in skilled nursing or health-related facilities now can live at home without having to fend for themselves. In Florida, one similar state-sponsored program, Community Care for the Elderly, has been so successful that it recently was helping over 35,000 old people stay out of institutions. These elderly people could have meals delivered to their homes, get assistance for personal care and homemaking or get transportation to needed medical services.

Many localities have set up agencies that find and match elderly roommates, something like a computer dating service. Also, there are agencies that make intergenerational match-ups between, say, a pensioner and a young couple who like the idea of having an extended family. Some state and private agencies pay the younger family for their care.

If you want to avoid a nursing home, you also should check into apartment buildings designed specifically for the elderly. Some are in so-called continuous-care communities and look like college campuses. They offer a variety of living choices: apartment house for people who are fit enough to live alone as well as an intermediate-care facility for those who need some medical attention and yet another facility that offers around-the-clock skilled care. Continuous care can be ideal for the elderly person who is independent but realizes that the day of infirmity inevitably will come.

Still, nursing homes may be the only choice for some families with elderly relatives. In general, those homes have improved significantly since the mid-1970s. The best tend to be nonprofit institutions sponsored by religious, union or fraternal organizations. At the finest homes, the byword is rehabilitation, regardless of the patient's age.

You can get names of such nursing homes in your area by asking your doctor or hospital social worker. Also, you can inquire at a senior-citizen center and your state chapter of both the American Health Care Association and the American Association of Homes for the Aging.

You should visit any homes you are considering at least twice —

once on an official tour and once as a surprise, if possible. Supervisors of a well-run home will welcome you and your questions. Make sure the residents seem content, clean and neat. Taste the food. To get free fact sheets on choosing a nursing home and finding financial aid, send stamped, self-addressed envelopes to the American Health Care Association, 1200 15th Street, NW, Washington, D.C. 20005, and the American Association of Homes for the Aging, Suite 400, 1129 20th Street, NW, Washington, D.C. 20036.

Inescapably, nursing homes are expensive: from $1,200 a month to $3,000, depending on the locality and the kind of accommodations. Medicare covers only part of the costs, and then only for 100 days. Private health insurance rarely pays for nursing home care. Medicaid can pay — but Medicaid patients usually must first use up all their own money. That means selling most of their assets to raise cash. Then they must sign over their Social Security benefits, plus all but a small monthly allowance.

Families pondering ways to care for aging relatives should take them into their deliberations from the start and should bear in mind their emotional as well as physical needs. If they know they have choices, they will be happier. And preventing depression and loneliness in the elderly goes a long way toward preventing physical decline.

The New Economics of Divorce

MARRIAGES may be made in heaven, but more and more divorces are being negotiated in accountants' offices. Because of a revolution in property settlements, splitting up a marriage is becoming much like the dissolution of a business partnership. Alimony is going out, a concept called "equitable distribution" is in, and court decrees are so unpredictable — and so expensive to obtain — that couples should go to extreme lengths to avoid trial.

Instead of fighting bitterly over who did what to whom, smart couples now are more likely to concentrate on tallying all the dollars and cents that were acquired during their life together so that they can be split equitably. State legislatures and courts across the country are acknowledging that both parties put effort into a marriage, so both are entitled to their fair share of the assets if they divorce. Both the spouse who pays the bills and the partner who works as a homemaker or who earns less are credited with their contributions.

Since 1970, most states have adopted new concepts of what marital property is and how it should be split. The new theory is that any property accumulated during a marriage should be divided not only fairly but also *finally* so that each partner can move on to the next stage of life, unencumbered by leftover financial ties. This is based on the two modern realities that many marriages do not last and that women are increasingly able to support themselves.

A decade ago, women could not count on receiving any assets that had not been held in their own names. Recently, though, more and more women have been getting at least half of the marital assets, even in the 41 states without community property laws on the books.

Now most states hold that all assets earned during a marriage, no matter by whom or in whose name they have been held, go into a common pot to be divided in whatever way a judge decides is fair. The only exceptions are anything that a spouse owned before marriage or received as an inheritance or a gift during the marriage. Such property continues to belong to him or her.

At the same time, though, women are getting less alimony. Just 15% of divorced wives receive these payments, and short-term alimony is becoming more common than long-term. In sum, courts no longer are burdening a husband with an ex-wife's maintenance until she remarries — if ever — and with an obligation to support the children until they are grown. It is expected that most women will work for pay and support themselves. So alimony usually is awarded just long enough for them to re-enter the work force or train for a better job. And support of children is considered the responsibility of *both* parents.

What are really on the rise are lump-sum, one-shot settlements. They are based on an analysis of the couple's financial assets. Figuring out the size of those assets, and just which partner is entitled to what, can mean lengthy litigation and high legal fees. Property judgments by a court are unpredictable at best, and sometimes downright unfair. If the couple cannot decide for themselves who gets what, the judge will. But these decisions are only as equitable and intelligent as the judge himself or herself.

Divorce is becoming so prevalent that more and more couples make an inventory of their assets every several years, just in case. They evaluate what they own, from cars and carpets to stocks and bonds. Then each partner outlines his or her individual contributions to this joint balance sheet, including the value of the wife's services if she is at home caring for children. Such written tabulations can save hours of high-priced legal time and help ensure a fairer division of property if a couple ever separates.

Because of the radical changes in the economics of divorce, anyone thinking about dissolving a marriage is well advised to do some serious financial planning first. Divorce lawyers now orchestrate elaborate financial settlements, and they often call in help from property appraisers, accountants, tax specialists and the like. The cost of divorce can easily run $5,000 for a middle-class couple with children, a house and other assets — and that is when they settle *out* of court. If they insist on going to trial, the fee can double or triple.

Couples facing a divorce can reduce cost and pain by using a professional mediator to help determine who gets what. Mediation is being offered by a growing number of specially trained lawyers, psychologists, social workers and marriage counselors. They have saved thousands of dollars in legal fees for many, many couples. Private mediators charge $70 to $150 an hour — and uncomplicated divorce settlements can be worked out in 12 hours or less. Or, put another way, for $1,800 — or much less.

The mediator asks each spouse about his or her assets and debts and meets with the couple together to help them resolve basic issues. But do not expect a mediator to replace an attorney. Most mediators recommend that their clients hire lawyers as soon as negotiation begins. That is because once the issues of the divorce have been worked out through mediation, any actual separation agreement must be drafted by a lawyer and reviewed by lawyers for both husband and wife.

How to locate a trained divorce mediator? The Academy of Family Mediators (P.O. Box 4686, Greenwich, Connecticut 06830) requires members to meet certain standards, and can provide names of those in your area. Or try the American Arbitration Association, listed in the Yellow Pages under "Mediation Services." It has offices in 33 cities and, for a $100 fee, will recommend a mediator who meets its professional standards. For a free pamphlet titled *Family Mediation Rules*, write to its headquarters at 140 West 51st Street, New York, New York 10020-1203.

Undoubtedly, the best divorce settlements come about when both partners are able to put aside personal squabbles and concentrate on what might be called enlightened self-interest. In such cases they accept the fact that neither will come out ahead but that both will be able to make a clean break and to start anew. Just remember: A peaceful divorce settlement is almost always better than a trial, because it is much cheaper.

The Tax Consequences of Divorce

I F YOU are estranged from your spouse, you may take comfort in the new federal laws affecting the tax consequences of broken marriages.

The Tax Reform Act of 1984 makes it much simpler for a divorcing couple to divvy up ownership of their property, such as houses and stocks. In the past, if a man transferred a house to his ex-wife upon their divorce, he would owe capital-gains taxes on any estimated appreciation in the property's value. Under the new rules, though, the man owes nothing. In fact, neither the man nor his ex-wife owes any taxes until the house is sold — perhaps many years from now. But when the ex-wife eventually sells the home, she will be liable for taxes on any rise in its value since its original purchase by the husband, although there are two ways she can avoid or defer paying Uncle Sam. First, if she is over 55, she can take advantage of a once-in-a-lifetime exclusion of up to $125,000 in capital gains on a primary residence. Or, she can purchase another home of equal or greater cost within two years of the sale, allowing her to save her exclusion for the future. Unfortunately, these special provisions do not apply to other property that one spouse transfers to another in a split-up, such as stocks. The ex-wife must still pay capital-gains taxes on these assets when she sells them.

Say a man owns a house that he bought for $100,000 but now is worth $150,000. Say, too, that he gets a divorce and puts the house in his ex-wife's name. Under the old rules, he would have to pay capital-gains tax on its estimated appreciation — that is, on $50,000. But according to the new law, he owes nothing. On the other hand, his ex-wife stands to end up owing more taxes than she would have before. If and when she sells the house, she now will have to pay tax on all its appreciation since her ex-husband first bought it.

The new law also changes the tax treatment of alimony. The basic rule remains this: If you receive alimony, the IRS considers it just like any other income, and you have to pay taxes on it. Similarly, if you pay alimony to an ex-spouse, the IRS considers it an expense, and you can deduct it from your taxable income.

Before 1985, you could count as alimony — and deduct — any money you gave your ex-spouse except for quite specific child-support payments. But the federal Tax Reform Act of 1984 changed that. It says that alimony in most cases is what goes clearly to the ex-spouse alone. The tighter new rules affect divorce or separation agreements signed on or after January 1, 1985. If yours became effective before that, then the old, more liberal rules probably still apply.

Here is how the new rules work: say you pay $1,500 a month to your ex-spouse, and she uses $500 of it for the children. You can deduct only $1,000 a month from your taxable income, but you cannot deduct the $500 that is spent for the children. This money is considered child support, and you have to pay taxes on it. There are some instances, however, when money that benefits *both* the ex-spouse and children can be considered alimony.

Among the other changes in the law, a nonworking spouse who receives alimony now can shelter as much as $2,000 of it annually in an Individual Retirement Account. Until 1985, only $1,125 a year in alimony could go into an IRA.

It is also easier to claim a share of your former spouse's pension. You now can start collecting as soon as your former mate reaches early-retirement age, normally 55. Or you can demand your share in a lump sum if the company pension plan allows it. You can postpone taxes on the lump sum by rolling it over into an IRA.

And deadbeats who miss child-support payments are in big trouble. In 1984 Congress called upon the states and territories to write child-support guidelines and set up get-tough collection programs by 1987. By mid-1988, all had adopted strict child-support enforcement methods, providing for withholding of wages, diversion of state tax refunds and placement of liens. In those states, frequently delinquent parents may be required to post a bond and could have their poor payment history reported to credit agencies. Furthermore, if a parent fails to pay the specified support, any federal, as well as state, tax refunds that he or she is entitled to could be diverted to help provide for the child.

Your Spending

How to Get Bargains

I F YOU plan your shopping carefully, you can buy the best of nearly everything at the top stores in the country for 15% to as much as 75% off the original prices. Everyone knows that department stores, specialty stores and manufacturers have sales from time to time. But the smartest shoppers track the sales systematically to learn in advance just which products and services will be discounted in just which months.

Seasonal markdowns now are likely to start earlier and last longer than they have in many years. The traditional white sale of household linens, for instance, often winds on for nearly two months. That is partly to justify the escalating cost of the accompanying catalogues and partly to counter competition from discount chains. Stores are under heavy pressure to turn over their merchandise quickly because high real interest rates make it costly to carry it on the shelves. Retailers estimate that only 20% to 25% of the total sales of high-fashion clothes in department stores are made at the original retail prices.

If you want to cash in on bargains, make a calendar of sales in your area. Very often stores have sales at the same time, year after year. For example, fall is a good season to check for promotional sales of brand-name china, glassware and silver. Storewide clearances of all kinds of merchandise regularly occur after Christmas, Easter and Independence Day. In department stores, men's clothing sales begin after Christmas and in late June, and last four weeks. Similarly, men's specialty stores schedule sales quite predictably — just after Christmas and Father's Day.

The most expensive brands of perfume, skin cream and cosmetics rarely go on sale in department and specialty stores. But promotional sales — for example giving away a travel pouch with the purchase of a bottle of perfume — are common before Mother's Day and Father's Day, at Christmas and in the spring, when cosmetics houses introduce new products and colors.

One cautionary note: Do not assume everything in a sale has been marked down for clearance. Even fancy stores stock special sale merchandise of inferior quality. And most stores have a stern policy of no refunds, no credits, no exchanges and no free alterations on sale items. If that blue silk tie has a greenish cast and the navy suit you hoped it would match runs to purplish, well, maybe you can give the tie to Uncle John for Christmas.

The New Discounts

A NEW breed of off-price stores is burgeoning across the country, making it easier to find bargains on clothing, housewares, furniture and electronic goods. Unlike old-style discount houses, the new off-price stores do not carry cheaply made merchandise but top-quality goods. You often can find items for 40% to 60% below regular retail prices. However, off-price outlets still tend to offer little personal service, few amenities, limited lines of merchandise and a frenetic atmosphere. To keep overhead down, they are often located on the wrong side of the tracks in low-rent districts. Among some first-rate off-price clothing marts with stores in various parts of the country are Judy Bond Blouses Factory Outlet, Calvin Klein Outlet Store and Burlington Coat Factory Warehouse.

Many traditional department stores are trying to capitalize on the trend by operating off-price outlets of their own. For example, Dayton Hudson, the big Minneapolis retailer, maintains a stable of off-price subsidiaries across the country, including Mervyn's and

Target stores. The May Department Stores Company recently bought Filene's Basement, a chain of 22 discount clothing stores in New England, Pennsylvania, New Jersey and New York. Until July 1988, it owned Loehmann's, which still has off-price outlets that reach customers in New York, Florida, through the Midwest and from Texas to California.

You can find off-price stores listed not only in newspapers but also in a number of national guidebooks. For example, Andrews McMeel publishes *The Third Underground Shopper* by Sue Goldstein; it sells for $8.95. Another is *S.O.S.: Save on Shopping Directory* by Iris Ellis; it is $10.95.

You also can pick up appliances and furniture at big discounts at special warehouses that many major retailers maintain in or near large cities. Prices are low — because items are often discontinued, slightly damaged or overstocked. For example, a Sears catalogue surplus store outside Seattle offered a Kenmore electric oven for $300, which was a $180 saving. And at a Macy's clearance center in San Jose, California, a slightly damaged $4,000 bedroom set sold for half its department-store price. To find such off-price outlets near you, telephone such major chain stores as Sears, J. C. Penney and Macy's.

In addition, many cities now have independent stores called membership warehouse outlets. Their prices are 20% to 40% below those in many regular retail stores. To find them, look in advertisements and the phone book for retailers with words such as "warehouse" and "wholesale club" in their names. Clubs carry thousands of products, including appliances, automotive supplies, clothes, food, furniture, liquor and toys.

Membership is restricted. To qualify, you must either own your own business or belong to or work for a designated organization. Such groups generally include labor unions, credit unions, hospitals, banks, savings and loan associations and local governments. Most customers own a small business and pay a yearly membership fee of about $25. There is usually no membership fee for nonbusiness customers. Most stores allow members to bring along a guest.

The key to success for warehouse outlets is volume. Their gross profit margins are thin — from 8% to 11% compared with 50% or more for department stores and 20% to 35% for discounters. Clubs have a no-nonsense decor. Towering banks of unadorned metal inventory racks rise from concrete floors. Most merchandise remains in the suppliers' cartons; only one sample of each is on display. You commandeer a wide-body shopping cart or a six-wheel dolly and wend your way through carton canyons of goods. At the checkout, you pay with cash or check. Credit cards are not accepted.

You can get further bargains on furniture by buying from discount stores in the big furniture-making state of North Carolina. Quite a few stores there will ship anywhere in the country, and your savings will pay many times over for the freight charges. A leather wing chair that retails nationally at $1,700 costs only $950 from a discounter in Greensboro named Barnes & Blackwelder. You will find comparable furniture deals at other North Carolina retailers. Many of them advertise in home-related magazines and take telephone orders on toll-free numbers. Avoid any dealer who asks for a deposit of more than 50%. Otherwise, you surrender your leverage if your order is long overdue or damaged in transit.

For many types of goods, some top stores and catalogue retailers have taken a tip from the airlines and are offering freebies to frequent buyers. Mark Cross, the leather goods chain, offers $100 gift certificates to anyone who buys $1,000 worth of its merchandise in a year. Really big spenders — those who purchase $10,000 or more — get the next $1,500 on the house. Purchase $3,000 a year on a Neiman-Marcus credit card, and you will qualify for free gift-wrapping for one year, free chocolates and more. The more you charge, the more you get. Run up a tab of $125,000, and Neiman-Marcus will give you a week-long vacation in London, Paris or the Jumby Bay resort in Antigua.

But remember: no matter how much you love an off-price item or how much you stand to save, a bargain is not a bargain under the following circumstances:

— If it does not fit you or the space it is intended for or your life-style. For example, no matter how low their price, those massive, heavily carved end tables will never look right flanking a light, graceful Louis XVI sofa.

— If you have to buy something else at full price to make use of it. A perfect plaid skirt marked down 70% is no buy if most of your blouses are prints.

— If it is not complete. Designer skirts or slacks missing their normal linings, top-notch camera bodies supplied with inferior lenses or furniture missing shelves can be fixed, but adding in the extra costs raises the ante sharply.

As a rule, never buy something just because the price is low. If you did not like it in the store, you will never be happy with it when you get it home.

The Fine Art of Haggling

M ANY shoppers find it hard to look a salesperson in the eye and ask a legitimate question: "Can you give me a break on the price?" The mere mention of the word *haggling* makes Americans tend to cringe or recall some quaint foreign bazaar where matching wits with shopkeepers is an official tourist sport. But bargaining for the best price is also a respectable stateside tradition, especially in individually owned stores and dealerships for big-ticket items such as cars, furniture, jewelry, VCRs and clothes.

The key to successful haggling is comparison-shopping to find out the fair market value of what you want to buy. You will also need an idea of the markup to see how much leeway you have to bargain. The typical markup on a new subcompact car, for example, is around 10%. On appliances, it is about 20% to 27%. Clothing is commonly 50%, while antiques dealers tend to build in a breath-taking 100% profit.

After asking for a break on the price, resist making the first offer yourself. If the price tag is $175, do not leap in with a $125 bid. Let the seller make the first offer. Then you can come in with a still lower one.

Do not make your bids in round numbers. If an item costs, say, $700, it is better to offer $485 than $500. Round numbers beg to be negotiated up by the seller. Odd numbers sound harder and firmer.

And take your time. If the seller quickly gives you a small price reduction, do not succumb to the natural tendency to breathe a sign of relief and accept the offer. When you feign indecision or voice a need to consult with your spouse, the merchant may be only too eager to sweeten the deal for fear of having no deal at all.

Discounts by Mail and Phone

Y OU do not have to live in a big city with a lot of discount houses to get some terrific bargains. Instead, you can consult several publications that list hundreds of discount mail-order items.

The Wholesale-by-Mail Catalog 1988, published by St. Martin's Press for $10.95, lists vendors of such diverse articles as reclaimed motorcycle parts and exotic coffees. The editors name more than 500 companies that trim 30% to 90% off suggested retail prices. For example, if you would like to buy a "reasonably" priced piano, you can write to Altenburg Piano House in Elizabeth, New Jersey, either for literature on its own line of pianos or to get prices at least 35% below list or suggested retail on such well-known lines as Baldwin, Mason and Yamaha.

If you are a gourmet cook and like Mexican food, a catalogue from the Mexican Kitchen/Cocina Mexicana in Brownsville, Texas, will show you how to save as much as 75% of what you would spend in specialty stores for dried chiles, ground chile powders, herbs and spices that are indispensable to authentic Mexican cuisine. You will also find tortilla presses and dried corn husks for tamales.

For savings of up to 50% on famous-label cigars and tobacco, ask Wally Frank in Middle Village, New York, for a 48-page color catalogue showing cigars by Don Diego, Dunhill, Lancer, Martinez, Montecruz, Te-Amo and other firms.

And anyone who needs to replace a lost sock or two can choose from popular brands such as Christian Dior, Bonnie Doon and Burlington, all offered by Socks Galore & More in Franklin, Tennessee.

You also can call thousands of businesses across the U.S. without paying a dime, or a quarter, thanks to toll-free numbers. Now you can let your fingers do the walking to them. AT&T has published a nationwide directory of toll-free 800 numbers for consumers. Many of the firms listed offer discounted merchandise. Just one example: the Albert S. Smyth Co. sells china, crystal and silverware at discounts of 25% or more. You can call it free by using the number in the 800 directory or by calling 800 information (800-555-1212). This toll-free directory costs $9.95, plus tax and shipping. But the call to place an order for it is *free*: dial 800-426-8686.

Smart Buys at Auctions

SHOPPING for artworks, antiques and other collectibles, more and more people are turning up at auctions in search of bargains. You don't have to be a high-roller or a big-time collector to get them. But the growing number of auction buyers has made those bargains harder to come by. Two places where you can still find them are at the charity auction and the old-fashioned country auction.

People who attend auctions held for charity or political fundraising are often more interested in the cause than in the merchandise. As a result, bidding seldom becomes heavy, and you can get some real buys. Similarly, most of the bargain hunters who show up at country auctions of estates are local folks interested in the land, the stock or the machinery on the block. That leaves the field clear for you, the seeker of antiques and other collectibles.

Wherever you go, the rules are fairly simple. All auctions display the merchandise before the bidding begins, so don't bid unless you have inspected an item thoroughly. You can get an idea of what an item will go for by studying the auction catalogue, if there is one. It gives high and low estimates of each item's worth, and bidding usually starts at about 70% of the lower figure.

It's best *not* to bid at the first auction you visit. Newcomers often get caught up in "auction fever" and bid too high. You would be wise to begin by observing the auction process. Visit the pre-auction exhibit, decide how much you would pay for an item, and then see what it actually goes for. Watch who the other bidders are and keep track of the winning prices in the auction catalogue. That way, when you spot something you might want at a future sale, you will have the price history of a similar item for reference. Put that together with some knowledge of regular retail prices, and you will know how far to go in your bidding.

At some auctions you will be given a paddle or a paper plate with a number on it. When the auctioneer calls out the price, just hold up the paddle, the plate or your hand if you want to bid. If you don't like the price, you can holler out something lower. Don't worry that you will wind up owning some larger expensive whatnot because you scratched your nose or tugged your earlobe. That just doesn't happen.

Try to arrive early at an auction. Bidding at the start often is on the low side as the audience and the auctioneer try to get the feel of each other. Before you bid on anything, set a mental limit on what you'll pay. And be careful that you don't bid against yourself. That is a mistake some beginners make. When the auctioneer calls for a higher price, they forget that the last bid was theirs.

Auctions, Government-Style

Y OU can get some exceptional deals when the government auctions off its surplus property. In fact, you can buy just about anything at cut-rate prices, from a bronze statue of a Buddha to a seaside house, a down vest to a private plane.

A government auction probably is going on in *your* area every week. Several thousand auctions are held throughout the country each year by the General Services Administration, the Department of Defense, the Customs and Postal Services and the Internal Revenue Service. The sales raise money for the Treasury and clean out the government's attics. Meanwhile, you can save an average 50% off the retail price, and often much, much more. And the government doesn't charge state or local sales taxes.

Virtually any item the government has ever bought, used or confiscated goes to the auction block. The Pentagon offers more than 400 classes of property, from used guided-missile launchers to guard dogs. The GSA traffics in office and hospital equipment, cars from the government motor pool and even Coast Guard lighthouses. A stream of civilian property that has been abandoned, confiscated or lost goes under the hammer at Postal and IRS auctions.

The quality of the offerings varies radically. Goods at GSA and Department of Defense auctions usually have seen better days. But the property at Postal and IRS auctions is newer.

To find out about sales, write or phone the agency whose auctions you want to attend and ask to be put on the free mailing list. The government can pack your mailbox every day with its sales catalogues and auction notices, so be selective. Some mail-order firms advertise that for $20 they will notify clients of forthcoming sales. But all they do is pass your name along to the appropriate government agency.

Government auctions often pit the amateur against the professional dealer. You can avoid competing with dealers if you look for the odd item in an auction that is dominated by another category. Wholesalers and retailers are not as likely to show up for a few pieces of jewelry or some fishing gear if the sale consists mainly of electronic parts. And if you are willing to travel, you are likely to find better buys because fewer people show up for sales at hard-to-find warehouses and military bases. For the same reason, you should try to attend the auctions that are held on weekdays rather than weekends.

A sparse audience, however, does not mean that the government will part with its property to the lowest bidder. It sets a so-called upset price, below which the property will not be sold. That price is usually at the low end of what the bureaucrats who run the auction figure the property would be worth on the open market. But such people are not always the best judges of value. So you might be as lucky as the sharp-eyed bidder who for $15,000 bought an entire lot of 94 miscellaneous furs at a GSA auction. She kept one of the sables she found in the lot and sold the others for $50,000.

To learn when auctions and sales of government-surplus property will take place, here is where to write:

— General Services Administration. For personal property, primarily manufactured goods, write to the General Services Administration, Federal Surplus Personal Property, in the region nearest to you. The regions are Atlanta (30303); Auburn, Washington (98002); Boston (02222-1076); Chicago (60604); Denver (80225); Fort Worth (76102); Kansas City, Missouri (64114); New York (10278); Philadelphia (19107); San Francisco (94105) and Washington, D.C. (20407). Ask for a copy of *Sale of Federal Surplus Personal Property*, which spells out the rules and procedures. Then ask to be put on the mailing list. Each region has its own.

The GSA also has a monthly catalogue listing all its real estate sales. Write to Consumer Information Center–F, Pueblo, Colorado 81002, and request a free publication called *Sales of Federal Surplus Real Estate*. If you want to be notified of real estate sales in a certain price range and location, write for an application form from the General Services Administration, Centralized Mailing Listing Service–8BRC, Building 41 Denver Federal Center, Denver, Colorado 80225.

— Department of Defense. Write to Bidders Control Office, Defense Reutilization and Marketing Service, Box 1370, Battle Creek, Michigan 49017-3092, for a copy of *How to Buy Surplus Personal Property from the Department of Defense*. It tells how to get on a bidder's list.

— U.S. Postal Service. Postal auctions take place in five cities. For information about the sales nearest you, write to the U.S. Post Office, Dead Parcel Branch, Atlanta (30304-9506); New York (10099-9543); Philadelphia (19104-9597); St. Paul (55101-9514) or San Francisco (94105-9501). Include a self-addressed, stamped envelope.

If you are interested in surplus postal equipment, inquire at a local post office for the address of the nearest Procurement Services office where these sales are held. Postal vehicles, such as the jeeps used by letter carriers, are sold at fixed prices by the vehicle maintenance facilities of local post offices.

— Internal Revenue Service. If the seizure of his property does not lead a recalcitrant taxpayer to pay his back taxes, the IRS auctions it off, although this rarely happens. Write to Chief of Special Procedures, Collection Division, at whichever of 63 IRS district offices is nearest you.

Your Charities

Guides to Sensible Giving

INDIVIDUAL Americans gave almost $77 billion to thousands of charities in 1987. The sum represented 2% of pre-tax income. That's much less than the biblical tithe of 10%, but much more than people in other countries contribute. If you want your donations to have the most effect, you should make a careful analysis before you give. Charity begins with homework.

The typical donor scatters relatively small contributions among a large number of charities. Yet it would make more sense for you to give fewer but bigger amounts. The smaller your gift, the larger the share that will be spent on fund-raising and overhead.

One charity that you might wisely include on your list is the United Way — the well-known coalition of many health and welfare groups in your community. Some critics argue that the United Way supports only established charities such as the Red Cross and the YMCA and excludes newer groups such as minority and women's organizations. If such complaints bother you, just ask your United Way solicitor for a list of the charities that the organization distributed money to last year. If you do not endorse some of those groups, you may be able to make a "negative designation" on your donation card. Groups you mark off will not get any of your contribution. But you are likely to endorse most United Way recipients. So unless you are planning to send separate checks to most of them, donating to the United Way is an efficient method of helping a wide variety of local groups.

Make sure that your contributions to individual charities are tax-deductible. The IRS will allow you to claim gifts to most religious, educational, social welfare and health groups. But several that solicit widely for funds — such as Handgun Control, Incorporated, and the Moral Majority — are classified as lobbying groups. They are tax-exempt themselves, but your donations to them are not tax-deductible. If you are in doubt about any group, just ask the IRS for a copy of a so-called determination letter, which will state whether or not your donations will be taxed.

You can write to any charity and request both an independently audited financial statement and an annual report of the programs that the charity sponsors. If any group fails to respond, you probably will not want to give money to it.

Once you get the data from a charity, a couple of independent watchdog groups can help you interpret them. One is the National Charities Information Bureau, which has thorough reports on hundreds of charities that solicit nationwide. The reports include analyses of balance sheets, income statements and activities.

By mailing a postcard to the National Charities Information Bureau, you can get a copy of its *Wise Giving Guide,* which lists the groups that either meet its standards, fail to meet them or have not responded to its requests for information. In a recent guide, for example, 209 groups — as disparate as the Sierra Legal Defense Club and the Puerto Rican Legal Defense and Education Fund — met the bureau's standards. But 76 charities did not meet them and another 56 groups did not provide adequate information to the bureau. If you request them, the bureau also will send you, free, up to three extensive reports on separate charities. The address is National Charities Information Bureau, 19 Union Square West, New York, New York 10003.

Another watchdog group is the Council of Better Business Bureaus' Philanthropic Advisory Service, or PAS. It scores thousands of national charities on reliability and responsiveness. For $1 and a self-addressed, stamped envelope, the PAS will send you its bimonthly guide to organizations that do or don't meet its standards. Its address is Philanthropic Advisory Service, 1515 Wilson Boulevard, Arlington, Virginia 22209. In addition, the Better Business Bureau in your own city often can give you similar information on local charities.

The Tax Benefits

BEGINNING with your 1987 taxes, you had to itemize your deductions in order to take any write-offs for charity. In the eyes of the tax collector, not all your charitable contributions are created equal. Some will save you more than others.

You can deduct all your donations when you give to organized charities such as churches, educational institutions and tax-exempt hospitals — just so the total does not exceed 50% of your adjusted gross income. You also can deduct all your contributions to veterans' organizations, fraternal associations and certain private foundations, just so they do not exceed 30% of your adjusted gross income. Don't worry, you probably will not top those limits unless you are a really big giver.

But you may be in trouble if you give to a foreign charity. You cannot take any deduction for that.

You can deduct only a limited amount when you stand to benefit from your contribution. For example, when you buy tickets to a theater benefit, you can deduct only the difference between what you actually paid and what you would have paid for the tickets at a regular performance.

Be sure to write down and take advantage of all the tax deductions you are entitled to. You can deduct not only your cash gifts but also the value of property you donate. That includes clothing, magazine subscriptions, stocks or other investments.

If you did volunteer work for a church, a synagogue or some other charitable organization, you can deduct the cost of traveling to meetings, fund-raisers or other events. The IRS permits you to write off 12 cents for every mile you drove to or from such charitable activities, plus parking fees and tolls. Bus, taxi and train fares are also deductible — if you have receipts to verify them. You also can deduct all your out-of-pocket expenses. They include the cost of telephone calls, stationery, stamps and uniforms. But you may not deduct the value of your work for charity.

Cash is almost never the smartest thing to give. If you have a choice between sending a $1,000 check or donating the same amount of stock or property that has appreciated, you will do more good at lower cost by giving the property. That way you will avoid paying the capital-gains taxes that would be due if you sold the property. You will need to plan more carefully if you want to donate tangible personal property, such as an art collection, instead of financial assets, such as stocks or bonds. For one thing, your gift must relate directly to the purpose of the charity in order for you to receive the largest tax benefit.

If you plan to will income-producing securities to charity, you can get the satisfaction of giving while you are still alive without losing any of the income. Just contribute the securities to a charitable remainder trust. Many universities and other charities set up such trusts. The charity agrees not to spend or otherwise use your full gift for an agreed-upon period of years, while you continue to collect the dividends or interest.

Some types of remainder trusts arrange to sell your low-yielding securities and reinvest the money in higher-yielding securities — so you actually collect more than if you had not made the gift. Part of your income from the trust may be sheltered from taxes. And you can increase your tax deduction by arranging to have the remainder trust pay its income to your parent or another person older than yourself. Ask a lawyer or tax accountant for particulars.

For example, a Connecticut widow gave the Nature Conservancy $27,000 worth of stock that had been paying her only 4½% a year in dividends. The Conservancy then sold the stock and reinvested it in a government securities fund that paid over 11%, which the widow then collected. So she more than doubled her income from her securities without paying any capital-gains taxes on the sale of them. Besides all that, she took a big deduction on her income taxes for making the gift.

Remember: It is better to give than to receive, but it is best to do both at once. And one more tip: Exceptionally large gifts by very wealthy people may be subject to the newly toughened alternative minimum tax. If you are one of these fortunate few individuals, be sure to consult an accountant or tax lawyer before making a particularly generous contribution.

How to Raise Money
for Your Favorite Cause

Raising money for your favorite charity takes the persuasiveness of a politician and the tough hide of a door-to-door salesman. Particularly in this time of tight budgets and federal cutbacks, any volunteer fund-raiser needs one other attribute as well: the ingenuity of an inventor to concoct clever ways to get donations.

If you are a volunteer, it will pay you to stage events that go beyond the standard charity ball. People around the country are raising money by sponsoring book fairs, art shows, auctions and much more. Whatever device you choose, it has to be something quite special. You have to have a gimmick.

A very successful one is the "no-dinner dinner." Rather than ask donors to pay hundreds of dollars to dress up and spend yet another Saturday night in a dull hotel ballroom, some charities let their supporters off the hook by telling them: "Just send the check and you can stay home."

When people support a nonprofit group, they usually get a warm feeling and a tax deduction. But it will not hurt your charity's bottom line to offer them something more. One such lure is the chance to purchase what money usually cannot buy. With a little digging you can discover priceless opportunities that can be sold for a price. For example, at a St. Louis Arts Council auction, several music lovers bid for a chance to conduct the St. Louis Symphony in one of its regular evening performances.

If your charity sells donated goods and services, anything from crocheted potholders to dinner with the mayor, the money that is raised generally is not taxed. But before your charity sells anything to the public, it's smart to check with an accountant or a lawyer. You may have to pay taxes on your profits if your enterprise is not *directly* related to the purpose for which your group was granted tax-exempt status.

One other tip: Most charities follow the 50% rule — if you do not earn at least a 50% profit on the revenues from your fund-raising event, you have not done your job efficiently.

A favorite means of achieving that profit — and more — is to hold an auction. The charity gets all the proceeds from the sale of donated items. When gathering goods and services to be auctioned off, ask for donations from as many individuals and businesses as possible — and nothing is too wild. Some auctions have included enough cement to repave a driveway (that was given by a construction firm) and even a gallbladder operation (that was contributed by a civic-minded surgeon). Entertainment and vacation offerings are popular. A couple might contribute the use of their faraway vacation home for a week or two. You might persuade a travel agency to donate air fare to the destination.

Some staples at charity auctions include dinners given by restaurants. But even dinners need not be routine. Volunteers in several charities have persuaded their city mayors or other local celebrities to cook and serve a meal in the home of the highest bidder. It's amazing how often celebrities will help out a worthy charity. Yes, you will have to spend something to stage your fund-raising event, but those headlinable outsiders can help reduce your expenses. Ideally, you should keep costs to about one-third of the amount of the total receipts — by begging and borrowing as much as you can.

Your Services

Appraisers

An appraiser can be a very important person in your financial life. If you are buying insurance to cover your jewelry or silverware, you will probably need an appraiser to certify their value. And you will want to hire an appraiser if you are buying or selling a house — or merely refinancing it. Countless people call themselves appraisers, but finding a knowledgeable and reliable one requires some effort.

To locate a real estate appraiser, ask your banker, lawyer or insurance agent for recommendations. Get the names of several candidates and then call each one. Ask him about his background and fees. Find out if he belongs to one of several appraisal associations. They include the American Institute of Real Estate Appraisers, the Society of Real Estate Appraisers and the National Association of Independent Fee Appraisers. Members tend to be trustworthy and experienced because each of these organizations screens and polices them to some degree. That is important because few states license real estate appraisers.

For personal property appraisers, once again seek advice from your banker, lawyer or insurance agent; museum curators also can suggest names. The two major associations are the American Society of Appraisers and the Appraisers Association of America. For jewelry alone, you might consider a member of the American Gem Society.

Appraisers use two measures to establish the value of your possessions. One is the replacement cost, which is what you would have to pay to replace the item. Usually you insure the property for the replacement cost. Then there is fair market value — it's the price a willing buyer would pay to a willing seller. The fair market value is used for settling an estate, dividing property for a divorce or donating a work of art for a tax deduction.

The fair market value is usually only half the replacement cost. That is because a dealer's markup is often 100%. An appraiser might tell you to insure a Chippendale highboy for $10,000 because it would cost that much to replace one. But if you wanted to sell the highboy, a dealer might pay you only $5,000.

An appraisal must be precise and explicit to back up an insurance or tax-loss claim. For jewelry, it should note size and weight of stones and their settings, as well as clarity, purity and color. Art and antiques should be evaluated for age, condition and any special factors, such as rarity.

What should you pay for an appraisal?

A real estate appraisal will cost you a fee of $200 to $300 or perhaps more. The price depends on the size and condition of your house, and on how long it takes to compare your property with others in your neighborhood.

To assess your jewelry, artwork or furniture, you should hire only an appraiser who charges by the hour or by the job. Most professionals believe that it is unethical to base fees on a percentage of the value of your goods, since there is an obvious temptation to overstate their worth. You also should avoid anyone who offers to appraise your belongings and buy them too. In that case, the appraiser may deliberately underestimate.

The cost of a personal property appraisal depends on how long the job takes, which can be from less than one hour to several days. For simple pieces of jewelry, you may pay $100 to $300 an hour. Even gemologists who are not certified appraisers can charge up to $150 an hour.

When a personal property appraiser comes to your house to evaluate your furniture, silverware and other property for insurance purposes, he will check each item's condition. He may also photograph your valuables. If he does not, then you should take photos yourself, including close-ups of any significant details.

Keep your appraisals current. The prices of jewelry, antiques and other collectibles fluctuate so sharply that you should have your insurance appraisals updated every two years.

298 | *Your Services*

Send one copy of your appraisal to your insurance agent. Hold all other copies and photographs of your belongings in a safe-deposit box or in your lawyer's office or another place that is fireproof and theftproof. One appraiser tells of a client who stored in his dining room sideboard a list of the values and locations of his most prized possessions. A thief found the list and neatly checked off the items as he loaded them aboard his truck. He then scrawled on the list, "thanks for the appraisal." It was just about the only thing he left behind.

Caterers

ENTERTAINING can be draining, but if you are thinking of having a party, you can save time and trouble by holding a catered affair. How do you keep the price within bounds?

It pays to bear in mind that small parties usually cost more per person than large ones with the same menu. A catered meal at home for fewer than 25 people approaches restaurant prices. In New York City, a trendy dinner at home for 12 could run $600, plus an additional $200 for three people to help serve; liquor and wine will be extra. The total easily could be well over $900. So if your group is smaller than a couple dozen, a restaurant might be cheaper.

Still, it is possible to treat yourself to the luxury of a catered affair without paying luxury prices. Avoid large caterers and those that emphasize exotic foods. They can charge $70 a person for food alone. Instead, seek out small caterers or those new to the business. They often give far better service at lower prices. And look for catering firms that will prepare dishes *you* can heat and serve yourself.

Don't rent china, silver or linen. You could pay about $6 to $10 a setting. You are better off borrowing, or even buying, your own.

Another way to pare costs is to get by with less help, particularly those bartenders and waiters who collect $80 to $120 for an evening's work. Instead of the caterer's workers, waitresses or bartenders, enlist some college students or neighborhood teenagers who serve for half as much.

Don't let caterers provide drinks or setups. The markups on them are intoxicating, so buy your own. And if you want music or live entertainment, you can save a lot when you hire talented students from a local college or music conservatory to do the playing.

Cocktail parties, of course, are cheaper than fancy dinners. You also can lower food costs by scheduling your cocktail party for a time when people tend to be less ravenous. Guests may only nibble at the hors d'oeuvres at an open house scheduled from 3 p.m. to 5 p.m., but a reception from 6 p.m. to 8 p.m. substitutes for dinner for many party-goers. Caterers estimate that most guests will down three or four drinks at a two-hour party.

Wedding receptions introduce special expenses. For 100 guests, a wedding cake might add $200 to $1,000. Champagne for a toast could mean at least 20 bottles — or at least $300 for an inexpensive kind.

The Yellow Pages list columns of "caterers." Still, the best way to find one is to ask people who have used caterers in the past. If you work for a company, check with the person there who arranges corporate entertainment. Sometimes officers of churches, temples and fraternal organizations also know the reputations of local firms that cater parties in their halls.

Once you have gathered a few recommendations, call and get a price estimate from each firm. Before you telephone, figure out what you can spend — and what kind of people will be at your party. If you have invited many big drinkers, for example, you can cut back on food. They tend to eat less than those who drink only a little.

Ask any caterer you are considering if you may observe — at a discreet distance — a party he has arranged. Most caterers will agree and also let you sample the food. Once you have chosen a firm, be prepared to sign a contract that protects both sides from surprises. For instance, taxes and tips are rarely included in the quoted price. Usually you will be required to pay a deposit of up to 50% with the balance due immediately before or after the party.

Book at least a month in advance for a cocktail party, and at least several months for a large wedding. You would be wise to call even earlier for a date in May, June, November or December — they are the peak seasons.

If you must cancel, call the caterer immediately. Each firm has its own refund policy but, with several days' notice, most will return all of your deposit in the hope that you will reschedule and call the caterer again.

Domestics

WITH the proliferation of two-income couples, more and more people find that they can afford — and in many cases absolutely need — household help. But how can you find and screen good applicants for domestic jobs?

First of all, recognize that you will have to pay a lot. Full-time domestics earn $200 to $450 a week and even more. New York City's Pavillion agency has placed a nanny who earns $800 a week. Day workers are paid $30 to $60, depending on what chores are involved.

One reason for the relatively high wage is the shortage of domestics. Their numbers decreased by almost 50% in the decade of the 1970s.

The best sources for candidates are newspaper ads, friends who have household help and employment agencies that specialize in placing domestic workers. The agencies will charge you a fee equal to two to four weeks' pay for the person you hire, and the workers tend to command top dollar. You can also ask at churches, colleges and senior citizens' centers for names of people looking for part-time or full-time employment.

If you advertise for help, try the small ethnic newspapers such as Chicago's Polish *Zgoda* or New York City's *Irish Echo,* as well as the large metropolitan dailies. If you live in a big urban area and are looking for live-in baby-sitters, consider advertising in small-town newspapers. Many young women are eager to spend a year or so in an exciting city but want to live in a secure household.

Whether you locate applicants yourself or get them through an agency, take the time to interview them thoroughly. Rely on your common sense and intuition, but also be sure to check references meticulously. That's the only way you can guard against hiring a thief. Call three former employers on the phone and ask pointed questions, such as: Did you like her personality? Did she smile a lot? Did she often skip work? And do you have any reason to doubt this person's honesty?

Home Movers

THE act of moving from one city or one neighborhood to another is among life's most stressful events, yet you can avoid the three major hassles of moving: delay, damage and overcharging.

How do you find a good mover? First, ask friends and co-workers who have moved recently, or your real estate agent or the person who arranges transfers at your company. Consider hiring only those firms that conform to government-regulated standards. If you are relocating to another state, your moving company should be certified by the Interstate Commerce Commission. If you are moving within the same city or state, choose a firm authorized by the appropriate state regulatory agency, usually the Public Utilities Commission or the state Department of Transportation.

Also check the reputation of the moving company's local agent, because he is the one you will be dealing with. Call your local Better Business Bureau or consumer-protection agency and ask whether complaints have been filed against the agent. Avoid anyone who has had 10 major complaints lodged against him over the past year.

Then solicit and compare written bids from several reputable agents. Make sure the bids include charges for extras, of which there are many. For example, if the movers do the packing, figure on paying up to $32 a box. Carefully read the mover's contract, or bill of lading, before you sign. The contract should include the total cost of the move, an inventory of goods to be shipped, the amount of liability insurance and the pickup and delivery dates you and the mover have agreed on.

Some movers "lowball" their bids by underestimating the weight of a shipment just to land a job. You can protect yourself against lowballing by getting a "binding estimate." This means that the mover charges you whatever he agrees to charge you. So it pays to get several estimates.

Before the move, make an inventory of your possessions, then check them off one by one as they go into the van. When the movers unload the truck at your new house, unpack dishes and other breakables right away. Note any damage on your inventory list and give one copy to the driver of the van.

If you are not satisfied with the mover's offer to repair or replace your damaged goods, look at your contract to see if the company has an informal dispute-resolution system. If you still have questions, then call your local branch of the American Arbitration Association, or write to the organization at 140 West 51st Street, New York, New York 10020-1203. If the move went well, you probably will want to tip the driver and each of his crew members $10 to $20 each.

It pays to read the Interstate Commerce Commission's booklet called *When You Move: Your Rights and Responsibilities.* For a free copy, write to the ICC, Office of Compliance and Consumer Assistance, 12th Street and Constitution Avenue, NW, Washington, D.C. 20423. Your mover is required by law to give you this booklet.

Many movers won't touch small shipments at all or will charge you as much as $1,000 to do so. One exception is Bekins' "you-don't-have-to-haul" service. It welcomes loads as small as 500 pounds or 34 cubic feet. Bekins charges from $175 to $400 anywhere in the continental U.S. Distance determines the exact fee.

To get the low rate, *you* have to do the heavy work. Pick up a special carton at the nearest Bekins outlet. Pack it and take it back to the mover's. The company guarantees doorstep delivery within 7 to 28 days.

Help When You Relocate

MOVING to a new state or city does not have to be a journey into the heart of darkness. However, you will have to do a fair amount of letter writing, library reading and talking to strangers. And eventually you should visit the place where you think you would like to live.

Anyone contemplating a move would do well to read *Places Rated Almanac,* published by Rand McNally for $14.95. This useful book compares the climates, crime rates, housing, education, recreation, arts, economic conditions and transportation systems in 329 metropolitan areas.

United Van Lines has free kits, each of which describes any one of 7,000 U.S. and foreign cities. Just call 800-325-3870 in most states. The company will give you two kits at a time. The *Book of the States,* which you can find in most libraries, gives you the tax rates of each state, county and municipality. The local Chamber of Commerce, of course, is another source of information.

To get a feel for life in a community, subscribe to local newspapers and city or state magazines and talk to people who live there. You can come closest to experiencing life in a strange city by visiting or becoming a paying guest of someone in town. One way is to seek commercial bed-and-breakfast accommodations in private homes.

Once you arrive, walk through the neighborhoods. A stroll past shuttered shops on Main Street may tell you more about the state of the economy than any Chamber of Commerce brochure. Seek out real estate agents. They know the virtues of various neighborhoods and they are willing to spend a lot of time with serious sales prospects.

When Your Employer Asks You to Relocate

So your employer has asked you to move to another plant or office. Resist rushing home breathlessly with the news. Instead, begin by finding out precisely what's being offered to you — and not just in terms of moving benefits. It is easy to underestimate the adjustment that a move will require. According to Eugene Jennings, a professor at Michigan State and an authority on relocation, you need to know three things.

First, the precise nature of your new assignment. Who, for example, will you be reporting to? Bad chemistry could more than wipe out any points you win by agreeing to relocate.

Second, the salary you will be making. A raise is the most sincere expression by your bosses that they really want you for this post.

Third, the opportunities for advancement that the new job will open up. The chance to make the first leap up the corporate ladder may come only once or twice in a career. Is the job being dangled before you such an opportunity?

The most serious portion of your analysis consists of exploring the possibilities with your family. You will, of course, want to look at the figures to see how the move would affect the family budget, both for the short and long haul. The company probably will cover the immediate costs of moving. But it may not be willing to cover the difference in housing prices here and there.

Your children may also be less than delighted with their prospects. To keep a move from being a childhood trauma, consult with your kids from the start.

Lawyers

WHETHER you are buying a house, making a will or filing a suit, sooner or later you will need a lawyer. Finding the right attorney at the right price can be a trial.

You are probably better off not to search in one of the large, wood-paneled law firms. Most of those partnerships specialize in corporate work, and even if their members agree to defend you in traffic court, the meter could start ticking at $100 an hour, or more. Instead, scout for a general practitioner in a moderate-size firm that handles personal and small-business affairs.

To locate one, the best advice is old-fashioned: ask people whose judgment you trust, for example, your banker, insurance agent or a member of your company's legal department. Make sure that the recommended attorneys have dealt with cases similar to yours. Your neighbor may have had a Perry Mason for his auto accident case, but that is probably not the right lawyer for your landlord-tenant dispute.

If you want additional recommendations, try your state or local bar association's lawyer referral service. The number is listed in the Yellow Pages. The referral service will give you the next name up on a list of participating attorneys. Trouble is, quality can vary widely. Some bar associations add the name of any attorney who wants to be included; others charge a fee or require only a minimum amount of experience. So ask the service what screening procedures are used. Also explain what kind of legal help you need, since many services break down their lists by specialties.

You can check the background of almost any attorney by consulting the *Martindale-Hubbell Law Directory,* available at most large public libraries. It describes the lawyers in your community and their educations. Sometimes it also gives evaluations by judges and fellow attorneys. If you need a foreign lawyer — to settle a relative's estate, for instance — write to the Overseas Citizens Services at the Department of State, Room 4800, Washington, D.C. 20520.

Lawyers typically charge $25 to $50 for an initial consultation, but many waive the fee if they do not take the case. Do not be shy about inquiring how much time and money your case will cost. Most attorneys charge by the hour; ask for an optimistic and a pessimistic price estimate.

For routine procedures, a lawyer may charge a flat rate — say, $50 to $200 for a simple will. For personal injury and damage cases, you might pay a contingency fee ranging from 20% to 50% of the amount finally collected, depending on how much work is required of your lawyer. Real estate closings are often charged as a percentage of the sales price or mortgage, typically 1%.

Remember that the fee is only one factor. Some of the least expensive advice can be as sound as the costliest. But $100 an hour for a tough, experienced specialist may be well spent — if you stand to lose heavily in a property settlement or child-custody battle.

When your problem is relatively simple, you might turn to a cut-rate legal clinic for no-frills assistance. But even clinics offer low prices only on high-volume procedures, such as wills. Handling extras might be charged by the hour — at $75 per hour in some cases.

Prepaid legal plans are an inexpensive alternative. Some are organized as benefits for groups such as labor or credit unions. For a yearly fee, a subscriber can get unlimited telephone consultations with a lawyer. Most prepaid plans will not cover criminal cases or litigation costs if you want to sue through the plan. But you can get valuable prevention advice that might keep down your costs. It is cheaper to ask a lawyer what your options are if you break a lease, for example, than to pay him to go to court when your former landlord sues for a year's rent.

Storefront and Prepaid Legal Services

IN shopping malls and storefronts, many discount law offices — called legal clinics — are springing up. A customer who knows what legal clinics can and cannot do, and follows a few simple rules in dealing with them, usually can get a genuine bargain.

Legal clinics generally work on routine personal law problems: uncontested divorces, simple wills, real estate closings, bankruptcies, uncomplicated personal injury suits, traffic violations and similar situations. Unlike traditional law firms, the clinics often advertise, and this generates high volume. Since most of the cases are similar, secretaries and paralegals can do the bulk of the paperwork with standardized forms. This lets the clinic's lawyers handle more clients more quickly.

As a result, prices can be much lower than those charged at traditional law firms. For example, at any of the 8 Murrin Metropolitan Attorneys-at-Law offices in the Minneapolis–St. Paul area, an uncontested divorce starts at $300 and a simple will at $85. Old-line law firms in the area charge in the range of $115 to $150 *an hour*. In general, the prices charged by conventional lawyers are three or four times greater than those of clinics.

Most clinics are open on evenings and weekends, so they also offer convenience. And most get good marks for competence. Yvonne Weight, a Virginia attorney who studied the discounters for three years as a member of a state bar disciplinary committee, says: "I don't recall a single neglect-of-legal-matter case on the part of clinic lawyers. They're efficient. They get their paperwork done." But she gives them lower marks for courtroom work.

Clinic lawyers did even better in a study by the University of Miami's Law and Economics Center. It found that 22 clients of California's Jacoby & Meyers clinics got cheaper, faster and better deals than 52 clients of more traditional Los Angeles law firms.

To locate clinic-style practices, thumb through the Yellow Pages for ads of law firms that list several offices and boast of low or flat fees for routine services. Then call around to comparison-shop. Unlike many traditional law firms, legal clinics usually will quote fees over the phone. Check out the firm by going in for an initial consultation — usually about $20 for a half an hour or so.

Of course, not every clinic delivers high quality for its discount rates. You would be wise to get a referral from someone who has used the clinic. Also check that your case fits into the limitations of the clinic's practice and ask for an estimate of the probable fee.

Prepaid plans can be fine for simple legal matters. A landlord who refused to return the security deposit on an apartment, for example, might change his mind if he received a letter written by a lawyer on your behalf. Or say your new car turns out to be a lemon. A prepaid service lawyer can help you get the manufacturer to make good on the warranty.

Complex issues such as a liability suit, divorce, bankruptcy or sophisticated mortgage arrangement are beyond the scope of prepaid packages. Also, the plans rarely cover court appearances. To make sure a plan suits you, you have to shop warily. Prepaid legal programs vary widely in their range of services.

Another way to save is to use one of the new prepaid attorneys' services. They are the legal profession's version of health insurance. You pay a fixed premium each year and are assured of at least basic legal care. The American Bar Association has strongly endorsed the idea, and quite a number of firms offer plans.

For example, for $96 to $175 a year you can buy a family plan from Nationwide Legal Services (475 Park Avenue South, New York, New York 10016; 800-ALL-LAWS or 212-889-6288 in New York State). It operates in 37 states, among them California, Illinois, Maryland, New Jersey and Texas. Members can call toll-free one of thousands of independent lawyers under contract with Nationwide to provide unlimited consultation. These lawyers will do such chores as review leases and other legal documents and draft a simple will.

Similarly, Lawphone (4501 Forbes Boulevard, Lanham, Maryland 20706) has member law firms in all 50 states, the District of Columbia and Puerto Rico. It offers phone consultations, review of documents and unlimited phone calls and letters on the client's behalf. Lawphone is available through various credit unions, bank credit cards and trade and professional associations. It may also be available as an employee benefit. Rates vary according to the region. For information, call 301-459-1333.

Legal service plans are available to individuals in every state. In some, including California, Colorado, New York and Pennsylvania, you can choose from up to 10 services. Usually you have a choice of four to six. For the programs in your state, send a stamped, self-addressed envelope to the National Resource Center for Consumers of Legal Services, 124-D East Broad Street, Falls Church, Virginia 22046.

Settling Out of Court

Americans seem to sue by reflex action when they believe they have been wronged. Yet, as Abraham Lincoln once noted, "The nominal winner is often a real loser — in fees, expenses and waste of time."

330 | Your Services

When your impulse is to sue, you don't necessarily have to go to court and tell it to a judge. There are better ways to settle legal disputes. For example, you can rent a judge who is sometimes called a "dispute resolver." Or you can go to a so-called dispute mediation center to have a quarrel settled. Such innovations are cheaper, faster and simpler than traditional litigation. Basically, they offer third-party mediation — help in resolving differences.

The best-known alternative to going to court is the American Arbitration Association. Its 33 regional offices handle 53,000 cases a year. People who seek arbitration agree to abide by the decision of a third party.

An increasingly popular device for business people is the mini-trial. The idea is to let companies settle their own fights out of court. Representatives of two disputing companies argue out their case before top executives of both of those companies. If they then cannot reach a compromise, they bring in a third party to help, often a retired judge.

Similar mini-trials also are well suited for disputes involving, say, a homeowner and a contractor over faulty bathroom plumbing; or the owner of a wrecked auto who is claiming more damages than an insurance company is willing to pay. They hire a retired judge — and often he can sit down with both sides and work out a settlement in an afternoon. The fee might run $150 to $200 an hour.

The savings are not only in money but also in damage to the disputants' feelings. An added benefit of resolving a case out of court is privacy. So is the fact that the remedy can be flexible, shaped by the plaintiff, the defendant and the dispute resolver. Although courts award money damages, they generally cannot order a contractor to fix a leaky roof.

Most out-of-court settlements involve mediation — that is, third-party help in settling disputes. The savings can be large. For instance, in Denver, a mediated divorce with no legal counsel usually costs about $800. A court divorce involving lawyers could run well into the thousands — for *each* side. Many of the divorce mediators around the country are lawyers with training in mediation.

To handle everyday disputes such as neighbor-against-neighbor and landlord-tenant disagreements, more than 350 mediation centers have popped up in every state in the country. They are sometimes called neighborhood justice centers, and they are usually state-supported. Not only are they fast, informal and effective, but they also charge nothing to iron out such problems as dogfights, broken windows and loud stereos.

For consumer complaints, state or local courts that hear small-claims cases often serve you well. The maximum claims range from $300 in Arkansas to $25,000 in Massachusetts. These courts are supposed to be simple, straightforward and sometimes free of lawyers. They are designed to make it easier for you to get justice, perhaps even without hiring an attorney, but because most states allow lawyers to represent either side, you might find that your opponent has hired one who outclasses you or ties you up in costly appeals. Even so, you might do very well on your own — and it will cost you only a few dollars to bring your complaint to court.

For more information on how you can get help in settling legal disputes out of court, look in the Yellow Pages under "Mediation Services." Or phone an organization named EnDispute, which has offices in Cambridge, Massachusetts; Chicago; and Washington, D.C. Or contact the American Arbitration Association.

Finally, the Better Business Bureau offers mediation and arbitration services to consumers at most of its 175 offices.

Package Delivery Services

SENDING a package overnight to almost any city in the country is a cinch these days. Several delivery services can do the job for you. But which does it best?

Among the overnight package couriers, probably the most esteemed is Federal Express. It has been in the business for a full 15 years and gained fame offering delivery before 10:30 a.m. the next day. Federal Express recently lost by a hair to United Parcel Service as the company with the widest reach. The longtime ground deliverer now boasts overnight air service to every address in the United States. Federal Express claims it serves areas containing 98% of the population.

There are three other major companies: Airborne Express, Emery and Flying Tigers. Like Federal and UPS, their guaranteed overnight deliveries are usually limited to certain origins and destinations.

Even the U.S. Postal Service has joined the race. It will take up to

70 pounds overnight between any of 26,000 post offices in the country that accept Express Mail. Like the commercial services, the postal people will make a special trip to pick up your package. But if your letter carrier works out of an Express Mail post office, you probably can leave a package in your mailbox stamped and ready for pickup.

In mid-1988, to send a two-pound package and get next-day delivery, the U.S. Postal Service charged $12; United Parcel Service charged $12.50; Federal Express and Emery Air Freight charged $23 and Airborne Express charged $25. Some of the services would deliver lighter-weight letters for still lower fees, but Flying Tigers' minimum was $20 for a package of five pounds or less.

Whatever service you choose, if you are sending a package to some out-of-the-way place, you will have to pay an additional fee. Post offices and delivery-service agents can tell you whether a town is on their regular rate list. Even so, it is wise to phone the person on the receiving end and find out whether one courier seems more reliable than others in her or his area.

Plumbers

FINDING a reliable, affordable plumber can be one of life's little challenges, and you should not wait for the pipes to burst before you begin looking. Every householder needs a list of good servicemen, including a plumber or two. The best way to avoid panic is to have them lined up before you need them.

When checking a plumber's reputation, you should ask how quickly he responds to emergencies, if he can be reached at night and on weekends and, of course, how much he charges. But how do you find the name of a plumber to check out? If asking your neighbors does not turn up a satisfactory specialist, the first place to try is the local affiliate of the National Association of Plumbing-Heating-Cooling Contractors (180 South Washington Street, Falls Church, Virginia 22046). Sometimes it is listed in the phone book as the Plumbing Contractors Association or the Master Plumbers Association. Most members are licensed and covered by liability insurance and workers' compensation. Their records probably will be fairly clear of complaints. The association often works with city agencies to resolve disputes that arise over a plumber's work or charges.

You pay less if you use an unlicensed, unaffiliated plumber, but if something goes wrong, you are more likely to be stuck.

So-called master plumbers are the most seasoned and best trained and can handle the toughest assignments. They have at least five to 10 years' experience and must pass a state exam. When you have a major job, the master plumber gets the appropriate building department permit. He also hires the apprentices and journeymen who do simpler repairs and installations, and he is responsible if anything goes wrong.

You also may locate reputable plumbers by calling the United Association of Journeymen and Apprentices of the Plumbing and Pipe Fitting Industry of the U.S. and Canada. In plain English, that is the plumbers' union. It will not recommend a specific plumber, but it will give you names of contractors who do use union plumbers.

Still another source is the building or plumbing inspection department at city hall. Inspectors see the work of every plumber in town, so they know good craftsmanship firsthand. If they do not want to recommend a plumber, at least they will give you an opinion about any whose names you have.

What can you expect to pay a reliable plumber? You have probably heard the old story of the brain surgeon who calls in a plumber to fix a leaky faucet. The plumber tinkers around for a few minutes and then announces, "That'll be $50."

"Heavens!" exclaims the customer. "I'm a brain surgeon, and I don't get $50 for a few minutes' work."

"Neither did I," says the plumber, "when I was a brain surgeon."

Plumbers have a well-earned reputation for high prices. You can expect to pay them between $25 and $55 an hour — and more than that at night and on weekends. That $25-to-$55 charge can be deceptive; often it applies to plumbers' travel time as well as the time they spent on the job. And rather than raise their already steep hourly rates to cover boosts in the cost of insurance and their other expenses, many plumbers choose the artifice of a so-called cartage charge of $2 to $3 tacked onto the bill for each visit. Not surprisingly, the prices are highest on the East and West coasts and lowest in the South and Midwest, notably in rural areas.

You will not be able to negotiate the price on an emergency repair job. But if you have work that can be planned in advance, you should get bids from several contractors. Plumbing is highly competitive, and you would be surprised how much the bids differ.

Some people try to save money by buying parts for their plumber. That makes no sense. You will have to buy at retail, and plumbers buy at wholesale. You will not save any money, but you will run the risk of buying the wrong parts.

Do not assume all plumbing repairs require a plumber. There are many jobs you can tackle yourself. Anyone mechanically inclined can patch small leaks, warm frozen pipes, unclog drains, repair faucet drips and replace ceramic tiles.

But beware of getting in over your head. A workman who did was cleaning the filters in a Cincinnati winery one December when he accidentally knocked open a water valve connected with the vats of wine. The rising pressure of fermenting wine caused a backflow into the municipal water system. The resulting Christmas present for the people of Cincinnati: sparkling Burgundy on tap, somewhat diluted.

Television Repairs

GETTING your television set repaired does not have to be as suspenseful or traumatic as an episode from "As the World Turns." Well-trained TV repairers abound, and here are some tips for finding a reasonably priced one.

Although TV sets are generally sturdy, they probably will malfunction once or twice during their average 10-year life span. If your set's problem is covered by a warranty, it must be repaired by one of the manufacturer's authorized service dealers. Their addresses usually come with the TV. But only a small percentage of TVs need repairs during warranty periods; that is normally 90 days for labor, one year for parts and two years for the picture tube.

Sometimes you can extend the free repair service by buying a service contract. It can cost up to $200 for 36 months of home service. But you are gambling that breakdowns will occur in the first few years and not later on.

Even if your warranty has expired, it is wise to use an authorized dealer for repairs because he stocks parts for your set and he has experience in fixing TVs like yours. You can find authorized dealers in the Yellow Pages under "Television Service" or "Television Repairs." If you cannot locate an authorized service dealer, make sure the repairer you choose has a place of business — not just a truck and phone number. Some elusive operators pick up sets and are never heard from again.

Membership in groups such as the International Society for Certified Electronics Technicians and the National Electronics Sales & Service Dealers Association provides some evidence that the repairer is competent, as well as interested in maintaining a reputation for reliability.

If possible, take your TV set to the repair shop to save on the house-call service charge. Ask for a written estimate of costs in advance.

When a repairer finishes work, he should give you an itemized bill and guarantee his work for at least 30 days. He should also return to you all parts he replaced, except the picture tube.

Above all, do not try to repair your TV yourself. For one thing, opening the back of your set can be dangerous because color picture tubes release electrical voltage for hours after the set has been unplugged.

Beware of Service Contracts

RIGHT after you agree to buy a car, refrigerator, TV set or other major appliance, the salesperson may startle you by warning that it could break down. Ah, but, he will add, you can insure against any repair cost by buying a service contract. Watch out: It may not be worth the money.

You generally can expect to pay far more for a service contract than for any repair bills it might cover. A study by the National Science Foundation showed that the cost of service contracts for color TV sets ran almost 10 times the probable cost of repairs for the average user. For refrigerators, service contracts cost 16 times as much as probable repairs.

If you feel that you must buy a service contract, the best time is a year or two *after* your purchase — once the warranty has run out and you have some idea of potential repair problems. Check newspaper ads for discounts that manufacturers sometimes offer. Be wary of contracts that are not sold by manufacturers. As one executive in the service contract trade warns, it is a fly-by-night business.

One way to avoid throwing away money is to compare the service contract with the manufacturer's warranty that comes with the product. Check the two for overlap, and satisfy yourself that you have complete protection.

A contract that covers only the power train of a car, for example, overlooks too many possible trouble spots. A useful service contract for autos does not exclude the electrical system and brakes. Also, it should allow you to get service at an independent repair shop in an emergency and reimburse you for towing costs. Many contracts sold by independent firms do not cover towing at all.

For TV sets, you will find that there is little advantage to buying a contract that starts before the year-long warranty expires. Read the fine print on TV contracts in any case — they may well require you to pay the first $75 for every repair job.

Service contracts are just not economical. They are a bargain only if you bought a lemon. When you buy a service contract, whatever its terms, you can be reasonably sure it is you who will be taking the financial risk.

Your Savings

How Much to Put Away

JUST a few years ago, savers were suckers because inflation ate up every penny of the interest you collected — and more. But all that has been turned around, and now your savings pay you more than inflation takes away. So this is the era of savers, and it is considerably smarter to save than to borrow. Yet Americans are not great savers. In the past decade, they have put aside anywhere from an average of 7.5% (in 1981) to 2.8% (in late 1987) of their after-tax income. Comparisons with people in other countries are difficult because methods of measuring savings vary, but according to their statistics, the West Germans save 14% and the Japanese 16% of their incomes. By any measure, they put away substantially more than Americans do.

Saving, of course, means accumulating money for a specific purpose — a down payment on a house, a college education, a comfortable retirement — or for use in an emergency. You put your savings in secure places that promise both to preserve your capital and pay you steady income. *Investing*, by contrast, involves accepting the risk of losing your money in exchange for a chance to earn richer gains. Thus, the amount that you should be saving depends on your age and your family situation. If you are reasonably young with few or no family responsibilities and face strong earning prospects in the future, you can afford to save relatively less and invest relatively more. But if you have children to educate or are rapidly approaching retirement, you should save more and invest less.

How much should you put away? One good but *bare minimum* plan is this:

— Between the ages of 30 and 40, save or invest 5% of your pre-tax income.

— Then, *increase* that amount by one percentage point a year between the ages of 40 and 45.

— After you are 45, aim to put away at least 10% a year.

Ways to Save More

Far too many Americans think they just cannot afford to save at all. If you are one of those who never seem to have anything left from your paycheck, examine your expenditures and see where you can cut back. If you are spending more than 15% to 20% of your take-home pay to meet installment debts beyond home mortgage payments, it is too much. Give the credit cards a rest.

Perhaps 20% of your after-tax income is going to groceries. Then you may have been eating too high on the hog. The national average is 15%. If you spend much more than 10% on clothing, consider slipping out of designer jeans and into less expensive models. Most people spend about 5% of their after-tax income on clothes.

But keep in mind that every family has unique needs. For example, if you live in an expensive city such as Los Angeles, your housing costs could be over 50% higher than they would be in Denver. The average U.S. family spends just over 30% of its income on housing.

After you have discovered the budget items you can reasonably trim, concentrate on the one area that you want to augment — your savings. Most families can comfortably save or invest 7% to 10% of their after-tax income.

The best way to build your savings is to treat them as a necessity. Put a fixed amount into savings each month. If doing that takes more discipline than you can muster, enroll in your company's payroll savings plan, which will deduct a regular amount from your salary before you ever see it. Or arrange with your bank or mutual-fund company to withdraw a certain amount from your checking account each month and automatically deposit it in a savings or investment account.

Aim to build an emergency cash reserve. It should equal three months of after-tax income, or at least enough to cover three months' worth of necessary expenses such as groceries, utilities, mortgage and car payments. Since this cash must be readily available, store it in a money-market mutual fund or bank money-market deposit account. A bank certificate of deposit usually will pay you more, but you will forfeit that difference — and then some — if you have to withdraw the cash early.

Once you have provided for emergencies, start saving for specific purposes. Saving is like dieting: it's tough to do unless you set goals. So set short-, medium-, and long-range goals. Short-term objectives could include saving for a summer holiday or for Christmas. A three-to-five-year target might be buying a vacation house or paying cash for a new car. The major long-term goals are educating the children and saving for a secure retirement.

What is the secret of saving more? Simply this: *Pay yourself first.* When you collect your paycheck, do not rush out and spend it all. Lay away a fixed amount every week or every month for your *own* savings or investments. That is paying yourself first — and it is smart.

Where to Put Your Savings Now

THIS is no time to be taking needless chances with your money. But it is possible to put your cash into institutions or instruments offering returns that are safe, big and guaranteed.

Where is the best place to put your savings now?

Among the many safe and rewarding places are money-market funds, bank money-market deposit accounts, bank certificates of deposit and U.S. Treasury securities. (All are discussed in the following chapters.) Bonds hold out tempting yields, too, but they are riskier because their face value — the price that you buy or sell them for — rises and falls along with the gyrations of interest rates.

When determining where to put your savings, you have to weigh and balance off three traditional concerns. They are: *yield* (How much am I earning on my money?), *liquidity* (How quickly can I withdraw my money if I need it?) and *safety* (Am I sure to get back every penny I put in?).

Considering all those factors, here are some guidelines:

The best all-around place to put short-term savings is in one of the money-market funds offered by mutual-fund companies and brokerage firms. They give you competitively high yields, instant liquidity and strong safety. For even more safety, you can deposit cash into two privately insured money funds: Vanguard Money Market Reserves-Insured Portfolio (P.O. Box 2600, Valley Forge, Pennsylvania 19482) and Capital T Insured Money Market Portfolio (The Travelers, 1 Tower Square, Hartford, Connecticut 06101).

If you have $500 to $1,000 to spare, you might as well put it in a federally insured bank money-market deposit account. It will pay you just a bit less than an ordinary money fund and offer you some additional benefits. You get government insurance on your deposits up to $100,000, plus the convenience of dealing face-to-face with your neighborhood bankers. Also, if you ever need a loan, it is often easier to get if you have some money on deposit in a bank.

If you are in a high tax bracket, you are probably best off in one of the tax-free money-market funds. They are offered by mutual-fund companies and in mid-1988 were paying about 4.25% — free of federal income taxes.

It does not make much sense to put much savings into an ordinary passbook account. You usually get only 5½% interest on it — all taxable — at a commercial bank, savings bank or savings and loan association. You can earn considerably more at the very same institution merely by switching to other forms of savings. As mentioned, with $1,000 or less, you can open a money-market deposit account. And you can buy a bank certificate of deposit for as little as $500 and keep it for as short a period as seven days. Some banks hold out for higher minimum deposits and longer maturities, so shop around.

If you do have a passbook account, make sure you are collecting the maximum legal interest on it. Since January 1984, the government has allowed banks to pay the same 5½% rate on passbook savings that S&Ls long had paid. But bankers know that once people put money into an account, they tend to keep it there. Consequently many banks still pay the same old 5¼% or less. Check into the interest that your bank is paying, and if it is not the maximum, seriously consider switching.

Even if your current bank does not offer the highest yields in your city, you are probably wise to stick with it if it provides convenient location, courteous service and easy loans when you need them. But if you do search around, you will discover that rates often vary by almost one percentage point within cities that have many competing banks. They also vary between the East and West coasts. Rates often are one-third to one-half a percentage point *higher* in California than in New York. Why the difference? Because California banks generally *charge* rates on unsecured consumer loans that are higher than those in the rest of the country.

If you have at least $5,000 to deposit, ask the banker if that will qualify you for a special bonus rate. Many banks and savings and loans pay their bigger savers more. S&Ls often pay slightly higher rates than banks do. You probably will find the steepest rates at suburban S&Ls and banks; they are trying to take money away from the big, downtown banks.

The longer you are willing to tie up your money, the better yield you will get. In mid-1988, six-month certificates yielded 7.11% on average. If you put some savings on ice for a year, you would have earned 7.45% on average.

Your Best Deals in Banking

A REVOLUTION is under way in the world of banking. The government is deregulating, meaning that financial institutions can compete more freely and fiercely than ever before and offer you more to get your business. The variety of their services, the size of the fees, the amount of interest rates — all these vary among financial institutions. Banks, savings and loan associations, credit unions and others are courting you. So, it cannot be repeated often enough: shop around for your best deals in banking.

The neighborhood bank is probably still the best place for your checking account, but not necessarily for your savings. You sometimes can earn more at no risk by putting your money into certificates of deposit sold not by banks but by stockbrokers. And you might be able to earn more by using the mail to put your savings in an out-of-state institution.

In many ways, it makes sense to give all your banking business to one institution. This is called "relationship banking," and in return for it, you often can get higher interest on your savings or lower fees on your checking or better terms on a loan. That's because when all your banking business is lumped together, you usually become a fairly big customer. For example, if your balance in a money-market deposit account or a SuperNOW account exceeds $5,000, you may earn a fraction of a percentage point more interest than do customers with smaller accounts. But relationship banking does cost you something. If instead you used many different financial institutions, each for a different service, you might get still better deals.

Your Best Deals in Checking Accounts

A GREAT place to put your money is in a checking account that also earns interest. That's just what you get with bank money-market accounts as well as NOW and SuperNOW accounts. But they all have limitations, and the NOW accounts can be downright tricky when it comes to figuring minimum balances and interest rates.

All banks used to require that you maintain balances of at least $1,000 if you wanted to earn the interest rates paid by money-market deposit accounts and SuperNOW accounts. There was no minimum for NOW accounts at first. That was federal law until 1986. Since then, banks can require any minimum balance they wish, or no balance at all. Some banks continue to require the old minimum and sometimes more. But minimums for a NOW or SuperNOW are commonly much less. Many banks give you interest on anything at all in your account.

But watch out: Most banks have monthly charges that can add up, especially if you are likely to keep only a small balance in your account. According to a survey by the Consumer Federation of America, a NOW account can cost small depositors as much as $189 a year, *after* interest income.

When you shop around among banks, the surest way to compare is to find out exactly how much money you will have in your account at the end of the year if you deposit, say, $100 on the first of the year. And be alert to differences between NOW and SuperNOW accounts offered by the same bank. Interest rates are often the same for the two. But a SuperNOW can require that a higher minimum be kept in the account to avoid a penalty charge, and the charge itself is typically more than a NOW account would impose. This means that if you duck under the necessary balance, the supposedly super account can cost more than a simple NOW.

Remember that bank money-market accounts pay higher interest — sometimes a full percentage point more — than NOW accounts. But bank money-market accounts let you write only three checks a month. The advantage of the NOW accounts is that you get unlimited checking.

Alas, writing a check isn't what it used to be. When you fail to hold your minimum balance, banks charge monthly or per-check fees, or both. To keep checking costs down you may prefer a noninterest, no-frills account. These basic accounts are increasingly popular today with low-balance depositors. Even most of these are not altogether free, though there is one kind aptly titled Totally Free Checking. This is one of the best accounts available for low balances.

And, it is quite possible to come out ahead with a NOW account if you're careful. You will probably make the best deal at a savings and loan association. If fees or balance requirements are low enough, you stand to earn some net income.

In any case, it's wise to call a half dozen banks and S&Ls and compare fees. When you are gathering information, be sure to ask how minimum balances are calculated and find out how much it costs if you slip under the minimum. Monthly fees range from $4 to $10 and per-check charges from about 15 cents to 30 cents.

Though you will certainly never bounce a check, you might be curious to know what the returned-check charges are for those unfortunate people who do. The cost now varies from $5 all the way to over $100. The average is $10 to $15. You also might be curious to know what a returned check actually costs your bank. According to the Federal Reserve Board, it's just 50 cents.

Automatic Teller Machines

MORE and more people are doing their banking through automatic teller machines, or ATMs. But if your automatic-teller-machine card is lost or stolen, and someone empties your checking account, are you liable for the losses? And what can you do to hold them down?

Under the federal Electronic Funds Transfer Act of 1978, you are liable for no unauthorized withdrawals if you report your ATM card lost or stolen before someone uses it. If you tell the bank within two business days of discovering the card's loss, your maximum liability is $50. After that it's $500. But if you still don't inform the bank of the loss within 60 days after it mails your statement listing any bogus withdrawals, you are liable for all money withdrawn after the 60th day — until you report the missing card.

Your bank may balk at replacing missing funds if it finds you negligent. But that will not relieve it of its legal obligations. If you have trouble with the bank, seek relief from one of the following four federal agencies in Washington, D.C.:

If the bank you deal with is a nationally chartered bank, write to the Comptroller of the Currency. If you have a problem with a state-chartered bank, contact the Federal Reserve Board. If your bank is state-chartered but not a Fed member, call or write to the Federal Deposit Insurance Corporation. If your automatic-teller difficulty is with a savings and loan association, write to the Federal Home Loan Bank Board. Give any of these agencies about four weeks to make decisions and get back to you.

Do not worry about using automatic banking tellers. You may be concerned that the impersonal machine will make an all-too-human mistake, that a $400 deposit will somehow show up on your statement as only $40. In a survey by the Federal Reserve Board, 6% of the people who used the electronic banking services claimed they had been victims of a machine error. But 95% of the grievances were settled satisfactorily. If your automatic teller blows a transaction, simply write the bank a note within 60 days of receiving your statement. By law, the bank must resolve the complaint within 45 days of getting your letter. And if it takes longer than just 10 business days, the bank must credit your account for the amount in dispute until any investigation ends. If you still have a grievance, write to the Federal Reserve Board's Division of Consumer and Community Affairs, 20th and C Streets, NW, Washington, D.C. 20551.

How Safe Are Banks and S&Ls?

MORE banks and savings institutions failed in 1987 than at any time since the Depression. The mounting cost to bail them out, as well as to shore up those near failure, is raising unsettling questions about insured deposits at banks, S&Ls and credit unions. S&Ls, the so-called thrifts, have suffered the greatest losses. In 1987, a third of them, mostly in Texas and California, lost $13.4 billion, or double the $6.6 billion profit made by the others. In 1988, hundreds were insolvent. By mid-August, 32 thrifts in Texas alone had been acquired or consolidated under the supervision of the Federal Savings and Loan Insurance Corporation. Total cost to the FSLIC for these rescue efforts could range from $6 billion to $9 billion.

Banks, too, have serious money woes. Their deposit insurer, the Federal Deposit Insurance Corporation, is wrestling with whether to close down or sell banks that have become insolvent. Problems facing the FDIC were starkly highlighted in July 1988 when it declared that the First RepublicBank Corporation of Dallas, the largest bank holding company in Texas, had failed. The bailout costs to the FDIC will also be huge.

Despite such adversities, banks have added more than $125 billion in new capital and reserves since 1980. Furthermore, almost all banks and S&Ls are now insured by the *federal* government — a result of crises in Ohio and Maryland in 1985 triggered by investors' mistrust of state-chartered privately insured thrifts.

There are other positive developments in the banking business as well. After large losses in 1987, profits at major banks took a sharp turn up in the first quarter of 1988. And thrifts reported more deposits than withdrawals. This is a different picture from 1987, when Americans depleted their savings to invest in the stock market. In the wake of the crash, they have flocked back to the plain Janes of the investment world with new appreciation for the safety of reasonably dependable rates and federal insurance.

If you are one of the returnees or a new saver, find out what kind of insurance your institution has. The Federal Deposit Insurance Corporation guarantees up to $100,000 per account in nearly 14,000 commercial and savings banks. You also get $100,000 of insurance coverage in about 3,000 S&Ls that are members of the Federal

Savings and Loan Insurance Corporation (this includes the insolvent ones) and in credit unions that belong to the National Credit Union Share Insurance Fund.

If you have money in one of these federally insured institutions and it should fail, you probably would not even feel it. Government regulators can arrange a takeover or merger so quickly that your bank's doors would never have to be closed. At worst, you might have to wait a few days to collect your money and forgo interest payments during that period. But remember — insurance will cover your deposits only up to $100,000. If you are fortunate enough to have more than that, open another insured account at another bank.

There are still other ways to expand the $100,000 limit. If you are married, you can have one account in your name, another in your spouse's name, and a third joint account. Thus a married couple between them could have $300,000 in federally insured deposits. But you can have no more than $100,000 under the same name even if you have more than one ordinary account. Say you have $70,000 in a money-market account and $40,000 in a certificate of deposit, both under your name at the same bank. Your combined $110,000 exceeds the insurance limit by $10,000.

As with most regulatory matters, there is an exception — and it concerns your Individual Retirement Accounts. If you have an IRA at a bank or S&L, any money-market deposit accounts or savings certificates in it will be insured separately. In this way, a married couple could have as much as $500,000 federally insured in the same institution: $100,000 in each of their regular accounts, $100,000 in their joint account and $100,000 in each of the IRAs.

Although the FDIC maintains a ratio of just 1 1/10 cents of insurance funds for every dollar on deposit, it can get additional money from the U.S. Treasury when it needs to. And the FSLIC goes to Congress for funds to help the ailing S&Ls.

Bank Money-Market Accounts

USUALLY, money-market deposit accounts at banks or savings and loan associations yield just slightly less than ordinary money-market mutual funds. Banks have considerable overhead — all those tellers and big buildings — and that makes it hard for them to pay more than the money funds.

If your savings are in a bank or savings and loan passbook account yielding only about 5½%, you may easily shift them to an insured, somewhat higher-yielding money-market deposit account at the same institution. Bank money-market accounts certainly offer convenience. Most banks let you write checks on them for any amount, although they limit the number of checks you can write each month to anybody except yourself. By contrast, the money-market funds often restrict you to checks of $250 or $500. Also, some merchants are readier to accept local bank checks than those drawn on a money-market fund in Moose Jaw.

If you are a particularly safety-minded person, then federal deposit insurance makes a bank money-market account or Super-NOW checking account attractive.

If you are invested in a so-called government-only money fund — the kind that buys U.S. government-backed issues — it might be worthwhile to move to a federally insured bank money-market account. You may be able to earn more interest, and the government protection is just as strong with one as the other. The government money funds earn about 1% less than regular money funds.

Certificates of Deposit

A RE you willing to tie your money up for a week or more? Then look into bank certificates of deposit. Deregulation has freed banks and savings and loans to set whatever maturity dates and interest rates they want on them. While ordinary passbook accounts usually yield only 5½% at best, CDs in mid-1988 were paying 6% to 9.4%.

Always check first whether the bank or savings institution will pay you simple interest or compound interest. The yield on a simple-interest CD is much lower than you might expect. Let's say you bought a $1,000 five-year simple-interest certificate paying 10%. It would give you $100 in interest every year, for a total of $500. Yet if that five-year CD paid the usual 10% a year, but the interest were compounded annually, you would end up with more interest — $610 — after five years.

Be sure to find out what the bank's penalties for early withdrawal are. Many banks are afraid of losing their CD funds, so they are discouraging early withdrawals by tacking on extremely stiff penalties. If you will be putting money into a CD but think you might need the cash soon, stick with a short-term certificate whose penalty is the loss of only one month's interest.

Also find out how you will be notified when your CD comes due. The bank should send you a reminder a few weeks before you have to decide whether to withdraw or redeposit the money.

You can usually get a little more interest by putting your money into a certificate of deposit at a brokerage house instead of a bank. Many stockbrokers buy small-denomination CDs in bulk from banks. The brokers then offer the certificates to the public in $1,000 units. Just like the CDs you get at a bank or savings and loan, brokered CDs have the ironclad backing of the Federal Deposit Insurance Corporation or some other federal agency.

When you buy a CD through a broker, you can sell it before it matures and not suffer the early withdrawal penalty you would pay if you cashed it at the bank. And you will not be charged a commission.

Brokers trade CDs the way they trade bonds. So, if interest rates rise after you buy a CD, your certificate's value falls. But if rates drop, you can sell out early at a profit. All in all, brokered CDs are usually a better deal than bank or savings and loan CDs.

Bargains by Buying in Bulk

SMART investors in certificates of deposit have learned a basic shopping lesson: It pays to buy in bulk. You can get more for your money if you band together with friends, neighbors or even co-workers to purchase jumbo CDs with face values of $100,000 or higher. That way, you can earn one and sometimes two percentage points above the rate offered on ordinary CDs.

For example, some time ago 129 residents of an apartment complex in Fort Lauderdale, Florida, pooled their savings and came up with close to $1 million. They used that to buy a seven-month CD paying 9% from a local savings and loan association. That was much better than the 7.7% they would have got if each had bought a $500 certificate.

To buy a jumbo CD, you will have to take the initiative and organize the group. You will also have to appoint one or more members as trustees. They do not have to be lawyers. They handle the paperwork and negotiate with the bank about the interest rate and the term of CD. It's usually six to 18 months. Trustees also collect the money and deliver it to the bank, along with a list of the depositors' names and Social Security numbers.

The bank then sets up a separate account for each saver for record-keeping purposes. That way, your deposit is fully covered by federal insurance up to $100,000 per account. Banks establish their own requirements about the minimum contribution per person — often it's $2,500. Most banks refuse to cash in jumbo CDs early for any reason. But some will let individual savers use their shares in the pool as collateral for loans.

Out-of-State Deposits

E VEN if banks and S&Ls in your state pay relatively low interest, you are free to get in on the highest rates, wherever you can find them. Just about every bank or savings and loan accepts out-of-state deposits. Institutions in states other than your own may pay a point or two more on your savings. You will have to deal with them by mail. That means, for a 25-cent stamp, you might earn an extra $100 or $200 a year on a $10,000 deposit.

To deposit your savings out-of-state is easy. Most banks will assign you an account number by phone. You then start the account by mailing in a check made out to your new account number. Be sure to endorse the check and write "For Deposit Only" on the back. And by all means make sure you know how long the quoted rate will be in effect. Some banks change their rates daily.

You will find higher rates and potential risks at state-chartered savings institutions than at federally insured ones. Watch out for those that insure themselves by pooling money in a fund. This insurance may not be enough in a pinch — as was shown in Ohio and Maryland, where some privately insured savings and loan associations briefly had to close or limit withdrawals in 1985. You are almost always safer doing business with a federally insured institution.

Federally insured banks in Texas have been paying unusually high rates. For example, on its money-market accounts, Champion Savings in Houston was paying an effective yield of 7.5% in mid-1988 for a minimum deposit of $5,000.

If you have savings that you can tie up a little while, consider putting them in a one-year certificate of deposit. In mid-1988 you could get an effective yield of 8.19% at Alamo Savings in San Antonio, Texas. Or, if you did not need the money for five years, you could have purchased CDs that yielded 9.25% at Brookside Savings in Kansas City, Missouri.

You can find out where the highest yields are now by looking in financial newspapers and magazines, such as the *Wall Street Journal*, *Barron's* and *Money*.

Three weekly banking newsletters can help your search for the best returns. One is called *100 Highest Yields* (P.O. Box 088888, North Palm Beach, Florida 33408-8888). It ranks only federally insured institutions, and it costs $84 for one year. Another newsletter is *Tiered Rate Watch* (P.O. Drawer 145510, Coral Gables, Florida 33114). It rates federally insured institutions that its publisher considers sound, and it costs $39 for three months, $59 for six months or $99 a year. A third weekly newsletter that lists the highest yields at federally insured banks across the country is *Banxquote Online*, published by Masterfund Inc. (575 Madison Avenue, New York, New York 10022; 212-605-0337). It costs $250 for 12 issues a year or $90 per quarter for PC on-line access plus a $200 registration fee.

Once you have selected several banks to explore, write or phone each of them for an application form and information on rates, minimum deposits and withdrawal penalties. To be on the safe side, request a copy of the institution's most recent financial statement. Compare its equity or net worth to assets. If you find a ratio of at least 5% at a bank or 3% at an S&L, the institution is probably solid.

Also ask about credit-card policies for nonresidents. A few banks offer no-fee Visa and MasterCards nationally, sparing you the usual annual fee of $15 to $45. Others charge a fee but keep interest rates on their cards at 11% to 17%.

Money-Market Mutual Funds

MONEY-MARKET funds that are sold by mutual-fund companies and brokerage firms have been a big bonanza for small savers. Although the yields from these funds have declined from their stratospheric levels of 1982 and 1983, they are still higher than the inflation rate.

The chief measure of a money fund's safety is the quality of investments that its managers make with your money. In effect, the funds make short-term loans to federal, state and local governments as well as to corporations and banks. Generally, the higher the risks that a fund takes, the higher the yields that it pays.

Some safety-first investors have flocked to money-market funds that buy only government securities, such as Capital Preservation Treasury Note Fund and Cardinal Government Securities Trust. These often pay a point or so less than do ordinary money funds and the bank money-market deposit accounts. Almost invariably, you can feel quite secure investing in a regular money fund, particularly if it is run by a well-established mutual-fund group or brokerage firm. But to sleep more soundly at night, check that the average maturity of the fund's securities is 60 days or less by asking the fund or looking at Donoghue's Money Fund Report, published in over 70 newspapers. Longer maturities do not give fund managers enough flexibility. If interest rates rise and the fund is locked into securities that pay lower rates, disgruntled shareholders might start a run for redemptions.

Choosing a money-market fund only because of its high yield can be a mistake. Since most ordinary money funds make the same kind of investments, their returns are usually within one or two percentage points of each other. You might be wiser to seek out money funds that let you shift your assets into *other* kinds of mutual funds when you think interest rates are heading down and the stock market is heading up. Some money funds have such exchange agreements with independent mutual funds. Other money funds belong to one of the many fund families. These families also have funds that invest in stocks, and sometimes in corporate, government and tax-exempt bonds.

Once you invest in a family, you usually can shift your cash from, say, a money fund into a stock mutual fund merely by making a phone call. Often the transfer costs nothing, and generally you can move your money around as frequently as you like. But a few fund families limit the switches in various ways to protect the fund against a sudden loss of assets in any one fund and to deter the shareholder from making hasty decisions.

A number of companies have good reputations for performance and offer a variety of funds. A sampling of the families that meet those criteria would include Fidelity, Kemper, Putnam, T. Rowe Price, Stein Roe & Farnham, Vanguard — and many more.

Your own selection of a mutual-fund family should be based chiefly on how well its stock funds have performed over the past decade. The most successful funds have been the so-called aggressive ones, which put shareholders' money in small or medium-size companies with big potential for growth. The time may come when you will want to transfer some assets from your money-market fund to your stock mutual fund. If you have chosen your fund group carefully, you will be able to keep it all in the family.

How Safe Are the Money Funds?

IF YOU have put cash in a money-market fund, not only are your savings collecting relatively high interest, but most probably they are also quite safe. Certainly, money funds have most of the convenient attributes of bank checking accounts. Almost always, you can take out, dollar for dollar, what you have put in, plus dividends. They are usually declared daily and automatically credited to your account.

However, there are some risks. Although investors look upon money-market funds as reliable alternatives to the friendly neighborhood bank, even the soundest of them are a bit chancier than banks. For one thing, money-fund interest rates can plummet. Back in 1976, for example, they even dropped below passbook savings rates. When interest rates fall, it is easy enough for you to pull your deposits from money funds. But this very freedom can hobble the funds' ability to pay off on the deposits. Indeed, when interest rates drop, some depositors tend to take flight like sparrows off a wire. In a few rare cases, this can cause you trouble; you may not necessarily get back every penny that you have put in.

Guardian angels do not watch over every money-market fund. In 1978, a small fund, the First Multifund for Daily Income, had to lower its share price from $1 to 93 cents. That was like a bank coldly telling its depositors: "Sorry, but we will now return only 93 cents of every dollar in your account." Redemptions began accelerating, and First Multifund eventually merged into another fund.

In 1980, another fund, Institutional Liquid Assets, came close to a similar experience. But then its distinguished sponsors, which included the First National Bank of Chicago and the Wall Street investment banking firm of Salomon Brothers, pumped in new money — and so, investors could collect 100 cents on the dollar.

The lesson for investors is not to abandon money funds but to choose them with care. Here are three guidelines:

First, know the manager or sponsor. You needn't entrust your money to complete strangers. You may already do business with a firm that sponsors a money fund, say, a brokerage house, a life insurance company or a mutual-fund group. A sponsor with an established reputation for financial responsibility will not jeopardize it by abandoning its customers. Strong sponsorship can give investors more peace of mind.

Second, go for funds that invest in securities that have a low average maturity — 45 to 60 days at most. That is the average length of time a fund has to hold on to an investment before cashing it in. As a rule, the shorter the average maturity, the safer the fund. The average maturities of large funds are published once a week in some newspapers. Also, most funds will supply the information via a toll-free telephone number.

Third — and to repeat — don't chase after the highest possible yields, or the hottest fund of the month. Over a year's time, the difference in interest payments between one fund and another is likely to be inconsequential. The customer shouldn't be greedy. He or she should expect a reasonable rate of return.

You can look up the rating of your money-market fund in a newsletter called *Income and Safety*. It ranks the 135 largest funds from AAA+ through BB on the basis of the diversification, maturity and quality of their investments. For a free copy of this newsletter, write *Income and Safety*, 3471 North Federal Highway, Fort Lauderdale, Florida 33306 (800-327-6720).

Treasury Securities

I F YOU are looking for the safest place in the world to invest your money, look to the federal government. Uncle Sam borrows more than $200 billion a year, and if he cannot pay his debts, he can always print more money.

The government securities with the most appeal for individual investors are Treasury bills, notes and bonds.

Bills are sold in minimum denominations of $10,000, and they come in three-, six-, and 12-month maturities.

Notes are usually sold in minimum denominations of $5,000 when they have maturities of less than four years — and in minimums of $1,000 when they have maturities of four years or more. You can get them in maturities ranging from one year to 10 years.

Bonds also sell in minimums of $1,000 but have maturities of more than 10 years. If you were grading these bonds on a report card, their yields of 8.8% for 30-year issues in mid-1988 would earn them marks of A-minus. They pay a percentage point or two less than similar debt issues of top-rated corporations. But all government securities rate an A-plus for safety.

You can buy Treasury issues through any of the 12 Federal Reserve banks or 25 branch offices. Or, you can order them by mail, using forms that you get from your local Fed bank.

The securities come to market at various intervals. For example, three- and six-month bills are auctioned off every Monday; 12-month bills are sold every four weeks on Thursday; two-year notes are generally sold at the end of each month; four-year notes are usually auctioned off in March, June, September and December; 10-year notes and 30-year bonds are usually sold in January, March, July and October.

You also can buy Treasuries from a commercial bank or your broker. This eliminates much of the hassle, but costs $25 to $50 and can wipe out a significant part of your return.

One problem: you will pay a rather stiff penalty if you ever want to sell your government securities before they mature. Just as brokers will charge a small investor substantially more than the market price if he is buying, so they will pay him substantially less if he is selling.

Thus, you are best off sticking to new government issues and holding them until they mature.

One big benefit: the interest you earn on Treasury securities is exempt from state and local taxes.

And when you buy a Treasury bill, you get another nice extra. Let's take one example with round numbers for easy calculation: If you bought, say, a $10,000 10% one-year bill, it cost you only $9,000 — that is, $10,000 minus 10%. A year later you will be paid the full $10,000. The real interest that you will collect is your $1,000 profit divided by your $9,000 investment. In fact, that's not 10%, but a fat 11.1%.

Your Borrowing

Your Best Deals in Loans

IT USED to be that borrowing could actually save you money in the long run. When inflation was running wild, it made sense to avoid future price increases by buying on credit. No longer. Inflation has been relatively moderate, so the real cost of borrowing has been at one of its highest points in years.

For example, in mid-1988 banks were charging an average 18.3% on your credit-card purchases. Well, subtract the 4.5% inflation rate from the 18.3% interest rate, and you see that you would be paying a real rate of almost 14% on your credit-card loan. Compare that with the real rate in 1980. Back then it was only 4%!

Moreover, since the beginning of 1987, interest on consumer loans such as car, college and credit-card loans has not been fully deductible, making borrowing all the more expensive. Deductions for the interest on these loans is being phased out: on your taxes for 1988, 40% will be deductible; for 1989, 20% will be; for 1990, 10%; and in 1991, the write-off will vanish altogether.

There is nothing wrong with borrowing — provided you do it wisely. Never borrow more than you can reasonably pay off. Never borrow for luxuries, such as gifts and vacation travel, if that means you will not be able to borrow for necessities, such as mortgage, medical or education expenses.

You should be sure, of course, that you are getting the most economical interest-rate deal. You may well be best off borrowing from a credit union, if you belong to one. Or taking out a lump-sum loan from a bank or a savings institution and paying it back in installments. In mid-1988 major banks in New York City, for example, were charging 10½% to 14% for personal loans that you could secure with collateral such as a savings account, stocks or bonds. For unsecured loans — which you often can get if you have a good job or regular income and can afford the repayments — they were charging about 16%. The rates are a couple of points less than the average for your credit-card debts. So, if you are paying interest on big credit-card balances, it may make sense to switch to an unsecured credit line and pay off your credit cards.

If you own publicly traded stocks or bonds, you can go to a stockbroker and take out a margin loan, commonly for half the value of your securities. He or she will charge you interest of generally ½% to 2½% above the rate that bankers charge brokers for loans.

The point is that when you are looking for money, you generally should canvass several different kinds of lenders. That's because no bank, savings and loan, credit union or finance company will have the lowest rate for every type of borrowing.

The best place to start searching for a general-purpose loan is where you keep your checking and savings accounts. Many banks charge as much as two percentage points less for loans to customers than to noncustomers.

If you are shopping for financing for a new car, you can often drive a better bargain on the showroom floor than at the bank. To move their cars, finance divisions of General Motors, Ford and Chrysler frequently charge several points less than banks do for car loans.

If you want to finance the purchase of a house or apartment, you will find that rates on mortgages do not vary a lot from lender to lender. Still, it pays to shop around because small variations can become significant over the long term of the mortgage. Generally, you will get the most competitive rates and terms at savings and loan associations and at mortgage banking firms.

If you already have bought a home, you can turn it into a piggy bank. You do that by applying for either a second mortgage or a home-equity line of credit.

The best place to get a second mortgage is a bank or savings and loan association. Recent rates have been between 11% and 13%. You can get a home-equity credit line from banks, savings and loans and brokerage firms. The rate in mid-1988 was about 11%.

Another source of cheap credit may be your life insurance policy. Whole life policies written before 1980 permit borrowing at 6% or even less; policies written after that have fixed rates of 8% or higher, or variable rates that in mid-1988 were around 10½%.

Many companies also let employees borrow from their assets in corporate profit-sharing or stock plans, and from corporate savings plans.

Finally, you can borrow money from your Individual Retirement Account once a year without penalty — just so long as you repay it within 60 days.

Many of these forms of borrowing are elaborated on in subsequent chapters in this section of the book.

Fast Ways to Raise Cash

Do you need to raise cash *quickly*? Perhaps you have a wedding to pay for, or some college tuition bills that are coming due soon. If so, you can still find loans that offer terms of endearment.

Start with your family. Loans from family members are inexpensive and need not be secured by collateral. If the loan is interest-free, it could be subject to federal gift tax laws. But under those laws, a relative can lend you up to $10,000 without incurring any gift tax.

Of course, in exchange for cheap credit, you run the risk of straining a family relationship. To lessen that possibility, you should draw up a promissory note. You can get preprinted forms at many stationery stores. The agreement should include a repayment schedule. If interest is charged, you should agree to an annual rate that is high enough to compensate your relatives for their forgone income. That figure might be as much as 10%.

In order to borrow against your life insurance policy you need the kind that has cash value, such as whole life. The amount you can borrow will depend on the number of years that the policy has been in effect, your age when it was issued and the size of the policy's death benefit. You do not have to disclose the reason for the loan, and you can repay at your own pace — or not at all. The interest rate probably will range between 5% and 8% per year. The longer you have been building your policy's cash value, the lower the rate.

More and more company-sponsored savings and profit-sharing funds also let vested employees borrow against the money they have in the plans. Typically, you can borrow up to $10,000 of your vested assets, plus half of your nonvested assets, with a limit of $50,000. How much interest will you pay? Companies usually base the charges on broad indexes of interest, such as those on long-term corporate bonds. In mid-1988, rates were slightly more than 10%. You usually make your repayments by payroll deductions.

Federal restrictions limit the maximum permissible loan to $50,000, and loans between $10,000 and $50,000 cannot exceed half your vested benefit in a company savings plan. Generally, with a company plan you are also required by federal law to repay the loan within five years. But if you are using the money to buy a house, you can get a payback period of from 10 to 25 years.

Banks and credit unions still are quick sources of loans — in the 10%-to-15% range in mid-1988. If you think those rates are high, just consider how steep they would be if government deregulation had not heightened competition.

The cheapest consumer loans typically are offered by credit unions. But the differences between their rates and those of other lenders is narrowing. That is one reason why you should shop around carefully before you sign any papers.

Another reason is that few credit unions make unsecured personal loans larger than $5,000. By contrast, many banks give their customers $10,000 credit lines secured only by a signature. To qualify, you will have to satisfy a series of income, net worth and length-of-employment requirements.

Often you can join a credit union by depositing a nominal sum — sometimes as little as $5. To qualify you generally must belong to the group whose members formed the credit union — a church, a labor union, a community or professional organization. But joining a credit union is a lot easier than it used to be. You may be eligible and not even know it. In 1982, the National Credit Union Administration liberalized its regulations. No longer do you have to work for the same company or belong to the same union as other members. For example, the First Community Credit Union in St. Louis previously could serve only employees of the Monsanto company. Now it is open to residents of three communities near the Monsanto headquarters and to employees of over 100 other companies in the area. Some credit unions now even permit members' distant relatives to join. For more information about credit unions in your area, write to Credit Union National Association, Box 431, Madison, Wisconsin 53701.

If you own stocks or bonds at a brokerage house, you can borrow on margin. You just pledge a portion of your holdings as collateral. The interest rates in mid-1988 were 9% to 10½%. Interest is usually charged to your account and compounded once a month.

The size of the margin loan you will qualify for depends on the type and market value of the securities you pledge, and the purpose for which you want to borrow. If you want $10,000 to buy stocks, for example, you must already own shares worth that amount. But if you want to borrow $10,000 on margin to buy something *other* than stocks and bonds, you will have to meet higher margin requirements ranging from $12,000 worth of U.S. Treasury notes to $20,000 in stock as collateral.

Now, say you have one of the new asset-management accounts at a bank or a brokerage house. You can borrow against your deposited assets by cashing checks drawn on the account. The rate in mid-1988 was 8¾% to 10¼%.

Another way to get a loan is to borrow against the equity you have built up in your home. Your choices include home-equity accounts, second mortgages and refinancing.

Of the three, home-equity accounts are probably the least costly. They are essentially overdraft checking accounts that you can open at a bank or brokerage firm, using the equity in your home to secure the credit. In mid-1988, the rates on such loans ranged from 10% to 13%. (For more, see "Your Borrowing: Getting Money from Your House.") Second mortgages have been available for between 11% and 13%. Rates for refinancing are somewhat lower, but stiff closing costs can sharply boost the total amount you will pay.

If other lenders will not oblige, then you can investigate consumer finance companies. Such firms make high-rate loans to high-risk customers.

Finally, if you need some money for just a short period of time, you can even consider borrowing from your Individual Retirement Account. No, you cannot permanently take money out of your IRA without paying income taxes on it and a 10% penalty. At least you cannot do it unless you are 59½ or older. But it is all right to withdraw some or all of your IRA funds once a year — if you make a rollover and replace them within 60 days. There is no penalty on that.

Just go to the bank or brokerage house or wherever you have your

IRA on deposit and take out some or all of your assets. If your IRA is invested in stocks or mutual funds, you may sell them. But be sure to replace all those assets within 60 days.

When you borrow from your IRA, you pay no interest on the loan, of course, because you are acting as your own banker. On the other hand, you will not collect any interest or dividends on your money so long as it is out of your Individual Retirement Account.

Getting Money from Your House

You can borrow against the equity in your house without suffering the hassle of a conventional second mortgage. Instead, many banks and brokerages offer a homeowner's equity account. An independent appraiser values your house, and then you can usually borrow up to 80% of your equity in it. You must borrow at least $1,000 and are likely to pay an interest rate about 2% above the prime rate, which is lower than the usual charge for second mortgages. There is no penalty if you pay off your loan early.

This type of loan is good for financing a child's education or an addition to the house. But because the funds are so accessible, beware of using a homeowner's equity account for risky investments. If you lose all your money, you lose your equity in the house, too!

If you are a retired homeowner, you can get monthly income from your property and still live in it. Look into a so-called reverse mortgage. It lets you borrow against your house and collect the loan proceeds — minus the interest — in the form of monthly payments. This goes on for a limited period, typically seven years. At the end of the term you have to pay off the loan, which can mean selling the house.

Then there's the shared-appreciation reverse mortgage. It assures you of income for the rest of your life or until you move. In one variation, you take out a loan against your house and pledge to give the mortgage company 50% or 100% of any future appreciation on the property. The more you pledge, the higher the monthly payments you collect. When you die, the mortgage company sells the house. The company then keeps the agreed-on share of any appreciation, plus an amount equal to all the monthly payments it made to you. Anything that is left over goes to your heirs.

How Much Debt Can You Handle?

Of ALL the financial mistakes imaginable, the grimmest is falling too deeply into debt. You do not have to be poor to get bogged down in excessive borrowing. Yet there is no reason to slip in beyond your means. Fortunately, there are ways to figure out how much debt you can comfortably handle.

Think hard about whether you really want to borrow at all. It is not cheap. Short-term rates on personal loans not backed by collateral averaged 16% in mid-1988. And with inflation at moderate levels, you no longer can count on paying back creditors in significantly cheaper dollars.

Most people, of course, do not have the luxury of avoiding debts altogether. So when you do borrow, remember: Necessities come first. These are followed by loans to finance long-term assets such as home improvements, major appliances, furniture and, most important, education for your children. Be sure to reserve some borrowing capacity for emergencies, such as unforeseen medical bills. Only after you have provided for necessities, long-term assets and emergencies should you even consider using credit for such indulgences as grand-luxe vacations.

Here is a test that can help tell you how much debt is too much for you:

First, estimate your current annual disposable income — that is all your income, minus your tax withholdings as well as contributions to various personal retirement, savings and investment plans.

Next, map out the year's expenses. Calculate how much of them will require various forms of debt, notably installment loans.

Debt counselors and credit managers generally agree that no more than 15% to 20% of your disposable income should be committed to installment debt, not counting home mortgage payments. Do not necessarily consider this your own upper limit. You may become nervous at only 10%, particularly if there is only one breadwinner in the family and you have a number of dependents.

How to Pay Off Your Debts

MEMBERS of Congress are not the only ones having trouble balancing a budget. Many families, too, are struggling to trim their own deficit spending. Just ask yourself:

— Am I borrowing to pay off old bills?

— Am I spending more than 15% to 20% of my take-home pay on monthly installment debts above and beyond my home mortgage?

— Am I constantly forced to dip into my checking overdraft and rarely able to bring it down?

— Do I find it hard to save regularly even a small part of my income?

A "yes" to any of those questions could be a warning that you are living beyond your means. If so, there are sensible steps you can take. It is precisely when they feel they are overwhelmed by bills and responsibilities that many people decide to plan for the future as they never have before.

Once you have concluded that you are in trouble, your first order of business is to determine exactly how much income you receive and itemize your monthly expenses. List all your monthly bills in their order of importance. Set priorities for paying them off. Probably the first priority will be to pay your home mortgage, and then your monthly utility and installment bills.

What if you find that you are still in debt over your head? Then it is wise to seek out your creditors and negotiate to stretch out your debts, that is, to arrange a longer term of repayment in smaller amounts each month. Creditors have a great deal of latitude to extend the due date on bills by up to 30 days. They possibly can refinance a debt to allow lower, though longer, payment — even if you are overdue 90 days.

If you have trouble meeting your same mortgage payments, go to your mortgage lender for help. The last thing a lender wants is to foreclose on your property. He would much rather have your cash. So, in most cases a loan can be rescheduled and payments reduced if necessary.

You might be tempted to sign up for a consolidation loan to pay off all your debts. That is simply not smart. The lure of a consolidation loan is that a bank or finance company will take over your many debts and you, in turn, will make payments to that one institution. The catch is that the interest rate on such a loan is likely to be high. So you could be replacing a heap of moderate debts with one big one that costs more to carry.

Even while working off your debt, you should plan to save. Setting aside as little as 3% to 5% of monthly income after taxes helps you start considering saving as an integral part of your budget.

Credit Counselors

PEOPLE who have trouble composing a debt-repayment schedule within a workable budget would do well to seek the guidance of a credit counselor. This professional will be sympathetic but firm. A counselor will ask you to provide intimate details about your total monthly income and expenses, a list of your outstanding bills and copies of any correspondence you have had with creditors about debts and loan. He or she will want to know whether you have been dunned by creditors or threatened with legal action, or whether a creditor has sought to have your pay garnished.

Next, the counselor will get in touch with your creditors. Counselors have more clout than you might, since creditors often prefer to deal with professionals. Your counselor will intercede on your behalf to reduce and stretch out monthly payments on debts while you organize your finances. The creditors may be in the mood to hold off for a while — because the *last* thing they want is for you to default and go bankrupt. They want to be sure to be repaid, and later is better than not at all. Sometimes, a counselor can even knock down the total balance due. Once you have renegotiated the debt terms through your counselor, you make your monthly payments to him or her. Your counselor then manages the debt for you.

Debtors who seek counseling actually may be rated better credit risks in the future. If a person completes a debt-repayment plan, lenders often consider him rehabilitated and will entertain other loan applications. Bankers do not believe that once a deadbeat, always a deadbeat.

Before you approach any credit-counseling agency for help, find out whether it is a nonprofit clinic or a for-profit company or simply a bill collector subsidized by your creditors. There are some 350 nonprofit credit-counseling organizations across the country. They are almost always better than the for-profit organizations, which charge much more. The National Foundation for Consumer Credit will direct you to nonprofit services in your state. Send a self-addressed, stamped envelope to NFCC, Suite 507, 8701 Georgia Avenue, Silver Spring, Maryland 20910. The phone number is 301-589-5600.

The nonprofit groups will ask for an initial contribution of an average of $10, although no one is turned away. Later they may request small fees for specific debt-repayment services. They also ask creditors to contribute 10% to 15% of the monthly payments that the counselors make on their client's behalf.

The American Association of Credit Counselors represents privately owned, for-profit companies. Twenty-five states specifically prohibit such operations. Where profit-making credit counseling is legal, state laws usually limit fees. They average about 12½% of the debt that a company manages for you, prorated over the term of your contract.

Scoring Points with Lenders

To DETERMINE whether or not you qualify for a loan, many lenders evaluate you according to a mysterious point system. That is why, whether you are applying for a loan or just a credit card, you will fill in dozens of blanks and answer enough questions to make you recall the Spanish Inquisition.

Lenders keep their credit rating systems secret, so it is difficult to find out what information is worth the most points in determining whether you get the credit you seek. Almost certainly, however, you will be scored on the number and types of existing loans and charge cards you list on your application. It helps a lot if you already have and use other forms of credit. The most desirable types you can have are the travel and entertainment cards, followed by bank credit cards and department-store charge cards. If you have a good record for paying credit-card bills and installment loans on time, that is a plus. But lenders do not like to see loans from finance companies on your application. A significant percentage of bad credit risks have been in debt to finance companies.

Your income may help you pass the credit test, but lenders know that someone who earns $40,000 a year is not necessarily twice as creditworthy as someone who makes $20,000. If more than 35% to 40% of your gross income goes to paying off current debts, including mortgage and auto loan payments, lenders are not likely to approve your application. In general, you are better off if you own your home rather than rent, and if you already have a checking or savings account.

If at first you don't succeed, apply and apply again. Ask why you were rejected and offer additional information. Or, go to another lender or credit-card issuer. Each one has different standards.

Checking Your Credit Rating

W HEN you apply for a loan, the prospective lender will probably check your credit record. But how can you ensure that this all-important record is fair and accurate?

Private credit bureaus are in the business of compiling the record of how promptly and fully you pay your bills. Then they sell this information to other companies — when you apply to those companies for a loan, for an insurance policy or even for a job.

If you get turned down for credit, the firm that refused you must tell you the name of the credit bureau it used in making its decision. You then should contact that bureau and ask for a copy of your report. The bureau is required by law to tell you what is in your file. If you request the information within 30 days of your having been denied credit, the bureau will charge you no fee. Otherwise, fees run about $10.

You can challenge any information in your file. If the credit bureau cannot confirm the disputed information, it must delete the information. If you request it, the bureau also must send a revised copy of your report to any credit grantor that received the report in the last six months.

Even if the credit bureau finds that the information is valid, you can write an explanation for anything you may have done that is considered wrong. The credit bureau should then attach your explanation, or a clear summary of it, to your report. That way, anyone who receives your credit history will also get your side of the story.

But what if you have made some very late payments or other credit bloopers in the past? How soon can you start with a clean slate? Most of your mistakes will be removed from your record within seven years after they occurred. The only incident that can remain longer is bankruptcy.

Finance Your Own Co-op

IF YOU operate a consumer co-op or would like to form one, a government-funded bank wants to lend you money.

Co-ops are hardly new. Farmers have banded together for more than a century to market their crops, and tenants have been forming co-ops for years to buy and run apartment buildings in New York City. But they have not caught on in many parts of the country, partly because conventional banks are wary of lending money to them.

The National Cooperative Bank in Washington, however, is eager to finance not only traditional cooperatives but also imaginative new ventures. For instance, the bank recently lent $3 million to Fastener Industries, a 100% employee-owned company in Berea, Ohio, to finance a leveraged buyout acquisition of a company in an unrelated business. The bank charges market rates. For more information, call the National Cooperative Bank at 202-745-4600.

What Credit Cards Do You Need?

THIS year alone, anyone with a good credit history could get in the mail as many as 10 invitations to sign up for different credit cards. But few people really need more than one or two. Keeping your credit cards to a minimum helps check impulse spending and reduces your risk if the cards are lost or stolen.

If you do not do considerable driving or traveling, you probably can get by with just one card. Your best bet would be a bank credit card, such as Visa or MasterCard. Both are honored at some 6 million establishments worldwide.

If you travel extensively or run up a large expense account, you need a travel-and-entertainment card, such as American Express, Diners Club or Carte Blanche. Such cards do not have any spending limits. By contrast, the credit line on a bank card can be eaten up quickly by an airline ticket and a few nights in a hotel.

Be careful of appeals to sign up for so-called premium cards. Annual fees may run from $35 to $250, compared with $15 to $45 for standard cards. You do get some extras with prestige plastic — often including higher credit limits, more generous check-cashing privileges and nonfee traveler's checks. But you may find that you do not make much use of the added attractions. In that case, you are just paying extra for snob appeal.

At the other end of the spectrum, a few banks still offer cards with no annual fee. A list of them is sold for $1.50 by BankCard Holders of America, Suite 1000, 460 Spring Park Place, Herndon, Virginia 22070. The association also sells for $1.50 a separate list of banks charging the lowest interest rates.

Before you sign up for any card, be sure you will not be cramped by a credit limit that is too low. Very important, find out what the interest rate is on unpaid balances. It typically ranges from 10½% to 22% a year, depending on the state where the card is issued. Of course, you can avoid finance charges if you pay your balances in full each month.

To get a bargain interest rate, you may have to deal with a bank outside your home state. And there is nothing wrong with that. Arkansas has the lowest credit-card rate ceiling, by state law. Banks there were charging about 10½% in mid-1987, and one bank issues cards nationwide.

The kind of card you pick should be determined by your payment habits. If you run up big bills and don't pay them right away, look for a card with the lowest interest rate. But if you pay off your bills promptly each month, pick one with no annual fee.

Quite a few credit cards now entitle you to a host of extras. Check closely before signing up for these cards. If the issuer is not charging you for the extras directly, you will probably pay for them through hefty annual fees and interest rates. While the prime rate was 9% in mid-1988, the average rate charged on credit-card balances was stuck at a steep 18.3%. That was about 3% more than most banks were demanding for unsecured personal loans.

If you are in the market for a new card, here are some of the enhancements you can expect to find:

For an extra $30 or so, many banks will enroll you in a toll-free telephone shopping service such as Comp-U-Store. It offers 250,000 items, from fresh flowers to cars, up to 50% below list price.

You also might be able to sign up for a toll-free message service. While traveling, you can leave or receive messages by calling an 800 number. This can be useful if you travel frequently and are hard to reach.

Some cards issue you checks, which you can fill out and use even at many stores that do not honor credit cards. But unlike most card purchases, you are charged for interest payments on the credit-card checks as soon as they clear the banks.

In general, big-city banks offer the most perks. For example, through Citicorp you can get $20 worth of credits with every $100 you charge. You can apply the credits to one of a dozen or so household products in a catalogue that the bank mails to cardholders four times a year. For an additional annual fee of $48, the California-based Bank of America offers a discount travel service called Trip-America. Meanwhile, the First National Bank of Chicago gives you automobile road service and $150,000 worth of travel and accident insurance for $34 extra a year.

Many banks are now issuing MasterCard and Visa as so-called debit cards. They look like credit cards, but they are not. With credit cards, you receive a bill every month for whatever you have charged. Then it is up to you to pay it. With a debit card, payments are taken automatically from your checking or savings account. They are transferred to the retailer's account as soon as his copy of your charge reaches the bank.

So if you choose to use a debit card, you should keep track of all your purchases with it. In fact, you should be as meticulous with your debit-card records as you are with your checkbook. And if your debit card is lost or stolen, be aware that you may well have greater liability for unauthorized charges on it than you would with a credit card.

Your Career

Defying the Common Myths

Ask a career counselor for the hottest job prospects, and you will hear that the future belongs to those who can command the computer. That's great news for anyone who cottons to modems and megabytes. The computer does indeed stand to create more careers than any invention since the wheel. But if you follow the herd to high-tech when your heart lies elsewhere, you may be making an expensive mistake. The wisest counsel in looking for a job is to pursue your own desires.

A surprising number of determined men and women are finding excellent jobs in fields that the career prophets have written off. They are doing it by challenging some of the common myths of job hunting. As writer Patricia O'Toole has observed, if you are determined to get into even the most glutted occupation, you cannot allow yourself to be daunted by common career myths.

Do not, for example, let Labor Department job projections be your guide. They are full of occupations that no longer exist and fail to mention many new fields, such as robotics or hazardous-waste management. National labor forecasts often obscure opportunities in your own community. For example, by tuning in to local trends, job hunters several years ago might have spotted how Connecticut, in the slow-growing Northeast, was making an economic comeback.

Spurred by the rise of high-tech and financial services businesses, the state now has one of the healthiest employment rates in the country. Job projections often underestimate the time it takes for new technologies to spread. For instance, genetic engineering is breeding considerably less employment than early enthusiasts had predicted.

Don't fret about getting caught in so-called female ghetto jobs. For example, social workers are finding terrific corporate jobs in employee counseling. And believe it or not, the world can use another writer — in fact, many of them. They will be needed to interpret and organize the computer data flood. Newsletters, TV cable services and trade journals all will require people who can convert raw data into readable English.

Don't accept the myth that a high-tech boom means a low-tech bust. Far from it. There is a surge in demand for personal services. As the population ages, one of the fastest-expanding careers will be geriatric nursing. But the real sleeper among service occupations may well be teaching. Millions of computer buyers will need instruction, and so will millions of semi-literate workers. Hundreds of corporations already run remedial English and math classes.

Don't fall for the line that it is better to be a specialist than a generalist. Across the country, Ph.D.'s are broadening themselves by enrolling in intensive short-term introduction to business courses — and becoming everything from factory managers to security analysts. Among the best-paid generalists are the so-called issues managers. They scan the horizons for developments that could affect a corporation's business. Issues managers have diverse backgrounds in the social sciences, hard sciences, finance, law, journalism and public relations.

Don't think you have to have an M.B.A. — a master's degree in business — to get ahead. The degree may get you in the door, but after that you will have to scramble like everybody else.

Don't assume that big corporations offer the most opportunities. During the 1970s, the 1,000 largest corporations created only 75,000 jobs. But small business generated 9.6 million jobs — most of them in enterprises with 20 or fewer employees.

Don't be afraid to start your own business. The hours are long and paupers outnumber princes, but working for yourself gives you the chance to do things your way.

Don't figure you have to go to the big city to find your fortune. From 1969 to 1984, the number of manufacturing jobs in metropolitan areas declined by 6.8%, but in rural areas it grew by 10.4%. Nor are factory jobs all that are cropping up in the country. The most plentiful jobs are in construction, transportation, finance and whole-sale trade. One reason for these new opportunities is that long distances between city and country just are not what they used to be. Telephone computer networks and improved trucking routes have shortened them. And many of the goods being produced in the country, such as products of microchip technology, are often light, compact and perfect for long-haul trips to market.

If you want to find employment and are willing to pick up and go, small towns and rural areas may offer your best chance.

Where the Opportunities Are

WHETHER you are self-employed or work for a company owned by others, you will find that the greatest job growth in the immediate future will occur in financial and business services, health care, recreation, engineering and, of course, telecommunications, computers and other high-tech businesses.

Accountants, financial analysts, personnel managers and other business specialists can look forward to keen demand for their services. Jobs for accountants alone will grow by as much as 40% in the next decade. Newcomers to accounting earn an average salary of $24,000 and as much as $32,000 in large companies. After three to five years, their paychecks climb to between $33,000 and $50,000. Promotion to corporate accounting manager, which may take six or more years, brings a jump to an average of $60,000 and can pay $80,000 or more.

Other business specialties require a combination of management and technical training, and their corporate status and salaries have been rising markedly. A benefits administrator in personnel with five years' experience can earn as much as $40,000. Personnel directors of major companies average more than $100,000 a year.

Careers in financial services are expanding because of the new attitude people have toward money. More Americans are willing to invest the effort and expense to plan their savings and investments. So brokerage houses and insurance companies are setting up financial-planning departments. In addition, banks, brokerage houses, real estate companies and other financial concerns will be hiring waves of analysts, portfolio managers, marketing specialists and, above all, salespeople. Some financial jobs will require M.B.A. degrees, but would-be stockbrokers who have sales experience in any area will be eligible for training programs at the brokerage firms.

In fact, the job prospects for salespeople are exceptionally bright in most industries. From 1986 to 2000, according to the Bureau of Labor Statistics, 3.7 million new sales jobs will open up; that is an increase of 30%. For example, Century 21, the real estate company, plans to hire 85,000 new people by 1990. The company's chiefs are looking for property managers and people to put together syndications and arrange mortgages. But most of the new jobs will be in real estate sales.

The increase in the number of two-career couples will provide more work for the relocation, personnel and headhunting firms that will have to solve the problems of moving an executive who also has a working spouse.

Another growing area will be child care. Ten million mothers with young children may well be working by 1990, and many of them will want day-care centers. Also, small businesses that help with time-consuming household chores should do well.

With the 65-and-over population rapidly expanding — some 35 million Americans will be in that age group by the year 2000 — there will be a need for business consultants who do retirement counseling and pension planning. To provide sufficient health care for the elderly, more and more other types of trained people will be required. Only several hundred doctors now are expert in geriatric medicine, but we will need some 9,000 of them by 1990 to serve an aging nation. That is only the beginning, and the field is by no means limited to doctors. According to some estimates, by the year 2000 there will be jobs for more than 500,000 therapists, researchers, nurses and workers in residential-care communities and group-living centers for older people.

The rising American concern with staying healthy will create still additional jobs. Medical centers will need technicians to run diagnostic equipment; office managers, marketing executives and accountants to handle the books; and nurses to treat patients.

A severe shortage of nurses pushed up entry-level pay about 40% from 1978 to 1988. Nursing-school graduates now start at $18,000 to $30,000 on hospital staffs, depending on the region. Head nurses are earning up to $42,000. Pay is highest on the East and West coasts. A master's degree improves earnings by as much as one-third. More than 800,000 nursing jobs will open up by the year 2000.

Computers will create new jobs — and not only where you expect them. More openings will come in banks, utilities and other businesses that use the mighty microchip than in those that manufacture it. Companies will be looking for programmers and systems engineers. And anyone who can develop software for micro- and personal computers will not have to hunt long for work.

The U.S. is in transition from an industrial society to an information society. In this new world, the individual and the computer will have to work together as a team. Everybody who wants to get ahead in this new society will need not only one skill but several skills. Humanists had better be able to communicate with technicians. Engineers should know how to read a balance sheet. In a world of expanded trade, people in business would be wise to know one or more foreign languages.

The workplace is shifting from emphasis on the narrow specialist who is in danger of becoming obsolete to the multiskilled generalist who can adapt. For people who can stay flexible in their jobs, the career paths of the future are wide open.

Here are some other ideas for careers in the 1990s:

— Career counselors. Because fewer young people will be coming along to enter the job market, there will be a labor shortage in some sectors. So companies will have to hire more young mothers and semi-retired people, and many of these workers will want career counseling.

— Water resource experts. The water shortage of the 1990s could become severe in many places. We shall require more hydrologists, environmental engineers and others to preserve our most important of all resources.

— Toxicologists. Business and government will want them to detect harmful effects of natural and man-made substances that pollute the environment.

— Molecular biologists and biological engineers. They will be hired by the biological engineering firms.

— Industrial relations specialists. With the new emphasis on enhancing industrial and office productivity, these experts will be called on to work out corporate agreements between management and labor.

— Development economists. People with college degrees in international economics and business will help to market American products abroad.

— Technicians, entertainers and writers. They will bring entertainment into the home by means of cable television and video cassettes.

— Entrepreneurs. The U.S. needs plenty of these daring risk takers to start new businesses. For anybody who has a marketable idea — from the highly technical world of electronics and computers to the everyday realm of retailing — entrepreneurship can offer one of the best careers of the era. (See "Your Enterprise.")

Where the Big Pay Is

How can you get the best salary — and where can you get it? Some companies have a tradition of paying well, notably those exploring the frontiers of science and the new technologies. But within any industry, salaries commonly are 15% higher at the most openhanded firms than at the most tightfisted ones. The principal factor is size: the higher a company's sales volume, the greater its pay is likely to be.

Many fields offer impressive rewards for accomplishment. Among the traditional standouts are law, investment banking, stock brokerage and executive recruiting. Yet in a number of fields, mostly those that are considered glamorous, starting salaries are small. But they climb sharply in the upper-middle to upper ranks. Television and advertising are examples.

Starting pay at law firms ranges all the way from the teens to the low fifties. Although a handful of big-city firms offer stratospheric salaries, that remuneration has less to do with an individual's immediate performance than his or her future promise.

Market conditions also influence pay. Partly because rich oil companies in the early 1980s bid up the going rate for secretaries in Houston to around $20,000, less lucrative businesses there were forced to pay more for secretaries, too. Geography, however, has less influence than it once did. More than three-quarters of all companies adhere to a national schedule, paying the same amount for the same job regardless of location.

Bigger companies tend to pay better than smaller ones. Low-profit companies pay low or give meager raises or both. Old companies or those in established fields such as steel and autos tend to offer a larger share of total pay in the form of fringe benefits than those in new businesses do. But the new ones give more stock bonuses and options.

It is unwise to sell your skills short, even in times when the economy is sluggish. In bureaucratic corporations with ossified pay systems, employees who start out cheap may never catch up.

Boomtowns

WHICH communities will offer you the best career opportunities in the future? You might well find that the most powerful factor behind the creation of jobs is the presence of prestigious, research-oriented universities. Their faculty members and graduate students often launch innovative companies, many in new high-tech realms.

Whole new industries spring up around university laboratories, according to David L. Birch, director of the Program on Neighborhood and Regional Change at MIT and the nation's leading authority on how jobs are created. His research concludes that the metropolitan areas where job growth promises to be brightest in the 1990s include those clustered around Los Angeles, New York, Dallas, San Francisco, Houston, Boston and Atlanta.

Fastest-growing of all should be the Los Angeles area, which is expected to top New York by the end of the 1990s as the nation's number-one job and population center. Much of the job activity in the region seems likely to move south to neighboring Orange County.

New York claims global preeminence in finance, advertising and the arts. After two decades of decline, the population of Manhattan is slowly climbing again. Still, the fastest job growth is occurring at the exurban fringes — in New Jersey, up the Hudson River valley as far as Poughkeepsie, and in Fairfield County, Connecticut.

Dallas, with its diversified economy, has been far less affected by falling oil prices than Houston. Economic expansion — and job growth — has shifted to the northern outskirts around Plano.

San Francisco has lost about 30,000 jobs in banking, finance and manufacturing since 1980. Big companies such as Pacific Bell, Bank of America and Chevron have moved thousands of employees to suburban locations to cut costs. But major job growth in the ten-county metropolitan area is under way in communities ringing San Francisco.

The Houston area, hit with job losses in the oil slump, is likely to rebound in the next four to five years on the strength of entrepreneurs in such fields as medical technology and computer software.

Boston has the nation's largest concentration of educational institutions, and they employ nearly 10% of its labor force. The area is loaded with young, fast-growing companies, many with university ties, and financial services, electronics, computers, software, medical research and consulting.

As for Atlanta, it is being transformed by fringe growth, notably in Gwinnett County, northeast of downtown. In addition, growing industries such as computer software are expected to generate many new jobs in the Washington, D.C., area, notably in the counties surrounding the city. And the well-diversified Phoenix area also continues to expand.

Three other areas that share extraordinary growth records and prospects are Austin, Texas, Raleigh-Durham, North Carolina and San Diego. All enjoy close ties to universities.

Does an M.B.A. Still Pay?

To earn one of those cherished master's degrees in business administration typically costs $10,000 to $20,000 a year in tuition and expenses for a full-time student. That is besides salary lost by studying rather than working for two school years. But does it still pay to get an M.B.A.?

The number of M.B.A.'s granted each year has more than tripled since 1970 to more than 67,000. Some 200,000 students, including part-timers, are enrolled in graduate business and management programs. Consequently, an M.B.A. no longer guarantees you an advantage in the race to top management positions. Tempting jobs open to graduates of even the most prestigious business schools are somewhat harder to get than they were in the late 1970s and early

1980s. Starting salaries are still high, but many no longer seem as startling as they did in the past. The average M.B.A. with little work experience and a nontechnical undergraduate degree got a job paying about $33,500 in 1988. That was not a great deal more than engineers with only bachelor's degrees got.

One way to gain the most benefit from an investment in an M.B.A. is to attend a first-rate graduate business school. The top ones include the schools at Stanford, Harvard, Chicago, Pennsylvania, Northwestern, Illinois, Texas, MIT, Berkeley, Michigan, Dartmouth, Columbia, Virginia and Carnegie-Mellon.

The payoff of attending one of those schools can be impressive: 26% of Harvard's graduates in 1988 took jobs in management consulting at a remarkably high median salary of $65,100.

It is also wise to earn a degree in science or technology *before* going to business school. The M.B.A.'s with undergraduate majors in engineering or hard sciences not only get jobs more easily than those without such backgrounds, but their starting salaries can be as much as 20% higher. Another smart move is to work for a few years before going to graduate business school.

The most successful combination for a new M.B.A. is to have a technical or scientific undergraduate degree *and* work experience. In 1988, such graduates with two to four years' work experience typically started at more than $45,000. That was about 35% higher than M.B.A.'s who majored in liberal arts as undergrads and had never held full-time jobs.

Opportunities Without College Degrees

THE Sunday papers are thick with openings for bank tellers, commercial artists, data processors, electronics technicians, medical technologists, nurses and secretaries. What's more, fewer and fewer of these classified ads stipulate a college degree as a requirement.

True though, graduates of four-year colleges still have a financial edge over workers without sheepskins. The latest statistics show that in 1986, the median earnings for 22- to 24-year-olds with a degree were $16,242 — 26% higher than wages earned by people with one to three years of college. And four-year grads earned a dramatic 39% more than those with only a high-school diploma.

Even so, many job openings call for skills that you are more likely to acquire in a technical school or on the job than on some ivied campus. Technical school graduates are routinely landing jobs with a higher starting pay than newly minted bachelors of arts can command. A computer programmer fresh from a six-month course can earn $21,000 a year while an English major is still home rewriting his résumé.

Technical training is expensive, but because it is condensed it costs far less than a $60,000 university degree. At one technical school, for example, a 12-month program to train electronic technicians is $6,560. Many two-year community colleges and private junior colleges offer vocational training at considerably lower cost than do private technical schools. Tuition averages about $680 a year for such job-oriented studies as data processing, police science, real estate sales and auto mechanics.

What is most valuable in vocational education — whether at a community college or a technical school — is hands-on training. When choosing a program, first visit the school and ask many questions. Inquire about the school's resources as well as about the time devoted to learning by doing. Also check to see which companies hire the most graduates. Then query those companies' personnel managers on how they rate the school's courses.

High-tech companies that need a competent work force often educate people in specialized skills. The list of such corporations includes AT&T, IBM, Xerox, Wang Laboratories and Control Data. A bachelor of science graduate of a 36-month course at the De Vry Institute of Technology in Chicago can get a job starting at about $22,000 a year. That's a fair return on an investment of $18,900 in tuition and registration fees.

The best deal, of course, is getting paid to learn a skill. Competition for on-the-job apprenticeships has always been stiff, but as business expands, so will the need for trainees. Along with the standard apprenticeships for plumbers, pipefitters and carpenters, there are programs in hundreds of other occupations, including biomedical equipment technician, meteorologist and chef.

The Labor Department's Bureau of Apprenticeship and Training supervises programs in 785 occupations. State agencies with information about apprenticeships are listed in the phone directory, usually under State Government, Employment Security Administration or the state's Department of Labor and Industry.

Even without training, high-school graduates can land worthwhile jobs in marketing, retailing and a few other fields. And in some government-regulated sales fields — particularly real estate, securities and insurance — a beginning file clerk can impress a boss by studying hard and passing a licensing exam.

Second Careers for Women

F OR many wives and mothers, work resumes at 40. But any woman who wants to re-enter the job market will find that she needs some shrewd strategies to do it.

The most serious difficulty confronting re-entry women is a lack of confidence and focus: too many of them tend to undervalue their previous experience. If you are one who does, you should know that many of the skills needed to manage a household or organize a charity bazaar can be transferred to business. Are ill-defined ambitions a problem? The solution may be career-planning workshops offered by countless nonprofit agencies, individual counselors and almost every university and community college. Courses vary from six weeks to six months and cost about $150 to $250.

An excellent source for women wanting to re-enter or advance in the job market is the nonprofit Catalyst organization's directory of 178 resource centers throughout the country. These offer career and educational counseling. Catalyst also provides briefs on 40 occupations for $4 each. You can write to Catalyst at 250 Park Avenue South, New York, New York 10003.

After determining your career objective, you may discover that you need to refurbish your skills before you try them out again. That's fine, but beware: some older women are tempted to dock in the safe harbor of academe. They go to college for year after year, stacking degree upon degree, never braving the rougher waters of the marketplace. Although men tend to think that they would not want a job if they already know how to do it, women often think that they have to be able to do a job before they can take it. Thus women tend to "overcredentialize" themselves and hold back from the day of reckoning.

As a first step back into the market, draft a résumé. You will want to present yourself in it in a way that is meant to fit your specific goal. Unless your educational credentials are recent or sterling, you probably will want to downplay them and play up your volunteer and other experience. Employers often are unimpressed with degrees or other credentials older than your teenage son.

Omit the personal details. Nobody is going to say her health is *terrible*. By law an employer cannot ask your age, marital status, or whether you have children. These same statistics are best left out of a résumé. When many an employer sees "children" written on a résumé, he or she thinks of "sick days."

Your instinct may be to run off 200 copies of your résumé and wallpaper the town. But, instead, you should treat this master copy as a draft and customize your résumé to correspond to the specific opening you are trying to fill.

To get a job interview, begin by telephoning friends and informing them that you are leaving the homestead for the wage-paying world. Use that grapevine of contacts you have developed — everyone from old school friends to members of clubs you have joined.

Even if you have had many years of significant but unpaid experience, your first re-entry job is likely to be on the lower rungs of the labor force. You should not be either insulted or excessively concerned if it is less glamorous, less responsible and lower paying than you expected. What is critical is that the job positions you for growth within the company or your chosen field.

One starting spot that rewards initiative handsomely is often overlooked — or looked down upon — by women. That position is sales. Insurance, brokerage and real estate firms will pay you at least a modest salary to learn the business. Commissions can quickly fatten the pay envelope once you master the skills. Most important, sales jobs provide avenues for advancement.

Part-Time Jobs for Professionals

A NEW class of high earners is working less and enjoying it more. The number of part-timers is fast expanding, and so is the list of employers welcoming them — and willing to pay them well.

In all, 20 million Americans work part-time — 17% of the nation's labor force. A surprising number of these are professionals, from surgeons to sales managers. To be a professional and a part-time worker was once a contradiction in terms. But no more. Today, about 2.2 million professionals choose to work part-time. Some do so voluntarily, others are motivated by economic forces. Whatever the reason, one out of every 11 professionals today has decided to forgo full-time employment.

Inventive variations in part-time work are becoming more common. Some people put in a full 40 hours or more a week but for, say, only six months or less a year. For some married couples or for two women who want to partially re-enter the workplace, job sharing makes a comfortable fit. What they do is divide one position's hours and responsibilities.

The part-time work that is easiest for professionals to get is in hard-to-find specialized skills. These include medicine, law, accounting, engineering and, especially, data processing. Professionals who have experience in these areas can find many jobs in federal agencies. The Federal Employees Part-Time Career Employment Act of 1978 opened 30,000 part-time positions, not only for scarce professionals but for middle managers as well. And all states now have policies permitting part-time positions in government.

Such jobs are harder to find in private industry because most corporations employ only a handful of part-time professionals. Yet some exceptional firms have large numbers of part-time posts, from engineer to loan officer. Among those employers have been the Equitable Life Assurance Society in New York City and the Bank of Boston.

Of course, the fewer hours you put in on the job, the less money you take out. About one-third of all part-timers get employer-provided health insurance. Typically, however, businesses prorate benefits or just don't provide any at all.

Since managers offer part-time work to hold on to valued employees, you may have more chances to reduce your hours on an existing job than to find a new part-time position. The most persuasive way to convince your boss to cut your hours is to keep a record for two or three months of exactly what tasks you do and how much time you need to do them. That will help you estimate how much you could get done with fewer hours and what responsibilities could be shifted to others.

You also should be able to show how you would keep up with responsibilities that normally require full-time hours, such as travel and staff meetings. Always stress the *quality* of your work above the money the company would save on your salary.

Tracking down a part-time job at another company will take considerably more time and effort. Such positions above the clerical level are rarely advertised, while ads that promise high earnings for part-time work at home are primarily misleading come-ons for such travails as pushing hard-to-sell goods.

Although employment agencies find jobs for part-time professionals, you will probably deal directly with a company if you want to become a permanent part-time employee. The wisest way to find a part-time job is to send a résumé with a brief cover letter stating your qualifications and what services you can provide — part-time. If you get an interview, be prepared to explain how you would handle specific problems that a job might present for someone working part-time. Also, volunteer to go full-time when emergencies arise. And offer to work a scaled-down schedule on a trial basis for a few months.

For more information on how and where to get part-time jobs, you can write to the Association of Part-Time Professionals, Inc., Flow General Building, 7655 Old Springhouse Road, McLean, Virginia 22102.

Making Moonlighting Pay

M ORE and more people hold down not one job but two. If you are one of these moonlighters, there are some rules you should follow to make the most of your second job and stay out of trouble with your primary employer, with the taxman and with your own family.

More than 5 million Americans work at second jobs, and they put in an average of 14 hours a week at them. They moonlight for many reasons: to earn more money, of course, but also because they may feel stuck on a plateau in their primary job, or because they want to lay the groundwork for a new career, or just because they yearn to exploit some skill or hobby and have fun.

They do a countless variety of things: a Long Island pediatrician conducts wine-appreciation courses on weekends and Wednesday evenings; a Kansas City, Kansas, family therapist is a weekend auctioneer; a New York civil engineer moonlights as a cabinetmaker and resurfacer of paddle-tennis courts.

If you want to take a second job, writer William C. Banks has suggested some rules to follow:

— Read a book for advice. A valuable one is Jay David's *How to Play the Moonlighting Game,* published by Facts on File, Inc.

— Tell your boss at your primary job that you are moonlighting, but assure him or her that your second career won't interfere with your regular work.

— Be sure to charge enough for your moonlighting. Bill any clients one-third to one-half *more* than your regular daytime wage. After all, you are working overtime, and you do have some expenses.

— Schedule your time so that you have some regular hours for relaxation and to spend with your family. If you find that you are having more than the usual tension on your regular job or that you are becoming tired or irritable, cut down on the moonlighting.

No one wants you to succeed in your part-time career more than the Internal Revenue Service. It defines moonlighting as a sideline business and demands a share of your take. As a self-employed moonlighter, you also will have to pay a Social Security tax of 13.02% on your net free-lance income, unless you earn $45,000 or more from your regular job and your employer has withheld from your paycheck the maximum Social Security contribution — just over $3,000 on income earned in 1988.

But the self-employed can get special tax breaks as well. If you show a profit in three years out of five, you are presumed to be running a business rather than a hobby, and you will be allowed to deduct from your entire taxable income any losses your enterprise generates. You must, however, keep detailed, accurate records of the income and expenses of your moonlighting activities.

First, you can deduct the cost of all supplies used in your venture, plus the business mileage on your car and parking fees and tolls.

Second, if you have an office or work space at home that you use *only* for business, you can deduct the portion of your rent, heat and utility costs that goes into maintaining the office. But you cannot deduct more than your net income from the business.

Third, you can deduct from your sideline income a certain amount of your business equipment purchases. The maximum deductible varies, depending on how you and your spouse file your taxes and other factors. You can deduct $10,000 as long as your business equipment purchases are less than $200,000 for the year. When you spend more than the deductible amount, you then can depreciate the excess cost.

Computer Jobs

THE belief is common that computers are wiping out countless traditional jobs, but in fact jobs created by the computer are going begging. Not enough people have the necessary skills. According to the Bureau of Labor Statistics, demand for people with the right training is expected to increase by 73% from 1986 to 2000. We shall need about 1.5 million specialists in computer fields.

Already there is call for whole new armies of trained workers to run computers; for systems analysts, who devise ways for computers to handle information; for programmers, who tell the machines what to do; for technicians, who maintain and repair the complex equipment. The need is also great for people who can teach others to use the machines. Thus, out-of-work schoolteachers are profiting from the new technology. After some retooling, many teachers are finding jobs training employees at companies that use computers. Small wonder that John Kemeny, former president of Dartmouth College, says, "It is as unforgivable to let a student graduate without knowing how to use a computer as it was in the past to let him graduate without knowing how to use a library."

People throughout the work force can improve their job status if they learn to adapt to computers. Word processors may put some typists out of work, but secretaries can use the machines to do the dull part of their jobs while they take on more responsibility. Similarly, the fastest moving business managers will be those who are the most creative in employing computers to streamline operations and save money.

If you do not know much about them, you can plug into the world of computers by taking night courses at community colleges that give you some experience with the machines. You also can learn to program computers by enrolling full-time at one of the schools that specialize in retraining. The price can be steep, $3,000 or $4,000. Often, however, your employer will pay for much or all of your retraining course.

The cheapest way to start learning about computers is by reading specialized magazines such as *Personal Computing*, which will set you back only $3. Or for a bit more you can buy a book on the subject. One thorough text that is easy to read is *Overcoming Computer*

Illiteracy: A Friendly Introduction to Computers by Susan Curran and Ray Curnow. It is put out by Penguin Publishing and costs $12.95.

Particularly rich career opportunities are opening up for computer systems analysts. They are the troubleshooters of the electronic age, working for most large companies as well as schools, hospitals and government agencies. The number of jobs in the field is expected to grow by the year 2000 to nearly 600,000 — a 76% increase over the number in 1986. A shortage of analysts is anticipated, and that would kick up their pay. It is already high, about $25,000 to $50,000, or more in some large cities.

Systems analysts seldom work directly on computers — some do not even know how to — but they have to understand what the machines can do. Their job is to figure out ways computers can solve problems. In brief, systems analysts are the human masters behind the electronic brains. They determine how to save a company time, effort and money. The analyst can streamline billing, keep track of inventory moving around the warehouse and devise ways to pull together a company's financial records.

Suppose a company wants to computerize its payroll department. Call for the systems analyst! He or she has to spend a few weeks in the department poring over records and interviewing people who work there. Next, the analyst makes up a list of all the pieces of raw data that go into calculating the payroll. For example, if the company has employees in more than one state, the details of each state's tax code have to be on the list. Finally, the analyst turns the list over to the computer programmer and gives him or her step-by-step instructions on how the computer is to put all that data together to produce the correct paycheck for each employee.

The instructions sound like gibberish. An opening sentence might read: "Build a table in working storage to accommodate 1,000 batch numbers." But that is as good as plain English to the programmer, who translates the instructions into terms the computer understands and does the physical work on the machine. Systems analysts can spend a whole year computerizing a payroll — and then come back if a major change is needed.

Suppose you or someone you know would like to become a computer analyst. To qualify, you usually need a few years' experience in the industry where you want to work. It helps considerably if you have had exposure to the company's financial dealings.

Many analysts have never attended college. They simply learned computer programming in night school, got jobs in a company's data-processing department and then moved up to the higher-paid post of systems analyst. True, companies are looking for people with a bachelor's or even a master's degree in business from a school with a well-regarded computer science curriculum. But given a choice, employers still prefer an analyst who knows the company's business to one whose computer training is strong.

The basic skill required by systems analysts is the ability to communicate well. That is because they have to find out from a company's employees what jobs they want done. Nonanalysts often have an exaggerated notion of the wonders that computers can perform. A wise analyst has to mesh these expectations with the realities of what computers actually can accomplish.

Are there any drawbacks to this career? The one serious complaint is that there are no well-traveled paths to top management. Usually the best an analyst can hope for is to become chief of computer operations. But analysts' jobs do take them around the company, from department to department. So a fortunate analyst may catch the eye of an executive who might offer him or her jobs that would move him or her into the company's mainstream.

Engineers

IN help-wanted ads around the country, one message is loud and explicit: engineers are needed — badly. The computer revolution and other high-tech developments will fuel a huge demand for them throughout the decade. The Labor Department estimates that the U.S. will need more than 500,000 more engineers in 1995 than it had in 1984. Colleges will be hard pressed to educate enough people to fill all the jobs. Even the civil engineering field, which had suffered during the construction slump of the late 1970s and early 1980s, is expected to boom. The government anticipates that 229,000 civil engineering jobs will be open in 1995 — 31% more than in 1984.

Spurred by equal-opportunity laws, companies are bidding up salaries for women and blacks and other minorities in engineering. In fact, women sometimes start out at higher pay than men. In the early 1970s, only 3% of all engineering students were women; today, they make up more than 15% of the undergraduate engineering students. Highly regarded engineering schools are at the University of California, Illinois, Michigan, MIT and Stanford. Of course, quality teaching is available in lesser-known schools, too.

For students coming straight from undergraduate school, engineering jobs offer the highest pay — for example, about $31,000 for entry-level chemical engineers in 1988. Generally, oil, chemical and drug companies pay the most; government agencies and colleges the least. In many companies, engineering is a route to the top. Recent chief executives at Exxon, Westinghouse and AT&T started as engineers.

The higher the climb, the less engineering is practiced. Some engineers who prefer the drawing board to administrative chores choose not to advance. So a number of companies promote pure technicians to some sort of consulting or distinguished fellow status. These jobs carry salaries of $70,000 to $80,000 and sometimes more — roughly equivalent to upper middle management.

With the rapid pace of technological change, engineers constantly have to re-educate themselves. They say that their usable knowledge has a half-life of eight years. That is, half of what an engineer knows when he starts out is obsolete in that time.

Financial-Services Jobs

THE financial-services business is changing as never before. So there are new job opportunities with banks and insurance companies, brokerage firms and mutual funds.

The best beginning jobs tend to go to people with a bachelor's degree in finance. But there also are openings for liberal-arts grads, for professionals who want to switch careers and for housewives returning to work. They can start out earning from $10,000 to $30,000. The lowest salaries are for jobs that involve selling, which many financial-services careers do. But salespeople also have the potential for the highest incomes because they collect commissions. The chief requirement for salespeople in brokerage houses and insurance companies is personality.

Demand is plentiful for people with technical training, too. Anyone who can write computer programs has a particular advantage in looking for a job. Liberal-arts majors can become securities analysts, investment managers and tax planners. They do not usually earn as much as top salespeople who are on commission, but analysts and managers can do very well.

The Bureau of Labor Statistics estimates that by the year 2000, banks will employ almost 2 million people in entry and managerial positions — over 13% more than they did in 1986. Generally you need a bachelor's degree, and often an M.B.A., for the good jobs.

For example, one large bank hired about 150 beginners in 1983. Those with undergraduate degrees were usually routed to accounting, auditing or marketing. They were paid $20,000 to start. But half of the newcomers were M.B.A.'s, expected to use their newly acquired skills in the bond, commercial lending, real estate, tax or trust departments. Their salaries were $30,000 to start.

People who do the hiring are not too impressed by flashy applicants. They are looking for the ability to persuade, negotiate and collaborate. That's because most banking jobs still involve some kind of selling. Lending officers in particular are expected to drum up new business.

While bankers usually earn only a salary, stockbrokers work almost entirely on commission. So there is no limit to what they can earn — if they are willing to work hard. But the money does not always come easily. Starting out as a securities salesman usually requires pursuing new accounts aggressively, making many cold calls all day long and having people — from close friends to total strangers — say "no" to you.

On the theory that clients prefer older account executives, most brokerage firms' personnel directors tell young people to get a couple of years' selling experience and then reapply. Those hired are paid $1,500 to $2,000 a month for the first year. Then their salary comes down, but their commissions pick up.

Some of the highest-salaried brokerage positions are held by securities analysts, who study companies for potential investment. Top analysts can earn well into six figures. Openings are few, and substantial experience is almost always required, but firms sometimes hire novices who show exceptional promise.

One way to take advantage of the bull market in financial-services jobs is to join the growing ranks of financial planners. These professionals analyze a client's entire financial situation and make recommendations about where he or she should invest and save his or her money. To become a fully trained financial planner, you have to pass six to 10 college-level courses. Two schools that offer the courses by mail are the College for Financial Planning (9725 East Hampden Avenue, Suite 200, Denver, Colorado 80231-4993) and the American College (270 Bryn Mawr Avenue, Bryn Mawr, Pennsylvania 19010).

Most planners come from large brokerage or insurance companies where they work on commission. Then they may set out on their own to become planners and charge a fee for their advice. Sometimes they also sell mutual funds, insurance and tax shelters and collect commissions.

Another career area to consider is insurance. Life insurance sales have grown strongly over the last decade and agents' commissions are up, thanks to the renewed popularity of permanent policies such as whole, universal and variable life. Full-time agents who have been in business three to five years or more average about $31,500 in earnings.

Many of the largest insurers hire people in their late 20s who have had a bit of experience selling. Salaries might start at around $20,000 and gradually decrease as the agents' commissions increase. Most insurance companies do not have their own sales corps but instead rely on independent agents. The independents offer customers a broad line of policies and annuities from any number of companies. The growth end of insurance now is selling policies not to individuals but to small businesses and big corporations or, through them, to large groups of employees.

Health Administrators

HEALTH-CARE administration is a flourishing profession that gives you the chance to do well by doing good. Managing a hospital or nursing home is much like managing any enterprise — except that the decisions can determine whether someone lives or dies.

What a health-care administrator does depends largely on the size of the institution he works for. A director of an 1,100-bed New York hospital spends his days and about a third of his evenings in meetings — on how to contain costs, raise funds, recruit specialists and whether to invest in the latest equipment. His salary is around $120,000 a year.

The administrator of a 70-bed hospital and nursing home in a small town in Idaho has plenty of meetings, too, but typically they are with surgeons about improving the light in the operating room or with the dietitian about how to contain the costs of meals. She also squeezes in visits to patients. Her salary is $39,000 — but, like her big-city counterpart, she also comes away with a sense of accomplishment.

As running medical institutions has become more complex, the administrative ranks have swelled to include not only the director or administrator, but also many middle managers who are skilled in accounting and market research. Some 336,000 people worked in the field in 1984; by 1995, almost 500,000 jobs are expected to be filled.

Many will be outside the medical institution — for example, in government agencies, where administrators may analyze regional needs for health care. Some experts also are hired by insurance companies, where they may design new types of coverage. Quite a few of the best opportunities are in the fast-expanding health maintenance organizations, which sell prepaid medical plans entitling subscribers to the services of a staff of salaried physicians.

Jobs in health administration can be both exciting and frustrating. At any moment, a hospital administrator is apt to get a call: a child needs a blood transfusion but her parents forbid it on religious grounds. On the spot, the administrator must decide whether to get a court order or go ahead with treatment.

These jobs call for stamina and patience. Administrators must wrestle with aggrieved patients and their relatives, feisty community groups, unions, demanding doctors and trustees. Administrators share chronic problems: too little money, too few nurses, constant turnover among low-paid aides, and strict, ever-changing government regulations. But the psychic rewards can be rich.

To land a job in the field, you usually have to have a bachelor of science degree or, for high-level positions, a master of business administration or a master of health administration. Some 30 schools offer undergraduate degrees in health-services administration; the two best regarded are at the University of New Hampshire and at Penn State. Among the outstanding graduate programs, all two-year courses, are those at the universities of Chicago, Michigan, Minnesota and Washington.

The starting salaries for an administrative assistant with a graduate degree range from $30,000 to $33,000, except in nursing homes, where the range is $25,000 to $28,000. After 10 years' experience, the figure jumps to anywhere from $45,000 for a nursing-home manager to $100,000 for the administrator of a hospital. Directors of hospital chains earn $125,000 or more.

People who want hospital careers can improve their prospects by joining chains such as the Hospital Corporation of America. And nursing-home administrators are in such short supply that a number of states allow them to head more than one nursing home.

Management Consultants

As corporate profits become harder to achieve, demand will rise for those corporate doctors, the management consultants. So business school graduates are rushing into the field. Consulting should flourish as clients seek help with lagging productivity, inflation and new product development.

Most of the best beginning positions are with consulting firms or with public accounting firms that offer consulting services. To land a job with a top outfit, you usually need an M.B.A. from a first-rate school. A few years' work experience also will get you in the door. People seeking a second career in management consulting can bring it off only if they offer solid grounding in a specialty. A product manager at a major consumer goods company, for example, could turn into a consumer marketing consultant.

It is not uncommon for high-ranking graduates of the best business schools to start in management consulting firms at $60,000 or more — sometimes much more. Since their services are so expensive, successful consultants must be able to get to the root of a problem and produce solutions quickly. A consultant must be articulate, assertive and versatile enough to sell his or her solution to the assistant plant managers, as well as the company president, without offending either.

One drawback, even for those who like consulting, is travel. Executives of big firms say their staff managers spend 30% of their time on the road. Another complaint is that consulting gives you influence but no real power to enforce decisions. But for bright young comers who are not sure where they want to work, consulting provides exposure within a corporation and a stepping-stone to a top-line job.

Military Officers

Long the nation's employer of last resort, the military is becoming downright upscale. To get a few good men and women, the Army, Air Force, Navy and Marines are offering sharply increased pay, abundant fringe benefits and generous pensions. From 1980 to 1988, military compensation soared 46%. Many people, particularly college graduates, can find remarkable opportunities as officers. A second lieutenant now can collect $25,000 a year, and a full colonel with 22 years of service easily commands $60,000. These earnings are made up of base pay plus tax-free allowances for housing and meals.

Then there are all the benefits: 30-day vacations, free family medical care, some free housing on base and a retirement plan paid for entirely by the government. The pension equals 45% of the base pay after 20 years of service, three-fourths after 30. Other benefits include discounts at commissaries and post exchanges, Veterans Administration mortgages, postgraduate scholarships with full pay and almost $11,000 for educational expenses. In addition, women are entitled to four weeks' paid maternity leave.

Although Uncle Sam may want you, he may not have room. Military commissions that were yours almost for the asking in the early 1980s are now hard to come by. Higher compensation is attracting heavy competition for commissions and is inducing officers to stay in the services. The attrition rate is the lowest since the Vietnam War.

There are three main routes to earning an officer's commission.

First are the officer candidate and training schools of the Army, Air Force, Navy and Marines. They fill most of their openings by recruiting people who are particularly qualified to become specialists, such as pilots or engineers. You can apply to any one of the 5,000 recruiting stations that the services maintain across the country. These schools once were the fast track into the military for college graduates. But now they are particularly difficult to enter. For example, in 1987 the Army received some 3,500 applications for 1,300 openings.

Second are the most prestigious sources of commissions: the Military Academy at West Point, the Air Force Academy at Colorado

Springs and the Naval Academy at Annapolis. Each pays cadets or midshipmen about $500 a month. After they are commissioned, they must serve at least five years on active duty.

Here is how to apply: In the fall of your junior year in high school, write to the academy of your choice for an application kit. Follow its instructions, then write to the U.S. congressman for your district and to both of your U.S. senators, asking them to nominate you. The legislators' staffs look for students with grades in the top fifth of their classes, good health, participation in athletics, leadership potential and gung-ho personalities. Each academy chooses enough candidates to fill the legislator's quota of five students in a school at any given time. Every year, about 1,100 freshmen enter each of the academies through congressional nomination.

Third, the broadest channel to a commission is college ROTC. It produces more than 12,000 officers a year. To become one of them, you take one to four years of military-science courses, drill periodically and show up for summer training. Almost 100,000 students are enrolled in ROTC. Many have scholarships, with the government picking up the bill for four years of college. But after they graduate, scholarship recipients must serve at least four years on active duty. (For more, see "Your Education: Financial Aid You Still Can Get.")

Paralegals

FOR a solid career in the law without spending the time and money to get a law degree, think about becoming a paralegal. The Bureau of Labor Statistics estimates that the number of paralegal jobs will more than double, to 125,000, from 1986 to the year 2000. The average starting salary is about $18,000.

Paralegals work for lawyers, researching cases and drafting documents. There is no standard licensing exam for them. Some law firms train their own paralegals, but many others prefer to hire graduates of certificate programs. These are usually one or two semesters long, and they are offered by colleges and vocational schools. For a list of such programs, contact your state bar association. Or write to the American Bar Association's Standing Committee on Legal Assistants, 750 North Lake Shore Drive, Chicago, Illinois 60611.

Secretaries

PARTLY because many women are turning their backs on traditional career roles, tens of thousands of secretarial jobs are wide open and waiting to be filled.

Not long ago, the Bank of America declared that on any given day it was advertising openings for 30 secretaries. Of those who responded, many were overqualified college graduates who could not find jobs in their chosen fields, so they were unhappy from the start. Quite a few of the rest were inadequately trained high school graduates. The shortage of competent secretaries remains severe, and it is likely to grow worse. The Department of Labor estimates that 478,000 secretarial jobs will open up every year through the mid-1990s. Employers probably will court secretaries by boosting pay and by making it easier to advance to better jobs.

A record 4 million secretaries are now employed, yet one out of five jobs that become available goes unfilled. Firms seeking women who will stay in secretarial positions often hire back-to-work housewives who got their training 20 years ago. Their skills, employers report, tend to be superb and their work ethic excellent.

The complaint is common that today's high school graduates do not have the basic skills. As the women's movement has dimmed the desire for secretarial work, the number of students who want to learn shorthand has diminished. Many schools offer only a beginning course, although it usually takes three semesters to become proficient. High schools do not emphasize spelling and grammar the way they used to, so many grads have trouble writing business letters.

Today, beginners start at $15,000 to $18,000 a year. Pay tends to be lowest in the South and Midwest and highest on the East and West coasts, and in large cities. The range for experienced secretaries in New York City, for example, is from $30,000 to $50,000, although some earn even more. Those who take shorthand can make $4,000 more than those who do not, and a bachelor of arts degree can command up to $5,000 more than a high-school diploma.

Job aspirants who can afford $6,495 may take an 8½-month course at Katharine Gibbs, the country's best-known secretarial school. The curriculum includes the usual skills plus electronic word processing and accounting. There is also a course in poise — called "professional development"—which requires students to observe themselves on videotape as they perform their duties. A dress code prevails, too: no jeans, sneakers or clogs.

Fewer than 1% of secretaries are men, and that is not expected to increase, because most think it's a woman's job. One man who disagrees is Herbert Nelson, secretary to the chairman of the *Bergen Record,* a New Jersey newspaper. After a quarter-century in this capacity, he draws an imposing salary of at least $60,000.

The payoff for top skills in many companies is that a secretary's career path follows her boss's. When he gets a promotion he takes her with him, a practice sometimes called "fate-sharing." Militant women complain that this reduces secretaries to appendages of their bosses. They urge management to post job openings scrupulously and to encourage women to apply for higher-ranking jobs. Indeed, many of them do move into management. With demand for competent secretaries at an all-time high, opportunities to advance should become greater than ever.

Secretaries who stay in their jobs say they enjoy them for two reasons. They get to know a lot about what is going on in a company without having to take the heavy responsibility for it, and they enjoy helping their bosses be more productive. They make it easier for him or her to succeed, and when he or she does, they share the satisfaction.

Teachers

MANY teachers are finding lucrative jobs outside the schools and colleges. They are switching from the schoolroom to the corporate-run training room.

During the late 1980s, millions of computer buyers will need instruction. So will millions of office and factory workers. More than 300 corporations run remedial classes in English and math. Large banks and insurance companies provide the most remedial education. The person likely to do the hiring of teachers is the director of training and development. The median salary is $38,000.

If you are a teacher, an essential strategy for making the switch is to develop—and use—acquaintances in business. Serve on school committees that have ties to local industry or participate in community organizations where you are likely to meet people in business. Once you are in the corporate door, you can pick up other industrial training specialties. And from there you might be able to move to a job in management.

The boom in adult education also has brought a roaring demand for part-time teachers of subjects as diverse as programming a computer or finding a mate. If you have a skill, you might be able to earn some extra money by teaching it.

Men and women are going back to school by the millions to study an enormous range of subjects. They are interested in courses from the practical, such as How to Live Well Without Going Broke, to the whimsical, such as The Art of Social Climbing. The teachers whom most adults prefer are not ivory-tower academics but those who have earned their knowledge on the job and have direct experience to share.

As a part-time teacher of an adult education course, you can expect to earn perhaps $18 to $20 an hour. But if your course is extremely popular, you can make as much as $400 an hour. All expenses connected with teaching are tax-deductible. There are non-monetary rewards, too, such as learning more about your field and gaining potential clients and business contacts.

The most popular adult education subjects are: starting a small business, making money in stocks and bonds, and how to buy, use and program computers. Demand is also brisk for courses in physical fitness, assertiveness training, practical topics such as plumbing and bicycle repair, and affairs of the heart, from divorce to middle-age dating.

The best places to get part-time jobs in adult education are at community colleges, municipal recreation agencies or the fast-spreading, noncredit independent learning centers. If you teach through a learning center, you usually will function as an independent contractor, taking 30% to 50% of the fees. Tuition generally ranges from $20 to $75 per student per course. For its cut of your fees, the center will promote your course in its catalogues, handle student registration and give both you and your curriculum a sense of legitimacy.

Successful Techniques for Job Hunting

JOB hunting is a skill, and it is fairly easy to learn how to do it right. Once you master a few techniques, you will substantially increase your chances of getting a job—whether you are entering the employment market for the first time or looking for a new position.

Take a case of how *not* to do it:

He seemed to have everything a job hunter could want: intelligence, charm and one of corporate America's prized credentials — a Harvard M.B.A. To distinguish himself, however, he wore a baseball cap as well as his three-piece suit to job interviews. He did indeed stick out — but he also struck out. Despite dozens of interviews, he got no offers.

The problem, of course, was the cap. Instead of marking him as a go-getting individualist, the hat told recruiters that he lacked self-confidence and was overly concerned with image. He had tried but misapplied the first rule of job hunting: Stand out from the pack. The way to do that is to do your own research into the company and its business, ask probing questions, and project certainty about yourself and your career goals without appearing smug.

The first hurdle in job hunting is to get an interview with prospective employers. Perhaps friends, business acquaintances or alumni of your high school or college can recommend you to employers whom they — or *their* friends — know personally. If all else fails, you might get an interview by writing directly to the employer. Send a forceful letter outlining your achievements and likely contributions to the company. But don't use such ruses as implying that you are something other than a job applicant.

Résumés are important, but they are not worth the incredibly long hours many job seekers invest in them. You probably can spend your time better in researching the company and thinking about how you specifically can be useful to it. The ideal résumé is no longer than one page. It should concentrate not on descriptions of your previous jobs but on your accomplishments: for example, "I increased sales 50% in six months." Do not exaggerate. An applicant who stretches the truth even about something innocuous will be branded as dishonest.

In preparing for your job interview, you have to look on yourself as a product for sale — cold-blooded as that may seem. First, you have to decide what the product is going to be — that is, what skills and qualities you have to offer an employer. The next step is to package your product well and to devise a strategy for selling it.

Like any salesman, you might practice your pitch on friends. But be prepared for the interviewer to throw some tough stock questions. One favorite is, "Tell me a little about yourself." A poor response to that begins, "Well, I was born on . . ." You would do much better to say something like: "Lately I've discovered that I can combine my abilities to . . ." and then go on to state specifically what you can do.

What you wear to the interview matters less than you may think. Of course, a serious applicant for a job at a traditional firm should not wear a scarlet jacket and white bucks or a diaphanous dress with a plunging neckline, not to mention a baseball cap. When in doubt, the best advice is to go conservative.

Since interviewers are impressed by applicants who ask sharp questions, it is wise to study the firm and its industry. You can read the company's annual report, ask a stockbroker for any written analyses of the firm and learn more about it in business reference books at a library.

Your sales presentation begins the moment you show up for the interview. Some personnel managers base their judgment partly on the office receptionist's reaction. If the applicant is rude to the receptionist, he will not get the job, no matter how smart he looks in the interview. It shows he is a two-class person.

Corporate recruiters recommend some techniques to help you stand out during an interview:

— Carry a folder marked with the company name — and take notes. That shows you are well organized.

— Convey enthusiasm. Try to turn your weaknesses into advantages. If an interviewer suggests that you lack qualifications, you can say that you are a fast learner who welcomes challenges — and then give an example.

— Prepare what vaudevillians used to call a "get-off line" — a parting comment that moves the recruiter closer to an offer. You might ask, for example, whether he sees any obstacles to hiring you.

Questions to Ask Your Prospective Employer

SWITCHING employers could be either the best decision of your working life — or a misstep that will make your old job seem like Paradise Lost. So, before you take a new job, you should ask a few crucial questions.

You might ask what happened to the last person who had the position you will be taking. If he or she was promoted, you will get some idea of where the job is likely to lead. If, instead, the person was fired, you may learn early on about a major stumbling block that could trip you up, too.

Ask to talk with someone at the company who is doing much the same job that you are being hired for. This person probably will be one of your soundest sources. Ask him or her whether your prospective boss is really as charming as he or she seems. Or ask about the *least* appealing aspect of working for the firm.

A good way to get general information about a company's style is by doing some research into the work histories and educational backgrounds of the top managers. Look them up in Dun & Bradstreet's *Reference Book of Corporate Managements* or in the *Standard & Poor's Register of Corporations, Directors and Executives*. They are available at major libraries. For example, if all top managers happen to have graduated from Ivy League colleges, that may tell you something about your chances for promotion. If you are a woman, you may want to find out how many women have advanced into upper management.

Find out as much as you can about the company's financial health. Is the firm growing? And where is this growth coming from? Your chances of advancement, of course, are greater if the company is expanding. Ask a stockbroker for research reports on the company. On the basis of its business outlook and strategy, consider where the company might be in five years.

Ask your prospective new boss or the person hiring you how and by whom your performance will be measured. You and your employer should agree on specific goals for you to accomplish — and a reasonable timetable for achieving them.

You will also want to know how the company will help you meet the goals you have agreed on. Your boss should stand ready to grant you powers commensurate with your responsibility. Will you have enough access to important support services, such as computers?

Ask what the salary range is for similar jobs in the organization. While you should aim to come in at the top of the range, this may still be too low. Many candidates will not consider changing jobs without a nice raise over their current pay.

What other compensation is the company willing to offer? This might include bonuses and benefits such as health plans and pension and profit-sharing programs. Your potential employer probably will be most impressed if you try to tie your compensation to your performance in as many ways as possible. Once you have worked out an agreeable compensation package, it is often a sound idea to have your prospective employer set down the details of the offer in a written memorandum.

Employment Contracts

EMPLOYMENT contracts are no longer just for movie stars. More and more managers are demanding — and getting — them. A survey of 500 big companies finds that nearly half have written understandings with their high-ranking employees. At some firms, executives down to assistant vice president have contracts.

You are most likely to get an employment contract if you are in an industry where competition for talent is fierce and ideas are at a premium. Many high-tech companies actually require employees to sign contracts that keep them from taking company secrets along with them if they leave.

The typical contract will guarantee you at least a certain minimum salary for two or three years, although you can be awarded raises that will increase it. A contract spells out your title, fringe benefits, bonuses, length of vacation and severance pay. In most cases, you agree not to quit during the term of the contract.

But if you are negotiating for a job, do not mention that you want a written agreement until an offer has been made and you agree to the terms of employment. In some cases it is enough to ask simply for a letter confirming the broad outlines of the terms. However, if you are dealing with complicated subjects such as stock options, you may want a more formal contract.

Pay particular attention to passages in the contract dealing with circumstances under which you may be fired. Avoid ill-defined words, such as "incompetence," which are subject to broad interpretation.

Be on the alert for contract provisions that could restrict your activities if you leave the company. Some employers may ask that you agree not to work for a competing firm. Make sure that what constitutes "competition" is defined as narrowly as possible.

And after you have struck a bargain, be sure to submit the proposed contract to your lawyer — *before* you sign it.

How to Move off a Plateau

BECAUSE of stiff competition in the job market, many people's careers are stalling at lower levels of work and at earlier ages than before. So, it takes more talent and drive to get ahead today than it has for many years. But by learning new skills and seeking added responsibilities, you can move up and off a career plateau. Several tactics:

Fortify yourself with knowledge. Take courses at a community college or specialized school to learn a new skill such as computer literacy or public speaking. It's quite possible that your company will subsidize your tuition.

Get involved in community or business projects. You can broaden your experience and increase your visibility by holding office in a professional group, writing an article in a trade journal or organizing a conference.

Look for new responsibilities to add to your job description. The delicate objective is to shine before superiors without alienating your immediate boss or co-workers. You don't want them to consider you an opportunist or a troublemaker. What you need is an idea that will make your superior's department look good and therefore win his blessing. Propose the plan to your immediate boss. With his approval, you can present it more formally to the company's higher-ups. If they let you try it and it works well, you're in a position to bargain for a new title or a raise or more authority. By showing eagerness to grow in your present job, you'll avoid being classified as deadwood.

Sometimes the best way to move a career off dead center is by trading your job for another at the same level. Many people now turn down transfers to other cities because they don't want to take on heavier mortgage costs or uproot a working spouse. Thus, it could pay for you to offer to move from headquarters to some distant branch office where opportunities may be richer.

Or you could talk to your boss about transferring to a different type of work in which you'd gain new skills. For example, an engineer who switches to a personnel job can acquire the managerial experience necessary for a higher-level technical assignment.

Another option is to continue doing the same job but in a department with room for advancement or with a specific need for your abilities. Even if such a horizontal shift doesn't lead to a promotion, the new challenges can get you out of a deadening routine.

To move sideways successfully, you need a history of creditable job performance, a sound plan and influential supporters. The first step is to zero in on the right department and job in your organization. Do not just listen for grapevine gossip. Check the employment office to find out who is hiring. Ask department heads to tell you their long-range plans. Scan trade magazines and securities analysts' reports to learn which parts of your industry are ripe for expansion.

Get help from insiders. Make lunch dates with people at your level or above. Ask about advancement opportunities and what it takes to land the job you're after. Only if every route off the plateau ends in a cul-de-sac should you look for a new employer.

Negotiating a Transfer

NEARLY half a million employees will be transferred away by their companies this year. If you are one of them, be careful to negotiate with your employer to get the best deal on moving expenses.

Most large companies have standard moving policies that supposedly leave little room for negotiation. But no matter how rigid the company position seems, employers are sometimes willing to make adjustments. If you know what to ask for, you can get more — and save yourself some unpleasant financial surprises.

The standard package begins with an agreement by the company to pay all the costs of transporting your household goods. If you own a house or condo, the company typically will arrange for the purchase of it at a price set by two or more local appraisers. If you sell the house yourself, your employer should pay for any real estate brokerage fees.

The company should cover any prepayment penalty on your old mortgage and pay for one or two house-hunting trips to the new location. Also ask for temporary living expenses for up to six weeks and up to three points for mortgage origination. And companies often provide interest-free or low-rate loans for down payments on your new house.

When you are negotiating a transfer, don't be afraid to ask for a raise at least large enough to offset any higher cost of living in the city where you are bound. Ask for an allowance of $1,000 to $5,000 to cover the costs of carpets, drapes and any other items you have to leave behind. These allowances are taxed as ordinary income by the federal, state and local governments. So, most companies give you still another allowance to offset that extra liability.

You should also get help in finding a job for a salaried spouse. Try to have the company hire a relocation firm to assist with résumés and to provide job counseling. And ask for compensation for child-care costs while your spouse is job hunting.

The Perils of Job Hopping

For those people who wonder whether the surest way to the top is to hop from job to job within a given field, or to stay with one company, here's a good word for fidelity. Job hopping may have its short-term attractions for ambitious people, but those at the top know it pays to stay with one employer. Eugene Jennings, a Michigan State University professor, tracked the careers of corporate presidents since 1953. He found that more than half of them remained loyal to one company.

True enough, job hopping can help you gain valuable training and experience in the early stages of your career. After that, the best reason to switch jobs is to overcome obstacles in your career path, such as a hostile boss or a demotion. Yes, job hopping is the accepted way to move up the ladder in a few volatile lines of work, such as advertising, television, fashion design, marketing, publishing and retailing. In recent years, the demand for hoppers has risen especially in high technology and information processing.

But elsewhere, restless job switchers sometimes are suspected of being merely opportunistic, perhaps unable to get along with co-workers or unable to complete a job. And the rewards of job hopping can be fleeting. Professor Jennings found that though managers increased their salaries by 35% on average when they changed companies, those of equal ability who stayed on did *even better*.

Some job hoppers may sacrifice substantial benefits. For example, a sound reason to stay with one company is that your pension increases with your years of service.

Jennings calls job hopping a "high-risk maneuver" that "fails as often as it works." New jobs sometimes do not turn out to be as alluring as first perceived, or new bosses as charming. Even if the hopper succeeds at fulfilling a specific new assignment, he risks being stereotyped as fit only for that role. Job hoppers sometimes deceive themselves into thinking they have improved their position. In one survey, 85% of those who changed their jobs thought that their moves had helped them, but their new bosses reported that only 46% had actually advanced. So executive recruiters warn that job hopping *within a field* often should be a last resort.

How to Change Your Career

AMERICA is still a land where opportunities abound to improve your economic situation — in fact, to change your life by starting an entirely new career or moving to a new community. We remain a nation of Daniel Boones looking for elbow room: Americans move an average of 11 times during their lives and switch jobs about six times. Each year, 2.5 million people enroll in courses designed to help them enter new professions.

Turnabouts in mid-career have been fairly common since colonial times. George Washington abandoned a long career as a surveyor to become a farmer. Jimmy Carter was 38 when he left peanut farming for the Georgia Senate. And Ronald Reagan was 55 when he gave up his movie career to enter full-time politics.

But today the reasons for veering off established career paths to explore whole new fields are often quite different from what they were just a few years ago. Career counselors say that mid-life job changers no longer complain about too little advancement or too little pay. Their reason for switching now is more likely to be a desire for personal satisfaction even though that often means lower pay and relocation to a job in another city.

People who have tired of commuter schedules and corporate politics often look for more autonomy. Teachers, social workers and doctors often say they reach a burnout point of physical or mental exhaustion; they tend to seek out less demanding professions. One teacher of emotionally disturbed children contends she felt guilty when she first took a job as a tour consultant for a motel chain. Now she wonders why she did not make the change several years ago.

Above all, the successful career changers are adaptable. Even though the switches do not always prove perfect, most people say the experience is worth the strain because it lets them regain control of their workaday destiny.

You can lessen your chances of making a big mistake in career switching if you turn to the right sources of information and counseling. For a good start, read a book called *Burnout: From Tedium to Personal Growth,* which is published by The Free Press and costs $28.95. *Burnout* provides a thoughtful description of this increasingly common problem and ways to deal with it.

The most popular book that coaches people in career switching is Richard Bolles's *What Color Is Your Parachute?* published by Ten Speed Press. This $8.95 paperback emphasizes self-evaluation and defining your goals.

For information about specific jobs, you can start in the reference section of the public library. Look for the Department of Labor's *Occupational Outlook Handbook* or *The Encyclopedia of Careers and Vocational Guidance.* Both tell you how to break into a field, and they explain the kind of work done in a variety of occupations. Then head again for a bookstore. For $12.95 you can buy the *American Almanac of Jobs & Salaries;* published by Avon, it lists pay scales in various fields. The *National Job Finding Guide,* published by Dolphin at $12.95, can help you determine if the career you are considering is thriving in the places where you might want to live.

If the change you are thinking about requires you to earn a college degree, shop for a school that will give you academic credit for your achievements in life. A directory called *Opportunities for College Credit* lists more than 1,200 colleges and universities that award credit for nontraditional academic work. You can order the directory for $5 plus postage from the Council for Adult and Experiential Learning, 10840 Little Patuxent Parkway, Suite 203, Columbia, Maryland 21044.

You cannot learn everything from books, of course, so speak with people in the fields you are considering. Professional and trade associations and college alumni groups will give you names. Use your free hours to work part-time in your new job before you plunge in. Even a pot-scrubber learns about such frustrations of running a restaurant as no-show reservations, late deliveries and long hours. And if you do better with a team than a tome, consider taking one of the courses or workshops in career change offered by community colleges and universities.

If you are thinking of making a change, some public libraries offer free courses in self-assessment and job evaluation. Universities, community colleges, YMCAs and YWCAs often have courses in career guidance for $200 or less. Private career counselors charge from $300 to $1,000 for several sessions.

Most of us also have undiscovered talents — artistic skills or money-making aptitudes — that we might not be aware of. If you want to make a career change and need help discovering a slumbering skill, consider having your abilities professionally tested. One of the oldest and best-known testers in the U.S. is the Johnson O'Connor Research Foundation. It charges $450 for 8½ hours of testing and evaluation of your aptitudes for logical analysis, artistic or musical talents and even executive ability. The foundation has 13 testing centers around the country. To get a list of them, write to Johnson O'Connor Research Foundation, 11 East 62nd Street, New York, New York 10021. Or call 212-838-0550.

What to Do If You Get Fired

GETTING fired does not have to be the end of the world. Hard as it is to maintain your composure while the blade is descending, it is imperative not to lose your head as you are getting the ax. Losing your job should lead you to reappraise your whole career, and that could open new vistas.

The chances of becoming re-employed improve significantly if you proceed in a businesslike way. Keep your emotions in check and your wits sharp. Remember, there is considerable truth in those counselors' platitudes that you should devote at least six hours a day to the search, write 15 to 20 letters each week and consider job hunting to be a job in itself.

One practical reason for keeping your cool is that the person firing you might give you good leads to other jobs. And he is sometimes in a position to sweeten the terms of separation.

Although most firms have well-defined termination benefits, there is often surprising latitude in practice. For example, if you are a manager of any kind, it is reasonable to ask for up to six months' salary. Also ask for extension of group life and health benefits for at least as many weeks as you are collecting severance pay.

As quickly as possible, you should try to have letters of recommendation written by the person of your choice in the company. In addition, request a desk, telephone and secretarial help somewhere in the company. But to save face, it is wise to leave your old desk quickly.

Prepare for a long job search, particularly if your salary needs are high. Figure on one month of hunting for each $10,000 of salary.

Most people are paralyzed by anxiety for the first week or two. After that, they should force themselves to start looking. Counselors warn that this is not the time for a vacation or other costly indulgence.

You should examine every option — such as moving to another city or changing careers. The biggest mistake some people make in their lives is to act as if they were born with a tag on their big toe that reads "I'm a middle manager" or "I'm an auto worker" or whatever.

But do not lurch into rash career decisions under pressure of finding another job. Do not switch careers out of anger at what has just happened to you. And do not go back to school simply to get away from the competitiveness of the job market.

You might browse through a book that career counselors recommend: *The Termination Handbook* by Robert Coulson. At the same time, update your résumé. List your objectives only in broad terms so as not to limit the kinds of openings interviewers might consider for you. A useful book is *The Perfect Résumé* by Tom Jackson.

A natural impulse is to call friends in other companies in the hope of immediately finding a new job. But that's simply trying to prove to your ex-boss and yourself that he had poor judgment in letting you go. The right time to begin calling around for leads is after you have a résumé and know where you would like to work.

Wangling job interviews is easier if you can use your friends for entrée. But if you have to start cold, one of the best devices is to write an enticing letter to the person who is in a position to hire. In four crisp paragraphs, outline why you are writing, who you are in terms of your previous titles and responsibilities, what you can do for the corporation you are writing to, and why you deserve a hearing.

Follow up your letter in a week or so with a phone call, but try not to sound too eager for the interview. If a potential employer senses that you are desperate, you've had it.

What do you say when a job interviewer asks whether you were fired from your last position? Don't hide it, lie about it or even dance around it. Being fired just does not carry the same stigma that it did 10 years ago. With so many mergers and corporate consolidations, it can mean simply that you were in the wrong place at the wrong time.

When you are looking for a new job, remember that personnel managers are impressed by someone who talks openly and honestly about himself. You can battle nervousness by rehearsing the job interview with a friend, preferably someone who personally has done some hiring. And although you want to cast yourself in a radiant light, managers really do appreciate a balanced self-appraisal. They like to hear a job applicant volunteer not just what he is good at, but where he is weak, too. Indeed, no one ever fits an employer's requirements perfectly.

It is equally important to have done your homework about the company and its field. Someone who has analyzed the firm's record and can speculate about its future impresses personnel executives much more than a job seeker who comes in asking, "What do you have open?"

Even if an interview goes splendidly, you probably will have to wait for a job to open. Without being overly pushy, the dedicated hunter finds reasons to keep in touch with potential employers. It is always wise to mail a thank-you note. You might even send along some new clippings or other information that might intrigue your interviewer.

But in the interview, don't be afraid to come right out and ask for a promising job. Like a salesman who is reticent about closing a sale, a job hunter who is squeamish can wreck his or her own carefully constructed campaign.

Tactics for Working Smarter

WHETHER you work at home juggling carpools and piano lessons or toil in an office trying to get everything done, you have probably vowed that someday — at long last — you will *get yourself organized*. In fact, as writer Marlys Harris has observed, with the help of a calendar, a notebook, a few file folders — and willpower — you can work not harder, but smarter.

The *principles* of good organization are the tried and tested clichés, and they really work: "First things first" and "One thing at a time" and, of course, "When in doubt, throw it out."

The *tactics* of sensible organization are just as obvious: make lists, plan ahead, avoid distractions, clear away clutter. But staying organized is a lifetime project. You must hew to it with the ardor of a 12th-century monastic as you avoid gossip sessions in the office, unnecessary phone calls and long, liquid lunches.

Where to begin? Most experts on organization believe you should start your program by tackling the most difficult problem — time management. There always seems to be too much to do and not enough time to do it.

First, you should unjam your schedule by taking on less. Have the nerve to say no to those requests to head the Chip-and-Dip Committee for the company picnic or write a memo on the Misuse of Company Stationery. Then there are the tasks that you can delegate to others. That is just what a Los Angeles career couple did when they went to the extreme measure of hiring a 22-year-old person to do their shopping, pick up their cleaning and perform other household chores. The couple called him their "wife."

No matter how much or how little you want to accomplish, getting it all done usually requires following the standard practice of making a list. Writing the list just before you leave work at the end of the day helps get you off to a fast start the next day. You might even keep a second list that would detail all the foreseeable tasks you want to accomplish. Each day you pick 10 items from that list and put them on your daily sheet.

You might be wise to construct a personal time log. Write down everything you do for two weeks. That way, you can get a sense of the amount of time you typically need to perform certain jobs. Try to drop or delegate those tasks that take huge amounts of time but produce small rewards. Concentrate on the chores that produce large benefits for the time you put in.

Do you keep putting off little tasks because they are boring and have nothing to do with your real goals in life? If so, make an appointment with yourself once a week when your energy is running low to get through all the niggling but necessary paperwork that has to be dealt with.

Are you the victim of unwelcome interruptions such as drop-in visitors who plunk down in a chair and keep you from accomplishing anything? Maybe you are encouraging them — for instance, by making eye contact as a co-worker passes your desk. Some time-management specialists recommend turning your desk around so that you sit sideways to the door. That should keep you from making the first fateful eye contact without alienating co-workers.

Is your desk a mess? Just throw out the clutter, the memos, clippings, reports and monthly summaries you keep. Chances are you will never look at most of what you save. If you could readily replace a document, then why not chuck it?

As for the material you do decide to keep, try sorting it into four piles: first, items that require your action; second, papers that must be referred to other people; third, all reading material; and fourth, items that have to be kept in your files because it is part of your job to keep them.

Unfortunately, each mail delivery brings with it more paper, including a request that you do something at a future date. To organize all those new piles, take an accordion-shaped file folder and number the compartments from one to 31, for each day in the month. File the papers in them. Then, first thing each morning, run through the file for that date and act on all those notes that say what you must do that day.

If you are really in a mess, you may have to seek professional help. It is available from specialists called time managers, who stand ready to sort out your schedule and your clutter. They are listed in the Yellow Pages under "Management Consultants," and the best way to sort them out from corporate consultants is simply to call around. Their fees are very negotiable: from $150 an hour down to $100 a day.

Your Health

How to Cut Your Medical Costs

THE price of a visit to the doctor has almost quadrupled since 1967, from an average of $11 to more than $40. In that period, the cost of a day in the hospital has gone up sixfold, leaping from $34 to $212. Although health insurance policies are more generous than ever, you may well face some sizable medical bills if you or a family member becomes ill or injured. But you can negotiate with your doctor, save on drugs and use other safe strategies to trim the bills that your insurance does not pay.

One means of cutting your costs is simply to ask your doctor to lower his price — if you consider it out of line or if you think your steady patronage entitles you to a discount. Physicians' fees are surprisingly negotiable.

Many hospitals offer discounts on the costs of fitness checkups. The examinations range from stress tests to full-scale physicals. To cite just a few examples from around the country: the Trinity Lutheran Hospital in Kansas City will test your fitness by checking such things as body fat, blood pressure and heart rate. The examination will cost you only $45, compared with $350 if you had all the tests done individually. At the Parkside Sports Fitness Center in Park Ridge, Illinois, you can also get a fitness profile for $45. Plus, they will give you a custom-designed exercise plan. If you live in California, the National Institute of Cardiovascular Technology periodically offers discounted fitness checkups at hospitals throughout the state. The tests cost $105, down from the usual $500.

You also can save on drugs. Health insurance may pay up to 80% of your prescription drug bill. But you will pay 20% of a smaller amount if you buy generic drugs. They are virtually identical to brand-name drugs in all but a handful of instances. Ask your doctor to write out the generic name or indicate on his prescription that the pharmacist is at liberty to substitute a generic equivalent of a brand-name drug.

When you buy either kind of drug, remember that you will likely get a better price from a chain drugstore than from an independent druggist. That's because chains can buy in bulk. So can mail-order outlets, which are another good alternative.

Only four out of 10 Americans have dental insurance, so it is helpful to know that comparison-shopping for a dentist can produce significant savings. In New York, for example, you can pay as little as nothing or as much as $65 for a routine cleaning.

One way to save, at least on simple procedures, is to let dental students practice their skills on your teeth at a clinic of any of the 60 U.S. dental schools. Clinics do work at fees that are roughly half what you would pay a regular dentist. Students are in the final two years of their four-year dental school education and you will be relieved to know that they are closely supervised. Trouble is, they may subject you to three times as much time in the chair as experienced dentists.

A less trying way to reduce costs may be to seek out a dental clinic run by a hospital. These clinics are staffed by new graduates. They are faster, less error-prone and command higher fees than students. Still, they charge as much as one-third less than private practitioners.

As for psychotherapy, medical insurance usually does not cover more than half the cost, and psychiatrists in private practice charge $50 to $100, sometimes even more, for a 45- to 50-minute session. Fortunately, there are less costly — and equally beneficial — options.

Psychologists and specially trained social workers can treat people with emotional problems for less than what psychiatrists charge. For anything other than private, individual treatment in the therapist's office, you usually can save money. The same therapist might charge you only half as much to treat you in a clinic as in his own private office.

Another way to save is group therapy. Many therapists and clinics hold group sessions, in which several patients talk with a professional for about 90 minutes. The cost may run from $15 to $60 a session, and group therapy is often used in conjunction with private sessions. If you suffer from a well-defined problem, such as anxiety about a new job, so-called brief psychotherapy might be your best course. The treatment aims to accomplish a specific goal in a limited number of sessions, typically 20.

Still another expense you can reduce is that for eyeglasses or contact lenses. Ophthalmologists provide the contact lenses that they prescribe, but usually you must take an ophthalmologist's prescription for eyeglasses to an optician. He or she grinds the lenses and sells frames but has no set training. Ophthalmologists charge $30 to $65 for a routine examination and up to $250 for a pair of soft lenses.

But if you don't have complex vision problems, investing in an exam by an ophthalmologist is like retaining a Nobel Prize–winning economist to figure your taxes. For a routine eye exam, an optometrist is good enough. Optometrists prescribe *and* sell both eyeglasses and contacts. Including eye exam, a pair of glasses bought through an optometrist is roughly 10% lower than a pair prescribed by an ophthalmologist and bought from an optician.

Checking Up on Your Health Insurance

Too many people who rely on their health insurance to pay their big medical bills are leaning on a rubber crutch. Even if you are among the nine out of 10 Americans covered by health insurance, you will find that almost no policy will pay all your medical bills all the time. That is why you should give your health insurance policy a thorough examination, diagnose its weaknesses and take steps to remedy them.

Many of your policy's ills can be cured with additional coverage. If you are hospitalized, for example, most policies will pick up 100% of the cost of your stay in a semi-private room up to a certain length of time. After that some will pay for 80%. But if your plan will not do that, your best protection against bankroll-breaking bills is to buy an individual major medical policy from Blue Cross/Blue Shield or one of the big private insurance companies.

This picks up where basic hospital and doctor-bill plans leave off.

Benefits usually range from $25,000 all the way to $1 million — and some policies provide unlimited coverage.

It is also wise to buy an individual major medical policy if your current plan has limits on how much it will pay for surgery. But do not waste your money on the so-called dread-disease policies, which insure you against specific illnesses such as cancer. That's like insuring only part of your car.

Most health plans have limits on the total benefits you can collect in your lifetime. The Health Insurance Association of America recommends at least $250,000 for each person covered. If you are ill at ease with your plan's maximum, you can supplement it at relatively low cost. For example, a family of four can buy a policy that pays all costs above $25,000 — up to a maximum $1 million. The average price is $360 to $500 a year.

About the only thing you cannot buy additional insurance for is your deductible for such outpatient expenses as doctor's appointments, prescription drugs, lab tests and private nurses. The deductible is the bare minimum you absolutely have to pay. These deductibles vary from $50 to $500 a year, although $200 seems to be the average these days.

When you give your health insurance policy its routine physical, you will discover that some expenses just are not covered. In addition, two-income couples with different employers have two policies to scrutinize. The strengths of one may make up for the weaknesses of the other.

Try to avoid so-called indemnity plans — which pay no more than the fixed and specified amount listed in the policy for particular operations or for a hospital bed. An indemnity policy that pays $100 a day for your room takes care of as little as a third of the cost. One exception to this is an indemnity plan that covers long-term care.

In group health plans, the insurer cannot cut off anybody's coverage, no matter how many claims he collects. But at the end of many an individual policy's term — usually once a year — the company can cop out. To head off cancellation of an individual policy, buy a guaranteed-renewable policy. It specifies that the company can neither cancel the coverage, so long as you pay the premiums, nor raise your rates merely because you have filed several expensive claims.

You should keep your policy up to date, especially at major mile-stones in your life. Will you or a family member soon reach age 65? Watch out! It is *your* responsibility to apply for Medicare at your local Social Security office no later than three months after you turn 65. Most group plans stop regular coverage at 65 and offer only a supplement to Medicare. If you do not apply and then become ill, you may have to pay your own medical bills.

If you are retiring before 65, make sure you are still covered under your group plan. Otherwise, you will have to buy a high-priced policy on your own. And if you are laid off or fired, ask your employer to continue your coverage for at least 30 to 90 days. If you do not get that protection, shop around for an interim policy to insure you for a few months.

When your child turns 19 years old — or 23 if he is a student — he will have to fend for himself. Your policy does not cover him. And remember, divorce ends a nonworking spouse's coverage. But laws in some 38 states allow him or her to convert readily to an individual policy with the same carrier — at his or her own expense. Also, if a working spouse dies, find out how long an employer will continue the widow's or widower's coverage.

One further tip on health insurance: Look for a policy with what is called stop-loss protection. That limits your maximum out-of-pocket medical expenses in any year, usually to $1,500 for a single person or $3,000 for a family. The policy pays for everything above that. If your group policy does not have a stop-loss clause, you can urge your employer to add it to the company policy. The cost is reasonable: about $60 for an individual, $180 for a family of four.

Prepaid Dental Plans

IF DENTIST bills are taking a big bite out of your family's budget, you may be able to chop these costs by joining a prepaid dental plan. It is a form of insurance that is typically limited to members of employee groups. But now individuals can buy into a few such plans. In exchange for your annual fees — $75 for individuals, $135 to $195 for a whole family at Northeast Dental in New York — these plans usually do not charge you any deductibles. Since they emphasize preventive dentistry, they also do not charge you for checkups.

While there are charges for procedures, they are generally 25% to 50% below what people covered by regular dental insurance must pay. For example, fillings often cost $20 or even less.

All prepaid plans place some restrictions on your choice of a dentist. Some plans provide a long list of private practitioners whom you can use. Others require you to select your dentist at a dental center that has a contract with the plan.

If your employer offers you the option of joining a prepaid plan, first ask your benefits counselor how many of the plan's dentists practice close to where you live or work. And inquire whether your whole family has to go to the same dentist. This could be a nuisance if you prefer to use one near your office and your family needs one close to home.

Ask the directors of the plan whether complicated dental work, such as a root canal or oral surgery, is handled by a specialist. Any dentist is licensed to perform such procedures. So make sure you will be referred to a specialist if you need periodontal, endodontic or orthodontic care.

Find out how the plan handles emergencies. The better prepaid plans guarantee 24-hour availability for care, even when your chosen dentist is not reachable. This service assures you that you will not be forced to pay for treatments by a dentist who is not part of the plan. Also ask about grievance procedures to settle possible disputes between you and your practitioner. The plan should offer arbitration by a patient-relations administrator, or, ideally, pay for a second opinion from an independent dentist.

Prepaid dental plans are available in most parts of the country. To find one in your area, check the Yellow Pages under "Dental Service Plans," or call your city or state dental society.

How to Find a Good Doctor

ONE of your most important investments, surely, is your investment in health care. So it is smart to spend at least as much time selecting a good doctor as it is, say, picking a new car or a house. Not all doctors are created equal. You can measure them against certain yardsticks of quality, but you must be willing to do some research.

Start your search by assembling a list of candidates. Ask neighbors, friends and fellow workers for recommendations. If you are moving to a new town or neighborhood, get a few names of prospective physicians from the doctor you have been seeing in your old town and neighborhood. You also can request referrals from your company's medical department; that is the simplest way to get the names of professionals who have earned reputations among patients for reliability. In addition, you can ask local medical and dental societies for the names of practitioners who take new patients.

You can consult the *Directory of Medical Specialists,* which is available in large public libraries. It lists the names, education and specialties of all U.S. doctors. Alternatively, you can telephone the internal-medicine or family-practice department of the nearest university-owned or university-affiliated teaching hospital and get the names of doctors who are on the staff. Finally, you might ask your pharmacist to suggest doctors who he feels are well qualified. He or she is in a good position to know which ones are up to date on the latest drugs.

Once you have found two or three candidates, call their offices and speak to the doctor if you can. Ask what he or she charges for some selected procedures such as a basic physical exam. If the physician will not say, move on to the next. You can even drop by for a get-acquainted interview. Doctors often do not charge for a few minutes' talk with a potential patient.

You will want to find out whether the doctor practices alone or as part of a group or in a health maintenance organization (HMO). This is a prepaid group health plan that provides physicians and hospitalization for its members as needed. There is little scientific evidence to suggest that your care will be any better or any worse in one type of practice or another. But many people feel that they get more individual attention — and hence better care — from a solo practitioner. (For more, see "Your Health: The Pros and Cons of HMOs.")

Studies indicate that the prestige of the doctor's medical school or its location — in the U.S. or abroad — makes little difference in the quality of care that he delivers. Two other criteria are far more important.

First, where did the doctor complete his residency? The best training programs generally are found at university-owned hospitals.

Second, has the doctor passed a certification exam given by the professional organization that oversees his specialty? Certification is no guarantee of excellence, but it is the best yardstick you have. Again, you can check the doctor's credentials in the *Directory of Medical Specialists.*

When you judge a doctor, also consider the hospitals he uses. You can't check into a hospital, except in an emergency, unless your doctor can admit you there. To do that, he must have been screened by its credentials committees and granted admitting privileges. Good doctors use good hospitals, so selecting the right physician can solve two potential problems.

When you are traveling and need medical care, you should call the county medical or dental society for names of available practitioners. The Travelers Aid Society will also give you the name and address of the nearest hospital. Be sure to take along an ample supply of any medication you may need. Carry it with you — not in a suitcase that might be lost. If you run out, you probably will need to see a local doctor for a new prescription.

When you are overseas, an American embassy or consulate can provide the names of English-speaking doctors, although the U.S. government does not guarantee their expertise. Doctors' and hospital bills overseas usually must be paid in cash, but your health insurance program may reimburse you — after you return home.

How to Find a Psychotherapist

M ANY thousands of Americans make a major and most important investment in psychotherapy. But picking a therapist can itself be a source of anxiety: psychotherapy is expensive and practitioners range from geniuses to charlatans.

More than 100,000 therapists practice in the U.S. today, offering more than 250 types of treatments. Anyone can hang out a shingle as a psychotherapist, and, with a little knowledge and a lot of brass, can succeed. Consequently, credentials are critical. Accredited mental-health professionals fall into five classes: psychiatrists, psychoanalysts, clinical psychologists, psychiatric social workers and psychiatric nurses.

Psychiatrists and most psychoanalysts have M.D.'s, which means they can prescribe drugs and hospitalization; they are needed to treat severe illness. Clinical psychologists have Ph.D.'s in psychology; clinical social workers must have at least a master's degree, and psychiatric nurses are registered nurses who have at least a master's degree in mental-health nursing.

The best way to find a therapist is to ask your family doctor for a referral. You also can consult state offices of professional societies, which give out the names of members by phone. Other good sources for specialists are mental-health associations, hospital clinics or self-help groups such as Alcoholics Anonymous or THEOS, which is a group for widowed people.

To check a therapist's credentials, contact the state chapter of the appropriate organization — for example, the American Psychiatric Association or the American Nurses Association. A few professionals might not belong, but it's safer to stick with those who do.

When you first meet a therapist, remember — you are a customer as well as a patient. Ask about credentials and fees. Some therapists will reduce charges if you are unable to pay the full rate. Feel free to get a second consultation or to change therapists.

Fees depend largely on the type of therapist the patient chooses. Psychiatrists charge the highest. In private practice, their sessions of 45 to 50 minutes cost $50 to $150 or even more. Psychologists with Ph.D's charge an average $50 to $90 for a session, while social workers bill $15 to $40.

Medical insurance coverage for psychotherapy can vary greatly, so before beginning treatment, it is smart to check with your insurer about what is reimbursed.

How to Pick a Hospital

WHEN you need to go to the hospital for medical care, it is not necessarily the best idea to head for the nearest one.

In judging a hospital, the basic gauge is whether it has the approval of the nonprofit Joint Commission on Accreditation of Hospitals. You can be sure that an accredited hospital has met certain standards of excellence in 23 categories.

For most medical problems, accredited community hospitals without teaching programs are good enough. Their staffs are competent, their costs tend to be about 15% lower than those of university hospitals and they have the reputation of being more hassle-free. For fairly routine treatment, it usually does not matter whether the hospital is municipally owned, or is privately owned and nonprofit, or is privately owned and for-profit.

However, for major surgery or serious illnesses, it just does not pay to be anywhere but in a university-owned hospital, or a hospital that conducts teaching programs for a university or a specialty center such as a children's hospital or an institute devoted to the treatment of a particular disease. Teaching and specialty hospitals tend to have doctors who are the most up to date. Another advantage of those institutions is that they generally see hundreds of patients a month. And, in medicine as in most disciplines, practice makes nearly perfect. Especially in surgery, volume is key. If the surgeons at a hospital do not perform 40 to 50 operations each year, they are probably not maintaining their skills. For heart surgeons, it should be closer to 200 or 300 operations annually.

How do you find out about a surgeon's or a hospital's volume? You have no choice but to ask. If your doctor does not want to tell you, try to gather information from local consumer groups, from insurance companies or from your state hospital association.

When surgery seems called for, a second opinion also makes financial sense. It can save your insurer money and you an operation. Many of the nonprofit insurers in the Blue Cross network have recognized the importance of second opinions. In some states, these organizations are encouraging them — and paying for them.

If you get a major hospital bill that is bigger than expected, check it carefully. Equifax Services Inc. is an Atlanta-based information service that conducted a multiyear study of large hospital bills for insurers. It reported that 97% of the many thousands of bills it scrutinized had errors. They resulted in overcharges of up to 15%. Among the most common mistakes are overstating services and charging for supplies and treatments that were never received.

When you or a relative is released from a hospital stay, insist on an itemized statement of charges. Ask for an explanation if you find items or services that you suspect weren't delivered. If you're still not satisfied, you can notify your insurance company, whose demands for an explanation will carry more clout. Some health insurers and employers are beginning to offer financial incentives to people who uncover excess charges on their medical bills.

Avoiding the High Cost of Hospitals

ONE reason for the rapid increase in medical costs is expensive, lengthy and sometimes unnecessary hospital stays. But you have several new ways to avoid the high price of hospitals.

In nearly half of all surgical operations, patients now can return home the same day. Today, surgical lasers have reduced hazardous bleeding, and lighter anesthetics eliminate the hours of grogginess and nausea. As a result, many routine procedures such as hernia repair and cataract removal are being done safely, efficiently — and economically — *outside* of hospitals.

These same-day operations are performed at hospital-affiliated clinics, as well as at independent surgical centers and even in doctors' offices. The doctors' fees are usually the same wherever an operation is performed, but *other* costs are 40% to 60% less than for a similar operation in a hospital. That's because the overhead in a clinic or office is lower and there are no room charges.

Some emergency-room treatment and many recuperative services also don't need the vast — and vastly expensive — resources of a fully equipped hospital. So entrepreneurs and hospitals have begun setting up independent emergency rooms. About 4,000 of them now exist across the country. They're staffed mainly by physicians specializing in emergency medicine or family practice. Some 50 million patients visited these centers in 1987. True, an emergency center is no place to go with a serious illness or injury. But for minor burns, sprains, cuts and colds, it can deliver faster, more convenient and often less expensive care.

Private business people also are offering home-care services that can be priced lower than the same care in a hospital. Some 11,000 agencies now provide home care, and 5,800 of them are Medicare-approved. They send out nurses, homemakers and even companions to people who are confined at home but don't need hospitalization.

So, if you are ever headed toward a hospital, you might pause a moment to consider your growing range of alternatives.

The Pros and Cons of HMOs

HEALTH maintenance organizations, or HMOs, are often called the best prescription for achieving high-quality, economical group health care. They are not like traditional group health plans. With a group plan, you pick your own doctors and send the bills to your insurance company for reimbursement. In an HMO, you — or more likely your employer — pay an annual fee, commonly about

$2,000 or so for a family of any size. Then the plan's doctors handle almost all your medical needs for no extra charge. HMOs usually cover a higher percentage of surgical and hospital costs than do group policies, and you do not have to pay any deductibles. As a result, you may save 10% to 40% a year. The HMO bets that it can keep you well. If it does, it comes out ahead. HMOs do whatever they can on an outpatient basis. And they often reward their doctors in the form of year-end bonuses and profit sharing if they succeed in keeping their clients out of the hospital.

A common criticism is that HMOs are too impersonal. At some of them, members cannot always count on seeing the same doctor every time. Indeed, unless you are willing to pay extra for private services, you must use not only the doctors employed by the HMO but also the hospitals, labs and other facilities with which your HMO has contracted. Another complaint is that too few specialists work for HMOs.

By and large, HMOs do provide good health care at reasonable prices — as their 30 million members can attest. A Johns Hopkins University survey in 1979 found that HMOs actually may offer *better* treatment than you will get through conventional health care.

Still, they can vary widely in quality. So, before signing up, ask friends or co-workers who belong how they rate the plan. You should phone the administration office of any HMO you are considering joining and ask if it is affiliated with a well-regarded local hospital and has more than half of its physicians certified by specialty boards.

It is a favorable sign if the HMO is a member of the Group Health Association of America, a trade organization that sets medical and financial standards for its 200 member plans. Also ask directors of the HMO whether it is federally qualified. That means it provides a specific range of services; about one-half of the 650 HMOs in the country do.

Because many HMOs are operating in the red, you also will want to conduct a financial checkup. Phone the state office that regulates HMOs for an opinion on the one you are considering. The HMO is probably sound if it has been in operation for at least three years, or if it is sponsored by a big insurance company or some other substantial institution.

Nonetheless, competition has become a threat to HMOs. Insurance companies, hospital chains and Blue Cross Associations are offering *different* kinds of plans. For example, big insurance companies also offer preferred provider organizations, or PPOs. They charge premium prices, but they allow you to choose not only your own family doctor but also your own specialists. And insurance companies and big HMOs are selling a so-called triple option — HMOs, PPOs and conventional policies, all in a single plan.

New Options in Births

A GROWING number of pregnant women do not want to give birth to their babies in a hospital delivery room. Those prospective parents now have several cost-saving options.

Certainly a hospital delivery room is the safest place to have a baby and the only wise choice for 20% of women who develop problems during pregnancy. But many women dislike the frequent use of anesthesia, the forbidding-looking equipment and what they see as the lack of personal attention. So they are choosing alternatives to the steel-and-tile delivery room.

For example, many women elect to have their babies in so-called hospital birthing rooms. Unlike the standard delivery room, these usually are furnished with beds, plants, stereos, and other comforts of home. Members of the family — including children — often can stay in the room with the mother. Labor, delivery and recovery all take place in the same congenial setting, where a nurse-midwife or obstetrician is in attendance. The cost for a routine delivery in a metropolitan hospital birthing room averages $2,680 versus the average $2,800 for a traditional delivery-room birth.

There are also 140 birthing centers away from hospitals that are licensed by 40 states. The centers usually are staffed by certified nurse-midwives, and all have consulting physicians on 24-hour call. They also have arrangements with nearby hospitals so that a woman who suddenly develops complications can be transferred quickly to a delivery room.

Some women want to have their babies in their own homes with the help of state-licensed midwives. A small number of the country's 3,000 certified midwives specialize in home births. They are trained to handle only routine deliveries. A home birth attended by a midwife could run $400 to $700. But it cannot be stressed enough that such procedures are *only* for women who have had an untroubled pregnancy and have received a doctor's fair assurance that they will have an uncomplicated birth.

Conquering Infertility

NEARLY one out of five young, married couples of childbearing age who try to conceive a child fail to do so. They know that the fight against infertility can be exasperating and expensive, but there are ways to hold down costs and increase your chances of success.

Thanks to modern therapies, couples battling infertility have about a 50-50 chance of parenthood once a diagnosis is made. And it is possible to identify the cause in 90% of the cases. The testing and treatment can cost $15,000 to $30,000 — and sometimes more. Insurers cover only part of this. Couples usually wind up paying at least 20% to 30% of the bill themselves.

If you are trying to overcome infertility, then above all get expert medical help. Your family doctor or gynecologist may be able to clear up minor difficulties. But if your doctor's treatments have had no effect after several months, see a fertility specialist. For the name of specialists and fertility clinics, write the American Fertility Society, 2140 11th Avenue South, Suite 200, Birmingham, Alabama 35205-2800.

Closely question any fertility specialist you are considering. Ask about the tests and treatments he or she usually performs, how long he or she has specialized in infertility, how successful he or she has been in helping couples conceive.

Check into your health insurance coverage. Some companies do not consider infertility to be an illness. But even they will pick up part of the bill for tests and treatment of conditions that may interfere with reproduction. Your compensation may depend on the wording a doctor uses when filling out insurance claim forms. One infertility specialist advises: "Insurance generally covers the cost, as long as you do not state that the work is being done for infertility per se, but instead use such terms as ovulation disorder, tubular obstruction or pelvic adhesion."

When Should You Have
Elective Surgery?

E VERY year, many thousands of Americans face a difficult choice: whether or not to have elective surgery. It can be costly, let alone painful. So when should you have elective surgery?

Aside from the usual fears, you have to consider many other factors, including lost income, uninsured medical expenses and extra outlays for convalescence. If you have any lingering doubts about undergoing a procedure, you will need a number of questions answered. Many of these should be directed to an internist or a family practitioner rather than a surgeon. That is because surgeons are oriented toward surgery. Find out the following:

— Can your condition be controlled by medication, diet or a medical device? If it can, are you likely to stay on the prescribed regimen?

— What are the chances that the disorder suddenly will get worse, resulting in emergency hospitalization?

— Will leaving your condition untreated limit your life-style, work or recreation?

If you decide on surgery, find out the chances of its success. You will also want a confirming second opinion before you proceed. Almost all health insurers will pay not only for a second opinion, but even for a third if the first two conflict. When seeking another opinion, avoid getting it from a colleague recommended by your surgeon. Instead, go to a doctor you have found independently.

To find another specialist on your own, phone the referral service of a major hospital, preferably one that has a medical school connected with it. Or call your county medical association, listed in the phone book. Pick a doctor who has diplomate status. That means he or she both has experience and has passed extensive exams in his or her specialty. The second doctor may insist you repeat the same tests you have already had, but if there is even a remote possibility that you do not need surgery, it is probably worth it.

The Costs of Plastic Surgery

PLASTIC surgery to fight sags, bags and wrinkles is performed on an astonishing half-million patients a year. But what are the costs — and the real value — of those operations?

Depending on the operation and the doctor, surgical fees vary widely. They generally range from $250 for common dermabrasion to $8,000 for body contouring. But a trend toward performing plastic surgery right in the doctor's office is eliminating steep hospital expenses for many patients. A single overnight stay in a hospital for a face-lift might easily cost $2,000 to $3,500 for operating room fees and a private room; in a surgeon's office the same patient might pay only $200 to $400 in fees for the room and various equipment — in addition to the doctor's bill, of course.

The operations now routinely done in doctors' offices include face-lifts, eyelid and nose surgery and hair transplants. An office nose job, for example, can take as little as an hour. Then the patient spends a couple of hours resting in a recovery room and goes home with a long list of dos and don'ts and a telephone number where the doctor can be reached, if necessary.

Beware, though, of heavily advertised cosmetic surgery clinics. In a few of these body shops, surgeons perform as many as 12 operations a day. This high-volume approach sometimes results in short-order workmanship.

At least 18% of cosmetic surgery patients are men, and the percentage is rising. Some of them hope to enhance their business careers by getting rid of a receding chin or an oversized nose; others simply want to smooth away the signs of aging. But, as one surgeon warns, "We can't make people into movie stars or mend broken marriages — the only way to get rid of every line and wrinkle is to embalm you."

How much do doctors charge? So-called tummy tucks are $750 to $4,000. Breast augmentation is typically $1,800 to $4,000. A face-lift can cost between $2,000 and $10,000. In one technique, the surgeon not only tightens the skin but also resculptures the jawline and neck by removing excess fat. Then he cuts and resews a neck muscle to form a kind of sling to support the neck and chin. Pain should be minimal and discoloration is gone in 10 days or so.

The news about nose jobs is that they are no longer the assembly-line reshapings of a decade ago. For a cost of between $1,500 and $6,000 you should get a nose that is natural and fits your face. The operation is done mostly from the inside out, so there is no visible scarring.

Hair transplantation is another growth business. You commonly will have to endure up to four painstaking — and often painful — sessions with a plastic surgeon or dermatologist. Sometimes the plugs of re-seeded hair do not take, or they sit in such neat rows that they look as if they have been sowed by John Deere. The bill can reach a hair-raising $20,000, though minor jobs are significantly less.

Whatever the estimated cost, a plastic surgeon will not raise his or her scalpel until you have paid in full. The doctors say that since the surgery is elective, high postponement and cancellation rates mess up their busy schedules. More likely, though, doctors fear that some patients would refuse to pay after seeing the results. If you are less than pleased, your only recourse now is to sue.

Even if you are satisfied with the surgery, medical insurance probably will not pay for it unless the work is considered health-related or rehabilitative, such as breast reconstruction. One uplifting note: plastic surgery often qualifies for a medical deduction on your income tax. But no matter how much you have to pay, do not expect the moon. While cosmetic surgery can help you turn back the clock, you cannot stop it forever.

If you pick a plastic surgeon, you should do it as though your life depended on it. In rare cases of complications, it might. An alarming number of practitioners are charlatans. There is nothing to prevent an M.D. from hanging out a shingle, calling himself a plastic surgeon and making extravagant advertising claims. According to the head of a plastic surgeons' watchdog committee in San Francisco, misleading advertising has resulted in numerous catastrophes and several known deaths in California.

One way to measure a surgeon's skill is to check his or her certification. If he does all kinds of cosmetic surgery, he should be certified by the American Board of Plastic Surgery. You can get a list of board-certified surgeons from the American Society of Plastic and Reconstructive Surgeons (233 North Michigan Avenue, Suite 1900, Chicago, Illinois 60601; 800-635-0635). If you tell the society what operation you are considering, it will provide the names of 10 board-certified doctors in your area who perform the procedure. A dermatologist doing hair transplants and skin peelings should be certified by the American Board of Dermatology.

Your surgeon should be affiliated with a reputable hospital or a medical school, even if he performs most of his operations in his office. Without the right qualifications, a hospital would not accept him. Moreover, doctors on hospital staffs are subject to review by their peers.

A plastic surgeon should be willing to spend plenty of time answering your questions. Some charge nothing for the first consultation, particularly if you decide to go ahead with surgery. Others ask for $35 to $60 as a consultation fee. If you do not think a surgeon is right for you, it is better to write off the consultation fee and find someone better.

The stakes in plastic surgery are always big. Your best protection is to put yourself in the hands of a responsible surgeon.

Selecting a Fitness Club

THE inalienable rights of Americans these days include life, liberty and the pursuit of fitness. If you are just discovering the exercise ethic, you are probably wondering what is the most effective and least expensive way to begin. True, you can pursue most exercise without spending a penny. But if you need instruction, discipline or just camaraderie, money spent on shaping up is a worthwhile investment. It need not cost you an arm and a leg.

More than 10,000 fitness clubs operate nationwide. Often the best are one-stop, full-service fitness facilities. They offer pools, indoor and outdoor tracks and aerobic equipment. Membership costs range from $400 a year at a first-class full-service club to several thousand dollars at ones that provide the toniest surroundings for toning. It is probably wise to enroll for a shorter period — say, six months — even at a more expensive rate. That way, you can test both your compatibility and commitment.

Before signing up, review the contract thoroughly. Ideally, you should be able to freeze your membership if you are traveling, get a prorated refund if you become temporarily disabled or simply cancel within 72 hours if you change your mind.

The emphasis at the best places is on exercise, not just relaxation and socializing. Saunas, whirlpools and steam baths are extras that can make you feel terrific but will soften your wallet before they harden your stomach.

The best way to begin evaluating a club is to examine it at lunchtime or other peak hours when its staff and facilities are taxed the most. Make sure there are enough professional instructors on hand and that they are willing — and able — to answer your questions. Check that the equipment is well maintained. And be sure to inspect the whirlpool. A sparkling, ringless tub with carefully regulated water indicates proper attention.

You do not have to join an expensive health club. Instead, consider the not-for-profit YMCAs and YWCAs. More than 1,000 Ys have fitness facilities. Membership rates are set by the local Ys. Many have family memberships and lower single-parent memberships in addition to individual memberships. The price often includes a profile of your current physical condition, and a training regimen taught by certified instructors and matched to your abilities.

Another economically sound choice for anyone who plays tennis, racquetball or squash are the court clubs. Look for a club that offers not only racquet games but other fitness equipment and facilities as well. Often you can buy à la carte what you plan to use, much the way you purchase court time. Clubs charge $10 to $40 an hour for singles tennis, $5 to $9 for racquetball.

Some people prefer to sign up for a series of exercise classes. The most important considerations are the qualifications of the teacher and the size of the class. The maximum should be 15 to 20 people.

If muscle-building is your forte, proper training is essential. Lifting free weights or using weight-resistant machinery can cause injury if you don't have sound instruction. You can get it at sleek Nautilus centers, which cost $200 to $900 a year. Or you can try the drabber but equally serviceable body-builders' gyms, which charge $100 to $250 on average.

Fitness takes time: 30 minutes to an hour, a minimum of three times a week. Keep in mind that your success in achieving your personal best has less to do with the cash you put down than with the dedication you keep up.

Where to Take a Drinking or Drug Problem

M ARY TYLER MOORE, Johnny Cash and Betty Ford have something in common with millions of other Americans. All have battled drinking or drug problems, or both — and won. If you or someone you know has such a problem, you can find effective treatment to fit just about every budget.

The number of treatment centers is huge and growing. Across the country, about 34,000 Alcoholics Anonymous groups and 4,500 rehabilitation clinics, hospitals, halfway houses and outpatient programs are offering help. The prognosis for those who seek help is good — recovery rates range from 50% to 85%, depending on the kind of patient a program caters to.

The costs range from nothing, in the case of AA, to $500 a day or even more. In fact, more and more people are getting the help they need at an affordable price. The reason is that treatment is increasingly being covered by health insurance.

In 1986 over two-thirds of the 21.3 million workers surveyed by the Bureau of Labor Statistics had group health insurance coverage for alcoholism or drug treatment. Medicare also covers up to 21 days per admission for inpatient treatment programs and, in 1989, up to $1,100 if outpatient psychiatric care is medically necessary.

The first step for alcoholics and addicts who recognize their problem and want help is detoxification, the elimination of alcohol and drugs from the blood. In the most serious cases, detoxification in a hospital usually lasts five to eight days and costs $300 to $500 a day. But it is covered by insurance even when policies don't pay for other aspects of treatment.

Once a patient has banished chemicals from his or her bloodstream, the roots of the addiction can be addressed. Specialists in treating addiction often recommend group therapy. They argue persuasively that confrontation with one's peers is an effective way to break down an alcoholic's or addict's denial of his or her disease. Here are the four basic treatment methods that use group therapy:

First, *self-help groups*. The most prominent of them is Alcoholics Anonymous. Health-care professionals praise AA — and it is absolutely free. Similar associations that have borrowed AA's tenets are Narcotics Anonymous and Pills Anonymous.

Second, *outpatient programs.* About 90% of all alcoholics or drug addicts who receive treatment get it from clinics and rehabilitation centers but don't stay there overnight. Many facilities charge $10 to $65 a visit, depending on the type of counseling provided and, in some cases, what the patient can afford.

Third, *inpatient clinics.* Most clinics charge $100 to $300 a day for typical 21- or 28-day stays. Generally, insurance reimbursement for inpatient care is limited to about one month per year. Although celebrities have gravitated to some clinics, everyone is treated as an equal.

Fourth, *halfway houses and therapeutic communities.* These provide extended inpatient care for people who would be likely to slip back into their old ways after a standard 30-day inpatient program. Room and board can cost $775 a month or more.

When you are ready to examine specific treatment programs, ask your doctor for recommendations. You also can get information from the 200 local chapters of the National Council on Alcoholism.

You would be wise to look for therapies that are conventional and well tested. For example, you're best off avoiding any doctor who tells you that alcoholism or drug addiction can be treated with prescriptions alone.

If you are considering a treatment program, here are some points to keep in mind:

When you meet with the administrator of a program, be wary if he or she suggests admittance before taking a complete case history. Also beware of any evasiveness about costs or a willingness to shave a few days off a program to match your insurance coverage.

Think of the interview as your chance to assess a program's quality. First ask if the clinic meets the approval of the Joint Commission on Accreditation of Hospitals, as well as state licensing agencies. Don't be afraid to ask what type of patients tend to use the program. Many of the best programs use group therapy. But if the other people in the program have radically different backgrounds from your own, you may find it difficult to identify with their problems. Also ask the administrator for recovery rates. A fair measure of success is one year of abstinence, but two years is better.

Your Education

Financial Aid You Still Can Get

PARENTS of teenagers who are heading toward college are becoming widely acquainted with a new American affliction: tuition shock. But there is some good news: despite cutbacks of federal aid, you still can get much help from other sources.

Financing a college education always has been tough, and it is certainly not getting any easier. Since 1980, the cost of a private-college education has risen about 85%, to a daunting $11,330 a year on average; the annual cost at public institutions is $4,445. No wonder parents with college-bound children feel caught in a budget supersqueeze.

Fortunately, though, you still have plenty of ways to ensure that your children get the education you want for them.

First, of course, start saving for college as soon as possible after your child is born.

Second, look for quality bargains in higher education. Many colleges manage to keep their academic standards up and their total costs down.

Third, press your hunt for financial aid. Sometimes it is available even to families with annual incomes of $100,000 or more. In fact, many colleges recently have changed their scholarship programs to attract high-schoolers regardless of their financial need. Any high-school student is in the running for an academic scholarship if he or she has at least a B average and College Board scores above the national norm. Don't necessarily put off applying to a prestigious university because you think you can't afford it. Sometimes the most expensive schools give the richest scholarships.

About half of all undergraduates on campuses in 1987 received financial aid. That was down slightly from 1980. Most of the aid originates in the federal government. The $18 billion pool of federal money for students in 1987 flowed mainly through six programs. They provide for grants, loans, work-study programs or some combination of the three.

The colleges themselves supplemented the federal programs with an estimated $4.5 billion of their own aid. It is often from colleges that middle- and upper-middle-income families receive their help.

To find out whether you qualify for aid, you go through a process called need analysis. Sometime after January 1 in the year your child heads for college, you fill out a form from either the American College Testing Program or the College Scholarship Service. It records your family size, income, assets, household expenses and other information.

The data then are analyzed in order to arrive at a figure known as your family contribution. That is the amount colleges will expect you to pay annually out of your own pocket. If college costs are more than that — and they usually are — the school's financial aid officers try to figure out ways to make up the difference.

Financial aid officers determine how large a loan each student is entitled to. They usually base their decision on something called the Uniform Methodology Formula, which takes into account not only a family's income but also its assets, such as the equity in the family house. Each financial aid administrator has the prerogative, under law, to make judgments in individual cases and can differentiate within the college's financial aid formula. If both parents are employed and, within a school year, one of them becomes unemployed or ill and unable to work, federal law allows them to reapply using a form for special conditions. The system *does* take into account unusual circumstances. Roger Koester, the financial aid analyst for Northwestern University, says, "A family can have an income in the $100,000 range and have five kids, three of them in college, and still show some eligibility. On the other hand, a family with one child in college, no unusual circumstances, and a $65,000 to $70,000 income will generally not be eligible for aid at most schools."

The cheapest money around is available through federally subsidized 5% Perkins Loans. Students can borrow up to $4,500 in each of their first two years, or a total of $9,000 over their entire undergraduate career. Repayment begins six months after the completion of studies and extends for up to 10 years.

The same repayment terms apply to the Guaranteed Student Loans. They are offered through lenders such as banks and credit unions. Students can qualify for a maximum of $2,625 for each of the first two years and an annual maximum of $4,000 for as many as three remaining years, or a total of $17,250 for an undergraduate education. Interest rates are set at 8% for the first four repayment years, 10% for the remainder.

As mentioned, families applying for almost all federal financial aid must submit to a financial needs test to determine whether their children are eligible for the loans. But a federal offering mercifully free of a needs test is the 10% Parent Loans for Undergraduate Students, known as the PLUS loan. The maximum is $4,000 a year and you get these loans through participating banks or other commercial lenders. But repayment — again, up to 10 years — begins within 60 days after you take out a PLUS loan.

Many states offer subsidized student loans to residents. Among the most generous are Alaska, Illinois, Maryland, Massachusetts, Minnesota, New York and Pennsylvania. To apply, see your college loan officer or go directly to your state education agency. Loan programs often are limited to in-state colleges, but students from New Hampshire and Pennsylvania can take a state loan along with them, wherever they enroll.

Another major source of help may be close to home — in the form of scholarships financed by local communities, clubs and other private organizations. Every year thousands of students win more than $100 million worth of scholarships sponsored by many noncollege organizations.

Some 400 companies, unions and trade organizations sponsor National Merit Scholarships worth up to $8,000 a year and covering all four years of college. In addition, if you are a veteran, you can ask at your local American Legion post about awards available for your children. Civic organizations and fraternal groups also dispense scholarship money. Just a few examples: The Knights of Columbus gives some four-year scholarships, each worth $1,000 a year, for children of members. Even a nonmember's child is eligible for scholarships from the Elks ($1,500 on average).

If your child is willing to spend four years after college in the armed services and another four years in the reserves, you might consider the Navy and Army Reserve Officer Training Corps. Or, you can look into Air Force ROTC, which requires at least four years of active duty and eight years in the reserves. All three programs can pay full tuition, fees and $100 a month at 520 participating colleges. Each year, about 6,000 high-school seniors are granted full four-year scholarships, but shorter-term awards are available to students who qualify after starting college. The three ROTC branches fund a total of more than 20,000 scholarships per year.

Parents are not the only ones suffering from rapidly escalating tuition costs. The schools themselves must work harder to attract students. Consequently, many colleges are developing attractive financing programs. They are offering more and more academic scholarships for students with top grades. These awards can range from a few hundred dollars to full tuition. For example, among the most generous and prestigious in 1988 are the University of North Carolina's 59 Morehead scholarships and the University of Virginia's 18 Jefferson scholarships. They pay the entire cost of attending their school.

A number of colleges also have adopted so-called guaranteed-tuition programs. With them, families can prepay all four years of tuition at the freshman rate. The University of Pennsylvania will even lend parents the money to do so — at favorable rates. Schools with guaranteed-tuition programs include Case Western Reserve University, Washington University in St. Louis and the University of Southern California. For families whose incomes are too high to qualify for existing programs, there are also new student-loan plans. Northwestern's Supplemental Parent Loan enables families with incomes over $30,000 to borrow up to the full tuition cost of $12,270 a year at 8¼%.

You can find out about scholarships of all kinds from high-school guidance counselors, college admissions officers and books such as Oreon Keeslar's *Financial Aids for Higher Education,* published by William C. Brown. Who knows? You might find a scholarship that few people compete for. At Harvard, for example, the William S. Murphy Fund divides nearly $11,000 each year among needy collegians named Murphy.

Do not fail to inquire whether any college your child is interested in offers an installment plan. Many do. Such programs often let you pay off a year's tuition bill month by month.

Another means of stretching your family's college dollars is to have your child substitute a job for a loan. Colleges are concerned about student debt, and thus they are expanding work-assistance programs. So is the federal government, despite cutbacks elsewhere. The government's college work-study programs can provide students with jobs that allow them to earn $600 to $1,000 a year.

Your child also can enroll in a school with a five-year cooperative education program that combines liberal arts with paid jobs. In the first year, the student takes a basic freshman curriculum of math and English along with courses in his or her major. Then for the next four years, the student alternates semesters of college study and paid work in a job. Usually the university lines up the job.

Some 1,000 colleges and universities offer co-op programs. Among the leaders are Drexel in Philadelphia, the University of Detroit and Northeastern University in Boston. For example, at Northeastern, tuition is about $7,380 a year and students can choose from a wide range of majors and paid jobs with more than 2,600 government agencies and private firms. Programs in engineering or computer science can be entered for an additional $800 a year. Engineering students usually earn enough money from their co-op jobs to pay for tuition, room, board, books, entertainment — and sometimes a car after graduation. (For more, see "Your Education: Co-op Programs.")

Finally, see whether it might be feasible for your child to accelerate his or her studies and graduate in three years instead of four. To do that, your child will need to take advance-placement exams in high school. If your youngster passes, he or she can skip some beginning college courses — and save a good deal of money along the way. Remember: Any child who graduates in three years can save a whole year's costs, and these days that can range anywhere from about $6,000 to nearly $12,000.

Financial Aid Consultants

To help determine a family's eligibility for college scholarships, grants, loans and other assistance, almost all U.S. colleges and universities use financial aid forms. But the forms are so troublesome to fill out that many parents are getting advice from academe's equivalent of tax advisers: college financial aid consultants.

This new breed charges fees from $20 to $350, depending upon how much individual attention you get. Consultants guide you through the aid application process and make sure no options and opportunities are overlooked. You may want to write to a national firm called Octameron (P.O. Box 3437, Alexandria, Virginia 22302). Many local consultants are also in the business.

A consultant typically begins by reviewing your finances. Then, using his or her knowledge of the schools' finances, he or she can figure out what kind of aid and how much you would get from colleges you are considering. He or she will also point you to money available from sources other than the schools — for example, state loan programs or private scholarships. Of course, the consultant will help you fill out the aid forms; you have to repeat that arduous task every year.

To find a consultant in your area, ask a financial aid officer at a local college or a high school guidance counselor. Check the references of all consultants you consider. Stay away from anybody who makes big promises about how much financial aid he or she can get for you or who urges you to misrepresent yourself on the forms. The applications you file *are* checked for accuracy.

Co-op Programs

I F YOU are looking for means to pay for a college education *and* get a career off to a good head start, look into an increasingly popular program called cooperative education. It is an excellent way for a student to help finance his or her own education while gaining expertise in a chosen field at the same time. Students alternate terms on campus with terms working at a real job. Last year, more than 200,000 young adults took advantage of such programs at some 1,000 colleges.

In a typical program a student takes a responsible job with a company that has agreed to participate in the arrangement. Students often work as trainees, and they earn up to $7,000 on the average for a year's work. Some of these earnings, minus taxes, are usually figured into the student's financial aid package back at school, and the grants and loans he would otherwise need may not be necessary.

The students commonly find that time spent on the job is a terrific boon to their careers. They usually receive no academic credit for their work, but they learn skills firsthand. Many positions become full-time after graduation, and pay a much higher salary than a less experienced applicant could expect.

Co-op jobs are scarcer, and salaries much lower, for humanities students than for technical students. Most co-op students are in business administration, computer science, other hard sciences and engineering. The biggest employer is the federal government. It put nearly 16,000 students to work in the 1987–88 school year. And the government usually keeps 68% of its students on the payroll after graduation.

To learn more about these programs, write to the National Commission for Cooperative Education, 360 Huntington Avenue, Boston, Massachusetts 02115.

Choosing the Right College

FULLY 60% of the students who enter a college as freshmen do not graduate from that school. Most leave early because they realize they simply chose the wrong college. It is easy to make that mistake — but it is also easy to avoid it. Your decisions about what college to attend will determine where you spend several years — and many thousands of dollars. The best way to select is to visit several schools, meet with faculty members, students and administrators — and make your own evaluations of some key points. For example:

Do the students share your talents and interests? To gauge the caliber of the competition you will face, compare your high-school grade point average with the average for this year's freshmen. College admissions officers will give you the data. If your scores are higher than the average for the entering class, you may find yourself underchallenged.

Consider the school's program in your planned major. If you intend to concentrate in science, for example, ask when the laboratories were last re-equipped. Find out where students who take your major go after graduation. It is a good sign if many get into prestigious graduate schools or win scholarships.

Take note of class sizes. At small colleges, the ratio of students to faculty members is a sound indicator of how much personal attention you will get. A ratio of 10 students per teacher is excellent. Ask an admissions officer to estimate the class sizes for courses in your major.

Find out about any special academic programs. You might be interested in completing your bachelor's degree in three years instead of four; more than 1,000 schools will let you do this. Or you might be interested in spending your junior year abroad — say, studying art in Italy. Many schools can accommodate you.

Determine what the total expenses are for the colleges you are considering, and decide whether you and your family can afford the price. You will not spend money just on tuition, room and board. You also will make at least one round-trip — and probably more — between your home and campus each year. And you will have to pay for books, entertainment and perhaps a personal computer.

If you think you will require financial aid, ask college officials how your needs will be met. See whether the college offers most of its assistance in the form of grants, loans or job opportunities. A school that can afford to give out most of its aid as grants is more financially attractive than one that cannot.

Ask yourself if graduating from a certain college will enhance your career. You can expect a precise answer if you have a specific goal. An aspiring engineer, for example, can find out the percentage of recent graduates in his or her field who received job offers — and how much those offers were for.

Try to get a feel for how loyal the college's alumni are. Ask college officials for evidence of old-boy and old-girl networks. This can help you get a job when you graduate.

Finally, find out about the school's financial condition. A school that must survive mostly on tuition because of its tiny endowment may well have crowded classes, run-down dormitories and outdated labs. To compare colleges fairly, divide endowment by the number of undergraduates, and determine which has the largest endowment per student.

Where to Get a Degree in Business

W HAT is the most popular undergraduate course on college campuses these days? It's *business*. One out of four students are aiming for a degree in business, and many hope it will be a ticket to job security after graduation. It can be — if you choose the right school.

You should carefully check out the quality of the school before enrolling because strong demand for business teachers in recent years has produced a serious shortage of them. Look very closely at who will be teaching you. At the best schools, at least 70% of the teachers hold Ph.D.'s. Also, look at what they will be teaching you. Highly specialized areas are often quickly outdated by technology. The association that accredits business programs has approved only 243 of the 1,200 or so colleges that offer undergraduate business degrees.

Money magazine has named nine schools that are generally considered the best places to study business at the undergraduate level:

The University of Virginia's McIntire School of Commerce is often considered the most elite undergraduate business school. Ninety percent of the graduates land jobs within three months of graduation.

At Bucknell University in Lewisburg, Pennsylvania, freshmen take an introductory course in management that lets them form their own companies, set corporate objectives, and then present final reports on how they met those goals.

The best schools attract hordes of recruiters. For example, at Indiana University, some 550 corporations send recruiters every year to meet promising students. And representatives from more than 600 companies visit the University of Texas.

If you are interested in accounting, check out the University of Michigan and the University of Illinois. Their accounting departments are among the best. For courses in marketing and information systems, consider the University of Minnesota.

If you want to study liberal arts as well, the University of North Carolina is one school that offers courses in logic, writing and public speaking. Finally, the Wharton School at the University of Pennsylvania offers the only Ivy League undergraduate business major. It's known for its expertise in accounting, applied economics and finance.

Other schools with strong, selective undergraduate business programs include the University of California at Berkeley, Carnegie-Mellon, MIT and the University of Wisconsin–Madison.

Cutting Costs at Community Colleges

YOU can get an effective and economical start toward earning a college degree by attending a two-year community college. Just over half of all freshmen and sophomores now attend such schools. Community colleges cost $700 a year on average; that is about half of what tuition and fees alone average at a state university. And you can economize on room and board by living at home and commuting.

Check the catalogue to make sure that your college has a transfer program to a four-year school. The college should be able to meet liberal-arts requirements for transfer and offer courses in English, math, history and science that look like the core curriculums at a state university.

You can judge academic merits by consulting *Peterson's Guide to Two-Year Colleges* to see how many students go on to four-year programs. Anything over 60% is encouraging. It is another sign of quality if the college has a chapter of Phi Theta Kappa, the honor society often considered the two-year counterpart of Phi Beta Kappa.

You also can earn a four-year bachelor's degree entirely by mail or phone. Most correspondence programs require some classroom attendance, but the Center for Distance Learning at Empire State College does not. The college is part of the State University of New York, and its correspondence program is accredited. Through the Center you can get a degree in business, human services, fire service administration or interdisciplinary studies. Each credit will cost you $47, and you need 128 credits to graduate. If you have had previous college experience, you can probably count some of it toward your degree. For more information, write to Empire State College, Center for Distance Learning, 28 Union Avenue, Saratoga Springs, New York 12866.

College Credit for Life Experience

You can earn college credits for learning you have acquired on your own — simply by taking a test. Quite a few accredited colleges administer such exams in what are generally called "external degree programs."

Two of the biggest and best known are at the University of the State of New York (Regents College, Cultural Education Center, Albany, New York 12230) and Thomas A. Edison State College (101 West State Street, Trenton, New Jersey 08625). Neither school has a residency requirement; both take students from all over the world.

To earn academic credit for work experience, you can take standardized tests. Or the college will tailor an exam to your special circumstances. To enroll in a Regents College degree program of the University of the State of New York, you pay $285 the first year plus a record-keeping fee of $200 to $215 each year thereafter and $25 to $125 for each three-credit exam.

For information on about 100 external degree programs, see *The Guide to External Degree Programs in the United States.* It is prepared by the American Council on Education, published by Macmillan and sold for $19.95.

Budgeting for Students

One extracurricular activity that every student should master when heading off to college is personal money management. But a student's day-to-day spending is typically as ad lib and unbuttoned as a fraternity beer blast. That does not mean you cannot keep your undergraduate from overspending.

During a school year, the average college student will lay out about $1,650 for books, other supplies, transportation and personal expenses at a state university. There is plenty of room for economizing, and the first place to look is at food and phones. Two surveys have illustrated that point. At Penn State, boarding students forked out an extra $415 a year for all those 2 a.m. pizzas and their accompaniments. And at the University of Connecticut, students spent more than $50 a month each on long-distance phone calls.

While many students seem to think that it costs less to live off campus than in a dorm, they may be wrong. In college towns with a lot of demand for off-campus housing, accommodations within walking distance of campus tend to be expensive. Of course, off-campus students can save money by sharing housing and doing their own cooking. If landlords demand a one-year lease, students should hold out for subleasing privileges.

Fraternity living is back in style on many campuses, and it is costly. Dues range from roughly $12.50 to $50 a month, plus another $60 to $200 or more a month for room and board. Onetime initiation fees add another $175 to $300, and once your child joins, there is a certain social pressure to do things with friends that usually involve spending money.

Most parents have to send money at one time or other. But doling out funds regularly by the week or month may tend to foster an unhealthy dependence. Instead, try giving your undergraduate a lump sum each semester and make it clear that the money will have to last. If you give your child spending money, be certain to sit down and discuss your mutual expectations. To avoid unnecessary strife, you need to know the student's assumptions about spending. And the student, in turn, should know when a check is coming, its amount and any rules about its use.

Whether students rely on parental subsidy, use their own money, or both, most have their own savings and checking accounts. Unhappily, few seem to know or care enough about how they work.

Many undergraduates keep their checking accounts in their home towns. But long-distance management of financial affairs is hard. For instance, it is tough to verify your balance quickly if you use an out-of-state bank. So it is a good idea to have an account on campus.

Some people strike a compromise by maintaining a checking account at school and a savings account at home. That can encourage self-discipline by making it difficult to dip into savings. Keeping a savings account far away is especially helpful for students who are tempted by automatic teller machines that make cash available at any hour, day or night.

Although some parents feel that a credit card might wrongly cushion a student who manages his or her affairs badly, others find that the piece of plastic can provide a good back-up for college kids.

It helps with car rentals, plane fares and railroad tickets. Trying to get money to college-age students in various locations can be frustrating. And it's often impossible for people of any age to cash personal checks away from home. Most parents who give their college-age children credit cards do so strictly for use in emergencies and they expect repayment.

Undergraduates who want to establish their own credit identity can open a charge account at a local store.

Ideally, college students should take full charge of a semester's spending. If the first semester seems too soon, put it off until the next term. But the parents' lives will not get any easier until the student runs his or her own finances.

Coaching Courses for the SATs

I F YOU are a high-school junior planning to take the all-important Scholastic Aptitude Test or the American College Testing Assessment, it makes sense to invest your time and money in a coaching school — particularly if a high score is crucial to your getting into the college of your choice.

Test results show that coaching *can* improve your SAT and ACT scores. True enough, designers of the tests measure the kind of reasoning ability developed over a long period of time. But leaders of the oldest and largest coaching school, the Stanley H. Kaplan Educational Center, claim their students raise their SAT scores by an average of 150 points.

Among those who stand to benefit most from coaching are first-time test takers. Familiarity with instructions, types of questions and time pressures help to improve your performance. Coaching also aids those who tend to "choke." They can learn how to pace themselves, make informed guesses and take shortcuts.

The best courses last for a month or more. But stay away from the so-called cram houses that offer three sessions or fewer, no matter how many hours they run. Before you sign up for any courses, be sure you sit in on a session and find out if students are satisfied with the instruction.

The Kaplan Center has 122 branches nationwide. You can call the toll-free number, 800-KAP-TEST, to find the location nearest you, or write the Kaplan Center at 131 West 56th Street, New York, New York 10019. The branches offer 40 to 50 hours of class in 11 sessions over six to 11 weeks for $495. Another reputable school with many branches is Sexton Educational Centers at 443 East Third Avenue, Roselle, New Jersey 07203.

If you do not feel the need for formal coaching, you might try examining two books. One is *How to Prepare for College Board Achievement Tests* (each subject sold separately), published by Barron's at $8.95, and another is called *10 SATs,* published by the College Board at $8.95.

Classes for the Elderly

MANY colleges are opening their classrooms to knowledge-hungry people aged 60 and up.

You can choose from thousands of quickie courses through a non-profit organization called Elderhostel. An average of $225 a week pays for anywhere from one to three courses taught by regular faculty members at U.S. colleges. That fee includes room and board, extracurricular films and parties. You can also sign up at universities in European and other countries, including Israel and Mexico. Two- and three-week foreign seminars range from about $1,000 to $3,600, including air fare.

Elderhostel enrolled about 142,000 students last year at 1,100 institutions. For information, write Elderhostel, 80 Boylston Street, Suite 400, Boston, Massachusetts 02116.

Courses in Public Speaking

IN A SURVEY, 2,500 Americans were asked, "What are you most afraid of?" The most frequent reply was not death, illness or poverty, but speaking before a group. Yet people in all types of jobs are asked routinely to speak at staff meetings, sales presentations and trade conventions. Their success or failure at the podium often influences their careers.

More and more people are signing up for courses that promise to help make them better public speakers. Fees range from $50 or even less for a course at a community college or YMCA all the way to $3,600 for a commercial course. If you can demonstrate that the course will help you perform better on the job, your company may be willing to pay for the instruction.

The grandfather of public-speaking courses is Dale Carnegie's Effective Speaking and Human Relations. It consists of 14 weekly evening sessions for about $700 to $1,000 (depending on region) and is offered at more than 1,100 locations across the country.

Another program, called Toastmasters, is not really a course but a series of meetings of a nonprofit organization of people interested in sharpening their public-speaking skills. You pay $25 to $50 a year, plus a onetime $12 fee to join. At meetings, there is no formal instruction. Instead, 20 or so members typically take turns giving five- to seven-minute speeches. Their peers then critique their performance.

Once you have picked a promising course, ask for the names of graduates in your field or profession. Call them and press for candid comments on the nature of the course, the quality of the instruction and the relevance of the program to your specific needs.

You may even become proficient enough to earn a second income as a professional lecturer. True enough, very few people can collect big money, but you still can make public speaking pay.

Try approaching schools, libraries, PTAs and other civic and business organizations, and offer your services. If you're good, your name will spread among local groups. At first, you may want to speak for free, and then as your reputation spreads you might start charging. When you can command perhaps several hundred dollars a speech, the smaller booking agencies may be willing to take you on.

Learning a Foreign Language

A LITTLE familiarity with a foreign language can go a long way when you are traveling abroad, whether on a weekend jaunt to Tijuana or a long business trip to Tokyo. The least expensive way to start learning is to take a self-taught course available on audio cassettes. These simple, repeat-after-me courses cost as little as $22. A company called Audio-Forum (96 Broad Street, Guilford, Connecticut 06437) markets sets of 45-minute cassettes in 50 languages. There are 135 courses, each in one of three categories: tourist, refresher or comprehensive. The tourist tapes teach the words and sentences you will need for such basic things as checking into and out of hotels and getting around on public transportation.

For more comprehensive courses, consider the cassettes sold by the Foreign Service Institute. It is the branch of the U.S. State Department that trains diplomats and other federal employees in languages. Instruction in one of some 20 languages costs $55 to $155 for a series of tapes lasting nearly seven hours. You can buy them through the National Audiovisual Center (Order Section, 8700 Edgeworth Drive, Capitol Heights, Maryland 20743).

Top-quality foreign language classes are offered by many colleges and continuing-education schools. The University of Houston, for instance, charges $180 for a 20-hour weekend mini-course in languages as varied as Arabic, French and Chinese. Also check out classes at cultural institutes sponsored by foreign governments and located in many major U.S. cities. For example, the Goethe Institute is a German cultural center with branches in many places. Its Chicago branch offers a German language course that meets once a week for 10 weeks. The cost is $120.

If you want the convenience that cassettes afford and the personalized attention you can get in a class, consider hiring a tutor. That will cost you $10 to $40 an hour, although an instructor from a commercial school will be much more expensive. The most affordable instructors are usually foreign exchange students or foreign language majors at local colleges. Ask instructors at such institutions to recommend tutors. You can also find teachers through the cultural institutes.

For a very intensive language-learning experience, go to classes offered by such chains as Berlitz and Inlingua. But be warned: Commercial courses can be costly. Expect to spend about $4,000 for a two-week total immersion course in any language at Berlitz. For that price, you will get day-long lessons from a private instructor.

To make your vacation a learning experience, enroll in a study-abroad program run by both U.S.-based and foreign schools. You can study as briefly as several days or as much as four weeks — or more. Many of these language classes for travelers are reasonably priced. In mid-1988, for example, at the Eurocentre in Paris, tuition for an intensive, four-week French course cost $836, plus $692 if you wanted to board with a family. In Moscow, the government-run Russian Language School will set you up in a 10-day group class at the Hotel Sevastopol. The cost is about $55 per day per person ($40 per day each for two people) and includes hotel room, transportation and excursions with an interpreter. You can locate programs abroad through colleges, commercial language schools, cultural institutes and foreign consulates in major U.S. cities.

Your Vacation

Saving by Swapping Homes

You can cut your holiday costs in half if you are willing to let another family use your house while you use theirs. Many thousands of Americans trade homes every year, often with foreign families. For a few weeks, they enjoy comfortable accommodations in each other's houses, often with a car at their disposal. And all that comes without worrying about hotel reservations, restaurant bills and rental cars.

Far more Americans than Europeans are looking for swaps. So you would be wise to begin searching for a desirable swap at least three months before your scheduled trip.

The best way to find out what is available is to join a vacation exchange organization. Get its directories and start writing the owners whose listings you like. Better yet, start telephoning them. You will find descriptions of houses up for exchange in places as diverse as Tasmania and Turkey.

Property owners pore over the directories for a house in the right spot and then negotiate trades with each other. Most clubs give advice on contracts, insurance and other details but otherwise aren't involved in exchanges. All allow members to advertise their homes for rent as well as exchange.

The largest of them, Vacation Exchange Club, lists about 6,000 homes in two general directories published during the year. For information, write to the club at 12006 111th Avenue, Youngtown, Arizona 85363. About half of its listings are in the U.S. and Canada, and the rest are in Europe, Australia and New Zealand, with British swappers particularly plentiful. It costs $24.70 to get both editions of the directory and to list your house in one of them. For $16 you get the directories without a listing; owners of Hawaiian beach houses, for instance, often prefer to initiate trades rather than list their homes and have to respond to sacks of mail.

Among the other clubs is Hideaways International (15 Goldsmith Street, P.O. Box 1270, Littleton, Massachusetts 01460), which focuses on U.S., Caribbean, Mexican and Hawaiian resort areas but also rents apartments and villas in London and Italy. Two directories and four newsletters a year, with some 2,000 listings, cost $65, which makes you a member. A black-and-white, quarter-page spread on your home, with photos, is $99. Hideaways also runs ads for weekly vacation-home rentals, as well as for yacht charters.

If you are reluctant to approach a foreign family yourself, try some services that will match you up with a European family for an added fee — usually $100 to $500. One such service is Home Exchange International, 22458 Ventura Boulevard, Suite E, Woodland Hills, California 91364.

A couple of tips: When you find a likely family to swap with, ask for references from people who have exchanged homes with that family in the past. And to avoid any unpleasant surprises, be sure to ask for a photograph of the house.

Rent-a-Villa Bargains

FOR a terrific vacation at a bargain price, consider *renting* apartments or houses in a tropical seaside resort. You can enjoy more privacy — at less cost — than at a big hotel. For a cold-weather week or two in the sun, rental apartments can be especially reasonable for a large family or several couples traveling together.

The best places go fast, so it is wise to book two or three months ahead. Hawaii and Mexico have the widest choice of medium-priced houses or condos. For example, on the Hawaiian island of Maui, six people can stay in a $500,000 beach-site condo for $33 a person per day. A luxury hotel nearby easily can cost twice as much.

The Caribbean has much to offer, too. Rents are fairly low on Barbados, St. Martin or Jamaica's north shore. You're likely to spend $50 to $75 a person per day for a two-to-five-bedroom house on or near the beach. Included may be a maid who cooks and a gardener who doubles as a houseman.

You can find a villa to rent through ads in two magazines, *Travel & Leisure* and *Town & Country*. Or look in such city magazines as *San Diego* or *New York*. The risks of renting someone's private home sight unseen are obvious. The best way to make sure you don't wind up spending a week in a tropical Gulag is to find a villa through a reliable rental agency. Among them are At Home Abroad (405 East 56th Street, Suite 6-H, New York, New York 10022) and Creative Leisure Corporation (951 Transport Way, Petaluma, California 94952).

Agents' fees typically are 20%, which you might pay in the form of a higher rent. But the charge may be worth it. A responsible agent won't handle a rental unless the owners have hired someone locally to maintain the place and take care of unexpected problems with plumbing, electricity or anything else that goes bump in the night.

Many owners of rental houses and apartments in popular vacation spots give big discounts to pilots and flight attendants stranded between trips. But you do not have to work for an airline to get the same cuts. You can qualify by joining an organization called Club Costa for $99 a year. Members receive quarterly issues of *Club Costa Magazine* and the *Hotline Update Newsletter*. The magazine lists available houses and apartments in Hawaii, the Bahamas, Spain, Portugal and elsewhere — at 10% to 70% off regular rates. For more information, write to Club Costa, 7701 College Boulevard, Suite 200, Overland Park, Kansas 66210. (For $49 a year, Club Costa also offers reduced rates at over 11,000 hotels worldwide.)

Time Shares

TIME sharing can offer great low-cost vacations. You pay a one-time fee for the right to go to the same place year after year for a week or two. But if you do not choose carefully, your bargain can become a burden.

More than 1 million Americans have been swept up in the vacation time-share boom. It began during the mid-1970s, when many builders of resort condominiums adopted the European idea of dividing expensive real estate among many buyers. Developers learned that they could double their profit by selling 52 weekly shares in every apartment. The time-share concept quickly spread to hotels and motels as well as to yachts and campgrounds. Meanwhile, exchange services sprung up that enabled buyers to swap their time shares in one resort for vacation weeks at another resort.

Prices of time-share vacation units vary from $3,000 for one week in an efficiency unit in New England to nearly $25,000 for a week in a luxurious three-bedroom condominium at Lake Tahoe. The average cost is $7,500 a week. Most buyers are middle-aged and middle-income, but many resorts attract other people. For example, time shares in Aspen are popular among young professionals, and those in the Florida Keys appeal to wealthy, older couples.

Competition for time-share customers is fierce, high-pressure sales are common and many states do not have adequate protection for customers. True, most time shares are sold fairly and most buyers are happy with them. Some, however, grow tired of spending year after year at the same place. In a 1983 survey, one-quarter of the 8,000 owners who were polled said they planned to sell their shares but not buy others.

Some of the resorts where you buy time have gone under in recent years because of shaky financing and inept management. To avoid such heartaches, take the trouble to investigate the deal thoroughly before you invest.

Start by being wary of a promoter's high-pressure sales tactics. Never, never, buy a time share on the spot. Instead, take home copies of the proposed contract, the schedule of maintenance fees and the disclosure statement, and study them carefully. Also, ask the salesman for customer references. It is best to buy from firms already running other resorts. The time-share owners at these locations can tell you how well the developer is meeting his or her obligations. Check the firm's reputation further with its banker or the state attorney general's office or, in some states, the special agency that regulates time-share offerings.

Look in the sales contract and other documents for a statement of your rights in the event the resort runs into financial trouble. If you are buying a so-called *right-to-use* time share, make sure the contract includes a nondisturbance clause. It obligates the developer's lender to recognize your occupancy rights in case of foreclosure. Ask the lender whether the same clause is in the mortgage or construction loan. If it is not, the clause — and your claim — are worthless.

In the disclosure statement and schedule of maintenance fees, see whether the developer is setting aside a part of the maintenance money for major repairs. If not, you could be socked for heavy special assessments in later years. And have a real estate attorney who is familiar with time shares review any documents before you sign them. Your own lawyer should be able to refer you to such a specialist. His or her fee for an hour or two of time will be money well spent.

If you buy a vacation time share but later become bored with visiting the same old resort, you have two options. The first is to exchange your time share for a share in another place at another time. Two services — Resort Condominiums International (3512 Woodview Trace, Indianapolis, Indiana 46268) and Interval International (6262 Sunset Drive, Penthouse I, Miami, Florida 33143) — work to find someone to trade with you. But you cannot swap an off-season week at an unknown beach resort for a snow-season week at a top ski resort. Swapping a time share can be tough unless you have one that is in a popular place at a desirable time of year.

The other option when you want to unload your time share is to sell. But selling the wrong season and the wrong resort may be next to impossible. So it's smart to think about the possibility of having to sell even before you buy. Some builders have resale brokerage offices, but they charge commissions of around 15%. The commission — coupled with closing costs of $250 to $500, paid by the seller — can make it difficult to turn a time-share unit into a profitable investment. Indeed, owners who sell sometimes lose 30% to 60%.

So if you are thinking of buying a vacation time-share unit, be sure to satisfy this all-important test: find a place you will love to be in that same time year after year. Here are some further guidelines to picking the right time share for you:

— If you buy a time-share unit in fee simple, which means you own it outright, brokers recommend you pay no more than 10 times the going rate for a comparable week in a hotel or rental apartment.

— If you buy the right to use, which in effect is a lease of 10 to 40 years, then divide the price by the number of years you get to use the property. If the amount is less than the cost of an equivalent rental unit, then the price is right.

— Buy one- or two-bedroom units. They are easier to resell than very small or very large ones.

— Buy time during the peak season at a popular area. This enhances your chance of swapping, renting or selling.

— Buy in a place that cannot be overbuilt because of geography, local building codes or moratoriums on further time shares.

— Buy your time share from an experienced builder. You will be less likely to wind up with poor maintenance, bad management or unforeseen liabilities. Also, big developers are more likely to help you rent or resell your time share.

— Buy in a place that is easy to reach. If it is not, that may discourage potential swappers or buyers.

— Buy a time share because you want a place to take a vacation. If you make the right choice — but only if you make the right choice — then you may have the double pleasure of regular access to a nice vacation spot plus a sound investment.

Hotel Time Shares

You know about buying time shares in condos and chalets at resort hideaways, but here is a new wrinkle. A few *hotels* around the country are selling off some of their rooms on a time-sharing basis.

For about $15,000 or so, plus a yearly maintenance fee, you get the right to use a room for a week of your choosing every year. Among the time-sharing hotels is the four-star Donatello in San Francisco.

Many buyers tend to be two-income couples in their 40s. Time-sharing a hotel isn't so much an investment that is likely to bring a profit soon; it is more a long-term commitment to a rather luxurious vacation home. With room service.

How to Get the Best, Cheapest Plane Rides

WHEN you buy an airline ticket, you enter a bazaar of wild negotiating and sometimes wonderful opportunities for bargains. Ticket prices vary sharply, depending upon how far in advance you make your reservation, what day and which time of year you take your flight and from whom you order. The person sitting next to you on the plane may have paid much more — or much less — than you.

Often you can get your lowest fares by ordering and paying for your ticket at least two weeks ahead of your departure and qualifying for supersaver fares. And travel agents frequently can get better deals than you alone can, so it pays to use them. Of course, agents collect their fees from airlines, so you pay no extra charge for their service. But just as one airline can give you lower prices on the same run than another line can, one travel agent can bring a nicer bargain than another. Obvious moral: It pays to shop around, among the air carriers and the travel agents.

U.S. regulations and international agreements are supposed to prohibit deep discounting of air fares on regularly scheduled flights, but it has flourished anyway because of simple economics. As one airline executive says, empty space on an airplane is "like overripe fruit in the supermarket — if you don't move it, it becomes worthless."

When the airlines anticipate empty seats on a flight, they quietly sell blocks of them at deep discounts to broker-dealers and to certain travel agencies. One of the fastest-growing discounters is named Access International, 250 West 57th Street, New York, New York 10107; (212-333-7280); in 1987 it sold $22 million worth of tickets to the public. It is based in New York City and also has offices in Chicago, Paris and London.

The British travel agency Thomas Cook has set up its own discounter, called Airfare Warehouse Ltd. It supplies Cook's 400 retail branches with tickets at steep discounts. Airfare Warehouse's lowest scheduled New York–London round-trip in mid-1988 was $500, but it was available only on Third World carriers such as Kuwait Airlines. Standard coach fare on a major carrier is $1,640.

Other typical *one-way* fares on Western carriers available in peak season from discounters around the country are New York to Paris for $225, versus the standard $700; Chicago to Rome for $280, versus the usual $900; and Los Angeles to Tokyo for $640, versus the standard $800.

Be aware that a ticket sold by a discounter will not be honored by other airlines. The ticket also is usually not refundable, and may carry other restrictions.

Once you have found the best price for a flight, buy your ticket right away. You then will avoid any fare increases before your departure date. Fares can and do go up overnight, sometimes sharply.

Several air carriers reduce their prices for night flights, usually beginning from 7 p.m. to 9 p.m. Be sure to check with the airlines.

Some travel agencies have begun to specialize in offering computerized services that track the very lowest airline fares. For instance, Traveltron, a free national service operated by a travel agent in Irvine, California, guarantees to locate the least expensive fares on flights between U.S. cities. Just one example: Fliers recently paid as much as $410 for one-way tickets between Los Angeles and Dallas. Traveltron directed callers to $129 fares. To use Traveltron, simply call 714-545-3335.

A decision by some of the nation's largest airlines will make it even easier to get better ticket prices. The computerized ticket reservation systems traditionally have steered travel agents and travelers to the big airlines that run the systems, creating a bias for their particular flights. Medium-size carriers criticized the practice as unfair competition. Now, passengers will be able to ask travel agents to book flights on the basis of the lowest fares, most convenient departure times and closest airports.

Some airlines offer special deals for passengers who meet certain age requirements. If you are at least 62, you can travel on any of Eastern Airlines' domestic routes, plus fly to Puerto Rico and Canada, by purchasing a Get Up and Go passport for $1,299. The passport is valid for a year, and for the price of an additional one, a companion of any age can travel with you, as long as you always fly together. When you are on the ground, you can stay at participating Omni, Hilton, Howard Johnson, Marriott or Vista International hotels at a reduced rate.

Whatever you pay, you can get the most for your money if you make some plans in advance.

Wise travelers always try to reserve their airplane seats well before the flight. If you have already bought your ticket, you can pick your seat as much as one year ahead of time on some major airlines. Also, ask for your boarding pass when you make your reservations. You will have a smoother flight if you avoid the rear of the plane. Tail winds cause the most turbulence there. On rear-engine planes like the 727 or DC-9, you will escape engine noise and vibration by sitting as far forward as you can. By doing that, you also avoid the crowds when you leave the plane. Being one of the first out the door can speed you on your way — provided you have only hand baggage and do not have to wait for checked luggage.

On any plane, you will get the most leg room by taking the seat next to an emergency exit, since there must be enough space in that area to permit easy exiting from the plane. In the coach section, another desirable seat is in the first row, behind a bulkhead. You usually have extra leg room and a good view out a window that is unobstructed by the wing. Sitting just behind the bulkhead also gives you more room above the waist because there is no seat in front of yours that can suddenly recline and slant back into your face.

Avoid, if possible, flying at the busiest times, which are the early mornings and late afternoons of weekdays. For reasons travel experts have not fathomed, the most crowded day of the week is Thursday. The least crowded days are Tuesday and Saturday. Take direct flights whenever possible, and if you must change planes, try to avoid delay-prone airports, such as those in Newark, Atlanta and Chicago.

When you make your reservation, ask whether the flight you want is often delayed. On the day of your trip, ask when the aircraft for your flight is expected to arrive, then allow an hour for turnaround time.

There is no foolproof way to avoid being "bumped" off an oversold plane. A wise plan is to call the airline the night before your flight and ask how full the plane is. If it is 60% full, don't worry. If it is full, and you absolutely have to make that flight, get to the airport at least an hour early.

Of the 430 million people who flew domestically in 1987, almost 900,000 were bumped. But if your plane is overbooked, do not fret. Before bumping anyone, the airline must ask for volunteers who are willing to give up their seats. The carrot may be cash or a later flight at no charge — basically anything you and the airline can agree to. If only a little money is offered, you may be able to bargain for more. Generally, the airline's ticket-counter people up the ante if there are not enough immediate volunteers. A free ride can be well worth a few hours' wait.

When you are bumped, the airline must get you on another flight that is scheduled to arrive within an hour of your original arrival time. If it cannot, it must pay you a penalty equal to your one-way fare up to a maximum of $200 and still fly you to your destination. If the airline cannot get you on a flight due to arrive within two hours of your original arrival time on a domestic flight or four hours on an international one, the penalty doubles to a maximum of $400. In cases when you are forced to make an overnight layover at a city not on your itinerary, the airline should pick up your hotel bill. But when the airline is not the culprit, you're on your own.

Every airline has its own "contract of carriage," in which it spells out its responsibility to you. You can get a copy simply by asking for it at the ticket counter or by writing to the airline.

Do not check any baggage you don't have to. When you make your reservations, ask how much you are allowed to carry on and pack accordingly. One more tip: You can improve your plane food — or at least have more choice — if you order a special meal by calling the airline at least a day in advance. Quite a few lines offer a remarkable array, from pasta to pastrami, but many veteran fliers say that you get the best deal, and the freshest food, by ordering a salad or vegetarian plate.

Finally, the ultimate bargain: Imagine getting a round-trip flight to Tokyo for 70% off the regular fare or a one-way ticket from Los Angeles to Honolulu for free. For such bargains, you just have to travel for one of several companies that use free-lance couriers.

Here's how it works. Some of the smaller overnight package express companies do not have their own fleet of planes. So they hire free-lancers to take commercial flights to destination cities, and use all or part of a free-lancer's baggage allowance to send their packages. The courier company pays at least half of the ticket price — and sometimes all of it. You can apply directly to one or more of the many courier companies around the country. Check in the Yellow Pages under "Air Courier Service."

Free Trips for Frequent Fliers

I F YOU travel often, it pays to become a steady customer of one or two airlines and enroll in their frequent-flier bonus programs. That way you can earn free trips, and you can even sell the travel awards that you do not have time to enjoy.

The awards commonly start after you have accumulated 10,000 miles, when you get an upgrade to first class for the price of a full-fare coach ticket. The free rides usually begin at 20,000 to 50,000 miles, and the rewards grow progressively richer. At the highest levels, quite a few airlines will take you to foreign countries, either on their own planes or through linkups with most European carriers, as well as Air New Zealand, Australia's Qantas and some Asian lines.

United Airlines gives two first-class round-trip tickets to the Orient or the South Pacific, plus 50% savings for up to seven nights in a Westin Hotel, and a one-week luxury car rental in the U.S., to passengers who have logged 150,000 miles. For 200,000 miles, Pan Am will give you *and* a companion unlimited business-class flights throughout its international and domestic system for 30 days. Having earned 60,000 miles on TWA, you *and* a companion can get round-trip coach-class tickets to anywhere in Europe the airline flies — and get 50% off regular room rates for two consecutive weekend nights at participating Hilton hotels, as well as four nights at participating Marriott hotels for 50% off regular room rates. In addition, you have free use of a midsize car for a two-day weekend. At 75,000 miles on American, you get two free first-class tickets anywhere the airline flies in the United States, including Hawaii. Just about all other big airlines, and some small ones, have similar deals.

When calculating your mileage for an award, many U.S. carriers will even count flights you have taken on other airlines, domestic or foreign. You also can earn mileage credits by staying at certain hotels, renting cars from designated firms or sailing on selected cruise lines. So whenever you take a flight, stop in a hotel, rent an auto or take a sea voyage, be sure to ask whether you can earn credits toward the frequent-flier program or programs in which you are enrolled.

If you do not have the time or the inclination to take the trips you have won, you can sell them through middlemen known as coupon brokers. Their advertisements appear in the classifieds of the *Wall*

Street Journal and many big-city newspapers under "Travel." But before you strike a deal, check out their reputations through local Better Business Bureaus.

Coupon brokering is perfectly legal, though the airlines dislike the practice. The price you will receive for your mileage credits is a function of supply and demand and the airlines' peak seasonal restrictions on bonus travel. Take, for example, the rights to a first-class round-trip seat on United Air Lines from the East Coast to Hawaii. The bonus could be sold to a broker for $500 or $600 and bought by a bargain hunter for $800 or $900; that is a savings of well over $1,500 on the full-fare price.

Special Deals in Hotels

THOSE lavish honeymoon packages at hotels and resorts are not only for newlyweds. Many times they are offered to anniversary celebrants as well — and it is a rare hotelier who will demand that you celebrate your wedding on its anniversary. Next time you book a room for two, simply ask for the hotel's anniversary or honeymoon rate.

For instance, the Westin Bonaventure Hotel in Los Angeles not long ago was offering one night's stay in a deluxe one-bedroom suite for about $210, or less than two-thirds the regular rate. Guests got champagne on arrival and breakfast the morning after.

For another kind of mini-vacation, check into the special weekend packages that many hotels offer. They usually include a double room for two nights with extras that can range from welcoming champagne to ballet tickets to a gourmet dinner by candlelight in your room. You pay one set price for all of this, and it is usually considerably less than everything would cost à la carte. In some cases, the saving can amount to 50%. Rates in top hotels for two people and two nights start at about $200 and run as high as $500.

A growing number of new hotels are offering suites — many at prices far below those in traditional hotels. Some suites also come with kitchens, so you can save still more by doing your own cooking. For instance, the Golden Strand Ocean Resort & Spa in Miami gives you a bedroom plus a sitting room with terrace, full kitchen and two bathrooms for $200 a night in the winter and — here's the bargain — $105 in the off-season. Some hotels charge at least twice as much. At the Hyde Park Suites in San Francisco, you pay $150 to $175 a night, which again is less than other hotels charge.

You can book at some 250 all-suite hotels through a service called the International Reservation System. From anywhere in the U.S. except New York State, you can call it toll-free at 800-231-0404. In New York State call 212-517-8886.

And whenever you stay in a hotel, be sure to ask if it gives travel bonuses for repeat customers. Members of Holiday Inns' Priority Club can stay with their family for the single-person corporate rate Monday through Friday, receive free coffee or tea and a newspaper and are given automatic upgrades when possible. Major credit-card holders can join Stouffer Hotels' Club Express. Members get free upgrades and certificates, which can be redeemed for free weekends, U.S. Savings Bonds and merchandise. If you pay $25 a year, you can join Hyatt's Gold Passport program and earn five points for every dollar charged to your room. For 5,000 points, the starting level, you are entitled not only to a room upgrade for as many as four nights but also to awards from Delta or Northwest Airlines and Hertz.

Bed-and-Breakfast Guest Houses

VACATIONERS find that staying in a big-city hotel can easily cost $100 a night or more. But there is a fast-growing alternative: guest houses that offer bed and breakfast. They have the comforts of home at truly down-home prices.

More and more private houses throughout America take in paying guests. Like the well-known European homes that offer tourists bed and breakfast for nominal fees, these guest houses flourish in many cities, towns and resort areas where they cater mostly to travelers who have given up on hotels because of their champagne prices and no-fizz accommodations.

These guest houses rent out an average of three rooms, and rates for a couple can range from $25 a night at a mansion in Geneva, New York, to $75 in Eureka, California. Breakfast and free parking are almost always part of the deal. There is no guilty fumbling for tips; hosts rarely accept them.

Most offer the kind of hospitality that is rare at hotels, eagerly sharing with you insiders' insights on fine restaurants and shopping bargains. But you may miss some amenities available at even moderately priced hotels. You probably won't have a TV or phone in your room. You may have to share a bathroom.

You can find a listing of more than 850 bed-and-breakfast hosts in a book, *Bed & Breakfast U.S.A.*, by Betty Revits Rundback and Nancy Kramer. It costs $10.95. If it is not readily available at your local bookstore, you can order it for $11.95 from the Tourist House Association of America at R.D. 2, Box 355-A, Greentown, Pennsylvania 18426.

Bed & Breakfast U.S.A. includes a chapter on how to start your own and lists over 140 bed-and-breakfast reservation agencies. They usually send free brochures describing members' houses and an application asking for your itinerary, how long you plan to stay and whether you insist on comforts such as air conditioning. Sometimes you can choose your house; other times you are assigned to one. These booking agencies may take a week or two to confirm reservations, so plan your trip in advance.

Dude Ranches

IF YOU are looking for a moderately priced family vacation, you might consider spending a week at one of America's 150 dude ranches. Each can offer a private cabin, three hearty meals a day and a companionable horse for the price of just a room in a big-city hotel. A week at a ranch typically costs around $450 to $800 per adult — with 10% or more off for children. The ranches are mostly in the open spaces of the West, but the East and South have a sprinkling of smaller spreads.

Many of the ranches still raise cattle for profit and let visiting dudes help round up the herd, brand a steer or lend a hand with chores. But the emphasis is on horseback riding. Ranches offer easy, medium and fast rides. Other activities can include fishing, hiking and swimming. The newest breed of ranches couples conventional resort fare such as tennis with an Old West setting. But the more frills a ranch offers, the more expensive it is likely to be.

To find a dude ranch, write or phone the tourist office in the state or states you would like to visit. If you are interested in the West, write the Dude Ranchers' Association at P.O. Box 471, Laporte, Colorado 80535.

Figuring your budget is simple because the rates are inclusive. You need add in only your transportation costs. It can cost less than $150 to outfit you from head to toe for a dude ranch. The biggest and most important investment is cowboy boots. They start at about $60. You'll also need a couple of pairs of broken-in jeans, flannel shirts and a warm jacket for cool morning or evening rides. A snug straw cowboy hat will shield your eyes from the sun and dust. The cheapest is about $20.

A warning about dude ranches: Do not expect luxurious rooms and gourmet meals. At all but the most expensive ranches, both rooms and meals are simple and basic.

Holding Down Costs of Foreign Travel

THE value of the dollar has fallen so much lately against the French franc, the British pound, the Italian lira and most other foreign currencies that travel abroad has become significantly more expensive than in recent years. So, to prevent any unexpected blows to your pocketbook, it pays to prepare a sensible travel budget in advance.

Before you go, read (or at least skim) one or two up-to-date guidebooks. They will help you arrive at a reasonable estimate of what your trip will cost. At least half a dozen travel newsletters also offer reliable cost information tailored to specific clients, such as retired travelers or singles. You can find out where to subscribe to them from travel agents, advertisements in travel magazines and your own special-interest groups.

After you have done your homework, sit down and make a daily budget. Add up the estimated costs of hotels, food, tips, taxis and incidentals. Then tack on at least 25% more for the unexpected.

Do not plan to spend the same amount each day. Try the "budget-splurge" method of travel. Cut back on certain days by eating delicatessen take-outs in the park for dinner. Then you can afford a really terrific restaurant the next day.

Prepay as much of your trip as you can before you leave. That avoids budget-busting surprises.

Package tours are surely the cheapest way to travel. But some stripped-down tours have more hidden costs than France has churches. Hotel and restaurant managers may ask you to pay extra for items you thought had been taken care of well in advance. You will have a hard time trying to collect when you get back home. Spare yourself grief by inquiring exactly what you are paying for before you leave. (For more, see "Your Vacation: Getting Good Value on Package Tours.")

The surest way to save money is to plan a trip as far ahead as possible. That way, you can get the cheapest air fares. If you do not want a package and are willing to lock in your plans 14 to 21 days ahead, buy an advance-purchase excursion ticket, called Apex. That almost always gives you the least expensive round-trip fare on regularly scheduled airlines. Any change made after purchase of the ticket may be costly.

Also, consider buying a one-way ticket to your destination and picking up your return ticket once you get there. If the local currency is on the decline against the dollar, the two one-ways may cost you less than a full-fare round trip bought in the U.S.

Plan to pay for your expenses abroad with a combination of traveler's checks and credit cards. Do not carry too much cash, because hotel thefts are on the rise. In a pinch, you usually can cash personal checks at top hotels and the offices of credit-card companies. But you need to have a credit card to do it.

If you enjoy train travel, one of the world's last great bargains is the Eurailpass. It allows you to travel first class as much as you want in sixteen European countries for $298 for 15 days. Children under 12 go half price; under four years old they ride free. Britain is not covered by the Eurailpass but has its own version, which allows an adult 15 days of unlimited first-class travel by railroads all over England, Scotland and Wales for $350. Children aged five through 15 travel for half fare.

European trains are usually fast, clean, comfortable — much better than most of their American counterparts. They are also good for stretching out and sleeping in — which is a clever way of saving a bundle on a hotel room every now and then.

Just about everywhere, you can save money by avoiding the costly capital cities and trekking off to the provincial centers and the countryside. For example, rural Britain is not only charming but also far less expensive than swinging London. But wherever you decide to go, you might follow the advice of the most savvy and seasoned travelers: take half of what you pack and twice as much as you have budgeted.

Getting Good Value on Package Tours

ALMOST every would-be tourist has heard horror stories about package tours. But you do not have to swear off those bargain deals if you want your vacation to go smoothly. You can get top value for your money provided you know how to examine your package tour in advance. Here are some of the questions you will want answered:

— Does the package include an inexpensive and convenient charter flight? Regular fares are down so much on some routes that you could wind up saving only about $25 on round-trip charters from New York City to London. When the savings are substantial, make sure that you do not have to stop en route in two or three other U.S. cities before heading for Rome — via London and Brussels.

— What do "first-class" accommodations really mean? The best European hotels are rated "deluxe." All that first class gets you is a clean bed-chamber with a private bath. You can determine if you are going first class or fleabag by looking up the amenities of your hotel in *The Official Hotel and Resort Guide,* available at travel agencies and libraries. The guide also lists the price you would pay for the room if you booked on your own. If the daily cost of the hotel on your package tour is *less* than the hotel's usual room rate, you know you are getting a deal.

— Will the meals consist of foie gras and roast pigeon, or tomato juice and roast chicken? Tour operators won't tell you what you will eat at meals included in the package, but they will give you hints. If you find you are to eat in hotel restaurants, remember that they seldom are great gastronomical palaces.

— What happens if you have to cancel? Read the brochure's fine print carefully. You will probably lose your hotel deposits, typically the cost of one to three nights. But most tour operators will refund the rest of your money, minus a fee of $25 to $100 depending on how close to the departure date you back out.

— One more important tip: You can check on the record of charter companies by phoning the U.S. Department of Transportation's Office of Intergovernmental and Consumer Affairs at 202-366-2220.

Shopping Bargains Overseas

DESPITE the dollar's decline in value, you still can find bargains when traveling abroad. With little effort, you can save 20% to 50% on some foreign purchases. You are likely to get the best buys on the specialties of each country, such as lace in Belgium, ceramics in Portugal and crystal in France. England has the top bargains in clothing and china; Italy is the place for fine leather goods. You can get diamonds in Amsterdam for up to 30% less than you might have to pay in the U.S. For furs, look to Scandinavia.

Europe is not the only mecca for American shoppers. Mexican leather and silver are reasonably priced, despite high inflation. Brazilian gemstones are as much as a third less in Rio de Janeiro than they are in the U.S. And Hong Kong is a bargain spot for jewelry, clothing, porcelain, Oriental rugs and native Chinese crafts and antiques.

Some other shopping advice:

— Look for bargains on products that have been brought in from countries outside the one you are visiting. A number of governments have lenient tax policies that make imported products less expensive than in the countries where they are manufactured. It is often cheaper to buy a Swiss watch in Copenhagen than in Geneva.

— Scout the big department stores, but only to determine the going prices for merchandise. Then buy the goods in the smaller boutiques and flea markets, where prices usually are lower.

— Haggle, when and where you can. Small retailers often are willing to haggle. Although that makes many Americans uncomfortable, a successful negotiation can save you plenty. Generally, the farther south you travel in Europe, the more acceptable it is to bargain. Always deal with the person in charge of a store and never in earshot of other customers. The more expensive an article, the more negotiable the price.

— Offer to pay cash for a discount. Stores have to pay fees of as much as 10% to credit-card companies for purchases on plastic.

— Don't get carried away with your bargains. Each U.S. traveler is allowed to take home $400 worth of goods duty-free. You will pay 10% duty on the next $1,000, and an average 12% on purchases beyond that. But there is no duty on gemstones.

How to Survive Customs Inspections

You are just back from a grand trip overseas, and the only obstacle between you and your waiting family is a cold-eyed U.S. customs agent. How can you best survive the customs inspection of your overstuffed baggage?

Even before they leave home, smart travelers write or visit an office of the U.S. Customs Service and get two of its leaflets. One is *Know Before You Go*, and, among other things, it lists the articles you cannot legally bring home. The second tells about goods that are duty-free if they are made and bought in any of more than 140 developing countries and territories. That leaflet is titled *GSP & the Traveler*. GSP stands for Generalized System of Preferences. You can also get these publications by writing to the U.S. Customs Service, P.O. Box 7407, Washington, D.C. 20044. Be sure to include the names of the leaflets — Customs publishes many more than these two.

A few items are duty-free no matter where they are bought. Among them are paintings; antiques; cut, unset diamonds and binoculars.

Each returning traveler, even an infant in diapers, is allowed $400 in duty-free merchandise or $800 if you are coming home from the Virgin Islands, Guam or Samoa. A family can pool their allowances. For example, a family of four — Mom, Dad and two children — get a total allowance of $1,600. If you go above your total, you are charged a flat 10% duty on the next $1,000 and up to 110% on everything else (though the average is 8%).

Customs agents are not easily fooled. They have price lists for popular goods such as French perfumes and Scottish woolens. They can spot amateurishly stitched American labels on clothes — a sure sign that somebody bought the garment abroad.

Inspectors are tougher at some gateways than others. The easiest entry into the country is often from Canada, since there is less concern about contraband traffic from the North. The toughest entry points are from the Orient, the Caribbean and South America because that is where the drugs come from. So it is small wonder that Honolulu and Miami have a well-earned reputation as the roughest U.S. customs checkpoints.

When you go through customs, you invite suspicion — and a search — if you act nervous or belligerent or carry something bizarre, such as a fur coat in summer. If an examiner finds an item you have not declared, he or she can charge you a fine equal to its wholesale price. On top of that, the agent can confiscate the item and charge you with a criminal offense.

So the best advice, of course, is to do your homework, keep your bills straight, tell the truth — and if you have overbought your $400 per-person limit, be prepared to pay your duty, which, after all, probably will not be very large.

Traveling Abroad with Children

You do not have to wait until your children have graduated from college to take a vacation in Europe. You can go now and take the children with you without breaking the bank at Monte Carlo. The money-saving trick is to stay away from places like the bank at Monte Carlo.

Peter Carry, executive editor of *Sports Illustrated* magazine, who has spent several summers in Europe with his wife and their young children, advises that the first rule of international travel with the under five-foot-tall set is: Don't travel. Rent a house and stay put except for family day trips and the occasional parental overnight. Hauling youngsters from one hotel to another and in and out of restaurants calls for the resources of the Aga Khan and the forbearance of Mother Teresa.

The key part of planning a family trip is finding the rental house. Avoid cities and well-known resorts. In a small town or village, your rent is likely to be relatively inexpensive, the chances will be good that you will have friendly neighbors and you can absorb local culture that isn't gussied up for tourists.

If you want to rent a house on fairly short notice, comb the classified ads in the Friday edition of the *International Herald Tribune*. You can buy it at major newsstands in large cities. The national tourist office of the country you want to visit, its consulate in your area or its embassy in Washington can also point you in the right direction.

When all else fails, get a guidebook to the country you would like to visit and select half a dozen or so towns that sound appealing. Then write to the local tourist office in each — most good guides like the Michelin include those addresses. You also can have your travel agent put you in touch with a rental agency. But once you have found your house, be sure to ask for photographs and a list of the contents before you consider renting.

Your largest single expense probably will be plane fares. But there are ways to hold down these and other costs. Sometimes the country where you will be staying is not necessarily the one you should fly to. For example, if you are traveling to the south of France, you may be wise to check to see if there is a specially inexpensive New York–to–London fare, and then pay extra to fly from London to Marseilles. Or you might want to fly to Barcelona because it is often cheaper to rent a car in Spain than in France.

But before you buy tickets on any cut-rate plane flights be sure they have reduced-cost seats for children; some of them do not. So more than ever, when flying to Europe with your family, you have to shop around.

You can carry more weight on a transatlantic flight than used to be allowed, because most carriers have replaced the 44-pound maximum with a system that limits each passenger to two bags of certain dimensions with a combined maximum weight of 140 pounds, plus a carry-on. This is a tremendous advantage if you are renting a house abroad.

Disposable plastic and paper household products are much more expensive in Europe than at home. So stuff all your leftover luggage capacity with them if you are renting a home for several weeks. And if you are traveling with infants, remember that an army duffel bag can hold more than 200 disposable diapers.

Consider springing for another plane ticket — and bring a baby-sitter along with you. That's right. If you usually have a mother's helper at home or often use baby-sitters, you probably can buy a seat to Europe for the same amount as these services cost. And because there seems to be an endless supply of bright, responsible American teenagers who will baby-sit in exchange for a chance to go to Europe, you need not pay more than expenses. A mother's helper means freedom for mother — and father — to get away, if only for an hour at the local café for coffee and a *digestif*.

How to Find a Reliable Travel Agent

I F YOU are planning a trip, a knowing travel agent can help guide you through the complexity of fares and the many package deals available. But how do you pick a good travel agent?

A travel agent, after all, is a double agent. He is engaged by you, the traveler, but he is paid by the airlines, hotels, tour operators and other travel services, which give him commissions — generally 10%. Thus, most travel agents prefer writing expensive international tours to planning a car trip to the nearest beach. Some may push hotels that offer better commissions than they do rooms, or package tours that are easier to arrange than customized itineraries.

But many travel agents do put their clients' needs first. For one thing, they thrive on repeat business and recommendations. The problem is not how to find an honest agent. What is most difficult is discovering one who is expert and experienced enough to guide you. You might test to see if his taste is compatible with yours by asking him for his favorite hotels and sights in places that you have visited and are well acquainted with.

Just about anyone can set himself up in the business. Window decals that boast affiliations with national travel agent associations guarantee that the agency meets some standards, but not very high ones. If the agent himself has completed a two-year course given by the Institute of Certified Travel Agents and has five years of travel industry experience, he can use the initials CTC after his name. This label at least suggests above-average commitment.

But the best guarantee to a competent agent is word of mouth. If you are trying an agent on someone else's recommendation, then tell that agent just who sent you. Agents work harder if they have to please old customers as well as new ones.

Solid professionals are interested in the outcome of trips. They usually take the initiative to call customers on their return. If you have complaints that are well founded, travel agents can help you get at least some of your money back.

Before settling on a travel agent, interview two or three on the telephone. Ask where each one has traveled in the past year. A conscientious agent can share first-hand experience of the places and services he recommends. He probably takes two or three week-long trips and several weekend excursions a year — just to keep his information up to date.

If an agent is unfamiliar with a destination, he should be willing to refer you to a colleague or another customer who has recently been there. You can tell an agent knows a place fairly well if he speaks authoritatively without continually consulting guidebooks and maps.

Do not hesitate to prod the agent to find the lowest fare. You will know he is really digging if he suggests times or dates that would result in cheaper tickets. On the other hand, be sure to investigate carefully any extremely low-priced package tours. Sometimes they cut so many corners that the hotel and meals aren't anything you would care to remember.

Travel agencies range from hometown mom-and-pop operations to the giant chains like American Express or Thomas Cook. Customers who want personal service often do better with small agencies with local reputations to protect. But large chains and agencies frequently offer a wider selection of services and a staff that knows about more areas of the world. Volume also breeds influence. Agencies that send planeloads of travelers to a destination can get scarce hotel rooms more easily in peak seasons.

Customers with particular travel needs should seek out specialized agents. Some are expert in exotic travel, in rail travel or freighter cruises, still others in the needs of singles or business travelers. Travel guidebooks are the places to find such specialists. And foreign airlines or national tourist offices also can be invaluable guides to agencies familiar with their countries.

What to Do If Your Baggage Is Lost

THE best-laid travel plans can be spoiled if your baggage is lost on an airline trip. One way to avoid this possibility is to carry all your luggage with you on board, as savvy air travelers have done at least since the invention of the hanging garment bag. Airlines usually place limitations on what you can carry with you, so if you must check a suitcase, don't pack anything in it you might need within 24 hours — or the only copy of your millionaire uncle's will.

The reassuring news is that less than 1% of all luggage is lost, even temporarily, and almost all bags that go astray are found, usually within a few hours. If you cannot locate your bag, your first step is to report the loss to the airline's representative immediately; the bag may still be on the plane you came in on. If a search turns up nothing, you will be given a form to fill out. Do not leave the airport without handing in the form — and keep a copy for your records.

If you will be bagless overnight, most airlines will give you either a toilet kit or the money to buy one. The airlines are stickier about replacing clothes. Many a week-long vacation has been hampered, if not ruined, because an airline did not pay for clothes until the vacation was almost over. Even then the carrier might pay only half the cost.

When luggage is lost, the airline is liable for damages, usually up to $1,250 per person on domestic flights and $9.07 a pound on international flights. Commuter lines are not liable for even that much, although many will pay anyway. If your luggage and its contents are worth more than the airline's liability limit, you can buy excess-valuation insurance from the airline when you check in. Carriers charge 10 cents to $1.25 for each $100 worth of coverage — up to $25,000. Even so, some airlines may refuse to insure jewelry, cash and breakable items, including antiques and camera equipment. Keep in mind that most homeowners or tenants insurance covers losses above an airline's liability limits.

Once your bag has been missing for four or five days, you should file a claim form. Extensive dickering over the worth of goods is fairly common. In the end, the airlines usually will reimburse you for your wayward belongings' fair market value, not the full replacement cost. So you stand to collect less than the original cost of your property. For expensive items, you may need to show receipts to prove how much you paid. Count on waiting six weeks for the payment. If you feel the settlement is unfair, take the matter to small-claims court — before cashing the airline's check. Also, you can complain to the Office of Intergovernmental and Consumer Affairs, Department of Transportation, 400 Seventh Street, SW, Washington, D.C. 20590.

The major causes of missing bags are mix-ups when they are moved from one place to another, failure to remove old airport tags and theft — usually by someone hanging around the baggage carousel. To avoid loss, always pull old airport tags off a bag before checking it; that avoids confusion about where it is heading. Learn the tag code letters for airports to which you often fly so that you can be sure your bag is properly ticketed. Make sure your name, address and phone number are marked on the outside of any checked luggage. If you do not have baggage tags, the airline usually will give you stick-on labels. In sum, bright, clear identification is your best guarantee that your bags will get to their destination.

Protecting Yourself Against Other Losses

VACATIONERS are easy marks for seasoned pickpockets and thieves, but you can take steps to make any loss you might suffer less harmful to your holiday. Before you leave home, prepare several lists of all important ID, credit card and telephone numbers. Photocopy key documents, such as your passport and plane tickets. If you are traveling abroad, also take along extra passport photos and a certified copy of your birth certificate. And leave a second set of copies with someone back home.

If your passport is stolen, go to a U.S. embassy or consulate. An officer there will ask you to present a police report of the theft and, if possible, to show proof of citizenship — for example, your birth certificate. A photocopy of your passport, or a written record of your passport number, place and date of issuance plus any personal information — exactly as it is written on the document — will also help. You should be able to get a new passport within a day or so. The fee is $42.

An American embassy or consulate also will help you if a thief takes your cash. For a one-time charge of $40, you can arrange for family or friends to wire money to the State Department in Washington. It will authorize the overseas office to give you the money, usually within 24 hours.

When traveler's checks or credit cards are stolen, report the theft to the issuing companies. If you have your receipt with the traveler's checks' serial numbers, you may be able to get some of your money as fast as you can make it to the company's nearest refund location. Often it is a local bank, travel service, hotel or rental car agency. Without the serial numbers, your refund could take hours or even days, while the company tries to verify your original purchase. Credit cards are tougher to replace. Only American Express promises to issue a new card through its local office by the end of the next business day.

Losing an airline ticket is costly. In the U.S., you have to wait several months for a refund to come through. There may be no refund at all if the stolen ticket was used. But an international passenger stands a better chance of receiving a new ticket at little or no additional cost. That is because all passengers have to show their passports before boarding.

What If Your Airline Is Grounded?

WHAT if you buy a plane ticket and your airline is grounded? It *could* happen. In 1987, 14 airlines went out of business.

Don't worry; your chances of getting your money back are excellent — *if* you have charged your ticket to a credit card. Under the Fair Credit Billing Act of 1974, a creditor cannot force you to pay for a service that you did not receive. Most credit-card issuers will refund your money promptly when you send them the invalid ticket.

If you buy your tickets from a travel agent you can purchase an insurance policy called Travel Guard Gold. One of its important benefits is a penalty waiver, which allows you to cancel a trip for any reason and reimburses you 50% or up to $400, whichever is higher. This provides a good hedge if you buy nonrefundable bargain tickets and then find you have to cancel your trip. The policy also covers your tickets if they lose their value, lost baggage, medical bills and accidental death while traveling. The minimum premium is $19 per trip.

Your Enterprise

The Art of Getting Rich

CAN you still get rich in America? Yes, you can — if you are willing to take some intelligent risks.

The quickest path to wealth will continue to be owning your own business. New opportunities will arise as the economy shifts away from the huge industrial companies to small and medium-size enterprises. Both the economic climate and social attitudes have warmed to entrepreneurs in recent years. You do not have to invent a marvelous new machine or master some obscure technology. All you have to do is devise a more efficient and profitable way of performing an old job.

Studies of entrepreneurs have shown that those who succeed share certain traits. They are able to take calculated risks and learn from their mistakes. Many of them stumbled along the way but then quickly picked themselves up, analyzed their errors and were smarter for having made them. They develop detailed business plans. They are persistent and patient. Often they begin with little money but considerable determination. They are also willing to devote themselves totally to the business.

For example, Sam Chavez, a high-school dropout from Denver, started 37 years ago by leasing a gas station. He worked 12 to 15 hours a day, seven days a week, to make it profitable — so profitable that the company leased out three more stations to him. He kept on working with a vengeance and saved enough money to open his own auto repair shop. Today, his four shops bring in about $11 million a year, and Chavez's net worth is more than $5 million.

Investing in real estate has been a road to fortune throughout American history. If you buy real estate now, you will probably find that giant returns will not come as easily in the years ahead as they did in the high-inflation 1970s. Still, you can make some gains if you equip yourself with knowledge by studying, and if you invest wisely in land or buildings with a future.

Take 40-year-old Tom Tinnin of Albuquerque. In just eight years, he turned a $26,000 stake into more than $750,000 worth of land-holdings. He began by buying lots at tax lien auctions — because he could count on getting discount prices. He looked for properties that lay in the path of what he felt would be the city's natural direction of expansion. One of his favorite strategies has been to buy raw land and then help persuade local zoning boards to approve it for residential building. He tries to become acquainted with everyone living near his land to sound out whether there is any opposition. Tinnin also likes to buy during economic recessions because sellers then are more likely to agree to low mortgage rates and small down payments.

Starting Your Own Business

AMERICA is a nation of small businesses — about 18 million of them. Many are extremely prosperous, and so are their owners. More millionaires come out of small businesses than big corporations. Of course, not every entrepreneur does so well. Of all new businesses, half fail in the first four years and 80% in the first 10 years, usually because their owners do not start out with enough capital or with a sound plan or simply because of bad management.

Still, a boom of sorts is under way in small businesses. The number of new firms with fewer than 20 employees increased by more than 220,000 in the past year. One reason is that many big and medium-size companies are cutting costs by farming out more and more office chores to small firms that specialize in them. This has created new opportunities for entrepreneurs in fields with low start-up costs, such as accounting, public relations, photocopying and credit reporting and collection services.

To start some of these service firms, you often need little more than a computer and a bank loan. For example, there is fast-growing demand for firms that provide financial services. With $5,000 to $10,000, it is possible to buy the computer equipment you need to do bookkeeping for bigger firms. And you can provide secretarial services with a word processor that costs $6,000 or more.

When starting your own business, the first two or three years are the critical period. To survive them, you will need to anticipate the problems that accompany each stage of the business. You can avoid or conquer difficulty with sound planning, ample capital, solid management skills and, of course, a well-conceived idea.

When you get that idea, it may seem so stunning to you, so can't-miss, that your first impulse will be to quit your job, remortgage the house and kiss your spouse and kids good-bye while you devote yourself to your brainstorm. But do not do anything of the kind. Instead, you should evaluate your drive, dedication and experience in estimating whether you can turn a pipe dream into a money-maker. Experience is the key.

Solid planning is also essential. You will need to draft a business plan itemizing the costs of developing your product or service, and projecting your company's share of market and sales over the next three to five years. This road map should be about 60 to 80 pages long and include weekly or monthly projections for the first two years and quarterly figures after that. Do the figuring yourself to become familiar with production, distribution and marketing.

To find out if your plan for a new business is realistic, you will need outside and impartial advice. Two SBA-affiliated volunteer groups, Service Corps of Retired Executives (SCORE) and Active Corps of Executives (ACE) work together at about 400 chapters throughout the U.S. to help fledgling businesses. The SBA also sponsors 50 Small Business Development Centers, which in turn direct 500 smaller groups. Do not overlook your local banker or lawyer for a critique of your business plan, but the most qualified source may be the president of a similar business. It is amazing how accessible these chief executives are.

You also can get help from a business incubator. That is a support center which provides fledgling entrepreneurs with inexpensive space and services, such as copy equipment and secretarial help.

These centers are often housed in old, renovated buildings and charge rents that are only a fraction of what businesses would have to pay elsewhere. Because overhead is so low, the business owners can devote more money to making their ventures succeed and grow. And most incubator businesses do succeed; some get so big that they eventually have to move out. More than 200 incubators operate in some 40 states. To get a free directory of them, write to the Office of Private Sector Initiatives, Small Business Administration, 1441 L Street, NW, Room 317, Washington, D.C. 20416.

You may be considering starting a new business all by yourself, but it pays to remember that teams have better odds for success than individuals do. The right combination brings more management skills and more money than you alone can.

But where do you find the right people to be your partners? Building an enterprise simply on blood ties, friendship or a shared enthusiasm for golf can be dangerous. True, your relatives and chums may have money to invest. Yet starting a company is strain enough without the added trauma of firing someone dear who does not work out. Or, worse yet, having to keep him or her.

Everyone tends to hire people like oneself, but you should seek those with complementary talents. An engineer who pairs up with a manufacturing or marketing person is better situated for success than a trio of engineers — even if their business is the next generation of computers. To ward off future difficulties, all partners should invest some capital in the business or at least forsake salary during the start-up phase. And you are much better off if you have worked with your new partners before.

Of course, money is supremely important when you start your business. Undercapitalization pits you against the clock in a losing race. To figure out how much capital you are going to need, hire an accountant — preferably one with experience in your industry. He can help show you how much money you would need either if heaven and Congress were on your side, or if Murphy's Law were in effect.

Even if you have the perfect partners and more than enough cash in the till, your new business still can be done in by poor record-keeping. Well before the day you first open, you will need to have sound financial information keeping you up to date on operating expenses, inventory costs, accounts receivable, debt obligations and income. Accurate financial records are an indispensable warning system.

With all that, if your small business then can survive two or three years of growing pains, the odds for continuing success will be in your favor.

Doing It at Home

STARTING a business right in your own home can be most reward-ing, both financially and in terms of life-style. Millions of Americans work at home ventures. The fastest-growing kinds of these enterprises are computer data and word processing, direct sales for commissions, and business services in general, including accounting, bookkeeping and typing.

If you want to start a business from your own home, first make sure you are allowed to do so. Zoning laws in many localities forbid it, as do some apartment leases and condominium bylaws. If you are in conflict with the rules, you can appeal for a permit or variance. Also make sure that you are operating within federal and state laws. Some laws, which were originally designed to prevent sweatshops, regulate what goods can be produced commercially at home.

Be certain to hire a lawyer who has worked with other home businesses. He or she can shepherd you through the several layers of bureaucratic formality that attend the birth of any business.

You also have to decide what legal form your business should take. Most small businesses start as proprietorships. They require little expense or government approval to set up.

One big advantage of a proprietorship is that both you and your business are taxed as individuals. Thus, if you have a full-time job and a part-time business that loses money, you usually can write off your losses against other income. Be careful, though: Tax reform stipulates that you must "materially participate" in a business in order to offset income from your full-time job. A major disadvantage of a proprietorship is that in case of a lawsuit, your personal liability is unlimited. That is just one reason why you should be sure to get adequate insurance. A regular homeowners or renters policy prob-ably is not enough. You doubtlessly will need extra personal liability coverage.

The biggest potential tax advantage of your home enterprise is that you are entitled to deduct not only for regular business expenses but also for a host of household expenses that you can prove are directly related to your work. Such deductions were once limited to the annual *gross* income from the business. Effective in 1987, the limit dropped to the annual *net* income from the business.

Putting your husband or wife on the payroll of your home business can be a tax saver, but you will need to follow some rules laid down by the IRS. By employing a spouse who has not previously been working for pay, many couples can increase their combined maximum annual contributions to their tax-saving Individual Retirement Accounts from $2,250 to $4,000. Your business can also deduct your spouse's salary, as well as any amounts it pays in for his or her pension or profit-sharing plans, worker's compensation, life insurance or health policies. Employing your husband or wife will not trigger a tax audit. But the IRS will not permit the extra deductions if it believes you hired your wife or husband solely for tax reasons.

If you are audited, you might be asked to prove that your spouse was hired for a legitimate business purpose. The more evidence you have that he or she is considered just another employee, the better. Many tax advisers recommend writing a job contract. It should cover your wife's or husband's duties, pay, benefits and the expected length of employment. Keeping a time sheet of his or her work hours and a description of the work will be useful as well.

Be certain that you are paying your spouse a reasonable salary. As evidence, clip newspaper advertisements for similar jobs. Or call a local employment agency and ask for the going wage. Try to get a letter from the agency documenting the quoted salary range, or at least keep legible notes on the conversation.

How to Learn to Be an Entrepreneur

THE orthodox wisdom until recently was that the only school for entrepreneurs was the school of hard knocks. But to survive in today's economy, small-business people — like the big — require management skills that are often best acquired through formal training.

More than 500 colleges and universities in the U.S. offer courses in starting a small business. Some, including Babson, Baylor, the

University of Southern California and the University of Pennsylvania, have introduced undergraduate majors in the field. If you have neither the time nor temperament to work toward a degree, you can choose from a variety of commercial and government-sponsored courses.

A good new-business course will cover such fundamentals as evaluating an idea for an enterprise, raising capital and dealing with supplies and customers. Students are frequently asked to prepare a detailed business plan for their firm's first five years.

You can size up a course's content by studying the catalogue or talking to faculty and former students. You usually can get names and phone numbers from those sponsoring the course.

The best and most accessible of the cram courses are those sponsored jointly by the Small Business Administration, Chambers of Commerce and community colleges. These courses meet at more than 300 community and junior colleges. They may last 50 hours — typically, for two hours on two nights a week. Usually they cost no more than $100.

The SBA also offers day-long seminars at 100 district and branch offices, where professionals such as accountants, bankers, marketing consultants and government officials meet to offer pointers to small-business people.

The nonprofit Center for Entrepreneurial Management offers courses to the public on audio and video tape at private clubs (such as the Harvard Club and Bohemian Club) around the U.S. For information on courses in your area, write to the Center at 180 Varick Street, 17th Floor, New York, New York 10014.

How to Raise the Money You Will Need

NEXT to a money-making idea, what you need most to get a new business off the ground is a talent for raising capital.

Even if your idea is brilliant, no backer will give you a dime until you have sunk in most of your own savings. So, the smart entrepreneur starts with as much of his own capital as possible, using all his sources of credit. If necessary, he will even remortgage his house. By maximizing his own stake in the business, he will impress other potential investors with his commitment. He also will retain tighter control of his enterprise.

When entrepreneurs need outside money, they begin by soliciting friends and relatives — and then go on to friends of friends and relatives. Close relatives usually are more willing than distant investors to wait for the profits to start rolling in.

Try to get this money as a loan rather than as an investment in return for a piece of your company. That way, you won't have to put up with Uncle Bill telling you how to run *his* business.

After you have approached friends and family, the best way to get names of potential investors you don't know is to ask accountants, bankers, lawyers, brokers and other business owners. They often know who has money to invest or lend. Local business groups like the Chamber of Commerce can provide more leads.

Once you have exhausted your individual financing sources, it is time to approach the institutions. If you need less than $100,000, the best sources are the banks, commercial finance companies, the Small Business Administration and business development companies. When you have to go to those outside capitalists and bankers for money, you may be rather pleasantly surprised. Though real interest rates are high, money to finance promising new businesses is fairly plentiful. Banks are making loans to small businesses again. Professional venture capitalists are loaded with cash, and they even complain they cannot find enough worthy enterprises to assist.

Venture firms like to invest close to home, and in amounts between $100,000 and $600,000. Sometimes they will lend the money. But more often than not, they want a piece of the business. No longer do venture capitalists concentrate their dollars on companies that have already proved that they will make it. Because of the unusual success of some recent new businesses, particularly in the realm of high technology and services, financiers are willing to take greater risks than just a few years ago — if they figure that they may also reap greater rewards.

You might also get help from interested local investors. Check to see if there is a venture capital club in your area. There are more than 90 such clubs in the U.S. They hold monthly luncheon meetings at which entrepreneurs and investors can discuss ideas for new products or businesses. Members include venture capitalists, bankers, attorneys and corporate executives. For more information, write to the International Venture Capital Institute, P.O. Box 1333, Stamford, Connecticut 06904.

For entrepreneurs in search of capital, a long, unblemished credit history is helpful. So is locating your business in California, Massachusetts, New York or Illinois — because that's where 74% of venture capital money goes.

Beyond friends, family members, banks, venture capitalists and the federal Small Business Administration, there are many other places to raise money for your new venture.

Among them, small-business investment companies, or SBICs, are private venture firms that borrow most of their funds from the Small Business Administration. Also, there are 128 Minority Enterprise SBICs that invest exclusively in concerns at least 51% owned by socially or economically disadvantaged people.

In about half the states, quasi-public business development corporations make loans to small businesses to create local jobs. You can get the details by asking your state's economic development agency where you can find a business development corporation, or BDC.

You also can turn to the little-known local development corporations, composed of local government officials and private citizens who borrow funds from the SBA and banks and then relend them to entrepreneurs in need of long-term financing.

Entrepreneurs searching for big money — say $500,000 or more for research and product development — should look into setting up limited partnerships. The people to speak with are local tax attorneys, accountants and brokers who have experience getting a group of high-bracket investors to invest money in a business in return for substantial tax write-offs.

You may even have to make a private offering of stock. The disadvantage is that it will reduce your stake in your own company. You could lose majority interest. The less you have to surrender, the more you can offer later to attract skilled managers and additional capital to your company.

In searching for financial help, be wary of firms that advertise that they are professional finders of money. Many of them charge high fees simply for sending out mass mailings to investors. But one reliable source of names of potential angels is the National Venture Capital Association. It will send you free copies of its membership directory if you send a self-addressed envelope with $1.50 postage on it to the National Venture Capital Association, 1655 North Fort Myer Drive, Suite 700, Arlington, Virginia 22209.

Plan to spend at least three months acquainting yourself with the sources of financing before you try to raise any substantial amount.

The bible for anyone planning to shop the venture capital firms is *Pratt's Guide to Venture Capital Sources,* published by Venture Economics, Inc., P.O. Box 81348, Wellesley Hills, Massachusetts 02181. Look for it in a good public library and save yourself the cover price of $130.

If you need help putting together your plan to start a small business, ask an accountant, lawyer or banker to refer you to a reliable professional consultant. Expect to pay your professional adviser at least $1,000. He may be able to show you how to use potential customers and suppliers as sources of financing and how to cut costs by leasing, rather than buying, equipment. So hiring a professional probably will be a sensible investment.

To increase your chances of raising money, start with the right source. If you want a bank loan, for example, call ahead to inquire whether the bank does the kind of lending you need. Then find out what your potential backers want — and deliver it. Ask a banker what it will take for him to lend you money. If you meet his standards, it will be hard for him to say no. Finally, if you are rejected, find out why. That way you can approach your next source with a better pitch.

How to Get the Right Franchise

You could have bought a fast-food franchise for peanuts a few years ago and sold it today for as much as half a million dollars. But it is not too late to be your own boss and perhaps take a ride to prosperity. You can do that by acquiring one of the many *new* franchises.

If you get into a strong franchising system, the odds of surviving and making good as a small-business man or woman multiply impressively. And some of the strongest new franchises are those that provide services to businesses that cannot themselves afford to hire the people and buy the expensive equipment to do the work.

You could provide such services for businesses as typing, copying, telexing and mail pickup. A fast-growing company that franchises these services is Mail Boxes Etc. USA, based in San Diego, California. Other promising franchise opportunities include photocopying and printing, specialized employment agencies and business brokers. These brokers bring together people who want to sell their small businesses and people who want to buy them. By doing just that, one Atlanta grandmother earned roughly $240,000 in commissions in only her second year of operation. Another group of franchises performs household services for people who are too busy to do them themselves. These chores run from housecleaning to protecting empty houses.

Service businesses have added a new dimension to franchising, but you also can find opportunities in its traditional backbone — retail stores. In fact, franchisers account for just over one-third of retail sales in the U.S. There is strong potential in stores that sell the more popular brands of home computers, TV equipment and inexpensive furnishings. Restaurants that serve ethnic specialties such as Greek or Mexican food are taking off as well.

According to the U.S. Department of Commerce, these should be excellent times to run a franchise. The reasons are an improving economy and greater public recognition of franchise trademarks. Revenues of some franchises are expected to grow much faster than the average in the immediate future. They include automobile repair and service chains, printing and copying services, home repair and maintenance firms, and temporary-employee agencies.

The Commerce Department puts out an excellent guide. It lists names and addresses of more than 1,400 franchise businesses, how much money a buyer has to invest in each and what kind of financial and managerial help he or she will get from the franchising company. The book is called *Franchise Opportunities Handbook 1987*. You can buy it for $16 from the Superintendent of Documents, U.S. Government Printing Office, Washington, D.C. 20402.

Another comprehensive list of the offerings is in *The 1988 Franchise Annual Handbook and Directory*. It costs $24.95, plus $3 postage, and you can get it from INFO Press, 728 Center Street, P.O. Box 550, Lewiston, New York 14092.

There are professional franchise consultants, but be careful in choosing one. According to the International Franchise Association in Washington, D.C., some people with little experience have set themselves up as franchise consultants and promise much more than they can deliver. Your best bet is to deal with a lawyer who is familiar with drawing up franchise contracts and with Federal Trade Commission rules on franchising. For a recommendation, try a franchise operator in your area or the local bar association. Before hiring a consultant, ask for the names of past clients and contact them.

Before you sign a contract to buy a franchise, the parent company must give you a disclosure statement. From it you can get the names and phone numbers of several franchises. You would be wise to phone them to find out how well they are doing.

When you buy a franchise, you pay the company an initial fee and later a continuing royalty that can vary from 3% to 12% of gross sales. In return, you can use the company's trademark and franchising services for a set period, usually 10 to 20 years. The basic service is to give operating instructions, often covering everything from sales tactics to the color of the office carpeting. Capable companies also help you pick a business location and buy equipment and inventory. Their representatives sit in with you when you hire your first employees. They also hold your hand through crises.

Instead of running franchises themselves, many investors hire managers to operate them. But franchisors usually feel that the owner's attention is crucial and therefore will not sell units to people who intend to be absentee owners. That is understandable: few salaried managers will put in the 60 to 80 hours of work each week that it takes to make a business succeed.

How to Get Your Invention to Market

AMERICAN ingenuity still thrives — and countless tinkerers are working in countless workshops and garages, hoping to become the Edisons of tomorrow. The lonely inventor who aims to make it big faces tremendous obstacles and risks. He also faces rousing rewards if he plays it right.

More than 88,000 patents were granted in 1987 (including one for a genetically altered mouse), but only 5% of all patented inventions ever make it to the marketplace, and scarcely 1% of them earn money for their originators. Still, individuals have brought forth plenty of recent products, from the CAT scanner to the laser amplifier.

Have you ever had an idea for a new product or some other invention? Not all bright ideas can be legally protected. But start by trying to get a copyright, a trademark or a patent.

For example, video or board games and computer software should be *copyrighted*. It costs $10 to register a copyright for your lifetime plus 50 years. Also, apply for a *trademark* as soon as you sell your product in more than one state. A trademark will keep other people from using your product's name.

Does your invention have a unique graphic or pictorial design? A *design patent* will protect the product's appearance against the idea pirates. And, if your creation is a useful new device or process, you will need a *utility patent*.

For a fee of $300 to $400, a patent attorney will conduct a search to see if your idea is already covered by one of the 4.7 million existing patents. If it is not, you then apply for a patent. After waiting an average of 23 months, and paying roughly another $1,000 to $5,000 in lawyer's fees, two out of three inventors get it. A patent protects your invention for 17 years and is not renewable. You will also need to apply for patents in other countries, at a cost of several hundred dollars each, or else you may find your idea exploited abroad.

After you get one or more patents, you will have to build a prototype of your invention; that can cost anywhere from $5,000 to $20,000. Before making such an investment, you would be wise to have your invention evaluated for its market potential. If the invention is energy-related, you can have it evaluated free of charge by the National Bureau of Standards in Washington, D.C.

A few universities also provide evaluation services. Baylor and the University of Wisconsin–Whitewater charge $100. In addition, the Small Business Administration has institutes at nearly 500 colleges that aid entrepreneurial inventors with such tasks as market research and feasibility analysis.

Once you have your invention patented and evaluated and build a prototype, you will face the really hard part: getting it produced and bringing it to market. You can accomplish that in many ways.

Arthur D. Little Enterprises, Inc., of Cambridge, Massachusetts, helps support inventions, but only those in the high-technology field. ADL typically pumps some $50,000 into research, development and market studies for each such product, although the amounts can range from $15,000 to $500,000. Then the company uses its considerable connections to bring the invention to market and shares equally in the revenues.

But beware of firms that want their money up front and often in alarming amounts. A number of so-called development companies promise to mount a marketing campaign that will turn the seed of a hopeless idea into a money tree. Such unscrupulous outfits prey on inventors' gullibility, vanity and pocketbooks. They extract $1,000 to $3,000 in exchange for little more than sending a form letter to prospective backers culled from the Yellow Pages.

Do not count on selling your invention to big corporations. They are seldom receptive to products that are N.I.H. — that is, "Not Invented Here." But small businesses are much more willing to buy a stake in outside innovations because it is cheaper than doing their own research. So roughly half of all new products and services are bought out by small businesses.

Making a Family Firm Succeed

M ANY of the almost 18 million small companies in the U.S. are family-dominated. But keeping a family business alive — and the family happy — takes work.

Family businesses do not have enviable survival rates. Only a third make it to the second generation, and only a tenth to the third generation. That's because of the difficulty of transferring control of the business from the founding father to his heirs.

Sibling rivalry among the heirs is a major problem. So is indulging a beloved relative. Profits fall and nonfamily employees are driven away when kith and kin monopolize important jobs despite poor performance.

Often parents do not parcel out enough authority to their children because they fear their own authority will be diminished. Conflicts between generations typically boil over when founding fathers are in their 60s and their children are in their 30s. At that point, the children need to assert themselves by taking risks — perhaps by introducing new products or otherwise expanding the business — but fathers want to protect their retirement security by keeping the business on a steady course.

Here are some tips on how to manage a successful succession in a family business:

— Heirs to the business first should get jobs outside the family firm. After they've proved themselves in these neutral surroundings, they can confidently return.

— When the time comes to pick a successor, the founder and his heirs should put family loyalty out of their minds. The big question is: Who can run the business best? It may not be the eldest son, but a daughter or an in-law or even a hired manager.

— If two or more heirs wind up sharing control of the business, they should agree ahead of time on some orderly way to settle disputes that may arise between them. They might agree to hire an independent arbitrator.

— Above all, the aging chief should gradually but steadily hand over control. The president of a family firm can do everything else right, but if he doesn't designate an heir, he has failed the business.

Profit from Your Leisure

To ENHANCE their incomes, more and more Americans are finding ways to get money from their fun. They are turning spare-time hobbies into ready cash. People are trading coins, playing the saxophone, performing magic, hybridizing plants — all for money.

Pastimes involving sports and entertainment seem most likely to turn into money-makers. One rewarding way for sports fans and aging athletes to stay close to the action is to become referees. A basketball ref can start out officiating at high schools for $20 to $40 a game. After a while he or she can graduate to college basketball for $45 to $450 a varsity match. Working just 50 nights a year, a college referee could earn as much as $22,500.

Some hobbies hardly ever work out well as profitable money-makers. Many indoor gardeners, for instance, try to convince themselves that cash can blossom on their blooms. In practice, the commercial growers offer such wide variety and low prices that you simply cannot compete with them from your home.

What is really blooming is the market for crafts. There are between 6,000 and 8,000 crafts fairs a year, and most of them are markets for amateurs. A growing number of boutiques and even department stores also provide outlets, but their standards for hand-made items are high.

A basic guideline for any hobbyist is that only quality sells. So whether you want to weave a rug or blow a trumpet for money, you have to do it well. Even the amateur has to be professional, businesslike and original. Countless talented people fail because they never grasp the importance of such basic business principles as sensible record-keeping or promotion.

Hobbies are treated under a special section of the tax code. Any expenses you incur can be deducted, but only from the income you derive from the hobby. Suppose you spend $1,000 to buy yak teeth. Later you find you have overestimated the market for yak-teeth bracelets and you can sell only one of them for $8.75. Result: You can deduct from your taxable income just $8.75 of the $1,000 you spent.

This hobby loss limit is waived when your pastime becomes a business. Then you can take deductions larger than your hobby income; that is, you can create a shelter for other income.

Before tax reform, if you could manage to make a profit in two out of five years, the IRS automatically assumed your hobby was a business. But beginning in 1987, the requirement rose to three out of five years. Even if you cannot pass the three-years-out-of-five test, you may still be able to convince the IRS that you are seriously trying to make a profit. You can help make a solid case by keeping accurate and up-to-date records, showing you work hard at your avocation and expend a serious effort to sell. If you are convincing, the tax court may let you claim losses for a decade or more, even though you cannot muster one profitable year.

In a cash business — most craft and part-time paid activities are strictly cash — the temptation to ignore the taxman is strong. Since there is no record of the transactions, the IRS probably will never hear of them. But your anonymity will not last long if you are determined to succeed in business. Then you will become profitable, maybe even rich and famous, and you can be sure that the taxman will not overlook you.

Publishing Your Own Newsletter

DO YOU want a nice small business? Why not start your own *newsletter?* The cost is low, and the payoff can be large.

There are some 13,000 newsletters in the country. Publishers range from husband-and-wife teams to corporate giants. Start-up costs generally are less than $10,000. Lately people have created successful newsletters on highly specialized subjects as diverse as recipes and shopping tips about chocolate, prescriptions for restoring old houses, advice on child development and where to find special and unspoiled vacation spots. And there are many letters on the subject of computers.

The field may seem crowded, but you can thrive — if you have an original idea. You can find out if your idea is original by consulting the *Oxbridge Directory of Newsletters, The National Directory of Investment Newsletters* or *Newsletter Yearbook Directory.* All are available at many libraries.

After choosing your subject, you will need to set a subscription price. Basically, your choice is between an expensive newsletter serving a limited audience and one with broader appeal and a lower price. Printing and postage costs make large-circulation newsletters much more expensive. That is why many publishers go for *limited* circulation — and *high* profit margins — with subscription prices ranging from $50 to more than $1,000 a year.

Next, you will want to test the market. Use direct mail to reach potential subscribers. It allows you to zero in on only those people you want to reach. You can rent mailing lists through list brokers. To find names of brokers, consult the guide called *Direct Mail List Rates and Data,* available in many libraries. Costs range from $25 to more than $100 per thousand names. A test mailing should cost a few thousand dollars at most. Ideally, it should yield a response of 1% to 3% and should bring in enough subscriptions to cover your direct-mail expenses.

How to Get Your Book Published

IT SEEMS that almost everyone wants to write a book. People read about an unknown author who sits down at the typewriter and then cashes in big with a best-seller — and they, too, want to get in on the money, and the fame.

Plotting to get your book published is frustrating, but talent and tenacity can lead to happy endings. Publishers receive more than 30,000 unsolicited manuscripts annually. They send nearly all of them back with the swiftness and compassion of John McEnroe returning a cream-puff serve. It is by no means impossible to get your first work of fiction or nonfiction published. To do it, though, you need to persuade a publisher or an agent at least to read your manuscript.

Most publishers urge that you do get an agent. You can find lists of well-known agents in two books at your public library. They are *Fiction Writer's Market* and *Literary Market Place*. Agents often act as informal editors and they can direct your book to a likely publisher. What's more, the fact that your book is being submitted by an agent known to the editor is a guarantee that the work will be considered.

If the publisher is interested, an agent probably will be able to get you a bigger advance. Don't expect anything more than $5,000. For their services, agents customarily charge 10% of whatever the writer receives.

Some agents also have a fee just for reading manuscripts. Before you agree to pay anything, find out what services you will be getting for your money. That's always a sound idea on any deal, of course. If an agent insists on a written contract, be sure you hire a lawyer to approve it before you sign.

It is perfectly legitimate for an unknown author who gets a nibble from a publisher to recruit an agent *before* proceeding further. The proper approach to an agent or to a publisher is to write a letter explaining the kind of book you have in mind. Enclose a chapter or at least a sample of your writing. Outline briefly what you have already published, if anything. Above all, include a self-addressed, stamped envelope if you want your chapter returned.

The easiest way to break into print is by writing what is known as popular fiction — that is, mystery stories, spy thrillers and adventure tales. Romances alone account for more than 40% of all fiction published between hard and soft covers. Advances on romances are relatively low. Harlequin Enterprises, which started the boom in romantic fiction, pays about $7,500 plus royalties of 6% to 8% of the book's wholesale price. But a highly successful writer who catches on and learns the formula can count on earning up to $50,000 a book.

In nonfiction, a fresh and sharply focused idea is more important than writing style. But the novice author had better be an expert in his subject. Readers want specific information on specific topics. Books on cooking and dieting do well, as does anything connected with ways to make money. And sex is definitely here to stay.

Beginning writers should take time to learn how books get published. Two monthly magazines often carry solid information for aspiring authors. They are called *Writer's Digest* and *The Writer*. Among the many books of advice, a good one is *How to Get Happily Published* by Judith Applebaum and Nancy Evans ($8.95, New American Library).

Literary Market Place also lists all the publishers. Check to see which houses are putting out books in your field. And be persistent. Many a best-seller was rejected by a score of publishers before finally being accepted.

If you cannot find a publisher who is captivated by your manuscript, don't despair. For a fee of $3,000 to $15,000, a so-called vanity publisher will design, print, bind and promote your book. Vanity books, however, are seldom taken seriously by other publishers. Or, you can do what Virginia Woolf, Walt Whitman and Mark Twain did, and publish your own book. A spectacular do-it-yourself story is that of Mary Ellen Pinkham. She began publishing her collection of helpful household hints in 1976 and so far she has earned more than $2.5 million.

Your Computer

Selecting a Personal Computer

THE personal computer, for better or for worse, is here. In 1980, not quite half a million personal computers were sold in the U.S. In 1987, after Santa sprinkled his share of chips, 8.7 million were sold in that year alone.

The decision to buy a computer should be made extremely cautiously. As writer Augustin Hedberg has observed, despite all the talk about computerizing your stamp collection or your Christmas-card list, you probably do not need a computer — *unless* you need it for at least one of three or four very specific applications. Those basic uses include word processing, personal financial or other record-keeping and bookkeeping for a small business. Of course, you might want to buy an inexpensive little computer to play games or just join the revolution.

When you give them jobs that are too simple, computers look silly. Many a potential computer buyer has sat patiently with a neighbor while he spent 15 minutes loading and reloading programs and trying to remember keyboard commands that would enable him to call up — wonder of wonders — his wife's birthday. But when computers get really complex tasks to handle or are called on for typing out long drafts of copy that you want to revise and edit, they shine.

If you decide to buy a computer, you will need a well-planned strategy. The best shopping rule is summed up in a newspeak aphorism: Software dictates hardware. What that means is that first you should find the program or kinds of programs you want. A software program usually comes in the form of a 5¼-inch or a 3½-inch diskette, often called a floppy disk because it is thin and flexible. The diskettes contain the instructions that will enable your computer to do the tasks you assign to it. Then — only after you determine what program you want — find the machine to run the program.

It may seem backward to select the program before you buy the computer. After all, you do not buy the phonograph records before you buy the stereo to play them on. But most stereos play all kinds of records. By contrast, personal computers are rigged to accept only certain kinds of software, and you could well discover that the marvelous application you read about in the newspaper is not available for the machine you just bought. For instance, many business people use the IBM PC for their personal computing needs while most schools use one of the Apple series. Of course, there are exceptions. Business schools tend to use IBMs, while many businesses that want what is called desktop publishing — the production of newsletters and brochures of high typographical quality — swear by the Apple Macintosh.

Do not allow yourself to be lured away from your primary use for a computer. For example, if you have decided that what you really want it to do is keep business inventories, do not be distracted by a machine that plays games. Get the computer — and the program to run on it — that does what you need to be done. It is better by far to buy a separate, inexpensive game machine and keep your serious hardware for serious uses.

When looking for software, do not buy anything until you see it work. Programs can sound better in conversation than they turn out to be in practice. Every system has its peculiarities. Take nothing for granted. And do not settle for a dealer demonstration. Would you allow a car salesman to give your new sedan its road test? Step right up and put your program through its paces. If you do not know how, have the dealer show you. Unfortunately, once you have bought and opened a program you usually cannot return it.

Before you buy any computer, find out how much ongoing help and support you can count on from your retail dealer. Visit a few dealers in your area and ask some questions to see if you can understand the dealer's answers. Many specialists know computers inside and out — but they do not know how to explain them to you.

Ask whether the dealer will help you learn how to use your computer. Does he or she hold classes for new users? Will he or she give you emergency answers to questions over the phone? Find out how well equipped the dealer is to repair any breakdowns. Don't forget: In deciding where to buy a personal computer — except those that sell for less than $500 — dealer support is the key.

The users' manuals that come with home computers are often written quickly and under great pressure. Many are nests of baffle-gab and glib misinformation. That is another reason why you may want to think twice before grabbing one of the tempting bargains that mail-order houses advertise in computer magazines. When you have bought a computer from an authorized dealer, you will have someone you can turn to for help.

He or she may also let you try before you buy. Many dealers are renting out personal computers for anywhere from a day to a year. In fact, as new machines reach the market, rentals become quickly available. In mid-1988, for example, the IBM PC-XT rented for $300 a month in Illinois. In Massachusetts, the Compaq Portable III went for $406 a month — or $264 a week or $60 a day. In Phoenix, the Apple Macintosh Plus rented for $230 a month. Most of the rental fee you pay is deductible from the price if you later choose to buy. Most dealers will also lease you such extras as a printer, color monitor and modem. A letter-quality printer might cost you $100 a month.

Students are especially heavy computer users, and they have special needs and opportunities. If you are a student shopping for a back-to-school computer — and the software to work on it — find out first if your college has already chosen a model to be used by all its students. Many schools are able to sell a particular brand at generous discounts. If your college does not have such a deal, begin your search by learning about the computer applications that are relevant to your major. If it is accounting, business or economics, you will want to know about the financial calculations that can easily be handled by a computer. If you are in the liberal arts, you will need a rundown on the capabilities of a basic word-processing program. More than any other application, word processing is the most popular campus use for personal computers.

Computer portability is an important factor to consider for the transient academic life. The Apple IIc, usually priced under $700, is a good, low-priced workhorse machine that is easily transported.

Other portables by IBM and Compaq are equally versatile but will cost at least twice as much. Both brands can use the software that has been written for the standard-setting IBM PC.

The fact that new computers, new software and new ways of joining the two come out every season may make you decide to wait a while before springing for a machine. Admittedly, a year from now the world of small computers will have evolved considerably — but the year after that, it will still be changing. If you decide to wait for the ultimate computer, you may wait forever.

How to Learn

COMPUTER illiterates, take heart. There is help out there in the form of books, magazines, courses and other computer users. Books are probably not the easiest way to learn about computers. After a few elementary chapters, you may be struggling in a postdoctoral spider's web of circuitry, machine architecture and computer languages. But two good reads are *Overcoming Computer Illiteracy: A Friendly Introduction to Computers,* published by Penguin Publishing for $12.95, and *Through the Micromaze: A Visual Guide from Ashton-Tate*, which sells for $9.95.

Beginners also can find reliable information in such computer magazines as *Personal Computing*. Or, you can try to learn from the machine itself by means of a learner's program, which flashes step-by-step instructions on the video screen. Two of the best such programs are Friendly Ware, a package for the IBM personal-computer user, and How to Program in the BASIC Language, a 12-lesson package with two diskettes that works on most major machines. For children, Rocky's Boots is an excellent introductory program.

If a course is what you want, be sure to find out if it is aimed at personal-computer users or at students planning careers in data processing. Courses are given at junior, community and technical colleges across the country. You will want to find out how big the class is — smaller is better, of course. Look into user groups as well. These are clubs of computer owners, and they offer members a chance to get together and discuss problems and programs. You can find the addresses of groups through dealers or computer magazines.

Using It to Help Manage Your Money

THOUGH computers cannot do everything, one chore they can do very well is help you manage your money and become a more successful investor. But it is not enough just to buy a computer. You will also have to buy a personal financial program — or several of them — written to fit your own situation.

The simplest programs help you balance your checkbook by comparing the checks you have written against the statements from your bank. You can get such software for less than $25. More elaborate products are known as personal finance programs. They let you keep a computerized tally of your assets and liabilities, your income and expenses. They also will provide you with a budget and print out your checks. One remarkably good program is Managing Your Money from MECA Software, which has a list price of $199, but is sold at many stores for about half that.

People increasingly are using personal computers to help keep track of their investments and analyze trends in the stock market. New software also will help you investigate individual securities. Within seconds these programs will let you size up a buying opportunity, or a must-sell situation. One program, called the Dow Jones Market Analyzer, can instantaneously turn a pile of statistics that might take several hours to plot by hand into a chart that can be read at a glance. It costs $350. With the Market Analyzer and a modem (a device that lets a computer receive information over the telephone lines) you can hook up your computer for a price to the Dow Jones data base and get all the financial statistics you need directly from the various exchanges.

Because computers are great organizers and calculators, they can save you money and time with your taxes — with a tax program. You can devise tax strategies, do all the calculations for your tax returns and then print out a completed 1040 form. *Turbo Tax* ($67.50) and Howard Soft's *Tax Preparer* ($239) are both excellent programs.

Remember, one of the first deductions on your computerized tax form should be for at least part of the cost of the computer and the software — as long as you use them for help with your taxes, investments or overall money management. Under the new rules of tax reform, this will count as one of your miscellaneous deductions.

You can deduct only the amount by which your total miscellaneous deductions exceed 2% of your adjusted gross income.

The Word on Word Processors

I F YOU are an executive, a scholar or anybody else who devotes more than four hours a week to writing or editing, you should seriously consider buying a word processor. It will let you write, revise and edit faster and more efficiently. Standard word-processing functions on most personal computers allow you to insert and delete words, sentences and paragraphs. You can move chunks of text around on an electronic screen and then check your spelling and syntax in an electronic dictionary.

What kind of word processor you should buy depends on the kind of wordsmithing you do. If you seldom write anything longer than memos or brief reports and do not need to revise your work heavily, then an electronic typewriter may handle all the word processing you need. Unlike your old electric typewriter, the new electronic has a microprocessor memory that stores characters for you to call up when you want them.

For maximum versatility look into a personal computer, such as the IBM PC or the Apple Macintosh. You can do word processing — not to mention figuring your taxes or playing video games — and sometimes for less than $2,000. Both Smith Corona and Magnavox have released small, inexpensive (both approximately $800) versions of dedicated word processors, computers that function only as word processors. If you want super-low-cost, no-nonsense word processing, you can make do handily with one of the book-size ultra-portable computers produced by Radio Shack. Most weigh less than five pounds, have their own built-in software programs and cost $500. Portables can also be hooked into printers when the time comes to commit your prose to paper.

Which word processor is best for you? One tip: If you work with people who use a particular brand of computer, you would be wise to look at machines that are compatible with theirs.

The brains of a PC word processor is the software you use with it. This is the disk containing the instructions that cause the computer to be so wonderfully useful when you want to write. More than 200 word-processing programs are on the market. They go by such names as WordStar, PFS:WRITE and Word Perfect #I. The best way to choose among them is by hands-on trial and error.

If you would like software that can do a bit of everything, with words *and* numbers, investigate the so-called integrated programs. Many of these let you do financial analysis, budgeting and record-keeping. Most also come with graphics and a word-processing program, so you can compose a caustic letter to your stockbroker, complete with charts. In mid-manuscript you can figure a budget and insert it as a statistical chart. Among the best integrated programs are Lotus Symphony and Framework (for the IBM PC) or Appleworks (for the Apple IIC).

Picking Educational Software

PITY the poor parents in this electronic age. Everywhere they turn they are told that their children should be learning on a personal computer. But with over 5,000 educational programs to choose from, which ones are best to buy?

Most educational software for grade-school children boils down to electronic flash cards: a question appears on the screen, the student answers it and the computer says whether he or she is right or wrong. These programs have proved highly effective. Other educational programs closely resemble games. Youngsters have to find their way through mazes or solve mysteries and thus learn how to develop strategies, organize their thoughts or simply take notes.

Among the better educational software programs are:

— Reader Rabbit, an early learning program featuring a dancing rabbit as a reward for correct answers, for those aged four to seven, sells for about $40.

— Math Blaster, which covers multiplication, division, subtraction, addition, percentages, fractions and decimals for kids six to 11, sells for about $50.

For $40 to $60 you can get Barron's SAT or Lovejoy's SAT, both of which will drill students for the big exam.

The Laptop Alternative

REMEMBER 1988 as the year the PC hopped off your desk and into your lap. The new lines of laptop computers — sleek, full-capability PCs that run on rechargeable batteries and can be comfortably balanced on your knee — have added a new dimension of convenience to computing. Several companies, including Datavue, NEC, Radio Shack, Sharp, Toshiba and Zenith, now field models that weigh less than 12 pounds and can be closed up and stored in a closet: perfect for a family that needs a computer but not a computer room. A new svelte challenger from Toshiba weighs only 6½ pounds. All are compatible with the IBM PC.

The laptops of yore often failed to please because their screens were dim enough to strain the eyeballs out of an owl. Recently, though, breakthroughs in LCD technology have yielded a generation of screens that are bright and clear. The new NEC MultiSpeed HD employs what's called a backlit electroluminescent screen that renders brilliantly crisp text. The MultiSpeed also houses a 20 megabyte hard disk, which boosts the machine's capacity well beyond that of an average desktop. Its price ($3,695) is also beyond that of most laptops.

For an excellent balance of price and performance, try the line of Zenith laptops. The Zenith SuperSport, at less than $2,000, is a great new arrival. Its rechargeable battery pack unclips from the back of the case and can be stored away when you want to plug the computer into an electrical outlet. The small machine's screen is clear and legible, and its weight, without the battery pack, is less than 10 pounds.

The Toshiba 1000, at 6½ pounds, is a good pick if you have to lug your machine around every day and don't mind a little squinting (the 9½-by-3-inch screen can be tough to read). But if you are not using it for heavy-duty word processing you may not care.

Your Auto

Getting the Most from Your Car

You may be thinking of trading in your auto and investing in a new one, but you often can get more mileage for your money by holding on to the reliable old car you already own. In fact, the best way to reduce your automobile costs is to drive a *safe* older car until just before it sputters to a permanent halt. Recognizing that moment takes skill, but here's a tip: Look for a sharp rise in repair costs.

Drivers who heed the maintenance instructions in their owner's manual usually can put 100,000 miles on their cars before facing transmission overhauls or other costly repairs. If you have been taking your car to a reliable mechanic for regular maintenance checkups, quiz him about what is likely to go wrong next.

Don't panic over a single big repair bill. Repair costs rise steadily through a car's first 10 years. But during that period, your insurance, depreciation and loan payments drop — or come to an end. The latest annual study by the Hertz car rental company showed that it costs $6,045 to own and operate a new compact model during its first year. By the 10th year, however, the cost drops to $2,568.

Maintain your old car faithfully, using a knowledgeable mechanic. See that brakes, tires and steering stay in top condition. Keep the body clean and well waxed. In high-pollution areas, keep your auto garaged as much as possible. Consider renting a car for longer trips, if you are worried about pushing your old auto to its limits. Review your repair records regularly. If costs suddenly shoot up, ask your mechanic whether it's time to trade in.

Try to nurse your car along until early spring. That's when nice weather and the thought of upcoming vacations lures buyers to used-car lots — and trade-in values start climbing. And spring is as smart a time as any to buy a new car. Auto makers now introduce new models all year round, so prices no longer fluctuate greatly with the seasons.

How to Find a Mechanic

To ENJOY years of trouble-free driving, finding the right auto mechanic can be almost as important as finding the right car. The best way to discover a competent mechanic is through a growing network of reputable service stations that are identified and appraised by the American Automobile Association. This is done through its Approved Auto Repair Service program.

The AAA's program is the first nationwide effort to separate reliable repair shops from problem-ridden ones. It covers every kind, from franchised dealers to independent neighborhood garages. The program includes more than 4,300 garages in 26 states and the District of Columbia, and is adding hundreds more each year.

Inspectors from the AAA apply rigorous standards. In fact, more garages fail than pass the first inspection. The repair bays, tools and mechanics' qualifications are checked. Then the AAA queries customers whose names an inspector picks from the shop's files.

You do not have to join the automobile association to take advantage of the program. Simply look for a garage with the AAA's red, white and blue sign and the inscription "Approved Auto Repair." Nonmembers can phone the local affiliated auto club for names of approved shops in the area.

One of the AAA's measures of a worthy shop is whether or not its mechanics are certified by the National Institute for Automotive Service Excellence, or ASE. The institute supports itself entirely from examination fees. To earn a certificate of competence, a mechanic or technician must have passed at least one of ASE's eight automobile specialty tests and have two years of hands-on experience.

Shops lacking AAA approval may still do first-rate work. Shops that display the blue and white ASE sign have at least one mechanic certified in one of the institute's specialties. Or go one step further and have the mechanic show you if he has an ASE certificate that says he is specially trained in repairing the system that you need to have fixed.

New-car owners are inclined to have repairs done by the dealer because that's where their warranty is honored. The dealer usually has good facilities and makes a special effort to please a customer who has bought one car and may buy another. But dealers tend to be expensive. For specific services, such as buying and installing a muffler, you may get the best price at a discount store, mass marketers such as Sears or Montgomery Ward or a specialty shop such as Midas. You could save 50% on a set of shocks by going to a specialist.

But don't let bargain prices take you away from an able general mechanic — if you have been lucky enough to find one. When you take a sick car to him, describe the symptoms in detail or even write them down. Request an estimate and ask him to call if something unexpected or expensive turns up. But don't offer your own diagnosis. That is *his* job.

Your Best Deals on Wheels

THE price that a dealer quotes to you for a new car represents only the first offer in a round of haggling. To negotiate with confidence, you need to know the dealer's cost or invoice price. It may be $500 to as much as $4,500 *less* than the car's sticker price.

The latest invoice figures can be found in a $3.50 guide titled *Edmund's New Car Prices,* sold at many bookstores and newsstands. What you do is total up the dealer's cost for your car, including all optional features. Then make your first offer, at $125 to $200 more than the invoice price. The dealer will bid that up, of course. But try to hold out for a price $200 to $500 over invoice for an American-made car — and at least $500 for a foreign one.

Also consider auto brokers, sometimes called buying services. In some cities, you can find them listed in the Yellow Pages under "Auto Brokers" or "Automobiles." In return for a fee of $20 to $400, they order cars through a network of dealers at prices as low as $75 over invoice.

For $20, a national car pricing and referral service called Car/ Puter will refer you to the nearest of more than 500 franchise dealers. They typically charge $50 to $150 over invoice for domestic cars and as low as $300 over invoice for imports. To use Car/Puter, call 800-221-4001, or 800-522-5104 in New York State.

A relatively stress-free way to get a used car is to buy one from a major car rental company. Avis, Hertz and National operate used-car lots made up of 10- to 18-month veterans of their fleets. Prices are nonnegotiable but well below retail for used cars. A complete maintenance record for each former rental is available.

Bargains on Demonstration Cars

AUTO dealers often offer their best deals on demonstration models. These are cars that have been lent to salespeople for their personal use or for showing to potential buyers. After three to six months and usually between 3,000 and 7,000 miles, the autos are sold at discounts of as much as 30%. Most demos are covered by what remains of manufacturer's warranties, and many dealers will extend those warranties for a small charge.

The cars also qualify for the special financing packages that are available on brand-new cars. Before you buy, compare the price of a demo with the price that the dealer may be offering on a *leftover* car from the *previous* model year that has not been driven at all. The leftover car may sell for slightly less. But the higher resale value of the previously driven but still newer demo probably will provide you with a better deal in the long run.

The Advantages of Leasing

PAYING cash is the cheapest way to buy a car. But if you are unable to lay out the money in one lump sum, you may want to take a look at leasing as an alternative to financing. It is no secret that leasing a car requires less cash up front than buying one. And monthly lease payments may be less than loan payments. What is not well known is that leasing also can be more economical in the *long* run — even when you figure in the resale value of the car that you buy. It depends on how you invest the money you would have spent on the down payment and sales tax.

Money magazine calculated several years ago that, for example, you could save $750 by leasing rather than financing a $46,000 Mercedes over four years. And, with an $11,000 Plymouth, you would have paid about only $85 more to lease than to finance.

You usually can get your best leasing deal from automobile dealers. Leasing companies are slightly higher. But it is generally more important for you to examine the deal than the dealer. Federal law requires any firm that leases you a car to tell you the size of the monthly payments, who is responsible for insurance and what the car's estimated value is. You should also ask about late-payment penalties and the cost of canceling the lease.

Both automobile dealers and leasing companies offer two broad categories of leasing contracts.

First, there is the closed-end, or walk-away, lease. With it, your monthly payments are based on the mileage you expect to put on the car. At the end of the lease, you turn the car in, and, if the car is in good condition, you owe nothing unless you exceed the agreed-upon mileage. In that case, you will have to pay up to 35 cents for each excess mile, depending on the wholesale value of the car.

Then there is the open-end lease, which gives you the option to buy the car at a preset price when the lease ends. The monthly payments are based on the estimated resale value of the car. If the car is worth more than that at the end of the lease, you pocket the excess. If it is worth less, you must make up the difference, up to a maximum of three times the monthly payment. One consequence is that you get your best deals — and lowest monthly payments — on cars that have the highest resale value.

Devices That Deter Theft

PROFESSIONAL car thieves are so swift and experienced that policemen, insurance underwriters and even manufacturers of anti-theft devices feel that it's hard to thwart them. But although alarms and other preventions are not foolproof, the right ones can save you anguish and expense.

If you own an expensive automobile and particularly if you live in a big city, your best protection against theft is never to leave your car on the street. Professional thieves are a match for almost any antitheft equipment. However, you should seriously consider buying alarms and locks to discourage joyriders and casual miscreants.

Antitheft devices now are so varied and sophisticated that you can outfit your car to do just about everything but roll over and play dead when it is attacked. One gizmo disengages the ignition and bolts the hood securely, another shuts off the fuel line and still others shriek if the car is molested. You can get these gadgets at stores that sell automotive accessories.

You are probably smart to start with an alarm because it will scare away the unprofessional thief. Typical alarm systems, such as those manufactured by Harrison Systems Corporation in Wilkes-Barre, Pennsylvania, cost anywhere from $125 to $275 installed. The least expensive type sets off a siren at a variety of intrusions — for example, if someone bangs a window or jolts the car.

If you figure an alarm may not be enough to scare the professionals off, you probably should invest in a device that stalls the engine before a thief can drive far. Fuel cutoffs made by Automotive Security Products, of Mount Vernon, New York, start at $80 for a basic device and rise to $280 for one that shuts off your fuel and ignition, sounds a siren alarm, prevents towing and protects all the locks on your car.

Less elaborate automobile protection devices also lock cars more tightly than usual. One of the best is the Medeco Super Lock, a heavy-duty ignition cylinder, made by C.E. Security Corp. of Long Island City, New York. It costs about $250 installed and $335 with a hood lock. Although professional thieves can bypass the ignition switch in most late-model cars, the Super Lock makes it impossible to start the car. However, a thief will not be put off by a cane lock, one end of which clamps to the steering wheel and the other to the brake pedal.

If what a thief wants is your wheels and tires, you can complicate his task by installing locking lugs. A set of four plus the special wrench needed to unlock them costs only about $15.

Choosing Among the Clubs

WORRIED about being stranded in a disabled car on a snowy night, millions of motorists have sought reassurance by joining an auto club. If you or other drivers in your family have any doubts about coping with breakdowns on your own, the question is probably not whether you should join a club but which one to join.

All auto clubs claim to offer the same basic services, and their annual fees range from $17 to $56. But these charges are no indication of the quality of what they provide. In fact, two basic services — trip planning and accident insurance — should not be important considerations when you choose a club. Your choice should be dictated by the quality of an auto club's road service.

Three national clubs offer so-called dispatch service. That means members have only to call the club's number and wait for help to arrive. The three are the American Automobile Association, Amoco and Sears Allstate Motor Club. If your club does not offer dispatch service, you will have to find help on your own.

Some other clubs provide a directory of affiliated service stations or a toll-free number for you to call to get the name of an approved station near where you've broken down. In most of these cases, the club pays for the emergency service, but that is usually limited to towing and minor roadside repairs, such as tire changing and battery recharging. Still other national clubs merely reimburse you for service you arrange on your own, which can be no boon to the panic-prone.

Whether the club pays directly or reimburses you later, the payments are often unrealistically low. For example, there is always either a dollar limit or a mileage limit for towing. The limit for road services generally ranges from $50 to $100, and if you exceed it, you pay the extra cost.

Be sure to read the fine print of any auto club's membership contract. Some demand an initiation fee and charge extra for a spouse, and others do not. Some clubs cover emergency service on any car you're driving; others limit coverage to cars you own or lease long-term. One tip: If you rarely travel far from home, you may find that regional auto clubs offer service equal to or better than many of the nationals.

Neo-Classic Cars

ALMOST nothing brings out the boy in a man so quickly as acquiring the car he yearned for in his youth. Now grown men — and women — are buying the automobiles of the 1950s and 1960s that they couldn't afford in adolescence. As a result, some neo-classic cars of relatively recent vintage are becoming valuable collector's items. People who own these autos can sell them for fancy prices at auctions and through ads in car-buff magazines.

For example, the 1963 Corvette Sting Ray was a design milestone with its split rear window and retractable headlights. It cost $4,257 when it was new but now is worth as much as $30,000. Ford introduced the Mustang in 1965 for $2,372; today a convertible could fetch as much as $15,000. Less sporty cars are worth large sums, too. A 1955 Chevrolet Bel Air two-door hardtop in excellent condition that cost $2,400 when it rolled off the assembly line commands as much as $20,000 now. Other valuable cars include the 1953 Studebaker Commander, the 1955 Chrysler 300 and the 1964 Pontiac GTO.

Not all cars of the 1950s and 1960s are valuable, of course. The ones that are represent a dramatic innovation in engineering or style. The closer a model is to its original condition, the higher the price it fetches. Ideally, a car should have all the same parts it had when it came out of the showroom.

Some of these machines sport protruding tail fins. Chrome drips off hoods and doors and dashboards light up like jukeboxes. To many people such excess was not Detroit's finest hour. But to others it is one more reason to own the cars they once drove only in their dreams.

Your Insurance

How Much Life Insurance
Do You Need?

INSURANCE agents offer formulas for how much insurance you need, but the formulas are flawed. The problem is that they cram many different kinds of people, with different requirements, into the same pigeonhole. How much coverage you really need hinges on what you want it to do for you. Do not make the mistake of expecting it to do too much. In fact, insurance should be designed to maintain, not to raise, the standard of living a family has achieved.

To figure out how much life insurance you need, estimate your family's living expenses. Then determine where that money will come from, if you should die. Include your Social Security benefits, savings, assets that can be sold and your spouse's income. The gap that's left between what costs you expect and what income you can count on is what you need to cover with life insurance. So, if you are a middle-income person with dependents, you are likely to need life insurance coverage in six figures. As a rule, you should buy enough so you could invest the proceeds and live off the interest or other income from them, assuming an 8% total yield. Thus, if you earn $32,000 a year now, you generally would want a policy for $400,000.

But you should use insurance *only* to protect dependents. Even if you are someone's provider, you may well need coverage for just a limited period, for example, until your children finish school or for the rest of your spouse's expected life. People without children often make the mistake of listening to agents who recommend buying policies while both the premiums and the risks of being medically uninsurable are low. Neither argument is convincing. If you cannot think of a beneficiary, you do not need life insurance.

When you are in the market for insurance, you can choose between two kinds of agents. The first is the captive agent; he or she is under contract to sell for just one company. The second is the independent agent; he or she can choose from among several companies to find a policy to suit each customer.

You might assume that an independent will get you the best possible deal. Don't count on it. Most independents, especially those who sell life insurance, represent only a handful of companies. And most companies pay higher commissions to agents who sell lots of policies. So you may be steered to a particular company even if it offers a less comprehensive or more expensive policy.

For that reason, when you want to buy insurance, visit *several* agents. Ask each one which companies he or she represents and tell him or her you are comparison shopping. If an agent knows there is the risk of losing a sale, he or she is much more likely to make a competitive recommendation.

How to Cut Your Costs

THESE DAYS insurance agents have something to say that is worth hearing: the cost of life insurance is plunging. Since 1980, according to the American Council of Life Insurance, the rates of 30 representative companies fell 15%. Rises in investment income and life expectancy allowed insurers to cut premiums.

The premium, however, is not totally reliable for comparing prices. There is a better way of stating your life insurance costs. It is called the interest-adjusted index, and all agents can quote it to you. This index takes into account three variables that affect your real insurance prices. Those three are the dividends on the policy, its cash value and the interest you could have earned if you invested your money elsewhere. Ask your agent for the interest-adjusted cost index of your policy and then compare it with those of policies offered by competing companies.

It pays to scout around for an insurance firm that provides special discounts. There are discounts on life insurance rates for women (because they live longer), for nonsmokers and for people who engage in regular exercise. (For more, see "Your Insurance: Discounts for Healthy Habits.")

Little-known discounts on other insurance can cut your bills. People who equip their homes with dead-bolt locks, smoke detectors and fire extinguishers pay about 5% to 10% less for homeowners insurance than their less vigilant neighbors. Allstate reasons that retirees 55 and older are often at home and gives them a 10% discount on homeowners insurance. And car owners who install antitheft devices can pay 5% to 15% less for auto coverage. (For more, see "Your Insurance: Auto Policies.")

Discounts for Healthy Habits

B EING conscientious about your health and fitness can trim not only your figure but also your insurance bill. For example, nonsmokers get 5% to 15% price breaks on their life insurance.

To qualify for the lower rates, you may have to pass a medical exam certifying that your weight, blood pressure and cholesterol levels are normal. You also will have to declare on a questionnaire that you exercise regularly. Allstate Insurance's 10-year term life policies, for instance, are 15% to 30% cheaper for physically fit nonsmokers who say they exercise three to five times a week. You will get the deepest discounts if you promise to use seat belts while driving or to avoid excessive salt in your diet. But you must not have a high-risk occupation or hobby, such as automobile racing.

ITT Life Insurance also offers premium discounts. For instance, a 35-year-old male smoker pays $720 a year for $100,000 worth of universal life insurance. But he can more than double his coverage for the same premium if he does not smoke and is certified by a doctor as being physically fit. Manhattan Life ranks individuals on a healthiness scale. For $100,000 of universal life coverage, a 40-year-old male smoker pays $816 a year, versus $732 for a nonsmoker.

If you suffer from hypertension, you can cut your premiums by as much as half by taking steps to correct your condition. Compared with those who have normal blood pressure, hypertensive people pay an average of 50% more for term insurance and up to 25% more for health policies. Both costs can drop if the policyholder's blood pressure comes down. A 30-year-old man with moderately high blood pressure will pay $285 annually for a $100,000 renewable term life policy with Allstate. If he reduces his blood pressure to normal for a year or two, his premiums will sink to about $195. Insurers are willing to offer lower rates because people who reduce their high blood pressure with medication and diet have a near-normal mortality rate.

Such incentives are beginning to show up in health insurance policies, too. A recent survey of 85 insurers found that a third of them give health-conscious policyholders discounts on disability, hospital and/or medical insurance. The discounts typically are smaller than those available on life insurance. But they can add up.

Three Kinds of Life Policies

You probably have heard a lot lately about the three kinds of life insurance policies. They are whole life, term and the relatively new universal life. Which of those three is best for you?

In pondering that question, bear in mind that you need life insurance early in your career, when your children are young and your assets are low. But if you plan properly as you grow older, your insurance needs should decline or even disappear.

The insurance that protects your family when you need it most for the lowest possible price is *term insurance*. Premiums are modest when you are young, but advance along with your age. Rates go up every year in the most popular plan. That's annual, renewable and convertible term. If you want, you can convert it automatically into whole life insurance.

Whole life insurance premiums, by contrast, never rise. But whole life buyers start out paying several times as much as they would for term. About $300 a year buys $100,000 worth of annual renewable term at age 40 for a man, and about $220 buys that amount for a woman. By contrast, $100,000 of whole life generally costs about $1,500 a year for males and $1,300 for females at age 40.

The excess premium goes into a whole life cash reserve. When you retire, you can surrender your policy and retrieve a fair amount of the cash in your reserve. If you have kept the policy 25 or 30 years, its cash surrender value will be about two-thirds the face value of the policy.

Whole life is a form of savings account. The tax-deferred earnings grow, but the policyholder usually collects just a modest interest rate on his savings. And whole life has other disadvantages. There are heavy sales charges, typically 55% of the first year's premium, plus 5% annually for the next nine years.

You cannot permanently withdraw any of your paid-in cash and still remain insured. So if you need the money, you will have to borrow against it, typically at 8% to 11% interest — or less if you bought the policy before 1980. You can't vary the premium or freely increase the insurance protection to suit your changing situation, either.

But you can do all that, and more, with universal life insurance. This policy combines term insurance with a tax-deferred savings account that pays about 9% interest. So, if you want to protect your family and build up tax-deferred savings, one way to do it is to buy a universal life policy.

One important warning: You have to shop for universal life with utmost care, because these policies can carry large sales commissions amounting to 50% or more of your first year's premium. Universal life does not always make sense for people who need less than $50,000 of insurance. It is often the case that the smaller the policy, the more burdensome the fees.

Variable Life Policies

VARIABLE life insurance is a relatively new type of policy that hitches an old-fashioned whole life policy to the unpredictable investment markets.

In many ways, variable life is like standard whole life. You pay fixed annual premiums. You can cash in your insurance anytime for its cash value. You can borrow against your policy at an interest rate stated in the contract. But unlike whole life, the cash value of your policy — and its death benefit — can sink as well as soar.

Why the difference? When you buy a whole life policy, part of your premium goes into investments chosen by the insurance company to yield a minimum *guaranteed* rate each year, usually 4% to 6%. Thus, the cash value of your policy and its death benefit rise steadily. Not so with variable life. Here, part of your premium goes into managed investment pools that *you* select. Depending on the company, you can put your money into a stock fund, a bond fund or a money-market fund. Or you can put some in each. With some restrictions, you can switch among funds in search of the highest yields.

If the investments behind your policy do well, both the cash value and the insurance value of the policy rise — potentially much faster than that of a standard whole life policy. Your gains, if any, are tax-deferred. If your investments lose value, so does your policy — although the benefit payable to your survivors will never fall below the amount of insurance you initially bought.

Is variable life sensible for you? Perhaps so, if you are in a high tax bracket. Then you can take fuller advantage of variable life's tax-deferred earnings status. The answer also might be yes if you plan on keeping the policy for 10 years or more. Otherwise, high fees and commissions — especially at the front end — will eat into any cash buildup.

There is also a kind of life insurance called variable universal life, and it combines some of the advantages of universal life and variable life. Ordinary universal life offers you so-called flexible-premium features, which allow you to vary from year to year the amount of your premium going into insurance coverage and the amount going into investments. Variable life allows you to switch the money in your investment account among a family of mutual funds and money-market funds.

This insurance offers you *both* the flexible-premium features of ordinary universal life and the fund-switching privileges of variable life. It thus gives you maximum control over where your insurance money goes. About 40 companies sell variable universal life, including Prudential, Equitable and John Hancock.

As with all life insurance that combines insurance with investment, any earnings are tax-deferred until you cash in the policy. If your beneficiary receives the earnings, they are exempt from federal income taxes. Still, variable universal life may not be a smart buy for you unless you plan to keep your policy at least 10 years. As with variable life, it will probably take that long for your tax-sheltered earnings to make up for heavy sales charges in the early years of the policy.

Avoiding Mistakes with Your Health Policy

How much should you be paying for health insurance, and what kind should you buy?

Unless you can join a group plan through your company or professional association, you will have to pay yearly premiums of $600 to $1,100 if you are a single male, $1,000 to $2,300 if you are a single female, and from $2,500 to $5,000 for a family of four. Policies that cost much less may provide poor coverage. Avoid insurance promising to pay a set amount for each day in the hospital instead of a portion of total expenses. A policy that pays for a single disease is also a mistake; it won't cover you for most forms of costly illness.

The indispensable coverage for most people is a Blue Cross hospital policy plus a major-medical or medical-catastrophe policy. They are available from nonprofit Blue Cross/Blue Shield and large commercial companies. The best policies make you pay a maximum of 20% of most expenses in addition to a certain deductible, but place *no* ceiling on benefits. (For more, see "Your Health: Checking Up on Your Health Insurance.")

Long-Term Care Insurance

A LONG stay in a nursing home can wipe out a lifetime of savings. Medicare does not pay many nursing-home bills, and the supplemental Medigap policies pay less. Even care in your own home can reduce you to a pauper's level, though not quite as rapidly.

But now more than 70 companies and seven Blue Cross plans are offering a number of types of long-term care insurance. Some of these policies pay as much as $120 a day toward the cost of skilled nursing care provided by a nurse or other medical professional. They also cover custodial care — that is, if you do not need medical attention but you do require some help in dressing, eating and walking. The best policies include home care and day care as well.

The cost of this insurance varies tremendously, from $100 all the way up to $15,000 a year, depending on your age when you buy the policy and the benefits you elect. Although nursing-home care is generally not needed for people in their 50s and 60s, the price is far lower during those years than it is if you wait until you are 70 and over. For example, the cost of one policy triples between 60 and 70. The same policy is ten times more expensive at the age of 80.

If you are interested in securing long-term protection, ask your insurance agent these key questions before you buy:

— Does the policy cover the whole spectrum of nursing care? Skilled care generally includes such services as giving injections that can be performed only by (or under the direct supervision of) nurses, physical therapists or other medically trained experts. Intermediate care must also be under the supervision of skilled medical personnel, but registered nurses are not required to be on 24-hour duty. Highly trained or licensed people are not required at all for custodial care. Most long-term nursing-home patients need custodial care, as do patients in their own homes. Day care is for people who live at home but need supervision, or company, while they are up and around. Look for a policy that provides all of these kinds of care, that will cover you even if you need *only* intermediate or custodial care and that allows you to enter a nursing home without a prior hospital stay.

— How generous is the daily benefit? It can range all the way from $20 to $120 a day. The nationwide average is $65 a day in a nursing home, or $24,000 a year. Home care including physical therapy, help with medication and preparation of food costs $30 to $50 a day.

— How long does a person have to be in a home before benefits begin? Some policies cover you from the moment you enter a nursing home. Others require that you be confined for a certain number of days, usually 20 to 100, before payments begin. You might want to remember that the longer the waiting period, the lower your insurance premiums will be.

— How long do benefits last? Plans typically cover you for two to six years.

— Are any illnesses, injuries or pre-existing conditions excluded from coverage? Don't buy a policy that excludes nursing-home stays due to mental or nervous disorders such as Parkinson's or Alzheimer's disease. And be sure the policy is guaranteed renewable.

Selecting the Best Disability Policy

THE biggest gap in many people's insurance protection is the absence of a disability policy. Don't rely on Social Security to replace your lost wages in case of serious illness or accident. You must be severely disabled to get Social Security disability benefits, and even then you will have to wait at least five months for payments to begin. The average benefit in 1988 was $919 a month for a family.

Even if you are young and healthy, the odds are uncomfortably short that someday you may need disability insurance. About a third of all people now aged 35 will be incapacitated for three months or longer before they're 65. So, for protection in case you are laid up, it makes sense to buy a disability insurance policy. It can cost from a few hundred dollars to $1,000 or more a year.

In tailoring your policy, aim to replace 50% to 60% of your current earnings before taxes. That should be enough to maintain most of your spending power, because disability benefits are tax-free if you have paid for your own insurance.

You are probably better off with coverage for a limited period of benefits. You can save hundreds of dollars a year in premiums by settling for five years of income instead of benefits until age 65.

An even better way to reduce premiums is to increase the number of weeks you must be disabled before the policy starts paying — the so-called waiting period. Take a man aged 35 who wants $1,000 a month in benefits. If they begin one month after he is disabled, his policy would cost him about $600 a year. But if he increases that waiting period to three months, the price falls to around $450.

Two things you don't want an insurer to do are raise your premiums or cancel your coverage. Any disability contract worth considering should be at least guaranteed renewable. The *best* type of policy is called *noncancelable*. It both guarantees renewal and freezes the premium at its original level for as long as you keep the insurance. Above all, buy a policy that covers all types of disabilities. Some weasel-worded contracts give the company an out by saying you are considered to be disabled only if confined to home.

The most important decision is to choose the right insurance company. If you become disabled you will be destined to have a relationship that may last for years. A few companies write most of the high-quality individual disability policies. The leaders include: Equitable, Guardian, Massachusetts Mutual, Minnesota Mutual, Monarch, Northwestern Mutual, Paul Revere, Provident Life and Accident and Union Mutual.

Help for the Hard-to-Insure

PEOPLE with health problems or dangerous jobs are considered bad insurance risks, but if you are one of them, do not despair. Some insurance companies are willing to take chances and sell you life, disability and health policies. The trouble is, they are so-called substandard policies. They cost you more, or give you less coverage than a regular policy. About 3% of all life insurance applicants must pay two to five times more for protection than people who do not pose extra risks.

The easiest and least expensive way to get insurance, of course, is to work for a company that offers group coverage. If you are not protected by a group, ask an insurance agent to refer you to a broker who specializes in high risks. Brokers usually deal only through agents, and each is familiar with a number of insurers. Have your agent put *several* brokers to work for you — and see who comes up with the broadest coverage for the lowest cost. Substandard-risk policies are not underwritten according to formulas, so there is always room for negotiation.

Even for a hard-to-insure person, term life insurance — straight protection without any cash value — is less expensive than whole life. But he will still pay more than a high-risk person would. A 26-year-old diabetic man, for example, can buy $100,000 of whole life insurance from one company for $1,688 a year; were he not diabetic, the same coverage would cost him $800.

Another option is to buy what is called a graded-death-benefit policy. With it, the death benefit gradually increases over a period of years until it equals the face value of the policy. The advantage of such coverage is that you do not have to answer any medical questions or undergo a physical exam. The disadvantage is that if you should die shortly after the policy is issued, your survivors will receive less than the policy's face value.

A word about disability insurance: If you are a high-risk person, expect to pay up to three times as much as usual for disability coverage. You can cut the cost by accepting lower monthly benefits. Or by collecting them for a shorter period of time or waiting longer for benefits to begin.

People who have medical problems also can reduce their premiums if they buy a policy that does not cover disabilities caused by their present infirmities. If such insurance does not offer you enough protection, look into policies with so-called limited exclusion riders. These plans cost only as much as the coverage sold to healthy people. Disabilities caused by medical problems that existed before the policy's purchase *are* covered. However, the policyholder has to wait longer for payments to begin after he or she has been disabled. Or he or she may collect benefits for a shorter period than if the disability had been caused by an illness contracted after he or she bought the insurance.

Auto Policies

CAREFUL shopping for car insurance is more important than ever because the cost keeps increasing. In the most recent year, the average auto insurance premium jumped more than 8%, to $475 in early 1988. What's more, the price of identical coverage can vary from company to company as much as 100%.

Insurance salesmen naturally try to sell their standard, fully loaded policy. It contains six basic types of coverage: bodily injury, property damage, uninsured motorist, medical payments, collision and comprehensive.

Don't skimp on bodily injury liability and property damage liability coverage. If you or anybody driving your car with your permission is in an accident in which someone is killed or injured, bodily injury liability coverage pays you for an attorney to defend against lawsuits by victims of the accident. It also pays other court costs and any judgments against you. Property damage liability covers property that you do not own. The average driver should carry a policy that would pay up to $100,000 for a single injury, but no more than $300,000 for all injuries in any one accident. It should also cover up to $50,000 in property damage. If you have substantial assets that could be seized in a court to pay off a judgment that exceeds your auto coverage, you should take out an additional umbrella policy. A $1 million umbrella policy costs about $150 to $200 a year in most states.

In some states, you are required to buy uninsured-motorist coverage. It pays you for injuries caused by a hit-and-run driver or someone who cannot pay a judgment. Yet if it is not required and if you have adequate health and disability insurance where you work, you may not need uninsured-motorist coverage, nor medical payments coverage. Both may largely duplicate protection already supplied by your regular medical policy.

Many are the ways to save on your policy. According to the Insurance Information Institute, you should take as large a deductible as you can afford on collision and comprehensive, which covers fire, theft and vandalism. The deductible is the amount you agree to pay before the insurance kicks in. For instance, increasing the deductible to $500 from the common $200 may reduce your collision premium about 20%. A $1,000 deductible can save you as much as 45%. If your car is more than five years old or its value is under $1,500, consider dropping collision and comprehensive coverage altogether. After five years, most American cars are worth no more than one-third their original value.

You can reduce your premium further through discounts. For example, companies may give you as much as 30% off if you have a good driving record or up to 15% off the comprehensive premium cost if your car has antitheft devices. Driver training could cut as much as 15% off your premium. And people aged 50 and over often can get discounts of 5% to 10%.

Once you understand your options, start canvassing companies for price quotes. To get a benchmark price, call State Farm. It's the nation's largest auto insurer and, in many areas, one of the least expensive. You also will want to learn about a company's reputation for service. To do that, check with your state's insurance department. The larger states, including Illinois, New York and California, publish annual lists of companies with the highest and lowest percentage of consumer complaints.

As you survey the insurance companies, be sure to learn which are most forgiving if you have an accident. For example, if you are at fault for an accident that results in a payment of more than $400, then the Nationwide Insurance Company usually will raise your rates 30%. State Farm generally increases its premium 10% after the first $400 property damage claim.

There are often significant differences in collision and comprehensive premiums for various car makes and models. So be sure to check this out when you buy a new car. Allstate, for instance, offers 25% to 55% discounts in most states on comprehensive and collision policies for cars that are least likely to be stolen — usually full-sized sedans and mini-vans.

Many states have drafted insurance companies into the war against auto theft. If you live in one of those states and you have installed special alarms or other antitheft devices, you can arrange for your premiums to be reduced. There are many other steps that drivers everywhere can take to improve their insurance against auto theft. (For more, see "Your Auto: Devices That Deter Theft.")

If you rent a car while waiting for the insurance settlement, you will probably have to bear some of that expense, too. Most policies pay about $15 a day toward a rental car. Renting is likely to cost you two or three times that much per day, and you probably will not get a settlement within a month. Thus, it is wise to buy a little-known rider that costs $15 to $40 a year and boosts rental coverage substantially. The rider also pays for transportation not only while your car is missing but also while it is in the shop for the repair of theft damage.

Your insurance coverage for the theft of accessories or possessions you have in the car may not be as extensive as you expect. Some insurance companies that classify removable radios as a portable accessory do not cover their theft. If you have resorted to toting your expensive stereo or radio around when you are out of the car, consider buying a disguise for it instead. For about $20, a plain plastic front gives your equipment the look of an ordinary factory-installed radio.

Neither your auto policy nor any extra coverage applies to other things that a thief might steal from your car, such as a $1,000 set of golf clubs or a $400 designer blazer. But you are probably covered anyway. Most homeowners policies apply to anything taken by someone who breaks into your car. There is a hitch, though: you have to *prove* that the doors were locked at the time of the theft.

Whatever kind of insurance you are buying, you can save money and worry by remembering this: Never risk more than you can afford to lose. But don't pay to insure what you can afford to risk.

Homeowners Policies

Every owner of a house or apartment needs insurance to protect his residence and its contents against calamity, but how much coverage is enough? The amount you should have depends on the *replacement cost* of your house. That is, what you would have to spend to rebuild your castle as it now stands.

Insurance companies like you to cover your home for 100% of its replacement cost. Total losses are rare, however, and you will be adequately insured for partial damage with 80% of the replacement cost. Be sure that your policy indexes the replacement cost to inflation. And if you make a substantial improvement to your house, raise your coverage to reflect its new replacement cost.

All homeowners policies cover your personal possessions. But they set limits on what you can claim and usually reimburse you only for what you paid for the item — minus depreciation — and not for what it would cost you to replace it today. To be sure that you are adequately covered when you make a claim for damage to a rug or furniture, add a *replacement cost rider* to your policy. Your yearly premium may go up about 10%, but the extra protection is worth it.

If you have a home-based business, you will need to add an *incidental business option* to your policy. It provides insurance for such property as personal computers or typewriters. The amount of coverage varies.

You can hold down your insurance costs by taking advantage of special deals offered by most companies. There are premium discounts of up to 20% on new homes, 5% for installing dead-bolt locks and smoke detectors and 20% if you put in an elaborate fire and burglar alarm. Increase your deductible to $250 from the standard $100, and you will lop 10% off your annual bill. But never scrimp on overall coverage in order to keep costs down.

No homeowners policy covers all perils. The best policies, however, are called HO-5 *with comprehensive coverage* or its equivalent, an endorsed HO-3. They may reimburse you not only for fire and windstorm, but also if, for example, your water pipes freeze and burst. Yet even these do not protect you against floods or earthquakes. For that, you need to seek extra coverage at higher cost.

If you live in an apartment, a co-op or condominium, you also need insurance to protect you from fire, burglary and even liability. True, landlords, co-op corporations and condo associations have insurance. But their policies cover only the building itself, and mishaps that occur in common areas. So you need your own policy.

It should cover excess living expenses. For example, if your apartment is damaged by fire, the insurance company will pay for your stay in a hotel. Your policy also should cover *full replacement costs* for articles that are stolen or destroyed. That will run you 10% to 15% more in premiums than *actual cash value* policies, but the extra benefit most likely is worth it. Apartment insurance generally costs anywhere from $100 to $200, with a standard deductible of $100. As with insurance on a house, you can lower your premium by 10% if you increase the deductible to $250.

Another point to remember is that homeowners and tenants policies set low limits on the payments for jewelry, furs, silverware and collectibles. But you can buy endorsements that protect your valuables at a small additional cost — for example, $10 to $15 for $1,000 of value on jewelry, $5 for $1,000 on silverware.

Your homeowners policy does include some liability coverage. That covers many claims against you for injuries to people on or off your property. But what if you get sued for ramming into a highly paid executive on a ski slope and crippling him for life? The possibility is remote, yet if you were hit by such a lawsuit, the $25,000 to $100,000 that most homeowners policies pay on such claims might not be enough. Get an excess liability or personal umbrella policy. It pays claims over the limit of your homeowners policy.

Excess Liability Insurance

Accidents can happen, and when they do, the law says that people who were to blame must pay the victims' financial losses. You can protect yourself against such damage suits by buying excess personal liability insurance. It is also called an umbrella policy. This supplements the protection you already have against injury claims as a standard part of your homeowners and automobile insurance.

Anyone could benefit from this extra protection. A judgment against you could lay claim to your future income for many years.

Liability policies cover you for accidents you might cause or be responsible for. You usually can buy a $1 million policy for $100 to $200 a year. But, since the excess liability policy takes over where auto or homeowners insurance ends, insurers will issue it only if you already have substantial primary coverage.

The best contracts cover almost every kind of liability claim except those related to business activities. For example, excess liability should also protect you if you are sued for libel, slander or invasion of privacy, malicious prosecution, wrongful eviction, defamation of character or discrimination. Some policies insure against bodily injury or property damage resulting from your use of reasonable force to protect persons or property. A good policy also pays for most of your legal defense. Your policy should extend to everyone in your household who is related to you by blood, marriage or adoption. That includes children away at school.

A sensible way to select a policy is with the help of an independent agent. He or she represents a number of companies and can help you sort through their policies. Choose the one with the most extensive coverage. Three companies that insurance consultants believe have the broadest policies are Crum & Forster, Kemper and St. Paul Fire & Marine.

Checking Your Insurer's Safety

You buy life insurance in case something happens to you. But what if something happens to your insurance company? If you worry that your firm might fail, you should heed the safety ratings of A. M. Best Company, a publisher of insurance data. Every year, it assigns insurance companies one of seven grades ranging from "A-plus" all the way down to "Omitted" — which means flunking.

A. M. Best bases its ratings on a thorough analysis of all factors affecting the insurer's financial stability, including policy renewal rates and performance of the firm's investments. An A-plus is the surest guarantee you can get that a life insurance company will not fail. Of the 1,548 companies Best reported on in 1987, 275 received an A-plus and 626 did not even qualify for a letter rating.

You can get ratings of the companies you are interested in by writing to them, or from *Best's Insurance Reports,* available at public libraries. Or ask an insurance agent. He or she probably has a condensed version of the reports called *Best's Agents Guide.* For your own copy, send $45 to A. M. Best, Ambest Road, Oldwick, New Jersey 08858.

Making a Household Inventory

CLOSE your eyes and try to list all your living-room furnishings or the contents of your jewelry box. If you have trouble coming up with a complete tally, imagine how hard it would be when you are upset, after a fire or burglary. Making a written inventory of your household goods can be one of the best money-saving steps you can take. A list not only guarantees that any insurance claim you submit after a burglary or a fire will be complete, but it also assures you of a smooth claims process. Your insurance company probably can give you an inventory form to fill out.

Insurers are not likely to question claims based on such inventories, especially if you submit them along with photos, receipts, or appraisers' statements for valuable items. You should leave a copy of your inventory of household goods with your insurance agent or in your safe-deposit box.

What should go into your inventory? Write down the date you bought each item of value in your name, plus its price. If an appraiser has estimated the value of any of your possessions, you should record the figure and the date. Make sure the appraisal is precise and explicit. Highly generalized descriptions will not back up a claim.

Describe each object as graphically as possible. Be sure to include its age, brand name, size, model number and other relevant details. For tableware, note the manufacturer, pattern and number of place settings. If your possessions are extensive and of particularly high quality, you might consider videotaping and recording your verbal descriptions of them.

In some categories of property, though, you may wish to lump together a number of articles and attach a single estimate of value. This is a particularly wise tactic with clothing. Unless you have closets full of designer evening gowns, there is no sense driving yourself crazy counting and describing everything in your wardrobe. Even a couple of priceless Hawaiian shirts should not be too hard to describe if an insurance company asks you to.

Your Personal Security

What to Do If You Are Ripped Off

W HEN your pocket has been picked, you are left with a purseful of problems. But there are ways to help your recovery from a rip-off.

Some 12 million Americans are victims of personal larceny each year. If you are one of them, chances are slim that your property will ever be recovered. Still, you should quickly inform the police about the theft. You will need a police report to prove your loss to the IRS, to your insurer and perhaps to your bank.

You also should immediately notify your bank and any of your credit-card issuers. A thief can swiftly begin using your checks and credit cards, and a few hours' delay increases the chances that he will get away with it. If you know the numbers of any stolen checks, your bank can stop payment. If not, you probably will have to close your account and open a new one. You are not liable for checks written by a thief, but if the signature closely matches your own, you will have to spend time proving to the bank it was a forgery.

Once you report the loss of your credit cards, you are not liable for any subsequent charges. If the thief gets away with using your cards before you report the loss, your liability is limited to $50 a card. But that amount adds up quickly if you have several cards. Many credit-card issuers have operators available around the clock. They also may provide toll-free numbers or accept collect calls.

One precaution is to sign up with a credit-card protection service offered through banks and credit-card firms. For $6 to $15 a year, a service will immediately contact all of your credit-card issuers after you notify it of the theft. The service pays any liabilities incurred after you call. Some services will even wire you money if you are robbed while traveling.

Another piece of plastic you may carry is a debit card used to operate the automatic teller machine at your local bank. If fraud is not involved, your liability is $50 if you notify the bank within two business days after theft; it jumps to $500 if you take three to 60 days. After that, liability is unlimited.

But what if your bank or credit union sends you a renewal card and it gets lost in the mail? Even if someone charges up a storm on the card, you wouldn't have to pay a penny. Federal law says that you have to "accept" the card first before you become liable for bad purchases. And if you didn't receive the card, you didn't accept it.

If you have any problems, be sure to state your case to your card issuer in writing. If that doesn't clear things up, contact the Federal Reserve Bank nearest you or, if you have a card issued by a credit union, write to the nearest office of the National Credit Union Administration.

Keeping Records to Reduce Your Loss

No one even wants to think about having his or her home burglarized. But if you confront the possibility beforehand, you can reduce your financial loss.

To prevent a burglary from leaving you broke, make an inventory of everything you have in your home. Your insurance company probably can give you a form to fill out. Then go through each room, opening drawers and cupboards and carefully listing every object of value. Record all identifying information, such as serial numbers of appliances and account numbers of credit cards. For tableware, note the manufacturers, pattern and number of place settings. Describe jewelry as fully as possible. It's also wise to photograph the contents of your house, item by item. Do this yourself with self-developing film that does not need to be processed by strangers. For art, antiques and family heirlooms you'll also need to cite estimates of each item's age and value. The best proof is an appraiser's dated statement. (See also "Your Insurance: Making a Household Inventory.")

Get receipts and appraisals for particularly valuable items. Without these documents, you will have to rely on what the insurance adjuster says your goods are worth. An appraisal must be precise and explicit to back up a claim. Don't accept any that give only highly generalized descriptions of your valuables.

Appraisers for your goods can be located through the American Society of Appraisers, P.O. Box 17265, Washington, D.C. 20041. It publishes a free directory of those members who are personal property appraisers, plus a free pamphlet, *Information on the Appraisal Profession.* For $5, you can get its *Directory of Professional Appraisal Services,* which includes appraisers in all fields. (See also "Your Services: Appraisers.")

You might even videotape your possessions. This technique lets you zoom in on details of antiques and fine artworks, highlighting makers' marks and signatures while commenting on their value. Videotaping services will do the job for you. But before you hire anyone to videotape your belongings, check his or her reputation with the Better Business Bureau and the local police.

If your home is burglarized, you will need accurate records for both the IRS and the police. These records will help you reduce your losses.

After a burglary, the criminals often melt down the precious metals in their loot and break up the jewelry to prevent its being traced. But most other stolen merchandise winds up back on the market intact. Police sweeps of pawnshops and suspected fences and crooked retailers sometimes turn up stolen property.

It's getting tougher to deduct burglary losses from your income taxes, so you may need more insurance coverage. Until 1982, you could deduct qualifying losses above $100 on your income tax form. Now you are allowed to deduct only those losses that exceed 10% of your adjusted gross income. And the loss must be figured as the lower of two amounts: the price paid for the item or its current value. So, if you lose something that is worth less today than when you bought it, you can deduct only its current market value. But if an item has grown in value since you bought it, you can deduct only its original, lower cost.

Protecting Yourself with Locks and Alarms

You can help make your home safe by installing the right locks and alarms, and it need not cost you a fortune or create a fortress. To stop a thief, first call the police — not for a squad car but for a free security checkup. Police departments often will send patrolmen to inspect your property and show you where it is vulnerable.

It is important to have reliable locks on all windows, since most burglars find it easier to break in through windows than to pick a lock on a door. Of course, do not forget to have strong locks on all doors, not just the front door. Crime prevention experts recommend replacing ordinary key-cylinder locks with pick-resistant ones. But for most residences, ultra-sophisticated locks that replace keys with magnetic cards, voice recognition or coded pushbuttons are expensive overkill.

Most good locks are secured by a rigid dead-bolt that extends at least one inch into the jamb. The Kentucky Department of Justice's Office of Crime Prevention has tested residential locks commonly available in the state. Among the manufacturers whose products were rated superior were Ideal, National Lock Hardware, MAG, Schlage, Emhart and Medeco.

Homeowners who want more protection than locks give can choose one of several alarm systems. It pays to check out the craftsman who puts in the system, since alarms are only as reliable as the people who install them. Be sure to get competitive bids, to ask for and check references and call your local Better Business Bureau to see if there have been any complaints about installers whom you are considering. You should shop as warily for an alarm system as for a used car.

Over 2,000 installers are members of either the National Burglar and Fire Alarm Association or the Central Station Electrical Protection Association. Both are in Washington, D.C., and each group will provide you with a list of its members in your town. To check out these candidates, request that the contractors give you the names and phone numbers of several recent customers. Then ask your state or local consumer protection agency whether complaints have been filed against the contractors' companies.

Expect to spend at least $1,500 for a contractor-installed alarm system. You often can get discounts on your property insurance if you put one in. The standard setup deploys two lines of defense. First, door and window trip switches detect break-ins. Second, interior sensors react to an intruder's movements, body heat or noisy forced entry.

Many such alarms also send out alerts by phone or cable-TV lines to the alarm company's local 24-hour monitoring center. Its staff responds to alarms by calling the customer to confirm an emergency or by immediately notifying the police. The charge for this service averages $20 to $25 a month. Nationwide companies that sell systems with 24-hour monitoring services include ADT, Honeywell Protection Services and Rollins Protective Services.

If you want to secure your home for much less money, you can buy basic, off-the-shelf alarms for a few hundred dollars and hook them up yourself. You get them in consumer electronics stores, though you do have to be handy around the house to properly install and fine-tune them.

One good home security device is Radio Shack's $100 indoor infrared detector. Its built-in alarm is triggered by a burglar's body heat.

A new generation of wireless alarm systems has recently come on the market. Schlage Lock Company's Keepsafer system is one of the least expensive and easiest to install. The basic system costs around $200 and consists of a central control console that has a built-in alarm horn and is plugged into a regular household outlet. The package also contains two transmitter sensor switches that you put on doors or windows.

Weekend or vacation houses that are often unoccupied are particularly vulnerable to break-ins as well as electrical or plumbing breakdowns. One early-warning system for both is Sensaphone. At $250, this plug-in, desktop unit monitors the status of a house's electricity supply, temperature and sound level.

Renting a Safe-Deposit Box

RISING crime has made more people than ever look for a safe place to put their valuables, whether they are jewelry, collectibles or important papers. Almost invariably, the most economical place to store precious possessions is a bank deposit box. The smallest cost $15 to $45 a year and are large enough for documents, securities and real estate deeds and appraisals. If you have anything else, you probably will want a bigger box. Those larger boxes are in short supply and anyone with a lot of jewelry, a stamp collection or anything bulky may face a long waiting list.

One solution is to find one of the many private safe-deposit companies. They have no connection with banks, but they do have security. To get in, you usually need to pass a complicated screening process.

Commercial vaults offer anonymity. But once the government receives information from another source, the vaults are subject to the same regulations as the banks.

The private vaults have the advantage of offering flexible storage space. Lockers can be fitted with special shelves and racks for stamp collections, rare books, wine, even computer tapes and disks. Works of art can be kept in rooms that have temperature and humidity controls and special fire-fighting systems designed not to damage art.

These commercial bulk storage facilities are sensible for two-home families who wish to lock up valuables when they are out of the area. Owners of vacation homes, for example, may want to store special possessions during the off-season.

Private vaults can be more expensive than banks for small spaces, but they are often cheaper for bulky storage. A private five-by-three-by-five-foot locker costs about $1,000 a year.

For more information about private vault companies, write to the National Association of Private Security Vaults, 3562 North Ocean Boulevard, Fort Lauderdale, Florida 33308.

Buying a Safe for Your Home

SINCE there are long waiting lists for safe-deposit boxes in banks, more and more people are searching for a secure place to store their valuables right in their own homes.

The biggest weakness of a home safe is its accessibility. If you take a weekend away from home, professional burglars have plenty of time to find and defeat your safe. So a safe-deposit box in a bank or a vault at a private safe-deposit company is the most secure place for jewelry, securities, coins and other valuables, but a home safe can be useful for documents and records.

When you buy a safe, be sure it has been rated by the Underwriters Laboratories for fire resistance. Say it is rated a class 150 two-hour safe. That means that temperatures inside will go no higher than 150 degrees Fahrenheit during a two-hour fire. A class 150 two-hour safe is a good one for protecting stamps and other expensive collectibles.

If you insist on keeping not only your documents but also tiaras and gold bullion in your home, then forget about a wall safe. A burglar can drill around the metal box and pull it free. What you will need is a so-called burglary-resistant safe. It should be anchored with bolts or embedded in a concrete floor and concealed by a rug. A floor safe the size of a file-drawer cabinet can cost up to $600.

Fancier, stronger safes can go for much more. You can easily pay more than $3,000 for a medium-size model with inch-thick steel walls, and an inch-and-a-half-thick door, a special locking mechanism in the door and an Underwriters Laboratories label marked TL-30. The TL number is an index of resistance to burglars' tools.

If you do not have a safe, the best protection for your valuables is ingenuity. Avoid the more common hiding places, like the toe of a shoe or the bottom of a sugar canister. Some people have foiled burglars by using false-bottom books, sewing jewelry into stuffed toys or pillows or even freezing diamonds in the ice tray. Just be careful of gulping them down with that one-too-many martini.

Your Consumer Problems

Gaining Through Complaining

For customers bedeviled by faulty products, snarled-up bills or late deliveries, a few well-chosen threats can succeed when all else fails. You can gain by complaining shrewdly. In fact, the U.S. Office of Consumer Affairs reports that consumers solve 88% of their grievances by lodging a complaint with somebody in authority at the offending company.

Any good gripe to a store or manufacturer, as writer Marlys Harris has observed, has five simple elements: a clear statement of the problem; facts that back up your story; a request for redress; a deadline by which the problem must be solved; and a threat that you are prepared to carry out if you do not get quick and complete satisfaction.

Many quite proper threats can produce results. For example, you can threaten to stop payment to the offending store or service person, to end your patronage or to tell other people how badly you have been treated. If all else fails, you can threaten a lawsuit. But use that as a last resort, for you often will have to be prepared to spend thousands of dollars on legal fees.

Face-to-face gripes frequently fail because you take out your anger on a clerk or bank teller who does not have the power to correct a problem. To get any results from an oral complaint, of course, you should ask to see the manager or whoever is in charge.

One successful face-to-face technique is called the broken record. It has been developed by specialists in assertiveness training. You drive your listener to distraction by tirelessly repeating your problem and your request for redress in a helpful and unctuous manner. Or you can take this technique another step by announcing, "I'm *not* moving until you straighten this out."

You may be tempted to make your gripe by telephone. That is less daunting than face-to-face complaining, but it often feels like punching a cloud. If you elect to fight that way, demand the name or employee number of the person with whom you speak. Write it down, along with any promises the complaint handler makes.

If the first person you speak with fails to solve your problem, ask to talk with a supervisor. Keep heading upward until you get some response. If you suspect a complaint handler is giving you the runaround by sending you to another department, threaten to get back to him. That is why you have asked for his name or number.

The telephone is particularly suited to solving delivery problems. You just threaten to call the dispatcher every 15 minutes until the truck arrives. After a few such distracting calls, he or she usually manages to work miracles.

If you have a gripe about snarled-up computers, immobile bureaucrats, snooty clerks or an unreliable product you have bought, the most effective way to complain is generally by writing a firm, effective letter. Aim your missive directly at the head of the company. Although he or she will probably pass it to a subordinate, the chief's interest is often enough to turn the laziest employee into a dynamo.

Since countless employees in large stores and companies must pore over letters that are usually boring, vague, abusive and lengthy, you have to make your letter stand out. One way to do that is simply to write plain, forceful English. The first paragraph should be brief — no more than two sentences of 10 or 15 words each. It should summarize the problem in a dramatic way — for example, "I'm very distressed by a billing problem that your company refuses to correct." And it should demand proper redress.

In the second paragraph pop a surprise: compliment the company. You might say that you have been delighted with its appliances over the years. In fact, those marvels have been joys to own. Then, in the next paragraph, go in for the kill. "So you can imagine my dismay," you might say, "when my latest purchase turned out to be a dud."

Move on to the facts, but omit unnecessary details. Since most people only scan letters you should state your demand twice — in the second sentence of the first paragraph and at the end. Also, try to establish a relationship with your reader to gain empathy. A businessman might say that he is in business, too, and would be upset to learn that one of his customers had been treated as poorly as he has.

A "P.S." is especially important. Tests have shown that a P.S. is one of the first things people read, so you want to make a statement that will get someone to read the rest of the letter. To a bank president, you might say you will be compelled to move your account elsewhere, notify the banking commission or take up the matter with your lawyer if you do not hear from the executive by a certain date.

If your complaint does not bring immediate results, step up your demands. Not only do you want your toaster replaced, but since you have had to put up with delay after delay, you think the company should throw in an electric can opener as well. When you keep raising the ante, management tends to become more eager to settle.

One further tip: The U.S. Office of Consumer Affairs has published a free, 92-page *Consumer's Resource Handbook*. It lists the names, addresses and phone numbers of consumer affairs directors at more than 700 corporations. If you do not get satisfaction from them, the booklet directs you to the addresses and phone numbers of other sources of help, such as local Better Business Bureaus and government consumer protection offices. To get the handbook, write to the Consumer Information Center–F, Pueblo, Colorado 81002.

Help from Better Business Bureaus

Now that the government is relaxing its regulation of business, where can consumers turn for help to settle their complaints against companies? More and more of them will be relying on the Better Business Bureau.

The nation's 175 Better Business Bureaus operate on funds contributed mostly by local firms. All the bureau members agree to respond promptly to consumer complaints, make fair adjustments when the customer has grounds for a gripe and advertise honestly. The most common complaints concern merchandise sold by mail, phone, radio or television.

How much a Better Business Bureau can help varies widely from community to community. For example, the Manhattan office, with a large full-time staff and budget, is one of the country's most pro-consumer bureaus. But some bureaus spend little time on investigations.

Probably the best time to call for help is before you make a deal. The bureau can tell you whether people have complained about a store or company and, if so, whether that business handled the complaint. But Better Business Bureaus won't ever give you lists of complaint-free companies. That's because recommendations of any kind are taboo. People who think they have been swindled or misled may get help, but it may take weeks to settle the case. It's best to put complaints in writing to give bureau specialists time to check out the facts.

Increasingly, the Better Business Bureau is resolving disputes by arbitration. All of its bureaus offer this service free to buyers and sellers willing to accept the results as legally binding. Most consumers who don't like an arbitrator's decision may have no further recourse, and in some states the courts will decline to hear their case. However, consumers who complain about their automobiles can reject an arbitrator's decision and go to court. If you win in a Better Business Bureau arbitration and your adversary doesn't pay up, the award is enforceable by the courts.

Your Retirement

Strategies to Start Saving Now

ALMOST everyone can look forward to an even longer average life span and better health than his or her forefathers. But if you are under 40, what you probably will not be able to do is retire as early as your parents could, or quit working completely when you do retire, or count on the government for as much of your support in your great age. Because you will have to do more to take care of yourself when you are old, you will have to start saving and investing while you are reasonably young.

Population trends will strain Social Security and private pensions, but only in the distant future. In the decade of the 1990s, the Social Security system will enjoy a huge surplus — some estimates run to *$1 trillion*. That is because the people who start retiring and tapping into Social Security benefits will come from the small generation that was born in the 1930s Depression. Meanwhile, the bulging generation of baby boomers born from the mid-1940s to the mid-1960s will be reaching their peak earning years and paying tremendous sums in Social Security taxes. Consequently, the Social Security system will have more than enough cash when today's 60-year-olds retire. It is *after* that when trouble may set in.

By the year 2010, half of all Americans will be 40 or older, whereas today the median age is 32. A major reason for the aging of America is the lengthening of life spans. If a man makes it to the age of 65 in the year 2010, he will have a 50-50 chance of living several years into his 80s; women will live even longer — into their late 80s. With fewer young people and many more elderly, the few will have to support the many through Social Security taxes. The U.S. probably will have to scale back government-paid retirement benefits. They will be lower in real dollars, and they will start later in life, perhaps at 67 instead of 65. Thus, your private pension — from either your employer or your Individual Retirement Account and Keogh plan, or from both — will become relatively more important than such sources are for contemporary retirees.

Today the combination of your pension and your Social Security benefits typically add up to 60% to 80% of your last few years' average salary. But pensions differ sharply from one industry to another. The best private pensions are provided by banking, chemical, insurance, petroleum and utility companies. Retailing, food-processing and garment-manufacturing firms tend to have the worst.

The very finest pensions go to government employees — military personnel and federal civil servants. A cost-of-living escalator makes many of their retirement plans especially generous. One study found that a federal civil servant who retired in 1969 at age 65 with a final salary of $25,000 had a pension that climbed to $35,000 in 10 years. Under similar circumstances, a person retired from a corporation would be collecting about $26,000, including Social Security. Almost no private plans are indexed to inflation, although some companies have given raises to their pensioners.

Happily, great new opportunities to save and invest for retirement are opening up. The number of tax-deferred corporate pension and savings plans has more than tripled since 1967, and new variations of those plans are appearing every day. IRAs, which let your savings grow tax-free, are now available to everyone who works for money, although not everyone can deduct his or her contributions. Meanwhile, the limit on tax-deductible contributions to Keogh plans for the self-employed has been raised dramatically. Add in the proliferation of new investments, from small bank certificates of deposit to zero-coupon bonds, and you have a wide assortment of investment opportunities that can provide for your later years.

Qualifying for a pension will be easier in coming years. Today, you usually have to work at the same company for 10 years to become vested, which means that you are guaranteed benefits when you retire. But beginning in 1989, tax reform cuts the time you must wait to five years. Under the new law, employers can choose an alternative plan that stretches out the process to seven years, by vesting 20% of your pension benefits after three years, and 20% in each of the subsequent four years. While the rule goes into effect in 1989, the years that you have logged with your company by then will count under the new law.

Even if you have only a meager company pension, there are ways to use whatever assets you have to achieve substantial gains.

You might start investing for retirement by putting a bit of money into a mutual fund that aims for growth. This type of fund invests in stocks of solid companies that offer better-than-average opportunities for capital appreciation. A mutual fund, of course, is an excellent place to put your yearly contribution to your Individual Retirement Account. You can find updated rankings of the best-performing mutual funds in the "Fund Watch" column in *Money* magazine.

You might further diversify your retirement fund by looking into real estate. Ask a stockbroker or financial planner to find you a real estate limited partnership that aims not for hefty deductions but for steady payments of income that is partially sheltered. Several years from now, when properties owned by the partnership are sold, you will also get a share of any profits on the deal. Or you might consider buying into one of the real estate investment trusts (REITs). They are public companies that invest in apartments and commercial developments. A portion of the income that REITs produce may be tax-sheltered.

Finally, keep a portion of whatever money you have in an asset-management account at a bank or brokerage house. Such an account allows you to trade stocks and bonds, buy money-market funds, write out checks and use a credit or debit card that permits you to borrow more than usual. Most important, any dividends or interest you collect will be put immediately into a money-market fund — and start growing right away.

To be financially secure later on, you will have to concoct a recipe for retirement income that will provide the same 60% to 80% of last earnings that are now typically provided by pensions and Social Security. The time to start saving and investing, of course, is now.

It is wise to get into the habit of investing in a tax-sheltered savings plan, such as an IRA, beginning at age 30, so that time and compound growth can work on your behalf. Aim to save and invest 5% of your pre-tax income between the ages of 30 and 40. Then, increase that amount by one percentage point a year between the ages of 40 and 45. After 45, save 10% a year.

If your employer offers you a savings plan where the company kicks in 50 cents or more for every dollar you invest, that is an offer you should not refuse. There are, however, two exceptions. First, if the plan invests exclusively in the company's own stock and you are not confident about your employer's future, you might be wise to put your money elsewhere. Second, don't rush to invest if you don't expect to become vested, which in such plans could take 10 years. Under the new tax law, many people will become fully vested in five years, effective in 1989.

In contrast to the safe and steady company savings plans, company profit-sharing plans can be chancy. The employer's contribution depends on the company's ability to turn a profit. As a result, there is no guarantee the plan will be funded from year to year. Even if you are sure about the profits, you still have to decide whether you could earn a higher return on the money you put in if you invested it on your own than if you left it with your employer's investment managers.

Nearly all companies with profit-sharing or savings plans let their vested employees leave with a lump-sum benefit. What comes next can be a real bonanza. The employee can take the employer's contributions plus any money that he has earned in the plan and defer paying taxes on the total by depositing all of it in an Individual Retirement Account. There the money can be invested, just like a regular IRA, and will compound tax-free until it is withdrawn.

How to Plan at Different Stages of Life

R EGARDLESS of your age, now is the time to figure out how much you will need to make retirement secure — and where that cash will come from.

Your first step is to calculate your anticipated income and expenses during your post-employment years. Usually it is unrealistic to aim for an annual income equal to your pay in the last year before you quit. You most likely will not need that much anyway, because your work-related expenses will disappear and your housing costs probably will fall. Your tax bill stands to decline, too, because Social Security benefits are largely tax-free, and there are special exemptions and tax credits for people 65 and older. So you should work toward building retirement income of between 60% and 80% of your pre-retirement earnings, before taxes.

After figuring out how much you will require each year, you should estimate your life expectancy. Use the national mortality tables that you can get from your insurance agent. But to be sure you will not run out of money, you should *double* the number of additional years the tables say you can expect to live.

To determine where your retirement income will come from, first estimate your Social Security benefit. When you turn 60, the local Social Security office will do that for you. If you expect to receive a company pension or money from a company savings plan, ask your employee benefits officer to rough out how much you might get. Also calculate what you can reasonably count on receiving regularly from your IRA and other savings and investments.

When you are in your 30s, start setting priorities for your spending, so that your major expenses will be paid off when you retire. At this age, it is a good time to buy a house or apartment, so your mortgage will also be paid off by the time you quit work. You should get into the savings habit. As mentioned earlier, try to save at least 5% of your pay. If you must, cut back on entertainment, travel and other discretionary expenses to find the extra money. It is when you are young that you should build an emergency fund equal to three to six months of living expenses. It should go into risk-free money funds or U.S. Treasury securities.

When you reach 45, aim to put away 10% of your income. Continue making the maximum contributions to tax-saving Individual Retirement Accounts, Keogh and 401(k) plans. Take full advantage of any of your company's savings and investment plans. If possible, do not switch jobs until you have worked for the same company long enough for your pension benefits to be vested.

Once you hit your 50s, try to save 10% to 15% of your gross income, especially in tax-deferred plans. Your investments should now tilt conservatively. Look for blue-chip stocks, conservative mutual funds and fixed-income investments, such as bonds and bank certificates.

When you reach your 60s, you probably soon will be collecting a Social Security check, and you should be aware of these points:

First, the government will not send you a check until you notify the local Social Security office that you are ready. So be sure to file an application three months before you want the first check to arrive.

Second, many couples do not realize that if only one spouse works for pay, Social Security will send you a monthly check equal to 1½ times the worker's entitlement — as long as the worker does not start collecting until age 65.

Third, Social Security may penalize you if you keep working in your 60s. The government cuts benefits by $1 for every $2 you earn beyond a certain amount when you are between age 62 and 70. But some good news: In 1990, the penalty will be reduced. Then, you will lose $1 for every $3 in earnings over the threshold. (For more, see "Your Retirement: Does It Pay to Work after You Retire?")

Annuities: Savings with a Tax Shelter

THE very mention of the word *annuity* may be enough to make your eyes glaze over. But consider these words: up to 9.6% interest, all of it tax-deferred; guaranteed principal; monthly checks for life. Now are you interested in annuities?

An annuity is a savings plan sponsored by an insurance company that offers some tax benefits. It is a contract promising to pay you a regular income, usually starting the day you retire and running for the rest of your life. Annuities are sold by brokers, financial planners and insurance agents, who charge fees ranging from nothing to 5% of your investment. Contracts called single-premium annuities generally require a deposit of $5,000 to $10,000 or more, but others called flexible premiums allow you to start with as little as $400 or less. The earnings on the money compound *tax-free*, just as with an IRA. And if you buy an annuity for your IRA, your contributions — up to $2,000 a year — may be *tax-deductible*.

The earnings on your annuity grow until sometime in the future, usually after you retire. Then you can either take one large lump sum or "annuitize" — that is, start collecting monthly payments that will continue either over a fixed period or for the rest of your life. Each payment is considered to be partly a return of principal, which will *not* be taxed, and partly your earnings or income on that principal, which *will* be taxed.

After you buy a contract, the insurance company may let you withdraw up to 10% of the value of your annuity each year without any penalties. But you do have to pay income tax on your withdrawals. If you want to take out more than 10%, the company will exact a surrender charge. Often it starts at 5% to 10% of the amount you are withdrawing during the contract's first year and declines until it disappears after five to 10 years. There are other fees as well. Many companies charge maintenance fees of $12 to $30 a year on fixed-rate and variable contracts.

Because of those penalties, annuities are not for you if you are seeking a convenient place to park your spare cash for just a short period. Nor are annuities sensible for very young adults who cannot afford to tie up capital. But disciplined savers in their mid-30s or older who seek tax relief should seriously consider annuities.

Say, for instance, a 35-year-old put a $10,000 inheritance into an annuity that paid an average 8% interest over the years. By the time he or she reached 65, the tax-deferred buildup would be $100,600. If the individual then took monthly payments for life, he or she might draw $1,100 each month from an insurance company with a generous payment schedule.

Different insurance companies make widely different monthly payments. Among various insurers, the lifetime payment for a man aged 65 lately ranged from $7.85 to $10.25 a month for each $1,000 of accumulated capital. In recent years, the rate has approximated the interest on long-term Treasury bonds. In mid-1988, that was 8.8%.

The sponsor of the annuity *guarantees* to pay you a certain interest rate on the money, generally for a year — and sometimes up to ten years. Lately that initial guaranteed rate has been typically 8%. After that, the rate moves up or down at the sponsor's discretion. Most insurance companies guarantee to pay you at least 3.5% to 5.5% a year, even if rates dip below that in the future.

The insurance company also guarantees to pay you back all the money you put into a fixed annuity. So, you would be wise to deal only with major insurers. Look for ones rated A-plus by *Best's Insurance Reports,* which objectively analyzes the companies. You can find *Best's Insurance Reports* in public libraries and, sometimes, at insurance agents' offices.

Variable annuities are riskier than fixed ones because your principal is not guaranteed. With a variable, the insurance company invests your money in stocks, bonds or money-market securities —

and some plans allow you to switch among them. Your returns fluctuate daily, along with their performance.

When shopping for a fixed-rate annuity, do not give in to the temptation to buy the one that promises the highest interest. Look instead for an escape or bailout clause. It will let you take out all your money in the future at no charge if the interest rate the company pays falls one or two percentage points below what it was when you bought the annuity. With such an escape clause, there is nothing to prevent you from switching tax-free from one annuity company to another, better-performing firm.

Before you buy any fixed-rate annuity, ask to see the interest rates that the insurance company has paid over the last 10 years. And you can find the best variable annuities by reading the performance data compiled by Lipper Analytical Services. Your insurance agent should have the latest Lipper survey.

Some company sponsors consistently outperform others in the Lipper Analytical survey. The fixed-income leaders based on total reinvested rate of return for 10 years have been NW Mutual VA C Bond Fund, Aetna Income Shares B NQ II and Aetna Income Shares C Q I. At the top of Lipper's money-fund variable annuity ratings for 10 years are Aetna Encore B NQ II, Aetna Encore D Q I and Aetna Encore C Q I.

The fixed-income leaders for five years are Compass II HY VA Account Q, Kilico Income NQ III and Kilico Income Q. Leading the money-fund variable annuity rankings for five years are Kilico Money Market Q, Kilico Money Market NQ and Monarch/Merrill-Money M.

How to Check Your Company Pension

IT IS too late to start preparing for your retirement on the day you pick up your gold watch. You should be looking into the pension plan that your employer provides right now.

Pension plans come in two kinds. First, there is the *defined benefit* plan. It promises you a fixed benefit upon retirement. Your pension is related to your salary and to the length of your employment, no matter what it costs the company to provide it. This means you can count on at least a certain minimum payment.

Second, there is the *defined contribution plan*. It promises you that your employer will invest a certain sum every year on your behalf. You are entitled to this money when you retire. Defined contribution plans are commonly company thrift or profit-sharing programs. Your employer agrees to match and invest a portion of your savings, or to set aside for you a percentage of profits pegged to your salary. If the company invests or performs poorly, the losses eventually come out of your own pocket. So it pays to monitor closely the income of a defined contribution plan.

Your pension is probably safer under a defined benefit plan than under a defined contribution plan. Even if your company runs into grave financial trouble, the Pension Benefit Guaranty Corporation, a government agency, insures defined benefit plans against termination. You are at least guaranteed to receive some pension. In 1988, the maximum insured benefit was $1,909 a month.

Even if your pension plan is well managed and adequately funded, you may be in for a shock when you retire. Your monthly payments could be substantially less than your individual benefit statement has led you to expect.

Typically, you will not get a company pension unless you work for the firm at least 10 years. In 1989, the usual minimum drops to five years. Then you are vested. That means you are entitled to keep the benefits you have built up even if you quit the company before retirement age. If you work for the same company for many years, you probably will be rewarded with a better pension than if you move around a lot. Mobile workers cut their odds of lasting at a firm long enough to become vested. Employees at small companies often get less generous pensions than their counterparts at major corporations. But if you work for a small, tightly controlled business such as a law firm or a dental practice, your pension benefit might vest within just six years.

If you are married, your original pension could well be 10% or more *less* than a single employee's. That is because employers pay insurance companies more for an annuity for a couple than for a single person, and the cost generally is passed on to the employee in the form of a smaller pension.

The best way to calculate your pension benefits is to read the summary plan description that your employer is obliged to give you once a year. Turn first to the summary plan's section on Social Security. You may discover that your company reduces your monthly pension benefit by a percentage of the amount you will receive from Social Security. That percentage could be as much as 83%.

If you are married, check out the joint and survivor benefits section of the plan. Provided you are vested, the law requires companies to give your spouse at least one-half of your pension benefits after you die, unless he or she waives this right. Your monthly payment probably will be reduced while you are alive — if you and your spouse have elected to let the spouse receive the pension after you die.

If you are thinking of taking a leave of absence or quitting and coming back, you had better examine the provisions for interrupted service. You want to be sure you do not jeopardize your vesting. And if you are considering collecting all your benefits in a lump sum, see if the actuarial assumptions are as favorable as if you choose monthly payments for life.

If you want to know more about your pension than what you can see in the summary plan description, ask your company for a copy of its fuller pension-fund tax return. It is called Form 5500. The Department of Labor also will send you that form if you phone 202-523-8771. You will need to know your employer's identification number and the plan identification number. You will have to get these from your company.

Once you have a copy of Form 5500, give it a careful reading. The first thing you want to know is, has the company told the IRS that it might terminate the plan? If so, the information will appear in item 9.

Item 12 gives the names of the fund's professional advisers. Watch out for lavish duplication of services — for example, four or five lawyers or actuaries. That costs you money.

Item 13 lists the fund's assets and liabilities. Notice if considerable sums languish in non-interest-bearing bank accounts. Look for diversification and degree of risk. More than a third of the assets invested in a single kind of real estate, for example, could be a sign of unnecessary risk.

Item 21 will tell you if the company is up to date on its payments to the fund. If it is not keeping current with its obligations, the next step could be termination of the plan.

Your company's employee benefit managers should be happy to answer any questions you have about Form 5500. Their attitude ought to be completely open and aboveboard. But if you get the feeling they are trying to hide something, take that as a warning about the future of your pension.

Should You Take Early Retirement?

COMPANIES are offering some tempting sweeteners these days to encourage employees to take early retirement. Rather than close plants or lay off people, hard-pressed corporations give financial inducements to employees who leave voluntarily, usually between the ages of 55 and 62. But you would do well to look hard before you leave. Early-retirement extras can carry you only so far. The pension that seems so high today may be gobbled up by inflation tomorrow.

Almost every company pension plan provides for early retirement. About 85% of major plans contain terms that cut early retirees' pension checks by *less* than the actuarial tables would mandate. Yet the difference in payments can be substantial. In some cases, if you quit at 55 — when your earnings may well be on the rise — you might get only 25% of the monthly pension you would have received had you worked to age 65.

When deciding whether to retire early, you have to figure out what you want to do and whether you can afford to do it. Sit down with a pencil and paper — or personal computer — and analyze expected income and outgo. Your company's personnel department should provide individual or group counseling to help you. But it's wise to beware of the arm-around-the-shoulder manner of some company-paid consultants. They may make retirement seem more flowery than it will be.

Most retirees need at least 60% to 80% of their pre-retirement salary to maintain their standard of living. To figure out how much money you'll need, draw up two scenarios — one assuming a relatively modest annual inflation rate of 3% to 4% and one with a high rate of 6% or more. You can shade toward the lower end of that spectrum if your major outlays, such as your housing costs, children's education expenses and medical bills, are under control. If not, you will need more. In any case, if the combination of your pension and Social Security falls short of your requirements, you will have to make up the difference through savings and investments or a second career.

Social Security penalizes workers for early retirement. At age 62 — the earliest you can begin drawing benefits — the monthly payment is about 20% less than it would be if it were started at age 65. And the gap is never closed. In 1988, the maximum annual benefit at 62 was $8,232 per worker, or $12,084 for a couple with a nonworking spouse also 62. However, if you are retiring early from one job but intend to keep working in another job, you can postpone receiving your Social Security benefits and thereby increase the size of checks when you start accepting them.

About 20% of pension plans permit you to take your pension in a lump, up front, and it's a good option. Quite often you also have the choice of taking any severance pay in installments or in a lump.

The lump-sum method is usually better. You can pay taxes on the money at a favorable rate, and then you can reinvest the rest or use it as seed money for a second career. If you invest this money prudently, its earnings can take the edge off future inflation.

One appealing investment choice is to roll the whole lump-sum payout, except for your contribution, into an Individual Retirement Account. This allows you to defer taxes on the money until you withdraw it later on. The IRA rollover is particularly attractive for the many early retirees who find that their biggest nest egg is in their company's tax-deferred thrift or profit-sharing plan. You can directly transfer the company's contributions and all the earnings from such a plan into an IRA.

But that is not your only tax-savings choice. You can take out all that money right away and reinvest it elsewhere — say, in real estate.

In any case, if you accept early retirement, you most likely will want to reorient your investments toward assured income instead of capital accumulation.

Making the Most of Your Nest Egg

I F YOU are nearing retirement, it is time to think about the best way to minimize taxes and maximize the income you will collect on the money you have been saving. Your first decision is how best to withdraw your money from tax-deferred accounts. You may have several such plans, including an IRA, and a company-sponsored profit-sharing or stock bonus program. Each presents its own special tax problems. So be sure to ask a lawyer, accountant or financial planner to guide you through the maze of regulations.

Most tax-deferred retirement accounts offer several choices of how you can withdraw your money.

If you take it all out in a *lump sum,* you often pay less tax than if you withdraw a series of smaller amounts. Most retirement plans, with the exception of IRAs, let you use forward averaging to calculate your taxes. On your 1986 income taxes, you could have used 10-year forward averaging. It allowed you to divide your lump sum by 10, and then pay taxes as if each 10th is the *only* income you will be collecting in each of the 10 years. This easily knocked two-thirds off what you owed to the IRS.

Unfortunately, tax reform reduced forward averaging to five years, beginning in 1987. However, if you turned 50 years old by January 1, 1986, you could use either 10-year or five-year averaging. The best method depends on the size of your lump sum. Under the two income tax brackets that went into effect in 1988, five-year averaging will usually result in lower taxes for amounts over $350,000; 10-year averaging will be best for smaller sums. For example, if you receive $200,000, you would pay $44,400 in taxes with five-year averaging and $36,900 using 10-year averaging.

You could get an even better tax break on a lump-sum withdrawal if you began participating in the plan before 1974. Before then, lump sums were taxed at low, long-term capital-gains rates. After 1974, you began paying ordinary income tax on the money. But you can divide the money according to how many years you participated in the plan before and after 1974. Say that you started just over 20 years ago, in 1969. Then one-quarter of your retirement fund will qualify for capital-gains treatment and three-quarters for forward averaging. Beginning in 1987, the low tax rates on your capital gains for the pre-1974 investments began to be phased out and they will be totally eliminated in 1993. But if you are 50 years old by January 1, 1986, you can still take advantage of the capital-gains rate on your pre-1974 portion.

Once you have your IRA, you will have to pay ordinary income taxes on the amount you take out. Withdrawals from your IRA can begin as early as age 59½, but starting at age 70½, the last deadline for IRA withdrawal, you must stick to a rigid withdrawal schedule based on life expectancy. At that point, a man would have up to 12 years to take out all his money and settle up with the tax collector. A woman would have 15 years. A husband and wife, each 70½ years old, would have 20 years. You will have to pay a stiff penalty in any year that you do not withdraw the required amount.

The only other way around the tax rules is to put your retirement funds into an annuity, because the earnings on it compound tax-free, just as with an IRA. Annuities provide assured income for the rest of your life. They also simplify withdrawals and eliminate further investment responsibilities. You just have to decide how you want to receive the payments.

One option is a lifetime income for you and your spouse. Another is to have payments continue to a beneficiary for a fixed period of time after your retirement, usually 10 to 20 years. Your income will vary depending on which plan you choose. But the difference is small, usually less than $100 a month.

If you want open-ended growth in your retirement account, consider either a variable annuity or a mutual fund. Many mutual funds will arrange a systematic withdrawal plan or a payout schedule that meets tax requirements for IRAs.

Does It Pay to Work after You Retire?

THE word "retirement" is no longer automatically associated with golf carts and golden-years cruises. More and more people are deciding to find another job after they retire. But after all the taxes you have to pay and all the Social Security benefits you stand to lose, does it really pay to take a job after retirement?

Your income after you retire includes your pension, Social Security benefits and any money you collect from IRA and Keogh plans and your investments. As long as you are not earning any money from a job, you can keep all of this, less the taxes you must pay. But if you are under 70 and start earning wages, you are in a different ball game. The more money you earn, the smaller your Social Security check will be. You will still have to pay Social Security taxes on your earnings. In 1988 retirees between the ages of 62 and 65 could earn up to $6,120 without jeopardizing their payments; people aged 65 to 70 could earn $8,400. And don't forget: Your new salary can throw you into a higher tax bracket and thus shrink the net return on your investments. The good news is that after you are 70 years old, you collect your full Social Security benefit no matter how much you earn from a job.

But if you plan to go on working after you retire, it is best to consult now with your company retirement counselor or an accountant and figure out how much you really will profit from your labors. Ideally, you also should start three years before retirement to investigate the job market, make contacts and take any necessary classes. If you have not applied for a job in 25 years, you will find it a much more competitive process.

One excellent place to start a post-retirement job search is with the Forty Plus Club, operating in 17 cities. These are self-help cooperatives staffed by job-seeking members. They run placement services, aid you in preparing your résumé and coach you in job-interviewing techniques.

If you do not want to work for pay but you do wish to keep busy, look for volunteer work. Two programs can help place you. One is the Retired Senior Volunteer Program, and the other is Voluntary Action. You can find them listed in the phone book or by calling your local Office for Aging. Also, check your city or county agency that directs services for the elderly; it may have lists of volunteer jobs for retirees.

Your Medical Care and Housing

MOST large corporations provide some medical insurance to their retirees, even early retirees. If your employer does not, you might be able to stay in its group plan by paying the full premium yourself. That is a better deal than you can get individually.

Medicare kicks in after you reach 65. But that alone will not be enough. You will need a comprehensive health insurance policy to bridge the gaps in Medicare's coverage. The cost of this so-called Medigap insurance varies from $300 to $1,250 a year, depending on your age, where you live and your health. You can lower costs by assuming more risk yourself. One way to do this is to get a policy with a fixed benefit limit. That means the insurer stops paying at a certain amount, usually $100,000.

The best Medigap policies, according to the National Insurance Consumer Organization, are offered by Blue Cross/Blue Shield and AARP. Other companies with good policies are Reserve Life and New York Life.

Another solution is to join a fixed-fee health maintenance organization, or HMO. But long-term, chronic problems requiring nursing-home care are usually beyond the scope of either HMOs or Medicare.

Besides arranging for medical care, one of the major financial decisions you will face when you near retirement is what to do with your house. Do you sell it? Or stay in it and tap your home equity?

If you are 55 or older, you probably can take the once-in-a-lifetime exclusion that exempts you from taxes on the first $125,000 gain from selling your home. But if you don't want to sell, you can tap into the equity that you have built up in your house by getting a so-called reverse mortgage. Many have terms of three to 10 years. During the agreed-upon period, you collect monthly payments, tax-free. At the end of the term you pay back principal and interest. Usually this is accomplished by selling the house. If you should die, or sell the house, before the term is up, principal and interest are due then.

Another form of reverse mortgage is being offered by American Homestead, a mortgage bank in Mount Laurel, New Jersey. Called the Individual Reverse Mortgage Account (IRMA), it is available in seven states: New Jersey, Pennsylvania, Ohio, Maryland, Delaware, Virginia and Connecticut. To be eligible, you must be 62 or older and own a house that is free and clear of mortgages and liens. If you have met these requirements, you can receive monthly payments based on all or part of the value of your house. IRMA keeps paying you no matter how long you live in your home. But when you eventually sell the house, or give it away or die, American Homestead gets principal, interest and a share of appreciation, based on how much of your home's value you mortgaged.

You also can sell your house and continue living there by using a sale-leaseback arrangement. For example, the buyer gives you a 10% down payment and you give him or her a 10- to 15-year mortgage at 10% to 11% interest. You also sign a lease granting you the right to rent the house for the rest of your life. During the term of the lease, the income from the mortgage should pay your rent and leave you with some extra cash, too. The buyer in a sale-leaseback deal is responsible for taxes, insurance and maintenance, which saves you money. Many parents have sold their houses to their grown children and then leased them back.

For information about where you can get reverse mortgages and how to arrange them, send a letter and a stamped, self-addressed envelope to the National Center for Home Equity Conversion, 110 East Main Street, Madison, Wisconsin 53703.

Continuing-Care Communities

I MAGINE yourself as a retired person enjoying safety and independence in comfortable surroundings with few worries about bills for catastrophic illness. A dream? Yes, but one already coming true for thousands of people who live in continuing-care communities.

There are now some 600 such communities in the United States, centered in Florida, California and Pennsylvania. For a one-time payment plus monthly maintenance you can get a contract that entitles you to an apartment, meals, medical service and, if necessary, nursing-home care until you die. One-time payments for this all-inclusive care range from about $20,000 for a studio to over $120,000 for a large apartment. Monthly fees run from $600 to $1,200. Costs are lower if you choose less nursing-home care and still lower if you pay for medical and personal services as needed and desired.

Continuing-care facilities are not new. The four oldest were established before 1900. But the bulk of them have appeared since 1960, and it's estimated that they will increase in number by the hundreds in the next ten years. Unfortunately, many of these facilities fell into bankruptcy, or suffered severe financial difficulties, in the 1970s and early 1980s. In the most egregious cases, the operators were con men. Other communities were run by people with the best of intentions but the worst of calculations. Victimized by circumstances beyond their control, elderly residents failed to get the homes and care for life that they had been promised. The money they paid was gone.

Today's picture is far brighter. Almost half the states now have laws regulating how continuing-care communities handle their financial obligations. And the nursing-home industry itself has tackled the job of inspection and accreditation.

But the job is far from completed. If you are considering this kind of retirement, check out all aspects carefully. You cannot judge by the depth of the carpeting in an apartment that you find attractive. For starters, restrict yourself to communities whose financial stability has been studied by an actuary. Read a copy of his or her report. If you can't get one, or if it says fees may be raised to cover cash shortfalls, strike the place from your list. Think twice about high up-front fees and lack of escrow accounts.

Ask for the biographies of the community's principal owners and operators. They should have solid experience in similar developments. Request the names of residents of these communities and then make some phone calls to investigate whether the projects are financially sound and deliver what they promise.

If you are thinking about a new project that is financed with state revenue bonds, ask for a copy of the prospectus and study it closely. The developer should allot more than 50% of the bond sale proceeds to land acquisition and construction costs. If he is spending anything less than 50% on these basics, that is clear warning that the developer is skimping — or skimming.

For information about continuing-care communities, write to the American Association of Homes for the Aging, Suite 400, 1129 20th Street, NW, Washington, D.C. 20036; the American Association of Retired Persons, 1909 K Street, NW, Washington, D.C. 20049; or the National Consumers League, 815 15th Street, NW, Washington, D.C. 20005.

Retiring to Foreign Countries

LIVING overseas can be a bargain, notably in countries where the dollar is still strong. More than 300,000 retired Americans live abroad. Over 65,000 Yankees live in Mexico alone. The largest cluster is in and around Guadalajara, in the state of Jalisco. Some estimate that their comfortable life costs 50% less than it would back home. If you are a retiree, there are some things to consider seriously before you move abroad.

Pick a country with topflight medical standards. Notable among them are Australia, Canada, Barbados, Costa Rica, West Germany, Britain, Sweden and Switzerland. Your American health-care coverage will be of little or no use overseas, and Medicare does not extend beyond U.S. territory. One company, the Copenhagen-based International Health Insurance Danmark, does offer several policies to expatriates. Its basic coverage costs about $875 a year per person. In countries with large expatriate enclaves you may find local private health insurance programs such as that of the American Society of Jalisco. The society's insurance costs from $87 to $318 a year. In some countries, your best opportunity may be a government-sponsored health program.

Then there is the matter of taxes. No matter where you go, the U.S. Internal Revenue Service takes its cut of your income. Your worldwide income is generally subject to the taxes of the country where you live as well. But the U.S. has tax treaties with many countries that let you credit one set of taxes against the other, so you don't pay twice.

Should you keep your money in the local currency or in U.S. dollars? As long as the dollar is more vigorous than the local currency, expatriate retirees should keep their money mainly in greenbacks. Some countries allow you to maintain a local bank account denominated in dollars or in another foreign currency of your choice.

Wherever you settle, you should have two wills: one covering property in the U.S., the other for assets in your adopted country. And each will should mention the other.

For further information on retiring to a foreign country, write or phone Jane Parker, Retirement Explorations, 19414 Vineyard Lane, Saratoga, California 95070; 408-257-5378.

Your Estate

Wills: Drafting Your Most Important Document

THE prolonged prosperity that many forecasters expect for the U.S. could have one unexpected consequence that would be a mixed blessing. It could swell the value of your investments, your company stock purchase and pension plans and your other assets so much as to create both a windfall and an estate tax headache for your heirs. In fact, you may have such a problem and not know it. Even if your income is modest, you may be building up great — and taxable — corporate benefits.

Because you will have more than you expected to leave to your heirs, it is increasingly important that you have a carefully prepared will. In fact, almost two-thirds of adult Americans do not have one. Yet there is no way without a will to leave your heirs exactly what you intend to leave them. Surely if you get your will in order, you can save your family considerable bitterness. No family situation brings more stress than divvying up Dad's or Mom's estate. One academic study shows that where there was no will, arguments among the heirs were four times as likely to occur.

You do not have to be super-rich to need a will. If you are middle-class, the value of your house, pension and personal property could easily run between $350,000 and $450,000 or more. You need a will to dispose of any property that is not jointly owned or that does not have a named beneficiary, as an insurance policy does. Only in a will can you appoint a guardian for your children or pass along Grandfather's favorite watch or make special provision for an aging relative or a handicapped child.

The federal tax act of 1981 allows you to leave your entire estate tax-free to your spouse. That is because there is now no limit on the so-called marital deduction. But when your widow or widower dies, the total amount that can go untaxed to your children or other heirs is limited. The maximum is $600,000 tax-free, over and above what you leave to your spouse. Even so, this limit is generous enough that the heirs to the vast majority of estates will not have to pay any federal taxes on them.

Many people think that writing a will is unnecessary because their surviving spouse will automatically inherit everything. But this is true in only a few states, and only if the assets are acquired during the marriage and are not gifts to or inheritances of one spouse. In most states, the law will make your spouse share your estate with your children, siblings or parents. And, since assets left to anyone other than a spouse are taxable if they are more than $600,000, the federal government becomes an unintended heir to part of your estate.

The tax changes of 1981 make it more important than ever to have a valid, updated will, even if it is only a simple will. This document can enable you to protect from the federal tax collector any sums above the $600,000 limit. In your will, leave to your spouse the maximum amount that can pass tax-free to your *other* heirs: that is, $600,000 in 1988. If the value of your estate is higher than that, put any amount above $600,000 into a so-called bypass trust. An experienced lawyer can explain in detail how this works and tell you if one makes sense for you — and then he or she can set it up. (For more, see "Your Estate: The Advantages of Trusts.")

If you still think you would never be worth enough to worry about making a will, you had better visit a lawyer anyway to find out how your *state* taxes will cut into your estate.

If you put off preparing and signing a will, then the state will carve up and parcel out what you leave — and quite possibly not the way you want to leave it. Usually the state gives one-third to one-half of your after-tax estate to the surviving widow or widower and the rest to the children. If you have no surviving spouse or children, then your estate goes to your parents, brothers and sisters and other blood relatives — or if you have none, then to the state itself. Unless you make proper provision in your will, your legacy will not be passed on to a friend or live-in lover whom you might have preferred to make your heir.

Most states do not accept wills that have not been vouched for by witnesses. Don't ask a beneficiary to be a witness; the will may be legal, but the beneficiary could lose his or her legacy.

It is wise to have a lawyer draft your will — and your spouse's. Resist the temptation to write one yourself following the instructions in a how-to book or using official forms published by some states. A technical slipup could make your homemade testament worthless. Only a lawyer knows what constitutes a valid document in your state. Some lawyers at legal clinics will draw up your will for as little as $50, but $200 is average for a simple document. The cost rises with the complexity of your finances. Don't be shy about interviewing a prospective lawyer and getting the cost in writing.

Lawyers admit that wills are loss leaders, and they hope to be made executors for the estate. Fees for executors typically are 2% to 5% of the gross estate. But you are under no obligation to do more than pay your lawyer for the will.

Once the will is drawn, sign only one copy and leave it with your lawyer. You can make minor changes with amendments at any time. Don't put your will in a safe-deposit box. Some states require that safe-deposit boxes be sealed on the holder's death, and it takes time to get the will released.

When drafting a will, people often make the mistake of trying to control their beneficiaries after they themselves have gone. For example, some time ago, one man set up a trust in his will but specified that the trust could hold only assets that yielded 4% to 8%. That was a reasonable return when the will was written — and anything above 8% was considered dangerously speculative. But when interest rates roared up, the trust manager was forced by the terms of the will to sell off many sound and high-yielding investments.

A sensible guideline when making bequests in a will is to use percentages rather than dollar amounts. If you do not, a lot can go wrong. Take the sorry case of a man who had a $100,000 estate and left all of it to his beloved sister, except for $10,000 that he willed to his nephew. But when the man died after a long illness, medical bills had shrunk his estate to only $12,000. The nephew got his promised $10,000, but the unfortunate sister collected only $2,000. The man would have been far wiser to have left his nephew 10% of the estate. In that case, the sister would have collected $10,800.

Dissolution of a marriage cancels any rights your ex-mate might have to your estate. But should you die before a separation agreement is signed, your soon-to-be ex probably will still inherit. And people will think it was very sporting of you not to hold a grudge.

Review your will at least once every three years, and keep it up to date. You may want to change some bequests, now that you can leave more money free of taxes. Be sure to revise your will if you move, particularly from a common-law state to a community-property state or vice versa. In a community-property state, any assets acquired during marriage are jointly owned by both partners — except for gifts and inheritances. But in a common-law state, assets are owned by whoever buys them.

If you drew up your will before September 13, 1981, when the old law was still in effect, and you used the conventional wording of that time, probate court would interpret your will to mean that you wanted only 50% of your estate to go to your spouse. Unless you change the wording now, your estate could be taxed on the other 50%. But a simple rewriting can reduce the tax to zero. So do not wait to write — or rewrite — your will.

You do not have to write a new will every time you want to make small changes, such as substituting a beneficiary or changing the amount of someone's bequest. In these cases, your lawyer usually will write a codicil, which must be witnessed and attached to your will. Whatever you do, don't write on the will itself. Such changes may invalidate it, reducing all your careful planning to ashes.

Another consequence of the 1981 tax act is that you may now have more insurance than you need. Because few people will pay estate taxes in the future, the necessity for that insurance coverage will fall off. There is also less reason to have your insurance policy assigned to your spouse. Assigning insurance usually is done to keep the proceeds of the policy out of the estate. But since it will be less important than in earlier years to reduce the size of your estate, the chief reason for assigning insurance disappears. By holding on to the policy yourself, you retain the right to change the beneficiary if and when you wish. But if you and your spouse want your heirs to avoid paying estate taxes on the proceeds from your insurance, you can assign the policy to your children, or to a trust for their benefit. (For more on trusts, see "Your Estate: The Advantages of Trusts.")

Finally, you may think a will is a statement of who gets what. But it may be just as important to state explicitly who does not get what — and why.

In most of the world, custom and law dictate that children automatically receive most of the parents' wealth when they die. That is, unless the kids have committed some awful crime. Only Britain and her former colonies give people the freedom to leave their heirs whatever they deem appropriate.

So leaving it to the kids or not leaving it to them is a choice Americans enjoy as a vestige of our colonial past. Let's say you have decided to exercise your option — you are going to leave it all to your darling daughter — but you want to cut off entirely your unworthy son. You had better say so in no uncertain terms in your will.

If you simply omit any reference to a child in your will, rather than specifically disinheriting him or her, that relative might be able to make a case that the drafting was flawed, that you "lacked testamentary capacity," or that people whom you left your money to exerted "undue influence."

Disenfranchised children are frequent will-challengers. One reason is that, if their claim is upheld in court, they stand to gain an inheritance equal to what state law provides if a parent dies intestate. That's usually one-half to two-thirds of the estate.

And squabbling is not limited to the rich. Fights over wills can be more a matter of frustrated expectations than anything else. One top estate lawyer tells the story of a widower who sought to leave 95% of his estate to his impoverished daughter and 5% to his son who was a wealthy doctor. The son challenged the will and settled out of court for another $5,000. Says the estate lawyer: "I guess he wanted to prove that Daddy loved him as much as his sister."

Should You Leave It All to Your Children?

NOWHERE but in America do so many parents enjoy the privilege of grappling with the question of what to leave their children. There are some 2 million U.S. households that enjoy a net worth of at least $1 million. Most of the millionaires inherited their wealth or built it on a business they founded. But plenty of corporate careerists also have created seven-figure estates by taking advantage of company profit-sharing and pension plans. In short, estate planning is fast becoming a major concern of the middle class.

And nowhere is the feeling about inherited wealth so ambivalent as in the U.S. Many people worry that Commodore Vanderbilt's grandson was right when he declared that "inherited wealth . . . is as certain death to ambition as cocaine is to morality."

Fortune magazine surveyed 30 multimillionaires on the subject of what they plan to leave to their heirs. One-fifth of them said their children will be better off with only minimal inheritances. And almost half plan to leave at least as much to charity as to their heirs.

For example, Warren Buffett, chairman of Berkshire Hathaway, is worth more than $1.6 billion. After putting his children through college, Buffett contents himself with giving them several thousand dollars each at Christmas. He plans to leave most of his money to his charitable foundation. Buffett says that setting up his heirs with a "lifetime supply of food stamps just because they came out of the right womb" can be "harmful" for them and is "an antisocial act."

T. Boone Pickens, the rich and famous oilman, warns, "If you don't watch out, you can set up a situation where a child never has the pleasure of bringing home a paycheck."

Yet there are sensible ways of passing on what you have without depriving the kids of their own feeling of achievement. Estate experts have some tips.

First, don't be so secretive with your heirs. As soon as the children begin to mature, bring the family finances into the daylight, so they will know approximately what they will get some day and have some idea how to hold on to it. They should also know, of course, if they will not be getting anything. Talks about family money, like those about sex, should begin as early as possible.

Second, shelve the silver spoon. No matter how well off you are, make sure your children go to work. Psychiatrists say that lack of work experience not only alienates heirs from humanity but also contributes to insecurity about their ability to survive without their inheritance.

Third, give later rather than sooner. Most estate advisers agree that the age of 21 is too early for children to reap a windfall. Businessman William Simon, the former U.S. treasury secretary, suggests that sensible parents put a reasonable amount in a trust that starts paying interest only when the child reaches 35 and then allows him or her to tap into the principal in two installments, at 40 and 45.

Above all, put child-rearing above estate planning. Psychiatrists say that wealthy parents in particular often pay too little attention to child-rearing. As billionaire Warren Buffett advises: "*Love* is the greatest advantage a parent can give."

The Advantages of Trusts

You probably think that trust funds are only for fabulously wealthy people, but you could easily be wrong. If you have children or substantial investments, you can add to your assets and reduce your taxes by setting up a trust.

The basic idea is simple: You transfer ownership of property or money to a trust on behalf of a beneficiary. Your beneficiary can be one or more persons — usually including your spouse or children. Or it can be an institution, such as a college or a church.

The person who contributes the assets is called the *grantor*. The grantor sets down instructions for the management of the trust and for passing out its income and principal. The grantor also chooses a trustee. That's a third party who holds title to the trust property and administers the trust. You can serve as trustee, or manager, of a trust you set up or you can name someone else to manage it for you. Of course, you will need to consult a lawyer about the proper way to establish a trust tailored to your needs.

There are two kinds of trusts. One is a *testamentary trust*. It is established in your will and starts paying off after you die. This trust is usually set up so a financially astute relative can manage the inheritances of youthful or potentially spendthrift heirs. Because testamentary trusts are part of your will, they do not avoid probate, which is the lengthy and sometimes expensive legal process by which estates are inventoried. The other kind of trust is a *living trust,* and it starts paying some income to your beneficiaries during your lifetime. After your death, the trust assets automatically pass to your chosen heirs — or remain in trust for their benefit. The assets also escape probate. That can be a big bonus. Probate can take months or years to complete, and the costs can be high. Lawyers' fees and probate expenses can slice 5% to 7% off a medium-sized estate that includes a house, some pension benefits and personal cash.

Furthermore, if you use an irrevocable living trust, you may be able to reduce your income taxes. That's because income earned by the assets you put in trust can be taxed not at your rate but at your beneficiary's rate. Those taxes are typically lower than yours.

If you are married, it is probably wise to have a lawyer set up what's called an irrevocable bypass trust. Here's how it works:

Suppose you and your spouse have $1 million in assets, which is not so unusual in these days of large pension benefits. In your will, do *not* leave the entire sum to your spouse. If you do, then when your spouse dies, your heirs will have to pay a stiff tax on any amount over $600,000. To avoid that, arrange in your will to leave $600,000 to your spouse, and put the remainder of your estate into a trust. In this case, the remainder is $400,000.

While your mate remains alive, he or she can receive the income earned by the trust and some of the principal. Upon your spouse's death, the money in the trust goes to the other heirs whom you have named as beneficiaries. They pay *no* estate tax on any amount below the $600,000 limit. Since the amount in the trust in this case is $400,000, they indeed pay no estate tax.

Beyond the bypass, there are other trusts you should consider. If you and your spouse have large life insurance policies, you may want to transfer ownership of them to something called an irrevocable life insurance trust. This also alleviates both income and estate taxes. A note of caution: An irrevocable trust, by definition, cannot be revoked or controlled by the grantor. If you desire to control the trust, give up the tax savings and make the trust revocable; never let a professional adviser talk you into making decisions for tax purposes if they do not coincide with your goals.

Minimizing Estate Taxes

L ET me tell you the true story of a millionaire who has set up his estate so that when he dies, his heirs will inherit his wealth without having to pay any taxes. You need not be a millionaire to learn a lesson or two for your own estate from Saul Jacobson.

An engineer from Delaware, who is now retired in Palm Beach, Florida, Jacobson is 77 and hopes to live to be at least 90. But just in case he doesn't, he has set up his estate so that his heirs will inherit it all — more than $1 million — without having to pay any taxes. He calls his planning "an enduring act of love."

Jacobson wisely sought advice from professionals — not just one but four of them: a financial planner, an accountant, a lawyer and a bank trust officer. All this cost him about $10,000, but he estimates that it will save his family at least half a million dollars.

His will states that half of Jacobson's assets will go directly to his son. The son could inherit up to $600,000 tax-free under federal law. To pay the taxes on any amount above that, Jacobson has bought life insurance.

In addition, he has set up what lawyers nickname a QTIP — that's a qualified terminable-interest property trust. The QTIP will provide for Jacobson's wife. If she survives him, she will collect the income from the QTIP as long as she lives. When she dies, the money in the trust will go to Jacobson's two grandchildren.

You might be able to draw a lesson from Saul Jacobson and leave the largest possible tax-free estate for your spouse and any children or grandchildren. Just consult a good lawyer and inquire whether it is worthwhile for you to set up a QTIP, a bypass or some other trust. And whatever you do, be sure you have a solid and up-to-date will. Remember to study the plan, trust instrument or will prepared by your professional advisers. Unless you strongly indicate otherwise, their proper goal will be to minimize your taxes. Only you know your true wishes — and maybe they will include giving an outright bequest of $10,000 to Aunt Mae or Cousin Charlie, with no strings attached.

Picking a Trustee

A NY trust needs a trustee who will take responsibility for the money. The trustee is both a watchdog and a safe-keeper. He or she protects the assets in the trust, collects any debts or dividends that are due, and pays a regular stipend to the heirs.

Very often people who write wills and set up trusts designate banks as the trustees. For honesty, impartiality and continuity, banks are hard to beat. Their fees as trustees are not high, usually 1% of the assets managed per year, up to $1,000,000. Above that amount, the percentage of assets lost to fees is even less. But how well do bank trust departments really do in managing estates and in guiding assets to growth?

In an earlier era of money management, bank trust departments minded the wealth of millionaires' widows and the heirs to great fortunes. The trust departments placed caution above all else, and so they invested in top-grade bonds and conservative stocks in order to produce returns of 3% a year or so. That hardly seems acceptable today.

Bank trust departments often sell off the assets in an estate and pool them in a much larger portfolio of common stocks, which they manage like a mutual fund. But a survey of such pools shows that during the decade of the 1970s they increased in value by only an average 110%, compared with 127% for the Standard & Poor's index of 500 stocks. So it is no surprise that, when choosing trustees, more and more people are turning away from bank trust departments and instead selecting lawyers, accountants and other private trustees. However, bank trust departments still offer a major advantage — they most likely will be around for many years, providing necessary continuity in the management of trust assets.

Most trusts designed to minimize estate taxes are irrevocable. Unless the trust specifically permits beneficiaries to switch banks, they can do little short of going to court, or threatening to do so, to upgrade performance or dismiss incompetent trustees. State and federal bank regulators are powerless to help. The courts can oust a trustee, but only on proof of fraud, incompetence or misappropriation of funds. So lawyers offer some advice to anyone putting a trust provision in one's will:

First, give beneficiaries an escape hatch by specifying their right to replace trustees. Do not retain any such rights yourself. You would be taxed under the grantor trust rules of the Internal Revenue Code — effectively defeating your original intentions in establishing the trust.

Second, appoint a co-trustee, preferably a friend or relative whom the bank would have to consult before changing investments and who would serve without fee.

Finally, spell out the trust manager's responsibilities; they can range from simple caretaking to complete control.

Above all, you might be wise to investigate now whether your spouse, your children or your other heirs would benefit by your setting up a trust and getting a trustworthy trustee.

Becoming an Executor

I T SEEMS like such an honor. A relative or close friend asks you to be the executor of his estate. You are flattered to be so trusted. But be warned: Estate administration is tough, time-consuming and sometimes even risky. You could wind up spending months, or even years, worrying about death, taxes — and greed.

The first rule of being the executor, as writer Evan Thomas has noted, is not to be one in the first place. Tell Aunt Sadie to get a lawyer or a seasoned bank officer who knows how to administer an estate. The only problem is that such a professional costs money, and Aunt Sadie didn't get to be rich by spending a cent she didn't have to. If you refuse the job, then the fees for a professional executor will reduce the estate by 2% to 5%.

If you do accept the request to become a nonprofessional executor, you will find that the job, for all its drawbacks, can be interesting. It is like having a person's life suddenly open before you. Of course, you may also find out a lot you didn't want to know.

Don't try to do the job by yourself. Get an expert lawyer to help, unless Aunt Sadie lived in Texas or one of the other few states that have fairly simple probate procedures. If the estate includes land, an ongoing business, a trust, substantial charitable bequests or anything else that could cause a tax problem, then whatever state you live in, hiring a lawyer is a must.

Finding that lawyer is not always easy. Start with the attorney who drafted the will. If he or she is not available, ask at your local bar association. Try to find a lawyer who is a fellow of the American College of Probate Counsel. The members of this organization have had at least 10 years' experience and are recommended by their peers.

When you become the executor of an estate, face up to the fact that you are going to be busy for quite a while. The very first thing an executor must do is find the will and read it. Next, have the lawyer whom you've hired get the will probated, that is, "proved" in the probate court as a valid will. The court will issue to you what's known as letters testamentary that give you authority as executor. You then have to notify all the heirs and any relatives who would have been entitled to inherit under state law if there had not been a will.

Your real chore will be finding and taking possession of the deceased person's property. Tangibles such as the house, car or jewelry should be locked up. An obituary is an advertisement for burglars. Buy or renew the insurance on all the property. If you don't, you could be personally liable for any loss.

Put any cash into a separate checking or savings account for the estate. Pay all the bills out of the estate checking account. Fortunately, it's usually the lawyer's job to pay any taxes, but you will need to give him a precise inventory of the assets and their value. And you — the executor — are responsible for seeing that the taxes are paid on time.

When the will has been probated and all taxes and debts have been paid, the executor prepares an accounting for the probate court of all assets received and sold, all claims and expenses paid and all amounts due to those who are to get the remaining estate. Then he is finally ready to distribute what is left to the heirs.

Sometimes the court will allow an executor to make distributions to needy heirs before the final accounting. Otherwise you allow at least four to six months for creditors to come forward before parceling out, say, the deceased person's pearls or the 300 shares of General Motors. If you do not wait and there is not enough money left in the estate to satisfy creditors, you could be held personally liable.

Probably the most trying aspect of your job as an executor is keeping meticulous records of the estate's expenses and receipts. That means more than just filling up a shoebox with check stubs and random bank statements. It might be worthwhile to pay the minimum annual fee of $500 to a bank trust department to act as custodian. The bankers will keep the records for you.

If the estate includes a large portfolio of securities, the executor will need astute investment advice to preserve and perhaps increase the assets before he or she hands them over to the heirs. Hiring a professional investment counselor means another fee, but may save the estate money in the long run.

Executors are held to a high standard of fiduciary responsibility. They run significant legal risks if they act in any way that could be considered contrary to the heirs' interests. So, there are a few things not to do. Don't deposit in your personal checking account any checks made out to you as executor, and never make yourself a temporary loan out of the assets of the estate. Also, you shouldn't buy anything from the estate without permission of all the other heirs and possibly the court.

Should you as the executor take a fee? In a few states, compensation is set by law — usually a one-time fee of 1% to 5% of the estate. In most states, though, an executor simply puts in for a "reasonable" fee and the court upholds it as long as no one objects.

For years it was traditional for executors who were family members to forgo a fee for their blood, sweat and tears. The fee might reduce the executors' own inheritance, and as ordinary income it would be taxed at higher rates than estate taxes. But now lawyers are urging executors to go ahead and take the money. Chances are, by the time you have made all the distributions and the court has discharged you from your responsibilities, you will have earned every cent.

Widows: Managing When Alone

IT IS sad but true that more than 11 million American women are widows. Those who are in the best financial shape are not necessarily the ones with the largest inheritances. Rather, they are the women who regularly, thoroughly and candidly discussed family finances with their husbands and, more important, what to do with their legacies if their husbands died first.

Because women live much longer than men, widows outnumber widowers by five to one. The average age at which all widows now living became widows is 53. Statisticians suggest that, thanks to higher life expectancy levels, that average will rapidly rise to 66 or 67. In any event, unless they remarry, widows face a decade or two — and sometimes more — of life on their own. Yet the overwhelming majority of them have never thought much about how to handle the family's assets or how their own economic needs would be met.

By contrast, the widows who cope the best are those who taught themselves — well in advance — how to manage money. The *wrong* time to start asking, say, the difference between money-market funds and stock-market mutual funds is when a woman has to start managing the family assets alone.

Wives should insist on periodically reviewing their family assets and liabilities with their husbands. Lynn Caine, author of the book *Widow*, suggests that a couple set aside an annual "contingency day" to assess what the surviving spouse would inherit and consider what he or she should do with it. They should discuss whether she or he ought to sell the major inherited assets, such as their house or art collection or business. The couple should also re-examine their wills *every* year and discuss where the widow or widower should seek financial advice.

Every married couple should update and put in writing all the information that can help the survivor and an executor settle the estate. This should include such basic facts as the names and phone numbers of the family attorney, accountant, stockbroker and insurance agent; also, the locations of bank accounts and safe-deposit boxes and important documents, such as wills, deeds and partnership agreements; and a list of assets and debts. Of course, all this information should be kept in one safe and convenient place.

Every married woman should regularly read the newspaper business pages and financial magazines. That is a necessary first step in planning for the possibility that someday she may have to direct her own financial affairs. A wife also should handle her own checking account, pay the bills periodically and take an active part in meetings with any of her husband's professional advisers, such as the stockbroker or insurance agent.

The first priority of a widow should be to preserve her inheritance. For instance, it may be foolish to sell off the family house, which is probably the best place for her to live today and may well be worth more tomorrow. She may be able to delay paying some bills so that the money can earn bank or money-fund interest. To guard against mistakes and con men, a new widow would be wise to double check whether questionable bills already have been paid.

She ought to wait six months or a year before considering investing her inheritance in anything that isn't safe and liquid. Quite often, she will not be thinking straight before then. Until the widow is ready to absorb the counsel of professionals and decide how to diversify her investments, any insurance money and other inherited cash can be kept safely in certificates of deposit, money-market funds or those mutual funds that invest in conservative stocks.

A new widow or widower can get wise counsel from a pamphlet called *What Do You Do Now?* It is available for $1 from the Life Insurance Marketing and Research Association, Order Department, P.O. Box 208, Hartford, Connecticut 06141. She or he also can get advice on additional sources of financial and emotional counsel by writing to the THEOS Foundation, 1301 Clark Building, 717 Liberty Avenue, Pittsburgh, Pennsylvania 15222.

Remember this: Eventually, a widow must assume responsibility for financial decisions. The sooner any married woman prepares for widowhood, the better. A much more secure legacy than money is knowing how to manage it.

Beware of State Taxes

A RE you planning to move to another state after you retire? If so, now is the time to confront the delicate subject of *state* death taxes.

As mentioned earlier, your estate would escape federal taxes if it were $600,000 or less in 1988. But 25 states and the District of Columbia collect death taxes independently of the IRS. A few even tax estates as modest as $100.

You pay no extra taxes in California, Florida, Nevada, Texas and 21 other states. Elsewhere you are socked for state taxes. For example, Minnesota, Mississippi, Oregon and South Carolina exempt anywhere from $120,000 to $600,000 from estate taxes. The remainder is taxed at rates from 1% to 16%, depending on the estate's size.

Often the amount of the tax depends on to whom you leave the money. For example, if you are a Delaware resident and you leave $400,000 to your spouse, he or she might owe no inheritance tax. But your child would pay around $19,000 on the same bequest. In Oklahoma, you can leave your entire estate to your spouse tax-free, but every cent you bequeath to a cousin or friend is taxable.

More than one state can tax your estate. Stocks, bonds and other paper assets are taxed in the state where you legally resided at the time of your death. But real estate, jewelry, furniture and other so-called tangible assets are taxed where they're situated. Most states will consider you a resident if you pay income tax there, or if you vote, do your banking, register your car, get a driver's license or have your primary home there.

You can cut the bill by taking full advantage of deductions. State laws generally give your spouse, children and grandchildren the most generous exemptions and the lowest tax rates. So, the more you give or leave to your immediate family, the less is owed to the state taxman.

You can also cut estate taxes by giving money to your heirs while you are still alive. You can give as much as $10,000 a year tax-free to each of as many people as you want. Married couples jointly may bestow as much as $20,000 a year.

In some states, if you and your spouse own property jointly, then it will not be hit by death taxes. In Michigan, all jointly held property is exempt. Maryland and Pennsylvania allow joint property to pass from one spouse to the other tax-free.

If you want to leave your entire estate to your spouse, you can do it in such a way that it will escape part or all of the state tax when he or she dies. To accomplish this, bequeath part of your property directly to your spouse and instruct that the rest be placed in an irrevocable trust from which your spouse can draw income after you die.

Most important, before making any estate-planning decisions, call your state tax department for detailed information. And be sure to consult an attorney.

Postscript

A Look Ahead to the Next Ten Years

Readers of previous editions of this book may recall that the author believes the United States is experiencing an unprecedented period of rapid social and political change, and that the changes will have profound effects upon our economy and our personal fortunes. I have received many requests for reprints of these thoughts. Here, then, I repeat them, substantially expanded and updated.

A s an editor travels across this great country of ours — and it is a great country — one word keeps echoing in his mind. That word is *revolution.*

It is absolutely indisputable that we live in revolutionary times. Just consider the many social upheavals that we Americans have lived through in the last 25 years: the youth revolution, the black revolution, the sexual revolution, the women's revolution and more. These upheavals have been generally peaceful, and most have passed their crest. But they have shaken our American society and economy so fundamentally that we shall never be the same again.

This should not surprise us overly much, because although we Americans are essentially a conservative people — we have had the same form of democratic government for more than two centuries — we are a people of the revolution. We were born of a rather long and violent revolution that began 213 years ago. And since then we have seen so many upheavals: the emancipation of the slaves, the enfranchisement of women, the rise to positions of power and influence of the later immigrants, the great wave of education and affluence and culture that swept over our country during and immediately after World War II.

It should never be forgotten that we Americans have a proud history and heritage of revolution, that ours is the land of the continuing revolution. And it is this rare capacity to change, to grow, to reform from within — peacefully, in an enduring democracy — that makes us the envy of the rest of the world.

My belief is not only that we are going through a series of revolutions that will profoundly affect our lives and our livelihoods, but also that in the immediate future the rate of change will accelerate and the degree of change will sharpen and in some cases become more shattering. If there is one certainty in our mercurial world, it is simply this: those of us who anticipate the changes and who sensibly act upon them not only will survive but also will prosper. And those of us who attempt to ignore the changes and conduct our activities as before will stagnate and wither.

This should not make us apprehensive. History's lesson is that it is precisely in times of wrenching change that humankind makes its most significant advances, that the largest enterprises are created, that the richest personal fortunes are built, that the most enduring achievements are recorded. More than that, all of us — you and I — can effect change. We can make things happen; we can make things happen for the better.

Just consider how much our world has changed in merely the past 15 years or so:

In the early 1970s, oil from Saudi Arabia cost $2.60 a barrel. A Chevy Malibu set you back $2,891, and a median-priced new house was $26,900. The Dow Jones industrials were heading toward their awesome closing high of 1051.7. Meanwhile, President Richard Nixon, having distanced himself from a third-rate burglary at the Watergate, was en route to re-election by a landslide.

Today's world is quite a different place. In the intervening period, we Americans have experienced four presidents, three recessions, two bouts of double-digit inflation and one frightening flare-up of interest rates that pushed the prime beyond 20%. Think about what is now common but then did not exist: money-market funds, specialty mutual funds, low-cost commodity funds, tax-exempt bond funds and bond unit trusts, tax-sheltered variable annuities and universal life insurance, stock futures contracts, asset management accounts and discount brokers. In that almost ancient age of the early 1970s, if any casual acquaintance had asked you about your very intimate experiences with savings or mortgage rates, stocks or Treasury bills, you would have thought him gauche, gross or slightly mad. But money has become the new sex, and such subjects have come out of the closet. They are the most intensely discussed topics among consenting adults.

People who consistently have anticipated the turns in the economy have usually managed to cope, and even prosper, better than those who have not. In the present uncertain era, when the only sure thing is that change will occur, nobody can anticipate precisely what the next 10 years may bring. But after weighing current trends and realities, we can make a fair estimate of the probable shape of at least some future developments.

We know, for example, that over the next decade some 75 million American baby boomers, now aged 25 to 43, will be passing through the time of life when people invariably spend the most for houses, cars, books, diapers and most other goods and services. So consumer demand stands to rise. We know that these young (or at least youngish) adults, millions of whom have fairly recently entered the labor force as raw beginners, will gain more experience and grow more skilled as time goes on. Consequently, America's productivity stands to increase. We know that far fewer people will be turning 18 and going to work in the next 10 years than the past 10. Thus, the labor problem of 1999 will not be unemployment but shortages of many kinds of skilled employees and of those willing to go to work on the lower-paying rungs of the service trades.

There are still other, broader developments that you can discern, developments that perhaps you can act upon to increase your earnings, enrich your investments and enhance your career. Given America's heritage of revolution and given the new power relationships in the world, let me suggest that there will be at least 10 major developments that will substantially change our country, our lives and our livelihoods in the next 10 years.

POINT ONE: The American nation, and much of the rest of the world, is now going through a conservative revolution of remarkable depth and breadth. This revolution extends far beyond the economy and into society and politics. The trend will continue regardless of which political party captures the White House. Furthermore, the revolution is only in its infancy. There is more to come.

The cause is clear: for the first time in history, after millennia of living as peasants or subsistence farmers, millions more people in many countries possess something in the way of material assets. They are struggling up into the broadening middle class. In the recent past, they have seen their assets eaten away by inflation, and so they are apprehensively fighting above all else to conserve those assets. As a consequence, they are changing their politics, their attitudes and their life-styles. They are shifting to support conservative policies and they are electing conservative governments.

You don't have to be an American chauvinist, a jingoist or even a capitalist to recognize the many countries where free electorates in just the last few years have changed their governments and moved their economies from the left to the center. Voters have done so in a dozen nations, including Britain and Jamaica, West Germany, Canada, the Netherlands and Belgium. Economic freedom is also spreading in Africa and Latin America. Even Socialist governments are rushing to unwind government regulation, reduce taxes and free up human enterprise.

Consider also: What if you and I were not Americans? What if we did not live in our home cities but instead in Caracas or Düsseldorf or Hong Kong? What would we be thinking? Somewhere in the backs of our minds we would be wondering: How can I transfer some of my money to the United States, because it is an island of political stability and economic vibrancy in an otherwise unstable, uncertain world?

That, in fact, is the kind of thinking that is taking place throughout the world. It is not because of our attractive interest rates that investment capital is flooding into the United States. Interest rates have plunged in the past several years, and still the capital keeps pouring in. The reason is that, whatever they can earn on their money, people know that so long as it is invested in the U.S. economy, it will be safe and secure.

In the U.S., a conservative revolution is obviously under way — in economics and society at large. My estimate is that this trend will continue.

In economic policy it will take the form of more movements toward freedom and away from government control. New businesses will rise rapidly, and competition will heighten — both competition at home and competition from abroad. With rare unanimity, Democratic and Republican leaders alike are speaking up for the need to stimulate enterprise.

A conservative revolution is also sweeping over, and sweeping up, our young people, those in their mid-30s and younger. They grew up in a rare time of declining expectations, and an era — some years ago — of oppressive inflation and scary unemployment. Consequently, they value a job and they put a premium on careers.

In the nation's universities, young people no longer automatically expect to rise to higher stations in life than their parents or their older siblings. They recognize that they have to work for their advance. Therefore, every freshman class is more conservative, realistic, moderate, than the previous one. The students are more conservative than their instructors and professors. In just the last several years, the whole situation on campus has been turned on its head.

POINT TWO: The most important social development in the United States will be the continuing rise to positions of power and influence of the nation's most important majority: American women.

As an editor goes around this country and speaks with hundreds upon hundreds of women, he recognizes that this absolutely revolutionary movement has spread: it has spread from the coasts inland, from the North to the South, from big cities to small communities. The consequence is that there is literally no woman in the country — whatever her position on such controversial issues as abortion or affirmative action — who remains unaffected.

Already the women's movement has profoundly changed our thinking on our basic economic policy-making. Take, for example, the way we think about such a sensitive and human issue as unemployment. So many women have come flocking into the labor force lately — 72.3% of all American women aged 20 to 54 are today at work in the paid economy or actively seeking paying jobs — that even liberal economists no longer consider full employment to be a 4% rate of unemployment but rather a 6% or even higher rate. By that measure, we have achieved full employment.

Also, more adult Americans are at work in our paid economy than at any other moment in our history. In just five years, while employment has been flat in most other Western economies, we have created 16 million new jobs, most of them in small entrepreneurial businesses, half of them filled by women.

As a consequence, we have only fairly recently begun to view unemployment as less of an economic threat than inflation. Now and in the future, regardless of which party is in power in the White House and the Congress, our economic policies will be directed more toward fighting inflation than fighting unemployment. Therefore, we can expect continued pressures to reduce the growth of government spending. And though interest rates may move sideways or even trend down over the next few years, they still will remain relatively high — that is, higher in real terms than we have been used to throughout most of our history.

What the women's revolution also portends is that future recessions will be milder and briefer than they otherwise would have been. That is because if one person in a household loses his or her paycheck, there is a much better than 50% chance that yet another person in that household will be bringing in full-time earnings. In part because we have so many multiple-earner families, purchasing power will continue to climb, and our buying of goods and services — particularly of quality goods and services — will be stronger than it otherwise would have been.

Young women who are members of multiple-paycheck families have a motivation to practice economic conservatism because they rather suddenly, surprisingly, find themselves quite affluent. It's not at all unusual for college-trained couples in their 20s or early 30s to be earning $40,000 a year, or much more. They are the new elite — people who find themselves with assets — and they want to conserve those assets from the twin depredations of inflation and high taxation. So, while women will remain a liberal force on social issues, it is quite likely that they will become a more conservative force in economic issues.

I cannot stress enough that the women's movement is a real revolution — and it is just beginning. In the past decade, the proportion of women among students graduating with master's degrees in business has doubled, from one in six to one in three; among law students it has gone from one student in four to two students in five.

Women soon will be rising to much higher positions of influence and power all around us. They will be knocking on the doors of real power. Most important, their revolutionary rise of consciousness, of self-awareness, of ambition and of demand will give the U.S. a significant edge in the intensifying global competition of the next 10 years. Whatever our shortcomings as a nation may be, we are far ahead of our allies and competitors in Europe, let alone Asia, Latin America and the Middle East, in at last beginning to admit women to positions of economic power and decision-making. This will significantly expand our pool of talent and merit — the group from which we draw our business, our political, our societal, our academic leaders — in the next decade. In short, with a larger group to choose from, we shall select better leaders. We have long since passed the day when we could afford the brutal luxury of shutting out of positions of leadership more than one-half of our American population.

POINT THREE: We are entering a technology- and service-oriented era.

The countries, the regions and the companies that master the new technologies or that develop the information services and the financial services that productively enhance the new technologies — those will be the countries, the regions and the companies that will prosper economically, will dominate politically, will inherit the future.

By contrast, the regions and companies that will sink into deeper trouble will be those that are unwilling to change and to modernize but instead seek through artificial means, such as import tariffs or quotas, to protect and prop up the outmoded and the inefficient industries. We will succeed only if we can out-compete lower-wage foreign producers — but we can do that only if we continue to invent, to innovate, and to offer high quality and reliability, excellent service and appealing design.

In the next 10 years, the computer's middle-age spread will revolutionize our job opportunities and the way we work. As demands increase for services, notably information delivery, jobs by the millions will be created for computer programmers, systems analysts and other service workers as disparate as secretaries and paralegals, financial advisers and nurses. Demand will be intense for the skilled, whether they wear white, blue or pink collars. But many unskilled assembly-line workers may have to step down to the lower-paying levels of the services, accepting jobs as restaurant workers or janitors. Increasingly, knowledge will be power: power to earn big, advance, enjoy autonomy and make decisions. The computer will become the great weapon to convey knowledge: to teach the old three Rs to schoolchildren and new skills to workers.

Industries based on resources — everything from agriculture to energy — have been battered lately. But as the Western economies continue to expand, rising demand will revive many resource-based industries and the regions dependent on them. Thus, in the early 1990s we may be entering a period in which the major growth sectors will be not only high technology and services but also energy and some other resources.

One consequence will be a marked shift of power within the United States. Already under way is a historic migration of jobs; and with that, a swing of economic and political power. The population is shifting to the West, the South and parts of the Northeast, where the high-tech is.

The problem is that, as the economy grows more competitive and complex, the U.S. is rapidly — and perhaps dangerously — becoming two countries: two countries in terms of its regions, its races and its economies. The recession and inflation of the early 1980s exacted their cruelest price on the people who are least prepared to cope — the poor. The educated, the skilled people, can take care of themselves. They ride the crest. They get jobs in the expansive new industries and services, they move to the booming regions, they put their money in all the fresh forms of high-reward investments, and their lives grow better. But the uneducated, the unskilled, fall further and further behind. The good life, the American dream, becomes ever more elusive for them.

Surely, one of the nation's most basic challenges over the next 10 years — and beyond — will be to find means for the members of the American underclass to lift themselves out of their economic and emotional slough. Many of our government programs and institutions have failed. Our public schools in a distressing number of communities have produced a generation of semi-literates. Our public housing has created public slums. Our public welfare has created despair, dependence and hopelessness among millions of our fellow Americans.

So, I believe that private enterprise — perhaps working with government tax incentives, credit and guarantees, but within the private economy — will have to take on more and more of the job of razing and then rebuilding the slums, of creating the factories and offices, and even, in some cases, of providing basic schooling to its employees. Surely all that will be a continuing challenge and opportunity for every American. We cannot allow ourselves to feel comfortable as long as so many of our fellow citizens remain so helplessly far behind.

POINT FOUR: In foreign affairs, the U.S. has the opportunity for a rather revolutionary change in its relations with those two superpowers, the Soviet Union and the People's Republic of China.

The Chinese, desperately trying to make their constricted economic system more efficient, are rushing to introduce some measures of freedom. The Soviets, paralyzed for so many years by illness, death and revolving-door succession among their geriatric leadership, have at long last turned to a new, younger generation of chiefs. So far, they have shown themselves to be more worldly than their very limited and xenophobic predecessors. Thus, they may be willing to open up their economy for more trade with us, and to slow the devastatingly expensive arms race in order to spend more for the modern technology that they can buy from us.

The chief executive with the toughest management problem in the world today is Mikhail Gorbachev, because he is trying to wrench a backward Soviet economy into the modern technological era without losing too much central control. His policy of *glasnost* — openness, freer discussion and internal criticism — appears to be drawing encouraging support within the Soviet Union, although there remains, of course, considerable bureaucratic opposition.

The Soviets and the Chinese urgently need our technology. Our policy should be to help induce them to free up their political and their economic systems, and to switch more of their limited capital resources out of arms and adventurism and into buying what we have to sell.

POINT FIVE: The U.S. and much of the developed world will continue to face a ticking time bomb because of the huge international debts that are being built by the developing nations.

The late senator Everett Dirksen, from my home state of Illinois, used to say, "You know, a billion here, a billion there. Soon it adds up to real money." Little more than a billion minutes ago, Christ was preaching peace in the Middle East. And the developing nations have built up a debt of more than *one thousand billion* dollars.

Bankruptcies of whole nations abroad are no longer unthinkable, but their consequences are unknowable. Nobody knows how Argentina, Brazil, Chile, Mexico, Peru, Venezuela, Sudan, Zambia, Zaire, Togo, Tanzania, Turkey, Poland, Romania and many another country ever will pay off their great and growing debts — or what would be the results of their failure to do so.

Yet if there are defaults on these loans and bankruptcies of whole nations, surely some major private banks could be brought under tremendous economic pressure. In that case, the Federal Reserve Board and other governmental authorities would be obliged to step in and bail them out. Thus, you and I, as citizens and taxpayers, ultimately would have to pay the bill.

Fortunately, a number of banks sensibly have begun to put aside reserves against likely future losses from shaky foreign loans. We probably will avoid catastrophe because all the major parties — the bank lenders, the debtor governments, the worldly institutions such as the International Monetary Fund — recognize that it is in their own best interests to take every possible step to prevent gross crisis. But along the way there will be many scares, shocks and short-term dislocations.

My point is this: All of us are part of this increasingly interdependent economic world. So we have to watch very carefully, we have to be exceedingly nimble for the indefinite future, to keep on top of and ahead of the changes in the economic news. Nobody can guess accurately to the penny what the dollar will be worth in the Frankfurt or Tokyo market, or estimate to the last quarter of a percentage point what the inflation rate or the prime interest rate will be even a few weeks from now. But if we are to survive, let alone to prosper, we all will have to educate ourselves about the basic economic and political tides that influence those all-important numbers that ripple on the surface. All of us will have to become armchair economists, or at least educated readers of the economic news.

POINT SIX: In the U.S., we face a period of rather prolonged, sustained economic expansion.

True enough, we have never seen such a spotty, fractionated economy. Some communities and businesses are thriving; others are taking it on the chin. It is hard to talk about the total economy without first recognizing that there are, and will continue to be, sharply differing performances among its varied parts.

But taking it as a whole, the U.S. economy has been enjoying a remarkably prolonged, sustained expansion, and I expect it to continue at least through the end of 1989. By that time, the expansion will be 85 months old, making it by far the longest in peacetime history. This economy has shown remarkable staying power. Just when it looked as if it might flag, the economy has picked up.

Fortune magazine's economists anticipate that the gross national product during 1989 will grow by 2½% or so after accounting for inflation. That would not be a boom, of course, but it would be moderate and, more important, sustainable expansion — the kind that can last longer than a boom.

What will power the economy?

— First, inflation will rise a bit but shows no signs of running away. The continuation of only moderate inflation will enhance the consumer's confidence and his or her spending power.

— Second, consumer purchasing power is also expanding because employment is heading up.

— Third, except for some overbuilding of office towers and apartments in parts of the Oil Patch and other areas of the Sun Belt, there are no dangerous excesses in the economy. We are not over-buying and over-stockpiling in such a way as to lead to a shattering plunge tomorrow.

POINT SEVEN: American business is going through a crash diet of cutbacks, spin-offs and restructurings that are *permanently* changing the structure of the economy. No less than 56% of the Fortune 500 companies have formally started the slimming-down process in the last five years. So far, the evidence overwhelmingly shows corporate restructuring to be a powerful force for economic improvement, despite its regrettable human costs.

The most visible consequence is that after years of stagnation, U.S. manufacturing productivity is rising sharply. In 1987 it went up about 3½%, which is more than double the rate of the mid- to late 1970s. (Productivity growth in the services is not sluggish, but that is another story.) The heroes are the smokestack industries — metals, textiles, tires, automobiles — where productivity is rising 5% or more.

We are just now beginning to benefit from the combination of three factors: the spurt in productivity, the decline in the dollar and some wage concessions by labor. Recently, U.S. productivity rose faster than Japan's or Germany's. Today, measured in dollars, compensation per hour in U.S. manufacturing is 18% less than in Germany and only 11% higher than in Japan. In some industries it is *less* than in Japan.

After years of stagnation and decline, a number of U.S. industries rather suddenly have become quite competitive in global markets. The U.S. now holds the lead in quality and technology in aircraft, pharmaceuticals, computers and agricultural equipment.

In other industries — such as cars, tires, chemicals and aluminum — we are not the world leaders, but our quality and efficiency are improving, and we can look for some export gains.

In fact, our volume of exports has risen more than 25% in the past year. The problem with our trade balance is not so much with our exports but with our imports. The rub is that import prices have not been going up as much as the value of the dollar has come down. But lately import prices have started to rise at a fairly rapid rate. Thus, the U.S. *trade* deficit should decline this year.

But what about the twelve-digit U.S. *budget* deficit? We probably will have the rare opportunity to save ourselves from ourselves in the 1990s, thanks to a lucky break of demographics. A very small generation of babies was born in the U.S. between 1930 (just after the Great Depression began) and 1946 (just after the boys marched home from World War II). Consequently, beginning about 1990 and continuing through about the year 2010, we will have a remarkably small generation of new retirees entering the Social Security system and claiming old-age benefits. Simultaneously, the post–World War II baby boomers will be reaching their peak earning years, and pouring huge sums into the Social Security coffers. The Social Security system may well be running a surplus of $200 billion a year late in the 1990s and a surplus of $1 trillion for the whole decade. The question, of course, is whether Congress will persist in being Congress and spend all that windfall, or will use it in creative ways both to narrow the budget deficit and to build up a big enough trust fund to provide Social Security benefits for the huge generation of baby boomers when they start to retire in large numbers around the year 2010.

The Social Security surplus will help considerably, but it alone cannot solve the basic problem that the U.S. government is spending much more than it is raising in operating revenues. What the nation needs — and what the world is crying out for — is a believable, practical *long-term* program that will progressively narrow the budget deficit over several years, a program that will bring the budget into balance in the economically expansive years of the early 1990s.

I take the contrarian view that Americans are in a mood to accept any deficit-reduction program that is both reasonable and equitable, that they are willing to accept sacrifices so long as they are convinced that *everybody* in our society will have to make some sacrifices.

Any new taxes should be leveled on consumption. People should be taxed less on what they put into the economy (in the form of work, saving and investment) and more on what they take out (in the form of consumption). So increases in taxes on whiskey, cigarettes and gasoline should be favored over growth-retarding increases in taxes on personal income or corporate profits.

Ideally, every dollar of additional tax revenue should be matched by two dollars of spending reductions. The great nut to crack immediately is defense. The U.S. just cannot afford to have a multitude of overlapping weapons systems, and it must close dozens of surplus military bases and munitions factories that Congress keeps open, not to protect the country but to protect jobs.

The most indefensible spending is that for people whose incomes are above the median. Spending of all kinds on the poor — for welfare, Medicaid, housing and food — adds up to just 7% of the budget. Though workfare can trim that a bit, the poor need most of what they get. But spending for subsidies to farmers who have gross incomes above $100,000 a year amounts to $8 billion. Medicare payments to people who are well-off run to further billions. Those are luxuries that the nation no longer can afford.

Eventually, most federal transfer payments must be subject to a means test. It is senseless for a person who retires with a plump pension to pay the same Medicare deductible as poorer citizens.

POINT EIGHT: The stock and bond markets should do well — over the intermediate term and the long term. I can absolutely guarantee you that at some point the market will fall, quite possibly by 10%, 20% or perhaps more. The trouble is, I cannot tell you when. As the economists say, "Give them a figure or a date, but never both."

I do not know — and I do not know anybody who knows — whether the stock market will be higher a week or a month from today than it is today. I do not believe that it matters very much, because almost all of us should be looking at the market from a long-term point of view. But I believe strongly that the market will be higher two years from now, and significantly higher five years from now, than it is today.

There are several reasons to expect that, even if stocks fall temporarily, the long-term bull market will resume: speculation in the market is certainly not excessive; recession in the economy is nowhere in sight; inflation and interest rates show no sign of roaring up in the near future; and the Dow Jones Industrial Average is substantially undervalued.

In terms of real purchasing power, in mid-1988 the Dow was much lower than it was a generation ago. Merely to match the record that it reached in 1965 in terms of real dollars — that is, after discounting for inflation — the Dow would have to hit nearly 3200. Surely our business leaders are wiser and our economic policies are more sensible today than they were in 1965.

Also, relative to real corporate earnings, the stock market in the U.S. over the past four years has risen much less than stock markets in many foreign countries. In short, our economy is significantly stronger than most of theirs are, but many of their stock markets have climbed much faster than ours has. It is likely that U.S. stocks are due for a rise, quite possibly a substantial rise over the long term.

POINT NINE: There will be a dramatic expansion of the quality market for goods and services. We Americans are coming to appreciate, as Europeans and the Japanese have so long appreciated, that smaller can be better, that less can be more if the goods and the services that one buys deliver real value for money. We also shall adopt — indeed, we are rapidly adopting — a conservation ethic.

You see this revolution going on in every aspect and facet of American life. You see people being more quality-conscious everywhere. They are not necessarily picking the fanciest designer label or paying the highest possible price, but they are showing a new sophisticated awareness that high quality is more efficient and therefore more economical in the long run.

A remarkable change is occurring in American marketing. As you go across the country and study markets, whether markets for magazines or cars or clothes or food, you see that the goods that are selling well are those that deliver real value for money: high quality, reliability, durability. And the goods that are selling poorly are those that do not have lasting value: the faddish, the flashy, the easily discarded goods.

We will buy fewer goods, but they will be better, higher-quality goods. We Americans shall adopt a European style of living, embracing the quality market. Our standards of living will not decline. Indeed, they will change, but they will rise. And business people — entrepreneurs, manufacturers, brokers, bankers, among others — who produce and deliver quality goods and quality services will surely prosper.

Before I go on to my final point, let me give you my own short list of superlatives — what may be the biggest, the best, the worst, the most, in the next 10 years.

Biggest-selling consumer goods: Anything that is high quality; also, convenience goods and services.

Biggest dogs on the market: Anything that stresses low price over high quality.

Biggest-spending consumer group: The aging youth market, the maturing baby-boom kids — many of whom are coming perilously close to 40 years of age. We might call them the over-the-thrill crowd.

There will not be a new baby boom, but there will be a parenting boom as more and more of the swelling generation of two-income working couples in their mid- to late 30s decide to have a child — but only one child, Superbaby! — or at most two.

Most significant demographic change: The number of people who are 65 or older and retired will surge. There may well be sharp generational conflicts between the retirees and the baby boomers. For example, the elders will want to collect ever more generous Social

Security benefits — including unlimited cost-of-living allowances — while the boomers will want to hold down the benefit payments and instead save and build up the funds for future years so that there will be enough left for the boomers when *they* start to retire.

The fastest-growing socioeconomic problem: Education — specifically, the crisis in public education, the harsh reality that our urban public schools are just not educating our young people to get jobs or even to cope with the increasingly complex demands of the economy. Consequently, business is more and more becoming the education of last resort — teaching new employees not only basic skills but also the three Rs, which the public schools are failing to teach them. In the years ahead, as it struggles to find enough able workers, business will become more deeply involved with education: teaching workers within companies, adopting schools with its communities, lending managers and technicians to become teachers.

Biggest social change: The continuing rise of women in the economy, in politics and in society at large. Women at work for pay represent a tremendous new bloc of consumers and decision-makers. They are a rich source of talent, and they will sharpen our productivity, our competitiveness in global markets and our leadership capabilities.

Strongest comeback by a currently depressed industry: Energy. It is ridiculous and dangerous to speak of an energy "glut" when the U.S. still must spend more than three-quarters of a billion dollars a week to import energy. Barring some unexpected breakthrough discovery, the world still will have a finite source of liquid energy, and as industry expands around the globe, demand for energy once again will scrape up against the limits of supply. Thus, we should be taking every sensible step now to explore for and develop energy and to conserve what we have.

Most promising energy source: Natural gas, because the U.S. possesses plenty of it, tucked away in relatively small but still economical pockets.

Least promising energy source: Solar power, a victim — so far — of extravagant hopes and disappointing performance.

Fastest-rising regions: Areas rich in technological enterprises, in services and, ultimately, in certain resources: specifically, the Southwest and the West for high-tech, services and eventually, too, for energy; the Southeast for much the same, except energy; and parts of the Northeast for communications, information and financial services.

Best investments: Growth stocks — and mutual funds concentrating on growth stocks. And, longer term, land — land in areas that hold resources, including energy resources and even farmland, which is now undervalued.

Surest political trend: The swing away from the left and to the center in many countries.

POINT TEN: In conclusion, let me observe that we are entering an era when the countries that possess the rare combination of human and material resources will prosper and inherit the future.

The next 10 years will provide more dangers and yet more opportunities than the last decade. In negotiating this period, it might be wise to recall history's lesson: this country has the unique capacity to change and to amaze. The nation also has the human *and* material resources to make life better.

The startling reality is that, for all its blemishes, the U.S. possesses unmatched and sometimes undervalued assets. Foreigners often see these visible advantages more clearly than we do, and so they are investing in America as if it were a high-growth stock. In record numbers, Europeans, Asians and Latin Americans are putting money into apartments in New York, office buildings in California, condominiums in Colorado, beachfronts in Hawaii, factories in South Carolina, banks in Florida and much more.

Increasingly, foreigners are also investing their lives in this country. The number of immigration visa applications is surging. The newcomers are not only the oppressed from Russia and Cuba, Poland and Cambodia, Nicaragua and Vietnam, but also educated, affluent people from all over. What these investors and immigrants are telling us should be clear: America is a stable, free land, and Americans who have some money to put aside might do well to invest in its future.

The nation's strengths range from enviable (and inexpensive) communications and transportation services to the world's most vigorous and most easily accessible venture capital markets. Beyond its rich resources of computers and other machines, the U.S. possesses fabulous amounts of raw materials — more, in many cases, than any other developed nation — and they are bound to pay rewards tomorrow to the investors of today.

It is not in industry or agriculture or the services that America has made its boldest advances: it is in society — and that societal progress stands to enrich and enlarge the nation's human capital. About 7.4 million Americans between the ages of 18 and 24 are now attending colleges and universities. This represents one in every four people in that age group, versus only one in seven in West Germany and one in eight in Britain. When they graduate, many of these students will go into business, industry and the sciences, and may well increase the value of your investments.

If I am right about our current problems (and they are many) as well as our future potentials (and they, too, are many), there will be five ingredients for the economic, the political and the social success of nations in the next 10 years. Societies, people, countries, will do well if they have a number of the following five characteristics:

First, a rich, modern, highly productive agricultural base, giving a country the capacity not only to feed its own people but also to export food — for economic gain, occasionally for political leverage, certainly for humanitarian purposes.

Second, an abundant base of energy-bearing raw materials — not only oil and natural gas, but also coal, hydroelectric power and all the rest.

Third, a vital, strong base of other, nonenergy raw materials — iron ore, copper, lead, phosphate, zinc and the like.

Fourth, an advanced, automated, highly developed technology and industry, including information- and financial-services industries.

Fifth, and most important, an educated, motivated, well-informed, skilled, sophisticated population.

I have gone down the list of all the member nations of the United Nations — 159 at latest count. It is fascinating and revealing if you try to apply these five criteria. You very quickly see that, for all of its vaunted military might, the Soviet Union qualifies under perhaps two of the five headings. But the Soviets suffer from grave problems because of their totally inefficient, bankrupt agriculture, because of the erratic nature of their industry, and because of the questionable skills and education of so much of their population.

China has a brilliant future, but a distant one. It suffers from severe problems and shortages, and will continue to do so for the rest of this century and probably well into the 21st century.

Germany and Japan are fairly well off, but only fairly so, because they lack the food and the fuel to supply their own populations, let alone to export.

The Netherlands, Norway and Britain have some significant problems at the moment. But, given their advanced industries, their energy resources and their skilled, educated populations, they face potentially very bright futures — *if* they choose the proper policies now.

But there are three, and only three, nations on the face of the earth that qualify by all five measures: rich agriculture, abundant energy and nonenergy resources, advanced industrial technology, and skilled, educated populations. Those three are Canada, Australia and, of course, the United States.

What our nation *lacks* is also apparent. It is the will, the methods, the procedures and often the institutions to exploit those resources. It is the leaders with skill and vision to rally the people. It is the resolve to overcome individual interests for the benefit of all. But those are purely psychological and institutional constraints, and thus they can be surmounted. That is where we come in. Surely we — you and I — can make a difference.

The U.S. has no major physical or material limitations. That is quite a superlative statement, but it is indisputably correct. So, despite all of our immediate and very visible problems, if we Americans follow sensible policies of government deregulation, of investment stimulation, of energy conservation and energy development, then the economic, the political and the social future of the United States in the rest of the revolutionary 1980s and the 1990s is absolutely dazzling.

Index

Home births, 402
Home businesses, 199, 212–214, 458–459
Home-care health services, 400
Home computers. *See* Personal computers
Home-equity accounts, 164, 193, 335–336, 338–339
Home Exchange International, 429
Home movers, 301–302
Homeowners insurance policies, 491, 501–506
Homes. *See* Houses and housing
Hospitals: careers as directors of, 370; checking out, 396–397; checkups in, 390; choosing, 398–399; and HMOs, 401; insurance policies by, 495; reducing costs in, 399–400
Hotels, 433, 439–440, 444
Hotline Update Newsletter, 430
Household services, franchises for, 464
Houses and housing: buying, 166–173, 181–182; equity from, 164, 193, 335–336, 338–339; expenses for, 20, 316; improvements for, 189–196; and interest rates, 48; inventories of property in, 505–506, 508–509; kits for, 182–183; and marriage, 252; in movies, 196–197; of parents, buying and renting of, 273; physicals for, 187–189; prices of, 164–165; renovation of, 158–159; resources for buying, 23; and retirement, 532–533; selling of, 171, 183–187, 255; as source of income, 270; transfer of, and divorce, 278. *See also* Mortgages; Moving; Real estate
How to Buy Stocks (Engel and Boyd), 23
How to Buy Surplus Personal Property from the Department of Defense, 288
How to Choose a Home Care Agency, 273
How to Get Happily Published (Applebaum and Evans), 471
How to Play the Moonlighting Game (David), 362
How to Prepare for College Board Achievement Tests, 424
H&R Block, 221
HSH Associates, 175
Hulber Financial Digest, The, 69
Humanistic mutual funds, 115–117
Hurried Child, The (Elkind), 266
Hypothecation, 187

Ibbotson, R., *Stocks, Bonds, Bills and Inflation* (SBBI), 56
Immigration of Adopted and Prospective Adoptive Children, The, 262
Import tariffs, 559
Income and Safety, 331
Income mutual funds for IRAs, 234
Income statements, 53

Income stocks, 33, 57
Income taxes. *See* Taxes
Income trusts, 13
Indemnity plans, 393
Index options, 87–88
Individual Retirement Accounts (IRAs), 4, 9, 229–233; alternatives to, 247–248; annuity plans for, 239–240; in banks, 237–239; and bonds, 240–241, 244; borrowing from, 336, 338; and child planning, 258; and company plans, 242–243; deadline for contributing to, 216; discount brokers for, 126; and divorce, 279; fees for, 244–245; for house down payments, 173; as investments, 37, 233–235; and Keogh plans, 205; and lump-sum payments, 529; mutual funds for, 107, 235–237; and profit-sharing plans, 521; and real estate plans, 241–242; for retirement, 519, 533; and rollovers, 245–247, 338–339, 529; safety of, 324; self-directed, 243–244; switching accounts of, 245–246; and taxes, 19, 42, 199; for windfalls, 30; withdrawing money from, 232; and zero-coupon bonds, 102
Individual Reverse Mortgage Accounts (IRMAs), 533
Industrial relations, careers in, 352
Information-processing industry: careers in, 352; job hopping in, 383
Infertility, dealing with, 403
Inflation: and bonds, 38; and gold, 114; indicators of, 50; for IRAs, 235; outlook for, 36, 562; and stocks, 38, 61; and tangible assets, 44; and women, 557–558
Information on the Appraisal Profession, 509
Information-processing industry: careers in, 352; job hopping in, 383
Information services, 559
Inherited wealth, 542
In-home services, 274
Inside tips and stock selection, 66–67
Insiders, The, 67
Insiders' Chronicle, 68
Installment debt, 18, 316, 340
Institute of Certified Travel Agents, 449
Institutional Brokers Estimate System, 62
Insurance: and appraisals, 297–298; auto, 499–502; for baggage, 451; for business liability, 458; careers in, 368; and child planning, 258; disability, 40, 497–499; executor responsibility for, 548; and financial planners, 25; for hard-to-insure, 498; for home buying, 172; homeowners, 491, 501–506; household, and alarm systems, 511; for legal services, 307; need for, 540; and risk, 32; as tax deduction, 212–213. *See also*